FAX 650.327.5497

Police
TEL 650.330.6300
FAX 650.327.4314

Transportation
TEL 650.330.6770
FAX 650.327.5497

THE·FAIRY·TALE
·OF·MY·LIFE·

HANS CHRISTIAN ANDERSEN, THE DANISH ROMANCE-WRITER.

THE·FAIRY·TALE OF·MY·LIFE

AN·AUTOBIOGRAPHY

HANS·CHRISTIAN·ANDERSEN

PADDINGTON PRESS LTD

THE TWO CONTINENTS
PUBLISHING GROUP

Library of Congress Cataloging in Publication Data

Andersen, Hans Christian, 1805-1875.
The fairy tale of my life.

Translation of Mit livs eventyr.
Reprint of the 1868 ed.
1. Andersen, Hans Christian, 1805-1875—
Biography. I. Title.
PT8118.A3E5   1975   839.8'1'36 [B]   75-11175

ISBN 0-8467-0074-3
Library of Congress Catalog Card Number 75-11175
Copyright 1975 Paddington Press Ltd
Printed in the U.S.A.

IN THE UNITED STATES
PADDINGTON PRESS LTD
TWO CONTINENTS PUBLISHING GROUP
30 East 42 Street
New York City, N.Y. 10017

IN THE UNITED KINGDOM
PADDINGTON PRESS LTD
231 The Vale
London W3 7QS

IN CANADA
distributed by
RANDOM HOUSE OF CANADA LTD
5390 Ambler Drive
Mississauga, Ontario LGW 1Y7

PUBLISHERS NOTE

Autobiography was an obsession for Hans Christian Andersen. The contrasts in his life of anonymity and celebrity, poverty and fortune, compelled him to constant self-review. He wrote his first autobiographical sketch in 1830 at the age of twenty-five before embarking on a tour of France and Italy, leaving instructions for its publication should he fail to return alive. By 1855, when he was known throughout Europe as the author of the Fairy Tales, he wrote his second autobiography for a Danish edition of his works. In 1868 Andersen submitted a continuation of this life story for an American edition of his complete works.

On the one-hundredth anniversary of Andersen's death we are pleased to reproduce here the English translation of 1871, which includes both the 1855 and 1868 texts.

CONTENTS.

CHAPTER I.
APRIL, 1805 — SEPTEMBER, 1819.

CHAPTER II.
SEPTEMBER, 1819 — OCTOBER, 1822.

CHAPTER III.
OCTOBER, 1822 — DECEMBER, 1828.

CONTENTS.

CHAPTER VII.

1835 — 1838.

CHAPTER VIII.

1839 — 1841.

CHAPTER IX.

1841 — MARCH, 1844.

CONTENTS.

CONTENTS.

CHAPTER XIII.

JULY, 1846 — DECEMBER, 1847.

CHAPTER XIV.

JANUARY, 1848 — MARCH, 1851.

CONTENTS.

CHAPTER XV.

1851 — APRIL 1855.

CONTINUATION.

APRIL, 1855, TO DECEMBER, 1867.

CONTENTS.

CONTENTS.

THE STORY OF MY LIFE.

CHAPTER I.

MY life is a lovely story, happy and full of incident. If, when I was a boy, and went forth into the world poor and friendless, a good fairy had met me and said, " Choose now thy own course through life, and the object for which thou wilt strive, and then, according to the development of thy mind, and as reason requires, I will guide and defend thee to its attainment," my fate could not, even then, have been directed more happily, more prudently, or better. The history of my life will say to the world what it says to me, — There is a loving God, who directs all things for the best.

In the year 1805 there lived at Odense, in a small mean room, a young married couple, who were extremely attached to each other ; he was a shoemaker, scarcely twenty-two years old, a man of a richly gifted and truly poetical mind. His wife, a few years older than himself, was ignorant of life and of the world, but possessed a heart full of love. The young man had himself made his shoemaking bench, and the bedstead with which he began housekeeping ; this bedstead he had made out of the wooden frame which had borne only a short time before the coffin of the deceased Count Trampe, as he lay in state, and the remnants of the black cloth on the wood-work kept the fact still in remembrance.

Instead of a noble corpse, surrounded by crape and wax-lights, here lay, on the second of April, 1805, a living and weeping child, — that was myself, Hans Christian Andersen. During the first day of my existence my father is said to have sat by the bed and read aloud in Holberg, but I cried all the

time. "Wilt thou go to sleep, or listen quietly?" it is re
ported that my father asked in joke; but I still cried on; and
even in the church, when I was taken to be baptized, I cried
so loudly that the preacher, who was a passionate man, said,
"The young one screams like a cat!" which words my mother
never forgot. A poor emigrant, Gomar, who stood as godfather, consoled her in the mean time by saying that the
louder I cried as a child, all the more beautifully should I
sing when I grew older.

Our little room, which was almost filled with the shoemaker's bench, the bed, and my crib, was the abode of my childhood; the walls, however, were covered with pictures, and
over the work-bench was a cupboard containing books and
songs; the little kitchen was full of shining plates and metal
pans, and by means of a ladder it was possible to go out on
the roof, where, in the gutters between it and the neighbor's
house, there stood a great chest filled with soil, my mother's
sole garden, and where she grew her vegetables. In my story
of the "Snow Queen" that garden still blooms.

I was the only child, and was extremely spoiled, but I continually heard from my mother how very much happier I was
than she had been, and that I was brought up like a nobleman's child. She, as a child, had been driven out by her parents to beg, and once when she was not able to do it, she had
sat for a whole day under a bridge and wept. I have drawn
her character in two different aspects, — in old *Dominica*, in
the "Improvisatore," and in the mother of Christian, in "Only
a Fiddler."

My father gratified me in all my wishes. I possessed his
whole heart; he lived for me. On Sundays he made me
perspective glasses, theatres, and pictures which could be
changed; he read to me from Holberg's plays and the "Arabian Tales;" it was only in such moments as these that I can
remember to have seen him really cheerful, for he never felt
himself happy in his life and as a handicraftsman. His parents had been country people in good circumstances, but upon
whom many misfortunes had fallen: the cattle had died; the
farm-house had been burned down; and lastly, the husband
had lost his reason. On this the wife had removed with him

to Odense, and there put her son, whose mind was full of intelligence, apprentice to a shoemaker ; it could not be otherwise, although it was his ardent wish to attend the grammar school, where he might learn Latin. A few well-to-do citizens had at one time spoken of this, of clubbing together to raise a sufficient sum to pay for his board and education, and thus giving him a start in life ; but it never went beyond words. My poor father saw his dearest wish unfulfilled ; and he never lost the remembrance of it. I recollect that once, as a child, I saw tears in his eyes, and it was when a youth from the grammar school came to our house to be measured for a new pair of boots, and showed us his books and told us what he learned.

"That was the path upon which I ought to have gone !" said my father, kissed me passionately, and was silent the whole evening.

He very seldom associated with his equals. He went out into the woods on Sundays, when he took me with him ; he did not talk much when he was out, but would sit silently, sunk in deep thought, whilst I ran about and strung strawberries on a bent, or bound garlands. Only twice in the year, and that in the month of May, when the woods were arrayed in their earliest green, did my mother go with us, and then she wore a cotton gown, which she put on only on these occasions and when she partook of the Lord's Supper, and which, as long as I can remember, was her holiday gown. She always took home with her from the wood a great many fresh beech boughs, which were then planted behind the polished stone. Later in the year sprigs of St. John's wort were stuck into the chinks of the beams, and we considered their growth as omens whether our lives would be long or short. Green branches and pictures ornamented our little room, which my mother always kept neat and clean ; she took great pride in always having the bed linen and the curtains very white.

One of my first recollections, although very slight in itself, had for me a good deal of importance, from the power by which the fancy of a child impressed it upon my soul ; it was a family festival, and can you guess where ? In that very

place in Odense, in that house which I had always looked on
with fear and trembling, just as boys in Paris may have looked
at the Bastile — in the Odense house of correction.

My parents were acquainted with the jailer, who invited
them to a family dinner, and I was to go with them.   I was at
that time still so small that I was carried when we returned
home.

The House of Correction was for me a great store-house of
stories about robbers and thieves ; often I had stood, but always at a safe distance, and listened to the singing of the men
within and of the women spinning at their wheels.

I went with my parents to the jailer's ; the heavy iron-
bolted gate was opened and again locked with the key from
the rattling bunch ; we mounted a steep staircase — we ate
and drank, and two of the prisoners waited at the table ; they
could not induce me to taste of anything, the sweetest things
I pushed away ; my mother told them I was sick, and I was
laid on a bed, where I heard the spinning-wheels humming
near by and merry singing, whether in my own fancy or in
reality, I cannot tell ; but I know that I was afraid, and was
kept on the stretch all the time ; and yet I was in a pleasant
humor, making up stories of how I had entered a castle full
of robbers.   Late in the night my parents went home, carrying me, the rain, for it was rough weather, dashing against
my face.

Odense was in my childhood quite another town from what
it is now, when it has shot ahead of Copenhagen, with its water
carried through the town and I know not what else !   Then it
was a hundred years behind the times ; many customs and
manners prevailed which long since disappeared from the
capital.   When the guilds removed their signs, they went in
procession with flying banners and with lemons dressed in
ribbons stuck on their swords.   A harlequin with bells and a
wooden sword ran at the head ; one of them, an old fellow,
Hans Struh, made a great hit by his merry chatter and his
face, which was painted black, except the nose, that kept its
genuine red color.   My mother was so pleased with him that
she tried to find out if he was in any way related to us, but I
remember very well that I, with all the pride of an aristocrat,
protested against any relationship with the " fool."

The first Monday in Lent the butchers used to lead through the streets a fat ox, adorned with wreaths of flowers and ridden by a boy in a white shirt and wearing wings.

The sailors also passed through the streets with music and flags and streamers flying; two of the boldest ended by wrestling on a plank placed between two boats, and the one that did not tumble into the water was the hero.

But what especially was fixed in my memory, and is very often revived by being spoken about, was the stay of the Spaniards in Funen in 1808. Denmark was in alliance with Napoleon, who had declared war against Sweden, and before anybody was aware of it, a French army and Spanish auxiliary troops, under command of Marshal Bernadotte, Prince of Pontecorvo, entered Funen in order to pass over into Sweden. I was at that time not more than three years old, but I remember very well those dark-brown men bustling in the streets, and the cannon that were fired in the market-place and before the bishop's residence; I saw the foreign soldiers stretching themselves on the sidewalks and on bundles of straw in the half-burned St. John's Church. The castle of Kolding was burnt, and Pontecorvo came to Odense, where his wife and his son Oscar were staying. The school-houses all about were changed into guard-rooms, and the mass was celebrated under the large trees in the fields and on the road. The French soldiers were said to be haughty and arrogant, the Spanish good-natured and friendly; a fierce hatred existed between them; the poor Spaniards excited most interest.

A Spanish soldier one day took me up in his arms and pressed against my lips a silvery image, which he carried on his breast. I remember that my mother became angry because, as she said, it was something Catholic, but I was pleased with the image, and the foreign soldier danced with me, kissed me, and shed tears; he had, perhaps, children himself at home. I saw one of his comrades carried to execution for having killed a Frenchman. Many years afterward, in remembrance of that, I wrote my little poem, " The Soldier," which, translated into German by Chamisso, has become popular, and is found in German " Soldier Songs " as an original German song.

Quite as lively as the impression of the Spaniards was a later event, in my sixth year, namely, the great comet of 1811 · my mother told me that it would destroy the earth, or that other horrible things threatened us, to be found in the book of "the prophecies of Sibylla." I listened to all these superstitious stories and fully believed them. With my mother and some of the neighboring women I stood in St. Canut's churchyard and looked at the frightful and mighty fire-ball with its large, shining tail.

All talked about the signs of evil and the day of doom. My father joined us, but he was not of the others' opinion at all, and gave them a correct and sound explanation ; then my mother sighed, the women shook their heads, my father laughed and went away. I caught the idea that my father was not of our faith, and that threw me into a great fright ! In the evening my mother and my old grandmother talked together, and I do not know how she explained it ; but I sat in her lap, looked into her mild eyes, and expected every moment that the comet would rush down, and the day of judgment come.

The mother of my father came daily to our house, were it only for a moment, in order to see her little grandson. I was her joy and her delight. She was a quiet and most amiable old woman, with mild blue eyes and a fine figure, which life had severely tried. From having been the wife of a countryman in easy circumstances she had now fallen into great poverty, and dwelt with her feeble-minded husband in a little house, which was the last, poor remains of their property. I never saw her shed a tear ; but it made all the deeper impression upon me when she quietly sighed, and told me about her own mother's mother, — how she had been a rich, noble lady, in the city of Cassel, and that she had married a " comedy player," — that was as she expressed it, — and run away from parents and home, for all of which her posterity had now to do penance. I never can recollect that I heard her mention the family name of her grandmother ; but her own maiden name was Nommesen. She was employed to take care of the garden belonging to a lunatic asylum, and every Sunday evening she brought us some flowers, which they gave her permis-

sion to take home with her. These flowers adorned my
mother's cupboard ; but still they were mine, and to me it
was allowed to put them in the glass of water. How great
was this pleasure ! She brought them all to me ; she loved
me with her whole soul. I knew it, and I understood it.

She burned, twice in the year, the green rubbish of the garden ; on such occasions she took me with her to the asylum,
and I lay upon the great heaps of green leaves and pea-straw
I had many flowers to play with, and — which was a circumstance upon which I set great importance — I had here better
food to eat than I could expect at home.

All such patients as were harmless were permitted to go
freely about the court ; they often came to us in the garden,
and with curiosity and terror I listened to them and followed
them about ; nay, I even ventured so far as to go with the
attendants to those who were raving mad. A long passage
led to their cells. On one occasion, when the attendants were
out of the way, I lay down upon the floor, and peeped through
the crack of the door into one of these cells. I saw within a
lady almost naked, lying on her straw bed ; her hair hung
down over her shoulders, and she sang with a very beautiful
voice. All at once she sprang up, and threw herself against
the door where I lay ; the little valve through which she
received her food burst open ; she stared down upon me, and
stretched out her long arm toward me. I screamed for terror
— I felt the tips of her fingers touching my clothes — I was
half dead when the attendant came ; and even in later years
that sight and that feeling remained within my soul.

Close beside the place where the leaves were burned the
poor old women had their spinning-room. I often went in
there, and was very soon a favorite. When with these people,
I found myself possessed of an eloquence which filled them
with astonishment. I had accidentally heard about the internal mechanism of the human frame, of course without understanding anything about it, but all these mysteries were very
captivating to me ; and with chalk, therefore, I drew a quan-
tity of flourishes on the door, which were to represent the
intestines ; and my description of the heart and the lungs
made the deepest impression. I passed for a remarkably

wise child, that would not live long; and they rewarded my eloquence by telling me tales in return; and thus a world as rich as that of the Thousand and One Nights, was revealed to me. The stories told by these old ladies, and the insane figures which I saw around me in the asylum, operated in the mean time so powerfully upon me, that when it grew dark I scarcely dared to go out of the house. I was therefore permitted, generally at sunset, to lay down in my parents' bed with its long, flowered curtains, because the press-bed in which I slept could not conveniently be put down so early in the evening on account of the room it occupied in our small dwelling; and here, in the paternal bed, lay I in a waking dream, as if the actual world did not concern me.

I was very much afraid of my weak-minded grandfather. Only once had he ever spoken to me, and then he had made use of the formal pronoun, "you." He employed himself in cutting out of wood strange figures, — men with beasts' heads and beasts with wings; these he packed in a basket and carried them out into the country, where he was everywhere well received by the peasant women, because he gave to them and their children these strange toys. One day, when he was returning to Odense, I heard the boys in the street shouting after him; I hid myself behind a flight of steps in terror, for I knew that I was of his flesh and blood.

I very seldom played with other boys; even at school I took little interest in their games, but remained sitting within doors. At home I had playthings enough, which my father made for me. My greatest delight was in making clothes for my dolls, or in stretching out one of my mother's aprons between the wall and two sticks before a currant-bush which I had planted in the yard, and thus to gaze in between the sun-illumined leaves. I was a singularly dreamy child, and so constantly went about with my eyes shut, as at last to give the impression of having weak sight, although the sense of sight was especially cultivated by me.

An old woman-teacher, who had an A B C school, taught me the letters, to spell, and "to read right," as it was called. She used to have her seat in a high backed arm chair near the clock, from which at every full stroke some little automata came out. She made use of a big rod, which she always carried with her. The school consisted mostly of girls. It was the custom of the school for all to spell loudly and in as high a key as possible. The mistress dared not beat me, as my mother had made it a condition of my going that I should not be touched. One day having got a hit of the rod, I rose immediately, took my book, and without further ceremony went home to my mother, asked that I might go to another school, and that was granted me. My mother sent me to Carsten's school for boys ; there was also one girl there, a little one somewhat older than I ; we became very good friends ; she used to speak of the advantage it was to be to her in going into service, and that she went to school especially to learn arithemetic, for, as her mother told her, she could then become dairy-maid in some great manor.

"That you can become in my castle when I am a nobleman ! " said I, and she laughed at me and told me that I was only a poor boy. One day I had drawn something which I called my castle, and I told her that I was a changed child of high birth, and that the angels of God came down and spoke to me. I wanted to make her stare as I did with the old women in the hospital, but she would not be caught. She looked queerly at me, and said to one of the other boys standing near, " He is a fool like his grandpapa," and I shivered at the words. I had said it to give me an air of importance in their eyes, but I failed and only made them think that I was insane like my grandfather.

I never spoke to her again about these things, but we were no longer the same playmates as before. I was the smallest in the school, and my teacher, Mr. Carsten, always took me by the hand while the other boys played, that I might not be run over ; he loved me much, gave me cakes and flowers, and tapped me on the cheeks. One of the older boys did not know his lesson and was punished by being placed, book in hand, upon the school-table, around which we were seated, but seeing me quite inconsolable at this punishment, he pardoned the culprit.

The poor old teacher became, later in life telegraph-director at Thorseng, where he still lived until a few years since. It is said that the old man, when showing the visitors around, told them with a pleasant smile : " Well, well, you will perhaps not believe that such a poor old man as I was the first teacher of one of our most renowned poets !   H. C. Andersen was one of my scholars ! "

Sometimes, during the harvest, my mother went into the field to glean.   I accompanied her, and we went. like Ruth in the Bible, to glean in the rich fields of Boaz.   One day we went to a place the bailiff of which was well known for being a man of a rude and savage disposition.   We saw him coming with a huge whip in his hand, and my mother and all the others ran away.   I had wooden shoes on my bare feet, and in my haste I lost these, and then the thorns pricked me so that I could not run, and thus I was left behind and alone.   The man came up and lifted his whip to strike me, when I looked him in the face and involuntarily exclaimed, — How dare you strike me, when God can see it ? "

The strong, stern man looked at me, and at once became mild ; he patted me on my cheeks, asked me my name, and gave me money. '

When I brought this to my mother and showed it her, she said to the others, " He is a strange child, my Hans Christian ; everybody is kind to him : this bad fellow even has given him money."

I grew up pious and superstitious ; I had not the least idea of what it was to be in want ; my father lived, as the saying is, from hand to mouth, but what we had was more than enough for me.   As to my dress I was rather spruce ; an old woman altered my father's clothes for me ; my mother would fasten three or four large pieces of silk with pins on my breast, and that had to do for vests ; a large kerchief was tied round my neck with a mighty bow ; my head was washed with soap and my hair curled, and then I was in all my glory.

In that attire I went with my parents for the first time to the theatre.   Odense at that time had already a substantial play-house built, I believe, for the company of Count Trampe or that of Count Hahn ; the first representations I saw were given in the German language.   Mr. Franck was the director ; he gave operas and comedies.   " Das Donauweibchen " was the favorite piece ; the first representation, however, that I saw was Holberg's " Village Politicians."

The first impressions which a theatre and the crowd assembled there made upon me was, at all events, no sign of anything poetical slumbering in me ; for my first exclamation on seeing so many people was, " Now, if we only had as many casks of butter as there are people here, then I would eat lots of butter ! " The theatre, however, soon became my favorite place, but, as I could only very seldom go there, I acquired the friendship of the man who carried out the play-bills, and he gave me one every day. With this I seated my-self in a corner and imagined an entire play, according to the name of the piece and the characters in it. That was my first, unconscious poetizing.

My father's favorite reading was plays and stories, although he also read works of history and the Scriptures. He pondered in silent thought afterward upon that which he had read ; but my mother did not understand him when he talked with her about it, and therefore he grew more and more silent. One day he closed the Bible with the words, " Christ was a man like us, but an extraordinary man ! " These words horri-fied my mother and she burst into tears. In my distress I prayed to God that he would forgive this fearful blasphemy in my father. " There is no other devil than that which we have in our own hearts," I heard my father say one day, and I made myself miserable about him and his soul ; I was there-fore entirely of the opinion of my mother and the neighbors, when my father, one morning, found three scratches on his arm, probably occasioned by a nail, that the devil had been to visit him in the night, in order to prove to him that he really existed.

My father had not many friends ; in his leisure hours he used to take me with him out into the woods. He had a great desire for country life, and it happened just at this time that a shoemaker was required at a manor house who would set up his bench in the neighboring village, and there have a house free of rent, a little garden, and pasture for a cow ; by perma-nent work from the manor and these additional helps one could manage nicely. My mother and father were very eager to have the place, and my father got a trial job to sew a pair of dancing-shoes ; a piece of silk was sent him, the leather he was to furnish himself. All our talk for a couple of days turned upon these shoes ; I longed so much for the little garden where we could have flowers and shrubs, and I would sit in the sunshine and listen to the cuckoo. I prayed very fervently to God that he would grant us our wishes, and I thought that no greater happiness could be bestowed upon us. The shoes were at last finished ; we looked on them with a solemn feeling, for they were to decide our future. My father wrapped them in his handkerchief and went off, and we waited for him with faces beaming with joy. He came home pale and angry ; the gracious lady, he said, had not even tried the shoes on, — only looked at them sourly, and said that the silk was spoiled and that he could not get the place. "If you have spoiled your silk," said my father, " I can be reconciled to spoiling my leather too," so he took a knife and cut off the soles.

There was no more hope of our getting into the country. We mingled our tears together, and I thought that God could easily have granted our wish. If he had done so, I had no doubt been a peasant all my life ; my whole future would have been different from what it has been. I have often since thought and said to myself: Do you think that our Lord for your sake and for your future has let your parents lose their days of happiness ?

My father's rambles in the wood became more frequent ; he had no rest. The events of the war in Germany, which he read in the newspapers with eager curiosity, occupied him completely. Napoleon was his hero : his rise from obscurity was the most beautiful example to him. At that time Denmark was in league with France ; nothing was talked of but war ; my father entered the service as a soldier, in hope of returning home a lieutenant. My mother wept, the neighbors shrugged their shoulders, and said that it was folly to go out to be shot when there was no occasion for it.

The morning on which the corps were to march I heard my father singing and talking merrily, but his heart was deeply agitated ; I observed that by the passionate manner in which he kissed me when he took his leave. I lay sick of the measles and alone in the room, when the drums beat, and my mother accompanied my father, weeping, to the city gate. As soon as they were gone my old grandmother came in ; she looked at me with her mild eyes and said it would be a good thing if I died ; but that God's will was always the best.

That was the first day of real sorrow which I remember.

The regiment advanced no further than Holstein ; peace was concluded, and the voluntary soldier returned to his work-stool. Everything fell into its old course. I played again with my dolls, acted comedies, always in German, because I had only seen them in this language ; but my German was a sort of gibberish which I made up, and in which there occurred only one real German word, and that was " *Besen*," a word which I had picked up out of the various dialects which my father brought home from Holstein.

" Thou hast indeed some benefit from my travels," said he in joke. " God knows whether thou wilt get as far ; but that must be thy care. Think about it, Hans Christian ! " But it was my mother's intention that, as long as she had any voice in the matter, I should remain at home, and not lose my health as he had done.

That was the case with him : his health had suffered. One morning he woke in a state of the wildest excitement, and talked only of campaigns and Napoleon. He fancied that he had received orders from him to take the command. My mother immediately sent me, not to the physician but to a so-called wise woman some miles from Odense. I went to her. She questioned me, measured my arm with a woolen thread, made extraordinary signs, and at last laid a green twig upon my breast. It was, she said, a piece of the same kind of tree upon which the Saviour was crucified.

" Go now," said she, " by the river side toward home. If your father is to die this time, then you will meet his ghost."

My anxiety and distress may be imagined, — I, who was so full of superstition, and whose imagination was so easily excited.

" And thou hast not met anything, hast thou ? " inquired my mother when I got home. I assured her, with beating heart, that I had not.

My father died the third day after that. His corpse lay on the bed ; I therefore slept with my mother. A cricket chirped the whole night through.

" He is dead," said my mother, addressing it ; " thou needest not call him. The ice maiden has fetched him."

I understood what she meant. I recollected that, in the winter before, when our window-panes were frozen, my father pointed to them and showed us a figure like that of a maiden with outstretched arms. " She is come to fetch me," said he, in jest. And now, when he lay dead on the bed, my mother remembered this, and it occupied my thoughts also.

He was buried in St. Knud's church-yard, by the door on the left-hand side coming from the altar. My grandmother planted roses upon his grave. There are now in the self-same place two strangers' graves, and the grass grows green upon them also.

After my father's death I was entirely left to myself. My mother went out washing. I sat alone at home with my little theatre, made dolls' clothes, and read plays. It has been told me that I was always clean and nicely dressed. I had grown tall ; my hair was long, bright, and almost yellow, and I always went bareheaded. There dwelt in our neighborhood the widow of a clergyman, Madame Bunkeflod, with the sister of her deceased husband. This lady opened to me her door, and hers was the first house belonging to the educated class into which I was kindly received. The deceased clergyman had written poems, and had gained a reputation in Danish litera-ture. His spinning songs were at that time in the mouths of the people. In my vignettes to the Danish poets I thus sang of him whom my contemporaries had forgotten, —

> Spindles rattle, wheels turn round,
>   Spinning songs depart ;
> Songs which youth sings soon become
>   Music of the heart.

Here it was that I heard for the first time the word *poet* spoken, and that with so much reverence, as proved it to be something sacred. It is true that my father had read Hol-berg's plays to me ; but here it was not of these that they spoke, but of verses and poetry. " My brother the poet," said

Bunkeflod's sister, and her eyes sparkled as she said it. From her I learned that it was a something glorious, a something fortunate, to be a poet. Here, too, for the first time, I read Shakespeare, — in a bad translation, to be sure ; but the bold descriptions, the heroic incidents, witches, and ghosts were exactly to my taste. I immediately acted Shakespeare's plays on my little puppet theatre. I saw Hamlet's ghost, and lived upon the heath with Lear. The more persons died in a play, the more interesting I thought it. At this time I wrote my first piece : it was nothing less than a tragedy, wherein, as a matter of course, everybody died. The subject of it I borrowed from an old song about Pyramus and Thisbe ; but I had increased the incidents through a hermit and his son, who both loved Thisbe, and who both killed themselves when she died. Many speeches of the hermit were passages from the Bible, taken out of the Little Catechism, especially from our duty to our neighbors. To the piece I gave the title " Abor and Elvira."

" It ought to be called ' Perch (Aborre) and Stockfish,' " said one of our neighbors wittily to me as I came with it to her after having read it with great satisfaction and joy to all the people in our street. This entirely depressed me, because I felt that she was turning both me and my poem into ridicule. With a troubled heart, I told it to my mother.

" She only said so," replied my mother, " because her son had not done it." I was comforted, and began a new piece, in which a king and queen were among the *dramatis personæ.* I thought it was not quite right that these dignified personages, as in Shakespeare, should speak like other men and women. I asked my mother and different people how a king ought properly to speak, but no one knew exactly. They said that it was so many years since a king had been in Odense, but that he certainly spoke in a foreign language. I procured myself, therefore, a sort of lexicon, in which were German, French, and English words with Danish meanings, and this helped me. I took a word out of each language, and inserted them into the speeches of my king and queen. It was a regular Babel-like language, which I considered only suitable for such elevated personages.

I desired now that everybody should hear my piece. It was a real felicity to me to read it aloud, and it never occurred to me that others should not have the same pleasure in listening to it.

The son of one of our neighbors worked in a cloth manufactory, and every week brought home a sum of money. I was at loose ends, people said, and got nothing. I was also now to go to the manufactory, "not for the sake of the money," my mother said, "but that she might know where I was, and what I was doing."

My old grandmother took me to the place, therefore, and was very much affected, because, said she, she had not expected to live to see the time when I should consort with the poor ragged lads that worked there.

Many of the journeymen who were employed in the manufactory were Germans; they sang and were merry fellows, and many a coarse joke of theirs filled the place with loud laughter. I heard them, and I there learned that, to the innocent ears of a child, the impure remains very unintelligible. It took no hold upon my heart. I was possessed at that time of a remarkably beautiful and high soprano voice, and I knew it; because when I sang in my parents' little garden, the people in the street stood and listened, and the fine folks in the garden of the states-councilor, which adjoined ours, listened at the fence. When, therefore, the people at the manufactory asked me whether I could sing, I immediately began, and all the looms stood still: all the journeymen listened to me. I had to sing again and again, whilst the other boys had my work given them to do. I now told them that I also could act plays, and that I knew whole scenes of Holberg and Shakespeare. Everybody liked me; and in this way the first days in the manufactory passed on very merrily. One day, however, when I was in my best singing vein, and everybody spoke of the extraordinary brilliancy of my voice, one of the journeymen said that I was a girl, and not a boy. He seized hold of me. I cried and screamed. The other journeymen thought it very amusing, and held me fast by my arms and legs. I screamed aloud, and was as much ashamed as a girl; and then, darting from them, rushed home to my mother, who immediately promised me that I should never go there again.

I again visited Madame Bunkeflod, for whose birthday I invented and made a white silk pincushion. I also made an acquaintance with another old clergyman's widow in the neighborhood. She permitted me to read aloud to her the works which she had from the circulating library. One of them began with these words : " It was a tempestuous night ; the rain beat against the window-panes."

" That is an extraordinary book," said the old lady ; and I quite innocently asked her how she knew that it was. "I can tell from the beginning," said she, " that it will turn out extraordinary."

I regarded her penetration with a sort of reverence.

Once in the harvest time my mother took me with her many miles from Odense to a nobleman's seat in the neighborhood of Bogense, her native place. The lady who lived there, and with whose parents my mother had lived, had said that some time she might come and see her. That was a great journey for me : we went most of the way on foot, and required, I believe, two days for the journey. The country here made such a strong impression upon me, that my most earnest wish was to remain in it, and become a countryman. It was just in the hop-picking season ; my mother and I sat in the barn with a great many country people round a great bin, and helped to pick the hops. They told tales as they sat at their work, and every one related what wonderful things he had seen or experienced. One afternoon I heard an old man among them say that God knew everything, both what had happened and what would happen. That idea occupied my whole mind, and toward evening, as I went alone from the court, where there was a deep pond, and stood upon some stones which were just within the water, the thought passed through my head, whether God actually knew everything which was to happen there. Yes, he has now determined that I should live and be so many years old, thought I ; but, if I now were to jump into the water here and drown myself, then it would not be as he wished ; and all at once I was firmly and resolutely determined to drown myself. I ran to where the water was deepest, and then a new thought passed through my soul. " It is the devil who wishes to have power over me ! " I uttered a loud cry, and, running away from the place as if I were pursued, fell weeping into my mother's arms. But neither she nor any one else could wring from me what was amiss with me.

" He has certainly seen a ghost," said one of the women, and I almost believed so myself.

My mother married a second time, a young handicraftsman ; but his family, who also belonged to the handicraft class, thought that he had married below himself, and neither my mother nor myself were permitted to visit them. My step-father was a young, grave man, who would have nothing to do with my education. I spent my time, therefore, over my peep-show and my puppet theatre, and my greatest happiness consisted in collecting bright colored pieces of cloth and silk, which I cut out myself, and sewed. My mother regarded it as good exercise preparatory to my becoming a tailor, and took up the idea that I certainly was born for it. I, on the contrary, said that I would go to the theatre and be an actor, a wish which my mother most sedulously opposed, because she knew of no other theatre than those of the strolling players and the rope-dancers. " Be sure, you will then get good whip-pings," said she ; " they will starve you to death to make you supple, and they will give you oil to eat to make your limbs soft ! " No, a tailor I must and should be. " You see how well Mr. Dickmann, the tailor, is getting on ! " Mr. Dickmann, was the first tailor in the town. " He lives in Cross Street, has large windows and journeymen on the table ; yes, if you could only be such a one ! " The only thing which in some meas-ure reconciled me to this prospect was, that I should then get so many fragments to make up for my theatre.

My parents moved to a street out of the Monk-Mill's gate, and there we had a garden ; it was a very little and narrow one, containing only one long garden-bed with currant and gooseberry bushes, and the path that led down to the river behind the monk-mill. Three great water-wheels were turn-ing round from the falling water, and stopped when the water-gates were closed ; then all the water ran out from the river, the bed dried up, the fishes plashed and jumped in its hollows so that I could catch them with my hands, and under the great water-wheels fat water-rats came forth to drink; suddenly the water-gates were opened and the water rushed roaring and foaming down: no rats were now to be seen, the river-bed was again filled, and I ran plashing through the water, as frightened as the amber-gatherers on the coasts of the western sea, when they happen to be far out and the flood sets in. I stood upon one of the big stones my mother used for wash-board and sang with all my might the songs I knew, and sometimes there was neither meaning nor melody in them, but still I sang my own self-made tunes as well as I could. The neighboring garden belonged to Mr. Falbe, whose wife Oehlenschläger mentions in his autobiography; she had formerly been actress, and was beautiful as *Ida Münster* in the drama " Herman von Unna ; " she was then Miss Beck.

When they had company in the garden they were always listening to my singing, and I knew it. All told me that I had a beautiful voice, which would bring me luck in the world. I often meditated how this luck should come, and as the wonderful has always been truth for me, so I expected the most marvelous things would happen.

An old woman who rinsed clothes in the river, told me that the Empire of China was situated straight under the very river of Odense, and I did not find it impossible at all that a Chinese prince, some moonlight night when I was sitting there, might dig himself through the earth up to us, hear me sing, and so take me down with him to his kingdom, make me rich and noble, and then let me again visit Odense, where I would live and build me a castle. Many evenings I was occupied with tracing and making ground-plans for it.

I was quite a child, and long afterwards when declaiming and reading my poems in Copenhagen, I still expected and hoped for such a prince among my auditors, who would hear me, understand me, and help me.

My passion for reading, the many dramatic scenes which I knew by heart, and my remarkably fine voice, had turned upon me in some sort the attention of several of the more influential families of Odense. I was sent for to their houses,

and the peculiar characteristics of my mind excited their interest. Among others who noticed me was the Colonel Hoegh-Guldberg, who with his family showed me the kindest sympathy; so much so, indeed, that he introduced me to Prince Christian, afterward King Christian the Eighth.

"If the prince should ask you what you have a liking for," said he, "answer him that your highest desire is to enter the grammar school." So I said this to the prince when he really asked me this question, and he answered me, that my singing and declamation of poetry was really good and beautiful, but for all that was no mark of genius, and that I must keep in mind that studying was a long and expensive course! in the mean time he would take care of me if I would learn a handy trade, for instance that of a turner. I had no inclination at all for it, and I went away very much disappointed, although this noble prince had spoken very naturally and was quite in the right. Since that, when my abilities were more clearly shown, he was, as we shall see, very kind and good toward me until his death, and he is held in my memory with the most tender feelings.

I grew rapidly, and was a tall lad, of whom my mother said that she could not let him any longer go about without any object in life. I was sent, therefore, to the charity school, but learned only religion, writing, and arithmetic, and the last badly enough; I could also scarcely spell a word correctly. I never studied my lessons at home; I used to learn them on the way to school and my mother boasting of my good memory at the expense of our neighbor's son, said, " He reads till it hums, but Hans Christian does not need to open his book and yet he knows his lesson." On the master's birthday I always wove him a garland and wrote him a poem; he received them half with smiles and half as a joke: the last time, however, he scolded me. His name was Velhaven and he was from Norway; he was no doubt a good man, but was of a violent nature, and seemed to be very unhappy. He spoke in earnest about religion, and when he went through our lessons in Biblical history he did it in such a vivid fashion that, listening to him, all the painted pictures on the wall-hangings representing scenes from the Old Testament, became full of life and had for me the same beauty, truth, and freshness that I afterwards found in the magnificent pictures of Raphael and Titian. Often I sat dreaming and gazing on the variegated wall, and he gave me a little reprimand because I was absent-minded. I told the boys curious stories in which I was always the chief person, but was sometimes rallied for that. The street lads had also heard from their parents of my peculiar turn of mind, and that I was in the habit of going to the houses of the gentry. I was therefore one day pursued by a wild crowd of them, who shouted after me derisively, "There runs the play-writer!" I hid myself at home in a corner, wept, and prayed to God.

My mother said that I must be confirmed, in order that I might be apprenticed to the tailor trade, and thus do something rational. She loved me with her whole heart, but she did not understand my impulses and my endeavors, nor indeed at that time did I myself. The people about her always spoke against my odd ways, and turned me to ridicule.

We belonged to the parish of St. Knud, and the candidates for Confirmation could either enter their names with the provost or the chaplain. The children of the so-called superior families and the scholars of the grammar school went to the first, and the children of the poor to the second. I, however, announced myself as a candidate to the provost, who was obliged to receive me, although he discovered vanity in my placing myself among his catechists, where, although taking the lowest place, I was still above those who were under the care of the chaplain. I would, however, hope that it was not alone vanity which impelled me. I had a sort of fear of the poor boys, who had laughed at me, and I always felt, as it were, an inward drawing towards the scholars of the grammar school, whom I regarded as far better than other boys. When I saw them playing in the church-yard, I would stand outside the railings, and wish that I were but among the fortunate ones — not for the sake of play, but for the sake of the many books they had, and for what they might be able to become in the world. At the provost's, therefore, I should be able to associate with them, and be as they were ; but I do not remember a single one of them now, so little intercourse would they hold with me. I had daily the feeling of having thrust myself in where people thought that I did not belong. One young girl, however, there was, and one who was considered, too, of the highest rank, whom I shall afterwards have occasion to mention ; she always looked gently and kindly at me, and even once gave me a rose. I returned home full of happiness, because there was one being who did not overlook and repel me.

An old female tailor altered my deceased father's great coat into a confirmation suit for me ; never before had I worn so good a coat. I had also, for the first time in my life, a pair of boots. My delight was extremely great ; my only fear was that everybody would not see them, and therefore I drew them up over my trousers, and thus marched through the church. The boots creaked, and that inwardly pleased me, for thus the congregation would hear that they were new. My whole devotion was disturbed ; I was aware of it, and it caused me a horrible pang of conscience that my thoughts should be as much with my new boots as with God. I prayed him earnestly from my heart to forgive me, and then again I thought about my new boots.

During the last year I had saved together a little sum of money. When I counted it over I found it to be thirteen rix dollars banco (about thirty shillings). I was quite overjoyed at the possession of so much wealth, and as my mother now most resolutely required that I should be apprenticed to a tailor, I prayed and besought her that I might make a journey to Copenhagen, that I might see the greatest city in the world.

" What wilt thou do there ? " asked my mother.

" I will be famous," returned I ; and I then told her all that I had read about extraordinary men. " People have," said I, " at first an immense deal of adversity to go through, and then they will be famous."

It was a wholly unintelligible impulse that guided me. I wept, I prayed, and at last my mother consented, after having first sent for a so-called wise woman out of the hospital, that she might read my future fortune by the coffee-grounds and cards.

" Your son will become a great man," said the old woman, " and in honor of him Odense will one day be illuminated."

My mother wept when she heard that, and I obtained permission to travel. All the neighbors told my mother that it
was a dreadful thing to let me, at only fourteen years of age,
go to Copenhagen, which was such a long way off, and such a
great and intricate city, and where I knew nobody.

"Yes," replied my mother, "but he lets me have no peace;
I have therefore given my consent, but I am sure that he will
go no further than Nyborg: when he gets sight of the rough
sea, he will be frightened and turn back again."

During the summer before my Confirmation, a part of the
singers and performers of the Theatre Royal had been in
Odense, and had given a series of operas and tragedies there.
The whole city was taken with them. I, who was on good
terms with the man who delivered the play-bills, saw the
performances behind the scenes, and had even acted a part
as page, shepherd, etc., and had spoken a few words. My
zeal was so great on such occasions, that I stood there
fully appareled when the actors arrived to dress. By these
means their attention was turned to me; my childlike manners and my enthusiasm amused them; they talked kindly
with me, and I looked up to them as to earthly divinities.
Everything which I had formerly heard about my musical
voice, and my recitation of poetry, became intelligible to me.
It was the theatre for which I was born; it was there that I
should become a famous man, and for that reason Copenhagen
was the goal of my endeavors. I heard a deal said about the
large theatre in Copenhagen, and that there was to be seen
what was called the ballet, a something which surpassed both
the opera and the play; more especially did I hear the
danseuse, Madame Schall, spoken of as the first of all. She
therefore appeared to me as the queen of everything, and in
my imagination I regarded her as the one who would be able
to do everything for me, if I could only obtain her support.
Filled with these thoughts, I went to the old printer Iversen,
one of the most respectable citizens of Odense, and who, as
I heard, had had considerable intercourse with the actors
when they were in the town. He, I thought, must of necessity
be acquainted with the famous dancer; him I would request
to give me a letter of introduction to her, and then I would
commit the rest to God.

The old man saw me for the first time, and heard my petition with much kindness ; but he dissuaded me most earnestly
from it, and said that I might learn a trade.

" That would actually be a great sin," returned I.

He was startled at the manner in which I said that, and it
prepossessed him in my favor ; he confessed that he was not
personally acquainted with the dancer, but still that he would
give me a letter to her. I received one from him, and now
believed the goal to be nearly won.

My mother packed up my clothes in a small bundle, and
made a bargain with the driver of a post carriage to take me
back with him to Copenhagen for three rix dollars banco.
The afternoon on which we were to set out came, and my
mother accompanied me to the city gate. Here stood my
old grandmother ; in the last few years her beautiful hair had
become gray ; she fell upon my neck and wept, without being
able to speak a word. I was myself deeply affected. And
thus we parted. I saw her no more ; she died in the following year. I do not even know her grave ; she sleeps in the
poor-house burial-ground.

The postilion blew his horn ; it was a glorious sunny afternoon, and the sunshine soon entered into my gay, child-like
mind. I delighted in every novel object which met my eye,
and I was journeying toward the goal of my soul's desires.
When, however, I arrived at Nyborg on the great Belt, and
was borne in the ship away from my native island, I then
truly felt how alone and forlorn I was, and that I had no one
else except God in heaven to depend upon.

As soon as I set foot on Zealand, I stepped behind a shed
which stood on the shore, and falling upon my knees, besought
of God to help and guide me aright ; I felt myself comforted
by so doing, and I firmly trusted in God and my own good
fortune. The whole day and the following night I travelled
through cities and villages ; I stood solitarily by the carriage,
and ate my bread while it was repacked. I thought I was
far away in the wide world.

CHAPTER II.

ON Monday morning, September 5th, 1819, I saw from the heights of Fredericksberg, Copenhagen for the first time. At this place I alighted from the carriage, and with my little bundle in my hand, entered the city through the castle garden, the long alley, and the suburb.

The evening before my arrival had been made memorable by the breaking out of the so-called Jews' quarrel, which spread through many European countries. The whole city was in commotion everybody was in the streets ; the noise and tumult of Copenhagen far exceeded, therefore, any idea which my imagination had formed of this, at that time, to me great city.

With scarcely ten dollars in my pocket, I turned into a small public-house. My first ramble was to the theatre. I went round it many times : I looked up to its walls, and regarded them almost as a home. One of the bill-sellers, who wandered about here each day, observed me, and asked me if I would have a bill. I was so wholly ignorant of the world, that I thought the man wished to give me one ; I therefore accepted his offer with thankfulness. He fancied I was making fun of him, and was angry ; so that I was frightened, and hastened from the place which was to me the dearest in the city. Little did I then imagine that ten years afterward my first dramatic piece would be represented there, and that in this manner I should make my appearance before the Danish public.

On the following day I dressed myself in my confirmation suit, nor were the boots forgotten, although, this time, they were worn naturally, under my trousers ; and thus in my best attire, with a hat on, which fell half over my eyes, I hastened to present my letter of introduction to the dancer, Madame Schall. Before I rung at the bell, I fell on my knees before

the door and prayed God that I here might find help and
support.   A maid-servant came down the steps with her basket in her hand ; she smiled kindly at me, gave me a skilling
(Danish), and tripped on.   Astonished, I looked at her and
the money.   I had on my confirmation suit, and thought I
must look very smart.   How then could she think that I
wanted to beg ?   I called after her.

"Keep it, keep it !" said she to me, in return, and was
gone.

At length I was admitted to the dancer ; she looked at me
in great amazement, and then heard what I had to say.   She
had not the slightest knowledge of him from whom the letter
came, and my whole appearance and behavior seemed very
strange to her.   I confessed to her my heartfelt inclination
for the theatre ; and upon her asking me what characters I
thought I could represent, I replied, *Cinderella.*   This piece
had been performed in Odense by the royal company, and
the principal characters had so greatly taken my fancy, that I
could play the part perfectly from memory.   In the mean time
I asked her permission to take off my boots, otherwise I was
not light enough for this character ; and then taking up my
broad hat for a tambourine, I began to dance and sing, —

"Here below, nor rank nor riches
Are exempt from pain and woe."

My strange gestures and my great activity caused the lady
to think me out of my mind, and she lost no time in getting
rid of me.

From her I went to the manager of the theatre, to ask for
an engagement.   He looked at me, and said that I was "too
thin for the theatre."

"O," replied I, "if you will only engage me with one hundred rix-dollars banco salary, then I shall soon get fat !"
The manager bade me gravely go my way, adding, that they
only engaged people of education.

I stood there deeply wounded.   I knew no one in all
Copenhagen who could give me either counsel or consolation.
I thought of death as being the only thing, and the best thing
for me ; but even then my thoughts rose upward to God, and
with all the undoubting confidence of a child in his father,

they riveted themselves upon Him. I wept bitterly, and then I said to myself, "When everything happens quite miserably, then He sends help. I have always read so. People must first of all suffer a great deal before they can bring anything to accomplishment."

I now went and bought myself a gallery ticket for the opera of " Paul and Virginia." The separation of the lovers affected me to such a degree, that I burst into violent weeping. A few women, who sat near me, consoled me by saying that it was only a play, and nothing to trouble one's self about ; and then they gave me a sausage sandwich. I had the greatest confidence in everybody, and therefore I told them, with the utmost openness, that I did not really weep about Paul and Virginia, but because I regarded the theatre as my Virginia, and that if I must be separated from it, I should be just as wretched as Paul. They looked at me, and seemed not to understand my meaning. I then told them why I had come to Copenhagen, and how forlorn I was there. One of the women, therefore, gave me more bread and butter, with fruit and cakes.

On the following morning I paid my bill, and to my infinite trouble I saw that my whole wealth consisted in one rix-dollar banco. It was necessary, therefore, either that I should find some vessel to take me home, or put myself to work with some handicraftsman. I considered that the last was the wiser of the two, because if I returned to Odense, I must there also put myself to work of a similar kind ; besides which, I knew very well that the people there would laugh at me if I came back again. It was to me a matter of indifference what handicraft trade I learned, — I only should make use of it to keep life within me in Copenhagen. I bought a newspaper, therefore, and found among the advertisements that a cabinet-maker was in want of an apprentice. The man received me kindly, but said that before I was bound to him he must have an attestation, and my baptismal register from Odense ; and that till these came I could remove to his house, and try how the business pleased me. At six o'clock the next morning I went to the workshop : several journeymen were there, and two or three apprentices ; but the master was

not come. They fell into merry and idle discourse. I was as
bashful as a girl, and as they soon perceived this, I was un-
mercifully rallied upon it.   Later in the day the rude jests of
the young fellows went so far, that, in remembrance of the
scene at the manufactory, I took the resolute determination
not to remain a single day longer in the workshop. I went
down to the master, therefore, and told him that I could not
stand it ; he tried to console me, but in vain : I was too much
affected, and hastened away.

I now went through the streets ; nobody knew me ; I was
quite forlorn. I then bethought myself of having read in a
newspaper in Odense the name of an Italian, Siboni, who was
the director of the Academy of Music in Copenhagen.   Everybody had praised my voice ; perhaps he would assist me for
its sake ; if not, then that very evening I must seek out the
master of some vessel who would take me home again. At
the thoughts of the journey home I became still more violently excited, and in this state of suffering I hastened to Siboni's house.

It happened that very day that he had a large party to dinner ; our celebrated composer Weyse was there, the poet Baggesen, and other guests. The housekeeper opened the door to
me, and to her I not only related my wish to be engaged as a
singer, but also the whole history of my life. She listened to
me with the greatest sympathy and then she left me. I waited
a long time, and she must have been repeating to the company the greater part of what I had said, for, in a while, the
door opened, and all the guests came out and looked at me.
They would have me to sing, and Siboni heard me attentively.
I gave some scenes out of Holberg, and repeated a few
poems ; and then, all at once, the sense of my unhappy condition so overcame me that I burst into tears ; the whole company applauded.

"I prophesy," said Baggesen, "that one day something
will come out of him ; but do not be vain when, some day,
the whole public shall applaud thee !." and then he added
something about pure, true nature, and that this is too often
destroyed by years and by intercourse with mankind. I did
not understand it all. I believed implicitly every man's word

and that all wished me well ; I did not keep a thought to myself, but always spoke it right out.

Siboni promised to cultivate my voice, and that I therefore should succeed as singer at the Theatre Royal.   It made me very happy ; I laughed and wept ; and as the housekeeper led me out and saw the excitement under which I labored, she stroked my cheeks, and said that on the following day I should go to Professor Weyse, who meant to do something for me, and upon whom I could depend.

I went to Weyse, who himself had risen from poverty ; he had deeply felt and fully comprehended my unhappy situation, and had raised by a subscription seventy rix-dollars banco for me.   I then wrote my first letter to my mother, a letter full of rejoicing, for the good fortune of the whole world seemed poured upon me.   My mother in her joy showed my letter to all her friends ; many heard of it with astonishment ; others laughed at it, for what was to be the end of it ?   In order to understand Siboni it was necessary for me to learn something of German. A woman of Copenhagen, with whom I travelled from Odense to this city, and who gladly would have supported me, had her means permitted, obtained, through one of her acquaintance, a language-master, who gratuitously gave me some German lessons, and thus I learned a few phrases in that language. Siboni received me into his house, and gave me food and instruction.   He had an Italian cook and two smart servant-girls ; one of them had been in Mr. Casorti's service and spoke Italian ; I spent the day with them, willingly ran their errands and listened to their stories ; but one day having been sent by them to the dinner-table with one of the dishes, Mr. Siboni arose, went out in the kitchen, and said to the servants that I was no " cameriére ; " and from that time I came oftener into the parlor, where his niece Marietta, a girl of talent, was occupied in drawing Siboni's picture as *Achilles* in Paer's opera ; I acted as model, dressed in a large tunic or toga, fit for the tall and strong Siboni, but not for me, a poor, lean, overgrown boy ; this contrast, however, amused the lively Italian lady, who laughed heartily and drew with great rapidity.

The opera singers came daily for practice, and sometimes I was allowed to be present.

" Il maestro " became sometimes under the singing so discontented that his Italian blood flew up into his cheeks, and
he burst out violently in German or in queer Danish.   Al
though it did not concern me, I was so frightened that I shivered in all my limbs.   He on whom I believed my whole future was depending, made me shake with fear, and sometimes,
when he was giving me a lesson, his severe look would make
my voice to quiver and bring tears into my eyes.

" Hikke banke Du " (I shall not beat you), said he in
broken Danish and let me go ; but calling me back again he
put some money into my hand, " to amuse yourself with," said
he, with a kind-hearted smile.

After all, I have since understood that Mr. Siboni was an
excellent singing-master, the founder of a good school of dramatic singing, but not so esteemed by the public as he deserved
to be.   Most people looked on him as a foreigner, who was
eating bread that might just as well have been given to a native, not knowing that among the natives there was not one
so good and able as he.

The Italian operas, which at that time had a great reputation throughout Europe, and were brought upon our stage by
Siboni, were received with hostility only because they were
Italian operas and Mr. Siboni an Italian.   " Gazza badra "
was hissed, also " La Straniera," and when Siboni at his benefit had chosen Paer's German opera, " Die Rache des Achilles," in which he played the chief part, he was hissed.   The
injustice of this and Siboni's great merit have been, since his
death, acknowledged by many, who at that time despised and
overlooked compositions of Rossini and Bellini, but a few
years after were applauding Verdi and Ricci, and it went so
far finally that no music or singing were of any value except
they were Italian ; but Mr. Siboni did not live to see that
change.

He tried with his whole soul to teach his pupils not only to
sing, but also to understand and conceive the character they
were representing.   He was in want of words to express himself in the German language, and the Danish he knew far less.
Most of the singers could only understand one of those languages, and this often occasioned comical scenes.

Half a year afterward my voice broke, or was injured, in consequence of my being compelled to wear bad shoes through the winter, and having besides no warm under-clothing. There was no longer any prospect that I should become a fine singer. Siboni told me that candidly, and counseled me to go to Odense, and there learn a trade.

I who in the rich colors of fancy had described to my mother the happiness which I actually felt, must now return home and become an object of derision! Agonized with this thought, I stood as if crushed to the earth. Yet, precisely amid this apparently great unhappiness lay the stepping-stones of a better fortune.

As I found myself again abandoned, and was pondering by myself upon what was best for me next to do, it occurred to me that the Poet Guldberg, a brother of the Colonel of that name in Odense, who had shown me so much kindness, lived in Copenhagen. He lived at that time near the new church-yard outside the city, of which he has so beautifully sung in his poems. I wrote to him, and related to him everything; afterward I went to him myself, and found him surrounded with books and tobacco pipes. The strong, warm-hearted man received me kindly; and as he saw by my letter how incorrectly I wrote, he promised to give me instruction in the Danish tongue; he examined me a little in German, and thought that it would be well if he could improve me in this respect also. More than this, he made me a present of the profits of a little work which he had just then published; it became known, and I believe they exceeded one hundred rix-dollars banco; the excellent Weyse and others also supported me. He and other good people subscribed a little sum for me, and the two servant-girls who lived at Siboni's also offered me kindly of their wages nine Danish marks quarterly; they only paid the first quarter, but still it proved their good-will toward me. I have never since seen these girls.

The composer, Mr. Kuhlau, with whom I never had spoken, was also among the subscribers; Kuhlau himself had known what it was to be a poor child; he was brought up in poverty, and it is told me, that he ran errands in the cold winter, and one evening, having gone for a bottle of beer, he fell and broke the bottle, and by the accident lost the sight of one of his eyes.

It was too expensive for me to lodge at a public-house ; I was therefore obliged to seek for private lodgings.   My ignorance of the world led me to a widow who lived in one of the most disreputable streets of Copenhagen ; she was inclined to receive me into her house, and I never suspected what kind of world it was which moved around me.   She was a stern but active dame ; she described to me the other people of the city in such horrible colors as made me suppose that I was in the only safe haven there.   I was to pay twenty rix-dollars monthly for one room, which was nothing but an empty store-room, without window or light, but I had permission to sit in her parlor.   I was to make trial of it at first for two days ; meantime, on the following day she told me that I could decide to stay or immediately go.   I, who so easily attach myself to people, already liked her, and felt myself at home with her ; but more than sixteen dollars per month Weyse had told me I must not pay, and this was the sum which I had received from him and Guldberg, so that no surplus remained to me for my other expenses.   This troubled me very much ; when she was gone out of the room, I seated myself on the sofa, and contemplated the portrait of her deceased husband. I was so wholly a child, that as the tears rolled down my own cheeks, I wetted the eyes of the portrait with my tears, in order that the dead man might feel how troubled I was, and influence the heart of his wife.   She must have seen that nothing more was to be drained out of me, for when she returned to the room she said that she would receive me into her house for the sixteen rix-dollars.   I thanked God and the dead man.

The following day I brought her all the money, very happy now at finding a home, but not leaving for myself a single skilling to buy me shoes, clothes, or other necessities, of which I was in great want.

I found myself in the midst of the mysteries of Copenhagen, but I did not understand how to interpret them.   There was in the house in which I lived a friendly young lady, who lived alone, and often wept ; every evening her old father came and paid her a visit. I opened the door to him frequently ; he wore a plain sort of coat, had his throat very much tied up, and his hat pulled over his eyes. He always drank his tea with her, and nobody dared to be present, because he was not fond of company : she never seemed very glad at his coming. Many years afterward, when I had reached another step on the ladder of life, when the refined world of fashionable life was opened before me, I saw one evening, in the midst of a brilliantly lighted hall, a polite old gentleman covered with orders : that was the old father in the shabby coat, — he whom I had let in. He had little idea that I had opened the door to him when he played his part as guest, but I, on my side, then had also no thought but for my own comedy-playing ; that is to say, I was at that time so much of a child that I played with my puppet theatre and made my dolls' clothes ; and in order that I might obtain gayly colored fragments for this purpose, I used to go to the shops and ask for patterns of different kinds of stuffs and ribbons. I myself did not possess a single skilling ; my landlady received all the money each month in advance ; only now and then, when I did any errands for her, she gave me something, and that went in the purchase of paper or for old play-books. I got many good and amusing books from the University Library. One day I went up to the University Dean, old Mr. Rasmus Nyrup, who was son of a peasant and had studied at Odense grammar school, and told him that I also was from Odense ; he was struck by my peculiarities, took me into his favor, and allowed me to go and look over the books in the library at the Round Church. He only commanded me to put them again in their right place, and that I did very conscientiously. He let me also take home with me many picture-books.

I was now very happy, and was doubly so because Professor Guldberg had induced Lindgrön, the first comic actor at the theatre, to give me instruction. He gave me several parts in Holberg to learn, — such as *Hendrik* and the *Silly Boy*, for which I had shown some talent. My desire, however, was to play the " Correggio." I obtained permission to learn this piece in my own way, although Lindgrön asked, with comic gravity, whether I expected to resemble the great painter ? I, however, repeated to him the soliloquy in the picture gallery with so much feeling, that the old man clapped me on the shoulder and said, " Feeling you have ; but you must not be an actor, though God knows what else. Speak to Guldberg about your learning Latin : that always opens the way for a student."

I a student ! That was a thought which had never come before into my head. The theatre lay nearer to me, and was dearer too ; yet Latin I had also always wished to learn. But before I spoke on the subject to Guldberg, I mentioned it to the lady who obtained for me gratuitous instruction in German ; she told me that Latin was the most expensive language in the world, and that it was not possible to gain free instruction in it. Guldberg, however, managed it so that one of his friends, Provost Bentzien out of kindness, gave me two lessons a week.

The dancer, Dahlen, whose wife at that time was one of the first artistes on the Danish boards, opened his house to me. I passed many an evening there, and the gentle, warm-hearted lady was kind to me. The husband took me with him to the dancing-school, and that was to me one step nearer to the theatre. There stood I for whole mornings, with a long staff, and stretched my legs ; but notwithstanding all my good-will, it was Dahlen's opinion that I should never get beyond a figurante. One advantage, however, I had gained ; I might in an evening make my appearance behind the scenes of the theatre ; nay, even sit upon the farthest bench in the box of the figurantes. It seemed to me as if I had got my foot just within the theatre, although I had never yet been upon the stage itself.

One night the operetta of the " Two Little Savoyards " was given ; in the market scene, every one, even the supernumeraries, might go up to help in filling the stage ; I heard them say so, and rouging myself a little, I went happily up with the others. I was in my ordinary dress, — the confirmation coat, which still held together, although, with regard to brushing and repairs, it looked but miserably, and the great hat which fell down over my face. I was very conscious of the ill condition of my attire, and would have been glad to have concealed it ; but, through the endeavor to do so, my movements became still more angular. I did not dare to hold myself upright, because, by so doing, I exhibited all the more plainly the shortness of my waistcoat, which I had outgrown. I had the feeling very plainly that people would make themselves merry about me ; yet, at this moment, I felt nothing but the happiness of stepping for the first time before the foot-lamps. My heart beat ; I stepped forward ; there came up one of the singers, who at that time was much thought of, but now is forgotten ; he took me by the hand, and jeeringly wished me happiness on my début. " Allow me to introduce you to the Danish public," said he, and drew me forward to the lamps. The people would laugh at me — I felt it ; the tears rolled down my cheeks ; I tore myself loose, and left the stage full of anguish.

Shortly after this, Dahlen arranged a ballet of " Armida," in which I received a little part : I was a spirit. In this ballet I became acquainted with the lady of Professor Heiberg, the wife of the poet, and now a highly esteemed actress on the Danish stage ; she, then a little girl, had also a part in it, and our names stood printed in the bill. That was a moment in my life, when my name was printed ! I fancied I could see in it a nimbus of immortality. I was continually looking at the printed paper. I carried the programme of the ballet with me at night to bed, lay and read my name by candle-light — in short, I was happy !

I had now been two years in Copenhagen. The sum of money which had been collected for me was expended, but I was ashamed of making known my wants and my necessities. I had removed to the house of a woman whose husband, when living, was master of a trading-vessel, and there I had only lodging and breakfast. Those were heavy, dark days for me. The lady believed that I went out to dine with various families, whilst I only ate a little bread on one of the benches in the royal garden. Very rarely did I venture into some of the lowest eating-houses, and choose there the least expensive dish. I was, in truth, very forlorn ; but I did not feel the whole weight of my condition. Every person who spoke to me kindly

I took for a faithful friend. God was with me in my little room; and many a night, when I have said my evening prayer, I asked of Him, like a child, "Will things soon be better with me?" I had the notion, that as it went with me on New Year's Day, so would it go with me through the whole year; and my highest wishes were to obtain a part in a play.

It was now New Year's Day. The theatre was closed, and only a half-blind porter sat at the entrance to the stage, on which there was not a soul. I stole past him with beating heart, got between the movable scenes and the curtain, and advanced to the open part of the stage. Here I fell down upon my knees, but not a single verse for declamation could I recall to my memory. I then said aloud the Lord's Prayer, and went out with the persuasion, that because I had spoken from the stage on New Year's Day, I should in the course of the year succeed in speaking still more, as well as in having a part assigned to me.

During the two years of my residence in Copenhagen I had never been out into the open country. Once only had I been in the park, and there I had been deeply engrossed by study-ing the diversions of the people and their gay tumult. In the spring of the third year, I went out for the first time amid the verdure of a spring morning. It was into the garden of the Fredericksberg, the summer residence of Frederick VI. I stood still suddenly under the first large budding beech-tree. The sun made the leaves transparent — there was a fragrance, a freshness — the birds sang. I was overcome by it — I shouted aloud for joy, threw my arms around the tree, and kissed it.

"Is he mad?" said a man close behind me. It was one of the servants of the castle. I ran away, shocked at what I had heard, and then went thoughtfully and calmly back to the city.

My voice had, in the mean time, in part regained its rich-ness. The singing-master of the choir-school heard it, offered me a place in the school, thinking that, by singing with the choir, I should acquire greater freedom in the exercise of my powers on the stage. I thought that I could see by this means a new way opened for me. I went from the dancing-school into the singing-school, and entered the choir, now as a shepherd, and now as a warrior. The theatre was my world. I had permission to enter the pit, and thus it fared ill with my Latin. I heard many people say that there was no Latin required for singing in the choir, and that without the knowledge of this language it was possible to become a great actor. I thought there was good sense in that, and very often, either with or without reason, excused myself from my Latin evening lesson. Guldberg became aware of this, and for the first time I received a reprimand which almost crushed me to the earth. I fancy that no criminal could suffer more by hearing the sentence of death pronounced upon him. My distress of mind must have expressed itself in my countenance, for he said, " Do not act any more comedy." But it was no comedy to me.

I was now to learn Latin no longer. I felt my dependence upon the kindness of others in such a degree as I had never done before. Occasionally I had had gloomy and earnest thoughts in looking forward to my future, because I was in want of the very necessaries of life ; at other times I had the perfect thoughtlessness of a child.

The widow of the celebrated Danish statesman, Christian Colbjörnsen, and her daughter, were the first ladies of high rank who cordially befriended the poor lad ; who listened to me with sympathy, and saw me frequently. Mrs. von Colbjörnsen resided, during the summer, at Bakkehus, where also lived the poet Rahbek and his interesting wife. Rahbek never spoke to me ; but his lively and kind-hearted wife often amused herself with me. I had at that time again begun to write a tragedy, which I read aloud to her. Immediately on hearing the first scenes, she exclaimed, " But you have actually taken whole passages out of Oehlenschläger and Ingemann."

" Yes, but they are so beautiful ! " replied I in my simplicty, and read on.

One day, when I was going from her to Mrs. von Colbjörnsen, she gave me a handful of roses, and said, " Will you take them up to her ? It will certainly give her pleasure to receive them from the hand of a poet."

These words were said half in jest ; but it was the first

time that anybody had connected my name with that of poet. It went through me, body and soul, and tears filled my eyes. I know that, from this very moment, my mind was awoke to writing and poetry. Formerly it had been merely an amuse- ment by way of variety from my puppet theatre.

One day I went out to Bakkehus believing myself very nicely dressed ; Edward Colbjörnsen had given me a very good blue dress-coat, better than I ever before had worn, but it was too large and wide for me, especially across the breast ; I could not afford to get it altered, and so I buttoned it close up to the neck ; the cloth looked quite new and the buttons were shining, but across the breast it was far too wide ; in order to remedy this want, I filled out the empty room with a heap of old theatre hand-bills ; they were loosely laid one upon another between the coat and the breast, and looked like a hump. In this attire I presented myself to Madame Colbjörnsen and Madame Rahbek ; they asked me if I would not unbutton my coat, it was so warm, but I took pretty good care not to for fear of dropping the hand-bills.

At Bakkehus lived also Professor Thiele, a young student at that time, but even then the editor of the Danish popular legends, and known to the public as the solver of Baggesen's riddle and as the writer of beautiful poetry. He was pos- sessed of sentiment, true inspiration, and heart. He had calmly and attentively watched the unfolding of my mind, until we now became friends. He was one of the few who, at that time, spoke the truth of me, when other people were making themselves merry at my expense, and having only eyes for that which was ludicrous in me. People had called me, in jest, the little orator, and, as such, I was an object of curios- ity. They found amusement in me, and I mistook every smile for a smile of applause. One of my later friends has told me that it probably was about this period that he saw me for the first time. It was in the drawing-room of a rich tradesman, where people were making themselves very merry over me. They desired me to repeat one of my poems, and, as I did this with great feeling, the merriment was changed into sym- pathy with me.

I must not forget to mention that I found a retreat, if I may call it so, — a cozy little room, where the voices of earlier days sounded in my heart; it was in the house of a worthy old lady, the mother of our renowned, now deceased, Urban Jürgensen ; she had a very clear judgment and was well educated, but belonged to the last generation, in which she still lived. Her father had formerly been castellan of the castle of Antvorskov, and Holberg used to come there on Sundays from Sorö ; he and her father would walk up and down the floor talking together about politics ; one day the mother sitting at the spinning-wheel undertook to share in the conversation : " I believe the distaff is talking," said Holberg, and her mother could never forgive the witty, coarse gentleman these words ! The one who was then a little child, now sitting an old, old woman by me, told me all these things.

The poet Wessel also resorted to her house, and made great fun of the fop, Mr. Reiser, whose horrible fire-stories we all know ; he let the poor man one day go home through the dirty streets in shoes and silk stockings.

She read daily her, classics, — Corneille and Racine, — and spoke with me of them, of their great thoughts and the characters they drew; she had no admiration for modern romantic poetry.

With a mother's warm affection she spoke of her exiled son, who in the war had so adventurously proclaimed himself King of Iceland, and therefore dared never return to Denmark ; she understood well how to describe his character and will as they showed themselves in his childhood.

How attractive that old woman's company was to me ! I listened to all she had seen, thought, and read, and I was in her house as a dear child whom she loved to have near her. I read her my first verses, and my tragedy, " Skovkapellet " (" The Chapel in the Wood "), and she said one day, with an earnestness that made me humble : " You are a poet, perhaps as good as Oehlenschlager ! in ten years — yes, when I am no longer here — please to remember me ! " I remember that tears rushed to my eyes, I was so solemnly and wonderfully touched by these words ; but I know also that I thought it impossible for me to reach so high as to be an acknowledged poet, and far less to be named with Oehlenschläger. " What a good thing it would be for you to study," said she ; "but many ways lead toward Rome! your way will no doubt also bring you there."

I heard it said every day, what a good thing it would be for me if I could study. People advised me to devote myself to science, but no one moved one step to enable me to do so ; it was labor enough for me to keep body and soul together. It therefore occurred to me to write a tragedy, which I would offer to the Theatre Royal, and would then begin to study with the money which I should thus obtain. Whilst Guldberg instructed me in Danish, I had written a tragedy from a German story, called "The Chapel in the Wood;" yet as this was done merely as an exercise in the language, and as he forbade me in the most decided manner to bring it out, I would not do so. I originated my own material, therefore ; and within fourteen days I wrote my national tragedy called the "Robbers in Wissenberg" (the name of a little village in Funen). There was scarcely a word in it correctly written, as I had no person to help me, because I meant it to be anonymous ; there was, nevertheless, one person admitted into the secret, namely, the young lady whom I had met with in Odense, during my preparation for Confirmation, — the only one who at that time showed me kindness and good-will. It was through her that I was introduced to the Colbjörnsen family, and thus known and received in all those circles of which the one leads into the other. She paid some one to prepare a legible copy of my piece, and undertook to present it for perusal. After an interval of six weeks, I received it back, accompanied by a letter which said that people did not frequently wish to retain works which betrayed, in so great a degree, a want of elementary knowledge.

It was just at the close of the theatrical season, in May, 1822, that I received a letter from the directors, by which I was dismissed from the singing and dancing school, the letter adding also, that my participation in the school teaching could lead to no advantage for me, but that they wished some of my many friends would enable me to receive an education, without which talent availed nothing. I felt myself again, as it were, cast out into the wide world, without help and without support. It was absolutely necessary that I should write a piece for the theatre, and that it *must* be accepted ; there was no other salvation for me. I wrote, therefore, a tragedy founded on a passage in history, and I called it " Alfsol." I was delighted with the first act, and with this I immediately went to the Danish translator of Shakespeare, Admiral Wulff, now deceased, who good-naturedly heard me read it. In Admiral Wulff's house and in his family circle I found a true home. Speaking of our first acquaintance, he told me many years afterward in joke, and exaggerating it a little, that I said entering the room : " You have translated Shakespeare ; I admire him greatly, but I have also written a tragedy : shall I read it to you ? "

Wulff invited me to breakfast with him, but I would not take anything, but read and read all the time, and having finished my reading I said : " Do you think I shall amount to anything, — I wish it so much ? " I put my papers into my pocket, and when he asked me to call again soon, I answered, " Yes, I will, when I have written a new tragedy." — " But that will be a long time," said he. " I think." said I, " that in a fortnight I may have another one ready," and with these words I was out of the door. In after years I met with the most cordial reception in his family. At that time I also introduced myself to our celebrated physicist Orsted, and his house has remained to me to this day an affectionate home, to which my heart has firmly attached itself, and where I find my oldest and most unchangeable friends.

A favorite preacher, the rural dean Gutfeldt, was living at that time, and he it was who exerted himself most earnestly for my tragedy, which was now finished ; and having written a letter of recommendation, he sent it to the managers of the theatre. I was suspended between hope and fear. In the course of the summer I endured bitter want, but I told it to no one, else many a one, whose sympathy I had experienced, would have helped me to the utmost of their means. A false shame prevented me from confessing what I endured. Still happiness filled my heart. I read then for the first time the works of Walter Scott. A new world was opened to me : I forgot the reality, and gave to the circulating library that which should have provided me with a dinner.

The present conference councilor, Collin, one of the most distinguished men of Denmark, who unites with the greatest ability the noblest and best heart, to whom I looked up with confidence in all things, who had been a second father to me, and in whose children I have found brothers and sisters, — this excellent man I saw now for the first time. He was at that time director of the Theatre Royal, and people universally told me that it would be the best thing for me if he would interest himself on my behalf : it was either Ørsted or Gutfeldt who first mentioned me to him ; and now for the first time I went to that house which was to become so dear to me. Carl Bernhard has in his novel, " Chronicles of the Time of Christian II.," given a description of that old house, from its first days until its last celebrity as Collin's home. Before the ramparts of Copenhagen were extended, this house lay outside the gate, and served as a summer residence to the Spanish Ambassador ; now, however, it stands a crooked, angular framework building, in a respectable street ; an old-fashioned wooden balcony leads to the entrance, and a great tree spreads its green branches over the court and its pointed gables. It was to become a paternal house to me. Who does not willingly linger over the description of home ?

I discovered only the man of business in Collin ; his conversation was grave and in few words. I went away, without expecting any sympathy from this man ; and yet it was precisely Collin who, in all sincerity, thought for my advantage, and who worked for it silently, as he had done for others, through the whole course of his active life. But at that time I did not understand the apparent calmness with which he listened, whilst his heart bled for the afflicted, and he always labored for them with zeal and success, and knew how to help them. He touched so lightly upon my tragedy, which had been sent to him, and on account of which many people had overwhelmed me with flattering speeches, that I regarded him rather as an enemy than a protector.

In a few days I was sent for by the directors of the theatre, when Rahbek gave me back my play as useless for the stage ; adding, however, that there were so many grains of corn scattered in it, they hoped that perhaps, by earnest study, after going to school and the previous knowledge of all that is requisite, I might, some time, be able to write a work which should be worthy of being acted on the Danish stage.

In order therefore to obtain the means for my support and the necessary instruction, Collin recommended me to King Frederick VI., who granted to me a certain sum annually for some years ; and, by means of Collin also, the directors of the high schools allowed me to receive free instruction in the grammar school at Slagelse, where just then a new, and, as was said, an active rector was appointed. I was almost dumb with astonishment : never had I thought that my life would take this direction, although I had no correct idea of the path which I had now to tread. I was to go with the earliest mail to Slagelse, which lay twelve Danish miles from Copenhagen, to the place where also the poets Baggesen and Ingemann had gone to school. I was to receive money quarterly from Collin ; I was to apply to him in all cases, and he it was who was to ascertain my industry and my progress.

I went to him the second time to express to him my thanks. Mildly and kindly he said to me, "Write to me without restraint about everything which you require, and tell me how it goes with you." From this hour I struck root in his heart ; no father could have been more to me than he was, and is ; none could have more heartily rejoiced in my happiness, and my after reception with the public ; none have shared my sorrow more kindly ; and I am proud to say that one of the most excellent men which Denmark possesses feels toward me as toward his own child. His beneficence was conferred without his making me feel it painful either by word or look. That was not the case with every one to whom, in this change of my fortunes, I had to offer my thanks ; I was told to think of my inconceivable happiness and my poverty ; in Collin's words was expressed the warm-heartedness of a father, and to him it was that properly I was indebted for everything.

The journey was hastily determined upon, and I had yet for myself some business to arrange. I had spoken to an acquaintance from Odense who had the management of a small printing concern for a widow, to get "Alfsol" printed, that I might, by the sale of the work, make a little money. Before, however, the piece was printed, it was necessary that I should obtain a certain number of subscribers; but these were not obtained, and the manuscript lay in the printing-office, which, at the time I went to fetch it away, was shut up. Some years afterward, however, it suddenly made its appearance in print without my knowledge or my desire, in its unaltered shape, but without my name.

The fictitious name which I took seems at first sight a great piece of vanity, and yet it was not so, but really an expression of love, — a childish love, such as the child has when it calls its doll by the name it likes best. I loved William Shakespeare and Walter Scott, and of course I loved also myself. I took therefore my name Christian, and so I assumed the fictitious name "William Christian Walter." The book exists still, and contains the tragedy " Alfsol," and a tale, " The Spectre at Palnatoke's Grave," in which neither the spectre nor Palnatoke play any part; it is a very rough imitation of Walter Scott. *Dana,* the speaker in the prologue, says that I am "only seventeen years old," and that I bring

— " a wreath of beech-roots and Danish flowers."

It is a very miserable production throughout.

On a beautiful autumn day I set off with the mail from Copenhagen to begin my school-life in Slagelse. A young student, who a month before had passed his first examination, and now was travelling home to Jutland to exhibit himself there as a student. and to see once more his parents and his friends, sat by my side, and exulted for joy over the new life which now lay before him; he assured me that he should be the most unhappy of human beings if he were in my place, and were again beginning to go to the grammar school. But I travelled with a good heart toward the little city of Zealand. My mother received a joyful letter from me. I only wished that my father and the old grandmother yet lived, and could hear that I now went to the grammar school.

CHAPTER III.

WHEN, late in the evening, I arrived at the inn in Slagelse, I asked the hostess if there were anything remarkable in the city.

"Yes," said she, "a new English fire-engine and Pastor
Bastholm's library," — and those probably were all the lions in
the city. A few officers of the Lancers composed the fine-
gentleman world. Everybody knew what was done in everybody's house, whether a scholar was elevated or degraded in
his class, and the like. A private theatre, to which, at general rehearsal, the scholars of the grammar school and the
maid-servants of the town had free entrance, furnished rich
material for conversation. In my "Picture Book without
Pictures," the fourth night, I have given a sketch of it.

I boarded with a respectable widow of the educated class,
and had a little chamber looking out into the garden and
field. My place in the school was in the lowest class, among
little boys : I knew indeed nothing at all.

I was actually like a wild bird which is confined in a cage ;
I had the greatest desire to learn, but for the moment I floun-
dered about, as if I had been thrown into the sea ; one
wave followed another ; grammar, geography, mathematics :
I felt myself overpowered by them, and feared that I should
never be able to acquire all these. The Rector, who took a
peculiar delight in turning everything to ridicule, did not, of
course, make an exception in my case. To me he stood there
as a divinity ; I believed unconditionally every word which he
spoke. One day, when I had replied incorrectly to his question, and he said that I was stupid, I mentioned it to Collin,
and told him my anxiety, lest I did not deserve all that people had done for me ; but he consoled me. Occasionally,
however, on some subjects of instruction, I began to receive
a good certificate, and the teachers were heartily kind to me ;

yet, notwithstanding that I advanced, I still lost confidence in myself more and more. On one of the first examinations, however, I obtained the praise of the Rector. He wrote the same in my character-book ; and, happy in this, I went a few days afterward to Copenhagen. Guldberg, who saw the progress I had made, received me kindly, and commended my zeal.

" I advise you as a friend not to make any more verses," said he, and the same advice was repeated on all sides. I did not write more verses, but reflected on my duties, and on the very uncertain hope I had of becoming a student. I paid a visit to the learned Mr. Bastholm of Slagelse, editor of a West Zealand newspaper, who lived in retirement devoted only to his studies.

I presented him a couple of my earlier writings and that gave him an interest in me. He also advised me to keep to my school-books, and wrote me a letter, in which he presented with true sentiment and sincere advice a truth, which may always have a place in many people's mind. He wrote : —

" I have read your prologue, my young friend, and I must confess that God has endowed you with a vivid imagination and a warm heart ; you still need cultivation of mind, but that may come, as you now have a good opportunity to procure it. Your constant aim should be to endeavor with the utmost zeal to finish your studies, and for that reason you should put aside all other things.

" I could wish that your juvenile essays were not printed, as I cannot see why the public should be incumbered with imperfections — we have plenty of that ; still they are so far good that they may serve to justify the support you receive from the public. The young poet must shun the infection of vanity, and watch over the purity and strength of his feelings. In the present period of your studies I advise you to write poems but seldom, and only when you need air for your feelings. Don't write anything for which you have to hunt after words and thoughts, but only when the soul is animated by an idea and the heart warmed by true feeling.

" Observe closely nature, life, and yourself, that you may

procure original material for your poetical pictures; make a
choice from the things that surround you; reflect from all
points of view on what you see; take up the pen, become
poet, as if you did not know that any poet had ever existed in
the world before you, or as if you had not to learn of anybody;
preserve that nobleness of mind, that purity and sublimity
of soul, without which the wreath of poetry never can crown
a mortal.   Your affectionate
    " SLAGELSE, *February* 1, 1823."   " BASTHOLM.

With the same sympathy I was followed by the before mentioned Colonel, now General Guldberg, of Odense ; he was
extremely happy at my admission into a higher school, wrote
frequently to me, and always encouraged and strengthened me ;
as the first summer vacation came on, he invited me to come
over to him, — nay, furnished me with the means to defray my
travelling expenses.   I had not been in my native town since
I left it to seek my fortune ; in that interval my old grandmother had died and also my grandfather.

My mother often told me, when I was a little boy, that I had
a fortune in prospect : that I should be heir of my grandfather,
who owned a house ; it was a little, poor wooden house, which
was sold after his death and immediately pulled down ; most
of the old man's money was applied to pay the taxes in ar-
rear, and the authorities had seized " the big stove with brass
drum," a piece worth owning, they said, and it was taken up
to the town-hall.   There was so much money that they could
have made a cart-load of the coins, but they were the old reduced coins, which the government no longer received.   In
1813, when these coins were reduced, the old insane man was
told that they were good for nothing.   " No man can reject
the King's money !" said he, " and the King won't reject his
own : " that was his whole answer.   " The big inheritance " I
had heard so much about was reduced to some twenty rix-
dollars and passed over to me.   I must however candidly
confess, that I did not care much about those riches ; my
thoughts were only lingering on my visit to my home.   I felt
rich and happy, and my mind was excited with expectation.

I crossed the Belt, and went on foot to Odense.   When

I came near enough to see the lofty old church tower, my heart was more and more affected ; I felt deeply the care of God for me, and I burst into tears.   My mother rejoiced over me.   The families of Iversen and Guldberg received me cordially ; and in the little streets I saw the people open their windows to look at me, for everybody knew how remarkably well things had fared with me ; nay, I fancied I actually stood upon the pinnacle of fortune, when one of the principal citizens, who had built a high tower to his house, led me up there, and I looked out thence over the city and the surrounding country, and some old women in the hospital below, who had known me from childhood, pointed up to me.   One afternoon, in company with the families of Guldberg and the Bishop, I sailed in a boat on the stream, and my mother shed tears of joy ; "for," as she said, "I was honored like the child of a count."

As soon, however, as I returned to Slagelse, this halo of glory vanished, as well as every thought of it.   I may freely confess that I was industrious, and I rose, as soon as it was possible, into a higher class ; but in proportion as I rose did I feel the pressure upon me more strongly, and that my endeavors were not sufficiently productive.   Many an evening, when sleep overcame me, I would wash my head with cold water, or run about the lonely little garden, till I was again wakeful, and could comprehend the book anew.   The Rector filled up a portion of his hours of teaching with jest, nicknames, and not the happiest of witticisms.   I was as if paralyzed with anxiety when he entered the room, and from that cause my replies often expressed the opposite of that which I wished to say, and thereby my anxiety was all the more increased.   What was to become of me ?

In a moment of ill-humor I wrote a letter to the head master, who was one of those who was most friendly inclined to me.   I said in this letter that I regarded myself as a person so little gifted by nature, that it was impossible for me to study, and that the people in Copenhagen threw away the money which they spent upon me : I besought him therefore to counsel me what I should do.   The excellent man strengthened me with mild words, and wrote to me a most friendly and consolatory letter : he said that the Rector meant kindly by me ; that it was his custom and way of acting ; that I was making all the progress that people could expect from me ; and that I need not doubt of my abilities. He told me that he himself was a peasant youth of three and twenty — older than I myself was — when he began his studies ; the misfortune for me was, that I ought to have been treated differently from the other scholars, but that this could hardly be done in a school ; still that things were progressing, and that I stood well both with the teachers and my fellow-students. I was always praised for Religion, Biblical History, and Danish themes : from all the classes, from the highest one too, one or another of the scholars used to come home to me to be helped in their Danish exercises, — "only not so well that it would be observed," was their request, — and I was again in turn helped by them in Latin. For "conduct," I got steadily every month from all the teachers the character "remarkably good ; " once it happened, however, that I only got "very good," and I was so troubled at the reduction that I immediately wrote a tragic-comical letter to Collin and told him that I was quite innocent, though I had only got the character "very good." In the mean time I knew that the Rector judged me otherwise than he reported ; now and then I discovered in him a gleam of kindness, and I was always among the scholars whom he invited to his house on Sundays ; and then he was quite another man, he was overflowing with jest and merriment, related funny stories, put up tin soldiers for us, and played with us and with his children.

Every Sunday we had to attend the church and hear an old preacher ; the other scholars learned their lessons in history and mathematics while he preached ; I learned my task in religion, and thought that by so doing it was less sinful. The general rehearsals at the private theatre were points of light in my school life ; they took place in a back building, where the lowing of the cows might be heard ; the street-decoration was a picture of the market-place of the city, by which means the representation had something familiar about it ; it amused the inhabitants to see their own houses.

On Saturday afternoons it was my delight to go to the castle of Antvorskov, at that time only half in ruins, and once a monastery, where I pursued the excavating of the ruined cellars, as if it had been a Pompeii.

In a little cottage there lived a young married couple, descended from a family of rank ; I believe they were married against the will of their parents ; they were truly very poor, but seemed happy, and the low-studded room with whitewashed walls had an air of comfort and beauty ; fresh-gathered flowers were placed on the table, where also books in luxurious bindings were scattered, and a harp stood ready for use.

I had accidentally made acquaintance with the young couple, and was always very kindly received by them ; idyllic beauty was spread over that little abode, which was situated below the lonely castle on the top of the hill. I often rambled also to the crucifix of St. Anders, which stands upon one of the heights of Slagelse, and is one of the wooden crosses erected in the time of Catholicism in Denmark. St. Anders was a priest in Slagelse, and travelled to the Holy Land ; on the last day he remained so long praying at the holy sepulchre, that the ship sailed away without him. Vexed at this circumstance, he walked along the shore, where a man met him riding on an ass, and took him up with him. Immediately he fell asleep, and when he awoke he heard the bells of Slagelse ringing. He lay upon the (Hvilehöi) hill of rest, where the cross now stands. He was at home a year and a day before the ship returned which sailed away without him, and an angel had borne him home. The legend, and the place where he woke, were both favorites of mine. On this hill I often sat in the evening and looked over meadow and cornfield down upon Corsoer where Baggesen was born. Here he might also have sat, when a scholar of Slagelse school, looking over the Belt to Funen. Upon this hill, I could indulge my fancies, and later, when passing here in the diligence, I often looked up to the hill with the cross, and thought of that portion of my life which was so closely attached to this spot.

The happiest time, however, was when, once on a Sunday, whilst the wood was green, I went to the city of Sorö, two (Danish) miles from Slagelse, which lies in the midst of

woods, surrounded by lakes. Here is an academy for the nobility, founded by the poet Holberg. Everything lay in a
conventual stillness. I visited here the poet Ingemann, who
had just married, and who held a situation as teacher ; he had
already received me kindly in Copenhagen ; but here his reception of me was still more kind. His life in this place
seemed to me like a beautiful story ; flowers and vines twined
around his window ; the rooms were adorned with the portraits of distinguished poets, and other pictures. We sailed
upon the lake with an Æolian harp made fast to the mast.
Ingemann talked cheerfully, and his excellent, amiable wife
treated me as if she were an elder sister : I loved these
people. Our friendship has grown with years. I have been
from that time almost every summer a welcome guest there,
and I have experienced that there are people in whose society
one is made better, as it were ; that which is bitter passes
away, and the whole world appears in sunlight.

Among the pupils in the academy of nobles, there were two
who made verses ; they knew that I did the same, and they
attached themselves to me. The one was Petit, who afterwards, certainly with the best intention, but not faithfully,
translated several of my books. He has also written a strange,
fantastical biography of me, in which, among other things, he
gives a description of my paternal home that seems to have a
great resemblance to that in "The Ugly Duckling." He makes
my mother a Madonna, lets me run with rosy feet in the evening sun, and more of the same kind. Petit was nevertheless
not without talent, and possessed of a warm, noble heart ; life
brought him many sorrowful days. Now he is among the dead,
and his vivacious spirit may have attained more serenity and
repose. The other was the poet Carl Bagger, one of the most
gifted of men who has come forward in Danish literature, but
who has been unjustly judged. His poems are full of freshness and originality ; his story, "The Life of my Brother," is a
clever book, by the critique on which the "Danish Monthly
Review of Literature" has proved that it does not understand
how to give judgment. These two academicians were very
different from me : life rushed rejoicingly through their veins ;
I was sensitive and childlike, while I was the most grown of

us three. The quiet Sorö, with its woody solitude, became thus for me a home of poetry and friendship.

An event that agitated much our little town was the execution of three criminals down at Skjelskjör. A rich young daughter of a farmer had induced her suitor to kill her father, who opposed their match ; an accessory to the crime was the man-servant, who intended to marry the widow. Every one was going to see the execution, and the day was like a holiday. The Rector dismissed the upper class from school, and we were to go and see the execution, for it would be a good thing for us to be acquainted with it, he said.

The whole night we drove in open carriages, and at sunrise we reached Skjelskjör. It made a very strong impression upon me. I never shall forget seeing the criminals driven to the place of execution : the young girl, deadly pale, leaning her head against the breast of her robust sweetheart ; behind them the man-servant, livid, his black hair in disorder, and nodding with a squinting look at a few acquaintances, who shouted out to him " Farewell ! " Standing at the side of their coffins, they sang a hymn together with the minister ; the girl's voice was heard above all the others. My limbs could scarcely carry me ! these moments were more horrible for me than the very moment of death. I saw a poor sick man, whose superstitious parents, in order to cure him of a fit, had given him to drink a cup of blood from the persons executed ; he ran away in wild flight till he sank exhausted on the ground. A ballad-maker was vending his " melancholy airs ; " the words were put in the mouth of the malefactors, and sounded comically to a well-known melody. The whole tragedy made such an impression upon my fancy that for a long time after I was persecuted by the memory of it ; and though many years have passed away, it is still as fresh to me as if it happened yesterday.

Events like this or other important incidents did not continue to happen ; one day after another glided away, but the less there is going on and the more quiet and monotonous one's life is the sooner one thinks of preserving what passes, — of keeping a diary, as it is called. At that time I also kept such a one, of which I have retained a couple of leaves, in which the whole of my strange, childish nature at that time is faithfully reflected. I insert here some passages from it, copying them literally.

I was then in the upper class but one, and my whole existence and happiness depended on being promoted to the highest class at the approaching examination. I wrote : —

" *Wednesday.* — Depressed in spirit I took up the Bible, which lay before me, for an oracle, opened it, pointed blindly at a place and read : ' O Israel, thou hast destroyed thyself ! but in me is thine help ! ' (Hosea.) Yes, Father, I am weak, but thou lookest into my heart and wilt be my help so that I can be promoted to the fourth class. Have answered well in Hebrew.

" *Thursday.* — Happened to pull off the leg of a spider ; went nicely through in mathematics. O God, God, to thee my heart's entire thanks.

" *Friday.* — O God, help me ! The night is so wintry clear. The examination is well over — to-morrow comes the result. O Moon ! to-morrow thou wilt behold either a pale, desperate being or one of the happiest. Read Schiller's ' Kabale und Liebe.'

" *Saturday.* — O God, now my fate is decided, but still hidden from me : what may it be ? God, my God ! do not forsake me ! my blood runs so fast through my veins, my nerves tremble with fear. O God, Almighty God, help me — I do not deserve it, but be merciful O God, God ! — (Later.) I am promoted — Is it not strange ? My joy is not so violent as I supposed it would be. At eleven o'clock I wrote to Guldberg and to my mother."

At that time I made a vow to the Lord in my silent thoughts that if He would let me be promoted to the fourth class, I would go to Communion the following Sunday, and that I also did.

You can see by this what trouble I had in my pious mind, and what degree of development I had reached, although at that time I was already twenty years old. How much better other young men at that age would have written in their diary !

The Rector grew weary of his residence in Slagelse ; he applied for the vacant post of Rector in the grammar school of Helsingör, and obtained it. He told me of it, and added kindly, that I might write to Collin and ask leave to accompany him thither; that I might live in his house, and could even now remove to his family; I should then in half a year become a student, which could not be the case if I remained behind, and that then he would himself give me some private lessons in Latin and Greek. I, of course, immediately received Collin's permission, and removed to the house of the Rector.

I was now to take leave of Slagelse: it was very hard for me to say good-by to my comrades and the few families whose acquaintance I had made: of course, I also on that occasion got an album, in which, amongst others, my old teacher Mr. Snitker wrote something: he had been Ingemann and Poul Möller's teacher when they were scholars there.

Carl Bagger wrote a poem addressed to me, which was more like a dedication to a young poet, than a poem to a boy going away to take his seat on a school-bench. And so I went thither, and approached heavy, wearisome days.

I accompanied the Rector to Helsingör; the journey, the first view of the Sound with its many sailing ships, the Kullen Mountains, and the beautiful country, all filled my mind with transport; I described it in a letter to Rasmus Nyrup, and as I thought it very well written, I sent the same letter to others, addressing it to each of them. Unfortunately it pleased Nyrup so well that he inserted it in the " Copenhagen Pictorial," so that each of them who had got the letter, or rather the copy of it, believed that he saw his letter printed in the news-paper.

The Rector's spirits were refreshed by the variety, the new company, and new activity, but only for a short time, and I soon felt myself forsaken; I became depressed and suffered much in mind. The Rector had sent Mr. Collin at that time an account of me, which I now have, in which he judges me and my abilities quite differently from what I and others had heard or could have believed him to say. If I had had any knowledge of it, I should have been strengthened: it would have made me healthier in mind, and would have acted beneficially upon my whole being.

I heard him every day condemn almost every intellectual faculty in me; he spoke to me as to an idiot, — to a perfectly brutish, stupid boy, — and at the same time he wrote earnestly about me to my patron Collin, who, on account of my fre-

quent reports of the Rector's dissatisfaction with me and my
poor abilities, had asked him for a statement.

" H. C. Andersen was, at the close of the year 1822, admitted to Slagelse grammar school, and being in want of the
most necessary preliminary knowledge, in spite of his pretty
advanced age, was put into the lowest class but one.

" Endowed by nature with a lively imagination and warm feelings, he attempted and acquired more or less completely the
different branches of instruction, and in general made such
progress, that it entitled him to be promoted successively from
the lower classes to the highest, to which he at present belongs, only with the difference that he has removed with the
undersigned from Slagelse to Helsingör.

" The kindness of others has until now maintained him in his
course of study, and I cannot refrain from saying that he is
perfectly worthy. His talents are good, and in one direction
even excellent ; his constant diligence, and his conduct, which
springs from an affectionate disposition, are such that he might
serve as a model for the pupils of any school. It may be
stated further, that, by continuing his praiseworthy assiduity,
he will, in October, 1828, be able to be promoted to the
Academy.

" Three qualities which a preceptor wishes for, but rarely
finds combined in the same pupil, namely, ability, diligence,
and excellent conduct, are assuredly to be found in H. C.
Andersen.

" In consideration of this, I must recommend him as very
worthy of any support which may be given to him to enable
him to continue his course, from which his advanced age will
not well allow him to retire. Not only the disposition of
mind, but also his faithful assiduity and undoubted talent, give
sufficient warrant that what may be bestowed upon him for his
welfare will never be lost.

S. MEISLING,
"Ph. Dr., and Rector of Helsingör's grammar school.
" HELSINGÖR, *July* 18, 1826."

Of this testimony which breathes so much goodness toward

me and which ought to be known, I had no sort of knowledge. I was entirely depressed, and had neither belief nor confidence in myself.   Collin sent me a few kind lines : —

"Don't lose courage, my dear Andersen! Compose your mind and be quiet and reasonable ; you will see that all will go well ; the Rector bears good-will to you. He takes perhaps another way of showing it from what others would, but still it leads to the same end.

"I may write more another time, to-day I am prevented.
"God bless you!   Yours,
"COLLIN."

The scenery here made a lively impression upon me, but I dared only to cast stolen glances at it.   When the school hours were over, the house-door was commonly locked ; I was obliged to remain in the heated school-room and learn my Latin, or else play with the children, or sit in my little room ; I never went out to visit anybody.   My life in this family furnishes the most evil dreams to my remembrance.   I was almost overcome by it, and my prayer to God every evening was, that He would remove this cup from and let me die. I possessed not an atom of confidence in myself.   I never mentioned in my letters how hard it went with me, because the Rector found his pleasure in making a jest of me, and turning my feelings to ridicule.

My letters to Collin at that period showed a dull and hopeless disposition of mind which deeply touched him ; I know that from himself, but there was nothing to be done.   He presumed and might presume that the real pressure was in my own mind, and in a nervous over-exertion, and did not come from without, as it really did.   My mind was very elastic and ready to receive every sunbeam, but these only reached me the few days once a year in my vacations, when I was allowed to go to Copenhagen.

What a change it was to get for a few days out of the Rector's rooms into a house in Copenhagen, where all was elegance, cleanliness, and full of the comforts of refined life! This was at Admiral Wulff's, whose wife felt for me the kindness of a mother, and whose children met me with cordiality; they dwelt in a portion of the Castle of Amalienburg, and my chamber looked out into the square. I remember the first evening there; Aladdin's words passed through my mind, when he looked down from his splendid castle into the square, and said, "Here came I as a poor lad." My soul was full of gratitude.

During my whole residence in Slagelse I had scarcely written more than four or five poems; two of which, "The Soul," and "To my Mother," will be found printed in my collected works. In my school-days in Helsingör I only wrote two poems, "New Year's Night" and "The Dying Child;" the last one was the first of my poems which gained attention and acknowledgment and was earliest published and translated. I read it to some acquaintance in Copenhagen; some were struck by it, but most of them only remarked my Funen dialect, which drops the *d* in every word. I was commended by many; but from the greater number I received a lecture on modesty, and that I should not get too great ideas of myself — I who really at that time thought nothing of myself.

One of my kind lady protectors said and wrote to me: "For God's sake don't believe that you are a poet because you can make verses! that might grow to a fixed idea. What would you say if I had got it into my head that I should become empress of Brazil! Would it not be a foolish thought? and so is also your belief that you are a poet!" But it was not at all my thought; it would however have been a playtime in my life, a consolation for me, if I had had such a thought.

During my stay in Copenhagen I was much blamed for my awkward manners, and next to it for always saying straight out what I was thinking.

At the house of Admiral Wulff I saw many men of the most distinguished talent, and among them all my mind paid the greatest homage to one, — that was the poet Adam Oehlenschläger. I heard his praise resound from every mouth around me; I looked up to him with the most pious faith: I was happy when one evening, in a large, brilliantly lighted drawing-room — where I deeply felt that my apparel was the shabbiest there, and for that reason I concealed myself behind

the long curtains — Oehlenschläger came to me and offered
me his hand. I could have fallen before him on my knees.
We saw each other often in Wulff's house, where also Weyse
used to come. He spoke very kindly to me and I heard him
improvise upon the piano. Bróndsted, who had returned to
Denmark, enlivened it by his eloquence. Wulff himself read
aloud his translations of Byron. The educated and refined
gentleman Adler, the friend of Christian VIII., completed
that social circle, where also the young daughter of Oehlenschläger, Charlotte, surprised me by her joyous, merry humor. What excellent days and evenings for me those days
in Copenhagen were!

From such a house as this I, after a few days, returned to
the Rector, and felt the difference deeply. He also came direct from Copenhagen, where he had heard it said that I had
read in company one of my own poems. He looked at me with
a penetrating glance, and commanded me to bring him the poem,
when, if he found in it one spark of poetry, he would forgive
me. I tremblingly brought to him " The Dying Child ; " he
read it, and pronounced it to be sentimentality and idle trash.
He gave way freely to his anger. If he had believed that I
wasted my time in writing verses, or that I was of a nature which
required a severe treatment, then his intention would have been
good ; but he could not pretend this. But from this day forward my situation was more unfortunate than ever ; I suffered
so severely in my mind that I was very near sinking under it.
That was the darkest, the most unhappy time in my life.

Just then one of the masters went to Copenhagen, and related to Collin exactly what I had to bear, and immediately he
removed me from the school and from the Rector's house.
When, in taking leave of him, I thanked him for the kindness
which I had received from him, the passionate man cursed me,
and ended by saying that I should never become a student,
that my verses would grow mouldy on the floor of the book-
seller's shop, and that I myself should end my days in a mad-
house. I trembled to my innermost being, and left him.

Several years afterward, when my writings were read, when
the " Improvisatore " first came out, I met him in Copenhagen ;
he offered me his hand in a conciliatory manner, and said that

he had erred respecting me and had treated me wrong; but it now was all the same to me. The heavy, dark days had also produced their blessing in my life.

A young man, who afterward became celebrated in Denmark for his zeal in the Northern languages and in history, became my teacher. I hired a little garret; it is described in the "Fiddler;" and in "The Picture Book without Pictures" people may see that I often received there visits from the moon. I had a certain sum allowed for my support; but as instruction was to be paid for, I had to make savings in other ways. A few families through the week-days gave me a place at their tables. I was a sort of boarder, as many another poor student in Copenhagen is still : there was a variety in it; it gave me an insight into the several kinds of family life, which was not without its influence on me. I studied industriously; in some particular branches I had considerably distinguished myself in Helsingör, especially in mathematics; these were, therefore, now much more left to myself: everything tended to assist me in my Greek and Latin studies; in one direction, however, and that the one in which it would least have been expected, did my excellent teacher find much to do; namely, in religion. He closely adhered to the literal meaning of the Bible; with this I was acquainted, because from my first entrance in the school I had clearly understood what was said and taught by it. I received gladly, both with feeling and understanding, the doctrine that God is love: everything which opposed this — a burning hell, therefore, whose fire endured forever — I could not recognize. Released from the distressing existence of the school bench, I now expressed myself like a free man; and my teacher, who was one of the noblest and most amiable of human beings, but who adhered firmly to the letter, was often quite distressed about me. We disputed, whilst pure flames kindled within our hearts. It was nevertheless good for me that I came to this unspoiled, highly-gifted young man, who was possessed of a nature as peculiar as my own.

That which, on the contrary, was an error in me, and which became very perceptible, was a pleasure which I had, not in jesting with, but in playing with my best feelings, and in regarding the understanding as the most important thing in the world. The Rector had completely mistaken my undisguisedly candid and sensitive character ; my excitable feelings were made ridiculous, and thrown back upon themselves ; and now, when I could freely advance upon the way to my object, this change showed itself in me.   From severe suffering I did not rush into libertinism, but into an erroneous endeavor to appear other than I was.   I ridiculed feeling, and fancied that I had quite thrown it aside ; and yet I could be made wretched for a whole day, if I met with a sour countenance where I expected a friendly one.   Every poem which I had formerly written with tears, I now parodied, or gave to it a ludicrous refrain ; one of which I called "The Lament of the Kitten," another, "The Sick Poet."   The few poems which I wrote at that time were all of a humorous character : a complete change had passed over me ; the stunted plant was reset, and now began to put forth new shoots.

Wulff's eldest daughter, a very clever and lively girl, understood and encouraged the humor, which made itself evident in my few poems ; she possessed my entire confidence ; she protected me like a good sister, and had great influence over me, whilst she awoke in me a feeling for the comic.

At this time, also, a fresh current of life was sent through the Danish literature ; for this the people had an interest, and politics played no part in it.

Heiberg, who had gained the acknowledged reputation of a poet by his excellent works, "Psyche" and "Walter the Potter," had introduced the vaudeville upon the Danish stage ; it was a Danish vaudeville, blood of our blood, and was therefore received with acclamation, and supplanted almost everything else.   Thalia kept carnival on the Danish stage, and Heiberg was her secretary.   I made his acquaintance first at Örsted's.   Refined, eloquent, and the hero of the day, he pleased me in a high degree : he was most kind to me, and I visited him ; he considered one of my humorous poems worthy of a place in his most excellent weekly paper, "The Flying Post."   Shortly before I had, after a deal of trouble, got my poem of "The Dying Child" printed in a paper; none of the many publishers of journals, who otherwise accept of the most lamentable trash, had the courage to print a poem by a school-boy. My best known poem they printed at that time, accompanied by an excuse for it. Heiberg saw it, and gave it in his paper an honorable place. Two humorous poems signed " H. " were truly my début with him.

I remember the first evening when the " Flying Post " appeared with my verses in it. I was with a family who wished me well, but who regarded my poetical talent as quite insignificant, and who found something to censure in every line. The master of the house entered with the " Flying Post " in his hand.

" This evening," said he, " there are two excellent poems : they are by Heiberg ; nobody else could write anything like them." And now my poems were received with rapture. The daughter, who was in my secret, exclaimed, in her delight, that I was the author. They were all struck into silence, and were vexed. That wounded me deeply.

One of our least esteemed writers, but a man of rank, who was very hospitable, gave me one day a seat at his table. He told me that a new year's gift would come out, and that he was applied to for a contribution. I said that a little poem of mine, at the wish of the publisher, would appear in the same new year's gift.

" What, then : everybody and anybody are to contribute to this book ! " said the man in vexation : " then he will need nothing from me ; I certainly can hardly give him anything."

My teacher dwelt at a considerable distance from me. I went to him twice each day, and on the way there my thoughts were occupied with my lessons. On my return, however, I breathed more freely, and then bright poetical ideas passed through my brain, but they were never committed to paper ; only five or six humorous poems were written in the course of the year, and these disturbed me less when they were laid to rest on paper than if they had remained in my mind.

In September, 1828, I was a student. Oehlenschläger, who was Dean at that time, pressed my hand and bid me welcome as *civis academicus :* that was an act of great importance for me. I was already twenty-three years old, but still much a child in my whole nature and my manner of speaking. A lit-

tle incident of these days will perhaps give you an idea of it.
Shortly before the examination day I saw a young man at the
dinner-table of H. C. Örsted : he looked very embarrassed and
retiring.   I had not seen him there before, and thought that
he had but just arrived from the country.   I asked him without ceremony, —

"Are you going up to the examination this year ? "

"Yes," he said with a smile, "I am going up there."

"I also," said I, and spoke now with him as a comrade a
good deal about this great event.   He was the professor who
was to examine me in mathematics, the richly gifted and excellent Von Schmidten, who in his external appearance was
so much like Napoleon, that in Paris he was taken for him.
When we met at the examination-table we were both very
much embarrassed ; he was as kind as he was learned, and
wished to encourage me, but did not know how to do it ; he
leaned over to me and whispered, —

"What is to be the first poetical work you will give us,
when you have finished your examination ? "

I gazed with astonishment on him and answered anxiously,—

"I don't know, sir, but be so kind as not to give me too difficult questions in mathematics ! "

"You know, then, something ? " said he, in a low voice.

"Yes, sir, I know mathematics tolerably ; in the Helsingör
school I often read 'the supplements' with the other scholars,
and I got the certificate 'remarkably good,' but now I am
afraid."   In that style the professor and the pupil conversed,
and during the examination, in which he tore all his pens to
pieces, he did not say anything, but only put one of the pens
aside to write down the result with.

When the examination (*Examen Artium*) was over, the
ideas and thoughts, by which I was pursued on the way to my
teacher, flew like a swarm of bees out into the world, and indeed, into my first work, "A Journey on Foot from the Holm
Canal to the East Point of Amack," — a peculiar, humorous
book, a kind of fantastic arabesque, but one which fully exhibited my own individual character at that time, my disposition to
sport with everything, and to jest in tears over my own feelings — a fantastic, gayly colored tapestry work was this poetical improvisation.

No publisher had the courage to bring out that juvenile work. I ventured therefore to do it myself, and in a few days after its appearance, the publisher Reitzel bought from me the copyright of the second edition, and after a while he had a third. In Fahlun, in Sweden, the work was reprinted in Danish, a thing which had happened only to the chief works of Oehlenschläger. A German translation was some years later published in Hamburg.

Everybody in Copenhagen read my book ; I heard nothing but praise, only a protector of rank gave me a severe lecture, but it struck me as rather comical. The man found in the "Journey on Foot" a satire of the Royal Theatre, which he not only considered as unseemly but also as ungrateful : unseemly because it was a royal theatre, or, as he said, the king's house ; and ungrateful because I had free admission to it.

This reproof of an otherwise reasonable man, was put out of mind by the triumph and praise the book received. I was a "student," a poet. I had attained the highest goal of my wishes. Heiberg noticed the book in a very kind and beautiful manner in the "Monthly Journal of Literature," and had earlier given extracts from it in his "Flying Post." The book was very much read in Norway, and that vexed Poul Möller, so that he criticised it without indulgence.

I did not know anything of it, and could not believe that anybody should not rejoice in the "Journey on Foot to Amack."

The same year about two hundred young men passed as "students," and among them were several who made verses, and had even got them published ; it was said in jest that that year four great and twelve minor poets were made students, and in truth, not counting it too exactly, we could get out that number. To the great ones belonged Arnesen, whose first vaudeville, "The Intrigue in the People's Theatre," was brought on the stage of the Royal Theatre ; F. J. Hansen, who at that time published "Readings for the Beau Monde ;" Hollard Nielsen ; and last, as the fourth poet, H. C. Andersen.

Among the twelve small ones was one who, later, unquestionably became one of the great in the Danish literature, — "Adam Homo's" poet, Paludan Müller. He had not yet published anything, and it was only known among his comrades that he made verses. One day I got a letter from him in which he proposed that we should publish a weekly paper together.

"You will perhaps be surprised to get such a proposition from me, from whom you have not yet seen anything which could induce you to suppose me equal to such an enterprise; yet I believe that I dare assure you with a certain kind of self-confidence that I am not the step-child of the Muses, as may be tested by the collection of poems I have written for my own pleasure, which are lying in my drawer at home." The plan and conditions followed; there were not to be translations or copying from other papers, but only original articles, etc. The letter was accompanied by his poem "The Smile," as a specimen. I had no fancy at all to be tied down to a newspaper, and so the matter was dropped.

Carl Bagger and I had, before the "Journey on Foot" was published, agreed to publish together our poems in one volume, but when my book met with so much praise and found so many readers, Bagger declared positively that our poems could not now go together, because it would be just as if his poems had to be brought forward by mine; the project was given up, but not our friendly relation.

I was received with great consideration by my fellow-students, and I was in a youthful poetical intoxication, in a whirl of joy, sporting and searching for the wrong side in everything. In this state I wrote in rhyme my first dramatic work, the vaudeville, "Love on the Nicholas Tower; or, What says the Pit?" which had one essential fault, noticed also in the "Monthly Journal," "that of satirizing what no longer existed amongst us, namely, the Fate tragedies of the Middle Ages."

My fellow-students received the piece with acclamation and shouted "Long live the author!" I was overwhelmed with joy, and thought it to be of more importance than it deserved. I could not contain myself. I rushed out from the theatre into the street, and then to Collin's house, where his wife was alone at home. I threw myself down upon a chair almost exhausted and wept in convulsions. The sympathizing lady did not know what to think, and trying to console me, said, —

" Don't let it grieve you so much. Oehlenschläger has also been hissed, and many other great poets." — " They have not hissed at all," exclaimed I sobbing : " they have applauded and cried *Vivat !* "

I was now a happy human being, thinking well of all mankind ; I possessed the courage of a poet and the heart of a youth.

All houses began to be open to me ; I flew from circle to circle in happy self-contentment. Under all these external and internal affections, I still however devoted myself industriously to study, so that without any teacher I passed my second academical examination, *Examen philologicum et philosophicum,* with highest marks.

A very peculiar scene passed at the examination by H. C. Örsted. I had answered all his questions very well, which pleased him, and when I had finished he called me back again, and said, — " I must ask you still one question more ; " and with a bright smile : " Tell me, what do you know about electro-magnetism ? " — " I have never heard that word," answered I. " Think a moment ! you have before answered so well, you must also know something of electro-magnetism ! "

" I have not read anything about it in your chemistry," said I with precision.

" I know it, but I have spoken about it at my lectures ! "

" I have been at all your lectures but one, and you probably spoke of it at that time, for I do not know a single bit of it, — not even the name."

Örsted smiled at that unusual confession, nodded and said,— " It is a pity that you did not know it — otherwise I should have given you ' præ,' now you can only get ' laud ;' for the rest, you have answered very well."

Later when I came home to Örsted, I asked him to tell me a little about electro-magnetism, and now I heard for the first time of it, and of his relation to it.

Ten years later, when the electro-magnetical thread was exhibited in the Polytechnic Academy in Copenhagen, I wrote an article, at Örsted's express wish, under the signature " Y," in the " Copenhagen Post," I believe, about the magnetic telegraph which was carried from the front to the back build-

ing of the Polytechnic Academy.   I drew the attention of the
citizens to that invention, which science owes to a Dane.

At Christmas I brought out the first collected edition of
my poems, which met with great praise.   I liked to listen to
the sounding bell of praise.   I had such an overflow of youth
and happiness.   Life lay bright with sunshine before me.

CHAPTER IV.

UNTIL now I had only seen a small part of my native land, — that is to say, a few points in Funen and Zealand, as well as Möen's Klint, which last is truly one of our most beautiful places ; the beech-woods there hang like a garland over the white chalk cliffs, from which a view is obtained far over the Baltic. I wished, therefore, in the summer of 1830, to devote my first literary proceeds to seeing Jutland, and making myself more thoroughly acquainted with my own Funen. I had no idea how much solidity of mind I should derive from this summer excursion, or what a change was about to take place in my inner life.

It was especially the heaths of Jutland that I rejoiced to see, and if possible I wanted to meet some gypsy family there. My interest had been excited by stories I had heard, and by the novels of Steen Blicher. The country was then not so much visited as it is now.

Steam-navigation had just been established ; a bad, slow-sailing ship called " Dania " made the voyage in about twenty-four hours, — an unheard of quick passage at that time.

The steamships had not yet come to be believed in. The year before I made a passage in such a ship, — " Caledonia," the first steamboat seen in our waters ; all the seamen ridiculed it and nicknamed it " Puddle-Malene."

H. C. Örsted was of course full of delight over this world-renowned invention, and it was very amusing to hear at a dinner where I was present, an old sailor, a relation of Mr. Örsted, who sat near him, arguing against these " smoke-ships."

" From the creation of the world," said he. " till this time, we have been satisfied with reasonable ships driven by wind, but now they are trying to make something better ; as often as one of those ' smoke-caps ' is passing, I cannot forbear taking my speaking-trumpet and scolding at it as long as it can hear me." It was a great event to go in a steamboat at that time, and it sounds almost incredible nowadays, when steamships are such every-day matters, that we think of their invention as something very remote ; to hear it said that Napoleon, when he took refuge with the English, saw for the first time a steamboat in motion.

A whole night in the Kattegat, on board this new kind of ship, made a deep impression on my fancy. We had rough weather indeed, and I was sea-sick ; it was only the next day in the evening that we reached Aarhuus. There, and in all the small towns of Jutland, my "Journey on Foot" was well known, as were also my humorous poems, and I was kindly received. I drove over the heath, where all was novel ; but it was bad weather, and having very light travelling clothes, the damp, chilly sea-wind affected me so severely that I was obliged to change my route from Viborg, where I stopped a few days, going southeast and giving up entirely the west coast ; that did not prevent me, however, from writing "Fancies by the Western Sea," and "Pictures of the West Coast of Jutland," which I never had seen, but only knew by others' verbal descriptions.

I saw now the country all round Skanderborg, Veile, and Kolding, and from there I went to Funen, enjoying the country-house life, and was received as a dear guest several weeks at the country seat "Maryhill," near the canal by Odense : the widow of the printer Iversen was my hostess.

This spot was in my earliest youth my ideal of a country-house. The little garden was plentifully supplied with inscriptions and verses, which told you what you were to think and feel at each place. Near the canal, where the ships passed, was built a little battery, mounted with wooden cannon ; there was also a watch-house and a sentry-box with a wooden soldier, all most childishly beautiful.

Here I lived with this intelligent, kind old woman, who was surrounded by a troop of bewitching, lovely grandchildren, all young girls. The oldest of these, Henriette, published at a later period two novels, "Aunt Anna," and "The Daughter of an Authoress."

The weeks passed with merriment and joy. I wrote a couple

of humorous poems, among which was "The Heart Thief," and occupied myself with a romance, "The Dwarf of Christian II.," for which I obtained some historical studies from the learned antiquary Vedel-Simonsen, of Elvedgaard, near Bogense. I went through about sixteen written sheets, which I read to Ingemann who seemed to like them. I may attribute to them the favorable recommendation he gave me when I offered my travelling petition.

Poems sprung forth upon paper, but of the comic fewer and fewer. Sentiment, which I had so often derided, would now be avenged. I arrived, in the course of my journey, at the house of a rich family in a small city ; and here suddenly a new world opened before me, — an immense world, which yet could be contained in four lines, which I wrote at that time : —

> A pair of dark eyes fixed my sight ;
> They were my world, my home, my delight ;
> The soul beamed in them, and childlike peace,
> And never on earth will their memory cease.

New plans of life occupied me. I would give up writing poetry, — to what could it lead ? I would study theology, and become a preacher ; I had only one thought, and that was *she.* But it was self-delusion : she loved another ; she married him. It was not till several years later that I felt and acknowledged that it was best, both for her and for myself, that things had fallen out as they had. She had no idea, perhaps, how deep my feeling for her had been, or what an influence it produced in me. She had become the excellent wife of a good man, and a happy mother. God's blessing rest upon her !

In my "Journey on Foot," and in most of my writings, satire had been the prevailing characteristic. This displeased many people, who thought that this bent of mind could lead to no good purpose. The critics now blamed me precisely for that which a far deeper feeling had expelled from my breast. A new collection of poetry, "Fancies and Sketches," which was published for the new year, showed satisfactorily what my heart suffered. A paraphrase of the history of my own heart appeared in a serious vaudeville, "Parting and Meeting," with this difference only, that here the love was mutual : the piece was not presented on the stage till five years later.

Among my young friends in Copenhagen at that time was Orla Lehmann, who afterwards rose higher in popular favor, on account of his political efforts, than any man in Denmark. Full of animation, eloquent and undaunted, his character of mind was one which interested me also. The German language was much studied at his father's; they had received there Heine's poems, and these were very attractive for young Orla. He lived in the country, in the neighborhood of the castle of Fredricksberg. I went there to see him, and he sang as I came one of Heine's verses, "Thalatta, Thalatta, du eviges Meer." We read Heine together; the afternoon and the evening passed, and I was obliged to remain there all night; but I had on this evening made the acquaintance of a poet, who, as it seemed to me, sang from the soul; he supplanted Hoffman, who, as might be seen by my "Journey on Foot," had formerly had the greatest influence on me. In my youth there were only three authors who as it were infused themselves into my blood, — Walter Scott, Hoffman, and Heine.

I betrayed more and more in my writings an unhealthy turn of mind. I felt an inclination to seek for the melancholy in life, and to linger on the dark side of things; I became sensitive, and thought rather of the blame than of the praise which was lavished on me. My late school education, which was forced, and my impulse to become an author whilst I was yet a student, make it evident that my first work, the "Journey on Foot," was not without grammatical errors. Had I only paid some one to correct the proofs, which was a work I was unaccustomed to, then no charge of this kind could have been brought against me. Now, on the contrary, people laughed at these errors, and dwelt upon them, passing over carelessly that in the book which had merit. I know people who only read my poems to find out errors; they noted down, for instance, how often I used the word *beautiful*, or some similar word. A gentleman, now a clergyman, at that time a writer of vaudevilles and a critic, was not ashamed, in a company where I was, to go through several of my poems in this style; so that a little girl of six years old, who heard with amazement that he discovered everything to be wrong, took the book, and pointing out the conjunction *and*, said, "There is yet a little word about which you have not scolded." He felt what a reproof lay in the remark of the child; he looked ashamed and kissed the little one. All this wounded me; but I had, since my school-days, become somewhat timid, and that caused me to take it all quietly: I was morbidly sensitive, and I was good-natured to a fault. Everybody knew it, and some were on that account almost cruel to me. Everybody wished to teach me; almost everybody said that I was spoiled by praise, and therefore *they* would speak the truth to me. Thus I heard continually of my faults, the real and the ideal weaknesses. In the mean time, however, my feelings burst forth; and then I said that I would become a poet whom they should see honored. But this was regarded only as the crowning mark of the most unbearable vanity; and from house to house it was repeated. I was a good man, they said, but one of the vainest in existence; and in that very time I was often ready wholly to despair of my abilities, and had, as in the darkest days of my school-life, a feeling as if my whole talents were a self-deception. I almost believed so; but it was more than I could bear, to hear the same thing said, sternly and jeeringly, by others; and if I then uttered a proud, an inconsiderate word, it was addressed to the scourge with which I was smitten; and when those who smite are those we love, then do the scourges become scorpions.

For this reason Collin thought that I should make a little journey, in order to divert my mind and furnish me with new ideas. I had by industry and frugality laid aside a little sum of money, so that I resolved to spend a couple of weeks in North Germany.

In the spring of 1831, I left Denmark for the first time. I saw Lübeck and Hamburg. Everything astonished me and occupied my mind. There were as yet no railways here; the broad, deep, and sandy route passed over the heaths of Lunenburg, which looked as I had read of them in the admired "Labyrinth" of Baggesen.

I arrived at Braunschweig. I saw mountains for the first time, — the Hartzgebirge — and went on foot from Goslar over the Brocken to Halle.

The world expanded so astonishingly before me my **good** humor returned to me as to the bird of passage, but sorrow **is** the flock of sparrows, which remains behind and builds in the nests of the birds of passage.

In the book at the summit of the Brocken, where so many travellers write down their names, thoughts, and sentiments, I also wrote down mine in a little verse : —

> Above the clouds I stand here,
> Yet must my heart confess
> That nearer far to heaven I was
> When I *her* hand could press.

Next year a friend told me that he had seen my verse, when he visited the Brocken, and a countryman had written below, " Poor little Andersen, save your verses for Elmquist's ' Reading book,' and trouble us not with them abroad, where they never find their way except when you come and write them down."

In Dresden I made acquaintance with Tieck. Ingemann had given me a letter to him. I heard him one evening read aloud one of Shakespeare's plays. On taking leave of him, he wished me a poet's success, embraced and kissed me ; which made the deepest impression upon me. The expression of his eyes I shall never forget. I left him with tears, and prayed most fervently to God for strength to enable me to pursue the way after which my whole soul strove — strength, which should enable me to express that which I felt in my soul ; and that when I next saw Tieck, I might be known and valued by him. It was not until several years afterward, when my later works were translated into German, and well received in his country, that we saw each other again ; I felt the true hand-pressure of him who had given to me, in my second father-land, the kiss of consecration.

In Berlin, a letter of Örsted's procured me the acquaint- ance of Chamisso. That grave man, with his long locks and honest eyes, opened the door to me himself, read the letter, and I know not how it was, but we understood each other immedi- ately. I felt perfect confidence in him, and told him so, though it was in bad German. Chamisso understood Danish ; I gave him my poems, and he was the first who translated any of them, and thus introduced me into Germany. It was thus he spoke of me at that time in the "Morgenblatt:" "Gifted with wit, fancy, and humor, and a national *naïveté,* Andersen has still in his power tones which awaken deeper echoes. He understands, in particular, how with perfect ease, by a few slight but graphic touches, to call into existence little pictures and landscapes, but which are often so peculiarly local as not to interest those who are unfamiliar with the home of the poet. Perhaps that which may be translated from' him, or which is so already, may be the least calculated to give a proper idea of him."

Chamisso became a life-long friend to me. The pleasure which he had in my later writings may be seen by the printed letters addressed to me in the collected edition of his works.

The little journey in Germany had great influence upon me, as my Copenhagen friends acknowledged. The impressions of the journey were immediately written down, and I gave them forth under the title of "Shadow Pictures." Whether I were actually improved or not, there still prevailed at home the same petty pleasure in dragging out my faults, the same perpetual schooling of me ; and I was weak enough to endure it from those who were officious meddlers. I seldom made a joke of it ; but if I did so, it was called arrogance and vanity, and it was asserted that I never would listen to rational people. Such an instructor once asked me whether I wrote *Dog* with a little *d ;* — he had found such an error of the press in my last work. I replied, jestingly, " Yes, because I here spoke of a little dog."

But these are small troubles, people will say. Yes, but they are drops which wear hollows in the rock. I speak of it here ; I feel a necessity to do so ; here to protest against the accusation of vanity, which, since no other error can be discovered in my private life, is seized upon, and even now is thrown at me like an old medal.

I willingly read for everybody whom I visited what I lately had written that pleased me. I had not yet learned by experience how seldom an author ought to do this, at least in this country. Any gentleman or lady who can hammer on a piano or sing a few songs, has no hesitation, in whatever

company they may enter, to carry their music-book with them
and place themselves before the piano ; it is but very seldom
that any remark is made on that ; an author may read aloud
others' poetical works but not his own — that is vanity.

That has been said many times about Oehlenschläger, who
was always willing to read his works in the different circles
where he went, and read them very beautifully too. How
many remarks I have heard about it from people who seemed
to think that they made themselves interesting thereby, or
showed their superiority to the poet : if they allowed themselves to do thus toward Oehlenschläger, how much further
could they not then go toward Andersen ?

Sometimes my good humor lifted me above the bitterness
that surrounded me ; I discovered weakness in others as well
as in myself. In such a moment I brought forth my little
poem, " Snik-snak," [1] which was printed, and I was made the
subject of many verses and poems in papers and periodicals.
A lady whom I used to visit sent for me, and catechised me
to know " if I ever visited houses where this poem had any
appropriateness ; she did not believe that it had anything
to do with the company that met at her house, but as I
was a guest there, people would imagine that her house
was the place I had aimed at," and then she gave me a good
lecture.

In the vestibule of the theatre one evening a well-dressed
lady, unknown to me, came up very near me, and with an expression of indignation looked me in the face and said, " Snik-
snak." I took off my hat : politeness does for an answer !

From the end of the year 1828, to the beginning of 1839, I
maintained myself alone by my writings. It was difficult for
me to pull through, — doubly difficult, because my dress must
in some measure accord with the circles into which I went.
To produce, and always to be producing, was destructive, nay
impossible. I translated a few pieces for the theatre, — " La
Quarantaine," and " La Reine de seize ans," — and wrote the
text for a couple of operas.

Through the writings of Hoffmann my attention had been
turned to the masked comedies of Gozzi, and finding among

---

[1] A popular expression for senseless gabble and chatter.

these " Il Corvo " to be an excellent subject for an opera text, I read Meisling's translation of it, became quite enraptured, and in a few weeks I wrote my opera text of " The Raven."

I gave it to a young composer, almost unknown at that time, but a man of talent and spirit, a grandson of him who composed the Danish folk's-song of " King Christian stood by the tall, tall mast." My young composer was the present Professor J. P. E. Hartmann.

It will sound strange to the ears of many, when I say that I at that time, in my letter to the theatrical directors, recommended him and gave my word for his being a man of talent, who would produce something good. He now takes rank among the first of living Danish composers.

My text to " The Raven " is without freshness and melody, and I have not inserted it in my collected writings ; only a chorus and a song are introduced among the poems.

I worked up also Walter Scott's " Bride of Lammermoor " for another young composer, Bredal. Both operas appeared on the stage ; but I was subjected to the most merciless criticism, as one who had stultified the labors of foreign poets. I have a reminiscence of Oehlenschläger at that time which not only displays his irritability, but also, in a high degree, his thoroughly noble nature.

The " Bride of Lammermoor " had appeared on the stage and was received with acclamation. I took the printed text to Oehlenschläger, who smiled and congratulated me on the great applause I had received, but said that it was easy for me to obtain it, as I had taken from Walter Scott, and had been assisted by the composer. It grieved me much to hear him say so, and tears came into my eyes ; when he saw that he embraced and kissed me, and said : " Other people are making me cross too ! " and now he was heartiness itself, presented me with one of his books, and wrote his and my name in it.

The composer Weyse, my earliest benefactor, whom I have already mentioned, was, on the contrary, satisfied in the highest degree with my treatment of these subjects. He told me that he had wished for a long time to compose an opera from Walter Scott's " Kenilworth." He now requested me to commence the joint work, and write the text. I had no idea of the summary justice which would be dealt to me. I needed money to live, and, what still more determined me to it, I felt flattered to have to work with Weyse, our most celebrated composer. It delighted me that he, who had first spoken in my favor at Siboni's house, now, as artist, sought a noble connection with me. I had scarcely half finished the text, when I was already blamed for having made use of a well-known romance. I wished to give it up ; but Weyse consoled me, and encouraged me to proceed. Afterward, before he had finished the music, when I was about to travel abroad, I committed my fate, as regarded the text, entirely to his hands. He wrote whole verses of it, and the altered conclusion is wholly his own. It was a peculiarity of that singular man that he liked no book which ended sorrowfully. Amy Robsart, in "Kenilworth," must marry Leicester. "Why make them unhappy, when one with only a few pen-strokes can make them happy !" said he. "But it is not historical," replied I. "What shall we then do with Queen Elizabeth ? " — "She may say : ' Proud England, I am thine ! ' " answered he. I yielded, and let him finish the opera with these words.

"Kenilworth" was brought on the stage, but was not printed, with the exception of the songs ; two of which have become very well known through the music. To this followed anonymous attacks : the city post brought me letters in which the unknown writers scoffed at and derided me. That same year I published a new collection of poetry, "The Twelve Months of the Year ; " and this book, though it was afterward pronounced to contain the greater part of my best lyrical poems, was then condemned as bad.

At that time "The Monthly Review of Literature," though it has now gone to its grave, was in its full bloom. At its first appearance, it numbered among its co-workers some of the most distinguished names. Its want, however, was men who were qualified to speak ably on æsthetic works. Unfortunately, everybody fancies himself able to give an opinion upon these ; but people may write excellently on surgery or pedagogical science, and may have a name in those things, and yet be dolts in poetry : of this proofs may be seen. By degrees it became more and more difficult for the critical bench to find a judge for poetical works., The one, however, who, through his extraordinary zeal for writing and speaking, was ready at hand, was the historian and states-councilor Molbech, who played, in our time, so great a part in the history of Danish criticism that I must speak of him rather more fully. He is an industrious collector, writes extremely correct Danish, and his Danish dictionary, let him be reproached with whatever want he may, is a most highly useful work ; but, as a judge of æsthetic works, he is one-sided, and even fanatically devoted to party spirit. He belongs, unfortunately, to the men of science, who are only one sixty-fourth of a poet, and who are the most incompetent judges of æsthetics. He has, for example, by his critiques on Ingemann's romances, shown how far he is below the poetry which he censures. He has himself published a volume of poems, which belong to the common run of books, — " A Ramble through Denmark," written in the *fade*, flowery style of those times, and " A Journey through Germany, France, and Italy," which seems to be made up out of books, not out of life. He sat in his study, or in the Royal Library, where. he has a post, when suddenly he became director of the theatre and censor of the pieces sent in. He was sickly, one-sided in judgment, and irritable : people may imagine the result. He spoke of my first poems very favorably ; but my star soon sank for another, who was in the ascendant, — a young lyrical poet, Paludan Müller ; and, as he no longer loved, he hated me. That is the short history ; indeed in the selfsame " Monthly Review " the very poems which had formerly been praised were now condemned by the same judge, when they appeared in a new enlarged edition. There is a Danish proverb, " When the carriage drags, everybody pushes behind ; " and I proved the truth of it now. People spoke only of my faults, and it certainly is human nature under such circumstances to feel badly. I showed this to my would-be friends, and from them it was told about the great city, which often ought rather to be called the little city. Even well-dressed people, passing me in the streets, made wry faces at me and threw out scoffing remarks.

The Danes are great mockers, or, to use a more polite expression, they have a great sense of the ludicrous, and that is the reason there are so many comedy poets among them.

It happened that a new star in, Danish literature ascended at this time. Henrik Hertz published his " Letters from the Dead " anonymously : it was a mode of driving all the unclean things out of the temple. The deceased Baggesen sent polemical letters from Paradise, which resembled in the highest degree the style of that author. They contained a sort of apotheosis of Heiberg, and in part attacks upon Oehlenschläger and Hauch. The old story about my orthographical errors was again revived ; my name and my school-days in Slagelse were brought into connection with St. Anders. I was ridiculed, or, if people will, I was chastised.

Hertz's book went through all Denmark ; people spoke of nothing but him. It made it still more piquant that the author of the work could not be discovered, People were enraptured, and justly. Heiberg, in his " Flying Post, " defended a few æsthetical insignificants, but not me.

To be scoffingly exposed in a public journal had then quite another side to it than now, when so many share the same fate. The predecessor of "The Corsair," "The Rocket," published by Mathias Winther, was then truly a kind of pillory, which gave a kind of importance to that side of the victim that was opposite the public, who then believed everything that got into print. There was only one, the student Drejer, under the ficticious name " Davieno," who supported me. He was a brother of the botanist, both now deceased, a very gifted man whose poems and biography are published, but not his more considerable poem, " A Versified Letter to Count Zealandsfar," which he wrote in my defense.

I could not say anything : I could only let the big heavy sea roll over me, and it was the common opinion that I was to be totally washed away. I felt deeply the wound of the sharp knife, and was upon the point of giving myself up, as I now already was given up by all others. There existed no other Allah than the author of " The Letters from the Dead," and Heiberg was his Prophet. I however, in a short time, published a little book, " Vignettes to the Poets," in which I characterized the dead and the living authors in a few lines each, but only spoke of that which was good in them. A little verse to me was printed in " The Day." It was signed " Count of Funen." People jibed at the new admirer and poet I had found, but they would not have done so if they had known that the author was the honorable old gentleman Mr. Wegener, director of the seminary for teachers at Jonstrup and publisher of the " House Friend." He was widely esteemed and honored. The book excited attention; it was regarded as one of the best of my works; it was imitated, but the critics did not meddle with it. It was evident, on this occasion, as had already been the case, that the critics never laid hands on those of my works which were the most successful.

My affairs were now in their worst condition; and precisely in that same year in which a stipend for travelling had been conferred upon Hertz, I also had presented a petition for the same purpose. I looked up to King Frederic VI. with true reverence and heartfelt gratitude. I had grown up with these feelings, and I felt a strong desire to give them expression. I could not do it in any other way than by presenting him a book, which he had allowed me to dedicate to him, "The Twelve Months of the Year."

A man, who meant well by me and was acquainted with what needed to be done, told me that I ought, in order to take proper measures to receive a stipend for travelling, to tell the King when I presented him my book, shortly and clearly who I was; that since becoming a student I had made my way without any support; and that travel would, more than anything else, serve to complete my education; then the King would probably answer, that I could bring him a petition, which I was to have by me and thereupon hand to him. I thought it monstrous that at the same moment when I presented him my book I should ask him a favor! "That is the way," said he; "the King is very well aware that you give him the book in order to ask for something!" This made me almost desperate, but he said, "That is the only way to do it," and I did it. My audience must have been very comical indeed; my heart was beating with fear, and when the King, in his peculiar manner, stepped abruptly toward me and asked what book I brought him, I answered, — " A cycle of poems!"

" A cycle, cycle — what do you mean?" Then I became quite disconcerted and said, —

"It is some verses to Denmark!" He smiled : —

"Well, well, it is very good, thank you!" and so he nodded and dismissed me. But as I had not yet begun on my real errand, I told him that I had still something more to say to him ; and now, without hesitation, I told him about my studies and how I had gone through them. " That is very praise-worthy," said the King ; and when I reached the point of a stipend for travelling, he answered, as I had been told he would : "Well, send me your petition ! "

"Yes, sire! exclaimed I in all simplicity. "I have it with me! but it seems to me so dreadful, that I should bring it along with the book ; they have told me that I ought to do so, that it was the right way, but I find it so dreadful : it is not like me!" — and tears rushed from my eyes. The good King laughed heartily, nodded in a friendly fashion, and took the petition. I made a bow and ran away at full speed.

The universal opinion was that I had reached the point of culmination, and if I was to succeed in travelling, it must be at this present time. I felt, what since then has become an acknowledged fact, that travelling would be the best school for me. In the mean time I was told that, to bring it under consideration, I must endeavor to obtain from the most distinguished poets and men of science a kind of rec-ommendation, because this very year there were so many dis-tinguished young men who were soliciting a stipend, that it would be difficult among these to put in an available claim. I therefore obtained recommendations for myself ; and I am, so far as I know, the only Danish poet who was obliged to produce recommendations to prove that he was a poet. And here also it is remarkable, that the men who recommended me have each one made prominent some very different quali-fication which gave me a claim : for instance, Oehlenschläger, my lyrical power, and the earnestness that was in me ; Inge-mann, my skill in depicting popular life ; Heiberg declared that since the days of Wessel, no Danish poet had possessed so much humor as myself ; Örsted remarked, every one — they who were against me as well as those who were for me — agreed on one subject, and this was that I was a *true* poet. Thiele expressed himself warmly and enthusiastically about the power which he had seen in me, combating against the oppression and the misery of life. I received a stipend for travelling — Hertz a larger and I a smaller one : and that also was quite in the order of things.

"Now be happy," said my friends, " make yourself aware of your unbounded good fortune ! Enjoy the present moment, as it will probably be the only time in which you will get abroad. You shall hear what people say about you while you are travelling, and how we shall defend you ; sometimes, however, we shall not be able to do that."

It was painful to me to hear such things said ; I felt a compulsion of soul to be away, that I might, if possible, breathe freely ; but sorrow is firmly seated on the horse of the rider. More than one sorrow oppressed my heart, and although I opened the chambers of my heart to the world, one or two of them I kept locked, nevertheless. On setting out on my journey, my prayer to God was that I might die far away from Denmark, or else return strengthened for activity, and in a condition to produce works which should win for me and my beloved ones joy and honor.

Precisely at the moment of setting out on my journey, the forms of those I loved arose in my heart. Among the few whom I have already named, there are two who exercised a great influence upon my life and my poetry, and these I must more particularly mention. A beloved mother ; an unusually liberal-minded and well educated lady, Madame Lässöe, had introduced me into her agreeable circle of friends ; she often felt the deepest sympathy with me in my troubles ; she always turned my attention to the beautiful in nature and the poetical in the details of life, and as almost every one regarded me as a poet, she elevated my mind ; yes, and if there be tenderness and purity in anything which I have written, they are among those things for which I have especially to be thankful to her. Another character of great importance to me was Collin's son Edward. Brought up under fortunate circumstances of life, he was possessed of that courage and determination which I wanted. I felt that he sincerely loved me, and I, full of affection, threw myself upon him with my whole soul ;

he passed on calmly and practically through the business of life. I often mistook him at the very moment when he felt for me most deeply, and when he would gladly have infused into me a portion of his own character, — to me, who was as a reed shaken by the wind. It was pleasure and happiness to me to recite either my own or others' poems. In a family circle, where I was present with my young friend, I was asked to recite, and I was ready to do it, but — knowing better than I just what the company meant, and that I was in their eyes nothing more than an object of ridicule — he came up to me, and said that if I recited a single piece he would go away! I was dejected, and the hostess and the ladies overwhelmed me with reproaches. It was only afterward that I saw things from his point of view and understood how, with his knowledge of the moment, he was my honest friend ; then it caused me tears, although I had the fullest confidence that he felt deeply for my interest. In the practical part of life, he, the younger, stood actively by my side, from the assistance which he gave in my Latin exercises, to the arranging the business of bringing out editions of my works. He has always remained the same ; and were I to enumerate my friends, he would be placed by me as the first on the list. When the traveller leaves the mountains behind him, then for the first time he sees them in their true form : so is it also with friends.

A little album of verses from many whose names were illustrious, was my little treasure ; it accompanied me on all my travels, and has since increased and become of very great value to me.

I left Copenhagen Monday, 22d April, 1833. I saw the steeples of the city dissolving from my view — we approached the promontory of Möen ; then the Captain brought me a letter and said jokingly : " It came just now down through the air." It was a few words more, an affectionate farewell from Edward Collin. Off Falster another letter from another friend. At bed-time a third, and early in the morning near Travemünde a fourth — all "through the air!" said the Captain. My friends had kindly and sympathetically filled his pockets with letters for me.

CHAPTER V.

IN Hamburg lived the poet Lars Kruse, author of the trag
edies, — "Ezzelin," "The Widow," "The Monastery,"
which I have seen performed at the Royal Theatre ; his novel,
"Seven Years," was much read ; the "Musenalmanach" of
Germany every year made a great show of his stories. Now
he is there as here almost entirely forgotten. He was an
amiable, well-meaning man, of a good-natured, fleshy appearance ; he spoke to me of his love for his country, and wrote
down in my album a little verse.

That was the first poetical greeting I received in a foreign
country, and therefore it was fixed in my memory. The next
lively impression of travel was formed in Cassel, upon seeing
a name in half-effaced letters on a street-corner, — the name
of Napoleon, for whom the street or place had been named.
That made a greater impression on me than all the glory of
"Wilhelmshöhe," with its artificial ruins and fountains. Napoleon was the hero of my youth and my heart.

In Cassel I saw for the first time Spohr, and was received
very kindly by him. He asked me many questions concerning music in Denmark and its composers. He knew something of Weyse's and Kuhlau's compositions.

A little theme of "The Raven," which Hartmann had written down in my album, captivated him much, and I know that
several years afterward he commenced a correspondence with
Hartmann, and made an attempt, yet without success, to put
"The Raven" on the stage at Cassel. He spoke of his own
works, and asked me which of them were given at the theatre
of Copenhagen, and I was obliged to answer "None at all,"
and must still say so.

His opera, "Zemire and Azor," seemed to be his best, and
was also so regarded by himself. He had a slight acquaintance with Danish literature, and knew something of Baggesen,
Oehlenschläger and Kruse.

Thorwaldsen had his highest admiration. I was touched at taking leave of him, for I thought that I was bidding farewell forever to a man, who by his works will be admired through generations. I did not think that we should meet each other again, and yet it happened many years afterward at London, where we met as old friends.

Nowadays we travel speedily through Germany to Paris, but it was not so in 1833. Then there were no railways, and we crept slowly forward, stowed away night and day in heavy, clumsy stage-coaches. After all that prose of travel, it was for me a kind of poetry to reach Frankfurt, Goethe's native town — the home in childhood, too, of the Rothschilds, where the rich mother of powerful men would not leave the little house in the Jew Quarter, where she had borne and brought up her rich and happy sons. The Gothic old gable-ended houses, the city hall of the Middle Ages, formed a page of pictures for me.

The composer Aloys Schmitt, known by his opera " Valeria," was the first abroad who asked me to write him an opera text. My smaller poems, which were translated by Chamisso, had shown him, as he expressed it, that I was the poet he wanted.

I saw the Rhine! Its banks appear least favorable at springtime, the vines looking meanly, as they rise toward the castle ruins. I had imagined it all much more grand. What I saw was below my expectation, and I think that I am not alone in that opinion ; the most beautiful point is undeniably Loreley, near St. Goar. The banks of the river Danube are more romantic, even the Rhone has points which surpass those of the Rhine. The traditions are the chief attractions of the Rhine. Tales and songs — those charming songs, which the German poets have sung to the honor of that mighty sea-green stream — are its highest beauty.

From the Rhine we continued our journey for three nights and days over Saarbrück, through the chalk district of Champagne, to Paris. I looked eagerly toward this " city of cities," as I then called it, and asked so many times if we should not soon be there that at last I stopped asking, and so we passed the very Boulevards even before I knew that we had reached that mighty city.

All my travelling impressions on my way from Copenhagen to Paris are presented in what I have here written, and but very little was I able to get hold of on this rapid passage. Still there were people at home who already expected to see something from me ; they did not consider that if even the curtain is raised the play is not immediately seen or clearly conceived.

I was now in Paris, but fatigued and sleepy. I descended at the Hôtel de Lille, Rue Thomas, near the Palais Royal. To go to bed and get a good sleep was the best thing for me, but I had not slept long before I was awakened by a dreadful noise ; it was light all around. I started to the window ; opposite, in the narrow street, was a large building. I looked through the windows : a crowd of people rushed down the stairs, crying and bellowing ; there was a great rush and rumble and flashing, and I, being still half asleep, thought of course that all Paris was in a revolution. I rang the bell and asked the waiter what the matter was. " C'est le tonnerre ! " said he ; " Le tonnerre ! " said the maid ; and seeing that I did not understand them, they rolled with the tongue, " Tonnerre-re-rrre ! " showing me how the thunderbolt beats down, and meanwhile it lightened and rumbled. It was the thunder, and the house opposite was the Vaudeville Theatre, where the play was just finished and people were rushing down-stairs ; that was my first awakening in Paris.

Now I was to see its grandeurs. The Italian opera was already closed, but the great opera was ablaze with brilliant stars. Madame Damoreau and Adolph Nourrit were singing. Nourrit was then in his full vigor, and was the favorite of the Parisians. I heard him, who had fought so bravely, and at the barricades had with his whole soul sung patriotic songs, exciting the enthusiasm of the fighters, and all was joy and jubilation. Four years more and I heard of his despair and death.

He went to Naples in 1837. His reception there was not what he expected ; even a hiss was heard, and that agitated much the singer who always had been admired. Once more, though sick at heart, he appeared in " Norma ; " one hiss was again heard, in spite of the stormy applause of all the rest.

Nourrit was deeply wounded ; he was up the whole night, and in the morning, the 8th of March, he precipitated himself from a window in the third story. His widow and six children were left to mourn him.

It was in his splendor and happiness, when living in a jubilee of admiration, that I heard him in Paris as *Gustavus the Third.* This opera was admired by all. The widow of the real Ankarström lived here and was an old woman ; she published a card in one of the best known journals, saying that the relations which Scribe had placed King Gustavus in, to her, were totally false, and that she had only seen the King once.

I saw the tragedy " Les Enfants d'Edouard," in the Theatre Français ; old Mademoiselle Mars played the part of the young sons' mother, and though I understood the French language very little, her acting made everything comprehensible to me ; a more beautiful voice in a woman I never have heard before nor since. When I was first living in Copenhagen the renowned Miss Astrup appeared on the Danish stage, and was admired by the Copenhagen public for her undying youthfulness ! I saw her as she appeared with feelings of piety in the tragedy " Selim, Prince of Algeria," where she acted the mother ; but for me she was an old, laced maid, stiff as a pin, with an unpleasant gaggling voice ; of her acting I could not judge. In Mademoiselle Mars in Paris I saw the true youthfulness, which did not consist in stays and struttings ; in her were youthful movements, a musical voice, and I could understand without being told that she was a true artist !

There were several of us Danes together that summer in Paris ; we all lived in the same hotel, and went in company together to restaurants, cafés, and theatres. Our own home-tongue was always spoken, letters were read by each other, views of home received and talked over, and at last we hardly knew whether we were in a foreign land or our own.

Everything was seen and had to be seen, for it was on this account we had come abroad. I remember that one of our dear friends one morning returning from museums and palaces almost exhausted, said : " I cannot help it, they must be seen ; for when I go home again I shall be ashamed to be asked and have to confess that I had not seen this or that ; there only remain a few places, and when they are done, I shall have a real good time!" This was the common talk, and will probably very often be repeated. I went out in company with the others and saw and saw, but most of it has long since been effaced from my memory.

The magnificent Versailles with its rich saloons and large paintings gave place in my mind to the Trianon. I entered Napoleon's bed-room with pious feelings ; all was there in the same state as when he lived : the walls had yellow tapestry and the bed yellow curtains ; a pair of stairs led up to the bed ; I put my hand on one of the steps which had been touched by his foot, and on his pillow. If I had been alone I should surely have knelt down. Napoleon was indeed the hero of my youth and also of my father. I looked up to him as the Catholic to his saint. I visited the little farm in the garden of Trianon, where Marie Antoinette, dressed as a peasant-girl, managed the dairy and all pertaining to it. I plucked a honeysuckle which climbed up to the window of the unfortunate Queen's room ; a little daisy, in all its simplicity, was in contrast preserved in memory of the mighty Versailles.

I saw, or rather I spoke, with few celebrities in Paris ; one of those, to whom I was introduced by a letter from the Danish ballet-master, Bournonville, was the vaudeville-poet, Paul Duport. His drama, " The Quaker and the Dancer," has been performed at our theatre, and was very well executed. The old man was much pleased to hear this information, and received me very kindly. A very comical scene, however, soon took place between us. I spoke French but poorly ; he thought that he could speak German, but he pronounced it s: that I could not understand him at all. He took a German dictionary, placed it on his lap and looked continually for words, but to speak by help of a dictionary is a very slow practice and suited neither a Frenchman nor me.

Another visit was to Cherubini, to whom I was, to speak properly, sent on an errand from Weyse. Many will still remember how poor an appreciation the ingenious Weyse got at home for his opera compositions. and yet among these were the melodious works, " The Narcotic Potion " and " The

Grotto of Ludlam." He lived and composed exclusively for us, but could never get into fashion. Only as composer of church music did he make his mark, and his "Ambrosian Hymn of Praise" was especially admired. It was that hymn I was charged by him to carry to Cherubini, the immortal composer of "The Two Days," and the master of so many excellent requiems. At this very time the attention of the Parisian public was attracted to him. He had then, after a long rest and in his old age, composed a new work for the great opera, "Ali Baba, or the Forty Thieves." It had no success, but was received with affectionate homage.

I went to Cherubini ; the old man looked like the pictures I had seen of him ; he sat before his piano and had a cat upon each shoulder. He had never heard of Weyse, not even of his name, and asked me of the music I brought him. The only Danish composer he knew was Claus Schall, who has composed the music for the ballets of Galeotti. Weyse never heard from Cherubini, and I never saw him again.

One day I entered " Europe Litteraire," a kind of Parisian " Athenæum," where Paul Duport had introduced me. A little man of Jewish cast came toward me. " I hear you are a Dane," said he ; " I am a German: Danes and Germans are brothers, therefore I offer you my hand ! "

I asked for his name, and he said: " Heinrich Heine ! " the poet whom, in my recent young erotic period of life, I had admired so much, and who had so entirely expressed my thoughts and feelings in his songs. There was no man I could have wished more to see and meet with than he, and so I told him.

" Only phrases ! " said he smiling ; "if I had interested you as much as you tell me, you should have sought me out before ! "

" I could not," replied I ; " you have so much sense of the ludicrous, that you might have thought it absurd in me, who am a Danish poet entirely unknown to you, to seek you. I know also that I should have behaved very awkwardly toward you, and if you had then laughed at me, or perhaps quizzed me, I should have been deeply wounded, for the very reason that I estimate you so highly ; so I should rather have missed seeing you at all."

My words made a good impression on him, and he was very kind and amiable. The next day he returned my visit in Hôtel Vivienne, where I lived. We met each other often, and sometimes we promenaded together on the Boulevard, but I did not then place full confidence in him, and I did not feel that hearty attraction which several years afterward I felt when we met again in Paris, and he had read my " Improvisatore " and some of my small stories. On my departure from Paris to Italy he wrote to me : —

" I should have wished, my dear colleague, to scribble some verses to you, but to-day I can hardly write tolerably in prose. Farewell ! I wish you a pleasant sojourn in Italy. Learn German well in Germany, and when you return to Denmark write down in German what you have seen and felt in Italy. That would make me very happy.

" H. HEINE.

"PARIS, *August* 10, 1833."

The first French book I tried to read in Paris was Victor Hugo's novel, " Notre Dame." I used daily to visit the cathedral and look upon the scenes depicted in that poetical work. I was captivated by those stirring pictures and dramatic characters, and what could I do better than go and see the poet, who lived in a corner-house in the Place Royale. They were old-fashioned rooms, hung with engravings, wood-cuts, and paintings of Notre Dame. He received me in his bed-gown, drawers, and elegant morning boots. Taking leave of him, I asked him for his name on a piece of paper ; he complied with my wishes, and wrote his name close up to the edge of the paper. I felt very badly, for it came immediately to my mind that he did this because he did not know me, and was cautious that no place should be left for me to write above his name. At a later stay in Paris I came to know the poet better.

During my journey to Paris, and the whole of the first month I spent there, I heard not a single word from home. I asked for letters at the post-office, but in vain. Could my friends, perhaps, have nothing agreeable to tell me ? Could it be that I still was envied the travelling stipend which the recommendations of so many had procured me? I was much depressed. At length, however, a letter arrived, — a large unpaid one, which cost a large sum in postage, but then it was such a splendid great one. My heart beat with joy and yearning impatience to read it; it was, indeed, my first letter from home. I opened it, but I discovered not a single written word, nothing but a printed newspaper, — "The Copenhagen Post," of Monday, May 13, 1833, containing a lampoon upon me; and that was sent to me all that distance with postage unpaid, probably by the anonymous writer himself.

That was to be my first greeting from home. This abominable malice wounded me deeply. I have never discovered who the author was; the verses betrayed a practiced pen; perhaps he was one of those who afterwards called me "friend" and pressed my hand. Men have base thoughts; I also have mine.

I remained in Paris till the July festivals were over; they were then in their first freshness, and I saw on one of the days the unveiling of Napoleon's pillar at the Place Vendôme.

The evening before, while the workmen were at work, the statue still covered, and people gathered in crowds on the place, a strange-looking, lean old woman came toward me, and with laughter and an expression of insanity said to me, "There they have placed him; to-morrow, perhaps, they take him down again. Ha, ha, ha! I know the French people!" I went away with sad thoughts.

The following day I had a seat upon a high scaffold at the corner of the place. I gazed on Louis Philippe, with his sons and generals. The "garde nationale" passed with music and with bouquets of flowers stuck in the gun-barrels; people shouted Hurra! but also "À bas les forts" was heard.

In the Hôtel de Ville was a people's ball in splendid style; all classes came together, from the royal family to the fishwomen. The crowd was so dense that Louis Philippe and his queen reached the seats arranged for them with considerable difficulty. It made a sad impression on me to hear the orchestra play the dance-music of the opera "Gustavus the Third," when the royal family entered. I looked to see in the face of Queen Amelie an impression similar to what I felt : she was deadly pale and clung tightly to Louis Philippe, who with a jovial smile saluted all and shook hands with several persons.

I saw the Duc d'Orleans, young and full of vigor, dancing with a poorly dressed young girl, — probably one of the lowest classes.

This feast and gayety continued through several days ; in the evenings funereal flambeaux burned upon the graves of the fallen citizens, which were adorned with wreaths of everlastings ; tournaments in boats were held in the Seine ; Danish sports in fine style were seen in Champs d'Elysées. All the theatres in Paris were open to the public, even in the middle of the day, and representations were given with open doors ; everybody could come and go as they liked. Sometimes the people interrupted the performance of tragedies and operas, and began to sing " La Parisienne " and " Allons Enfants." In the evenings rockets and fire-works flashed and cracked in the air, and there were brilliant illuminations of churches and public buildings.

Thus ended my first visit to Paris, and the finale could not have been more grand and festive.

As to my French, I had not improved much in the nearly three months I spent here. It is a weakness of the Danes that they here live together, — exclusively together, and I had given way to the same weakness. I felt a necessity to learn a little more of that language, and therefore determined to board for a while in some quiet place in Switzerland so as to be compelled to speak French ; but I was told that such a stay would be very expensive for me.

" If you would condescend to visit a little city up in the Jura Mountains, where it snows even in August, you would there find a cheap place and many friends too," said a Swiss to me, with whom I had made acquaintance through his family in Copenhagen. After Paris and all its pleasures, a stay in those solitary mountains would be very refreshing to me. I wished there in quiet to finish a poem, which now occupied my thoughts. The plan for the journey was laid, and the route fixed by Geneva and Lausanne to the little city of Le Locle, in the Jura Mountains.

Among my compatriots in Paris were two who belonged to Denmark's renowned men, both of whom had received me very kindly. One of them was the author of the "Vons and Vans," and the "Laterna Magica," the poet Peter Andreas Heiberg, who at a period, so different from ours, was exiled from Denmark, and had chosen Paris for his new home; his life is well known to all Danes. I sought him out; he lived in one of the smaller hotels, and was an aged and almost blind man.

His son, John Ludvig Heiberg, our present director of the theatre, had then recently married Johanne Louise, Denmark's, and, I am bold to say, one of the world's most honored and estimated actresses of the age. It greatly interested the old Heiberg to hear of her, but I understood that he still held to his old fashioned, or perhaps Parisian opinions, regarding scenic artists.

He did not like it that his son's wife should be governed by the theatre director, whom he considered to be a kind of a tyrant; meanwhile he was glad to hear from me, and, as he said, from all the Danes, that she was such a respectable girl, endowed with real talent. It is a pity that he never himself learned to know her talent, her important place on the Danish stage, and her noble character. He seemed to feel very desolate, and it was pitiful to behold the half-blind man feeling his way along through the well-known arcades of the Palais Royal. At my departure he wrote in my album : —

" Receive a blind man's friendly farewell !

" P. A. HEIBERG.

" PARIS *August* 10, 1833."

The other famous Dane who favored me was the counselor of state Bröndsted, with whom I became acquainted at the house of Admiral Wulff; he came from London, where he had read my book, " The Twelve Months of the Year." He had not before read anything of mine; my verses pleased him, he became interested in me, and was my intellectual guide and good friend. Some days before I left Paris he sent me, one morning, a poem he had written.

For several days and nights I now travelled, squeezed in dusty diligences. The small adventures of a travelling life were served up for me, and I have kept some of them in remembrance and will here give you one.

We had left the flat plains of France and reached the Jura Mountains ; here in a little village, late in the evening, the conductor helped two young farmer's daughters to get into the diligence, where I was the only passenger.

" If we do not let them drive with us they will be obliged to walk two hours on a desert road," said the conductor; they whispered and tittered together ; they knew that a gentleman was in the coach, but could not see me ; at last they took courage and asked me if I was a Frenchman, and learning that I was from Denmark, they made me believe that they knew that country. They recollected from the geography that Denmark was the same as Norway. Copenhagen they could not pronounce, but always said " Corporal," and so forth.

They asked me whether I was young, and married, and how I looked. I kept quiet in a dark corner, and gave them as ideal a description as I could ; they understood the sport, and when in turn I asked them of their appearance, they made themselves out to me real beauties.

They urged me to show my face when we arrived at the next station ; I would not yield to their wishes, and so they covered their faces with their handkerchiefs and alighted, and, laughing merrily, held out their hands to me ; they were young and had very beautiful figures. Those two unknown, invisible, gay girls represented a laughing image of my travelling life.

The road led along deep precipices ; the peasants' houses down in the valleys were like playthings, and the forests like potato-fields ; suddenly a view opened between two rocks — to me it seemed like misty forms or swimming, aerial mountains. It was the Alps with Mont Blanc, which I now beheld for the first time. The road passed downward always along the precipice; it was as if we were lowered down through the air. All was seen as in a bird's-eye view. A thick smoke ascended from far below; I thought it was a coal-mine, but it was a cloud ascending toward us, and when it reached us

we beheld before us Geneva with its lake, the whole Alpine
range, — the lowest parts in a blue mist, the highest mountain-
forms sharp and dark, and the glaciers glittering in the sun.
It was a Sunday morning ; a holy religious feeling filled my
breast in this grand church of nature.

I knew that old Purari with his family was living in Geneva.
He came as an emigrant to Copenhagen and stayed there for
several years ; Danes were always well received by him. I
asked a man in the street for Purari's house ; he proved to be
one of his friends, and accompanied me immediately to those
kind-hearted folks. The daughters spoke Danish ; our conversation turned on Denmark, Henrik Hertz, who had been
Purari's scholar, and of the great success and renown " Letters from the Dead " had excited at home. Purari told of his
stay in Copenhagen, where he carried on a hardware trade
and gave instructions in French, and spoke of Louis Philippe's
stay there at the house of the merchant De Coninck, under
the name of Mr. Müller, on a voyage to North Cape as a
botanist. Purari was one day invited to dine with him at the
palace ; no waiters were present, Louis Philippe arranging
himself all that belonged to the table.

The Alps appeared to lie so near the town that I wished to
take a morning walk up to them ; but it was as if the mountains kept retiring. I walked and walked ; it was noon before
I reached the foot of the first rock, and evening before I came
back to Geneva.

Past Lausanne and Vevay I reached Chillon, — the old,
picturesque castle, which had so much excited my interest
before by Byron's poem of " The Prisoner of Chillon." The
whole country made an impression on me as if I were in the
South, although the mountains of Savoy before me glittered
with snow ; but below by the deep green lake, where the
castle was situated, vine and corn fields stretched ; stout old
chestnut-trees cast a shade and bent their branches in rich
abundance over the water. I walked over the draw-bridge
into the darksome yard of the castle ; I perceived some small
apertures in the wall, from which in former times they poured
hot oil and water over the assailants.

In the chambers of the castle were trap-doors, which, when

stepped upon, whipped round, and the poor victims were precipitated down into the deep sea or were spitted on iron nails,
fastened in the rock below. In the cellars were rusting the
iron rings to which the prisoners' chains had been fastened;
a flat stone had served as couch. On one of the pillars Byron
had, in 1826, carved his name. The woman, who was my
guide, told me that she did not know him, and had tried
to hinder him from doing it, but in vain; and now every
one looks on those letters, for " it was such an extraordinary
person, that gentleman," said she, and nodded very signifi-
cantly.

From Chillon commenced the ascent of the Jura Mountains,
always higher and higher up, until I reached my new home
the watch-making city Le Locle.

This little city is situated in a valley of the Jura Mountains,
where in former ages the sea had been, and petrifactions of
fishes were still to be seen. Often the clouds floated below
us, and there was a repose and stillness among the dark pine-
trees, the grass was freshly green, and round about glittered the
juicy violet-colored crocus. The peasants' houses were white
and clean, and each of them was stocked with watches. The
bilberry bushes with their red clusters recalled me the pictures
in an A B C book, and the berries were beautifully red and
reminded me of my home.

Le Locle is a pretty important town, and here I found
a blessed home in an amiable family of a wealthy watch-maker,
the family Houriet; the man was a brother-in-law of our deceased, skillful Urban Jürgensen. I was received like a dear
relation, and they would not hear a word about payment. " It
is an invitation," said the man and wife; they pressed my
hands and I became good friends with all, and with the children too.

There were two old aunts in the house, Rosalie and Lydia,
and it was a good exercise for me to talk to them in French
of Denmark, and of their dear sister, whom they had not seen
since she went away, quite young, with her husband. They
spoke only French and did not understand other languages,
and though I spoke it but very poorly they understood me
well, and I them.

Although it was August they made fire in my stove every morning and evening; some days it snowed, but I knew that below the Jura Mountains it was still warm and delicious summer weather. I was only two hours distant from it. In the evenings, in that elevated region, there was a solemn repose in nature, and the sound of the evening-bells ascended to us from the French frontier beyond the river. At some distance from the city stood a solitary house, painted white and clean. On descending through two cellars, the noise of a mill-wheel was heard, and the rushing waters of a river which flowed on, hidden here from the world. I often visited this place and the beautiful Doub-fall some distance off. In my novel "O. T." I have described the scenery and the recollections of my stay in Le Locle.

Political agitation had also found its way to this little city high up on the mountains and shut in by forests, — this home of my repose. The canton of Neufchatel belongs to Prussia, and from being good neighbors, the Prussian party and the Swiss party among the peasants opposed each other, shunned each other, and each sang their own songs. Sometimes it came to small railleries. I heard from a genuine Switzer, who had in his bedroom a framed picture of William Tell shooting the apple off his son's head, that one of the Prussian party had destroyed it by pressing his elbow against the glass, and thus spoiled the engraving: " He did it on purpose ! " said he. All those political clouds passed lightly over me. I lived a happy family life and was a dear guest. I got a far better insight into the domestic life and the customs and manners of the country than travellers generally do.

Besides this I was occupied in writing a new poem. During my journey from home, and while staying in Paris, the idea of a poem fixed itself firmer and firmer in my mind, and I hoped, as it became more clearly worked out, to propitiate my enemies by it, and get their recognition as being a true poet. The old Danish folk-song of " Agnete and the Merman " was the subject I meant to treat.

In Paris I wrote the first part of it, and in Le Locle I finished my poem and sent it home. I accompanied it with prefatory remarks, which I should not now write as I then did, nor should I treat the subject of Agnete as then. The preface is very characteristic of me at that time : —

"Even as a child, the old story of 'Agnete and the Merman,' representing the double world, the earth and the sea, took hold of me. When grown up I beheld in it a great image of life, with the never satisfied desire of the heart, and its strange longing after another new existence. It had long been my thought to express what so occupied my soul. The old song from my home resounded in my ear in the midst of the excitement of Paris ; it went with me on the gay Boulevard and among the treasures of art at the Louvre. The whole grew out of my heart before I was aware of it myself.

"Far from Paris, high up in the Jura Mountains, in a northern clime, among dark forests of pines silent as death, is Agnete's birthplace, but it is Danish in soul and mind. I send my dear child to my father-land, where it belongs. Receive her kindly ; she brings my greetings to all of you.

"As abroad all Danes become friends and brothers, so she also goes toward kindred and friends. Snow falls at my window, heavy winter clouds hover over the forest, but below the mountain are summer, grapes and corn. To-morrow I journey over the Alps to Italy ; perhaps there I shall dream a beautiful dream, which I then will send to my dear Denmark, for the son must tell the mother his dreams. Farewell !

"H. C. ANDERSEN.

"LE LOCLE, IN THE JURA MOUNTAINS, 14 *September, 1833*."

My poem reached Copenhagen, and was printed and sold. They sneered at the passage in the preface of "Agnete " : " The whole grew out of my heart before I was aware of it." It was coldly received, and people said that I had done it in imitation of Oehlenschläger, who at one time used to send home masterpieces. At the same time that " Agnete " was published, Paludan Müller published also his poem " Amor and Psyche," which captivated every one.

By comparison with this the weakness in my book was felt the more. It was noticed in the " Monthly Review of Literature," but not praised. The poem did not produce the effect on H. C. Örsted that I expected ; in a long and very amiable letter, dated March 8, 1834, which I received in Italy, he spoke freely and justly of my poem, and many years afterward I was ready to acknowledge that he was right.

My poem, " Agnete," with all its faults, was, however, a step forward ; my purely subjective poetical nature tried here to display itself objectively. I was in a transition period, and this poem closed my pure lyrical phasis. It has been also of late critically said in Denmark, that notwithstanding the fact that on its first appearance it excited far less attention than some of my earlier and less successful works, yet in it the poetry is of a deeper, fuller, and more powerful character than any which I had hitherto produced.

The producing it on the stage in a shorter form and with some alterations was an experiment aimed at attracting a large audience to a summer performance ; it was given twice, but I was abroad then also. Notwithstanding Mrs. Heiberg played the part of *Agnete* very genially and touchingly, and that Nils Gade had composed pretty music for the single songs and choruses, it could not be kept up. " Agnete " was sent home ; she was for me a beautiful statue seen only by me and God !. Hope and dreaming clung closely to this poem, which took its way northward. The following day I set out for the South, for Italy, where a new portion of my life was to begin.

At my departure from those dear people in Le Locle the children wept. We had become friends, although I could not understand their *patois :* they shouted loudly into my ear, because they fancied I must be deaf, as I could not understand them. Even the servants wept and squeezed my hands. The old aunts had knit woolen cuffs to wear on the cold passage over the Simplon.

" Agnete " and my stay in Le Locle close one portion of my poetical life.

CHAPTER VI.

ON the 5th of September, 1833, I crossed the Simplon on my way to Italy. On the very day on which, fourteen years before, I had arrived poor and helpless in Copenhagen, did I set foot in this country of my longing and of my poetical happiness.

What grandeur of nature ! Our heavily laden coach with its team of horses was like a fly on a gigantic block ; we crept along the rocky road which, at Napoleon's command, had broken through this spine of the earth ; the glass-green glaciers shone over us ; it grew colder and colder ; the shepherds were wrapped in cowhides, and the inns kept up good fires in their stoves ; it was full winter here, but in a few minutes the coach was rolling along under chestnut-trees, whose long and green leaves glittered in the warm sunshine. Domo d'Ossola's market-places and streets gave us in miniature a picture of the national street-life.

Lago Maggiore shone between the dark-blue mountains ; beautiful islets, like bouquets, floated upon the water : but it was cloudy ; the skies were gray, as in Denmark. When evening came, all was again whiffed away ; the air shone transparent and serene, and the skies seemed to float thrice as high as at home. The vines hung in long trails along the road, as for a feast. Never since have I seen Italy so beautiful.

The Cathedral of Milan was the first work of art I beheld in Italy. I climbed the marble-rock that art has hollowed out and formed into arches, towers, and statues, rising in the clear moonlight, and had there a view of the Alps with their glaciers, and of the whole green, fertile Lombard country. Porta Sempione, called by the people after Napoleon's name, was still in course of erection. In La Scala were given operas and ballets ; all was visited and seen, but the cathedral of

Milan, was, however, the place where the heart was elevated in devotional tranquillity by listening to the beautiful church music.

I left this magnificent city in company with two country-men ; our vetturino carried us through the country of the Lombards, which was as flat as our green islands at home, and as fertile and beautiful as they. The rich maize-fields, the beautiful weeping-willows, were new to us. The moun-tains we passed seemed, however, insignificant after seeing the Alps. At last we got a view of Genoa, and also of the sea, which I had not seen since I left Denmark. The Danes feel the same affection for the sea as the mountaineers feel for their mountains. From my balcony I could look out over that new, yet familiar, dark-blue, level stretch.

In the evening I went to the theatre in the main street, the only large street in Genoa. As a great public building, I thought it must be very easy to find, but it was not so ; one pal-ace more magnificent than the other lay side by side ; at last a huge marble Apollo, shining white as snow, showed me where the place was.

A new opera was presented for the first time : it was Donizetti's " Elisire d'Amore ; " after that was given a comic ballet, " Il Flauto Magico." The sound of the flute compelled all to dance ; at last even the supreme council itself and all the old pictures on the walls of the city hall, — an idea I have later applied in the comedy " Ole Luköie."

A written permit of the Admiralty got us admission into the Arsenal, where the galley-slaves, then about six hundred in number, lived and worked.

We visited the inner prisons, the dormitory with large barrack beds along the walls, furnished with iron chains, to which the prisoners were attached when they went to bed. Even in the sick rooms some of the prisoners were chained to their beds.

Three agonizing prisoners with livid faces and bursting eyes made a dreadful impression on me. They observed my emotion, and one of the prisoners looked at me with a sinister look. I understood him. I was here only out of curiosity to see their sufferings. He burst out into a coarse laugh, half rising up in the bed, and fixing his evil eyes diabolically upon me. Here, loaded down with chains, lay a blind old man with silvery hair.

In the yard were different working-rooms ; several of the galley-slaves were chained together, two and two. I saw one prisoner, dressed of course as the others, in white pantaloons and red shirt, but the stuff was finer ; he was young and with-out chains. They told us that he was a man from the city, who had done a large business, but had stolen enormous sums and otherwise cheated the city ; now he was sentenced to stay two years in the galleys : he did not work, nor was he in irons during the day, but in the night he was locked in together with the others, and like them chained to the bed. His wife frequently sent him money ; he lived sumptuously within these walls ; but what was that when he was always with these criminals, and in the night chained with them and forced to listen to their ribaldry and wickedness ?

The first day's journey from Genoa along the shore south-ward is one of the finest journeys one can make. Genoa is situated on the slopes of the mountains and surrounded by green olive woods. Oranges and pomegranates hung in the gardens ; grass-green, shining lemons heralded the spring; while the inhabitants of northern countries now were looking for winter.

One picture of beauty followed another ; all was new and ever memorable to me. I still see the old bridges covered with ivy, and the Capuchins and crowds of Genoese fisher-men with their red caps.

The whole sea-coast with its beautiful villas, and the sea white with sailors and steamers, produced a grand effect. Later I discovered far away bluish mountains : they were those of Corsica, the cradle of Napoleon.

At the foot of an old tower, under a large shady tree, sat three old women, with long silvery hair falling over their brown shoulders, spinning on distaffs. Huge aloes grew at the road-side.

The reproach will perhaps be cast at me, in relating the story of my life, that I dwell too long on Nature in Italy, and perhaps, not without reason, may apprehend that the ac-count of my travels will come to abound in descriptions ; but it will soon be seen that I was more occupied with persons whom I met than with things. On the other hand, nature and art were most prominent in my mind during this first visit to Italy.

What a fascinating evening I spent in Sestri di Levante! The inn lies near the sea, which sends its waves in great rollers over the beach. The sky was brilliant with fiery red clouds, the mountains changing with new colors. The trees were like great fruit-baskets, filled to overflowing with heavy grapes from the creeping vines. Suddenly the scene changed as we went higher up the mountains. All was then dry and ugly for a long while. It was as if fancy, forming Italy into a wonderfully beautiful garden, had thrown away upon this spot all its weeds. The few scattered trees were without leaves; here were neither rocks nor mould, only mud, gravel, and quarry stones; and again, as if by enchantment, all was lying in a Hesperian loveliness. The Bay of Spezzia we saw before us.

Bewitching blue mountains overhung a most fertile and beautiful valley, which was as an overflowing horn of plenty; the grapes hung heavy and juicy around the shady trees; oranges and olives mingled their branches with them, and the vine drooped luxuriantly in long trails from tree to tree. Black, shining swine, without bristles, sprang about like goats, and made the donkeys kick even when ridden by a Capuchin with his huge green umbrella.

We reached Carrara on the birthday of the Duke of Modena; the houses were hung with garlands, the soldiers had stuck myrtle-branches in their caps, and the cannon thundered. But it was the marble quarries we wished to see; they lie outside of the city; a clear stream near the road slipped over the shining snow-white marble stones.

The quarry was of white and gray marble, containing crystals. It seemed to me as if it were a bewitched mountain, where the gods and goddesses of antiquity were bound in the stones, and now were waiting some mighty magician — a Thorwaldsen or a Canova — who could set them free and give them to the world.

Notwithstanding all the novelty and the beauty of nature, I and my travelling companions very often had the spirit of

Nicholas toward Italy, the mode of travelling was so entirely different from what we ever had known : the eternal cheatings at the inns ; they were continually asking for our passports, which were examined and signed more than fifteen times in a few days ; our vetturino did not know the way, we got lost, and instead of reaching Pisa in the day-time, we arrived there in the middle of the night. After being searched and annoyed we drove through the dark streets, which were without lanterns ; the only light we had was a big burning candle which our driver had bought at the city gate, and which he now held before him. At last we reached our destination, " Albergo del Ussaro." " One day like Jeppe we lie on a dung-hill, the next in the castle of the baron," I wrote home, and here was the baron's castle.

We were in want of rest, in want of a real *dolce far niente,* before we could begin to see the curiosities of the city, the Church, the Baptistery, Campo Santo, and the Leaning Tower.

Our theatre painter usually represents Campo Santo in the scene of the monastery hall in " Robert le Diable." In the archway there stood monuments and bass-reliefs, — one of those by Thorwaldsen, representing " Tobias's Recovery," and the artist has portrayed himself as the young Tobias. The Leaning Tower was not very inviting to ascend, yet we mounted its stairs. It is a cylinder surrounded by pillars ; there are no rails at the top of it. The side which turns to the sea, under the effect of the sea-winds, is in a state of dilapidation. The iron has crumbled, the stones have lost their solidity, and all has a dirty yellow color. I could look from here over a level country as far as Leghorn, which now can be reached in a short time by the railway ; but at that time there was no railway, and we were obliged to go with a vetturino. He was but a poor guide, who did not know anything, and would show us nothing that we cared to know about.

" There," he said, " lives a Turkish merchant, but his shop is closed to-day ; there is a church with beautiful pictures, but they are now taken away ; that man who just passed is one of our richest merchants ; " and everything he told us was about as interesting as that. Then he carried us to the synagogue, " the most beautiful and rich in Europe ; " it made anything but a religious impression upon us.   The interior was like an exchange-hall, and the unusual sight of worshippers with hats on, and speaking to each other in a high key, was very unpleasant.   Filthy Jewish children stood upon the chairs ; some old Rabbis were grinning from a kind of pulpit and enjoying themselves with some old Hebrews.   Up by the tabernacle they pushed and elbowed each other, and there was a general crowding and cuffing.   There seemed to be no thought of devotion, and there could not well be either.   Overhead on a large gallery the women were almost hidden behind a close frame.

The most beautiful sight I saw in Leghorn was a sunset ; the clouds glittered like flame ; the sea shone, the mountains shone ; it was like a frame around this filthy city, — a decoration which gave it Italian splendor.   Soon, however, this splendor was turned into the magnificence of art, for we had come to Florence.

I had never had an eye for sculpture ; I had seen almost nothing at home ; in Paris I had certainly seen many statues, but my eyes were closed to them ; but here when visiting the magnificent galleries, the rich churches with their monuments and magnificence, I learned to understand the beauty of form — the spirit which reveals itself in form.   Before the " Venus de Medici " it was as if the marble eye had acquired the power of sight ; a new world of art revealed itself to me, and I could not escape from it.

I visited the galleries daily, and a new world was opened to me.   I went oftenest to the Church of Santo Croce with its magnificent marble monuments.   Sculpture, Painting, and Architecture sit personified around the coffin of Michel Angelo.   The corpse of Dante is kept in Ravenna, but Santo Croce possesses his monument ; Italia points at the poet's colossal statue, while Poetry mourns over his sarcophagus. There is a monument to Alfieri here, from the hands of Canova, adorned with a mask, a lyre, and a crown of laurel. The tombs of Galileo and of Machiavel are not so noticeable, but the places are no less sacred.

One day three of us fellow-countrymen went in search of a fourth, the engraver Sonne, and arriving at the quarter where we were told he lived, we were talking loudly with each other, when a man in shirt-sleeves and apron came up to us and asked us in Danish, "Gentlemen, for whom are you looking?" He was a locksmith from Copenhagen, who had settled here, married a French girl, and had been away from Denmark nine years. He told us his history, and we in turn told him about home; in beautiful Florence he was still longing for "Mönter Street."

Upon leaving Florence, we wished to go by Terni to see the waterfall, and thence to Rome. We had a most wretched time: in the day burning sunshine, in evening and night venomous flies and gnats; added to that a disagreeable vetturino, and the annoyances that such a man can inflict on a traveller.

The sentences glorifying the beauty of Italy, which we saw written on the window-panes and on the walls of the inns, appeared to us to be travesties. I did not think then how dearly my heart would cling to that memorable and beautiful country. While still in Florence, on entering the coach which the vetturino had procured us, our torments began. At the coach door stood a human figure who, like Job, scraped himself with potsherds. We shook our heads when he touched the coach door; he went round to the other side and got the same warning there; he came back again, and was again sent away; at last our vetturino appeared and told us that the man was a passenger, a nobleman from Rome; that took us aback, and we let him in.

But his filthiness of body and clothes determined us at last to tell the vetturino we could not make the journey with the man as long as he should be inside the coach, and so, after a good deal of talk and gesticulating, we saw the "nobleman" climbing up to the driver. The rain fell in torrents, and I was sorry for the poor man; but really it was not possible for us to take him in to us, and so we let the rain wash him clean.

The road was romantically beautiful, but the sun was burning hot; the flies hummed around us, and we tried to defend ourselves by myrtle branches; the horses were so beset with flies that they looked like carcasses. We passed the night in a dreadful house at Levane. I saw the "nobleman" standing up by the fire-place drying his clothes, while he helped the hostess pluck the chickens we were to eat, and all the time giving vent to his anger against us, — the heretical Englishmen as he called us, promising us a speedy punishment, which we really did get this very night ; for we left our windows open to get fresh air, and were so attacked by flies and gnats that our faces and hands swelled and bled ; one of my hands had no less than fifty-seven stings, and I suffered much from pain and fever.

The following day we passed Castiglione, going through a luxuriously beautiful country with olive woods and vines ; fine-looking, half-naked children, and old women with silvery hair tended swine, that were shining and black as coal. At the Lake of Thrasymene, where Hannibal fought, I saw on the road-side the first native laurel-tree. We entered now the Papal States, and after having gone through an examination of our passports and trunks at the custom-house, we enjoyed the most beautiful sunset ; such a gorgeousness of colors I never shall forget. But the inn where we stayed was horrid ; the floor was broken, cripples gathered outside the door ; the hostess, dressed in a dirty wrapper, came grinning like an ugly witch and spat on the floor every time she brought in to us a dish of meat.

I have recalled that place in " The Galoshes of Fortune," and given a picture of it, and how uncomfortable one may be in the " Bella Italia." The next forenoon we reached Perugia, the city where Raphael was the pupil of Perugino, and where we saw pictures by the scholar and the master.

We had a beautiful view over the extensive olive woods, and beheld the same scenery which was reflected in the eyes of Raphael, as also once in the eyes of the Emperor Augustus, when the arch of triumph, built of freestone, was erected for him, and is still in the same state as if finished yesterday.

In the evening we arrived at Foligno. The city was in a very dilapidated state ; almost all the houses in the main street were supported by beams from the opposite houses. A short time since an earthquake occurred here ; the walls had great cracks, and some of the houses lay in ruins. It began to rain ; the inn was but a very poor shelter, and the meat could not be eaten even by us, who were almost starving from our long fast.

" Kennst du das Land " —

sang a young German in parody, while the wind and rain shook the miserable windows. We said to ourselves, if now a new earthquake should come, the whole town would tumble down ; but that did not happen, and we slept safely.

The next afternoon we were in Terni, at that magnificent waterfall in the midst of laurel and rosemary, away up in great olive groves, among all the splendors of Italy. A little stream rushing headlong from the rock, — that is all, but it is a most charming sight ; the water-dust rose like vapor far up in the air ; the sun shone upon all with intensely red rays, then it set, and suddenly it became dark.

It was deep night when I wandered through the dark olive woods, separated from my comrades, in company with a lively young American gentleman, who told me of Niagara, of Cooper, and the great prairies.

The next day was rainy, the road was bad, the environs did not have anything new to show us, and we were tired to death. The filthy Nepi offered us a dirty hotel ; but rambling about in the evening, I came by accident upon some ruins out of town, where a waterfall rushed foaming down into an abyss. I have recalled it in my " Improvisatore, " where Antonio for the last time sees the features of Fulvia.

The day at last came when we were to see Rome. We drove in rain and mud ; we passed by " Monte Soracte," celebrated by Horace's song, through the Campagna of Rome ; but none of us felt its grandeur, nor were captivated by the colors and beautiful outlines of the mountains ; we only thought how soon we were to get there, and of the repose we should then have. I must confess that when we came to the hill of La Storta, where those coming from the north get the first sight of Rome, I felt indeed happy ; but the impression was not that of a poet : at the first sight of Rome and St. Peter's I exclaimed : " God be praised ! now we can soon get something to eat ! "

ROME !

It was the 18th of October, in the middle of the day, when I arrived at Rome, the city of cities, where I soon was to feel as if I had been born there and was in my own house. I reached the city in time to witness a most rare event — the second funeral of Raphael. The Academia St. Luca had kept for many years a skull which was asserted to be the head of Raphael ; but in later years, its genuineness being called in question, Pope Gregory XVI. gave permission to have the grave opened in the Pantheon, or, as the place is now called, Santa Maria della Rotunda. The dead man was found safe and sound, and the corpse was again to be deposited in the church.

When the grave was opened and the bones brought forth, the painter Camuccini had sole permission to paint the whole scene. Horace Vernet, who lived in the French Academy at Rome and knew nothing about it, took his pencil and made a sketch. The papal police present forbade it ; he looked surprised at them, and said very quietly : " But at home I can do it from memory ? " Nobody could say anything against that, and in the time from twelve o'clock at noon until six o'clock in the evening he painted a beautiful and very truthful picture, and had it engraved afterward ; but the plate was immediately seized by the police and confiscated. Thereupon Vernet wrote a violent letter and demanded that they should deliver him the plate within twenty four hours ; that art was not a monopoly, like salt and tobacco. They sent it back, and he broke it in pieces and dispatched them with a letter to Camuccini, written in a very fiery style, telling him that he might know by this that he was not going to make use of it to Camuccini's detriment. Camuccini had the plate put together again and sent it, accompanied with a very friendly letter, to Horace Vernet, declaring that he had entirely given up publishing his drawing. After that everybody was allowed to take a drawing of the grave, and in consequence there was a host of pictures.

Our countrymen procured us tickets for the festival, and so our first entrance into Rome was to attend the funeral of Raphael.

Upon a platform, covered with black cloth, stood a coffin of mahogany with cloth of gold. The priests sung a *Miserere*, the coffin was opened, and the reports read were deposited in it.

The singing from an invisible choir sounded strangely beautiful, while the procession was moving around in the church. The most eminent artists and men of rank followed. Here I saw again, for the first time in Rome, Thorwaldsen, who, like the others, marched step by step bearing his taper. The solemn impression was rather disturbed, however, by the carelessness with which they lifted the coffin on end to get it through a small opening, so that we could hear the bones and joints rattle together.

I was at last in Rome, and very happy. Of all my countrymen, Mr. Christensen, the engraver, received me most kindly. We had not before been personally acquainted, but I had become dear to him through my lyric poems. He took me at once to Thorwaldsen, who lived in his old place in Via Felice ; he was just then occupied with his bass-relief, " Raphael." Raphael is seen sitting upon some ruins, where we see in bass-relief the Graces ; he is drawing from nature. Love holds the tablet for him, while at the same time she reaches him the poppy, an emblem of his early death ; the Genius with the torch looks sorrowfully upon him, and Victory stretches a wreath over his head.

Thorwaldsen spoke with great liveliness of his idea, of the feast of yesterday, and of Raphael, Camuccini, and Vernet. He showed me many magnificent pictures, which he had bought of masters still living, and intended to give after his death to Denmark. The plain straightforwardness and heartiness of this great artist affected me so that I almost shed tears when I took leave of him, although he said we must see each other now every day.

Among other countrymen who were associated directly with me was Ludvig Bödtcher, from whom we have several beautiful poems, Italian in feeling. He lived a retired life in Rome, devoted to art, nature, and an intellectual *dolce far niente :* he had spent many years here — knew of all that was interesting and beautiful. In him I found a guide who had intellect and knowledge.

There was another with whom I associated on even more cordial terms ; that was the painter Küchler, who was at that time still young, bodily and spiritually, and not without humor. I did not then foresee what has since happened, that he would

end his life as a mendicant friar in a little monastery in Silesia.
When several years after I visited Rome for the second time,
the youthful temperament was gone.   It was very seldom
that the humor again flashed up ; and in 1841, when for the
third time I saw Rome, he had become a Catholic, and painted
now only altar-pieces and religious pictures.   He was, as we
know, a couple of years since, ordained by Pio Nono as
mendicant friar, and as such a one he wandered barefooted
through Germany up to a poor monastery in the Prussian
states.   He was no more the painter Albert Küchler, but the
Franciscan Pietro di Sante Pio.   May God grant him that
peace and happiness which he, misunderstanding the loving
God, is surely seeking in a bewildered way, and — will find !

It was still as in the most beautiful summer season at
home, and although Rome with all its splendors was entirely
new to me, I could not help visiting the country in such
charming weather.   A trip to the mountains was agreed upon.
Küchler, Blunck, Fearnley, and Bödtcher, who were as natives
here, acted as leaders.   Their knowledge of the Italian people,
and of the manners and habits of the country, not only made
the trip very cheap, but I acquired also such a clear and profound apprehension of all that I became acclimatized intellectually ; the first germ of my pictures of Italian nature and life
was planted within me, and sprung forth in my " Improvisatore."
I had not yet thought of writing such a book, — not even any
sketches of travel.

This week's ramble was my most happy and most enjoyable
time in that charming country.   Across the Campagna, passing by graves of antiquity, picturesque aqueducts, and groups
of shepherds with their herds, we kept on to the Albanian
Mountains, whose blue and charming undulating outlines
seemed so near in the transparent air.

At Frascati, where we took our breakfast, I saw for the first
time a really popular " osterie," crowded with peasants and
ecclesiastics.   Hens and chickens ran about on the floor, the
fire burned on the hearth, and the ragged boys dragged our
donkeys up to the door ; we mounted them, and continued
our way on a trot or at an ambling pace, as it pleased them,
always climbing, — passing the ruins of Cicero's villa to the an-

cient Tusculum, which now offered to the sight only paved streets, but no houses, only fragments of walls among laurel and chestnut-trees.

We visited Monte Pozio, where there was a well with such a resonance that it seemed to hide the source of music, — that sounding depth, from which Rossini poured out his laughing and triumphant melodies, and where Bellini shed his tears and sent out over the world his melancholy tones.

We had the good fortune to be witnesses of more scenes of popular life than travellers nowadays are likely to see. We saw the golden-laced Dulcamara himself upon his medical car with his attendants, dressed as for a masquerade, making his quack-speech.

We met with bandits chained to a cart drawn by oxen, and surrounded by gens-d'armes; we saw a funeral, where the corpse lay uncovered upon the bier: the evening glow fell on the white cheeks, and the boys ran about with paper-horns, gathering up the wax that dripped from the monks' tapers. The bells rung, the songs resounded, the men played at morra, and the girls danced the Saltarello to the sounds of the tambourine. I have never since seen Italy more festive and beautiful; I had Pignelli's pictures before me in nature and reality.

We returned to Rome, to its magnificent churches, to the glorious galleries, and to all its treasures of art; but the continually charming summer weather, although we were in the middle of November, recalled us again to the mountains, and this time we started for Tivoli.

The morning hours in the Campagna were cool as in autumn; the peasants made fires at which they warmed themselves; we met with country-people on horseback, dressed in wide, black, sheep-skin fur coats, as if we were in the country of Hottentots; but when the sun rose we had again warm summer weather. It was fresh and green about Tivoli, the city of cascades; the olive woods were decked with bouquets of cypresses and red vine leaves.

The great waterfalls rushed like masses of clouds down into the green; it was a hot day, and we should have liked much to get a shower-bath under the fountain of Villa d'Este.

Here grow the tallest cypresses in Italy, as mighty as those of the Orient.   In the darkness of the evening we descended to the foot of the high waterfall ; our torches threw a wavering light on the close laurel hedges ; we listened to the thundering water rushing headlong, and the depth seemed to be not only greater but also nearer than it really was.   We set fire to some bundles of straw, by which the old temple of Sibyl was illuminated, and with its colonnade made a background to the trembling flame.

Once more in Rome, where the life of the people was as stirring as in Goethe's time, and where the artists met more kindly and tenderly than I have since known them to.   The Scandinavians and Germans formed one circle ; the French, who had their own academy under the direction of Horace Vernet, formed another.   At the dinners in the osterie " Lepre," each nationality had its own table ; in the evening Swedes, Norwegians, Danes, and Germans came together in society, and here were still seen notabilities of former days.   I saw the two old landscape-painters — Reinhard and Koch, as well as Thorwaldsen.

Christmas was our most beautiful feast.   I have mentioned it in " A Poet's Bazaar," but it has never since been so joyous, so fresh and bright as it was in 1833.   We were not allowed to have our frolic within the city, and therefore we hired a large house in the garden of Villa Borghese, near the Amphitheatre.   The flower-painter Jensen, the medal-engraver Christensen, and I went out there early in the morning, and in our shirt-sleeves, in the warm sunshine, bound wreaths and garlands.   A large orange-tree hung with fruit served for our Christmas-tree.   The best prize, a silver cup, with the inscription, " Christmas Eve in Rome, 1833," I was happy enough to win.   Each of the guests gave a present, and one or another funny thing was chosen.   I had brought with me from Paris a pair of big yellow collars, which were not fit for anything but a carnival sport.   These I wished to use, but my jest took a turn that might easily have ended in quarrel and anger.   I had no idea that there existed another opinion than that of Thorwaldsen being the most eminent one present, and that I could therefore present him the wreath.   The collar, which bore the color of envy, was thus taken along with me in jest. I did not know what we now can read in Thiele's "Life of Thorwaldsen," that there had once been a quarrel between Byström and Thorwaldsen as to their respective abilities. Byström believed that Thorwaldsen surpassed him in bass-reliefs but not in groups. Thorwaldsen grew passionate and exclaimed : " You may tie my hands, and I will with my teeth bite the marble better than you can hew it ! "

At the Christmas-feast both Thorwaldsen and Byström were present. I had made a wreath for my great countryman and written a little verse. The present was for him, but the yellow collar which lay at the side of it was for the one who, by drawing lots, accidentally got this parcel. The lot was drawn by Byström, and the contents of the verse to the winner was : "You may keep Envy's yellow collar, but the wreath you must hand to Thorwaldsen ! " In a moment there was great confusion at such an ill-mannered act, but when it was found that the package had fallen accidentally into the hands of Byström, and that it came from me, all was smoothed over and good-humor was restored.

I very seldom received letters from home, and except one or two they were all written with the intent to instruct me, and were often very inconsiderate. They could not help grieving me, and they affected me so much that the Danes whom I liked here in Rome, and with whom I associated, always exclaimed : " Have you got another letter from home ? I would not read such letters, and I would give up friends who only pain and plague me ! " Well, I needed to be educated and they took me in hand, but harshly and unkindly. They did not reflect how much a thoughtlessly written word could affect me ; when enemies smite with scourges, friends' whips are scorpions.

I had not yet heard anything of " Agnete." The first report of it was from a " good friend." His judgment of the poem will give you an idea of me as I was at that time : —

" You know that your, I dare almost say, unnatural sensibility and childishness make you very different from me — and I must tell you that I had expected something else ; another spirit, other ideas and images, and the least of all, such a character as that of *Henning;* in short, ' Agnete ' seems to be like your other poems (N. B. like the best of your poems), although I had hoped here and there to perceive some intellectual change in you, as a result of your travelling. " I have talked with —— about it, and he agrees with me ; and as he, who is not only your friend but also a kind of mentor to you, has written to you concerning it, you shall be delivered from my advice. . . . . Dear friend, chase away these money troubles and home thoughts, and turn your present journey to its full profit ! A little more manliness and power ; a little less childishness, eccentricity, and sentimentality ; a little more study and depth — and I shall congratulate Andersen's friends on his return, and Denmark at receiving her poet ! "

That letter was from a man who was dear to me, who was among my true friends, younger in years, but in happy circumstances and of ability ; one of those who would most gently express his opinion, because I was " so sensitive, so childish." I am surprised that he and other reasonable people could expect to discover a great change in me in " Agnete," under the influence of travel, which, as I have before said. only consisted in my journeying by steamer from Copenhagen to Kiel ; by the diligence to Paris, and, later, to Switzerland ; and as soon as four months after my departure, I had sent the poem home. It required more time than that to see any results of my travel, and in the course of a year I brought forth my " Improvisatore."

I felt so depressed by this and other letters still more painful that I was in despair and on the point of forgetting God, and giving up Him and all mankind. I thought of death in an unchristian manner. You will, perhaps, ask me if there were none at that time who could say any kind and encouraging word of my " Agnete," — the poem which had sprung out of my very heart, and not, as they wrote to me, " scribbled in a headlong fashion." Yes, there was one, and that one was Madame Lässöe. I am going to quote a couple of words from her letters : —

. . . . " I must confess that ' Agnete ' has not met with great success, but to drag it down in the way you have heard is the work of malice. There are many great beauties in it, but I think that you have made a great mistake in the treatment of that subject. ' Agnete ' is a butterfly, which we well may look at but may not touch. You have treated her very airily, but you have surrounded her with clumsy objects, and made her circle too small to flutter in."

When I was thus depressed at the judgment passed upon me at home, I received information of the death of my old mother. Collin informed me of it, and my first exclamation was : " O God, I thank Thee ! Now her poverty is at an end, and I could not relieve her from it ! " I wept, but could not familiarize myself with the thought that I now possessed not a single one in the world who would love me because I was of the same kith and kin. That new impression brought forth tears, which I shed profusely, and I had a perception that that which had happened was the best for her. I had never been able to make her last days bright and free from sorrow. She died in the happy belief of my success, and that I had become famous.

The poet Henrik Hertz was among those who had lately arrived at Paris. He was the one who had attacked me severely in the " Letters from the Dead." Collin wrote to me that Hertz would come, and that he would be glad to hear we had met as friends.

I was in " Café Græco " when Hertz one day entered ; he gave me his hand kindly, and I took great pleasure in conversing with him. As soon as he perceived my sorrow, and understood my sufferings, he spoke very consoling words. He spoke of my works, of his opinion of them, hinted at the " Letters from the Dead," and, strange to say, begged me not to disregard harsh criticism, asserting that the romantic sphere in which I moved drove me into extravagances. He liked my pictures of nature, in which my humor was especially manifested, and as for the rest, he was sure it must be a consolation to me that almost all true poets had gone through the same crisis as I, and that after this purgatory I would come to a sense of what was truth in the realm of art !

Hertz, together with Thorwaldsen, heard me read " Agnete," and remarked that he had not well caught the whole poem, but had found the lyric passages very successful, and thought that what they at home called errors of form were what the romance lost by being treated dramatically. Thorwaldsen did not say much, but sat and listened attentively with a serious, thoughtful face while I read. When his look met mine, he nodded kindly and cheerfully. He pressed my hand and praised the melody. "It is so real Danish," said he, "and springs from the woods and the sea at home."

It was in Rome that I first became acquainted with Thorwaldsen. Many years before, when I had not long been in Copenhagen, and was walking through the streets as a poor boy, Thorwaldsen was there too : that was on his first return home. We met one another in the street. I knew that he was a distinguished man in art ; I looked at him, I bowed ; he went on, and then, suddenly turning round, came back to me and said, "Where have I seen you before ? I think we know one another." I replied, "No, we do not know one another at all." I now related this story to him in Rome ; he smiled, pressed my hand, and said, "Yet we felt at that time that we should become good friends." I read " Agnete " to him ; and that which delighted me in his judgment upon it was the assertion, " It is just," said he, " as if I were walking at home in the woods, and heard the Danish lakes ; " and then he kissed me.

One day, when he saw how distressed I was, and I told him about the pasquinade which I had received from home in Paris, he gnashed his teeth violently, and said, in momentary anger, " Yes, yes, I know the people ; it would not have gone any better with me if I had remained there ; I should then, perhaps, not even have obtained permission to set up a model. Thank God that I did not need them, for there they know how to torment and to annoy." He desired me to keep up a good heart, and then things could not fail of going well ; and with that he told me of some dark passages in his own life, where he in like manner had been mortified and unjustly condemned.

After the Carnival I left Rome for Naples. Hertz and I travelled together. My intercourse with him was of great value to me, and I felt that I had one more generous critic. We travelled over the Albanian Mountains and through

the Pontine Marshes, and reached Terracina, where the oranges
grow, where we saw our first palm-trees in the gardens near
the road ; the Indian fig spreads its heavy leaves along the
rocks, where we see the ruins of Theodoric's Castle ; Cyclopean
walls, laurel and myrtle became soon an every-day sight. We
saw from Cicero's villa in Mola di Gaeta the open Garden of
the Hesperides. I strolled in the warm air under the large
lemon and orange-trees, and threw the yellow, shining fruits
into the charming blue sea, which gleamed and broke in gentle waves.

We remained here a day and night, and arrived at Naples
in time to see the full eruption of Vesuvius. Like long roots
of fire from a pine-tree of smoke the lava flowed down the
dark mountain.

I went with Hertz and some other Northmen to visit the
eruption. The road winds through vineyards and by the side
of lonely buildings, the vegetation changing soon into mere
rushes ; the evening was infinitely beautiful.

From the hermitage we wandered on foot up the mountain
ankle-deep in ashes ; I was in a happy humor, sang loudly
one of Weyse's melodies, and was the first to reach the summit. The moon shone directly upon the crater, from which
ascended a pitch-black smoke ; glowing stones were thrown
up in the air and fell almost perpendicularly down again ; the
mountain shook under our feet. At each eruption the moon
was covered by smoke, and as it was a dark night we were
obliged to stand still and hold on by the big lava blocks. We
perceived that it was gradually growing warmer beneath us.
The new lava stream burst forth from the mountain out toward
the sea. We wished to go thither, and we were obliged to pass
over a lava stream recently hardened ; only its upper crust was
stiffened by the air, red fire gleamed forth from rifts here and
there. Led by our guide we stepped upon the surface, which
heated us through our boot-soles. If the crust had broken, we
should certainly have sunk down into a fiery abyss. We advanced silently and reached the lava blocks that had been
hurled down, where we met with many travellers, and from here
we looked out over the stream of fire that was breaking forth
and rolling down — a sort of fiery gruel ! The sulphurous

vapor was very intense; we could scarcely endure the heat under our feet, and were not able to stand here more than a few minutes; but what we saw is burned into our thoughts. We saw round about us abysses of fire, and out of the crater it whistled as if a mighty flock of birds were flying up from a wood.

We could not mount to the very cone, because red-hot stones were continually raining down. About an hour was occupied in the short but heavy climbing up to the place where we stood, while it only took ten minutes to descend. We went at a flying pace; for to keep from falling upon our face we had to drive our heels in constantly; often we fell flat upon our backs in the soft ashes. The descent was a merry fall through the air. It was charming, tranquil weather; the lava shone from the black ground like colossal stars. The moonshine was clearer than it is at home in the North at noon-time on a gloomy autumn day.

When we came down to Portici we found all the houses and doors shut, not a man to be seen, and no coaches to be had, and so the whole company went home a-foot; but Hertz was obliged to lag, as on the descent he had bruised his foot; so I stayed by him, and we walked slowly and soon were both quite alone. The flat-roofed white houses shone in the clear moonshine; we did not meet nor see a man: Hertz said, that it seemed to him as if we were passing through the extinct city in the "Arabian Nights."

We spoke of poetry and of eating. We were indeed uncommonly hungry, and every osterie was closed, so we were compelled to endure it until we should reach Naples. The large undulating outlines were broken in the moonlight as if it were blue fire; Vesuvius cast up its pillar of fire, the lava was reflected as a dark-red stripe in the quiet sea. Several times we stopped in silent admiration, but our conversation always turned again upon a good supper, and that late in the night was the bouquet of the whole.

Later I visited Pompeii, Herculaneum, and the Grecian temple at Pæstum. There I saw a poor little girl in rags, but an image of beauty, a living statue, yet still a child. She had some blue violets in her black hair; that was all her ornament.

She made an impression upon me as if she were a spirit from the world of beauty. I could not give her money, but stood in reverence and looked at her, as if she were the goddess herself appearing from that temple upon the steps of which she was seated among the wild figs.

The days were like the beautiful summer of the North, and we were in the month of March. The sea looked very inviting, and I sailed with a party in an open boat from Salerno to Amalfi and Capri, where the Blue Grotto some years ago had been discovered, and was now the great attraction to all travellers here. The witch-hole, as it was called here, had become the wonderful grotto of the fairies. I was one of the first who described it; years have since elapsed, but storm and undulation have always since prevented me from again visiting this magnificent spot; yet once seen it never can be forgotten. I was not so much taken with Ischia, and subsequent visits have not been able to put it beside the island of the Tiber, the wooden-shoe-shaped Capri.

Malibran was in Naples; I heard her in "Norma," "The Barber," and "La prova." And so from the world of music Italy disclosed a wonder to me; I wept and laughed, and was raised to a pitch of excitement. In the midst of the enthusiasm and applause I heard a hiss thrown at her, — only a single hiss. Lablache made his appearance as *Zampa* in the opera "Zampa," but he was ever memorable as *Figaro*, — what liveliness, what gayety!

On the twentieth of March we returned for Easter week to Rome. The mountains were dressed in winter garments. We visited Caserta to see the great royal castle there, with its rich saloons and pictures from the time of Murat; we went to see the amphitheatre at Capua, with its vaults under the floor, — huge openings, which have been furnished with contrivances so that one can go up and down. All was seen.

The Easter Feast kept us in Rome. At the illumination of the dome I was separated from my company. The great crowd of people carried me away with them over the Angelo bridge, and when I had reached the middle of it I came near fainting; a shivering went through me, my feet shook under me, and could not longer carry me. The mass pressed on; I was

overwhelmed with a trembling sensation ; it grew black before
my eyes ; I had a feeling of being trampled under foot ; but
by an exertion of soul and body I kept up : they were terrible
seconds, that dwell in my thoughts more than the splendor
and magnificence of the feast.

Meanwhile I reached the other side of the bridge and felt
much better. Blunck's studio was near by, and from here, with
the Angelo castle in front, I saw to the end the grand Girandola, surpassing all the fire-works I ever before had seen. The
fire-works at the July feast in Paris were but poor in comparison with Rome's splendid cascades of fire.

In the Osterie my countrymen drank my health, bidding
me farewell, and sang a travelling song. Thorwaldsen hugged
me and said that we should see each other again in Denmark
or in Rome. My second of April I spent at Montefiascone.
An Italian married couple, very amiable people, were my travelling companions. The young wife was very much afraid of
robbers, as the country was said to be unsafe ; the burned
tracts of woodland, with their black stumps of trees, did not
enliven the scenery ; the mountain roads were narrow, with
black deep abysses ; and now there rose a tempest so violent
that for several hours we were compelled to take shelter in a
little inn at Novella. The storm raged, the rain drove down ;
the whole scene was like that of a robber-story, but the robbers were wanting, and the end of the story was that we
reached Siena, and later also Florence, safe and sound. Florence was now an old acquaintance of mine, together with all
that it possessed, — even from the metal pig to its churches
and galleries.

In the director of the *Cabinet Literaire*, Wieusseux, I learned
to know a man who, sixteen years ago, had been in Denmark
and lived there in the house of the authoress Madame Brun.
He knew Oehlenschläger and Baggesen, talked of them and of
Copenhagen and its life. When we are abroad and hear people talk of home, we feel then how dear it is to us. I did
not feel however any home-sickness, and had not felt it during
my whole journey. I looked anxiously toward the time of returning home, as if I were then to be awakened from a beautiful dream to heavy reality, to suffering and patience. And

now my face was turned homeward. Spring went with me ; in Florence the laurel-trees were in bloom. Spring was round about me, but it dared not breathe into my soul. I went northward over the mountains to Bologna. Malibran sung here, and I was to see Raphael's " Saint Cecilia," and then again by Ferrara to Venice, the withered lotus of the sea.

If one has seen Genoa with its magnificent palaces, Rome with its monuments, and has wandered in the sunny, laughing Naples, Venice will only be a step-child ; and still this city is so peculiar, so different from all other cities of Italy, that it ought to be seen, but before the others, and not as a *triste vale* at the departure from Italy. Goethe speaks of that sepulchral spectacle, the Venetian gondola. It is a swift, swimming mortuary bier, pitch-black with black fringes, black tassels, and black curtains. At Fusina we went on board such a one, and passing between an interminable range of poles, through muddy water and clearer water, we entered the silent city. Only the Place of St. Mark with its variegated church of Oriental architecture, and the wondrous Doge Palace with its dark memories, the prison and the Bridge of Sighs, were lively with people. Greeks and Turks sat and smoked their long pipes, doves flew by hundreds round the trophy poles, from which waved mighty flags.

It seemed to me as if I were on the wreck of a spectral, gigantic ship, especially when it was day-time. In the evening, when the moon shines, the whole city seems to rouse ; then the palaces stand out more squarely and look more noble. Venetia, the queen of Adria, that in the day-time is a dead swan upon the muddy water, gets then life and beauty.

A scorpion had stung my hand, and this made my stay here a painful one. All the veins in my arm swelled. I had paroxysms of fever, but fortunately the weather was cold, the sting not very venomous, and in the black, sepulchral gondola I left Venice without regret, to go to another city of graves, — that where the Scaligers repose, and where is the tomb of Romeo and Juliet, — the city of Verona.

My countryman, the painter Bendz, born like myself in Odense, left his home in youth and freshness ; his talent was acknowledged, he had a faithful bride, and hastened joyfully to Italy, climbed the Alps, saw the Canaan of art lying before him, and suddenly died in Vicenza. I sought his grave, but nobody could tell me where it was. The memory of this brother from the same native town, came vividly before me on this spot. His lot seemed to me so happy, that I could have wished my own the same! my mind became more and more depressed as I ascended the Alps, toward the North, homeward.

I travelled in company with a young Scot, Mr. Jameson from Edinburgh; he found that the Tyrol Mountains bore a great resemblance to the heights of his own home, and tears came into his eyes, for he felt home-sick; I did not know that disease. I only felt an increasing depression in thinking of all I was to meet with. anticipating the bitter cup I certainly would have to drink. Besides, I was sure I never again should see this beautiful country I now was leaving.

The Alps lay behind us, and the Bavarian table-land stretched before us. The last of May I arrived at Munich. I took a room in the house of an honest comb-maker on Carl Square. I had no acquaintances, but these were soon made. In the street I immediately met with my countryman Birch, who married Charlotte Birch-Pfeiffer, renowned as an authoress and actress. She was at that time directress of the City Theatre in Zurich, and therefore I could not then make her acquaintance. I had formerly often seen Birch in Siboni's house; he knew me, and showed me much attention and kindness. We saw each other often, and he was frank and sociable.

The philosopher Schelling was then living in Munich. I had heard much about him from H. C. Örsted. I can add another kind of connection too. My landlady in Copenhagen had told me that Schelling, during his stay there, had lived in her house, and that the bed I occupied had been his. I had no letters of recommendation, nobody who could introduce me to him; therefore I went without ceremony to his house, announced myself, and was very well received by the old man. He conversed a long time with me about Italy; I did not speak German well, one Danish idiom followed another; but just that was what interested him most, — the

Danish element shone through, he said; it seemed to him so strange and yet so familiar. He invited me to see his family and talked with me very kindly. Several years afterward, when I had acquired a name in Germany, we met in Berlin as old friends.

My stay at Munich was very pleasant, but the days pointed more and more toward my real home, Copenhagen. By careful economy I tried to extend the time of my stay, for I was afraid that once home I should grow fast there, and the rolling seas would pass over me.

From letters I learned how entirely I had been given up and blotted out as poet; the " Monthly Journal of Literature " had publicly stated this as a plain fact. It was my " Collected Poems," published during my absence, which had separately met with great success, and the "Twelve Months of the Year," that served as proof of my intellectual death. A travelling friend brought me the " Monthly Journal ; " of course it was well that I should see it with my own eyes.

I left Munich. In the coach was a lively man who was going to the bath of Gastein; at the city gate the poet Saphir came and shook hands with him. My companion was very interesting ; the theatre was soon made the subject of our conversation ; we spoke of the last representation of " Götz von Berlichingen," where Esslair had the principal part and was several times called out ; but he did not please me ; I told my companion so, and said that I liked Mr. Wespermann, who played the part of *Selbitz*, best of all. " I thank you for the compliment!" exclaimed the stranger. It was Wespermann himself; I did not know him ; my joy at being in company with that able artist drew me nearer to him, and the journey made us friends.

We reached the Austrian frontier. My passport from Copenhagen was in French, the frontier guard looked at it, and asked for my name. I answered, " Hans Christian Andersen ! "

" That name is not in your passport, your name is Jean Chrétien Andersen ; so you travel under another name than your own ? "

Now commenced an examination, which became very amusing. I, who never carried either cigars or other prohibited articles with me, had my trunk searched through and through, and I myself was scrupulously examined ; all my letters from home were looked through ; they made me declare on oath whether they contained anything beside family affairs ; after that they asked me what my "chapeau bras" was. I answered, "A hat for society."—"What kind of society?" asked they,—"a secret society?" My ivy wreath from the Christmas Feast in Rome seemed very suspicious to them. "Have you been in Paris?" they again asked. "Yes!" And now they let me know that all was as it ought to be in Austria, that they were not going to have revolutions, and were very well contented with their Emperor Franz. I assured them that I was of the same mind, and that they might be entirely at rest ; I hated revolutions, and was a tiptop kind of subject. That all went for nothing ; I was more severely searched than all the others, and the only reason was that the officer in Copenhagen had translated the Danish name Hans Christian by Jean Chrétien.

In Salzburg, near my lodging, was an old house with figures and inscriptions ; it had belonged to Doctor Theophrastus Bombastus Paracelsus, who died there. The old serving-woman in the inn told me that she also was born in that house, and that she knew about Paracelsus ; that he was a man who could cure the disease among men of quality called gout, and on that account the other doctors grew angry and gave him poison ; he discovered it, and was skillful enough to know how to drive the poison out. He therefore locked himself in the house, and ordered his servant not to open the door before he called him ; but the servant was very curious, and opened the door before the time, when his master had not got the poison higher up than into the throat, and seeing the door open, Paracelsus fell dead on the floor. That was the popular story I got. Paracelsus has always been to me a very romantic and attractive personage, and no doubt could be made use of in a Danish poem, for his wandering life carried him up to Denmark. He is spoken of as surgeon in the allied army there, and is mentioned during the reign of Christian II. as giving Mother Sigbrith in Copenhagen a kind of physic in a vial, which cracked and let the contents out with a noise like a clap of thunder. Poor Paracelsus! he was called a quack, but was a genius in his art before his time : but every one who goes before the coach of Time gets kicked or trampled down by its horses.

When one is in Salzburg one must also see Hallein, go through the salt works, and pass over the cover of the salt-boiling, huge iron pan. The waterfall at Golling foams over the blocks of stone, but I have forgotten all impressions save that made by the smiles of a child. I had for guide a little boy who possessed in a singular degree the seriousness of an old man, a look which we sometimes perceive among children; an air of intelligence, a certain seriousness, was spread over the little fellow, not a smile was seen upon his face. Only when we arrived at the foot of the foaming, rushing waters, which resounded in the air, his eyes began to beam, and the little chap smiled so happily and said proudly, " That is Golling Fall!" The waters foam and foam still; I have forgotten them, but not the smile of the boy. It often happens that we notice and retain in our memory some little thing about places we see, which many may call unessential or accidental. The magnificent monastery at Mölk on the Danube, with its splendor of marble and its magnificent view, has only left in my mind one permanent, fresh remembrance — that of a large, black, burnt spot on the floor. It was caused during the war in 1809; the Austrians were encamped on the northern bank of the Danube ; Napoleon had taken up his quarters in the monastery. A dispatch which in a fit of anger he had set fire to and thrown away, had burnt that hole in the floor.

At last I came in sight of the steeple of St. Stephen's Church, and soon I stood in the Imperial City. The house of the Sonnenleitners was at that time a true home for all Danes. We always found countrymen here, and many notabilities used to meet here in the evening : Captain Tscherning, the doctors Bendz and Thune, the Norwegian Schweigaard. I did not go there very often, as the theatre had more attraction for me. The Bourg Theatre was excellent. I saw Anschütz as *Götz von Berlichingen ;* Madame von Weissenthurn as *Madame Herb* in " The Americans." What a play it was ! A

young girl, Mathilde Wildauer, who has since acquired the
name of an artist, made her first appearance on the stage in
these days as *Gurli* in the " Indians in England." Several
comedies of Kotzebue were given here in a very excellent way.
Kotzebue had good sense, but no great fancy ; he was the
Scribe of his time ; he could write unpoetical pieces, but his
good sense gave them all admirable dialogues.

In Hitzing I saw and heard Strauss ; he stood there in the
middle of his orchestra like the heart in that waltz organism ;
it seemed to me as if the melodies poured through him and
escaped out of all his members ; his eyes flashed, and it was
easy to see that he was the life and soul of the orchestra.
Madame von Weissenthurn had her villa in Hitzing, and I made
the acquaintance of this interesting lady. I have since, in
" A Poet's Bazaar," given a kind of silhouette of this amiable
and gifted lady. Her comedies, " Which is the Bride," and
" The Estate of Sternberg," have been received with great success on the Danish stage. Our younger people, I suppose, do
not know Johanne von Weissenthurn ; she was daughter of an
actor, and appeared on the stage while quite a child. In the
year 1809, she played *Phædra* for Napoleon in Schönbrunn,
and was presented by him with a gift of full three thousand
francs. She wrote on a wager in eight days, when twenty-five
years old, the drama " Die Drusen " ; since that she has written more than sixty dramatic pieces ; and after forty years activity the Emperor Franz bestowed upon her the " golden civil-
honor medal," which had not been given to any actress before,
and which procured her the Prussian golden medal for arts
and sciences. She left the theatre in 1841, and died in Hitzing the 18th of May, 1847. Her comedies are published in
fourteen volumes. I spoke for the first time with her at her
villa in Hitzing ; she was a great admirer of Oehlenschläger.
" The great one " she always called him, whom she had learnt
to know and estimate, when he as a young man was in Vienna.
She liked to listen to my narratives from Italy, and said that
my words gave her a clear perception of that country, so that
she seemed to be there with me.

In Sonnenleitner's house I learned to know Mr. Grillparzer,
who had written " The Ancestress," and " The Golden Fleece."

In true Viennese fashion he shook my hand and greeted me as a poet.

I saw Castelli very often. He is undoubtedly the type of a true Viennese, and is in possession of all the excellent and peculiar qualities of such a one, — namely, good-nature, brilliant humor, faithfulness and devotion to his emperor. "The good Franz," said he, "I have written a petition to him in verse, and begged him when we Vienneses meet him and salute him not to answer our salutations by taking off his hat in this cold weather!" I saw all his *bijouterie* — his collections of snuff-boxes; one of them, in the shape of a snail, had belonged to Voltaire! "Bow and kiss it," said he.

In my "Only a Fiddler," where Naomi appears in Vienna, I have made Castelli one of the actors, and the verse which stands at the head of the chapter was written for me by the poet before we separated.

After spending a month in Vienna I commenced my journey homeward by way of Prague, enjoying "the poetry of travelling life" as people call it. A crowd of people were squeezed together, the coach jerked and rattled, but this brought out some droll characters that helped to keep up the good humor in the coach. Among others we had an old gentleman who was displeased with everything; he had been the victim of extortion, and was continually calculating how much money he had spent, and he found that it was always too much; first it was for a cup of coffee that was not worth the money, then he was vexed by the degeneracy of the young people nowadays, who had too much to do with everything, even with the fate of the world. A dirty Jew who was seated at his side, prattled all the time and told ten times over his journey to Ragusa in Dalmatia! he would not, he said, be a king, — that was too much; but he would like to be a king's valet, like one he had known, who had grown so fleshy that he could not walk, and was obliged to have a valet for himself. He was nasty from head to foot, and yet he was continually talking of cleanliness. He was indignant at hearing that in Hungary they used to heat the ovens with cow's dung! he served up old anecdotes to us. Suddenly he became absorbed in thought, drew a paper out of his pocket, rolled his

eyes about, and wrote.   He had ideas ! he said, and asked me
to read what he had written down.

There were no reserved seats in the coach, and we had to
agree the best way we could ; but the two best places were after
all taken away from us by two new travellers, who stepped in
at Iglau while we, weary and hungry, went to the supper-
table.   They were a young woman with her husband ; he was
already asleep when we reëntered the coach ; she was awake
enough for both of them, and loquacity itself; she spoke of
art and literature, of refined education, of reading a poet and
comprehending him, of music and plastic art, of Calderon and
Mendelssohn.   Sometimes she stopped, and sighed at her
husband, who leaned his head upon her : " Raise your angelic
head, it crushes my bosom ! " said she.   And now she talked
about her father's library, and of the meeting she was again to
have with him ; and when I asked her of the Bohemian literature, she was intimately acquainted with all the authors of note
in the country, — they came to her father's house, who had in
his library a complete collection of books belonging to modern
literature, etc.   When day broke I perceived that she and her
husband were a fair Jewish couple ; he awoke, drank a cup of
coffee, and fell asleep again, leaned his head against his wife,
opened his mouth only once to utter a wornout witticism, and
so slept again — that angel !

She wanted to know about us all, what our positions and
conditions were, and learning that I was an author, she took
much interest in me.   When we gave our names at the gates
of Prague, an old deaf gentleman said that his name was
" Professor Zimmermann ! "   " Zimmermann ! " she cried out ;
" Zimmermann's ' Solitude ! '   Are you Zimmermann ? "   She
did not know that the author she meant had been dead a long
time.   The deaf gentleman repeated his name, and now she
burst out into lamentations that only at the hour of separation
she had learned with whom she had been travelling.

I had told her that I meant to go early next morning to
Dresden ; she said that she was very sorry for it, because she
would have invited me to see her father and his library, and,
perhaps, meet with people of sympathetic mind !   " We live in
the largest house of the place ! "   She pointed it out to me

and I saw that both she and her husband entered it. When they took leave, the husband gave me his card. The next morning I decided to stay two days in Prague, so I could pay my travelling companions a visit, and take a view of the library with its Bohemian literature.

I went to the large house where I had seen the couple enter. In the first story nobody knew anything of the family, nor in the second story ; mounting the third, I mentioned the great library that was said to be there! no, nobody knew of it. I reached the fourth story, but neither here was any information to be had, and they said that no other families lived in the house except those I had seen ; there lived, to be sure, an old Jew in a couple of garrets in the top of the house, but they were sure that I could not mean him. Nevertheless I mounted the stairs, — the walls to the staircase consisting of rough boards ; there was a low door at which I knocked. An old man dressed in a dirty night-gown opened it, and I stepped into a low-studded room ; in the middle of the floor stood a large clothes-basket filled with books. " It is not possible that family lives here ! " said I.

" My God ! " cried a female voice from a little side-chamber. I looked in that direction and beheld my travelling lady in *negligée,* balancing her fine, black silk travelling gown over her head in order to get it on, and in the opposite chamber her husband gaped in a sleepy fashion, drowsily nodding his " angel head." I stood amazed : the lady stepped in, the dress open in the back, an untied bonnet on the head, and her cheeks blushing with surprise. " Von Andersen ! " said she, and uttered an excuse. All was out of order here, and her father's library — she pointed at the clothes-basket. All the boasting in the travelling coach was reduced to a garret and a bag filled with books !

From Prague I went by Toeplitz and Dresden home to Denmark. With mingled feelings in my heart I went ashore, and not all the tears I shed were tears of joy. But God was with me. I had no thought or affection for Germany ; my heart was attached to Italy, which was a paradise lost to me, where I should never again go. With dread and anxiety I looked toward the future at home.

Italy, with its scenery and the life of its people, occupied my soul, and toward this land I felt a yearning. My earlier life and what I had now seen, blended themselves together into an image — into poetry, which I was compelled to write down, although I was convinced that it would occasion me more trouble than joy, if my necessities at home should oblige me to print it. I had already in Rome written the first chapter, and others afterward in Munich. It was my novel of "The Improvisatore." In a letter I received in Rome, J. L. Heiberg wrote that he considered me as a kind of an improvisatore, and that word was the spark which gave my new poem its name.

At one of my first visits to the theatre at Odense, as a little boy, where, as I have already mentioned, the representations were given in the German language, I saw the "Donauweibchen," and the public applauded the actress of the principal part. Homage was paid to her, and she was honored; and I vividly remember thinking how happy she must be. Many years afterward, when, as a student, I visited Odense, I saw, in one of the chambers of the hospital where the poor widows lived, and where one bed stood by another, a female portrait hanging over one bed in a gilt frame. It was Lessing's "Emelia Galotti," and represented her as pulling the rose to pieces; but the picture was a portrait. It appeared singular in contrast with the poverty by which it was surrounded.

"Whom does it represent?" asked I.

"O!" said one of the old women, "it is the fáce of the German lady, — the poor lady who was once an actress!" And then I saw a little delicate woman, whose face was covered with wrinkles, and in an old silk gown that once had been black. That was the once celebrated singer, who, as the *Donauweibchen*, had been applauded by every one. This circumstance made an indelible impression upon me, and often occurred to my mind.

In Naples I heard Malibran for the first time. Her singing and acting surpassed anything which I had hitherto either heard or seen; and yet I thought the while of the miserably poor singer in the hospital of Odense: the two figures blended into the *Annunciata* of the novel. Italy was the background for that which had been experienced and that which was imagined.

My journey was ended. It was in August of 1834 that I returned to Denmark. I wrote the first part of the book at Ingemann's, in Sorö, in a little chamber in the roof, among fragrant lime-trees. I finished it in Copenhagen.

" To the Conference Councilor Collin and to his noble wife, in whom I found parents, whose children were brethren and sisters to me, whose house was my home, do I here present the best of which I am possessed." So ran the dedication.

The book was read, the edition sold, and another one printed. The critics were silent, the newspapers said nothing, but I heard in roundabout ways that there was an interest felt in my production, and that many were much pleased with it. At length the poet Carl Bagger wrote a notice in the " Sunday Times," of which he was editor, that began thus : —

" 'The poet Andersen does not write now as well as formerly ; he is exhausted : that I have for a long time expected.' In this fashion the poet is spoken of here and there in some of the aristocratic circles, perhaps in the very place where on his first appearance he was petted and almost idolized. But that he is not exhausted, and that he now, on the contrary, has swung himself into a position altogether unknown to him before, he has by his 'Improvisatore' shown in a most brilliant way."

People laugh now at me, but I say frankly I wept aloud, I cried for very gladness, and was moved to thankfulness toward God and man.

CHAPTER VII.

MANY who formerly had been my enemies, now changed their opinion; and among these one became my friend, who, I hope, will remain so through the whole of my life. That was Hauch the poet, — one of the noblest characters with whom I am acquainted. He had returned home from Italy after a residence of several years abroad, just at the same time when Heiberg's vaudevilles were intoxicating the inhabitants of Copenhagen, and when my "Journey on Foot" was making me a little known. He commenced a controversy with Heiberg, and somewhat scoffed at me. Nobody called his attention to my better lyrical writings; I was described to him as a spoiled, petulant child of fortune. He now read my "Improvisatore," and feeling that there was something good in me, his noble character evinced itself by his writing a cordial letter to me, in which he said that he had done me an injustice, and offered me now the hand of reconciliation. From that time we became friends. He used his influence for me with the utmost zeal, and has watched my onward career with heartfelt friendship. But so little able have many people been to understand what is excellent in him or the noble connection of heart between us two, that not long since, when he wrote a long novel, and drew in it the caricature of a poet, whose vanity ended in insanity, the people in Denmark discovered that he had treated me with the greatest injustice, because he had described in it my weakness. People must not believe that this was the assertion of one single person, or a misapprehension of my character; no: and Hauch felt himself compelled to write a treatise upon me as a poet, that he might show what a different place he assigned to me.

But to return to "The Improvisatore." This book raised my sunken fortunes, collected my friends again around me, nay, even obtained for me new ones. For the first time I felt that

I had obtained a due acknowledgment. The book was translated into German by Kruse, with a long title, " Jugendleben und Träume eines italienischen Dichter's." I objected to the title ; but he declared that it was necessary in order to attract attention to the book.

Bagger had, as already stated, been the first to pass judgment on the work ; after an interval of some time a second critique made its appearance, more courteous, it is true, than I was accustomed to, but still passing lightly over the best things in the book, and dwelling on its deficiencies, and on the number of incorrectly written Italian words. And as Nicolai's well-known book, " Italy as it really is," came out just then, people universally said, " Now we shall be able to see what it is about which Andersen has written, for from Nicolai a true idea of Italy will be obtained for the first time."

I presented my book to Christian VIII., at that time Prince Christian. In the antechamber I met with one of our lesser poets, who is in possession of a high rank in the state calendar ; he was so condescending as to speak to me. Well, we exercised the same trade, we were both poets, and now he delivered a little lecture for my benefit to a high personage present on the word " Collosseum." He had seen that word spelled by Byron " Coliseum," — that was terrible ! The same blunder kept recurring, and made one forget what there might be of good in the book. The lecture was delivered in a loud voice for the benefit of the whole assembly. I tried to demonstrate that I had written it in exactly the right way and Byron not ; the noble gentleman shrugged his shoulders and smiled, handed me my book, and regretted " the bad misprint in that beautifully bound book ! "

The " Monthly Review of Literature " noticed many little now forgotten pamphlets and comedies, but did not deign to bestow on " The Improvisatore " a single word, perhaps because it already had a great public ; a second edition of the book was published. Only when I had a firm footing and wrote my next novel, " O. T.," — it was in the year 1837, — was " The Improvisatore " mentioned by the " Monthly Review : " then how I was scolded and reproved ! But this is not the place to speak of that.

It was from Germany that there came the first decided acknowledgment of the merits of my work, or rather, perhaps, its over-estimation. I bow myself in joyful gratitude, like a sick man toward the sunshine, when my heart is grateful. I am not, as the Danish " Monthly Review," in its critique of " The Improvisatore," condescended to assert, an unthankful man, who exhibits in his work a want of gratitude toward his benefactors. I was indeed myself poor Antonio, who sighed under the burden which I had to bear, — I, the poor lad who ate the bread of charity. From Sweden also, later, resounded my praise, and the Swedish newspapers contained articles in praise of this work, which within the last two years has been received with equal warmth in England, — where Mary Howitt, the poetess, has translated it into English. Everywhere abroad was heard the loudest acknowledgment of its excellence.

"This book is in romance what 'Childe Harold' is in poetry," — so it was criticised in England; and when, thirteen years after, I came for the first time to London, I heard of a generous criticism in the " Foreign Review," attributed to the son-in-law of Walter Scott, the able and critical Lockhart. I did not know anything about it ; I could not at that time read English ; and although it appeared in one of the most read and best known reviews that come to Copenhagen, it was not mentioned in any Danish newspaper.

In North America also some English translations were afterward published, and in 1844 there followed in St. Petersburg a Russian, translated from the Swedish, and another translation into Bohemian was also made. The book was warmly received in Holland, and the well known monthly " De Tijd " contained a very complimentary critique of it.

In 1847 it was published in French, translated by Madame Lebrun, and was very favorably criticised ; its purity was especially taken notice of.

There are in Germany seven or eight different editions of this romance, with various imprints. I must furthermore refer to the well known Hitzig's edition of Chamisso's works, in which the poet expresses his delight at my book, and ranks it higher than such works as " Nôtre Dame de Paris," " La Salamandre," etc.

Then and during the years following, it was from without, so to speak, that the most hearty recognition came, and kept me up in spirit. If Denmark really had a poet in me, then no one at home took any heed to my need of nourishment. While people frequently set out carefully in the hot-house some little blade of what they believe may come to have some sort of value, almost every one has done, as it were, everything to prevent my growing. But our Lord willed it thus for my development, and therefore He sent the sun's rays from without, and let what I had written find its own way.

There exists in the public a power which is stronger than all the critics and cliques. I felt that at home I stood on firmer ground, and my spirit again had moments in which it raised its wings for flight.

A few months only after the publication of " The Improvisatore " I brought out the first part of my " Wonder Stories," but the critics would not vouchsafe to me any encouragement ; they could not get away from their old preconceived notions. The " Monthly Review " never deigned to mention them at all, and in " Dannora," another critical journal, I was advised not to waste my time in writing wonder stories. I lacked the usual form of that kind of poetry ; I would not study models, said they — and so I gave up writing them ; and in this alternation of feeling between gayety and ill-humor I wrote my next novel, " O. T." I felt just at the time a strong mental impulse to write, and I believed that I had found my true element in novel-writing.

There were published successively " The Improvisatore " in 1835, " O. T. " in 1836, and " Only a Fiddler " in 1837. Many liked my " O. T.," especially H. C. Örsted, who had a great appreciation of humor. He encouraged me to continue in this direction, and from him and his family I met with the kindest acknowledgments.

At Sibbern's, with whom I now had a personal acquaintance, I read " O. T." Poul Möller, who had just arrived from Norway, and was no admirer of my " Journey on Foot to Amack," was present at one of my evening readings, and listened with great interest. The passages concerning Jutland, the heath, and the Western Sea pleased him especially,

and he praised them warmly. Some translations of " O T."
into German were afterward again translated into Swedish,
Dutch, and English. " O. T." was read and again read, the
book had its partisans, but the newspaper and journal critics
did not show me any encouragement; they forgot that with
years the boy becomes a man, and that people may acquire
knowledge in other than the ordinary ways.

Many who had perhaps never read my last greater works,
were the most severe judges, but not quite so honest as
Heiberg, who, when I asked him if he had read these novels,
answered me jokingly, " I never read great books ! "

The year after (1837) appeared my romance, " Only a Fiddler," a spiritual blossom sprung out of the terrible struggle
that went on in me between my poet nature and my hard
surroundings. Yet it was a step in advance. I understood myself and the world better, but I was ready to give up expecting to receive any kind of true recognition of that which God
had bestowed upon me. In another world it might be cleared
up — that was my faith. If " The Improvisatore " was a real
improvisatore, " Only a Fiddler " was then to be understood
as struggle and suffering: this production was carefully
wrought, and, looked at from without, it was conceived and
executed with the greatest simplicity. The opposition that
had stirred in me against injustice, folly, and the stupidity
and hardness of the public, found vent in the characters of
Naomi, Ladislaus, and the godfather in Hollow Lane.

This book also made its way at home, but no word of thanks
or encouragement was heard; the critics only granted that I
was very fortunate in trusting to my instinct, — an expression
applied to animals, but in the human world, in the world of
poetry, it is called genius; for me instinct was good enough.
There was a constant depreciation of all that was good in me.
A single person of distinction told me once that I was treated
very hardly and unjustly, but nobody stepped forward to de-
nounce it.

The novel " Only a Fiddler " made a strong impression for
a short time on one of our country's young and highly gifted
men, Sören Kierkegaard. Meeting him in the street, he told
me that he would write a review of my book, and that I should

be more satisfied with that than I had been with the earlier, because, he said, they had misunderstood me! A long time elapsed, then he read the book again, and the first good impression of it was effaced. I must almost believe that the more seriously he examined the story, the more faults he found ; and when the critique appeared, it did not please me at all. It came out as a whole book, the first, I believe, that Kierkegaard has written ; and because of the Hegelian heaviness in the expression, it was very difficult to read, and people said in fun that only Kierkegaard and Andersen had read it through. I learned from it that I was no poet, but a poetical figure that had escaped from my group, in which my place would be taken by some future poet or be used by him as a figure in a poem, and that thus my supplement would be created ! Since that time I have had a better understanding with this author, who has always met me with kindness and discernment. That which contributed likewise to place this book in the shade was the circumstance of Heiberg having at that time published his " Every-day Stories," which were written in excellent language, and with good taste and truth. Their own merits, and the recommendation of their being Heiberg's, who was the beaming star of literature, placed them in the highest rank.

I had, however, advanced so far that there no longer existed any doubt as to my poetical ability, which people had wholly denied to me before my journey to Italy. Still not a single Danish critic had spoken of the characteristics which are peculiar to my novels. It was not until my works appeared in Swedish that this was done, and then several Swedish journals went profoundly into the subject, and analyzed my works with good and honorable intentions. The case was the same in Germany ; and from this country, too, my heart was strengthened to proceed. It was not until last year that in Denmark a man of influence, Hauch the poet, spoke of the novels in his already mentioned treatise, and with a few touches brought their characteristics prominently forward.

" The principal thing," says he, " in Andersen's best and most elaborate works, in those which are distinguished for the richest fancy, the deepest feeling, the most lively poetic spirit, is of talent, or at least of a noble nature, which will struggle its way out of narrow and depressing circumstances. This is the case with his three novels, and with this purpose in view it is really an important state of existence which he describes — an inner world, which no one understands better than he, who has himself drained out of the bitter cup of suffering and renunciation painful and deep feelings, which are closely related to those of his own experience, and from which Memory, who, according to the old significant myth, is the mother of the Muses, met him hand in hand with them. That which he, in these his works, relates to the world, deserves assuredly to be listened to with attention ; because, at the same time that it may be only the most secret inward life of the individual, yet it is also the common lot of men of talent and genius, at least when these are in needy circumstances, as is the case of those who are here placed before our eyes. In so far as in his 'Improvisatore,' in 'O. T.,' and in 'Only a Fiddler,' he represents not only himself, in his own separate individuality, but at the same time the momentous combat which so many have to pass through, and which he understands so well, because in it his own life has developed itself ; therefore in no instance can he be said to present to the reader what belongs to the world of illusion, but only that which bears witness to truth, and which, as is the case with all such testimony, has a universal and enduring worth.

"And still more than this, Andersen is not only the defender of talent and genius, but, at the same time, of every human heart which is unkindly and unjustly treated. And whilst he himself has so painfully suffered in that deep combat in which the Laocoön snakes seize upon the outstretched hand, — whilst he himself has been compelled to drink from that wormwood-steeped bowl which the cold-blooded and arrogant world so constantly offers to those who are in depressed circumstances, he is fully capable of giving to his delineations in this respect a truth and an earnestness, nay, even a tragic and a pain-awakening pathos, that rarely fails of producing its effect on the sympathizing human heart. Who can read that scene in his 'Only a Fiddler,' in which the 'high-bred hound,' as the poet expresses it, turned away with disgust from the broken victuals which the poor youth received as alms, without recognizing, at the same time, that this is no game in which vanity seeks for a triumph, but that it expresses much more — human nature wounded to its inmost depths, which here speaks out its sufferings ? "

Thus is it spoken in Denmark of my works, after an interval of nine or ten years ; thus speaks the voice of a noble, venerated man. It is with me and the critics as it is with wine, — the more years pass before it is drunk, the better is its flavor.

During the year in which the " Fiddler " came out, I visited for the first time the neighboring country of Sweden. I went by the Göta canal to Stockholm. At that time nobody understood what is now called Scandinavian sympathies ; there still existed a sort of mistrust inherited from the old wars between the two neighbor nations. Little was known of Swedish literature, and yet it required little pains for a Dane easily to read and understand the Swedish language ; people scarcely knew Tegnér's " Frithiof and Axel," excepting through translations. I had, however, read a few other Swedish authors, and the deceased, unfortunate Stagnelius pleased me more as a poet than Tegnér, who represented poetry in Sweden. I, who hitherto had only travelled into Germany and southern countries, where by this means the departure from Copenhagen was also the departure from my mother tongue, felt, in this respect, almost at home in Sweden : the languages are so much akin, that of two persons each might read in the language of his own country, and yet the other understand him. It seemed to me, as a Dane, that Denmark expanded itself ; kinship with the people exhibited itself in many ways, more and more ; and I felt in a lively degree how near akin are Swedes, Danes, and Norwegians.

I met with cordial, kind people, and with these I easily made acquaintance. I reckon this journey among the happiest I ever made. I had no knowledge of the character of Swedish scenery, and therefore I was in the highest degree astonished by the Trollhätta voyage, and by the extremely picturesque situation of Stockholm. It sounds to the uninitiated half like a fairy tale, when one says that the steamboat goes up across the lakes over the mountains, from whence may be seen the outstretched pine and beech woods below. Immense sluices heave up and lower the vessel again, whilst the travellers ramble through the woods. None of the cascades of Switzerland, none in Italy, not even that of Terni, have in them anything so imposing as that of Trollhätta. Such is the impression, at all events, which it made on me.

On this journey, and at this last-mentioned place, commenced a very interesting acquaintance, and one which has not been without its influence on me, — an acquaintance with the Swedish authoress, Fredrika Bremer. I had just been speaking with the captain of the steamboat and some of the passengers about the Swedish authors living in Stockholm, and I mentioned my desire to see and converse with Miss Bremer.

" You will not meet with her," said the captain, " as she is at this moment on a visit in Norway."

" She will be coming back while I am there," said I in joke ; " I always am lucky in my journeys, and that which I most wish for is always accomplished."

" Hardly this time, however," said the captain.

A few hours after this he came up to me laughing, with the list of the newly arrived passengers in his hand. " Lucky fellow," said he aloud, " you take good fortune with you ; Miss Bremer is here, and sails with us to Stockholm."

I received it as a joke ; he showed me the list, but still I was uncertain. Among the new arrivals I could see no one who resembled an authoress. Evening came on, and about midnight we were on the great Wener Lake. At sunrise I wished to have a view of this extensive lake, the shores of which could scarcely be seen ; and for this purpose I left the cabin. At the very moment that I did so, another passenger was also doing the same, — a lady neither young nor old, wrapped in a shawl and cloak. I thought to myself, if Miss Bremer is on board, this must be she, and fell into discourse with her ; she replied politely, but still distantly, nor would she directly answer my question whether she was the authoress of the celebrated novels. She asked after my name ; was acquainted with it, but confessed that she had read none of my works. She then inquired whether I had not some of them with me, and I lent her a copy of " The Improvisatore," which I had destined for Beskow. She vanished immediately with the volumes, and was not again visible all morning.

When I again saw her, her countenance was beaming, and she was full of cordiality ; she pressed my hand, and said that she had read the greater part of the first volume, and that she now knew me.

The vessel flew with us across the mountains, through quiet inland lakes and forests, till it arrived at the Baltic Sea, where islands lie scattered, as in the Archipelago, and where the most remarkable transition takes place from naked cliffs to grassy islands, and to those on which stand trees and houses. Eddies and breakers make it here necessary to take on board a skillful pilot ; and there are indeed some places where every passenger must sit quietly on his seat, whilst the eye of the pilot is riveted upon one point. On shipboard one feels the mighty power of nature, which at one moment seizes hold of the vessel, and the next lets it go again. Miss Bremer related many legends and many histories which were connected with this or that island, or those farm premises up aloft on the main land.

In Stockholm the acquaintance with her increased, and year after year the letters which have passed between us have strengthened it. She is a noble woman ; the great truths of religion, and the poetry which lies in the quiet circumstances of life, have penetrated her being.

It was not until after my visit to Stockholm that her Swedish translation of my novel came out ; my lyrical poems only, and my " Journey on Foot," were known to a few authors ; these received me with the utmost kindness, and the lately deceased Dahlgrén, well known by his humorous poems, wrote a song in my honor — in short, I met with hospitality, and countenances beaming with Sunday gladness.

I had brought with me a letter of introduction from Ör-sted to the celebrated Berzelius, who gave me a good reception in the old city of Upsala. From this place I returned to Stockholm. City, country, and people were all dear to me ; it seemed to me, as I said before, that the boundaries of my native land had stretched themselves out, and I now first felt the kindredship of the three peoples, and in this feeling I wrote a Scandinavian song. In this poem there was nothing of politics : politics I have nothing to do with. The poet is not to serve politics, but go before movements like a prophet. It was a hymn of praise for all the three nations, for that which was peculiar and best in each one of them.

" One can see that the Swedes made a deal of him," was the first remark which I heard at home on this song.

Years pass on ; the neighbors understand each other better ; Oehlenschläger, Fredrika Bremer, and Tegnér cause them to read each other's authors ; and the foolish remains of the old enmity, which had no other foundation than that they did not know each other, vanished. There now prevails a beautiful, cordial relationship between Sweden and Denmark. A Scandinavian club has been established in Stockholm ; and with this my song came to honor ; and it was then said, " It will outlive everything that Andersen has written : " which was as unjust as when they said that it was only the product of flattered vanity. This song is now sung in Sweden as well as in Denmark.

On my return home I began to study history industriously, and made myself still further acquainted with the literature of foreign countries. Yet still the volume which afforded me the greatest pleasure was that of nature ; and during a summer residence among the country seats of Funen, and more especially at Lykkesholm, with its highly romantic site in the midst of woods, and at the noble seat of Glorup, from whose possessor I met with the most friendly reception, did I acquire more true wisdom, assuredly, in my solitary rambles, than I ever could have gained from the schools.

The house of the Conference Councilor Collin in Copenhagen was at that time, as it has been since, a second father's house to me, and there I had parents, and brothers, and sisters. It was here that the humor and love of life observable in various passages of the novel " O. T.," and in the little dramatic pieces written about this time, for instance, " The Invisible at Sprogö," had their origin, and where much good was done to me in this respect, so that my morbid turn of mind was unable to gain the mastery of me. Collin's eldest daughter, Madame Ingeborg Drewsen, especially exercised great influence over me, by her merry humor and wit. When the mind is yielding and elastic, like the expanse of ocean, it readily, like the ocean, reflects its surroundings.

I was very productive, and my writings, in my own country, were now classed among those which were always bought and read ; therefore for each fresh work I received a higher payment. Yet truly, when you consider what a circumscribed world the Danish reading world is, and that I was not, when looked at from Heiberg's and the " Monthly's " balcony, acknowledged as a poet of the time, you will see that this payment could not be the most liberal. Yet I had to live. I call to my mind how astonished Charles Dickens was at hearing of the payment I had received for " The Improvisatore."

" What did you get ? " asked he. I answered, " Nineteen pounds ! " — " For the sheet ? " he inquired. " No," said I, " for the whole book." — " We must be misunderstanding each other," continued he ; " you don't mean to say that for the whole work, 'The Improvisatore,' you have only nineteen pounds ; you must mean for each sheet ! " I was sorry to tell him that it was not the case, and that I had only got about half a pound a sheet.

" I should really not believe it," exclaimed he, " if you had not told it yourself."

To be sure, Dickens did not know anything about our circumstances in Denmark, and measured the payment with what he got for his works in England ; but it is very probable that my English translator gained more than I, the author. But after all, I lived, though in want.

To write, and always to write, in order to live, I felt would be destructive to me, and my attempts to acquire some kind of situation failed. I tried to get a situation in the royal library. H. C. Örsted supported warmly my petition to the director of the library, the grand-chamberlain Hauch. Örsted ended his written testimony, after having mentioned H. C. Andersen's " merits as a poet," by — " He is characterized by uprightness, and by a regularity and exactness which many think cannot be found in a poet, but will be conceded to him by those who know him ! "

These words of Örsted about me did not, however, produce any effect; the grand chamberlain dismissed me with great politeness, saying that I was too highly endowed for such a trivial work as that in the library.   I tried to form an engagement with the Society for promoting the Liberty of the Press, having planned and made a design for a Danish popular almanac, like the very renowned German one of Gubitz: no Danish popular almanac existed here at that time.   I believed that my pictures of nature in "The Improvisatore" had proved my capability for this kind of productions, and that my "Wonder Stories," which I had then commenced to publish, might show them that I could tell stories too.

Örsted was very well pleased with the plan, and supported it in the best way, but the committee decided that the work would be burdened with too many and too great difficulties for the society to engage in it.   In other words, they had no confidence in my ability; but afterward such an almanac was published by another editor, under the auspices of the society.

I was always forced, in order to live, to think of the morrow.   One hospitable house more was in these days opened for me, that of the old, now deceased, widow Bügel, *née* Adzer.   Conference Councilor Collin was, however, at that time, my help, my consolation, my support, and he is one of those men who do more than they promise.   I suffered want and poverty — but I have no wish to speak of it here.   I thought, however, as I did in the years of my boyhood, that when it seems to be hardest for us, our Lord brings us help! I have a star of fortune, and it is God!

One day, as I sat in my little room, somebody knocked at the door, and a stranger with beautiful and amiable features stood before me: it was the late Count Conrad Rantzau-Breitenburg, a native of Holstein and Prime Minister in Denmark. He loved poetry, was in love with the beauty of Italy, and was desirous of making acquaintance with the author of "The Improvisatore."   He read my book in the original; his imagination was powerfully seized by it, and he spoke, both at court and in his own private circles, of my book in the warmest manner.   He was of a noble, amiable nature, a highly educated man, and possessed of a truly chivalrous disposition.   In his youth he had travelled much, and spent a long time in Spain and Italy; his judgment was therefore of great importance to me. He did not stop here; he sought me out. He stepped quietly into my little room, thanked me for my book, besought me to visit him, and frankly asked me whether there were no means by which he could be of use to me.

I hinted how oppressive it was to be forced to write in order to live, and not move free from care, to be able to develop one's mind and thoughts. He pressed my hand in a friendly manner, and promised to be an efficient friend, and that he became. Collin and H. C. Örsted secretly associated themselves with him, and became my intercessors with King Frederick VI.

Already for many years there had existed, under Frederick VI., an institution which does the highest honor to the Danish government, namely, that beside the considerable sum expended yearly for the travelling expenses of young literary men and artists, a small pension shall be awarded to such of them as enjoy no office emoluments. All our most important poets have had a share of this assistance, — Oehlenschläger, Ingemann, Heiberg, C. Winther, and others. Hertz had just then received such a pension, and his future subsistence was made thus the more secure. It was my hope and my wish that the same good fortune might be mine — and it was. Frederick VI. granted me two hundred rix-dollars banco yearly. I was filled with gratitude and joy. I was no longer *forced* to write in order to live; I had a sure support in the possible event of sickness ; I was less dependent upon the people about me.

A new chapter of my life began.

CHAPTER VIII.

FROM this day forward, it was as if a more constant sunshine had entered my heart. I felt within myself more repose, more certainty; it was clear to me, as I glanced back over my earlier life, that a loving Providence watched over me, that all was directed for me by a higher Power; and the firmer such a conviction becomes, the more secure does a man feel himself. My childhood lay behind me, my youthful life began properly from this period; hitherto it had been only an arduous swimming against the stream. The spring of my life commenced; but still the spring had its dark days, its storms, before it advanced to settled summer; it has these in order to develop what shall then ripen.

That which one of my dearest friends wrote to me on one of my later travels abroad, may serve as an introduction to what I have here to relate. He wrote in his own peculiar style : " It is your vivid imagination which creates the idea of your being despised in Denmark ; it is utterly untrue. You and Denmark agree admirably, and you would agree still better, if there were in Denmark no theatre — *Hinc illæ lachrymæ !* This cursed theatre. Is this, then, Denmark? and are you, then, nothing but a writer for the theatre? "

Herein lies a solid truth. The theatre has been the cave out of which most of the evil storms have burst upon me. They are peculiar people, these people of the theatre ; from the first pantomimist to the first lover, every one places himself systematically in one scale, and puts all the world in the other. The pit's circle is the boundary of the world ; the critiques in the newspapers are the fixed stars of the universe ; if applause now resounds, soon it is only idle babble and the repetitions of what others have said ; is it not, then, natural and pardonable to grow giddy over a reputation which is really sound ?

As politics at that time did not play any part with us, the theatre furnished the chief topic of the daily and nightly conversations. The royal Danish theatre might indeed be placed on a level with the first theatres in Europe ; it possessed eminent talent. • Nielsen was then in the vigor of youth, and besides his ability as an artist he possessed an organ of speech which was like very music, delivering the words in a way to bewitch one. The Danish stage had then Dr. Ryge, who by his person, genius, and voice, was especially fitted to act in the tragedies of Oehlenschläger. The stage possessed in Frydendal a rare impersonation of wit and humor, characterized by education and gentility. Stage was a complete cavalier, a true gentleman, and had a ready wit in playing comic *rôles.* Besides those, we possessed actors of talent still living, — Madame Heiberg, Madame Nielsen, Mr. Rosenkilde, and Mr. Phister. We had at that time an opera, and the ballet began to flourish under the leading of Bournonville.

As I have before said, our theatre was one of the first stages of Europe, but we cannot therefore assert that all who gave it direction were true leaders, although some of them assumed to be such ; at least so it seemed to me, because they did not pay much regard to authors. I believe that the Danish theatre always has been in want of a kind of military discipline, and this is absolutely necessary where many interests have to be combined into a whole, — even when that whole is an artistic one. I have always observed the same dissatisfaction on the part of the public toward the directors of the theatre, especially as regards the choice of pieces, as exists between the directors and the actors. It could not be, perhaps, otherwise, and all young authors, who like me do not enjoy the favor of the hour, will have to suffer and struggle under the same circumstances. Even Oehlenschläger suffered much, was overlooked, or, it seemed to me, was at least not treated as he ought to have been. The actors were applauded, he was hissed. How have I not heard my countrymen speak of that genius ! Well, it may perhaps be so in all countries, but how sad that it should be so. Oehlenschläger relates himself that his children at school had to listen to the unkind words of the other boys at having such a father as he was ; and they talked only as they heard their parents talk.

Those actors and actresses who, through talent or popular favor, take the first rank, very often assume to be above both the directors and authors ; these must pay court to them, or they will ruin a part, or, what is still worse, spread abroad an unfavorable opinion of the piece previous to its being acted ; and thus you have a coffee-house criticism before any one ought properly to know anything of the work. It is moreover characteristic of the people of Copenhagen, that when a new piece is announced, they do not say, " I am glad of it," but " It will probably be good for nothing ; it will be hissed off the stage." That hissing off plays a great part, and is an amusement which fills the house ; but it is not the bad actor who is hissed ; no, the author and the composer only are the criminals ; for them the scaffold is erected. Five minutes is the usual time, and the whistles resound, and the lovely women smile and felicitate themselves, like the Spanish ladies at their bloody bull-fights.

For a number of years November and December were always the most dangerous time for a new piece, because the young scholars were then made " Students," and, having cleared the fence of " artium," were very severe judges. All our most eminent dramatic writers have been whistled down, — as Oehlenschläger, Heiberg, Hertz, and others ; to say nothing of foreign classics, as Molière.

In the mean time the theatre is and was the most profitable sphere of labor for the Danish writer. When I stood without help and support this induced me to make a trial, and to write the opera text already spoken of, — for which I was so severely criticised ; and an internal impulse drove me also to try my powers in writing vaudevilles. The authors were then poorly paid, until Collin took charge of the theatre as manager. There are things we call facts, which cannot be effaced, and I must mention them. A well known, very able business man, was made director of the theatre. A good arrangement in many things was looked for because he was a clever accountant ; and there was also an anticipation that the opera would flourish because he had a good ear for music, sang in musical circles, and thus energetic changes were expected ; among these changes was a regulation as to the pay for the pieces,

As it was a difficult matter to judge of their value it was decided that they should be paid for according to their length ; at the first representation of a piece, the manager stood with a watch in his hand and noted down how many quarters of an hour it took to go through with it ; these were added together, and the payment was regulated by the sum.   If the last quarter of an hour was not all taken by the piece it fell to the theatre : was not that a very business-like and well contrived plan ?   Everybody thinks of number one, and that was the case with me.   I needed every shilling, and therefore I suffered a heavy loss when my vaudeville, " Parting and Meeting," which was divided into two acts, with separate titles, was considered as two vaudevilles, and according to the manager's opinion could even as well be given separately.   But " we must not speak evil of our magistrate," and the directory of the theatre is the dramatic poet's magistrate, whereas some of the personages — but I will let them speak for themselves !

Collin was no longer manager of the theatre, — Counselor of Justice Molbech had taken his place ; and the tyranny which now commenced degenerated into the comic.   I fancy that in course of time the manuscript volumes of the censorship, which are preserved in the theatre, and in which Molbech has certainly recorded his judgments on received and rejected pieces, will present some remarkable characteristics.   Over all that I wrote the staff was broken !   One way was open to me by which to bring my pieces on the stage ; and that was to give them to those actors who in summer gave representations at their own cost.   In the summer of 1839 I wrote the vaudeville of " The Invisible One at Sprogö," to scenery which had been painted for another piece which fell through ; and the unrestrained merriment of the piece gave it such favor with the public that I obtained its acceptance by the manager ; and that light sketch still maintains itself on the boards, and has survived such a number of representations as I had never anticipated.

This approbation, however, procured me no further advantage, for each of my succeeding dramatic works received only rejection, and occasioned me only mortification.   Nevertheless, seized by the idea and the circumstances of the little

French narrative, " Les Épaves," I determined to dramatize
it ; and as I had often heard that I did not possess the assiduity sufficient to work my *matériel* well, I resolved to *labor*
this drama — " The Mulatto " — from the beginning to the
end in the most diligent manner, and to compose it in alternately rhyming verse, as was then the fashion. It was a foreign subject of which I availed myself ; but if verses are
music, I at least endeavored to adapt my music to the text,
and to let the poetry of another diffuse itself through my spiritual blood ; so that people should not be heard to say, as
they had done before, regarding the romance of Walter Scott,
that the composition was cut down and fitted to the stage.

The piece was ready and was read to several able men, old
friends, and to some of the actors also who were to appear in
it ; they declared it excellent, and very interesting ; especially
Mr. William Holst, whom I wished to act the principal part ;
he was one of the artists on the stage who met me kindly and
generously, and to whom I ought to express my thanks and
acknowledgment.   In the antechamber of Frederick VI. one
of our government officers from the West Indies spoke against
the piece, saying that he had heard it ought not to be admitted
on the royal stage, because it might have a pernicious influence upon the blacks of our West Indian islands.   " But this
piece is not to be represented at the West Indies," was the
reply.

The piece was sent in, and was rejected by Molbech.   It
was sufficiently known that what he cherished for the boards,
withered there the first evening ; but that what he cast away
as weeds were flowers for the garden — a real consolation for
me.   The assistant-manager, Privy Counselor of State Adler,
a man of taste and liberality, became the patron of my work ;
and since a very favorable opinion of it already prevailed with
the public, after I had read it to many persons, it was resolved
on for representation.

Before the piece was represented on the stage there occurred a little scene, as characteristic as amusing, which I will
relate here.   There was a very brave man, but a man of no
artistic knowledge, whose judgment of the piece, however,
might turn the scale : he told me that he was well disposed

toward me, but that he had not yet read my piece ; that there were many who spoke well of it, but that Molbech had written a whole sheet against it. " And now I must also tell you," he added, " that it is copied from a novel. You write novels yourself; why do you not yourself invent a story for your piece ? Then I must remind you that to write novels is one thing and to write comedies another. In these there must be theatrical effect ; is there any such in ' The Mulatto,' and if so is it any thing new ? " I tried to enter into the ideas of the man, and answered, — " There is a ball ! "

" Yes, that is very well, but that we have in ' The Bride : ' is there not something brand-new ? " — " There is a slave-market ! " said I. " A slave-market : that I think we have not had before ! Well, that is something, I shall be just toward you. I like that slave-market ! " And I think that this slave-market threw the last necessary *yes* in the urn for the acceptance of " The Mulatto."

I had the honor to read it before my present King and Queen, who received me in a very kind and friendly manner, and from whom, since that time, I have experienced many proofs of favor and cordiality. The day of representation arrived ; the bills were posted ; I had not closed my eyes through the whole night from excitement and expectation ; the people already stood in throngs before the theatre, to procure tickets, when royal messengers galloped through the streets, solemn groups collected, the minute guns pealed — Frederick VI. had died that morning !

The death was proclaimed from the balcony of the palace of Amalienborg, and hurrahs were given for Christian VIII., the gates of the city were closed, and the army swore allegiance. Frederick VI. belonged to the patriarchal age ; the generation that had grown up with him had not before suffered the loss of a king, and the sorrow and seriousness were great and sincere.

For two months more was the theatre closed, and was opened under Christian VIII., with my drama, " The Mulatto " ; which was received with the most triumphant acclamation ; but I could not at once feel the joy of it, I felt only relieved from a state of excitement, and breathed more freely.

This piece continued through a series of representations to receive the same approbation ; many placed this work far above all my former ones, and considered that with it began my proper poetical career.   It was soon translated into Swedish, and acted with applause at the royal theatre in Stockholm.   Travelling players introduced it into the smaller towns in the neighboring country ; a Danish company gave it in the original language, in the Swedish city Malmö, and a troop of students from the university town of Lund welcomed it with enthusiasm.   I had been for a week previous on a visit at some Swedish country-houses, where I was entertained with so much cordial kindness that the recollection of it will never quit my bosom ; and there, in a foreign country, I received the first public testimony of honor, which has left upon me the deepest and most inextinguishable impression.   I was invited by some students of Lund to visit their ancient town. Here a public dinner was given to me ; speeches were made, toasts were pronounced ; and as I was in the evening in a family circle, I was informed that the students meant to honor me with a serenade.

I felt myself actually overcome by this intelligence ; my heart throbbed feverishly as I descried the thronging troop, with their blue caps, approaching the house arm-in-arm.   I experienced a feeling of humiliation ; a most lively consciousness of my deficiencies, so that I seemed bowed to the very earth at the moment others were elevating me.   As they all uncovered their heads while I stepped forth, I had need of all my thoughts to avoid bursting into tears.   In the feeling that I was unworthy of all this, I glanced round to see whether a smile did not pass over the face of some one, but I could discern nothing of the kind ; and such a discovery would, at that moment, have inflicted on me the deepest wound.

After a hurra, a speech was delivered, of which I clearly recollect the following words : "When your native land and the nations of Europe offer you their homage, then may you never forget that the first public honors were conferred on you by the students of Lund."

When the heart is warm, the strength of the expression is not weighed.   I felt it deeply, and replied, that from this moment I became aware that I must assert a name in order to render myself worthy of these tokens of honor. I pressed the hands of those nearest to me, and returned them thanks so deep, so heartfelt, — certainly never was an expression of thanks more sincere. When I returned to my chamber, I went aside, in order to weep out this excitement, this over-whelming sensation. " Think no more of it, be joyous with us," said some of my lively Swedish friends ; but a deep earnestness had entered my soul. Often has the memory of this time come back to me ; and no noble-minded man who reads these pages will discover vanity in the fact that I have lingered so long over this moment of life, which scorched the roots of pride rather than nourished them.

My drama was now to be brought on the stage at Malmö ; the students wished to see it ; but I hastened my departure, that I might not be in the theatre at the time. With gratitude and joy fly my thoughts toward the Swedish University city, but I myself have not been there again since. In the Swedish newspapers the honors paid me were mentioned, and it was added that the Swedes were not unaware that in my own country there was a clique which persecuted me ; but that this should not hinder my neighbors from offering me the honors which they deemed my due.

It was when I had returned to Copenhagen that I first truly felt how cordially I had been received by the Swedes : amongst some of my old and tried friends I found the most genuine sympathy. I saw tears in their eyes, — tears of joy for the honors paid me ; and especially, said they, for the manner in which I had received them. There is but one manner for me ; at once, in the midst of joy, I fly with thanks to God.

There were certain persons who smiled at the enthusiasm, and others who liked to turn it into ridicule. The poet Heiberg said ironically to me, — "When I go to Sweden you must go with me, that I also may get a little attention ! " I did not like the joke, and answered, — " Take your wife with you and you will get it easier."

From Sweden there came only enthusiasm for " The Mulat-to," while at home certain voices raised themselves against it : " the material was merely borrowed, and I had not mentioned

that on the printed title-page." That was an accidental fault.
I had written it upon the last page of the manuscript, but as
the drama itself closed with the printed sheet, a new sheet
would have had to be printed in order to include that note.   I
consulted one of our poets, who thought it entirely superfluous,
because the novel " Les Épaves " was much read and known.
Heiberg himself, when he wrote over again " The Fairies," by
Tieck, did not mention with a single word the rich source from
which he took it.   But here he laid hands on me ; the French
narrative was scrupulously studied and compared with my
piece.   A translation of " Les Épaves " was sent to the editor
of " The Portefeuille," with urgent request that it should be
inserted.   The editor let me know of it, and I begged him of
course to publish it.   The piece continued to have a good run
on the stage, but the criticism diminished the value of my work.
That exaggerated praise which I had received, now made me
sensitive to the blame ; I could bear it less easily than before,
and saw more clearly that it did not spring out of an interest
in the matter, but was only uttered in order to mortify me.
In the newly published novel, also, by the author of " Every-
day Stories," the admiration for " The Mulatto " was laughed
at.   The idea of the victory of genius, which I had expressed
there, was considered only an idle fancy.

   For the rest, my mind was fresh and elastic ; I conceived
precisely at this time the idea of " The Picture-Book without
Pictures," and worked it out.   This little book appears, to
judge by the reviews and the number of editions, to have obtained an extraordinary popularity in Germany.   One of those
who first announced it, added, — " Many of these pictures
offer material for narratives and novels — yes, one gifted with
fancy might create romances out of them."   Madame von
Göhren has in her first romance, " The Adopted Daughter,"
really borrowed the material from " The Picture-Book without Pictures."   In Sweden, also, was my book translated, and
dedicated to myself; at home it was less esteemed, and so far
as I remember it was only Mr. Siesby, who, in the " Copenhagen Morning Journal," granted it a few kind words.   A
couple of translations appeared in England, and the English
critics gave the little book very high praise, calling it " an

Iliad in a nutshell!" From England, as also later from Germany, I have seen a proof-sheet of the same book in a splendid edition, which changed it to a "Picture-Book without
Pictures" with pictures.

At home people did not set much store by the little book,
they talked only of "The Mulatto;" and finally, only of the
borrowed *matériel* of it. I determined, therefore, to produce
a new dramatic work, in which both subject and development,
in fact everything, should be of my own conception. I had
the idea and now wrote the tragedy of "The Moorish Maiden,"
hoping through this to stop the mouths of all my detractors,
and to assert my place as a dramatic poet. I hoped, too,
through the income from this, together with the proceeds of
"The Mulatto," to be able to make a fresh journey, not only to
Italy, but to Greece and Turkey. My first going abroad had
more than all beside operated toward my intellectual development; I was therefore full of the passion for travel, and of
the endeavor to acquire more knowledge of nature and of
human life.

My new piece did not please Heiberg, nor indeed my
dramatic efforts at all; his wife — for whom the chief part
appeared to me especially to be adapted — refused, and that
not in the most friendly manner, to play it. Deeply wounded
I went forth. I lamented this to some individuals. Whether
this was repeated, or whether a complaint against the favorite
of the public is a crime, — enough : from this hour Heiberg
became my opponent, — he whose intellectual rank I so highly
estimated, — he with whom I would so willingly have allied
myself, — and he who so often — I will venture to say it — I
had approached with the whole sincerity of my nature. I
have constantly declared his wife to be so distinguished an
actress, and continue still so entirely of this opinion, that I
would not hesitate one moment to assert that she would have
a European reputation, were the Danish language as widely
diffused as the German or the French. In tragedy she is, by
the spirit and the geniality with which she comprehends and
fills any part, a most interesting artist; and in comedy she
stands unrivaled.

The wrong may be on my side or not, — no matter : a party

was opposed to me. I felt myself wounded, excited by many coincident annoyances there. I felt uncomfortable in my native country — yes, almost ill. I therefore left my piece to its fate, and, suffering and disconcerted, I hastened forth. In this mood I wrote a prologue to "The Moorish Maiden," which betrayed my irritated mind far too palpably. If I would represent this portion of my life more clearly and reflectively, it would require me to penetrate the mysteries of the theatre, to analyze our æsthetic cliques, and to drag into conspicuous notice many individuals who do not belong to publicity. Many persons in my place would, like me, have fallen ill, or would have resented it vehemently : perhaps the latter would have been the most sensible. The best thing for me was to go away, and that was also the wish of my friends. "Be of good cheer, and try as soon as possible to get away from that gossip!" wrote Thorwaldsen to me from Nysö. "I hope to see you here before you go away ; if not, then we must see each other in Rome!" — "For heaven's sake, set out!" said my sincere and sympathizing friends, who knew how I suffered. H. C. Örsted, also, and Collin fortified me in my purpose, and Oehlenschläger sent me in a poem his greeting for the journey.

My friend, the poet H. P. Holst, was also going abroad ; his poem, "O my country, what hast thou lost!" was in every one's mouth ; he had in a few affectionate and plain words told what every one felt. The death of King Frederick VI. was a national grief, a family sorrow, and this beautiful poem, which so naturally expressed it, took a strong hold of the people. Holst was the happy poet of the day ; without any difficulty, without offering any testimonies, he got a travelling pension. This is said without any bitterness against him. His many friends in the Students' Union got up a good-by supper for him, and this suggested the same compliment to me ; and amongst the elder ones who were present to receive me were Collin, Oehlenschläger, and Örsted. This was somewhat of sunshine in the midst of my mortification ; songs by Oehlenschläger and Hillerup were sung ; and I found cordiality and friendship, as I quitted my country in distress. This was in October of 1840.

For the second time I went to Italy and Rome, to Greece and Constantinople — a journey which I have described after my own manner in " A Poet's Bazaar."

In Holstein I continued some days with Count Rantzau-Breitenburg, whose ancestral castle I now for the first time visited. Here I became acquainted with the rich scenery of Holstein, its heath and moorland. Although it was late in the autumn we had fine days. One day I visited the neighboring village of Münsterdorph, where the author of " Siegfried von Lindenberg," Müller von Itzehoe, is buried.

A railway between Magdeburg and Leipsic was now built. It was the first time I had seen and travelled upon such a one, and it was a real event in my life. In my " Poet's Bazaar " you may read of the powerful impression it made on me.

Mendelssohn-Bartholdy lived in Leipsic, and I wished to pay him a visit. Collin's daughter and his son-in-law, Counselor of State Drewsen, had the year before brought me a greeting from Mendelssohn. When on the Rhine they heard that he was aboard the steamer, and as they knew and loved him as a composer they spoke to him. When he heard that they were Danes his first question was whether they knew the Danish poet, Andersen. " I consider him as my brother," said Madame Drewsen, and that was a point of connection. Mendelssohn told them that they had read to him while he was sick my novel, " Only a Fiddler." The book had amused him and awakened an interest in the author. He begged them to give me his best compliments, and added that I must not fail to come and see him when I passed through Leipsic. Now I arrived here but only to stay one day. I went in search of Mendelssohn immediately : he was at rehearsal in the " Gewandhaus." I did not send in my name, only that a traveller was very anxious to call on him; and he came, but was, I observed, very much vexed, for he was in some perplexity about his work. " I have but very little time, and I really cannot talk here with strangers ! " said he. " You have invited me yourself," answered I ; " you have told me that I must not pass through the city without seeing you ! " — " Andersen ! " cried he now, " is it you ? " and his whole countenance beamed ; he embraced me, drew me into the concert-room, and urged me to be present at the rehearsal of the Seventh Symphony of Beethoven.   Mendelssohn wished to keep me to dinner, but I was to dine with my older friend, Brockhaus.   Immediately after dinner the diligence started for Nürnberg.   But I promised him to stay on my return a couple of days in Leipsic, and I kept my promise.

In Nürnberg I saw for the first time daguerreotype pictures : they told me that these portraits were taken in ten minutes ; that seemed to me a bit of witchcraft ; the art was new then, and far from what it is nowadays.   Daguerreotypes and the railway were the two new flowers of the age.

By the railway I started for Munich, to see old acquaintances and friends.   I met with many countrymen here : Blunck, Kiellerup, Wegener, the animal painter Holm, Marstrand, Storch, Holbech, and the poet Holst, with whom I was from here to travel to Italy.

We remained a couple of weeks in Munich and lodged together. He was a very good comrade, affable and sympathizing. With him I visited sometimes the artists' coffee-house, — a Bavarian reflex of the life in Rome ; but there was no wine, only beer which frothed in the glasses.   I had no great pleasure here, and among my countrymen were none who interested me ; and I was no doubt judged as a poet much after the Copenhagen scale.

Holst was, however, better treated by them.   I therefore usually went alone my own solitary walk, sometimes in full strength of body and mind, but often again despairing of my powers.   I had a certain disposition to dwell upon the shady side of life, to extract the bitter from it — just tasting it ; I understood very well how to torment myself.

If I received little attention from my countrymen in the couple of weeks I remained in Munich, yet I found it in a high degree among foreigners.   My " Improvisatore " and " Only a Fiddler " were known to several people here.   The renowned portrait painter, Stieler, sought me out, opened his house for me, and there I met Cornelius, Lachner, and Schelling, with whom I was acquainted before.   Soon more private houses stood open for me.   My name reached the ears of the theatre intendant, and I got a free place in the theatre, just by the side of Thalberg.

In "A Poet's Bazaar" I have told of my call on Kaulbach, an artist who was then little esteemed by other artists, but whom the world has now justly learned to value as a great one. I saw then in a cartoon his magnificent picture, " The Devastation of Jerusalem," and sketches of his " Battle of the Huns ; " he showed me also the charming drawings of his " Reinecke Fuchs," and of Goethe's " Faust."

I was as happy as a child at going with my friend H. P. Holst to Italy, for I could show him that beautiful country and all its grandeur, but our countrymen in Munich would not let him go ; his portrait must be taken ; the time was always deferred for some reason or other, and at last, not able to tell me when he could depart, I set off alone, and had to give up the pleasure of travelling with the poet in that country which I loved and knew as the beautiful land of art. In the mean time we agreed to lodge together in Rome, when he arrived there, and to travel together to Naples.

I left Munich the second of December, passed over the Tyrol by Innsbruck, crossed the Brenner, and entered Italy, the land of my longings and dearest thoughts. So I had then really come back again, and it was not as they once said to me, " it would be the only time that I should have the chance."

I was in a tremor of happiness ; in a moment the sorrows which crushed my mind were dispersed, and I prayed earnestly and fervently to God that he would grant me health and power to live a true poet. I reached Rome the nineteenth of December, and the pictures and events of the journey are given in " A Poet's Bazaar." The same day I arrived I got a good lodging with some respectable people on " Via Purificatione," a large apartment, a whole story, for Holst and myself, who I expected would soon come.

But he did not come for a long time. I was obliged, therefore, to wander about alone in that large, empty dwelling. I had hired it at a very low rate, and this winter there were but very few foreigners in Rome, the weather being very bad and a malignant fever raging.

A little garden belonged to my house, in which was a large

orange-tree, covered with fruit. Blooming monthly roses crept up the wall in rich abundance, and monkish songs solemnly resounded from the monastery of the Capuchins, — the very same in which I had made the *Improvisatore* spend his boyhood. I visited again churches and galleries, and I saw again all the treasures of art. I met several old friends, and spent a Christmas Eve ; if not so gay a festival as the first one, yet a Christmas in Rome. I once more went through Carnival and Moccoli. But not only was I myself ill, all nature about me appeared likewise to sicken ; there was neither the tranquillity nor the freshness which attended my first sojourn in Rome. The earth quaked, the Tiber rose, flooding the streets, where they rowed in boats ; fever snatched numbers away. In a few days Prince Borghese lost his wife and three sons. The weather was sleety and windy ; in short, it was dismal.

I sat many an evening in my large chamber ; a cold draught came from windows and doors ; scanty brushwood burned in the grate, and while the heat from it warmed one side, the other felt the cold air ; I dressed myself in a cloak and sat with warm travelling boots on within doors, and suffered, besides, the most violent toothache for weeks, which I have tried to make fun of in the tale " My Boots."

Holst did not arrive until the month of February, a little before the Carnival. I suffered in body and in mind, but he showed me much sympathy, and that was a real blessing to me.

Rain and wind prevailed. And now came letters from home. My letters told me that " The Moorish Maiden " had several times been acted through, and had gone quietly off the stage ; but, as was seen beforehand, a small public only had been present, and therefore the manager had laid the piece aside. Other Copenhagen letters to our countrymen in Rome spoke with enthusiasm of a new work by Heiberg, — a satirical poem, "A Soul after Death." It was but just out, they wrote ; all Copenhagen was full of it, and Andersen was famously handled in it.

The book was admirable, and I was made ridiculous in it. That was the whole which I heard, — all that I knew. No one told me what really was said of me, wherein lay the amusement and the ludicrous. It is doubly painful to be ridiculed when we don't know why we are. The information operated like molten lead dropped into a wound, and agonized me cruelly. It was not till after my return to Denmark that I read this book, and found that what was said of me in it was really nothing in itself which was worth laying to heart. It was a jest over my celebrity, " From Skaane to Hundsrück," which did not please Heiberg ; he therefore sent my " Mulatto " and " The Moorish Maiden " to the infernal regions, where — and that was the most witty conceit — the condemned were doomed to witness the performance of both pieces in one evening ; and then they could go away and lay themselves down quietly. I found the poetry, for the rest, so excellent that I was half induced to write to Heiberg, and to return him my thanks for it ; but I slept upon this fancy, and when I awoke and was more composed, I feared lest such thanks should be misunderstood, and so gave it up.

In Rome, as I have said, I did not see the book ; I only heard the arrows whiz and felt their wound, but I did not know what the poison was which lay concealed in them. It seemed to me that Rome was no joy-bringing city ; when I was there before I had also passed dark and bitter days. I was ill, for the first time in my life, truly and bodily ill, and I made haste to get away.

It was near Carnival tide that Holst arrived, and with him came our friend, Conrad Rothe, now minister of Our Lady's Church in Copenhagen. We three made the journey together to Naples in the month of February.

There is an old saying, a tradition among the foreigners in Rome, that the evening before departure from Rome one ought to go to the Fontane del Trevi and drink of its water, and then one would be sure of coming to Rome again. The first time I went away from here I was prevented from going to the fountain ; I kept thinking of it the whole night : in the morning the man came who carried my luggage, I followed him and accidentally passing by the Fontane del Trevi, I dipped my finger into the water, tasted it, and had faith — " I shall come here again ! " and I did. This time at our departure I disregarded the superstition ; we started, when suddenly the diligence turned out from Il Corso, as we were to call for an ecclesiastic in a monastery, and we passed Fontane del Trevi, and it proved that for the third time I came to Rome. The ecclesiastic was a chapel-master, a lively man, who at Albano threw off the clerical dress and became a gay and genteel gentleman. H. P. Holst has introduced his character in his Italian sketches.

It was very cold in Naples ; Vesuvius and the hills about were covered with snow. There was fever in my blood, and I suffered in soul and body ; a toothache for several weeks had made me very nervous ; I tried to keep up as well as I could, and drove with my countrymen to Herculaneum, but while they rambled about in the excavated city, I kept still, oppressed with fever ; it chanced that they made a mistake in the railway-trains, and instead of going to Pompeii we returned to Naples. I found myself so prostrated by the fever, that only by being bled freely was my life saved. The next week I grew sensibly better ; and I proceeded by a French war-steamer, the *Leonidas*, to Greece. On the shore the people sang " Eviva la Gioia ! " Yes, long live joy ! if we only could reach it.

It was now as if a new life had risen for me, and in truth this was the case ; and if this does not appear legibly in my later writings, yet it manifested itself in my views of life, and in my whole inner development. As I saw my European home lie far behind me, it seemed to me as if a stream of forgetfulness flowed over bitter and rankling remembrances : I felt health in my blood, health in my thoughts, and freshly and courageously I again raised my head.

Naples lay in the sunlight, the clouds hung about Vesuvius down to the hermit's hut, the sea was almost calm. The night following I was roused to see Stromboli vomiting fire and mirrored in the water.

In the morning we passed Charybdis, and saw the surf at Scylla. Sicily, with its low rocks and the smoking Ætna sprinkled with snow, was before us.

I have in my " Bazaar " spoken of the voyage along the sea-coast, my stay at Malta, and the brilliant nights and days I spent on the calm Mediterranean Sea, whose long waves sparkled in the night. The splendor of the stars astonished me and filled me with admiration ; the light of Venus was like that of the moon in our North, and made the objects cast a shade ; on the surface the big dolphins tumbled ; on the ship all was gayety. We frolicked, sung, danced, played at cards, and chatted together, — Americans, Italians, and Asiatics ; bishops and monks, officers and travellers.

A few days of living together on the sea make close fellowship. I was as at home, and it was therefore a real grief to me to leave the ship at Syra. The French steamboat line from Marseilles to Constantinople crosses at the island of Syra that of the line between Alexandria and Piræus. I must therefore here go on board a ship from Egypt, and was the only one, except a Persian from Herat, who left the *Leonidas* at Syra.

The city looked like a city of tents, — like a camp, — for large sails to keep off the sun were stretched from one house to another. The shore had a pretty white and red aspect, for a crowd of Greeks with red jackets and white " fostanelles " were gathered there. The Greek steamer which usually makes the passage between Syra and Piræus was repairing, and therefore I went on board that from Alexandria which had just arrived, and would not stay in quarantine more than a couple of days on its arrival at Piræus. In my " Bazaar " I have given a series of pictures of the voyage, to which I must refer, and may therefore here make a quicker flight through the countries.

In the harbor of Piræus, where we had dropped anchor and passed quarantine, a boat came up to the ship filled with Danes and Germans. The " Allgemeine Zeitung " had told them that I was to arrive ; they rowed up to the ship to bring me their welcome, and when the quarantine was finished they called for me at Piræus, and with a Greek servant in national dress we drove through the olive woods up to Athens, whose Lycabettos and Acropolis I had already had in view for a long time. The Dutch Consul, Travers, was also Danish Consul, and spoke Danish. The chaplain to the King, Lüth, was from Holstein : he had married a young Danish lady from Fredensborg, and was also among my new friends.

Lüth told me that he had learnt Danish by reading my

" Improvisatore " in the original. I met here our countryman Koeppen, the architects, the brothers Hansen, and the Holsteiner Professor Ross. The Danish language was heard in the royal city of Greece, and champagne popped for Denmark and for me.

I remained a month at Athens. My friends would have arranged a feast for me on my birthday, the second of April, by visiting Mount Parnassus ; but winter had set in, a heavy snow had fallen, and I celebrated my birthday on the Acropolis. Among the dearest and most interesting acquaintances I made at Athens was that of Prokesch-Ostens, the resident Austrian minister, already at that time known by his " Memories of Egypt and Asia Minor," and his " Travels in the Holy Land." Consul Travers presented me to the King and Queen. I made several very interesting trips from here ; I spent the Greek Easter here, and the Feast of Liberty, of which I have tried to give a picture.

Like another Switzerland, with a loftier and clearer heaven than the Italian, Greece lay before me : nature made a deep and solemn impression upon me. I felt the sentiment of standing on the great battle-field of the world, where nation had striven with nation, and had perished. No single poem can embrace such greatness ; every scorched-up bed of a stream, every height, every stone, has mighty memoirs to relate. How little appear the inequalities of daily life in such a place. A kingdom of ideas streamed through me, and with such a fullness that none of them fixed themselves on paper. I had a desire to express the idea, that the godlike was here on earth to maintain its contest ; that it is thrust backward, and yet advances again victoriously through all ages ; and I found in the legend of the " Wandering Jew " an occasion for it. For twelve months this fiction had been emerging from the sea of my thoughts ; often did it wholly fill me ; sometimes I fancied with the alchemists that I had dug up the treasure ; then again it sank suddenly, and I despaired of ever being able to bring it to the light. I felt what a mass of knowledge of various kinds I must first acquire. Often at home, when I was compelled to hear reproofs on what they call a want of study, I had sat deep into the night, and had studied history in

Hegel's "Philosophy of History." I said nothing of this, or other studies would immediately have been spoken of, in the manner of an instructive lady, who said, that people justly complained that I did not possess learning enough. "You have really no mythology," said she; "in all your poems there appears no single god. You must pursue mythology; you must read Racine and Corneille." *That* she called learning; and in like manner every one had something peculiar to recommend. For my poem of "Ahasuerus" I had read much and noted much, but yet not enough; in Greece, I thought, the whole will collect itself into clearness. The poem is not yet ready, but I hope that it will become so to my honor; for it happens with children of the spirit as with the earthly ones, they grow as they sleep.

The twenty-first of April I again sailed from Piræus to Syra, where I went on board the French steamship *Rhamses*, from Marseilles to Constantinople. We had very rough weather in the Archipelago; I thought of shipwreck and death, and having the conviction that all was over, I was filled with a strange feeling of rest, and lay down in my berth, while others around me were moaning and praying. All was crashing and cracking, but I fell asleep, and when I awoke we were safe and sound at Smyrna. Another quarter of the globe lay before me. In truth I felt a devotion at treading it like that which I felt as a child when I entered the old church of Saint Knud at Odense. I thought on Christ, who bled on this earth; I thought on Homer, whose song eternally resounds hence over the earth. The shores of Asia preached to me their sermons, and were, perhaps, more impressive than any sermon in any church can be.

Smyrna looked very grand with its pointed, red roofs, as in the North; there were but few minarets; the streets were narrow, like those of Venice. An ostrich and a camel came along, and for both the people were compelled to step aside into the open houses. There was a swarming crowd of people in the streets: Turkish women, who only showed their eyes and tip of the nose; Jews and Armenians, with white and black hats, some of which had the form of a bean-pot upside down. The consuls had run out from their houses the re-

spective flags of their countries; in the bay lay a smoking
Turkish steamer, with the crescent on its green flag.

In the evening we left Smyrna: the new moon threw its light
upon the mound of Achilles's tomb on the plains of Troy. At
six o'clock in the morning we entered the Dardanelles: upon
the European side lay a red-roofed town with windmills and a
fine fortress; upon the Asiatic side a smaller fortress. The
distance between these two parts of the world seemed to me
to be that of the Sound between Helsingör and Helsingborg.
The captain judged it to be two and three quarters *lieus.*
Gallipoli, where we entered the Sea of Marmora, has an
entirely Northern, gloomy look: there were old houses with
balconies and wooden terraces; the rocks around were low,
but had a naked, wild aspect; there was a heavy sea, and toward the evening rain fell.   The next morning the magnificent
city of Constantinople lay before us, — a Venice risen out of
the sea. One mosque more splendid than another rose to our
view; the Seraglio lay light and swimming before us. The
sun burst forth and shone upon the Asiatic shores, the first
cypress woods I had seen, and upon the minarets of Scutari.
It was an enchanting view! There was a crying and halloaing
of people in the small, rocking boats with which it swarmed;
majestic looking Turks carried our baggage.

In Constantinople I passed eleven interesting days; and
according to my good fortune in travel, the birthday of
Mohammed itself fell exactly during my stay there. I saw the
grand illumination, which completely transported me into the
"Thousand and One Nights."

Our Danish ambassador lived several miles from Constantinople, and I had therefore no opportunity of seeing him; but
I found a cordial reception with the Austrian internuncius,
Baron Stürmer. With him I had a German home and friends.
I contemplated making my return by the Black Sea and up
the Danube; but the country was disturbed; it was said there
had been several thousand Christians murdered. My companions of the voyage, in the hotel where I resided, gave up this
route of the Danube, for which I had the greatest desire, and
collectively counseled me against it.   But in this case I must
return again by Greece and Italy — it was a severe conflict.

I do not belong to the courageous ; I feel fear, especially in little dangers ; but in great ones, and when an advantage is to be won, then I have a will, and it has grown firmer with years. I may tremble, I may fear ; but I still do that which I consider the most proper to be done. I am not ashamed to confess my weakness ; I hold that when out of our own true conviction we run counter to our inborn fear, we have done our duty. I had a strong desire to become acquainted with the interior of the country, and to traverse the Danube in its greatest expansion. I battled with myself ; my imagination pointed to me the most horrible circumstances ; it was an anxious night. In the morning I took counsel with Baron Stürmer, and as he was of opinion that I might undertake the voyage, I determined upon it. From the moment that I had taken my determination I had the most immovable reliance on Providence, and flung myself calmly on my fate. The fourth of May I went on board the ship, which lay by the garden of the Seraglio.

Early in the morning, when we weighed anchor, we heard the sad news that the large Austrian steamship, which we had expected to meet us, had struck upon a rock the night before in the fog in the Black Sea, and was totally wrecked. We passed through the strange-looking Bosphorus, suffered heavy seas and foggy weather, stopped one day at the city of Kostendsche, near the decayed rampart of Trajan, and rode in big carriages of basket-work, drawn by white oxen, along the desolate country, where wild dogs were strolling about. Only the tumbled down tombstones of two cemeteries showed us that here had been towns, which were burnt by the Russians in the War of 1809. It was the city of Dobrudscha. We spent two days in passing over the whole remarkable seat of war of the Russians and Turks. I have thus in my head the best map I could obtain of the Danube territory, — the clearest idea of the miserable small towns and ruined fortresses ; I saw whole ruins of fortifications, built of earth and basket-work. We did not hear anything of the disturbances in the country until we reached Rustschuk, with its many minarets. The shore was crowded with people : two Frankish-dressed young men were thrown into the Danube ; they swam toward land ; one of them reached it, but the other, who was stoned, swam out toward us and cried out : " Help ! they are killing me ! " We stopped in the middle of the river, got him up, and made signals by a cannon-shot. The pasha of the city came on board and took the poor Frank under his protection.

From the ship we saw next day the Balkan Mountains, covered with snow ; between them and us the revolt was raging. In the night we heard that an armed Tartar, who carried letters and dispatches from Widdin to Constantinople, was attacked and killed ; another, I believe, had the same fate. The third got his escort scattered, escaped from it himself, and came down to the Danube, where, hidden among the reeds, he had awaited the arrival of our steamship. The man, in his sheep-skin clothes, just coming out of the mire, and armed to the teeth, as we call it, looked horribly when we at lamp-light be-held him coming on board ; he travelled with us a whole day up the Danube.

At Widdin, the strong fortress of the Turks, we went ashore, but not before we were well fumigated so that we might not bring any contagions from Constantinople. Hussein-Pasha, who resided here, sent us all the last copies of " Allgemeine Zeitung," so that we got our best information about the condi-tion of the country from the German side. Servia looked like a primitive woodland ; we travelled in small boats for many miles the rushing and foaming Danube, — through the " iron gate," as they call that part of the river. I have in my " Ba-zaar " given a picture of it.

At Old Orsova we had to pass quarantine. The building was only arranged to receive Wallachian peasants, and not travellers with more wants ; almost all the rooms were paved ; the provisions horrid, the wine still worse. I shared a room with the Englishman, Mr. Ainsworth, a brother of the writer, who was on his way home from his travels in Kurdistan. When " A Poet's Bazaar " was published afterward in Lon-don, Mr. Ainsworth wrote in the " Literary Gazette " of 10th October, 1846, at the editor's suggestion, an account of our stay in quarantine, where his appreciation of me is very kindly expressed, and places me, perhaps, in too good a light. He re-lates that I was " very skillful in cutting out paper. The drawings of the Mewlewis, or leaping dervishes, in my Asiatic travels, are from cuttings of his."

After having passed quarantine we crossed the military frontier, under lofty chestnut-trees ; past relics of the time of the Romans, by ruins of bridges, towers, and the grand "Trajan tablet" in the rocky wall. Picturesque groups of Wallachian peasants were varied by Austrian soldiers in great numbers, and gypsy bands encamped in caves of the rocks. One picture followed another, but when we came again on board the steamship, it was so thronged with people that we could scarcely move. All were going to the great fair at Pesth ; the passage was a long, sleepless, and difficult one, but we had a good view of the Hungarian people. The country became more and more flat, and had no longer its former rich variety, which it again displayed afterward nearer Presburg. The town of Theben was in flames when we passed. I arrived at the imperial city of Vienna on the twenty-first day of the journey, and landed at the Prater. I visited old friends, and soon, by way of Prague and Dresden, the journey turned homeward.

It seemed to me very characteristic that during the whole journey from Italy by Greece and Turkey to Hamburg my trunk was only twice searched, namely, at the Austrian and the German frontier, while it was examined not less than five times before I entered my room at Copenhagen. They searched it first on my arrival in Holstein, then at Aroesound, again at my landing in Funen, next at Slagelse, when I left the diligence, and at last when I came with the stage-coach to Copenhagen ; such was the custom at that time.

On my arrival at Hamburg there was a great musical festival. I met many countrymen at the table d'hôte, and while speaking to my friends of the beautiful Greece, of the rich Orient, an old Copenhagen lady addressed me with the words : —

"Mr. Andersen, have you on your many and long travels ever seen anything abroad so beautiful as our little Denmark ?"

"Indeed I have !" answered I : "I have seen many things far more beautiful ! "

"Fie ! " exclaimed she, "you are no patriot ! "

I passed through Odense just at the time of St. Knud's Fair. "I am very glad," said a respectable lady of Funen, "that you have arranged your great journey so as to come to the fair. I see that you keep to Odense: that I have al-ways said!" So there I passed for a patriot!

Arriving at Slagelse, the town of my school days, I was strangely affected and surprised at meeting with some old friends. When I was scholar there I used to see Pastor Bastholm with his wife every evening taking the same walk, — from the back gate of their garden along the pathway over the corn-field, and returning by the great road. Now, several years after, returning from Greece and Turkey, and driving on the highway of Slagelse, I saw the old couple taking their usual little walk through the corn-field. It affected me strangely. They went there still year after year the same way, and I had flown so far, far about. The great contrast between us was strangely brought into my thoughts.

In the middle of August, 1841, I was again in Copenhagen, and this time without anxiety or suffering, as on my first return from Italy. I was very glad to see again all my dear friends, and with a sincere heart I exclaimed : " The first moment of return is the bouquet of the whole journey!" There I wrote my recollections of travel, under the title of "A Poet's Bazaar," in several chapters, according to the countries. In various places abroad I had met with individuals, as at home, to whom I felt myself attached. The poet is like a bird ; he gives what he has, and he gives a song. I was desirous of giving every one of those dear ones such a song. It was a fugitive idea, born, may I venture to say, in a grateful mood. Count Rantzau-Breitenburg, who had resided in Italy, who loved the land, and was become a friend and benefactor to me through my " Improvisatore," must love that part of the book which treated of his country. To Liszt and Thalberg, who had both shown me the greatest friendship, I dedicated the portion which contained the voyage up the Danube, because one was a Hungarian and the other an Austrian. With these indications, the reader will easily be able to trace out the thought which influenced me in the choice of each dedication. But these appropriations were, in my native country, regarded as a fresh proof of my vanity : " I wished to figure with great names, — to name distinguished people as my friends."

The book has been translated into several languages, and the dedications with it. I know not how they have been regarded abroad ; if I had been judged there as in Denmark, I hope that this explanation will change the opinion concerning them. In Denmark my " Bazaar " procured me the most handsome remuneration that I had as yet received, — a proof that I was at length read there. No regular criticism appeared upon it, if one excepts notices in some daily papers, and afterward in the poetical attempt of a young writer who, a year before, had testified in writing his love for me, and his wish to do me honor ; but who now, in his first public appearance, launched his satirical poem against his friend. I was personally attached to this young man, and am so still. He assuredly thought more of the popularity he would gain by sailing in the wake of Heiberg, than on the pain he would inflict on me.

The newspaper criticism in Copenhagen was infinitely stupid. It was set down as exaggerated, that I could have seen the whole round blue globe of the moon in Smyrna at the time of the new moon. That was called fancy and extravagance which there every one sees who can open his eyes. The new moon has a dark-blue and perfectly round disk.

The Danish critics have generally no open eye for nature : even that very cultivated " Monthly Periodical of Literature " in Denmark censured me once, because in a poem I had described a rainbow by moonlight. That too was my fancy, which, said they, carried me too far. When I said in the " Bazaar," " If I were a painter, I would paint this bridge ; but, as I am no painter, but a poet, I must therefore speak," etc : the critic says, " He is so vain, that he tells us himself that he is a poet." There is something so pitiful in such criticism, that one cannot be wounded by it ; but even when we are the most peaceable of men, we feel a desire to flagellate such wet dogs, who come into our rooms and lay themselves down in the best places there. There might be a whole Fool's Chronicle written of all the absurd and shameless things which, from my first appearance before the public till this moment, I have been compelled to hear.

In the mean time the "Bazaar" was much read, and made what is called a hit. I received, connected with this book, much encouragement and many recognitions from individuals of the highest distinction in the realms of intellect in my native land.

Several editions of that book have since been published, and it has been translated into German, and into Swedish and English, and it has been received with great favor. The English edition in three volumes, with my portrait, was published by Richard Bentley in London, and was very generously noticed in English papers and reviews. The English publisher sent to Christian VIII. a beautifully bound copy of that book and of my earlier published writings. They did the same in Germany, and the king appreciated highly the great consideration they' showed me abroad. I know that he expressed it to H. C. Örsted and many others, while he uttered his astonishment at the opposition I still met at home, at the constant effort to bring into prominence my weak side and efface the impression of the good, and at the pleasure people took in mocking at and depreciating my activity. It made me happy to hear this, and the more as it came from H. C. Örsted, the only man of all my intimate and sympathizing friends who clearly and distinctly expressed his appreciation of my poetical ability and strongly encouraged me, while he predicted that there ought to come and would come a better time for me at home, when I should be acknowledged, and should feel myself as well satisfied with the judgment I received as I now ought to be at that which came from abroad.

We often talked together of what was the real cause that I must struggle so much and so long, and we agreed touching many probable causes. The fault might perhaps lie in my poverty at first, and my desponding tone to people. They could not forget, as was also remarked abroad, that they had seen me as a poor boy running about and growing up. Some fault might perhaps also lie, as remarked by my biographer in the "Danish Pantheon," in that I did not know of, nor use the means most authors make use of in order to profit by society ; add to this, what also H. C. Örsted deplored, that the highly esteemed Monthly showed severity and want of good-will toward me ; and finally the contempt of the "Letters from the Dead," the critiques in the newspapers, which followed the fashion ; in short, the printed public judgment, which used its power among us and made us bow to its authority. Besides, we have all a great sense of the ludicrous, and I had the ill fortune to be set in a ridiculous light by several awkward but very well meant articles.

It was a time when the newspapers in my native city, Odense, always called me " Our city's child," and gave information about me which could not be of any interest to the public. Extracts were given from my private letters when I was abroad, which became ridiculous when given in the newspaper : thus, for instance, when I once wrote home from Rome that I had seen Queen Christina in the chapel of Pope Sixtus, and added that she put me in mind of the wife of the composer Hartmann, it was reported in the Funen newspaper that "Queen Christina resembled a certain lady in Copenhagen." Of course they laughed at that. How often have I experienced the awkward friendship that vexes us. From that time until now I have always feared to speak of such things to a thoughtless news-writer, and yet I have not escaped. I was afterward again ridiculed when it was no fault of mine. I was on a journey, and stopped for half an hour at the Odense post-office, where a news-writer asked me, —

" Are you going abroad now ? "

" No," I answered.

" Do you not expect to ? "

" It depends on whether I can get money. I am writing a piece for the theatre ; if it proves successful I presume I shall go away."

" Where will you then go ? "

" I do not yet know ; either to Spain or to Greece, I think."

The same evening I read in the newspaper a paragraph to the effect that — " H. C. Andersen is writing a piece for the theatre : should it prove to be successful he is going abroad, either to Spain or to Greece."

Of course I was ridiculed, and a Copenhagen newspaper was right in saying that my journey was rather a distant prospect. The piece was to be written, played, and have its success, and then one could not be sure whether my journey would be to Spain or Greece. People laughed, and one who is laughed at has lost his cause. I became depressed and took no pains to conceal it. When boys throw stones at a poor dog which is swimming against the stream, it is not because they are wicked but because they think it fun, and people had similar sport with me. I had no defenders, I did not belong to any party, I had no newspaper-writing friends, and therefore I was compelled to do as I did. In the mean time it was said and written and frequently repeated, that I lived only in the company of my admirers! How little they knew about it. What I here must present is no complaint ; I will not cast a particle of shade over the many whom I really love ; I am sure that if I had fallen into great need and trouble, they would have put forth all their endeavor not to let me go under, but a poetic nature needs sympathy of another kind, and of that I have been very much in want. My dearest friends have as severely and loudly as any critic expressed their surprise at the appreciation my works have received abroad. Fredrika Bremer discerned it and was very much astonished. We were in company together in Copenhagen at a house where it was said that I was a spoiled child. She thought she was telling something agreeable when she said : " It is almost incredible how Andersen is loved in Sweden from south to north ; in almost every house we see his books ! "

" Don't make him believe such things ! " was the answer, and said in real earnest. Much has been said about the fact that to be noble or of high birth has no longer any significance : that is only nonsense. The able but poor student is not received in what we call good houses with the same kindness as the well-dressed child of nobility, or the son of a public functionary. I could illustrate it by many examples, but I will only give one, which may stand for all, — one out of my own life. The guilty is or was — I will not say which — a person highly honored, whose name I will omit.

When Christian VIII., for the first time as king, visited the theatre, " The Mulatto " was played. I was seated in the parquette by the side of Thorwaldsen, who, when the curtain fell, whispered to me : " The King is bowing to you ! "

"It must be for you!" I answered; "it cannot concern me!" I looked up to the royal box: the King again bowed, and plainly it was intended for me ; but I felt that a possible misunderstanding on my part would lead to my being laughed at by the public, and therefore I sat quietly, and the next day I went to the king to give him my thanks for that unusual favor, and he teased me for not returning his greeting on the spot. A few days after there was a grand *bal parée* at the castle of Christiansborg for all classes of the community. I had received a card of invitation.

"What shall you do there?" asked one of our elder men of learning, when I spoke of the festival to him. "What do you have to do with such places!" repeated he.

I answered in joke, — "Well, it is because I am always so well received in that circle!"

"But it is not your place there!" said he angrily.

There was nothing for me but to answer freely and laughingly, as if I did not feel the sting, —

"The king himself has in the theatre saluted me from his box, so I think I may also go to his *bal parée!*"

"Saluted you from his box, you say!" exclaimed he: "but that does not prove that you have any right to intrude!"

"But people of the same class that I belong to will be at the ball!" added I more earnestly ; "students will be there!"

"Yes, but what students?" he asked. I named a young student of the gentleman's own family.

"Yes, but that is different!" replied he then: "he is the son of a Counselor of State! What was your father?"

My blood boiled at that. "My father was a tradesman!" said I. "I have, by the help of God and by my own work, acquired the position I now have, and which you think honorable enough I make no doubt!" He never apologized to me for his rudeness.

It is very difficult to tell in a roundabout way of wrong that one has suffered, when the wrong has not been malicious, and I have throughout my book felt this difficulty, and therefore I have refused to show the full cup of bitterness : I have only let fall some drops from it. The journey had strengthened me and I began to show indications of a firmer purpose, a more certain judgment. Many heavy seas still followed, but from that time I steadily advanced through smooth water toward the recognition I could wish for and claim of my own country, — such also as Örsted had predicted in his comforting words.

CHAPTER IX.

POLITICAL life in Denmark had, at that time, arrived at a higher development, producing both good and evil fruits. The eloquence which had formerly accustomed itself to the Demosthenic mode, — that of putting little pebbles in the mouth, the little pebbles of every-day life, — now exercised itself more freely on subjects of greater interest. I felt no call thereto, and no necessity to mix myself up in such matters; for I then believed that the politics of our times were a great misfortune to many a poet. Madame Politics is like Venus: they whom she decoys into her castle perish. It fares with the writings of these poets as with the newspapers: they are seized upon, read, praised, and forgotten. In our days every one wishes to rule; the subjective makes its power of value; people forget that that which is thought of cannot always be carried out, and that many things look very different when contemplated from the top of the tree, to what they did when seen from its roots. I will bow myself before him who is influenced by a noble conviction, and who only desires that which is conducive to good, be he prince or man of the people. Politics are no affair of mine. God has imparted to me another mission: that I felt, and that I feel still.

I met in the so-called first families of the country a number of friendly, kind-hearted men, who valued the good that was in me, received me into their circles, and permitted me to participate in the happiness of their opulent summer residences; so that, still feeling independent, I could thoroughly give myself up to the pleasures of nature, the solitude of woods, and country life. There for the first time I lived wholly among the scenery of Denmark, and there I wrote the greater number of my fairy tales. On the banks of quiet lakes, amid the woods, on the green grassy pastures, where the game sprang past me, and the stork paced along on his red legs, I heard nothing of politics, nothing of polemics ; I heard no one practicing himself in Hegel's phraseology.   Nature, which was around me, and within me, preached to me of my calling.   I spent many happy days at the old house of Gisselfeld, formerly a monastery, which stands in the deepest solitude of the woods, surrounded by lakes and hills.   The possessor of this fine place, the old Countess Danneskjold, mother of the Duchess of Augustenburg, was an agreeable and excellent lady.   I was there not as a poor child of the people, but as a cordially received guest.   The beeches now overshadow her grave in the midst of that pleasant scenery to which her heart was allied.

Close by Gisselfeld, but in a still finer situation, and of much greater extent, lies the estate of Bregentved, which be-belongs to Count Moltke, Danish Minister of Finance.   The hospitality which I met with in this place, one of the richest and most beautiful of our country, and the happy, social life which surrounded me here, have diffused a sunshine over my life.

It may appear, perhaps, as if I desired to bring the names of great people prominently forward, and make a parade of them ; or as if I wished in this way to offer a kind of thanks to my benefactors.   They need it not, and I should be obliged to mention many other names still if this were my intention.   I speak, however, only of these two places, and of Nysö, which belongs to Baron Stampe, and which has become celebrated through Thorwaldsen.   Here I lived much with the great sculptor, and here I became acquainted with one of my dearest young friends, the future possessor of the place.

Knowledge of life in these various circles has had great influence on me : among princes, among the nobility, and among the poorest of the people, I have met with specimens of noble humanity.   We all of us resemble each other in that which is good and best.

Winter life in Denmark has likewise its attractions and its rich variety.   I spent also some time in the country during this season, and made myself acquainted with its peculiar characteristics.   The greatest part of my time, however, I passed in Copenhagen.   I felt myself at home with the married sons and daughters of Collin, where a number of amiable children were growing up. Every year strengthened the bond of friendship between myself and the nobly gifted composer Hartmann : art and the freshness of nature prospered in his house. Collin was my counselor in practical life, and Örsted in my literary affairs. The theatre was, if I may say so, my club. I visited it every evening, and in this very year I had received a place in the so-called court stalls. An author must, as a matter of course, work himself up to it. After the first accepted piece he obtains admission to the pit ; after the second greater work, in the stalls, where the actors have their seats ; and after three larger works, or a succession of lesser pieces, the poet is advanced to the best places. Here were to be found Thorwaldsen, Oehlenschläger, and several older poets ; and here also, in 1840, I obtained a place, after I had given in seven pieces. Whilst Thorwaldsen lived, I often, by his own wish, sat at his side. Oehlenschläger was also my neighbor, and in many an evening hour, when no one dreamed of it, my soul was steeped in deep humility, as I sat between these great spirits. The different periods of my life passed before me : the time when I sat on the hindmost bench in the box of the female figurantes, as well as that in which, full of childish superstition, I knelt down there upon the stage and repeated the Lord's Prayer, just before the very place where I now sat among the first and the most distinguished men. At the time, perhaps, when a countryman of mine thus thought of and passed judgment upon me, — " There he sits, between the two great spirits, full of arrogance and pride ; " he may now perceive by this acknowledgment how unjustly he has judged me. Humility and prayer to God for strength to deserve my happiness, filled my heart. May He always enable me to preserve these feelings ! I enjoyed the friendship of Thorwaldsen as well as of Oehlenschläger, — those two most distinguished stars in the horizon of the North. I may here bring forward their reflected glory in and around me.

There was in the character of Oehlenschläger, when he was not seen in the circles of the great, where he was quiet and reserved, something so open and child-like, that no one could help becoming attached to him. He was of great importance

to the nation, to the whole North, and that is well known ;
he was the true-born poet, always appearing young, and when
the oldest of all, surpassing all in the fertility of his mind.
He listened in a friendly spirit to my first lyrical productions ;
followed me with sympathy, and when the critics and people
judged me harshly and ungenerously, he was the man who
opposed them with genuine fervor. One day he found me
deeply depressed at the severe and bitter treatment I was receiving ; he pressed me to his bosom, —
"Do not mind those bawlers !" said he ; "I tell you, you are
a true poet !" Then he expressèd passionately and warmly
his judgment of poetry and poets, of our criticism at home,
giving me his full sympathy. He appreciated earnestly and
kindly the poet who told fairy tales ; and I remember one day,
when a man tried to lower me by pointing out what he called
orthographical sins which he had discovered in one of my
books, Oehlenschläger exclaimed with animation : "But they
shall be there, they are little characteristics which belong to
him, and yet are not at all the principal marks. The great
Goethe said about just such a little error, — 'Let the little
wretch stay !' and would not even correct it."

I will further on give a few traits of his character and of our
intercourse in the last few years of his life. My biographer
in the "Danish Pantheon" brought me in contact with Oehlenschläger, when he said : "In our days it is becoming more and
more rare for any one, by implicitly following those inborn impulses of his soul, which make themselves irresistibly felt, to
step forward as an artist or a poet. He is more frequently
fashioned by fate and circumstances than apparently destined
by Nature herself for this office. With the greater number of
our poets an early acquaintance with passion, early inward experience, or outward circumstances, stand instead of the original vein of nature, and this cannot in any case be more incon-
testably proved in our own literature than by instancing
Oehlenschläger and Andersen. And in this way it may be
explained why the former has been so frequently the object
for the attacks of the critics, and why the latter was first properly appreciated as a poet in foreign countries, where civiliza-
tion of a longer date has already produced a disinclination for

the compulsory rule of schools, and has occasioned a reaction toward that which is fresh and natural ; whilst we Danes, on the contrary, cherish a pious respect for the yoke of the schools and the worn-out wisdom of maxims."

Thorwaldsen, whom, as I have already said, I had become acquainted with in Rome in the years 1833 and 1834, was expected in Denmark in the autumn of 1838, and great festive preparations were made in consequence. A flag was to wave upon one of the towers of Copenhagen as soon as the vessel which brought him should come in sight. It was a national festival. Boats decorated with flowers and flags filled the Rhede ; painters, sculptors, all had their flags with emblems ; the students' bore a Minerva, the poets' a Pegasus. It was misty weather, and the ship was first seen when it was already close by the city, and all poured out to meet him. The poets, who, I believe, according to the arrangement of Heiberg, had been invited, stood by their boat ; Oehlenschläger and Heiberg alone had not arrived. And now guns were fired from the ship, which came to anchor, and it was to be feared that Thorwaldsen might land before we had gone out to meet him. The wind bore the voice of singing over to us : the festive reception had already begun.

I wished to see him, and therefore cried out to the others, " Let us put off ! "

" Without Oehlenschläger and Heiberg ? " asked some one.

" But they are not arrived, and it will be all over."

One of the poets declared that if these two men were not with us, I should not sail under that flag, and pointed up to Pegasus.

" We will throw it in the boat," said I, and took it down from the staff ; the others now followed me, and came up just as Thorwaldsen reached land. We met with Oehlenschläger and Heiberg in another boat, and they came over to us as the enthusiasm began on shore.

The people drew Thorwaldsen's carriage through the streets to his house, where everybody who had the slightest acquaintance with him, or with the friends of a friend of his, thronged around him. In the evening the artists gave him a serenade, and the blaze of the torches illumined the garden under the large trees ; there was an exultation and joy which really and truly was felt. Young and old hastened through the open doors, and the joyful old man clasped those whom he knew to his breast, gave them his kiss, and pressed their hands. There was a glory round Thorwaldsen which kept me timidly back : my heart beat for joy of seeing him who had met me when abroad with kindness and consolation, who had pressed me to his heart, and had said that we must always remain friends. But here in this jubilant crowd, where thousands noticed every movement of his, where I too by all these should be observed and criticised — yes, criticised as a vain man who now only wished to show that he too was acquainted with Thorwaldsen, and that this great man was kind and friendly toward him — here, in this dense crowd, I drew myself back, and avoided being recognized by him. Some days afterward, and early in the morning, I went to call upon him, and found him as a friend who had wondered at not having seen me earlier.

In honor of Thorwaldsen a musical-poetic academy was established, and the poets, who were invited to do so by Heiberg, wrote and read each one a poem in praise of him who had returned home. I wrote of Jason who fetched the golden fleece — that is to say, Jason-Thorwaldsen, who went forth to win golden art. A great dinner and a ball closed the festival, in which, for the first time in Denmark, popular life and a subject of great interest in the realms of art were made public.

From this evening I saw Thorwaldsen almost daily in company or in his studio : I often passed several weeks together with him at Nysö, where he seemed to have firmly taken root, and where the greater number of his works executed in Denmark had their origin. He was of a healthful and simple disposition of mind, not without humor, and, therefore, he was extremely attached to Holberg the poet : he did not at all enter into the troubles and the disruptions of the world.

One morning at Nysö — at the time when he was working at his own statue — I entered his work-room and bade him good morning ; he appeared as if he did not wish to notice me, and I stole softly away again. At breakfast he was very parsimonious in the use of words, and when somebody asked

him to say something at all events, he replied in his dry
way : —

"I have said more during this morning that in many whole
days, but nobody heard me. There I stood, and fancied that
Andersen was behind me, for he came and said Good-morn-
ing! so I told him a long story about myself and Byron. I
thought that he might give me one word in reply, and turned
myself round ; and there had I been standing a whole hour
and chattering aloud to the bare walls."

We all of us besought him to let us hear the whole story yet
once more ; but we had it now very short.

"O, that was in Rome," said he, "when I was about to
make Byron's statue ; he placed himself just opposite to me,
and began immediately to assume quite another countenance
to what was customary to him. 'Will not you sit still?' said I ;
'but you must not make these faces.' — 'It is my expression,'
said Byron. 'Indeed?' said I, and then I made him as I
wished, and everybody said, when it was finished, that I had
hit the likeness. When Byron, however, saw it, he said, 'It
does not resemble me at all ; I look more unhappy.'

"He was, above all things, so desirous of looking extremely
unhappy," added Thorwaldsen, with a comic expression.

It afforded the great sculptor pleasure to listen to music
after dinner with half-shut eyes, and it was his greatest delight
when in the evening the game of lotto began, which the whole
neighborhood of Nysö was obliged to learn ; they only played
for glass pieces, and on this account I am able to relate a peculiar characteristic of this otherwise great man — that he
played with the greatest interest on purpose to win.

He would espouse with warmth and vehemence the part of
those from whom he believed that he had received an injustice ; he opposed himself to unfairness and raillery, even
against the lady of the house, who for the rest had the most
childlike sentiments toward him, and who had no other thought
than how to make everything most agreeable to him.

In his company I wrote several of my tales for children —
for example, "Ole Lucköie" ("Ole Shut Eye"), to which
he listened with pleasure and interest. Often in the twilight,
when the family circle sat in the open garden parlor, Thor-

waldsen would come softly behind me, and, clapping me on the shoulder, would ask, " Shall we little ones hear any tales to-night ? "

In his own peculiarly natural manner he bestowed the most bountiful praise on my fictions, for their truth ; it delighted him to hear the same stories over and over again.   Often, during his most glorious works, would he stand with laughing countenance, and listen to the stories of " The Top and the Ball," and the " Ugly Duckling."   I possess a certain talent of improvising in my native tongue little poems and songs. This talent amused Thorwaldsen very much ; and as he had modeled, at Nysö, Holberg's portrait in clay, I was commissioned to make a poem for his work, and he received, therefore, the following impromptu : —

> "No more shall Holberg live," by Death was said :
> " I crush the clay, his soul's bonds heretofore."
> " And from the formless clay, the cold, the dead,"
> Cried Thorwaldsen, " shall Holberg live once more."

One morning, when he had just modeled in clay his great bass-relief of the " Procession to Golgotha," I entered his study.

" Tell me," said he, " does it seem to you that I have dressed Pilate properly ? "

" You must not say anything to him," said the Baroness, who was always with him : " it is right ; it is excellent ; go away with you ! "

Thorwaldsen repeated his question.

" Well then," said I, " as you ask me, I must confess that it really does appear to me as if Pilate were dressed rather as an Egyptian than as a Roman."

" It seems to me so too," said Thorwaldsen, seizing the clay with his hand, and destroying the figure.

" Now you are guilty of his having annihilated an immortal work ! " exclaimed the Baroness to me with warmth.

" Then we can make a new immortal work," said he, in a cheerful humor, and modeled Pilate as he now remains in the bass-reliefs in Our Lady's Church in Copenhagen.

His last birthday was celebrated there in the country.   I had written a merry little song, and it was hardly dry on the paper when we sang it in the early morning, before his door, accompanied by the music of jingling fire-irons, gongs, and bottles rubbed against a basket. Thorwaldsen himself, in his morning gown and slippers, opened his door, and danced round his chamber ; swung round his Raphael's cap, and joined in the chorus. There was life and mirth in the strong old man.

On the last day of his life I sat by him at dinner ; he was unusually good-humored ; repeated several witticisms which he had just read in the "Corsair," a well-known Copenhagen newspaper, and spoke of the journey which he should undertake to Italy in the summer. After this we parted ; he went to the theatre, and I home.

On the following morning the waiter at the hotel where I lived said, "that it was a very remarkable thing about Thorwaldsen — that he had died yesterday."

"Thorwaldsen ! " exclaimed I ; "he is not dead ; I dined with him yesterday."

"People say that he died last evening at the theatre," returned the waiter.

I fancied that he might be taken ill ; but still I felt a strange anxiety, and hastened immediately over to his house. There lay his corpse stretched out on the bed ; the chamber was filled with strangers ; the floor wet with melted snow ; the air stifling ; no one said a word : the Baroness Stampe sat on the bed and wept bitterly. I stood trembling and deeply agitated.

Thorwaldsen's funeral was a day of mourning for the nation. Men and women dressed in crape stood at windows and in the streets ; they uncovered their heads involuntarily when the coffin passed by. There was a calmness even among the most wild boys ; the poorest children held each other's hands and formed ranks, through which the great funeral procession moved from Charlottenborg to Our Lady's Church, where King Christian VIII. came to meet the procession.

From the organ was played a funeral march, composed by Hartmann ; the tones were so powerful that we felt as if the great invisible spirits joined the procession. A good-night hymn which I had written, and to which also Hartmann had set music, was sung by Danish students over his coffin.

CHAPTER X.

IN the summer of 1842, I wrote a little piece for the summer theatre, called " The Bird in the Pear-tree," in which several scenes were acted up in the pear-tree. I had called it a dramatic trifle, in order that no one might expect either a great work or one of a very elaborate character. It was a little sketch, which, after being performed a few times, was received with so much applause, that the directors of the theatre accepted it; nay, even Mrs. Heiberg, the favorite of the public, desired to take a part in it. People had been amused; had thought the selection of the music excellent. I knew that the piece had stood its rehearsal — and then suddenly it was hissed. Some young men, who gave the word to hiss, had said to some others, who inquired of them their reasons for doing so, that the trifle had too much luck, and then Andersen would be getting too mettlesome.

I was not, on this evening, at the theatre myself, and had not the least idea of what was going on. On the following evening I went to the house of one of my friends. I had headache, and was looking very grave. The lady of the house met me with a sympathizing manner, took my hand, and said, "Is it really worth while to take it so much to heart! There were only two who hissed, the whole house beside took your part."

"Hissed! My part! Have I been hissed?" exclaimed I.

It was quite comic; one person assured me that this hissing had been a triumph for me; everybody had joined in acclamation, and "there was only one who hissed."

After this, another person came and I asked him the number of those who hissed. "Two," said he. The next person said "three," and said positively there were no more. One of my most veracious friends, the *naïve*, worthy Hartmann, now made his appearance; he did not know what the others had said, and I asked him, upon his conscience, how many he had heard ; he laid his hand upon his heart, and said that, at the very highest, there were five.

"No," said I : "now I will ask nobody more ; the number grows just as with Falstaff ; here stands one who asserts that there was only one person who hissed.

Shocked, and yet inclined to set it all right again, he replied, "Yes, that is possible,' but then it was a strong, powerful hiss."

"The Bird in the Pear-tree" was ridiculed in several newspapers, and "A Poet's Bazaar" was noticed again only to be made sport of. I remember well that Oehlenschläger praised them both at this time. Heiberg, on the contrary, wrote in his journal of my dramatic trifle : —

"It belongs to that kind of small creatures whose admission into our theatre cage it would be pedantic to oppose ; for we may say of it, that if it does no good, it does no harm either ; it is too little for that, too insignificant, and too innocent. As a piece to fill up an evening's entertainment, of which a theatre is in want, it may perhaps please many, and certainly will not hurt any one. It is, to be sure, not without some artless and lyric beauty."

Heiberg, as manager of the Royal Theatre, and as proprietor of the rejected piece, allowed the Casino Theatre ten years afterward to perform it. I had then grown up into a kinder generation. My little work was performed with great and lively acclamation, and it has often since been played.

On the eighth of October, 1842, Weyse died ; he was my first noble protector. In earlier days we often met at Wulff's ; we worked together on "Kenilworth," but we never became intimate friends. His life was as solitary as mine, and yet people liked to see him as well as I dare believe they liked to see me ; but I have the nature of a bird of passage, and fly over Europe ; his longest trip was to Roeskilde, where, in a certain family circle, he found a home, and where he could play fantasies on the great organ of the cathedral. At Roeskilde is his grave. He could not bear travelling, and I remember his humor when, upon returning from Greece and Constantinople, I made him a call.

"See now, you have not been any further than I !" said

he ; " you have reached Crown-Prince Street, and looked out
on the royal garden ; I do the same ; and you have thrown
away ever so much money. Would you travel ? Go to Roeskilde ; that is enough, until we visit moons and planets ! "

The first time that " Kenilworth " was performed, I received
a characteristic letter from him which begins thus : " *Caris-
sime domine poeta !* The dull-minded people in Copenhagen
cannot understand what we are driving at in the finale of the
second act of our opera," etc. " Kenilworth " was appointed
for the funeral festival at the theatre ; it was Weyse's last and
perhaps favorite work ; he had chosen the subject himself ; he
had himself written some parts of the text, and I am convinced that if his immortal soul in the other world still had
his earthly thoughts, he would have enjoyed seeing this work
brought him as a flower of honor ; but it was abandoned, and
Shakespeare's tragedy, " Macbeth," for which Weyse had composed the music, was given ; yet I don't think it is the most
characteristic of his compositions.

On the day of burial, strangely enough, the corpse was not
yet quite cold near the heart. I heard of it as I came with
the funeral train to the house of mourning, and asked the physicians for heaven's sake to examine it, and do all that they
could to bring him to life again; but they assured me after a
close examination that he was dead and would stay dead ;
that this kind of warmth was not unusual ; but I asked them
finally to sever his arteries before they closed the coffin ; they
would not do it. Oehlenschläger heard of it and came up to
me, saying, " What ! would you have him dissected ! " — " Yes,
rather than that he should awaken in the grave, and you too
would rather have them do so to you when you die ! " — " I ! "
exclaimed Oehlenschläger, and drew back. Alas ! Weyse was
dead.

By my last works, and by prudent economy, I had now
saved a small sum of money, which I set apart for the purpose
of a new journey to Paris. At the end of January, 1843, I left
Copenhagen. In consideration of the advanced season, I took
the route by Funen, through Sleswick and Holstein. It was a
wearisome and difficult journey until I reached Itzehoe and
Breitenburg. Count Rantzau received me very heartily and

kindly; I spent a few pleasant days with him at the old castle. The vernal storms raged, but the sun burst forth with its warm rays, and the larks sung over the marshy green. I visited all the places in the vicinity which I had before known. The days and evenings were a continual feast.

I who always lived without thinking of politics or political parties, observed now for the first time a kind of variance between the duchies and the kingdom. I had thought so little about the relation of these countries to each other, that in my "Bazaar" I had written in the dedication: "To my fellow-*countryman* the Holsteiner, Professor Ross;" but I felt now that this matter of nationality was not as I had supposed it to be. I heard a lady talking of "our duke," meaning the King. "Why do you not call him king?" I asked in my ignorance of hostilities.

"He is not our king, but our duke!" replied she. Petty political irritations occurred. Count Rantzau, who loved the King, Denmark, and the Danes, and was besides a very attentive host, smoothed over what was said in a jesting manner. "They are silly fools!" he whispered to me, and I thought that it was eccentricity that I had met with, and not the prevailing opinion, which I began to fear.

We learned that a conflagration had raged in Hamburg, which had ravaged the whole portion of the city near the Alster. A few new houses had since been rebuilt, but the most part lay still in ruins, with burnt beams and crumbling towers. At the "Jungfernstieg" and the "Esplanade" were erected rows of small brick shops, where the merchants, who had suffered by the fire, had their salesrooms. It was difficult for foreigners to find shelter. But I was fortunate enough to find entertainment under the best and most comfortable of roofs, that of Count Holck, who was Danish postmaster, and I was received in his family as a dear guest.

I spent happy hours here with the genial Speckter. He had just begun to draw those pictures for my tales, which are so admirable, so full of genius and humor; they are to be seen in one of the English editions, and in one of the less fortunate German translations, where "The Ugly Duckling" is translated by "The Green Duck," and has since passed in a French translation as "Le petit Canard vert."

There was not yet any railway over the Lunenburg heath ; we rode a whole night and day in the slow stage-coach by bad roads from Haarburg over Osnabrück to Düsseldorf, where I arrived on the very last day of the carnival, and saw in German shape what I had before seen in Roman. Cologne is said to be, among German towns, the place where they have the most magnificently arranged street processions. In Düsseldorf the festival was favored by most lovely weather, as the reporters would say. I saw a funny parade : a cavalry troop of boys on foot, who managed the horses they made believe to ride on ; a comic Hall of Fools, — a parody on "The Walhalla," which was open for visitors ; they told me that the painter Achenbach, whom I learned to know and appreciate, arranged the festival. Among the masters of the Düsseldorf school I recognized several old friends whom I knew on my first stay at Rome.

I met a countryman, a native of Odense, Mr. Benzon. At home, as soon as he began to paint, he painted my portrait. It was the first one that had been made of me, and was quite horrible ; it looked like the shadow of a man, or like one who has been pressed between some leaves for several years, and was now taken out and found to be as dry as a mummy. The book-seller, Reitzel, bought it of him. Benzon had here in Düsseldorf risen to a place among artists, and had recently finished a beautiful picture, " Saint Knud," who was slain in the church of St. Albani, in Odense.

I made a quiet journey by diligence, and by railroad, which was but partially finished, to Brussels, by way of Cologne and Lüttich. Here I heard Alizard in Donizetti's " La Favorita." I wearied of seeing in the Gallery Rubens's fleshy, fair-haired women, with homely noses and faded clothes ; I felt solemnly affected in the magnificent churches, and lingered before the old, memorable Hôtel de Ville, where Egmont was beheaded. The tower lifts itself up with its garniture and its points, — a wonderful, grand piece of Brussels lace.

On the railway from here to Mons I leaned against the door to look out of the window, when it sprung open, for it was not locked ; and if my neighbor had not seen it and immediately grabbed me and held on tight, I should certainly have been hurled out; as it was, I escaped with the fright only. It was spring-time in France; the fields were green, the sun warm; I caught sight of St. Denis, passed the new fortifications of Paris, and soon was seated in my room in the Hôtel Valois, Rue Richelieu, opposite the Library.

Marmier had already, in the " Révue de Paris," written an article on me, " La Vie d'un Poète." He had also translated several of my poems into French, and had actually honored me with a poem which is printed in the above named " Révue." My name had thus reached, like a sound, the ears of some persons in the literary world, and I here met with a surprisingly friendly reception.

I often visited at Victor Hugo's and enjoyed great kindness there, — a reception which Oehlenschläger in his " Life " complains that he did not find; so I ought to feel flattered. At Victor Hugo's invitation I saw at the Théatre Français his abused tragedy, " Les Burggraves," which was every evening hissed and parodied at the smaller theatres. His wife was very handsome, and possessed that amiability so peculiar to French ladies which makes foreigners so entirely at home with them.

Mr. and Mrs. Ancelot opened their house to me, and there I met Martinez de la Rosas and other remarkable men of these times. I was greatly taken with De la Rosas a long time before I knew who he was. His whole appearance, and the impression his conversation had made upon me, induced me to ask Madame Ancelot who that gentleman was.

"Have I not presented you to him?" said she; " he is the statesman, the poet Martinez de la Rosas!" She brought us together, told him who I was, and he asked after old Count Yoldi at Copenhagen; and described then to the whole circle how beautifully and sympathizingly Frederick VI. had cared for the Spaniard, when he had asked his advice as to what party at home he ought to join, and when that which he joined lost power, the Danish king bestowed upon him an office and home in Denmark. The conversation turned soon entirely upon Denmark. A young diplomat, who had just returned from being present at the coronation of Christian VIII., gave us a peculiar, very kind, and animated description of Frederick's

Castle and the festival there, but a description which sounded oddly to a Dane. He spoke of the mighty beech woods, the old Gothic castle built in the midst of the water, the richly gilt church, and — what sounded very droll since it seemed as if he believed it to be a custom in every-day life — that all the grand functionaries wore yellow and white silk-clothes, with feathers stuck in the barrettes and long trailing velvet mantles, which they throw over the arm when walking in the street. He had seen it himself! and I admitted that it was so at the coronation.

Lamartine seemed to me, in his domestic and in his whole personal appearance, to be the prince of them all. On my apologizing because I spoke such bad French, he replied that he was to blame, because he did not understand the northern languages, in which, as he had discovered in late years, there existed a fresh and vigorous literature, and where the poetical ground was so peculiar that you had only to stoop down to find an old golden horn. He asked about the Troll-hätta canal, and avowed a wish to visit Denmark and Stockholm. He recollected also our now reigning king, to whom, when as prince he was in Castellamare, he had paid his respects ; besides this, he exhibited, for a Frenchman, an extraordinary acquaintance with names and places in Denmark. On my departure he wrote a little poem for me, which I preserve amongst my dearest relics.

I generally found the jovial Alexandre Dumas in bed, even long after mid-day ; here he lay, with paper, pen, and ink, and wrote his newest drama. I found him thus one day ; he nodded kindly to me, and said, " Sit down a minute ; I have just now a visit from my muse ; she will be going directly." He wrote on ; spoke aloud ; shouted a *viva !* sprang out of bed, and said, " The third act is finished ! "

He lived in the Hôtel des Princes in Rue Richelieu, his wife was at Florence, his son, Dumas junior, who has since followed in his father's literary footsteps, had his own house in the city. " I live quite *à la garçon*," said Dumas, " so you must put up with what you find ! " One evening he escorted me about to the various theatres, that I might see life behind the scenes. We were at the Palais Royal, talked with Dejazet

and Anais, wandered then, arm in arm, along the gay Boulevard to the Théatre St. Martin. " Now they are just in the
short petticoats ! " said Dumas ; " shall we go in ! " That we
did, and behind scenes and curtains we wandered through
the sea in the " Thousand and One Nights." There was a
crowd of people, machinists, choristers, and dancers, and Dumas carried me into the middle of the noisy crowd. When we
returned home along the Boulevard we met a young man, who
stopped us. " That is my son ! " said Alexandre Dumas : " he
was born when I was eighteen years old ; now he is of the
same age and has no son ! " He was in later years the well
known " Dumas fils ! "

I also have to thank him for my acquaintance with Rachel.
I had not seen her act, when Alexandre Dumas asked me
whether I had the desire to make her acquaintance. One
evening, when she was to appear as *Phædra*, he led me to
the stage of the Théatre Français. The representation had
begun, and behind the scenes, where a folding screen had
formed a sort of room, in which stood a table with refreshments, and a few ottomans, sat the young girl who, as an
author has said, understands how to chisel living statues out
of Racine's and Corneille's blocks of marble. She was thin
and slenderly formed, and looked very young. She looked to
me there, and more particularly so afterward in her own house,
as an image of mourning ; as a young girl who has just wept
out her sorrow, and will now let her thoughts repose in quiet.
She accosted us kindly, in a deep, powerful voice. In the
course of conversation with Dumas she forgot me. I stood
there quite as one outside. Dumas observed it, said something
handsome of me, and on that I ventured to take part in the
discourse, although I had a depressing feeling that I stood
before those who perhaps spoke the most beautiful French in
all France. I said that I truly had seen much that was glorious and interesting, but that I never yet had seen a Rachel,
and that on her account especially had I devoted the profits
of my last work to a journey to Paris ; and as, in conclusion,
I added an apology on account of my French, she smiled and
said, " When you say anything so polite as that which you

have just said to me, to a Frenchwoman, she will always think that you speak well."

When I told her that her fame had reached us in the North, she declared that it was her intention to go to St. Petersburg and Copenhagen. "And when I come to your city," she said, "you must be my defender, as you are the only one there whom I know ; and in order that we may become acquainted, and as you tell me that you have come to Paris especially on my account, we must see one another frequently. You will be welcome to me. I see my friends at my house every Thursday. But duty calls," said she, and offering us her hand, she nodded kindly, and then stood a few paces from us on the stage, taller, quite different, and with the expression of the tragic muse herself. Joyous acclamations ascended to where we sat.

As a Northlander I cannot accustom myself to the French mode of acting tragedy. Rachel plays in this same style, but in her it appears to be nature itself ; it is as if all the others strove to imitate her. She is herself the French tragic muse, the others are only poor human beings. When Rachel plays, people fancy that all tragedy must be acted in this manner. It is in her truth and nature, but under another revelation from that with which we are acquainted in the North.

At her house everything is rich and magnificent, perhaps too *recherché*. The innermost room was light-green, with shaded lamps and statuettes of French authors. In the *salon*, properly speaking, the color which prevailed principally in the carpets, curtains, and book-cases was crimson. She herself was dressed in black, probably as she is represented in the well-known English steel engraving of her. Her guests consisted of gentlemen, — for the greater part artists and men of learning. I also heard a few titles amongst them. Richly appareled servants announced the names of the guests : tea was drunk and refreshments handed round, more in the German than the French style.

Victor Hugo had told me that he found she understood the German language. I asked her, and she replied in German, " Ich kann es lesen ; ich bin ja in Lothringen geboren ; ich habe deutsche Bücher, sehn Sie hier ! " and she showed me Grillparzer's " Sappho," and then immediately continued the conversation in French. She expressed her pleasure in acting the part of *Sappho,* and then spoke of Schiller's " Marie Stuart," which character she has personated in a French version of that play. I saw her in this part, and she gave the last act especially with such a composure and tragic feeling, that she might have been one of the best of German actresses ; but it was precisely in this very act that the French liked her least.

" My countrymen," said she, " are not accustomed to this manner, and in this manner alone can the part be given. No one should be raving when the heart is almost broken with sorrow, and when he is about to take an everlasting farewell of his friends."

Her drawing-room was, for the most part, decorated with books, which were splendidly bound and arranged in handsome book-cases behind glass. A painting hung on the wall, which represented the interior of the theatre in London, where she stood forward on the stage, and flowers and garlands were thrown to her across the orchestra. Below this picture hung a pretty little book-shelf, holding what I called " the high nobility among the poets," — Goethe, Schiller, Calderon, Shakespeare, etc.

She asked me many questions respecting Germany and Denmark, art and the theatre ; and encouraged me with a kind smile around her grave mouth, when I stumbled in French and stopped for a moment to collect myself that I might not stick quite fast.

" Only speak," said she. " It is true that you do not speak French well. I have heard many foreigners speak my native language better ; but their conversation has not been nearly as interesting as yours. I understand the sense of your words perfectly, and that is the principal thing which interests me in you."

The last time we parted she wrote the following words in my album : " L'art c'est le vrai ! ' J'espère que cet aphorisme ne semblera pas paradoxal à un écrivain aussi distingué que M. Andersen."

I perceived amiability of character in Alfred de Vigny. He has married an English lady, and that which is best in both

nations seemed to unite in his house. The last evening which
I spent in Paris, he himself, who is possessed of intellectual
status and worldly wealth, came almost at midnight to my
lodging in the Rue Richelieu, ascended the many steps, and
brought me his works under his arm. So much cordiality
beamed in his eyes, and he seemed to be so full of kindness toward me, that I felt affected by our separation.

I also became acquainted with the sculptor David. There
was a something in his demeanor and in his straightforward
manner that reminded me of Thorwaldsen and Bissen, especially of the latter. We did not meet till toward the conclusion
of my residence in Paris. He lamented it, and said that he
would execute a bust of me if I would remain there longer.

When I said, "But you know nothing of me as a poet, and
cannot tell whether I deserve it or not," he looked earnestly
in my face, clapped me on the shoulder, and said, " I have,
however, read you yourself before your books. You are a
poet."

At the Countess Bocarme's, where I met with Balzac, I
saw an old lady, the expression of whose countenance attracted my attention. There was something so animated, so
cordial in it, and everybody gathered about her. The Countess introduced me to her, and I heard that she was Madame
Reybaud, the authoress of " Les Épaves," the little story which
I had made use of for my drama of " The Mulatto." I
told her all about it, and of the representation of the piece,
which interested her so much that she became from this
evening my especial protectress. We went out one evening
together and exchanged ideas. She corrected my French,
and allowed me to repeat what did not appear correct to her.
She is a lady of rich mental endowments, with a clear insight
into the world, and she showed maternal kindness toward me.

Balzac, with whom, as I have already said, I made acquaintance in the saloon of the Countess Bocarme, was an elegant
and neatly dressed gentleman, whose teeth shone white between his red lips ; he seemed to be very merry, but a man
of few words, at least in society. A lady, who wrote verses,
took hold of us, drew us to a sofa, and placed herself between
us ; she told us how small she seemed to be when seated be-

tween us. I turned my head and met behind her back Balzac's satirical and laughing face, with his mouth half open and pursed up in a queer manner; that was properly our first meeting.

One day I was going through the Louvre, and met a man who was the very image of Balzac in figure, gait, and features, but the man was dressed in miserable tattered clothes, which were even quite dirty; his boots were not brushed, his pantaloons were spattered with mud, and the hat was crushed and worn out. I stopped in surprise; the man smiled at me: I passed him, but the resemblance was too strong; I turned, ran after him, and said: "Are you not M. Balzac?" He laughed, showed his white teeth, and only said, "To-morrow Monsieur Balzac starts for St. Petersburg!" He pressed my hand, — his was soft and delicate, — nodded, and went away. It could not be other than Balzac: perhaps in that attire he had been out on an author's investigation into the mysteries of Paris; or, was the man perhaps quite another person, who knew that he resembled Balzac strongly, and wished to mystify a stranger? A few days after I talked with Countess Bocarme, who gave me a message from Balzac — he had left for St. Petersburg.

I also again met with Heine. He had married since I was last here. I found him in indifferent health, but full of energy, and so friendly and natural in his behavior toward me, that I felt no timidity in exhibiting myself to him as I was. One day he had been telling his wife in French my story of "The Constant Tin Soldier," and, whilst he said that I was the author of this story, he introduced me to her.

"First, are you going to publish your travels?" he asked; and when I said No, he proceeded, "Well then I will show you my wife." She was a lively, pretty young lady. A troop of children — "Some we've borrowed of a neighbor, not having any of our own," said Heine — played about in their room. We two played with them whilst Heine copied out one of his last poems for me.

I perceived in him no pain-giving, sarcastic smile; I only heard the pulsation of a German heart, which is always perceptible in the songs, and which *must* live.

Through the means of the many people I was acquainted with here, — among whom I might enumerate many others, as, for instance, Kalkbrenner, Gathy, etc., — my residence in Paris was made very cheerful and rich in pleasure. I did not feel myself like a stranger there : I met with a friendly reception among the greatest and best. It was like a payment by anticipation of the talent which was in me, and through which they expected that I would some time prove them not to have been mistaken.

Whilst I was in Paris, I received from Germany, where already several of my works were translated and read, a delightful and encouraging proof of friendship. A German family, one of the most highly cultivated and amiable with whom I am acquainted, had read my writings with interest, especially the little biographical sketch prefixed to " Only a Fiddler," and felt the heartiest good-will toward me, with whom they were not then personally acquainted. They wrote to me, expressed their thanks for my works and the pleasure they had derived from them, and offered me a kind welcome to their house if I would visit it on my return home. There was something extremely cordial and natural in this letter, which was the first that I received of this kind in Paris, and it also formed a remarkable contrast to that which was sent to me from my native land in the year 1833, when I was here for the first time.

In this way I found myself, through my writings, adopted, as it were, into a family to which since then I gladly betake myself, and where I know that it is not only as the poet, but as the man, that I am beloved. In how many instances have I not experienced the same kindness in foreign countries ! I will mention one for the sake of its peculiarity.

There lived in Saxony a wealthy and benevolent family ; the lady of the house read my romance of " Only a Fiddler," and the impression of this book was such that she vowed that if ever, in the course of her life, she should meet with a poor child which was possessed of great musical talents, she would not allow it to perish as the poor Fiddler had done. A musician who had heard her say this, brought to her soon after, not one, but two poor boys, assuring her of their talent

and reminding her of her promise. She kept her word : both
boys were received into her house, were educated by her, and
are now in the Conservatorium ; the youngest of them played
before me, and I saw that his countenance was happy and
joyful. The same thing, perhaps, might have happened ;
the same excellent lady might have befriended these children without my book having been written : but notwithstanding this, my book is now connected with it as a link in the
chain.

On my return home from Paris, I went along the Rhine ; I
knew that the poet Frieligrath, to whom the King of Prussia
had given a pension, was residing in one of the Rhine towns.
The picturesque character of his poems had delighted me
extremely, and I wished to talk with him. I stopped at several
towns on the Rhine and inquired after him. In St. Goar, I
was shown the house in which he lived. I found him sitting
at his writing table, and he appeared annoyed at being disturbed by a stranger. I did not mention my name ; but
merely said that I could not pass St. Goar without paying my
respects to the poet Frieligrath.

" That is very kind of you," said he, in a very cold tone ;
and then asked who I was.

" We have both of us one and the same friend, Chamisso ! "
replied I, and at these words he leapt up exultantly.

" You are then Andersen ! " he exclaimed ; threw his arms
around my neck, and his honest eyes beamed with joy.

" Now you will stop several days here," said he. I told
him that I could only stay a couple of hours, because I was
travelling with some of my countrymen who were waiting for
me.

" You have a great many friends in little St. Goar," said
he ; " it is but a short time since I read aloud your novel of
" O. T." to a large circle ; one of these friends I must, at all
events, fetch here, and you must also see my wife. Yes,
indeed, you do not know that you had something to do with
our being married."

He then related to me how my novel, " Only a Fiddler," had
caused them to exchange letters, and then led to their acquaintance, which acquaintance had ended in their being a

married couple. He called her, mentioned to her my name, and I was regarded as an old friend.

In Bonn, where I passed the night, I called on old Moritz Arndt, he who afterward became so bitter against the Danes. Then I only knew him as the author of the beautiful and powerful song: "What is the German father-land?" I saw before me a vigorous, ruddy old man with silvery hair; he spoke Swedish to me, a language which he had learnt, when, as refugee on Napoleon's account, he visited our neighboring country; he was a youthful and brisk old man; I was not unknown to him, and it seemed to me that he took so much interest in me because I was a Scandinavian. In the course of our conversation a stranger was announced: neither of us heard his name; he was a young, handsome man with a bold, sunburnt face. He sat quietly down by the door and did not speak until Arndt showed me out, when he rose, and Arndt exclaimed joyfully, "Emanuel Geibel!" Yes, it was he, the young poet from Lübeck, whose fresh, beautiful songs in a short time echoed through the German countries, and to whom the King of Prussia had given a kind of pension as well as to Frieligrath: Geibel was just going to visit Frieligrath at St. Goar, and was to spend several months with him. Now he would not let me go till I had made acquaintance with the poet. Geibel was a very handsome, powerful, and fresh young man; as he stood by the side of the hale old poet, I saw in those two, the young and the old, the picture of Poetry always blooming.

"The child of fortune," an English author once called me, and I must gratefully acknowledge all the blessings I have enjoyed during my life; the great opportunity I have had to meet with and become acquainted with the most noble and best men of my time. I tell all this as I have told before that which was miserable, humiliating, and depressing; and if I have done so in the spirit which was at work in my soul, it will not be called pride or vanity; neither of them would assuredly be the proper name for it. It is from abroad that I have received acknowledgment and honor; but people may perhaps ask at home, Has he then never been attacked in foreign countries? I must reply, No!

No regular attack has been made upon me, at least they have never at home called my attention to any such, and therefore there certainly cannot have been anything of the kind, — with the exception of one which made its appearance in Germany, but which originated in Denmark, at the very moment when I was in Paris.

A certain Mr. Boas made a journey at that time through Scandinavia, and wrote a book on the subject. In this he gave a sort of survey of Danish literature, which he also published in the journal called "Die Grenzboten;" in this I was very severely handled as a man and as a poet. Several other Danish poets also, as, for instance, Christian Winther, have an equally great right to complain. Mr. Boas had drawn his information out of the miserable gossip of every-day life; his work excited attention in Copenhagen, but nobody there would allow themselves to be considered as his informants; nay, even Holst the poet, who, as may be seen from the work, travelled with him through Sweden, and had received him at his house in Copenhagen, on this occasion published, in one of the most widely circulated of our papers, a declaration that he was in no way connected with Mr. Boas.

Mr. Boas had in Copenhagen attached himself to a particular clique consisting of a few young men; he had heard them, full of lively spirits, talking during the day of the Danish poets and their writings; he had then gone home, written down what he had heard, and afterward published it in his work. This was, to use the mildest term, inconsiderate. That my "Improvisatore" and "Only a Fiddler" did not please him, is a matter of taste, and to that I must submit myself. But when he, before the whole of Germany, where probably people will presume that what he has written is true, if he declare it to be, as is the case, the universal judgment against me in my native land; when he, I say, declared me before the whole of Germany to be the most haughty of men, he inflicts upon me a deeper wound than he perhaps imagined. He conveyed the voice of a party, formerly hostile to me, into foreign countries. Nor is he true even in that which he represents; he gives circumstances as facts, which never took place.

In Denmark what he had written could not injure me, and many have declared themselves afraid of coming into contact with any one who printed everything which he heard. His book was read in Germany, the public of which is now also mine ; and I believe, therefore, that I may here say how faulty is his view of Danish literature and Danish poets — in what manner his book was received in my native land, and that people there know in what way it was put together. But after I have expressed myself thus on this subject I will gladly offer Mr. Boas my hand; and if, on his next visit to Denmark, no other poet will receive him, I will do my utmost for him ; I know that he will not be able to judge me more severely when we know each other than when we knew each other not. His judgment would also have been quite of another character had he come to Denmark but one year later ; things changed very much in a year's time. Then the tide had turned in my favor ; I then had published my new children's stories, of which from that moment to the present there prevailed, through the whole of my native land, but one unchanging honorable opinion. When the edition of my collection of stories came out at Christmas, 1843, the reaction began ; acknowledgment of my merits was made, and favor shown me in Denmark, and since that time I have no cause for complaint. I have obtained and I obtain in my own land that which I deserve — nay, perhaps much more.

I will now turn to those little stories which in Denmark have been placed by every one, without any hesitation, higher than anything else I had hitherto written.

In my book " In the Hartz Mountains " one finds properly my first wonder story, in the section " Brunswick," where it appears as a bit of irony in the drama " Three Days in the Life of a Looking-glass ; " in the same book one also finds the first suggestion of " The Little Mermaid ; " the description of the Elves belongs quite to this class of writing. Only a few months after the " Improvisatore " appeared, in 1835, I brought out my first volume of " Wonder Stories," [1] which at that time

[1] The Danish term *Eventyr*, used by Andersen, is not properly rendered by any one word in English ; it includes those stories in which the marvelous and superhuman predominate, just as *Historier*, used by Andersen

was not so very much thought of. One monthly critical journal even complained that an author who had taken such a step forward in the "Improvisatore," should immediately fall back with anything so childish as the tales. I reaped a harvest of blame, precisely where people ought to have acknowledged the advantage of my mind producing something in a new direction. Several of my friends, whose judgment was of value to me, counseled me entirely to abstain from writing tales, as these were a something for which I had no talent. Others were of opinion that I had better, first of all, study the French fairy tale.

The "Monthly Journal of Literature" paid no attention to the book, nor has it done so since. "Dannora," edited and published by J. N. Höst, was in 1836 the only one that gave a notice, which reads amusingly now, though at the time it naturally grieved me. The reviewer says that "These 'Wonder Stories' will be able to amuse children, but they are so far from containing anything instructive that the critic hardly ventures to recommend them as harmless reading ; at least nobody will maintain that a child's sense of decency will be sharpened when it reads about a princess who rides in her sleep on a dog's back to a soldier who kisses her, after which she herself, wide-awake, tells of this fine adventure — as a wonderful dream," etc. The story of the "Princess on Pease," the reviewer finds, has no wit, and it strikes him "not only as indelicate but positively without excuse, as putting the notion into a child's head that a lady of such rank must always be excessively refined." The reviewer concludes with the wish that the author may not waste any more time in writing wonder stories for children. I would willingly have discontinued writing them, but they forced themselves from me.

In the volume which I first published, I had, like Musäus, but in my own manner, related old stories, which I had heard as a child. The tone in which they still sounded in my ears

for certain other of his stories, denotes those which are more matter of fact, more what we call *narrative*. The title *Wonder Stories* has been used in this edition of Andersen's writings, though with regret, for it is a somewhat awkward and affected term. Under this conviction the title of this autobiography has been made to read *The Story of My Life*, instead of, more exactly, *The Wonder Story of My Life.* — EDITOR.

seemed a very natural one to me, but I knew very well that
the learned critics would censure the style of talk, so, to quiet
them I called them "Wonder Stories told for Children," although my intention was that they should be for both young
and old. The volume concluded with one which was original,
"Little Ida's Flowers," and seemed to have given the greatest pleasure, although it bore a tolerably near affinity to a
story of Hoffman's, and I had already given it in substance
in my "Foot Journey." In my increasing disposition for
children's stories, I therefore followed my own impulse, and
invented them mostly myself. In the following year a new
volume came out, and soon after that a third, in which the
longest story, "The Little Mermaid," was my own invention.
This story, in an especial manner, created an interest which
was only increased by the following volumes. One of these
came out every Christmas, and before long no Christmas-tree
could exist without my stories.

Some of our first comic actors made the attempt of relating
my little stories from the stage ; it was something new, and a
complete change from the declamatory poetry which had been
heard to satiety. "The Constant Tin Soldier," therefore, "The
Swineherd," and "The Top and Ball," were told from the
royal stage, and from those of private theatres, and were well
received. In order that the reader might be placed in the
proper point of view, with regard to the manner in which I
told the stories, I had called my first volume "Stories told for
Children." I had written my narrative down upon paper,
exactly in the language, and with the expressions in which I
had myself related them, by word of mouth, to the little ones,
and I had arrived at the conviction that people of different
ages were equally amused with them. The children made
themselves merry for the most part over what might be called
the actors ; older people, on the contrary, were interested in
the deeper meaning. The stories furnished reading for children and grown people, and that assuredly is a difficult task
for those who will write children's stories. They met with
open doors and open hearts in Denmark ; everybody read
them. I now removed the words, "told for children," from
my title, and published three volumes of "New Stories," all

of which were of my own invention, and were received in my own country with the greatest favor. I could not wish it greater; I felt a real anxiety in consequence, a fear of not being able to justify afterward such an honorable award of praise.

A refreshing sunshine streamed into my heart ; I felt courage and joy, and was filled with a living desire of still more and more developing my powers in this direction, — of studying more thoroughly this class of writing, and of observing still more attentively the rich wells of nature out of which I must create it. If attention be paid to the order in which my stories are written, it certainly will be seen that there is in them a gradual progression, a clearer working out of the idea, a greater discretion in the use of agency, and, if I may so speak, a more healthy tone and a more natural freshness may be perceived.

As one step by step toils up a steep hill, I had at home climbed upward, and now beheld myself recognized and honored, appointed a distinct place in the literature of my country. This recognition and kindness at home atoned for all the hard words that the critics had spoken. Within me was clear sunshine ; there came a sense of rest, a feeling that all, even the bitter in my life, had been needful for my development and my fortune.

My " Stories " were translated into most of the European languages ; several versions in German, as also in English and French, followed and continued still to be issued ; translations have been published also in Swedish, Flemish, Dutch etc., and by following the path our Lord has shown me, I have been favored more than if I had followed the way of criticism, that advised me " to study French models." If I had done so, I should scarcely have been translated into French, or, as now is the case, been compared in one of the French editions with Lafontaine and my " Stories " with his " fables immortelles," — " Nouveau Lafontaine, il fait parler les bêtes avec esprit, il s'associe à leurs peines, à leurs plaisirs, semble devenir leur confident,leur interprète, et sait leur créer un langage si naïf, si piquant, et si naturel qu'il ne semble que la reproduction fidèle de ce qu'il a véritablement entendu ; " neither should I have attained, at least in one direction, that influence upon the literature of my country which I hope I have.

From 1834 till 1852, wonder stories followed in various volumes and in several different publications, when they were issued in one collection in an illustrated edition, — the later ones classed under the title "Tales" (*Historier*), a name not chosen arbitrarily; but of this I will say a few words further on.

CHAPTER XI.

A T this period of my life I made an acquaintance which
was of great moral and intellectual importance to me.
I have already spoken of several persons and public characters who have had influence on me as a poet; but none of
these have had more, nor in a nobler sense of the word, than
the lady to whom I here turn myself, — she, through whom I,
at the same time, was enabled to forget my own individual
self, to feel that which is holy in art, and to become acquainted with the command which God has given to genius.

I now turn back to the year 1840. One day in the hotel in
which I lived in Copenhagen, I saw the name of Jenny Lind
among those of the strangers from Sweden. I was aware at
that time that she was the first singer in Stockholm. I had
been that same year in this neighbor country, and had there
met with honor and kindness : I thought, therefore, that it
would not be unbecoming in me to pay a visit to the young
artist. She was, at this time, entirely unknown out of Sweden,
so that I was convinced that, even in Copenhagen, her name
was known only by few. She received me very courteously,
but yet distantly, almost coldly. She was, as she said, on a
journey with her father to South Sweden, and had come over
to Copenhagen for a few days in order that she might see this
city. We again parted distantly, and I had the impression of
a very ordinary character which soon passed away from my
mind.

In the autumn of 1843, Jenny Lind came again to Copenhagen. One of my friends, our clever ballet-master, Bournonville, who has married a Swedish lady, a friend of Jenny Lind,
informed me of her arrival here, and told me that she remembered me very kindly, and that now she had read my writings.
He entreated me to go with him to her, and to employ all my
persuasive art to induce her to take a few parts at the Theatre

Royal ; I should, he said, be then quite enchanted with what I should hear.

I was not now received as a stranger ; she cordially extended to me her hand, and spoke of my writings and of Miss Fredrika Bremer, who also was her affectionate friend. The conversation soon turned on her appearance in Copenhagen, and of this Jenny Lind declared that she stood in fear.

"I have never made my appearance," said she, "out of Sweden ; everybody in my native land is so affectionate and kind to me, and if I made my appearance in Copenhagen and should be hissed ! — I dare not venture on it ! "

I said, that I, it was true, could not pass judgment on her singing, because I had never heard it, neither did I know how she acted, but nevertheless I was convinced that such was the disposition at this moment in Copenhagen, that only a moderate voice and some knowledge of acting would be successful ; I believed that she might safely venture.

Bournonville's persuasion obtained for the Copenhageners the greatest enjoyment which they ever had.

Jenny Lind made her first appearance among them as *Alice* in "Robert le Diable ; " it was like a new revelation in the realms of art ; the youthfully fresh voice forced itself into every heart ; here reigned truth and nature ; everything was full of meaning and intelligence. At one concert Jenny Lind sang her Swedish songs ; there was something so peculiar in this, so bewitching ; people thought nothing about the concert room ; the popular melodies uttered by a being so purely feminine, and bearing the universal stamp of genius, exercised their omnipotent sway ; the whole of Copenhagen was in raptures. Jenny Lind was the first singer to whom the Danish students gave a serenade : torches blazed around the hospitable villa where the serenade was given : she expressed her thanks by again singing some Swedish songs, and I then saw her hasten into the darkest corner and weep for emotion.

"Yes, yes," said she, " I will exert myself, I will endeavor ; I will be better qualified than I am when I again come to Copenhagen."

On the stage she was the great artiste who rose above all those around her ; at home, in her own chamber, a sensitive young girl with all the humility and piety of a child.

Her appearance in Copenhagen made an epoch in the history of our opera; it showed me art in its sanctity; I had beheld one of its vestals. She journeyed back to Stockholm, and from there Fredrika Bremer wrote to me : " With regard to Jenny Lind as a singer, we are both of us perfectly agreed ; she stands as high as any artist of our time can stand ; but as yet you do not know her in her full greatness. Speak to her about her art, and you will wonder at the expansion of her mind, and will see her countenance beaming with inspiration. Converse then with her of God, and of the holiness of religion, and you will see tears in those innocent eyes ; she is great as an artist, but she is still greater in her pure human exist-ence ! "

In the following year I was in Berlin ; the conversation with Meyerbeer turned upon Jenny Lind ; he had heard her sing her Swedish songs and was transported by them.

" But how does she act ? " asked he.

I spoke in raptures of her acting, and gave him at the same time some idea of her representation of *Alice.* He said to me that perhaps it might be possible for him to induce her to come to Berlin.

It is sufficiently well known that she made her appearance there, threw every one into astonishment and delight, and won for herself in Germany a European name. Last autumn she came again to Copenhagen, and the enthusiasm was incredible ; the glory of renown makes genius perceptible to every one. People bivouacked regularly before the theatre, to obtain a ticket. Jenny Lind appeared still greater than ever in her art, because one had an opportunity of seeing her in many and such extremely different parts. Her *Norma* is plastic ; every attitude might serve as the most beautiful model to a sculptor, and yet people felt that those were the inspiration of the moment, and had not been studied before the glass. *Norma* is no raving Italian ; she is the suffering, sorrowing woman — the woman possessed of a heart to sacrifice herself for an unfortunate rival — the woman to whom, in the violence of the moment, the thought may suggest itself of murdering the children of a faithless lover, but who is immediately dis-armed when she gazes into the eyes of the innocent ones.

"Norma, thou holy priestess!" sings the chorus, and Jenny Lind has comprehended and shows to us this holy priestess in the aria, "Casta diva." In Copenhagen she sang all her parts in Swedish, and the other singers sang theirs in Danish, and the two kindred languages mingled very beautifully together; there was no jarring; even in the "Daughter of the Regiment," where there is a deal of dialogue, the Swedish had something agreeable: and what acting! nay, the word itself is a contra- diction — it was nature; anything as true never before ap- peared on the stage. She shows us perfectly the true child of nature grown up in the camp, but an inborn nobility per- vades every movement. *The Daughter of the Regiment* and the *Somnambule* are certainly Jenny Lind's most unsurpass- able parts; no second can take their places in these beside her. People laugh, they cry; it does them as much good as going to church; they become better for it. People feel that God is in art; and where God stands before us face to face there is a holy church.

"There will not in a whole century," said Mendelssohn, speaking to me of Jenny Lind, "be born another being so gifted as she;" and his words expressed my full conviction; one feels, as she makes her appearance on the stage, that she is a pure vessel, from which a holy draught will be presented to us.

There is not anything which can lessen the impression which Jenny Lind's greatness on the stage makes, except her own personal character at home. An intelligent and child- like disposition exercises here its astonishing power; she is happy, — belonging, as it were, no longer to the world; a peace- ful, quiet home, is the object of her thoughts; and yet she loves art with her whole soul, and feels her vocation in it. A noble, pious disposition like hers cannot be spoiled by homage. On one occasion only did I hear her express her joy in her talent and her self-consciousness. It was during her last residence in Copenhagen. Almost every evening she appeared either in the opera or at concerts; every hour was in requisition. She heard of a society, the object of which was to assist un- fortunate children, and to take them out of the hands of their parents by whom they were misused, and compelled either to

beg or steal, and to place them in other and better circumstances. Benevolent people subscribed annually a small sum
each for their support, nevertheless the means for this excellent
purpose were small.

"But have I not still a disengaged evening?" said she;
"let me give a night's performance for the benefit of these
poor children ; but we will have double prices ! "

Such a performance was given, and returned large proceeds ; when she was informed of this, and that, by this
means, a number of poor children would be benefited for several years, her countenance beamed, and the tears filled her
eyes.

"Is it not beautiful," said she, "that I can sing so ! "

I value her with the feeling of a brother, and I regard
myself as happy that I know and understand such a spirit.
God give to her that peace, that quiet happiness which she
wishes for herself !

Through Jenny Lind I first became sensible of the holiness
there is in art ; through her I learned that one must forget
one's self in the service of the Supreme. No books, no men
have had a better or a more ennobling influence on me as the
poet, than Jenny Lind, and I therefore have spoken of her so
long and so warmly here.

I have made the happy discovery by experience, that inas-
much as art and life are more clearly understood by me, so
much more sunshine from without has streamed into my soul.
What blessings have not compensated me for the former dark
days ! Repose and certainty have forced themselves into my
heart. Such repose can easily unite itself with the changing
life of travel ; I feel myself everywhere at home, attach myself
easily to people, and they give me in return confidence and
cordiality.

In the summer of 1844 I once more visited North Germany.
An intellectual and amiable family in Oldenburg had invited
me in the most friendly manner to spend some time at their
house. Count von Rantzau-Breitenburg repeated also in his
letters how welcome I should be to him. I set out on the
journey, and this journey was, if not one of my longest, still
one of my most interesting.

I saw the rich marsh-land in its summer luxuriance, and made with Rantzau several interesting little excursions. Breitenburg lies in the middle of woods on the river Stör; the steam voyage to Hamburg gives animation to the little river; the situation is picturesque, and life in the castle itself is comfortable and pleasant. I could devote myself wholly to reading and poetry, because I was just as free as the bird in the air, and I was as much cared for as if I had been a beloved relation of the family. Alas! it was the last time that I came hither; Count Rantzau had, even then, a presentiment of his approaching death. One day we met in the garden; he seized my hand, pressed it warmly, expressed his pleasure in my talents being acknowledged abroad, and his friendship for me, adding, in conclusion, "Yes, my dear young friend, God only knows, but I have the firm belief that this year is the last time when we two shall meet here; my days will soon have run out their full course." He looked at me with so grave an expression that it touched my heart deeply, but I knew not what to say. We were near to the chapel; he opened a little gate between some thick hedges, and we stood in a garden, in which was a turfed grave and a seat beside it.

"Here you will find me, when you come the next time to Breitenburg," said he, and his sorrowful words were true. He died the following winter in Wiesbaden. I lost in him a friend, a protector, a noble, excellent heart.

When I, on the first occasion, went to Germany, I visited the Hartzgebirge and Saxon Switzerland. Goethe was still living. It was my most heartfelt wish to see him. It was not far from the Hartz to Weimar, but I had no letters of introduction to him, and, at that time, not one line of my writings was translated. Many persons had described Goethe to me as a very proud man, and the question arose whether indeed he would receive me. I doubted it, and determined not to go to Weimar until I should have written some work which would convey my name to Germany. I succeeded in this, but alas! Goethe was already dead.

I had made the acquaintance of his daughter-in-law, Mrs. von Goethe, born Pogwitsch, at the house of Mendelssohn-

Bartholdy, in Leipsic, on my return from Constantinople ; this *spirituelle* lady received me with much kindness. She told me that her son Walter had been my friend for a long time ; that as a boy he had made a whole play out of my " Improvisatore " ; that this piece had been performed in Goethe's house ; and lastly, that Walter had once wished to go to Copenhagen to make my acquaintance. I thus had now friends in Weimar.

An extraordinary desire impelled me to see this city where Goethe, Schiller, Wieland, and Herder had lived, and from which so much light had streamed forth over the world. I approached that land which had been rendered sacred by Luther, by the strife of the Minnesingers on the Wartburg, and by the memory of many noble and great events.

On the 24th of June, the birthday of the Grand Duke, I arrived a stranger in the friendly town. Everything indicated the festivity which was then going forward, and the young prince was received with great rejoicing in the theatre, where a new opera was being given. I did not think how firmly the most glorious and the best of all those whom I here saw around me would grow into my heart ; how many of my future friends sat around me here — how dear this city would become to me — in Germany, my second home. I was invited by Goethe's worthy friend, the excellent Chancellor Müller, and I met with the most cordial reception from him. By accident I here met, on my first call, with the Kammerherr Beaulieu de Marconnay, whom I had known in Oldenburg ; he was now living in Weimar. He invited me to remove to his house. In the course of a few minutes I was established as his guest, and I felt " it is good to be here."

There are people whom it only requires a few days to know and to love ; I won in Beaulieu, in these few days, a friend, as I believe, for my whole life. He introduced me into the family circle ; the amiable chancellor received me equally cordially ; and I who had, on my arrival, fancied myself quite forlorn, because Mrs. von Goethe and her son Walter were in Vienna, was now known in Weimar, and well received in all its circles.

The reigning Grand Duke and Duchess gave me so gra-

cious and kind a reception as made a deep impression upon
me. After I had been presented, I was invited to dine, and
soon after received an invitation to visit the hereditary Grand
Duke and his lady at the hunting seat of Ettersburg, which
stands high, and close to an extensive forest. The old fashioned furniture within the house, and the distant views from
the park into the Hartz Mountains, produced immediately a
peculiar impression. All the young peasants had assembled
at the castle to celebrate the birthday of their beloved young
Duke ; climbing-poles, from which fluttered handkerchiefs and
ribbons, were erected ; fiddles sounded, and people danced
merrily under the branches of the large and flowering lime-
trees. Sabbath splendor, contentment, and happiness were
diffused over the whole.

The young and but new married princely pair seemed to be
united by true heartfelt sentiment. The heart must be able
to forget the star on the breast under which it beats, if its
possessor wishes to remain long free and happy in a court ;
and such a heart, certainly one of the noblest and best which
beats, is possessed by Karl Alexander of Saxe-Weimar. I
had the happiness of making a long enough stay to establish
this belief. During this, my first residence here, I came
several times to the happy Ettersburg. The young Duke
showed me the garden, and the tree on the trunk of which
Goethe, Schiller, and Wieland had cut their names ; nay even
Jupiter himself had wished to add his to theirs, for his thun-
der-bolt had splintered it in one of the branches.

The intellectual Mrs. von Gross (Amalia Winter), Chancellor von Müller, — who was able to illustrate the times of
Goethe and to explain his " Faust," — and the soundly honest
and child-like minded Eckermann, belonged to the circle at
Ettersburg. The evenings passed like a spiritual dream ;
alternately some one read aloud ; even I ventured, for the
first time in a foreign language to me, to read one of my own
tales, — " The Constant Tin Soldier."

Chancellor von Müller accompanied me to the princely
burial-place, where Karl August sleeps with his glorious wife,
— not between Schiller and Goethe, as I believed when I wrote,
— " The prince has made for himself a rainbow glory, whilst

he stands between the sun and the rushing waterfall." Close beside the princely pair, who understood and valued that which was great, repose these their immortal friends. Withered laurel garlands lay upon the simple brown coffins, of which the whole magnificence consists in the immortal names of Goethe and Schiller. In life, the prince and the poet walked side by side ; in death, they slumber under the same vault. Such a place as this is never effaced from the mind ; in such a spot those quiet prayers are offered, which God alone hears.

I remained above eight days in Weimar ; it seemed to me as if I had formerly lived in this city ; as if it were a beloved home which I must now leave. As I drove out of the city, over the bridge and past the mill, and for the last time looked back to the city and the castle, a deep melancholy took hold on my soul, and it was to me as if a beautiful portion of my life here had its close ; I thought that the journey, after I had left Weimar, could afford me no more pleasure. How often since that time has the carrier-pigeon, and still more frequently, the mind, flown over to this place! Sunshine has streamed forth from Weimar upon my poet-life.

From Weimar I went to Leipsic, where a truly poetical evening awaited me with Robert Schumann. This great composer had a year before surprised me by the honor of dedicating to me the music which he had composed to four of my songs ; the lady of Dr. Frege, whose singing, so full of soul, has pleased and enchanted so many thousands, accompanied Clara Schumann, and the composer and the poet were alone the audience : a little festive supper and a mutual interchange of ideas shortened the evening only too much. I met with the old, cordial reception at the house of Mr. Brockhaus, to which from former visits I had almost accustomed myself. The circle of my friends increased in the German cities ; but the first heart is still that to which we most gladly turn again.

I found in Dresden old friends with youthful feelings ; my gifted half-countryman Dahl, the Norwegian, who knows how upon canvas to make the waterfall rush foaming down, and the birch-tree to grow as in the valleys of Norway, and Vogel von Vogelstein, who did me the honor of painting my portrait, which was included in the royal collection of portraits. The theatre intendant, Herr von Lüttichau, provided me every evening with a seat in the manager's box ; and one of the noblest ladies, in the first circles of Dresden, the worthy Baroness von Decken, received me as a mother would receive her son. In this character I was ever afterward received in her family and in the amiable circle of her friends.

How bright and beautiful is the world ! How good are human beings ! That it is a pleasure to live becomes ever more and more clear to me.

Beaulieu's younger brother, Edmund, who is an officer in the army, came one day from Tharand, where he had spent the summer months. I accompanied him to various places, spent some happy days among the pleasant scenery of the hills, and was received at the same time into various families.

I visited with the Baroness Decken, for the first time, the celebrated and clever painter Retsch, who has published the bold outlines of Goethe, Shakespeare, etc. He lives a sort of Arcadian life among lowly vineyards on the way to Meissen. Every year he makes a present to his wife, on her birthday, of a new drawing, and always one of his best ; the collection has grown through a course of years to a valuable album, which she, if he die before her, is to publish. Among the many glorious ideas there, one struck me as peculiar ; the " Flight into Egypt." It is night ; every one sleeps in the picture, — Mary, Joseph, the flowers, and the shrubs, nay even the ass which carries her — all, except the child Jesus, who, with open, round countenance, watches over and illumines all. I related one of my stories to him, and for this I received a lovely drawing, — a beautiful young girl hiding herself behind the mask of an old woman ; thus should the eternally youthful soul, with its blooming loveliness, peep forth from behind the old mask of the fairy tale. Retsch's pictures are rich in thought, full of beauty, and a genial spirit.

I enjoyed the country life of Germany with Major Serre and his amiable wife at their splendid residence in Maxen ; it is not possible for any one to exercise greater hospitality than is shown by these two kind-hearted people. A circle of intelligent, interesting individuals, were here assembled ; I remained among them above eight days, and there became acquainted with Kohl the traveller, and the clever authoress, the Countess Hahn-Hahn, in whom I discerned a woman by disposition and individual character in whom confidence may be placed. Her novels and travels at that time were much read, and she has since, on account of her conversion to the Catholic faith and her " From Babylon to Jerusalem," been again talked about. It is said that her father is famous for his unbounded love of the dramatic art, so that at last he was almost always absent from his estates going about with his company of comedians. She married her cousin, the wealthy Count Hahn-Hahn, but a divorce followed, and from that time she published poems, novels, and travels. Much is said and said in blame about the prominent characteristics of her novels, especially their air of superiority, and people have accused her of introducing thus her own personality, but that is not the impression made upon me. She travelled and always lived with the Baron Bystram, a very amiable gentle- man. Every one said and believed that they were married, and as such they were also received in the very highest so- ciety. When I once asked the reason why the marriage was kept concealed, they gave as a probable reason, that if she married again, she would lose the large annuity she drew from her first husband, and without that sum she could not get along. As authoress she has been harshly attacked ; her position as a writing nun, or, if you will, a Catholic missionary woman, has something about it very unnatural and unhealthy, but she is truly of a noble nature and a rarely gifted woman. It is a pity that the talents she received from God have not brought forth here the flowers and fruits which they might perhaps have produced under other circumstances. Toward me she was considerate and kind. It was through the dark glass of my " Only a Fiddler " and my " Wonder Stories " that she thought me a poet.

Where one is well received, there one gladly lingers. I found myself unspeakably happy on this little journey in Ger- many, and became convinced that I was there no stranger. It was heart and truth to nature which people valued in my writings ; and, however excellent and praiseworthy the exterior beauty may be, however imposing the maxims of this world's wisdom, still it is heart and nature which have least changed by time, and which everybody is best able to understand.

I returned home by way of Berlin, where I had not been for several years; but the dearest of my friends there — Chamisso, was dead.

> The fair wild swan which flew far o'er the earth,
> And laid its head upon a wild swan's breast,

was now flown to a more glorious hemisphere; I saw his children, who were now fatherless and motherless. From the young who here surround me, I discover that I am grown older; I feel it not in myself. Chamisso's sons, whom I saw the last time playing here in the little garden with bare necks, came now to meet me with helmet and sword: they were officers in the Prussian service. I felt in a moment how the years had rolled on, how everything was changed, and how one loses so many.

> Yet is it not so hard as people deem,
> To see their souls' belovéd from them riven;
> God has their dear ones, and in death they seem
> To form a bridge which leads them up to heaven.

I met with the most cordial reception, and have since then always met with the same, in the house of the Minister Savigny, where I became acquainted with the clever, singularly gifted Bettina, and her lovely, spiritual-minded daughters, — the youngest of whom had written the poetic fairy tale, "The Mud King's Daughter." They introduced me to their mother with "Now, what do you say of him!" Bettina scanned me, and passed her hand over my face: "*Passable!*" said she, and went away, but came back again, affectionate and full of originality. One hour's conversation with Bettina, during which she was the chief speaker, was so rich and full of interest, that I was almost rendered dumb by all this eloquence, this fire-work of wit. In the evening when the company broke up, she let her carriage return empty while we walked together up the street "*Unter den Linden;*" the prince of Wurtemberg gave her his arm, while I went with the young girls. At

Meinhardt's Hotel, where I lived, we stopped, Bettina placed herself before the staircase, made a military salute with the hand, and said : " Good-night, comrade : sleep well ! " A few days after, visiting her in her home, she appeared then in another way, quite as lively, but not so outward in her jests ; she impressed me as profound and kind. The world knows her writings, but another talent which she is possessed of is less generally known, namely her talent for drawing. Here again it is the ideas which astonish us. It was thus, I observed, she had treated in a sketch an accident which had occurred just before, — a young man being killed by the fumes of wine. You saw him descending half-naked into the cellar, round which lay the wine casks like monsters : Bacchanals and Bacchantes danced toward him, seized their victim, and destroyed him ! I know that Thorwaldsen, to whom she once showed all her drawings, was in the highest degree astonished by the ideas they contained.

It does the heart much good when abroad to find a house, where, when immediately you enter, eyes flash like festal lamps, a house where you can take peeps into a quiet, happy domestic life, — such a house is that of Professor Weiss. Yet how many new acquaintances which were found, and old acquaintances which were renewed, ought I not to mention ! I met Cornelius from Rome, Schelling from Munich, my countryman I might almost call him — Steffens the Norwegian, and once again Tieck, whom I had not seen since my first visit to Germany. He was very much altered, yet his gentle, wise eyes were the same, the shake of his hand was the same. I felt that he loved me and wished me well. I must visit him in Potsdam, where he lived in ease and comfort. At dinner I became acquainted with his brother the sculptor.

From Tieck I learnt how kindly the King and Queen of Prussia were disposed toward me ; that they had read my romance of " Only a Fiddler," and inquired from Tieck about me. Meantime their Majesties were absent from Berlin. I I had arrived the evening before their departure, when that abominable attempt was made upon their lives.

I returned to Copenhagen by Stettin in stormy weather, full of the joy of life, and again saw my dear friends, and in a few days set off to Count Moltke's in Funen, there to spend a few lovely summer days. I here received a letter from the minister Count Rantzau-Breitenburg, who was with the King and Queen of Denmark at the watering-place of Föhr. He wrote, saying that he had the pleasure of announcing to me the most gracious invitation of their Majesties to Föhr. This island, as is well known, lies in the North Sea, not far from the coast of Sleswick, in the neighborhood of the interesting Halligs, those little islands which Biernatzki described so charmingly in his novels. Thus, in a manner wholly unexpected by me, I should see scenery of a very peculiar character, even in Denmark.

The favor of my king and queen made me happy, and I rejoiced to be once more in close intimacy with Rantzau. Alas, it was for the last time !

It was just now five-and-twenty years since I, a poor lad, travelled alone and helpless to Copenhagen.   Exactly the five-and-twentieth anniversary would be celebrated by my being with my king and queen, to whom I was faithfully attached, and whom I at that very time learned to love with my whole soul.   Everything that surrounded me, man and nature, reflected themselves imperishably in my soul.   I felt myself, as it were, conducted to a point from which I could look forth more distinctly over the past five-and-twenty years, with all the good fortune and happiness which they had evolved for me.   The reality frequently surpasses the most beautiful dream.

I travelled from Funen to Flensborg, which, lying in its great bay, is picturesque with woods and hills, and then immediately opens out into a solitary heath. Over this I travelled in the bright moonlight. The journey across the heath was tedious ; the clouds only passed rapidly. We went on monotonously through the deep sand, and monotonous was the wail of a bird among the shrubby heath. Presently we reached moorlands. Long-continued rain had changed meadows and corn-fields into great lakes ; the embankments along which we drove were like morasses ; the horses sank deeply into them. In many places the light carriage was obliged to be supported by the peasants, that it might not fall upon the cottages below the embankment. Several hours were consumed over each mile (Danish). At length the North Sea with its islands lay before me. The whole coast was an embankment, covered for miles with woven straw, against which the waves broke. I arrived at high tide. The wind was favorable, and in less than an hour I reached Föhr, which, after my difficult journey, appeared to me like a real fairy land.

The largest city, Wyck, in which are the baths, is built exactly like a Dutch town. The houses are only one story high, with sloping roofs and gables turned to the street. The many strangers there, and the presence of the court, gave a peculiar animation to the principal street. Well-known faces looked out from almost every house ; the Danish flag waved, and music was heard. It was as if I had come to a festival ; the sailors from the ship carried my luggage to the hotel. Not far from the landing-place, near the one-story dwelling where the royal couple lived, we saw a large wooden house, at the open windows of which ladies were moving about ; they looked out and shouted : "Welcome, Mr. Andersen ! Welcome." The sailors bowed low, and took off their hats. I had all along been an unknown guest to them, now I became a person of consideration, because the ladies who saluted me were the young Princesses of Augustenburg and their mother, the Duchess. I had just taken my place at the table d'hôte, and was, as a new guest, an object of curiosity, when a royal footman entered with an invitation from their Majesties to dinner, which had begun, but the king and queen had heard of my arrival, and had kept a place at table ready for me.

Their Majesties had provided lodging for me ; during my whole stay there I took breakfast, dinner, and supper with the royal family, and Rantzau-Breitenburg. These were beautiful and bright poetical days for me, — days that will never come back. It is so good to see a noble human nature reveal itself where one might expect to find only the king's crown and the purple mantle. Few people could be more amiable in private life than the then reigning Majesties of Denmark. May God bless them, and give them joy, even as they filled my breast with happiness and sunshine ! On several evenings I read aloud some of my little stories ; "The Nightingale " and " The Swineherd " seemed to please the King most, and were

therefore repeated several evenings.   My talent of extemporiz-
ing was discovered one evening.   One of the courtiers recited
in joke a kind of jingle for the young Princesses of Augustenburg ; I stood near by and added in fun, " You do not say
your verse rightly : I know it better ; you must say " — and
now I made an impromptu.   They jested and laughed ; it was
heard in the next room where the King sat at the card-table;
he asked what was the matter, and I repeated my impromptu.
Now they all tried to extemporize and I helped them along.
" And have I not made a poem all alone ? " asked General
Ewald, who was playing at cards with the King ; " will you not
be so kind as to recite for me one of my best ? "

"Ewald's poems are well known to the King, and to the
whole country ! " said I, and turned away, when Queen Caroline Amelia said, " Do you not remember something that
I have thought and felt ? "   I wished to recite some worthy
lines, and answered, " Certainly, your Majesty : I have written
something down, and will bring it to-morrow."

" You remember it, I am sure ! " she repeated.   They urged
me, and I extemporized the following strophe, which is printed
among the shorter verses in my poems : —

PRAYER.

O God, our Rock when storms do rage,
  Thou art our Sun, our life the shade :
Strengthen the King in this tempestuous age,
  For Denmark's hope on him is stayed.
May his hand wreath the flag with flowers,
  And honor Love and every purpose grand ;
And when Thou judgest this great world of ours,
  Pure as a lily may sea-girt Denmark stand.

I sailed in their train to the largest of the Halligs, — those
grassy runes in the ocean, which bear testimony to a sunken
country.   The violence of the sea has changed the main-land
into islands, has riven these again, and buried men and villages.   Year after year are new portions rent away, and, in
half a century's time, there will be nothing here but sea.   The
Halligs are now only low islets covered with a dark turf, on
which a few flocks graze.   When the sea rises these are driven
into the garrets of the houses, and the waves roll over this lit-

tle region, which is miles distant from the shore. Oland, which we visited, contains a little town. The houses stand closely side by side, as if, in their sore need, they would all huddle together. They are all erected upon a platform, and have little windows, as in the cabin of a ship. There, in the little room, solitary through half the year, sit the wife and her daughters spinning. There, however, one always finds a little collection of books. I found books in Danish, German, and Frisian. The people read and work, and the sea rises round the houses, which lie like a wreck in the ocean. Sometimes, in the night, a ship, having mistaken the lights, drives on here and is stranded.

In the year 1825, a tempestuous tide washed away men and houses. The people sat for days and nights half naked upon the roofs, till these gave way ; nor from Föhr nor the main-land could help be sent to them. The church-yard is half washed away ; coffins and corpses are frequently exposed to view by the breakers : it is an appalling sight. And yet the inhabitants of the Halligs are attached to their little home. They cannot remain on the main-land, but are driven thence by homesickness.

We found only one man upon the island, and he had only lately arisen from a sick-bed. The others were out on long voyages. We were received by girls and women. They had erected before the church a triumphal arch with flowers which they had fetched from Föhr ; but it was so small and low that one was obliged to go round it ; nevertheless they showed by it their good-will. The Queen was deeply affected by their having cut down their only shrub, a rose-bush, to lay over a marshy place which she would have to cross. The girls are pretty, and are dressed in a half Oriental fashion. The people trace their descent from Greeks. They wear their faces half concealed, and beneath the strips of linen which lie upon the head is placed a Greek fez, around which the hair is wound in plaits.

On our return, dinner was served on board the royal steamer ; and afterward, as we sailed in a glorious sunset through this archipelago, the deck of the vessel was changed to a dancing room. Young and old danced ; servants flew

hither and thither with refreshments; sailors stood upon the
paddle-boxes and took the soundings, and their deep-toned
voices might be heard giving the depth of the water. The
moon rose round and large, and the promontory of Amron
assumed the appearance of a snow-covered chain of Alps.

I visited afterward these desolate sand hills : the King went
to shoot rabbits there. Many years ago a ship was wrecked
here, on board of which were two rabbits, and from this pair
Amron is now stored with thousands of their descendants.
At low tide the sea recedes wholly from between Amron
and Föhr, and then people drive across from one island to
another ; but still the time must be well observed and the
passage accurately known, or else, when the tide comes, he
who crosses will be inevitably lost. It requires only a few
minutes, and then where dry land was large ships may sail.
We saw a whole row of wagons driving from Föhr to Amron.
Seen upon the white sand and against the blue horizon, they
seemed to be twice as large as they really were. All around
were spread out, like a net, the sheets of water, as if they
held firmly the extent of sand which belonged to the ocean
and which would be soon overflowed by it. This promontory
brings to one's memory the mounds of ashes at Vesuvius ;
for here one sinks at every step, the wiry moor-grass not being
able to bind together the loose sand. The sun shone burn-
ingly hot between the white sand hills : it was like a journey
through the deserts of Africa.

A peculiar kind of rose and the heath were in flower in the
valleys between the hills ; in other places there was no vegetation whatever ; nothing but the wet sand on which the
waves had left their impress ; the sea on its receding had
inscribed strange hieroglyphics. I gazed from one of the
highest points over the North Sea ; it was ebb-tide ; the sea
had retired about a mile ; the vessels lay like dead fishes
upon the sand, awaiting the returning tide. A few sailors
had clambered down and moved about on the sandy ground
like black points. Where the sea itself kept the white level
sand in movement, a long bank elevated itself, which, during
the time of high water, is concealed, and upon which occur
many wrecks. I saw the lofty wooden tower which is here

erected, and in which a cask is always kept filled with water, and a basket supplied with bread and brandy, that the unfortunate human beings who are here stranded may be able in this place, amid the swelling sea, to preserve life for a few days until it is possible to rescue them.

To return from such a scene as this to a royal table, a charming court concert, and a little ball in the bath-saloon, as well as to the promenade by moonlight, thronged with guests, a little Boulevard, had something in it like a fairy tale, — it was a singular contrast.

As I sat on the above-mentioned five-and-twentieth anniversary, on the 5th of September, at the royal dinner-table, the whole of my former life passed in review before my mind. I was obliged to summon all my strength to prevent myself from bursting into tears. There are moments of thankfulness in which, as it were, we feel a desire to press God to our hearts. How deeply I felt, at this time, my own nothingness ; how all, all, had come from him. Rantzau knew what an interesting day this was to me. After dinner the King and the Queen wished me happiness, and that so — graciously, is a poor word — so cordially, so sympathizingly ! The King wished me happiness in that which I had endured and won. He asked me about my first entrance into the world, and I related to him some characteristic incidents.

In the course of conversation he inquired if I had not some certain yearly income : I named the sum to him.

" That is not much," said the King.

" But I do not require much," replied I, " and my writings procure me something."

The King, in the kindest manner, inquired further into my circumstances, and closed by saying, —

" If I can, in any way, be serviceable to your literary labors, then come to me."

In the evening, during the concert, the conversation was renewed, and some of those who stood near me reproached me for not having made use of my opportunity.

" The King," said they, " put the very words into your mouth."

But I could not, I would not have done it. " If the King,"

I said, "found that I required something more, he could give it to me of his own will."

And I was not mistaken. In the following year King Christian VIII. increased my annual stipend, so that with this and that which my writings bring in, I can live honorably and free from care. My King gave it to me out of the pure good-will of his own heart. King Christian is enlightened, clear-sighted, with a mind enlarged by science; the gracious sympathy, therefore, which he has felt in my fate is to me doubly cheering and ennobling.

The 5th of September was to me a festival day: even the German visitors at the baths honored me by drinking my health in the pump-room.

So many flattering circumstances, some people argue, may easily spoil a man, and make him vain. But, no; they do not spoil him, they make him on the contrary — better; they purify his mind, and he must thereby feel an impulse, a wish, to deserve all that he enjoys. At my parting audience with the Queen, she gave me a valuable ring as a remembrance of our residence at Föhr; and the King again expressed himself full of kindness and noble sympathy. God bless and preserve this exalted pair!

The Duchess of Augustenburg was at this time also at Föhr with her two eldest daughters. I had daily the happiness of being with them, and received repeated invitations to take Augustenburg on my return. For this purpose I went from Föhr to Als, one of the most beautiful islands in the Baltic. That little region resembles a blooming garden; luxuriant corn and clover-fields are inclosed with hedges of hazels and wild roses; the peasants' houses are surrounded by large apple orchards, full of fruit. Wood and hill alternate. Now we see the ocean, and now the narrow Lesser Belt, which resembles a river. The castle of Augustenburg is magnificent, with its garden full of flowers, extending down to the very shores of the serpentine bay. I met with the most cordial reception, and found the most amiable family life in the ducal circle. I spent fourteen days here, and was present at the birthday festivities of the Duchess, which lasted three days;

among these festivities was racing, and the town and the castle were filled with people.

Happy domestic life is like a beautiful summer's evening; the heart is filled with peace ; and everything around derives a peculiar glory. The full heart says, "It is good to be here ;" and this I felt at Augustenburg.

CHAPTER XII.

IN the spring of 1844 I had finished a dramatic tale, " Fortune's Flower." The idea of this was, that it is not
the immortal name of the artist, nor the splendor of a crown
which can make man happy ; 'but that happiness is to be found
where people, satisfied with little, love and are loved again.
The scene was perfectly Danish, an idyllian, sunbright life, in
whose clear heaven two dark pictures are reflected as in a
dream ; the unfortunate Danish poet Ewald, and Prince Buris,
who is tragically sung of in our heroic ballads. I wished to
show, in honor of our times, the Middle Ages to have been
dark and miserable, as they were, but which many poets only
represent to us in a beautiful light.

Professor Heiberg, who was appointed censor, declared himself against the reception of my piece. During the last years
I had met with nothing but hostility from this party : I regarded
it as personal ill-will, and this was to me still more painful
than the rejection of the pieces. It was painful for me to be
placed in a constrained position with regard to a poet whom I
respected, and toward whom, according to my own conviction,
I had done everything in order to obtain a friendly relationship. A further attempt, however, must be made. I wrote
to Heiberg, expressed myself candidly, and, as I thought,
cordially, and entreated him to give me explicitly the reasons
for his rejection of the piece and for his ill-will toward me.
He immediately paid me a visit, which I, not being at home
when he called, returned on the following day, and I was received in the most friendly manner. The visit and the conversation belong certainly to the extraordinary, but they occasioned an explanation, and I hope led to a better understanding for the future.

He clearly set before me his views in the rejection of my
piece. Seen from his point of sight they were unquestionably

correct ; but they were not mine, and thus we could not agree. He declared decidedly that he cherished no spite against me, and that he acknowledged my talent. I mentioned his various attacks upon me, for example, in the " Intelligencer," and that he had denied to me original invention : I imagined, however, that I had shown this in my novels ; " But of these," said I, "you have read none ; you yourself have told me so."

" Yes, that is the truth," replied he ; " I have not yet read them, but I will do so."

" Since then," continued I, "you have turned me and my "Bazaar" to ridicule in your poem called " Denmark," and spoken about my fanaticism for the beautiful Dardanelles ; and yet I have, precisely in that book, described the Dardanelles as not beautiful ; it is the Bosphorus which I thought beautiful ; you seem not to be aware of that ; perhaps you have not read ' The Bazaar ' either ? "

" Was it the Bosphorus?" said he, with his own peculiar smile ; "yes, I had quite forgotten that, and, you see, people do not remember it either ; the object in this case was only to give you a stab."

This confession sounded so natural, so like him, that I was obliged to smile. I looked into his clever eyes, thought how many beautiful things he had written, and I could not be angry with him. The conversation became more lively, more free, and he said many kind things to me ; for example, he esteemed my stories very highly, and entreated me frequently to visit him. I have become more and more acquainted with his poetical temperament, and I fancy that he too will understand mine. We are very dissimilar, but we both strive after the same object. Before we separated he conducted me to his little observatory ; now his dearest world. He seems now to live for poetry and now for philosophy, and — for which I fancy he is least of all calculated — for astronomy. Recent years, in which I have acquired so many blessings have brought me also the appreciation of that gifted genius.

But to follow the succession of time : the dramatic tale was brought on the stage, and in the course of the season was performed seven times and was then laid to rest, at least under that theatrical management. I have often asked myself the question, Is it because of special weakness in my dramatic works or because I am the author of them, that they are judged so harshly and are attacked on every occasion? I could discover this only by writing an anonymous work and let that take its course; but could I keep my secret? No, all agreed that I could not, and this opinion worked to my advantage. During a short visit at Nysöe I wrote "The King Dreams;" nobody except Collin knew that I was the author. I heard that Heiberg, who just at that time was using me very sharply in the "Intelligencer," interested himself very much for the anonymous piece, and, if I am not mistaken, he put it on the stage. I must however add that afterward he gave it a beautiful and generous critique in the "Intelligencer," and that too after he had caught the notion that it might be written by me, — which almost all doubted.

A new experiment procured for me still greater pleasure and fun, because of the situation I fell into and the judgments I heard. At the very time I was having so much trouble in getting my "Fortune's Flower" represented, I wrote and sent in "The New Lying-in Room."[1] The little comedy was at that time performed most exquisitely. Madame Heiberg played with life and humor the part of *Christina;* she gave an air of freshness and charm to it all, and the piece met, as is well known, with great success. Collin was initiated into the secret, as also H. C. Örsted, to whom I read the piece at my own home, and he was pleased with the praise that the little work received. Nobody anticipated that it came from me. Returning home the evening after the first representation of the piece, one of our young, clever critics came to my rooms; he had been at the theatre, and expressed now the great pleasure he had found in the little comedy. I was rather embarrassed and feared I might betray myself by words or aspect, so I said immediately to him : " I know its author!"— "Who is it?" asked he. "It is you!" said I, "you are in such agitation, and much of what you say betrays you! Do not see anybody

---

[1] There is a comedy by Holberg called "The Lying-in Room," founded, as this also, on the custom in Denmark of a woman receiving the congratulation of her friends shortly after the birth of a child, — a custom which has fallen into disuse from its manifest imprudence. — ED.

else this evening and speak as you have been speaking to me, for you will be discovered!" He blushed and was quite astonished, laid his hand upon his heart and assured me solemnly that he was not the author. "I know what I know!" said I laughingly, and begged him to excuse my leaving him. It was not possible for me to hold in longer, and so I was compelled to speak as I did, and he did not suspect any deceit.

I went one day to the director of the theatre, the Privy Counselor Adler, to hear of my "Fortune's Flower."

"Well," said he, "that is a work with considerable poetry in it, but not of the kind that we can make use of. If you could only write a piece like "The New Lying-in Room!" That is an excellent piece, but does not lie within reach of your talent; you are a lyrist, and not in possession of that man's humor!"

"I am sorry to say that I am not!" I answered, and now I also praised "The New Lying-in Room." For more than a year the little piece was played with great success, and nobody knew its author's name; they guessed Hostrup, and that was no damage to me; afterward one or another guessed me, but it was not believed. I have seen how those who have named me have been set right, and one of the arguments used was: "Andersen could not have kept still after such a success!" — "No, that would have been impossible," said I, and I made a silent vow not to reveal myself as its author, for several years, when it should have no more interest for the public, and I have kept my word. Only last year I revealed it, by inserting the piece among my "Collected Writings," as also the piece "The King Dreams." Several characters in the novel "O. T.," as also some in "Only a Fiddler," *e. g.* Peter Vieck, might have put them on the scent that I was the author. I had thought that people might have found some humor in my stories, but it was not so; it was only found in my "New Lying-in Room."

It was this characteristic of my writing which especially pleased H. C. Örsted, who was the first that spoke of it and bade me believe that I really had humor. He perceived it in some of my earlier works, and in several traits of my character. When my first collection of poems appeared in 1830, of which several had been printed separately, I tried to find a motto for the whole collection, but I could not find anything striking, so I made one myself.

"Forgotten poems are new!" — JEAN PAUL.

And I had the fun afterward to see other authors, men of erudition, quoting the same motto of Jean Paul ; I know from what source they had it, and Örsted also.

There was a time when I suffered so very bitterly from a too severe and almost personal criticism, that I was often at the point of giving up, but then there came moments where humor, if I dare call it so, raised me from the sadness and misery into which I had sunk ; I saw clearly my own weakness and wants, but also what was foolish and absurd in the insipid rebukes and learned gabble of the critics.

Once in such a moment I wrote a critique upon H. C. Andersen as an author ; it was very sharp, and finished by recommending study and gratitude toward those who had educated him. I took the conceit with me one day to H. C. Örsted's, where a company was gathered for dinner. I told them that I had brought with me a copy of a shameless and harsh criticism, and read it aloud. They could not imagine why I should copy such a thing, but they also condemned it as harsh.

"It is really so," said Örsted, "they are severe against Andersen, but yet it seems to me that there is something in it, some arguments which are really striking and give us an insight into you!"

"Yes," I answered, "for it is from myself!" and now there was surprise, and laughter and joking ; most of the company wondered that I could have been able to write such a thing myself.

"He is a true humorist!" said Örsted, and that was the first time that I discovered for myself that I was in possession of such a gift.

As people grow older, however much they may be tossed about in the world, some one place must be the true home ; even the bird of passage has one fixed spot to which it hastens : mine was and is the house of my friend Collin. Treated as a son, almost grown up with the children, I have become a member of the family ; a more heartfelt connection, a better home have I never known : a link broke in this chain, and precisely in the hour of bereavement, did I feel how firmly I have been engrafted here, so that I was regarded as one of the children.

If I were to give the picture of the mistress of a family who wholly loses her own individual *I* in her husband and children, I must name the wife of Collin ; with the sympathy of a mother, she also followed me in sorrow and in gladness. In the latter years of her life she became very deaf, and beside this she had the misfortune of being nearly blind. An operation was performed on her sight, which succeeded so well, that in the course of the winter she was able to read a letter, and this was a cause of grateful joy to her. She longed in an extraordinary manner for the first green of spring, and this she saw in her little garden.

I parted from her one Sunday evening in health and joy ; in the night I was awoke ; a servant brought me a letter. Collin wrote, " My wife is very ill ; the children are all assembled here ! " I understood it, and hastened thither. She slept quietly and without pain ; it was the sleep of the just ; it was death which was approaching so kindly and calmly. On the third day she yet lay in that peaceful slumber : then her countenance grew pale — and she was dead !

> Thou did'st but close thine eyes to gather in
> The large amount of all thy spiritual bliss ;
> We saw thy slumbers like a little child's.
> O Death! thou art all brightness and not shadow.

Never had I imagined that the departure from this world could be so painless, so blessed. A devotion arose in my soul ; a conviction of God and eternity, which this moment elevated to an epoch in my life. It was the first death-bed at which I had been present since my childhood. Children, and children's children were assembled. In such moments all is holy around us. Her soul was love ; she went to love and to God!

At the end of July the monument of King Frederick VI.

was to be uncovered at Skanderborg, in the middle of Jutland. I had, by solicitation, written the cantata for the festival, to which Hartmann had furnished the music, and this was to be sung by Danish students. I had been invited to the festival, which thus was to form the object of my summer excursion.

Skanderborg lies in one of the most beautiful districts of Denmark. Charming hills rise covered with vast beech woods, and a large inland lake of a pleasing form extends among them. On the outside of the city, close by the church, which is built upon the ruins of an old castle, now stands the monument, a work of Thorwaldsen's. The most beautiful moment to me at this festival was in the evening, after the unveiling of the monument ; torches were lighted around it, and threw their unsteady flame over the lake ; within the woods blazed thousands of lights, and music for the dance resounded from the tents. Round about upon the hills, between the woods, and high above them, bonfires were lighted at one and the same moment, which burned in the night like red stars. There was spread over lake and land a pure, a summer fragrance which is peculiar to the North, in its beautiful summer nights. The shadows of those who passed between the monument and the church, glided gigantically along its red walls, as if they were spirits who were taking part in the festival.

A royal steamship was ordered to bring home the students, and before our departure the citizens of Aarhuus got up a ball for us. We arrived in a long procession of carriages at the city, but earlier than they had expected, and as we were to have a very elegant reception we were advised to wait a little. So we stopped in the hot sun a long time out of the city, all for the honor of it, and when we entered the city we were drawn up in rows on the market-place ; the good citizens each took a student to entertain. I stood among the students, and several citizens, one after another, came up to me, bowed, asked my name, and when I told it them they asked, "Are you the poet Andersen?" I said "Yes!" They bowed again and went away ; all went away ; not one of them would have the poet, or perhaps they wished me so good a host, the very best one, that at last I did not get any at all. I stood forsaken and alone, like a negro at a slave-market whom nobody will buy. I alone was obliged to find a hotel in the good city of Aarhuus.

We went homeward over the Kattegat with song and laughter. The Kullen lifted its black rocks, the Danish shores stood fresh and green with their beech woods ; it was a journey for the musician and the poet. I returned home to literary activity. In this year my novel of "The Improvisatore" was translated into English by the well-known authoress Mary Howitt, and was received by her countrymen with great applause. "O. T." and "Only a Fiddler" soon followed, and met with, as it seemed, the same reception. After that appeared a Dutch, and lastly a Russian translation of "The Improvisatore." That which I should never have ventured to dream of was accomplished ; my writings seem to come forth under a lucky star ; they have flown over all lands. There is something elevating, but at the same time something terrific, in seeing one's thoughts spread so far, and among so many people ; it is, indeed, almost a fearful thing to belong to so many. The noble, the good in us becomes a blessing ; but the bad, one's errors, shoots forth also, and involuntarily the thought forces itself from us : God ! let me never write down a word of which I shall not be able to give an account to Thee. A peculiar feeling, a mixture of joy and anxiety, fills my heart every time my good genius conveys my fictions to a foreign people.

Travelling operates like an invigorating bath to the mind, — like a Medea-draught which always makes one young again. I feel once more an impulse for it — not in order to seek material, as a critic fancied and said, in speaking of my "Bazaar ; " there exists a treasury of material in my own inner self, and this life is too short to mature this young existence ; but there needs refreshment of spirit in order to convey it vigorously and maturely to paper, and travelling is to me, as I have said, this invigorating bath, from which I return as it were younger and stronger.

By prudent economy, and the proceeds of my writings, I was in a condition to undertake several journeys during the last year. That which for me is the most sun-bright, is the one in which these pages were written. Esteem, perhaps over estimation, but especially kindness, in short, happiness and pleasure, have flowed toward me in abundant measure.

I wished to visit Italy for the third time, there to spend a summer, that I might become acquainted with the South in its warm season, and probably return thence by Spain and France. At the end of October, 1845, I left Copenhagen. Formerly I had thought when I set out on a journey : God ! what wilt Thou permit to happen to me on this journey ? This time my thoughts were : God ! what will happen to my friends at home during this long time ? And I felt a real anxiety. In one year the hearse may drive up to the door many times, and whose name may be read upon the coffin ! The proverb says, when one suddenly feels a cold shudder : " Now death passes over my grave." The shudder is still colder when the thoughts pass over the graves of our best friends.

I spent a few days at Count Moltke's, at Glorup ; strolling players were acting some of my dramatic works at one of the nearest provincial towns. I did not see them ; country life firmly withheld me. There is something in the late autumn poetically beautiful ; when the leaf is fallen from the tree, and the sun shines still upon the green grass, and the bird twitters, one may often fancy that it is a spring-day ; thus certainly also has the old man moments in his autumn in which his heart dreams of spring.

I passed only one day in Odense. I feel myself there more of a stranger than in the great cities of Germany. As a child I was solitary, and had therefore no youthful friend ; most of the families whom I knew, have died out ; a new generation passes along the streets ; and the streets even are altered. Later burials have concealed the miserable graves of my parents. Everything is changed. I took one of my childhood's rambles to the Marian-heights, which had belonged to the Iversen family ; but this family is dispersed ; unknown faces looked out from the windows. How many youthful thoughts have been here exchanged !

One of the young girls, Henriette Hanck, who at that time sat quietly there with beaming eyes and listened to my first poem when I came here in the summer time as a scholar from Slagelse, sits now far quieter in noisy Copenhagen, and has thence sent out her first writings into the world; the romances, "Aunt Anna" and "An Author's Daughter," both were published in Germany. Her German publisher thought that some introductory words from me might be useful to them; and I, the stranger, but perhaps the too hospitably entertained, have introduced the works of this clever girl into Germany. I visited her childhood home; was by the Odense Canal when the first little circle paid me homage and gave me joy. But all was strange there, I myself a stranger; neither was I to see her more, for when, the year after, I came home from my travels, I received the news of her death, in July, 1846. She was an affectionate daughter to her parents, and was, besides this, possessed of a deeply poetical mind. In her I have lost a true friend from the years of childhood, one who had felt an interest and a sisterly regard for me, both in my good and my evil days.

The ducal family of Augustenburg was now at Castle Gravenstern they were informed of my arrival, and all the favor and the kindness which were shown to me on the former occasion at Augustenburg, were here renewed in rich abundance. I remained here fourteen days, and it was as if these were an announcement of all the happiness which should meet me when I arrived in Germany. The country around here is of the most picturesque description; vast woods, cultivated uplands in perpetual variety, with the winding shore of the bay and the many quiet inland lakes. Even the floating mists of autumn lent to the landscape a picturesqueness, a something strange to the islander. Everything here is on a larger scale than on the island. Beautiful was it without, glorious was it within. I wrote here a new little story, — "The Girl with the Matches;" the only thing which I wrote upon this journey. Receiving the invitation to come often to Gravensteen and Augustenburg, I left, with a grateful heart, a place where I had spent such beautiful and such happy days.

Now no longer the traveller goes at a snail's pace through the deep sand over the heath; the railroad conveys him in a few hours to Altona and Hamburg. The circle of my friends there is increased within the last years. The greater part of my time I spent with my oldest friends, Count Holk, and the resident Minister Bille, and with Zeise, the excellent translator of my stories.   Otto Speckter, who is full of genius, surprised me by his bold, glorious drawings for my stories ; he had made a whole collection of them, six only of which were known to me.   The same natural freshness which shows itself in every one of his works, and makes them all little works of art, exhibits itself in his whole character.   He appears to possess a patriarchal family, an affectionate old father, and gifted sisters, who love him with their whole souls. I wished one evening to go to the theatre : it was scarcely a quarter of an hour before the commencement of the opera : Speckter accompanied me, and on our way we came up to an elegant house.

" We must first go in here, dear friend," said he ; " a wealthy family lives here, friends of mine, and friends of your stories ; the children will be happy."

" But the opera," said I.

" Only for two minutes," returned he ; and drew me into the house, mentioned my name, and the circle of children collected around me.

" And now tell us a tale," said he ; " only one."

I told one, and then hastened away to the theatre.

" That was an extraordinary visit," said I.

" An excellent one ; one entirely out of the common way ! " said he exultingly.   " Only think : the children are full of Andersen and his stories ; he suddenly makes his appearance amongst them, tells one of them himself, and then is gone ! vanished !   That is of itself like a fairy tale to the children, that will remain vividly in their remembrance."

I myself was amused by it.

In Oldenburg my own little room, home-like and comfortable, was awaiting me.   Hofrath von Eisendecher and his well-informed lady, whom, among all my foreign friends, I may consider as my most sympathizing, expected me.   I had promised to remain with them a fortnight, but I stayed much longer.   A house where the best and the most intellectual people of a city meet, is an agreeable place of residence, and such a one had I here.   A deal of social intercourse prevailed in the little city; and the theatre, in which certainly either opera or ballet was given, is one of the most excellent in Germany. The ability of Gall, the director, is sufficiently known, and unquestionably the nomination of the poet Mosen has a great and good influence. I have to thank him for enabling me to see one of the classic pieces of Germany, "Nathan the Wise," the principal part in which was played by Kaiser, who is as remarkable for his deeply studied and excellent tragic acting as for his readings.

Mosen, who somewhat resembles Alexandre Dumas, with his half African countenance and brown, sparkling eyes, although he was suffering in body, was full of life and soul, and we soon understood one another. A trait of his little son affected me. He had listened to me with great devotion, as I read one of my stories; and when, on the last day I was there, I took leave, the mother said that he must give me his hand, adding that probably a long time must pass before he would see me again, the boy burst into tears. In the evening, when Mosen came into the theatre, he said to me, "My little Erick has two tin soldiers ; one of them he has given me for you, that you may take him with you on your journey."

The tin soldier has faithfully accompanied me; he is a Turk : probably some day he may relate his travels.

Mosen wrote in the dedication of his "John of Austria," the following lines to me : —

"Once a little bird flew over
    From the North Sea's dreary strand ;
Singing, flew unto me over,
    Singing Märchen through the land.
Farewell ! yet again bring hither
Thy warm heart and song together."

Here I again met with Mayer, who has described Naples and the Neapolitans so charmingly. My little stories interested him so much that he had written a little treatise on them for Germany. Kapellmeister Pott and my countryman Jerndorff belong to my earlier friends. I made every day new acquaintance, because all houses were open to me through the family with whom I was staying. Even the Grand Duke was so generous as to have me invited to a concert at the palace the day after my arrival, and later I had the honor of being asked to dinner. I received in this foreign court, especially, many unlooked-for favors. At the Eisendeckers and at the house of the parents of my friend Beaulieu, — the Privy-Councilor Beaulieu, at Oldenburg, — I heard several times my little stories read in German.

I can read Danish very well, as it ought to be read, and I can give to it perfectly the expression which ought to be given in reading: there is in the Danish language a power which cannot be transfused into a translation ; the Danish language is peculiarly excellent for this species of fiction. The stories have a something strange to me in German ; it is difficult for me in reading it to put my Danish soul into it ; my pronunci-ation of the German also is feeble, and with particular words I must, as it were, use an effort to bring them out ; and yet people everywhere in Germany have had great interest in hearing me read them aloud. I can very well believe that the foreign pronunciation in the reading of these tales may be easily permitted, because this foreign manner approaches, in this instance, to the child-like ; it gives a natural coloring to the reading. I saw everywhere that the most distinguished men and women of the most highly cultivated minds listened to me with interest; people entreated me to read, and I did so willingly. I read for the first time my stories in a foreign tongue, and at a foreign court, before the Grand Duke of Oldenburg and a little select circle.

The winter soon came on ; the meadows, which lay under water, and which formed large lakes around the city, were already covered with thick ice ; the skaters flew over it, and I yet remained in Oldenburg among my hospitable friends. Days and evenings slid rapidly away ; Christmas approached, and this season I wished to spend in Berlin. But what are distances in our days ? — the steam-carriage goes from Han-over to Berlin in one day! I must away from the beloved ones, from children and old people, who were near, as it were, to my heart.

I was astonished in the highest degree, on taking leave of the Grand Duke, to receive from him, as a mark of his favor and as a keepsake, a valuable ring. I shall always preserve it, like every other remembrance of this country, where I have found and where I possess true friends.

When I was in Berlin on the former occasion, I was invited, as the author of "The Improvisatore," to the Italian Society, into which only those who have visited Italy can be admitted. Here I saw Rauch for the first time, who, with his white hair and his powerful, manly figure, is not unlike Thorwaldsen. Nobody introduced me to him, and I did not venture to present myself, and therefore walked alone about his studio, like the other strangers. Afterward I became personally acquainted with him at the house of the Prussian Ambassador in Copenhagen. I now hastened to him.

He was in the highest degree captivated by my little stories, pressed me to his breast, and expressed the highest praise, which was honestly meant. Such a momentary estimation or over-estimation from a man of genius erases many a dark shadow from the mind. I received from Rauch my first welcome in Berlin : he told me what a large circle of friends I had in the capital of Prussia. I must acknowledge that it was so. They were of the noblest in mind as well as the first in rank, in art, and in science — Alexander von Humboldt, Prince Radziwil, Savigny, and many others never to be forgotten.

I had already, on the former occasion, visited the brothers Grimm, but I had not at that time made much progress with the acquaintance. I had not brought any letters of introduction to them with me, because people had told me, and I myself believed it, that if I were known by anybody in Berlin, it must be the brothers Grimm. I therefore sought out their residence. The servant-maid asked me with which of the brothers I wished to speak.

"With the one who has written the most," said I, because I did not know, at that time, which of them had most interested himself in the "Märchen."

"Jacob is the most learned," said the maid-servant.

"Well, then, take me to him."

I entered the room, and Jacob Grimm, with his knowing and strongly marked countenance, stood before me.

"I come to you," said I, "without letters of introduction,

because I hope that my name is not wholly unknown to you."

" Who are you ? " asked he.

I told him ; and Jacob Grimm said, in a half-embarrassed voice, " I do not remember to have heard this name : what have you written ? "

It was now my turn to be embarrassed in a high degree ; but I now mentioned my little stories.

" I do not know them, " said he ; " but mention to me some other of your writings, because I certainly must have heard them spoken of."

I named the titles of several ; but he shook his head. I felt myself quite unlucky.

" But what must you think of me," said I, " that I come to you as a total stranger, and enumerate myself what I have written : You must know me ! There has been published in Denmark a collection of the " Märchen " of all nations, which is dedicated to you, and in it there is at least one story of mine."

" No," said he good-humoredly, but as much embarrassed as myself ; " I have not read even that, but it delights me to make your acquaintance. Allow me to conduct you to my brother Wilhelm ? "

" No, I thank you," said I, only wishing now to get away ; I had fared badly enough with one brother. I pressed his hand, and hurried from the house.

That same month Jacob Grimm went to Copenhagen ; immediately on his arrival, and while yet in his travelling dress, did the amiable, kind man hasten up to me. He now knew me, and he came to me with cordiality. I was just then standing and packing my clothes in a trunk for a journey to the country ; I had only a few minutes' time : by this means my reception of him was just as laconic as had been his of me in Berlin.

Now, however, we met in Berlin as old acquaintance. Jacob Grimm is one of those characters whom one must love and attach one's self to.

One evening, as I was reading one of my little stories at the Countess Bismark-Bohlen's, there was in the little circle one person in particular who listened with evident fellowship of feeling, and who expressed himself in a peculiar and sensible manner on the subject. This was Jacob's brother, Wilhelm Grimm.

"I should have known you very well, if you had come to me," said he, "the last time you were here."

I saw these two highly gifted and amiable brothers almost daily. The circles into which I was invited, seemed also to be theirs ; and it was my desire and pleasure that they should listen to my little stories, that they should participate in them, — they whose names will be always spoken as long as the German "Volks Märchen" are read.

The fact of my not being known to Jacob Grimm on my first visit to Berlin had so disconcerted me, that when any one asked me whether I had been well received in this city, I shook my head doubtfully and said, "But Grimm did not know me."

I was told that Tieck was ill — could see no one ; I therefore only sent in my card. Some days afterward I met at a friend's house, where Rauch's birthday was being celebrated, Tieck, the sculptor, who told me that his brother had lately waited two hours for me at dinner. I went to him, and discovered that he had sent me an invitation, which, however, had been taken to a wrong inn. A fresh invitation was given, and I passed some delightfully cheerful hours with Raumer, the historian, and with the widow and daughter of Steffens. There is a music in Tieck's voice, a spirituality in his intelligent eyes, which age cannot lessen, but, on the contrary, must increase. "The Elves," perhaps the most beautiful story which has been conceived in our time, would alone be sufficient, had Tieck written nothing else, to make his name immortal. As the author of "Märchen," I bow myself before him, the elder and the master, and who was the first German poet who many years before pressed me to his breast, as if it were to consecrate me to walk in the same path with himself.

The old friends had all to be visited ; but the number of new ones grew with each day. One invitation followed another. It required considerable physical power to support so much good-will. I remained in Berlin about three weeks, and

the time seemed to pass more rapidly with each succeeding
day. I was, as it were, overcome by kindness. I, at length,
had no other prospect for repose than to seat myself in a railway carriage, and fly away out of the country.

And yet amid these social festivities, with all the amiable
zeal and interest that then was felt for me, I had one disengaged evening, — one evening on which I suddenly felt solitude
in its most oppressive form, — Christmas Eve, that very evening
of all others on which I would most willingly witness something festal, willingly stand beside a Christmas-tree, gladden-
ing myself with the joy of children, and seeing the parents
joyfully become children again. Every one of the many families in which I in truth felt that I was received as a relation,
had fancied, as I afterward discovered, that I must be invited
out ; but I sat quite alone in my room at the inn, and thought
on home. I seated myself at the open window, and gazed up
to the starry heavens, which was the Christmas-tree that was
lighted for me.

"Father in heaven !" I prayed, as the children do, "what
dost Thou give to me ? "

When the friends heard of my solitary Christmas night,
there were on the following evening many Christmas-trees
lighted ; and on the last evening in the year there was planted
for me alone a little tree with its lights and its beautiful presents — and that was by Jenny Lind. The whole company
consisted of herself, her attendant, and me ; we three children
from the North were together on Sylvester Eve, and I was the
child for whom the Christmas-tree was lighted. She rejoiced
with the feeling of a sister in my good fortune in Berlin ; and
I felt almost pride in the sympathy of such a pure, noble, and
womanly being. Everywhere her praise resounded, not merely
as a singer, but also as a woman ; the two combined awoke a
real enthusiasm for her.

It does one good, both in mind and heart, to see that which
is glorious understood and beloved. In one little anecdote
contributing to her triumph I was myself made the confidant.

One morning as I looked out of my window "*Unter den
Linden*," I saw a man under one of the trees, half hidden, and
shabbily dressed, who took a comb out of his pocket, smoothed

his hair, set his neckerchief straight, and brushed his coat with his hand ; I understood that bashful poverty which feels depressed by its shabby dress. A moment after this, there was a knock at my door, and this same man entered. It was W ——, the poet of nature, who is only a poor tailor, but who has a truly poetical mind. Rellstab and others in Berlin have mentioned him with honor ; there is something healthy in his poems, among which several of a sincerely religious character may be found. He had heard that I was in Berlin, and wished now to visit me. We sat together on the sofa and conversed : there was such an amiable contentedness, such an unspoiled and good tone of mind, about him, that I was sorry not to be rich in order that I might do something for him. I was ashamed of offering him the little that I could give ; in any case I wished to put it in as agreeable a form as I could. I asked him whether I might invite him to hear Jenny Lind.

"I have already heard her," said he smiling ; "I had, it is true, no money to buy a ticket ; but I went to the leader of the supernumeraries, and asked whether I might not act as a supernumerary for one evening in 'Norma.' I was accepted, and habited as a Roman soldier, with a long sword by my side, and thus got to the theatre, where I could hear her better than anybody else, for I stood close to her. Ah, how she sung, how she played ! I could not help crying ; but they were angry at that : the leader forbade, and would not let me again make my appearance, because no one must weep on the stage."

Jenny Lind introduced me to Madame Birch-Pfeiffer. "She taught me German," said she ; "she is as good as a mother to me ! You must make her acquaintance !" I was very glad to do so. We went through the street in a drosky. The world-renowned Jenny Lind in a drosky ! somebody will perhaps say, as it was said in Copenhagen, when she was seen once riding in such a carriage with an older lady friend : "It is not respectable for Jenny Lind to ride in a drosky ; things must be in keeping !" What strange notions some people have of what is proper ! Thorwaldsen once said at Nysöe, when I was going to the city by the omnibus, "I'll go with you !" and the people exclaimed : "Thorwaldsen in an omni-

bus! that is not seemly!" — "But Andersen is also going with
me!" said he, innocently. "That is quite another thing," said
I to him. Thorwaldsen in an omnibus would be scandalous,
and so it was with Jenny Lind in a drosky. She rode, however, in Berlin within such a one, which we engaged in the
street, and so we reached Madame Birch-Pfeiffer.

I had heard of the ability of this artist as an actress; I knew
her talent *à la* Scribe for presenting in dramatic form what has
had a home in romance, and I knew with what harshness
criticism had almost always treated the highly gifted lady.
At first sight it seemed to me as if this had given her a little
smile of bitterness; I perceived it in her salutation: "I have
not yet read your books, but I know that you are criticised
very favorably: that I cannot say of myself!"

"He is like a good brother to me!" said Jenny Lind, and
laid my hand in hers. Madame Birch-Pfeiffer bid me a kind
welcome; she was all life and humor. The next time I called
on her she was reading my "Improvisatore," and I felt that I
had one more friend among women.

With the exception of the theatre, I had very little time to
visit collections of any kind or institutions of art. The able
and amiable Olfers, however, the Director of the Museum,
enabled me to pay a rapid but extremely interesting visit to
that institution. Olfers himself was my conductor; we delayed
our steps only for the most interesting objects, and there are
here not a few of these; his remarks threw light into my mind,
— for this therefore I am infinitely obliged to him.

I had the happiness of visiting the Princess of Prussia
many times; the wing of the castle in which she resided was
so comfortable, and yet like a fairy palace. The blooming
winter-garden, where the fountain splashed among the moss at
the foot of the statue, was close beside the room in which the
kind-hearted children smiled with their soft blue eyes. One
forenoon I read to her several of my little stories, and her
noble husband listened kindly; Prince Pückler-Muskau also
was present. On taking leave she honored me with a richly
bound album, in which, beneath the picture of the palace, she
wrote her name. I shall guard this volume as a treasure of
the soul; it is not the gift which has a value only, but also the
manner in which it is given.

A few days after my arrival in Berlin, I had the honor to be invited to the royal table. As I was better acquainted with Humboldt than any one there, and as it was he who had particularly interested himself about me, I took my place at his side. Not only on account of his high intellectual character, and his amiable and polite behavior, but also from his infinite kindness toward me, during the whole of my residence in Berlin, is he become unchangeably dear to me.

The King received me most graciously, and said that during his stay in Copenhagen he had inquired after me, and had heard that I was travelling. He expressed a great interest in my novel of "Only a Fiddler;" her Majesty the Queen also showed herself graciously and kindly disposed toward me. I had afterward the happiness of being invited to spend an evening at the palace at Potsdam; an evening which is full of rich remembrance and never to be forgotten! Besides the ladies and gentlemen in waiting, Humboldt and myself were only invited. A seat was assigned to me at the table of their Majesties, exactly the place, said the Queen, where Oehlenschläger had sat and read his tragedy of "Dina." I read four little stories, "The Fir-Tree," "The Ugly Duckling," "The Top and the Ball," and "The Swineherd." The King listened with great interest, and expressed himself most wittily on the subject. He said how beautiful he thought the natural scenery of Denmark, and how excellently he had seen one of Holberg's comedies performed.

It was deliciously pleasant in the royal apartment, — gentle eyes were gazing at me, and I felt that they all wished me well. When at night I was alone in my chamber, my thoughts were so occupied with this evening, and my mind in such a state of excitement, that I could not sleep. Everything seemed to me like a fairy tale. Through the whole night the chimes sounded in the tower, and the aerial music mingled itself with my thoughts.

I received still one proof more of the favor and kindness of the King of Prussia toward me, on the evening before my departure from the city. The order of the Red Eagle, of the third class was conferred upon me. Such a mark of honor delights certainly every one who receives it. I confess can didly that I felt myself honored in a high degree. I discerned in it an evident token of the kindness of the noble, enlightened King toward me: my heart was filled with gratitude. I received this mark of honor exactly on the birthday of my benefactor Collin, the 6th of January; this day has now a twofold festal significance for me. May God fill with gladness the mind of the royal donor who wished to give me pleasure!

The last evening was spent in a warm-hearted circle, for the greater part, of young people. My health was drunk; a poem, " Der Märchenkönig," declaimed. It was not until late in the night that I reached home, that I might set off early in the morning by railroad. In Weimar I was again to meet Jenny Lind.

I have here given in part a proof of the favor and kindness which was shown to me in Berlin: I feel like some one who has received a considerable sum for a certain object from a large assembly, and now would give an account thereof. I might still add many other names, as well from the learned world, as Theodor Mügge, Geibel, Häring, etc., as from the social circle; the reckoning is too large. God give me strength for that which I now have to perform, after I have, as an earnest of good-will, received such a richly abundant sum.

After a journey of a day and night I was once more in Weimar, with the noble hereditary Grand Duke. What a cordial reception! A heart rich in goodness, and a mind full of noble endeavors, live in this young prince. I have no words for the infinite favor which, during my residence here, I received daily from the family of the Grand Duke, but my whole heart is full of devotion. At the court festival, as well as in the familiar family circle, I had many evidences of the esteem in which I was held. Beaulieu cared for me with the tenderness of a brother. It was to me a month long Sabbath festival. Never shall I forget the quiet evenings spent with him, when friend spoke freely to friend.

My old friends were also unchanged; the wise and able Schöll, as well as Schober, joined them also. The intellectual, venerable Madame von Schwindler, an intimate friend of Jean Paul in his younger days, received me with sympathy and maternal kindness ; she told me that I put her in mind of that great poet ! She told me much of him that I had not heard before.

Jean Paul or Frederick Richter, which was his true name, was so poor when he was young that in order to get money to buy paper to write his first work, he was obliged to write copies of " The Village Gazette " for the peasants in the village where he lived. She told me that the poet Gleim was the first who noticed him, and wrote to her about the gifted young man, whom he had invited to his house, and to whom he had sent five hundred thalers. Madame von Schwindler had lived here at Weimar in the days of its glory ; she had been a visitor at the court in the evening along with Wieland, Herder, and Musæus ; of them and of Goethe and Schiller she had much to relate. She presented me with one of Jean Paul's letters to her.

Jenny Lind came to Weimar ; I heard her at the court concerts and at the theatre ; I visited with her the places which are become sacred through Goethe and Schiller : we stood together beside their coffins, where Chancellor von Müller led us. The Austrian poet, Rollet, who met us here for the first time, wrote on this subject a sweet poem, which will serve me as a visible remembrance of this hour and this place. People lay lovely flowers in their books, and as such, I lay in here this verse of his : —

" WEIMAR, 29*th January,* 1846.

" Märchen rose, which hast so often
    Charmed me with thy fragrant breath ;
  Where the prince, the poets slumber,
    Thou hast wreathed the hall of death.

" And with thee beside each coffin,
    In the death-hushed chamber pale,
  I beheld a grief-enchanted,
    Sweetly dreaming nightingale.

" I rejoiced amid the stillness ;
    Gladness through my bosom past,
  That the gloomy poets' coffins
    Such a magic crowned at last.

"And thy rose's summer fragrance
    Floated round that chamber pale,
  With the gentle melancholy
    Of the grief-hushed nightingale."

It was in the evening circle of the intellectual Froriep that I met, for the first time, with Auerbach, who then chanced to be staying in Weimar. His "Village Tales" interested me in the highest degree; I regard them as the most poetical, most healthy, and joyous production of the young German literature. He himself made the same agreeable impression upon me; there is something so frank and straightforward, and yet so sagacious, in his whole appearance, I might almost say that he looks himself like a village tale, healthy to the core, body and soul, and his eyes beaming with honesty. We soon became friends — and I hope forever.

My stay in Weimar was prolonged; it became ever more difficult to tear myself away. The Grand Duke's birthday occurred at this time, and after attending all the festivities to which I was invited, I departed. I would and must be in Rome at Easter. Once more in the early morning, I saw the hereditary Grand Duke, and, with a heart full of emotion, bade him farewell. Never, in presence of the world, will I forget the high position which his birth gives him, but I may say, as the very poorest subject may say of a prince, I love him as one who is dearest to my heart. God give him joy and bless him in his noble endeavors! A generous heart beats beneath the princely star.

Beaulieu accompanied me to Jena. Here a hospitable home awaited me, filled with beautiful memories from the time of Goethe, — the house of the publisher Frommann. His kind, warm-hearted sister had shown me much sympathy in Berlin; the brother was not here less kind.

The Holsteiner Michelsen, who has a professorship at Jena, assembled a number of friends one evening, and in a graceful and cordial toast in my honor, expressed his sense of the importance of Danish literature, and the healthy and natural spirit which flourished in it.

In Michelsen's house I also became acquainted with Professor Hase, who, one evening having heard some of my little stories, seemed filled with great kindness toward me. What he wrote in this moment of interest on an album leaf expresses this sentiment : —

"Schelling — not he who now lives in Berlin, but he who lives an immortal hero in the world of mind — once said : 'Nature is the visible spirit.' This spirit, this unseen nature, last evening was again rendered visible to me through your little tales. If on the one hand you penetrate deeply into the mysteries of nature ; know and understand the language of birds, and what are the feelings of a fir-tree or a daisy, so that each seems to be there on its own account, and we and our children sympathize with them in their joys and sorrows ; yet, on the other hand, all is but the image of mind ; and the human heart, in its infinity, trembles and throbs throughout. May this fountain in the poet's heart, which God has lent you, still for a time pour forth this refreshingly, and may these stories in the memories of the Germanic nations become the legends of the people!" That object, for which as a writer of poetical fictions, I must strive after, is contained in these last lines.

It is also to Hase and the gifted improvisatore, Professor Wolff of Jena, to whom I am most indebted for the appearance of a uniform German edition of my writings.

This was all arranged on my arrival at Leipsic: several hours of business were added to my traveller's mode of life. The city of book-selling presented me with her bouquet, a sum of money ; but she presented me with even more. I met again with Brockhaus, and passed happy hours with Mendelssohn, that glorious man of genius. I heard him play again and again ; it seemed to me that his eyes, full of soul. looked into the very depths of my being. Few men have more the stamp of the inward fire than he. A gentle, friendly wife, and beautiful children, make his rich, well-appointed house, blessed and pleasant. When he rallied me about the stork, and its frequent appearance in my writings, there was something so childlike and amiable revealed in this great artist!

I also met again my excellent countryman Gade, whose com-positions have been so well received in Germany. I brought him the text for a new opera which I had written, and which

I hope to see brought out on the German stage. Gade had written the music to my drama of " Agnete and the Merman," compositions which were very successful. Auerbach, whom I again found here, introduced me to many agreeable circles. I met with the composer Kalliwoda, and with Kühne, whose charming little son immediately won my heart.

On my arrival at Dresden I instantly hastened to my motherly friend, the Baroness von Decken. That was a joyous, hearty welcome ! One equally cordial I met with from Dahl. I saw once more my Roman friend, the poet with word and color, Reineck, and met the kind-hearted Bendemann. Professor Grahl painted me. I missed, however, one among my olden friends, the poet Brunnow. With life and cordiality he received me the last time in his room, where stood lovely flowers ; now these grew over his grave. It awakens a peculiar feeling, thus for once to meet on the journey of life, to understand and love each other, and then to part — until the journey for both is ended.

I spent, to me a highly interesting evening, with the royal family, who received me with extraordinary favor. Here also the most happy domestic life appeared to reign — a number of amiable children, all belonging to Prince Johann, were present. The least of the Princesses, a little girl, who knew that I had written the history of the " Fir-tree," began very confidentially with, — " Last Christmas we also had a Fir-tree, and it stood here in this room ! " Afterward, when she was led out before the other children, and had bade her parents and the King and Queen good-night, she turned round at the half closed door, and nodding to me in a friendly and familiar manner, said I was her Fairy-tale Prince.

My story of " Holger Danske " led the conversation to the rich stores of legends which the North possesses. I related several, and explained the peculiar spirit of the fine scenery of Denmark. Neither in this royal palace did I feel the weight of ceremony ; soft, gentle eyes shone upon me. My last morning in Dresden was spent with the Minister von Könneritz, where I equally met with the most friendly reception.

The sun shone warm : it was Spring who was celebrating her arrival, as I rolled out of the dear city. Thought as-

sembled in one company all the many who had rendered my
visits so rich and happy : it was spring around me, and spring
in my heart.

In Prague I had no acquaintance. But a letter from Dr.
Carus in Dresden opened to me the hospitable house of Count
Thun. The Archduke Stephan received me also in the most
gracious manner ; I found in him a young man full of intellect
and heart. I visited Hradschin and Wallenstein's palace, but
these splendid places had all been supplanted by — the Jews'
quarter ! It was horrid ; it swarmed with women, old men,
and children, laughing, crying, chaffering, and at every step
the street became narrower ; the ancient synagogue, in imitation
of the Temple of Jerusalem, is placed as if squeezed between
the houses. In the lapse of time a layer of earth had gathered
on its wall. I was obliged to step down before I could enter,
and here were ceiling, windows, and walls all begrimed with
smoke ; an odious smell of onion and other bad vapors
reached me, so that I was compelled to go out into the open
place, the burying-ground. Tombstones with Hebrew inscriptions were standing and lying in confusion under a grove
of elder-trees, — stunted, unhealthy looking, almost sapless.
Cobwebs were hanging like rays of mourning-crape among
the dead, black graves. Besides it was a very interesting
point of time when I left Prague. The military, who had been
stationed there a number of years, were hastening to the railway, to leave for Poland, where disturbances had broken out.
The whole city seemed in movement to take leave of its
military friends ; it was difficult to get through the streets
which led to the railway. Many thousand soldiers were to be
accommodated ; at length the train was set in motion. All
around the whole hill-side was covered with people ; it looked
like the richest Turkey carpet woven of men, women, and
children, all pressed together, head to head, and waving hats
and handkerchiefs. Such a mass of human beings I never
saw before, or at least, never at one moment surveyed them :
such a spectacle could not be painted.

We travelled the whole night through wide Bohemia : at
every town stood groups of people ; it was as though all the
inhabitants had assembled themselves. Their brown faces,

their ragged clothes, the light of their torches, their, to me, unintelligible language, gave to the whole a stamp of singularity. We flew through tunnel and over viaduct; the windows rattled, the signal whistle sounded, the steam horses snorted; I laid back my head at last in the carriage, and fell asleep under the protection of the god Morpheus.

At Olmütz, where we had fresh carriages, a voice spoke my name — it was Walter Goethe! We had travelled together the whole night without knowing it. In Vienna we met often. Noble powers, true genuis, live in Goethe's grandsons, in the composer as well as in the poet; but it is as if the greatness of their grandfather pressed upon them. Liszt was in Vienna, and invited me to his concert, in which otherwise it would have been impossible to find a place. I again heard his improvising of *Robert*. I again heard him, like a spirit of the storm, play with the chords : he is an enchanter of sounds who fills the imagination with astonishment. Ernst also was here ; when I visited him he seized the violin, and this sang in tears the secret of a human heart.

I saw the amiable Grillparzer again, and was frequently with the kindly Castelli, who just at this time had been made by the King of Denmark Knight of the Dannebrog Order. He was full of joy at this, and begged me to tell my countrymen that every Dane should receive a hearty welcome from him. Some future summer he invited me to visit his grand country-seat. There is something in Castelli so open and honorable, mingled with such good-natured humor, that one must like him : he appears to me the picture of a thorough Viennese. Under his portrait, which he gave me, he wrote the following little improvised verse in the style so peculiarly his own : —

> "This portrait shall ever with loving eyes greet thee,
>   From far shall recall the smile of thy friend ;
> For thou, dearest Dane, 'tis a pleasure to meet thee,
>   Thou art one to be loved and esteemed to the end."

Castelli introduced me to Seidl and Bauernfeld. At the Danish ambassador's, Baron von Löwenstern, I met Zedlitz. Most of the shining stars of Austrian literature I saw glide past me, as people on a railway see church towers ; you can

still say you have seen them ; and still retaining the simile of
the stars, I can say, that in the Concordia Society I saw the
entire galaxy. Here was a host of young, growing intellects,
and here were men of importance. At the house of Count
Szechenyi, who hospitably invited me, I saw his brother from
Pesth, whose noble activity in Hungary is known. This short
meeting I account one of the most interesting events of my
stay in Vienna ; the man revealed himself in all his individuality, and his eye said that you must feel confidence in him.

At my departure from Dresden her Majesty the Queen of
Saxony had asked me whether I had introductions to any one
at the court of Vienna, and when I told her that I had not,
the Queen was so gracious as to write a letter to her sister,
the Archduchess Sophia of Austria. Her imperial Highness
summoned me one evening, and received me in the most
gracious manner. The dowager Empress, the widow of the
Emperor Francis I., was present, and full of kindness and
friendship toward me ; also Prince Wasa, and the hereditary
Archduchess of Hesse-Darmstadt. The remembrance of this
evening will always remain dear and interesting to me. I
read several of my little stories aloud. When I wrote them,
I little thought that I should some day read them aloud in the
imperial palace.

Before my departure I had still another visit to make, and
this was to the intellectual authoress, Frau von Weissenthurn.
She had just left a bed of sickness and was still suffering,
but wished to see me. As though she were already standing
on the threshold of the realm of shades, she pressed my hand
and said this was the last time we should ever see each other.
With a soft motherly gaze she looked at me, and at parting
her penetrating eye followed me to the door.

With railway and diligence my route now led toward Trieste. With steam the long train of carriages flies along the
narrow rocky way, following all the windings of the river.
One wonders that with all these abrupt turnings one is not
dashed against the rock, or flung down into the roaring
stream, and is glad when the journey is happily accomplished.
But in the slow diligence one wishes its more rapid journey
might recommence, and praise the powers of the age.

At length Trieste and the Adriatic Sea lay before us ; the Italian language sounded in our ears, but yet for me it was not Italy, the land of my desire. Meanwhile I was only a stranger here for a few hours ; our Danish Consul, as well as the consuls of Prussia and Oldenburg, to whom I was recommended, received me in the best possible manner. Several interesting acquaintances were made, especially with the Counts O'Donnell and Waldstein, the latter for me as a Dane having a peculiar interest, as being the descendant of that unfortunate Corfitz Ulfeldt and the daughter of Christian IV., Eleanore, the noblest of all Danish women. Their portraits hung in his room, and Danish memorials of that period were shown me. It was the first time I had ever seen Eleanore Ulfeldt's portrait, and the melancholy smile on her lips seemed to say, " Sing, poet, and free him for whom it was my happiness to live and suffer, from the chains which a hard age has him cast upon ! " Before Oehlenschläger thought of writing his " Dina," which treats of an episode in Ulfeldt's life, I was at work on this subject, and had collected considerable historical material : I wished to bring it on the stage, but it was then feared this would not be allowed ; that the time lay too near ours, and that King Frederick VI. would not give permission to have any of his ancestors, later than Christian IV., brought on the stage. Count Rantzau-Breitenburg assured me that it was so. Christian VIII. who was then prince, encouraged me, however, to elaborate that poetical work, " it could at any rate be read ! " he said, but I gave it up.

When King Christian VIII. ascended the throne, all these reasons fell to the ground, and one day Oehlenschläger said to me : " Now I have written a ' Dina,' which you also once have thought of." His drama had a plan and character quite different from mine. One may understand thus how everything connected with Ulfeldt and his descendants interested me. Count Waldstein told me that there were still in his father's castle in Hungary or Bohemia, I do not remember exactly where, many letters and papers concerning Corfitz and Eleanore. Another descendant of Ulfeldt I made acquaintance with in Sweden, namely Count Beck-Friis ; the picture of Christian IV., the head of the family, hangs in the dining hall. Now they besought me to relate what I knew of that family and of all existing memories at Copenhagen, from " the blue tower" to the monument in Ulfeldt's Square. That monument has just been removed by order of the King.

On the Adriatic Sea I was carried in thought back to Ulfeldt's time and the Danish islands. This meeting with Count Waldstein and his ancestors' portrait brought me back to my poet's world, and I almost forgot that the following day I could be in the middle of Italy. In beautiful mild weather I went with the steamboat to Ancona.

It was a quiet starlight night, too beautiful to be spent in sleep. In the early morning the coast of Italy lay before us, the beautiful blue mountains with glittering snow. The sun shone warmly, the grass and the trees were splendidly green. Last evening in Trieste, now in Ancona, in a city of the Papal States, — it was almost like enchantment! Italy in all its picturesque splendor lay once more before me ; spring had ripened all the fruit trees so that they had burst forth into blossom ; every blade of grass in the field was filled with sunshine, the elm-trees stood like caryatides enwreathed with vines, which shot forth green leaves, and above the luxuriance of foliage rose the wavelike blue mountains with their snow covering. In company with Count Paar from Vienna, the most excellent travelling companion I have ever had, and a young nobleman from Hungary, I now travelled on with a vetturino for five days.

The Bohemians like all other travellers when they come to Italy for the first time, expect to be attacked by banditti, as I also in my earlier days feared, and carry weapons and pistols with them. "They are loaded with double shots!" said he. " But where are they ? " I asked, as I could not discover any. "I have them in my portmanteau!" And that was placed under my seat. As I did not like that, and could also assure them that the robbers would hardly wait until I got up, got the portmanteau opened, and the murderous weapons out, they were taken out and fastened over our heads in the carriage, and placed before us in all the inns on our way. We visited Loretto, saw the pious people kneeling in the holy house, which angels had carried through the air ; we passed through solitary, romantic countries among the Apennines. We did not meet with other robbers than some in chains on a cart escorted by soldiers. Solitary, and more picturesque than habitable inns among the Apennines were our night's quarters. At length the Campagna, with its thought-awakening desolation, lay before us.

It was the 31st of March, 1846, when I again saw Rome, and for the third time in my life I reached this city of the world. I felt so happy, so penetrated with thankfulness and joy; how much more God had given me than a thousand others — nay, than to many thousands! And even in this very feeling there is a blessing — where joy is very great, as in the deepest grief, there is only God on whom one can lean! The first impression was — I can find no other word for it — adoration. When day unrolled for me my beloved Rome, I felt what I cannot express more briefly or better than I did in a letter to a friend: " I am growing here into the very ruins ; I live with the petrified gods, and the roses are always blooming, and the church bells ringing — and yet Rome is not the Rome it was thirteen years ago when I first was here. It is as if everything were modernized, the ruins even, grass and bushes are cleared away. Everything is made so neat ; the very life of the people seems to have retired ; I no longer hear the tambourines in the streets, no longer see the young girls dancing their Saltarella: even in the Campagna intelligence has entered by invisible railroads ; the peasant no longer believes as he used to do. At the Easter festival I saw great numbers of the people from the Campagna standing before St. Peter's whilst the Pope distributed his blessing, just as though they had been Protestant strangers. This was repulsive to my feelings ; I felt an impulse to kneel before the invisible saint. When I was here thirteen years ago, all knelt ; now reason had conquered faith. Ten years later, when the railways will have brought cities still nearer to each other, Rome will be yet more changed. But in all that happens, everything is for the best ; one always must love Rome ; it is like a story book : one is always discovering new wonders, and one lives in imagination and reality."

The first time I travelled to Italy I had no eyes for sculpture ; in Paris the rich pictures drew me away from the statues ; for the first time when I came to Florence and stood before the "Venus de Medici," I felt, as Thorwaldsen expressed it, "the snow melt away from my eyes ;" and a new world of art rose before me. And now at my third sojourn in Rome, after repeated wanderings through the Vatican, I prize the statues far higher than the paintings. But at what other places as at Rome, and to some degree in Naples, does this art step forth so grandly into life ! One is carried away by it, one learns to admire nature in the work of art ; the beauty of form becomes spiritual.

Among the many clever and beautiful things which I saw exhibited in the studios of the young artists, two pieces of sculpture were what most deeply impressed themselves on my memory ; and these were in the studio of my countryman Jerichau. I saw his group of " Hercules and Hebe," which had been spoken of with such enthusiasm in the " Allgemeine Zeitung " and other German papers, and which, through its antique repose, and its glorious beauty, powerfully seized upon me. My imagination was filled by it, and yet I must place Jerichau's later group, the " Fighting Hunter," still higher. It is. formed after the model, as though it had sprung from nature. There lies in it a truth, a beauty, and a grandeur which I am convinced will make his name resound through many lands !

I have known him from the time when he was almost a boy. We were both of us born on the same island : he is from the little town of Assens. We met in Copenhagen. No one, not even he himself, knew what lay within him ; and half in jest, half in earnest, he spoke of the combat with himself whether he should go to America and become a savage, or to Rome and become an artist — painter or sculptor : that he did not yet know. His pencil was meanwhile thrown away : he modeled in clay, and my bust was the first which he made. He received no travelling stipendium from the Academy. As far as I know, it was a noble-minded woman, an artist herself, unprovided with means, who, from the interest she felt for the spark of genius she observed in him, assisted him so far that he reached Italy by means of a trading vessel. In the begin-

ning he worked in Thorwaldsen's atelier. During the labor
of several years, he has doubtless experienced the struggles
of genius and the galling fetters of want ; but now the star of
fortune shines upon him. When I came to Rome, I found
him physically suffering and melancholy. He was unable to
bear the warm summers of Italy ; and many people said he
could not recover unless he visited the North, breathed the
cooler air, and took sea-baths. His praises resounded through
the papers, glorious works stood in his atelier : but man does
not live on heavenly bread alone. There came one day a
Russian prince, I believe, and he gave a commission for the
"Hunter." Two other commissions followed on the same day.
Jerichau came full of rejoicing and told this to me. A few
days after he travelled with his wife, a highly gifted painter,
to Denmark, from whence, strengthened in body and soul, he
returned, with the winter, to Rome, where the strokes of his
chisel will resound, so that, I hope, the world will hear them.
My heart will beat joyfully with them !

I also met in Rome, Kolberg, another Danish sculptor,
until now only known in Denmark, but there very highly
thought of, a scholar of Thorwaldsen's and a favorite of that
great master. He honored me by making my bust. I also
sat once more with the kindly Küchler, and saw the forms
fresh as nature spread themselves over the canvas.

I sat once again with the Roman people in the amusing
puppet theatre, and heard the children's merriment. Among
the German artists, as well as among the Swedes and my own
countrymen, I met with a hearty reception. My birthday
was joyfully celebrated. Frau von Goethe, who was in Rome,
and who chanced to be living in the very house where I
brought my "Improvisatore" into the world, and made him
spend his first years of childhood, sent me from thence a
large, true Roman bouquet, a fragrant mosaic. The Swedish
painter, Södermark, proposed my health to the company
whom the Danes, Swedes, and Norwegians had invited me to
meet. From my friends I received some pretty pictures and
friendly keepsakes.

Constantly in motion, always striving to employ every moment and to see everything, I felt myself at last very much

affected by the unceasing sirocco. The Roman air did not agree with me, and I hastened, therefore, as soon as I had seen the illumination of the dome and the *girandola*, immediately after the Easter festival, through Terracina to Naples. Count Paar travelled with me. We entered St. Lucia : the sea lay before us ; Vesuvius blazed. Those were glorious evenings ! moonlight nights ! It was as if the heavens had elevated themselves above and the stars were withdrawn. What effect of light ! In the North the moon scatters silver over the water : here it was gold. The revolving lanterns of the light-house now exhibited their dazzling light, now were totally extinguished. The torches of the fishing-boats threw their obelisk-formed blaze along the surface of the water, or else the boat concealed them like a black shadow, below which the surface of the water was illuminated. One fancied one could see to the bottom, where fishes and plants were in motion. Along the street itself thousands of lights were burning in the shops of the dealers in fruit and fish. Now came a troop of children with lights, and went in procession to the Church of St. Lucia. Many fell down with their lights ; but above the whole stood, like the hero of this great drama of light, Vesuvius with his blood-red flame and his illumined cloud of smoke.

The heat of the sun became more and more oppressive, the sirocco blew dry and warm. As an inhabitant of the North, I thought that heat would do me good ; I did not know its power, and when the Neapolitans wisely kept themselves indoors or crept along in the shadows of the houses, I ran boldly about to Molo, to Musæo Bourbonico ; but one day, in the midst of Largo di Castello, it was as if my breathing would suddenly stop, as if the sun was sinking down into my eyes ; its rays went through my head and back, and I fainted away. When I recovered I found I had been carried into a coffee-house ; they had laid ice upon my head ; I was lame in all my limbs, and from that time I did not venture out in the day-time ; the least exertion affected me, and the only exercise I could bear was to take a drive in a carriage up to Camaldali, and to spend the evenings on the large, airy terraces at the sea-shore with the Prussian ambassador, the Baron Brockhausen.

I visited the islands of Capri and Ischia once more. My compatriot, the *danseuse* Miss Fjeldsted, visited the baths there, and had improved so much that in the evenings she danced the Saltarello with the young girls under the orange-trees, and had so enchanted the young folks that they gave her a serenade. Ischia has never had that charm for me that it has for many travellers ; the sun was too hot, and every one, advised me to go to Sorrento, Tasso's city, where the air appeared lighter.

In company with an English family whose acquaintance I had made at Rome, I hired a couple of rooms out of Sorrento in Camello, near the sea, which rolled its waves into the caverns beneath our little garden. The heat of the sun compelled me to stay in the whole day, and here I wrote "Das Märchen meines Lebens."[1] In Rome, by the bay of Naples, and amid the Pyrenees, I wrote and completed those sketches which were to serve as a commentary to my writings in the German edition. They were sent sheet by sheet in letters to Copenhagen, where one of my clever friends had free scope with the manuscript, and, after perusing it, sent it to my publisher at Leipsic, and not a sheet was lost on the way.

My stay in Camello was very agreeable, and the view from my windows and the loggia, unsurpassed. Vesuvius and the Mediterranean lay before me, but there was no other walk than the long, narrow way between the high walls, which surround and almost hide the stony gardens. One would have to be a lizard to endure that burning heat, where not a breath of air stirred, and I should have been obliged to get a pair of stilts before I could look over the walls. I moved, therefore, into the city of Sorrento, where the composers, the Swede Josephson and the Dutch Verhulst, both friends of mine, lived and kept their summer cottage. The very day I arrived here a great festival was celebrated : three young girls, daughters of a rich merchant, took the veil. The church was adorned in the most fantastical way, an orchestra performed music, and real opera buffo music too. We heard from " The Barber of Seville " the whole aria of Don Bazile about slander, and meanwhile the cannons were thundering outside. The

[1] The German brief, of which this book is a fuller narrative.

excess of variety destroyed the pious feeling I had brought with me! an old, queer officer, who with great difficulty tried to kneel down, did not help to make it more solemn for me ; only when the mass was read by one of the young girls, and her voice sounded tenderly and with a thrill in it, a more holy feeling again took possession of me.

At Josephson's there was, beside his personal amiableness, something else that drew us nearer together, namely, our common friendship for Jenny Lind. She had been his god-mother when he was converted from the Jewish to the Christian faith, and she had always since shown him true sympathy and friendship. When travelling abroad he had called upon her at Berlin, and had daily visited her in her home ; he was there called a " Swedish theological student," which they soon changed to a " village parson." The rumor ran that he was betrothed to the Swedish Nightingale ; everybody has read and heard that story ! We often had our laugh at the genius and inventive faculty which Rumor possesses.

The well-known festival of the Madonna dell' Arco called me again to Naples, where I took up my quarters at a hotel in the middle of the city, near Toledo Street, and found an excellent host and hostess. I had already resided here, but only in the winter. I had now to see Naples in its summer heat and with all its wild tumult, but in what degree I had never imagined. The sun shone down with its burning heat into the narrow streets, in at the balcony door. It was necessary to shut up every place : not a breath of air stirred. Every little corner, every spot in the street on which a shadow fell, was crowded with working handicraftsmen, who chattered loudly and merrily ; the carriages rolled past ; the drivers screamed ; the tumult of the people roared like a sea in the other streets ; the church bells sounded every minute ; my opposite neighbor, God knows who he was, played the musical scale from morning till evening. It was enough to make one lose one's senses !

The sirocco blew its boiling-hot breath and I was perfectly overcome. There was not another room to be had at St. Lucia, and the sea-bathing seemed rather to weaken than to invigorate me. I went therefore again into the country ; but the sun burned there with the same beams ; yet though the air there was more elastic, for all that it was to me like the poisoned mantle of Hercules, which, as it were, drew out of me strength and spirit. I, who had fancied that I must be a true child of the sun, so firmly did my heart always cling to the South, was forced to acknowledge that the snow of the North was in my body, that the snow melted, and that I was more and more miserable.

Most strangers felt as I myself did in this, as the Neapolitans themselves said, unusually hot summer ; the greater number went away. I also would have done the same, but I was obliged to wait several days for a letter of credit ; it was more than three weeks since it was due.

"There is no letter for you ! " always said the mighty Rothschild, to whom my letters were addressed ; and one day, tired of my continual asking, he gave a vigorous pull at the drawer where all the letters for foreigners were kept who had letters of credit upon the banker. " Here is no letter ! " but as he pushed the drawer back again a little angrily, a letter fell on the floor, which was sealed with wax and had become glued on the hind-part of the drawer. The letter was for me and contained a letter of credit ; more than a month had it lain here, and would have remained there longer had he not pulled out the drawer so violently ; now then I could get away ! Yet there was a deal for me to see in Naples ; many houses were open to me. I tried whether my will were not stronger than the Neapolitan heat, but I fell into such a nervous state in consequence, that till the time of my departure I was obliged to lie quietly in my hot room, where the night brought no coolness. From dawn to midnight roared the noise of bells, the cry of the people, the trampling of horses on the stone pavement, and the before-mentioned practicer of the scale — it was like being on the rack ; and this caused me to give up my journey to Spain, especially as I was assured, for my consolation, that I should find it just as warm there as here. The physician said that, at this season of the year, I could not sustain the journey.

I took a berth in the steamboat *Castor* for Marseilles ; the vessel was full to overflowing with passengers ; the whole quarter-deck, even the best place, was occupied by travelling carriages ; under one of these I had my bed laid ; many people followed my example, and the quarter-deck was soon covered with mattresses and carpets. One of the first of the English nobility, the Marquis of Douglas, married to the Princess of Baden, was on board with his wife. We conversed together ; he learned that I was a Dane but did not know my name. We talked of Italy and of what had been written about that country ; I named " Corinna," by Madame de Staël-Holstein ; he interrupted me by saying : —

" You have a countryman who has still better described Italy for us ! "

" The Danes do not think so ! " I answered.

He spoke in high praise of " The Improvisatore " and its author. " It is a pity," said I, " that Andersen had been there so short a time when he wrote his book ! "

" He has lived there many years ! " answered the Marquis.

" O no," I assured him, " only ten months ; I know it exactly ! "

" I should like to know that man," said he.

" That is very easy ! " continued I, " he is here on board," and now I told him whom I was.

It blew strongly ; the wind increased, and in the second and third night raged to a perfect storm ; the ship rolled from side to side like a cask in the open sea ; the waves dashed against the ship's side, and lifted up their broad heads above the bulwarks as if they would look in upon us. It was as if the carriages under which we lay would crush us to pieces, or else would be washed away by the sea. There was a lamentation, but I lay quiet, looked up at the driving clouds, and thought upon God and my beloved.

When at length we reached Genoa most of the passengers went on land : I should have been willing enough to have followed their example, that I might go by Milan to Switzerland, but my letter of credit was drawn upon Marseilles and some Spanish seaports. I was obliged to go again on board. The sea was calm ; the air fresh ; it was a most glorious voyage along the charming Sardinian coast. Full of strength and new life I arrived at Marseilles, and, as I here breathed more easily, my longing to see Spain was again renewed. I had laid the plan of seeing this country last, as the bouquet of my journey. In the suffering state in which I had been I was obliged to give it up, but I was now better. I regarded it, therefore, as a pointing of the finger of Heaven that I should be compelled to go to Marseilles, and determined to venture upon the journey. The steam-vessel to Barcelona had, in the mean time, just sailed, and several days must pass before another set out. I determined therefore to travel by short days' journeys through the South of France across the Pyrenees.

Before leaving Marseilles, chance favored me with a short meeting with one of my friends from the North, and this was Ole Bull! He came from America, and was received in France with jubilees and serenades, of which I was myself a witness. At the table d'hôte in the Hôtel des Empereurs, where we both lodged, we flew toward each other. He told me, what I should have expected least of all, that my works had also many friends in America, that people had inquired from him about me with the greatest interest, and that the English translations of my romances had been reprinted, and spread through the whole country in cheap editions. My name flown over the great ocean! I felt myself at this thought quite insignificant, but yet glad and happy ; wherefore should I, in preference to so many thousand others, receive such happiness? I had and still have a feeling as though I were a poor peasant lad over whom a royal mantle is thrown. Yet I was and am made happy by all this ! Is *this* vanity, or does it show itself in these expressions of my joy?

Ole Bull went to Algiers, I toward the Pyrenees. Through Provence, which looked to me quite Danish, I reached Nismes, where the grandeur of the splendid Roman amphitheatre at once carried me back to Italy. The memorials of antiquity in the South of France I have never heard praised as their greatness and number deserve ; the so called Maison Quarrée is still standing in all its splendor, like the Theseus Temple at Athens : Rome has nothing so well preserved.

In Nismes dwells the baker Reboul, who writes the most charming poems ; whoever may not chance to know him from these, is, however, well acquainted with him through Lamartine's "Journey to the East." I found him at his house, stepped into the bakehouse, and addressed myself to a man in shirt sleeves who was putting bread into the oven ; it was Reboul himself! A noble countenance which expressed a manly character greeted me. When I mentioned my name, he was courteous enough to say he was acquainted with it through the "Revue de Paris," and begged me to visit him in the afternoon, when he should be able to entertain me better. When I came again I found him in a little room which might be called almost elegant, adorned with pictures, casts, and books, not alone French literature, but translations of the Greek classics. A picture on the wall represented his most celebrated poem, "The Dying Child," from Marmier's "Chansons du Nord." He knew I had treated the same subject, and I told him that this was written in my school days If in the morning I had found him the industrious baker, he was now the poet completely ; he spoke with animation of the literature of his country, and expressed a wish to see the North, the scenery and intellectual life of which seemed to interest him. With great respect I took leave of a man whom the Muses have not meanly endowed, and who yet has good sense enough, spite of all the homage paid him, to remain steadfast to his honest business, and prefer being the most remarkable baker of Nismes to losing himself in Paris, after a short triumph, among hundreds of other poets.

By railway I now travelled by way of Montpellier to Cette, with that rapidity which a train possesses in France ; you fly there as though for a wager with the Wild Huntsman. I involuntarily remembered that at Basle, at the corner of a street where formerly the celebrated "Dance of Death" was painted, there is written up in large letters, "Dance of Death," and on the opposite corner, "Way to the Railroad." This singular juxtaposition just at the frontiers of France, gives play to the fancy ; in this rushing flight it came into my thoughts ; it seemed as though the steam whistle gave the signal to the dance. On German railways one does not have such wild fancies.

The islander loves the sea as the mountaineer loves his

mountains ! Every seaport town, however small it may be,
receives in my eyes a peculiar charm from the sea. Was it
the sea, in connection perhaps with the Danish tongue, which
sounded in my ears in two houses in Cette, that made this
town so homelike to me ? I know not, but I felt as if I were
in Denmark rather than in the South of France. When far
from your country you enter a house where all, from the master
and mistress to the servants, speak your own language, as was
here the case, these home tones have a real power of enchantment : like the mantle of Faust, in a moment they transport
you, house and all, into your own land. Here, however, there
was no northern summer, but the hot sun of Naples ; it might
even have burnt Faust's cap. The sun's rays destroyed all
strength. For many years there had not been such a summer, even here ; and from the country round about came
accounts of people who had died from the heat: the very
nights were hot. I was told beforehand I should be unable
to bear the journey in Spain. I felt this myself, but then
Spain was to be the bouquet of my journey. I already saw
the Pyrenees ; the blue mountains enticed me — and one
morning early I found myself on the steamboat.

The sun rose higher ; it burnt above, it burnt from the
expanse of waters ; myriads of jelly-like medusas filled the
river ; it was as though the sun's rays had changed the whole
sea into a heaving world of animal life ; I had never before
seen anything like it. In the Languedoc Canal we had all to
get into a large boat which had been constructed more for
goods than for passengers. The deck was covered with boxes
and trunks, and these again occupied by people who sought
shade under umbrellas. It was impossible to move ; no
railing surrounded this pile of boxes and people, which was
drawn along by three or four horses attached by long ropes.
Beneath in the cabins it was as crowded ; people sat close to
each other, like flies in a cup of sugar. A lady who had
fainted from the heat and tobacco smoke, was carried in and
laid upon the only unoccupied spot on the floor ; she was
brought here for air, but air there was none, spite of the
number of fans in motion ; there were no refreshments to be
had, not even a drink of water, except the warm, yellow water

which the canal afforded. Over the cabin windows hung
booted legs, which at the same time that they deprived the
cabin of light, seemed to give a substance to the oppressive
air. Shut up in this place one had also the torment of being
forced to listen to a man who was always trying to say something witty; the stream of words played about his lips as the
canal water about the boat. I made myself a way through
boxes, people, and umbrellas, and stood in a boiling-hot air ;
on either side the prospect was eternally the same : green
grass, a green tree, flood-gates — green grass, a green tree,
flood-gates — and then again the same ; it was enough to
drive one insane.

At the distance of a half-hour's journey from Béziers we
were put on land ; I felt almost ready to faint, and there was
no carriage here, for the omnibus had not expected us so
early ; the sun burnt infernally. People say the South of
France is a portion of Paradise ; under the present circumstances it seemed to me a portion of hell with all its heat.
In Beziers the diligence was waiting, but all the best places
were already taken ; and I here for the first, and I hope for
the last time, got into the hinder part of such a conveyance.
An ugly woman in slippers, and with a head-dress a yard high,
which she hung up, took her seat beside me ; and now came
a singing sailor who had certainly drunk too many healths ;
then a couple of dirty fellows, whose first maneuver was to
pull off their boots and coats and sit upon them, hot and dirty,
whilst the thick clouds of dust whirled into the vehicle, and
the sun burnt and blinded me. It was impossible to endure
this further than Narbonne ; sick and suffering, I sought rest,
but then came gens-d'armes and demanded my passport, and
then just as night began, a fire must needs break out in the
neighboring village ; the fire alarm resounded, the fire-engines
rolled along, it was just as though all manner of tormenting
spirits were let loose. From here as far as the Pyrenees
there followed repeated demands for your passport, so wearisome that you know nothing like it even in Italy : they gave
you as a reason, the nearness to the Spanish frontiers, the
number of fugitives from thence, and several murders which
had taken place in the neighborhood : all conduced to make
the journey in my then state of health a real torment.

I reached Perpignan. The sun had here also swept the
streets of people ; it was only at night time that they came
forth, but then it was like a roaring stream, as though a real
tumult were about to destroy the town. The human crowd
moved in waves beneath my windows, a loud shout resounded ;
it pierced through my sick frame. What was that? — what
did it mean? " Good evening, M. Arago!" resounded from
the strongest voices, thousands repeated it, and music sounded ;
it was the celebrated Arago, who was staying in the room
next to mine : the people gave him a serenade. Now this
was the third I had witnessed on my journey. Arago addressed them from the balcony, the shouts of the people filled
the streets. There are few evenings in my life when I have
felt so ill as on this one ; the tumult went through my nerves ;
the beautiful singing which followed could not refresh me.
Ill as I was, I gave up every thought of travelling into Spain ;
I felt it would be impossible for me. Ah, if I could only
recover strength enough to reach Switzerland ! I was filled
with horror at the idea of the journey back. I was advised
to hasten as quickly as possible to the Pyrenees, and there
breathe the strengthening mountain air : the baths of Vernet
were recommended as cool and excellent, and I had a letter
of introduction to the head of the establishment there. After
an exhausting journey of a night and some hours in the morning, I reached the place. The air was cool, and more strengthening, than I breathed for months. A few days here entirely
restored me, my pen flew again over the paper, and my
thoughts toward that wonderful Spain.

Vernet as yet is not one of the well-known bathing places,
although it possesses the peculiarity of being visited all the
year round. The most celebrated visitor last winter was
Ibrahim Pacha ; his name still lives on the lips of the hostess
and waiters as the greatest glory of the establishment ; his
rooms were shown first as a curiosity. Among the anecdotes
current about him is the story of his two French phrases, *merci*
and *très bien*, which he pronounced in a perfectly wrong manner.

In every respect, Vernet among baths is as yet in a state of
innocence ; it is only in point of great bills that the Command-

ant has been able to raise it on a level with the first in Europe. As for the rest, you live here in a solitude, and separated from the world as in no other bathing-place; for the amusement of the guests nothing in the least has been done; this must be sought in wanderings on foot or on donkey-back among the mountains; but here all is so peculiar and full of variety, that the want of artificial pleasures is the less felt.

It is here as though the most opposite natural productions had been mingled together — northern and southern, mountain and valley vegetation. From one point you will look over vineyards, and up to a mountain which looks like a sample card of corn-fields, and green meadows where the hay stands in cocks; from another you will only see the naked, metallic rocks, with strange crags jutting forth from them, long and narrow as though they were broken statues or pillars; now you walk under poplar-trees, through small meadows, where the balm-mint grows, as thoroughly Danish a production as though it were cut out of Zealand; now you stand under shelter of the rock, where cypresses and figs spring forth among vine leaves, and see a piece of Italy. But the soul of the whole, the pulses which beat audibly in millions through the mountain chain, are the springs. There is a life, a babbling in the ever-rushing waters! It springs forth everywhere, murmurs in the moss, rushes over the great stones. There is a movement, a life which it is impossible for words to give; you hear a constant rushing chorus of a million strings; above and below you, and all around, you hear the babbling of the river nymphs.

High on the cliff, at the edge of a steep precipice, are the remains of a Moorish castle; the clouds hang where hung the balcony; the path along which the ass now goes, leads through the hall. From here you can enjoy the view over the whole valley, which, long and narrow, seems like a river of trees, which winds among the red, scorched rocks; and in the middle of this green valley rises, terrace-like on a hill, the little town of Vernet, which only wants minarets to look like a Bulgarian town. A miserable church with two long holes as windows, and close to it a ruined tower, form the upper portion, then come the dark brown roofs, and the dirty gray houses with opened shutters instead of windows ; but picturesque it certainly is.

But if you enter the town itself — where the apothecary's shop is, as also the book-seller's — poverty is the only impression. Almost all the houses are built of unhewn stones, piled one upon another, and two or three gloomy holes form door and windows, through which the swallows fly out and in. Wherever I entered, I looked through the worn floor of the first story down into a chaotic gloom beneath. On the wall hangs generally a bit of fat meat with the hairy skin attached ; it was explained to me that this was used to rub their shoes with. The sleeping-room is painted in the most glaring manner with saints, angels, garlands, and crowns *al fresco*, as if done when the art of painting was in its greatest state of imperfection.

The people are unusually ugly ; the very children are real gnomes ; the expression of childhood does not soften the clumsy features. But a few hours' journey on the other side of the mountains, on the Spanish side, there blooms beauty, there flash merry brown eyes. The only poetical picture I retain of Vernet was this. In the market-place, under a splendidly large tree, a wandering peddler had spread out all his wares, — handkerchiefs, books, and pictures, — a whole bazaar, but the earth was his table ; all the ugly children of the town, burnt through by the sun, stood assembled round these fine things ; several old women looked out from their open shops ; on horses and asses the visitors to the bath, ladies and gentlemen, rode by in long procession, whilst two little children, half hid behind a heap of planks, played at being cocks, and shouted all the time " Kekkeriki ! "

Far more of a town, habitable and well-appointed, is the garrison town of Villefranche, with its castle of the age of Louis XIV., which lies a few hours' journey from this place. The road by Olette to Spain passes through it, and there is also some business ; many houses attract your eye by their beautiful Moorish windows carved in marble. The church is built half in the Moorish style, the altars are such as are seen in Spanish churches, and the Virgin stands there with the Child, all dressed in gold and silver. I visited Villefranche one of the first days of my sojourn here ; all the visitors made the excursion with me, to which end all the horses and asses far and near were brought together ; horses were put into the Commandant's venerable coach, and it was occupied by people within and without, just as though it had been a French public vehicle. A most amiable Holsteiner, the best rider of the company, the well-known painter Dauzats, a friend of Alexandre Dumas's, led the train. The forts, the barracks, and the caves were seen ; the little town of Cornelia also, with its interesting church, was not passed over. Everywhere were found traces of the power and art of the Moors ; everything in this neighborhood speaks more of Spain than of France ; the very language wavers between the two.

And here in this fresh mountain nature, on the frontiers of a land whose beauty and defects I am yet to become acquainted with, I will close these pages, which will make in my life a frontier to coming years, with their beauty and defects. Before I leave the Pyrenees these written pages will fly to Germany, a great section of my life ; I myself shall follow, and a new and unknown section will begin. What may it unfold ? I know not, but thankfully, hopefully, I look forward. My whole life, the bright as well as the gloomy days, led to the best. It is like a voyage to some known point, — I stand at the rudder, I have chosen my path, but God rules the storm and the sea. He may direct it otherwise ; and then, happen what may, it will be the best for me. This faith is firmly planted in my breast, and makes me happy.

The story of my life, up to the present hour, lies unrolled before me, so rich and beautiful that I could not have invented it. I feel that I am a child of good fortune ; almost every one meets me full of love and candor, and seldom has my confidence in human nature been deceived. From the prince to the poorest peasant I have felt the noble human heart beat. It is a joy to live and to believe in God and man. Openly and full of confidence, as if I sat among dear friends, I have here related the story of my life, have spoken both of my sorrows and joys, and have expressed my pleasure at each mark of applause and recognition, as I believe I might even express it before God himself. But then, whether this may be vanity? I know not: my heart was affected and humble at the same time, my thought was gratitude to God. That I have related it is not alone because such a biographical sketch as this was desired from me for the collected edition of my works, but because, as has been already said, the history of my life will be the best commentary to all my works.

In a few days I shall say farewell to the Pyrenees, and return through Switzerland to dear, kind Germany, where so much joy has flowed into my life, where I possess so many sympathizing friends, where my writings have been so kindly and encouragingly received, and where also these sheets will be gently criticised.

When the Christmas-tree is lighted, — when, as people say, the white bees swarm, — I shall be, God willing, again in Denmark with my dear ones, my heart filled with the flowers of travel, and strengthened both in body and mind: then will new works grow upon paper: may God lay his blessing upon them! He will do so. A star of good fortune shines upon me; there are thousands who deserve it far more than I; I often myself cannot conceive why I, in preference to numberless others, should receive so much joy: may it continue to shine! But should it set, perhaps whilst I conclude these lines, still it has shone, I have received my rich portion; let it set! From this also the best will spring. To God and men my thanks, my love!

CHAPTER XIII.

NINE years have elapsed, — years rich for history ; serious but great days for Denmark ; sorrowful, but at the same time also happy ones for me. They have brought me my country's full acknowledgment ; they have, it is true, made me older, but still they have kept me young ; they have brought me repose and serenity. I am here going to unfold this new period of my life !

Strengthened by the mountain air, and having regained my vigor for the homeward journey, I intended to go from Vernet to Switzerland, arranging it so that I only travelled nights in the diligences and remained the hot days in Perpignan and Narbonne. Still it seemed to me as if I was transferred from the life-nourishing air to an element where the vital substance was wanting. A heavy, dull, and gloomy air surrounded me, producing real suffering, and I soon felt as if every nerve were on fire. The nights brought no freshness except for the flies, which now gathered strength for their round-dances. A couple of days' or rather of nights' repose at Cette, where I slept on my mattress on the balcony of the house under a starlit heaven, kept me up. All that I know about the beauty of Montpellier is that it lay in sunbeams, which burnt me through My room, closed with tight shutters, was the common abode for all the travellers, who were dressed as if going to take a bath.

During our swift flight on the railroad we got information of a horrible disaster which had occurred on the northern railway of France. At any other time, had I been well, this would have stirred my fancy, but now I was so affected by the burning sun of Southern France, that I felt a kind of sea-sickness ; I was in a state of depression that made me indifferent to all that happened. The railroad stopped at

Nîmes, and we were obliged to take the crowded and dusty diligence for Avignon.

The almond-trees stood laden with ripe fruit, and almonds and figs were almost the only things I lived on. Resting, and that always behind closed window-shutters, is a very sad travelling life! The Pope's castle here resembled a fortress; it had been transformed to a barrack, and the cathedral looked as if it were only a little wing of it. In the museum was Vernet's statue of Thorwaldsen, on which some wiseacre had erased with a lead-pencil the word " danois " from his name. Two pictures of Vernet, given by him " to the good city of Avignon," hung here, representing " Mazeppa," but a little different from the engravings. There was life and movement in the streets in the evening ; a mountebank on horseback with a drum cried his wares, like another Dulcamara. Vine leaves were profusely twined about the windows, like awnings stretched out to shelter from the sunbeams. I was very near Vaucluse, but I had not strength enough to make a trip thither ; all that I had was to be saved for getting me to Switzerland, where I expected to find coolness among the mountains. So I was not to see the celebrated fountain of Vaucluse, the stream that bore the image of Laura, — that image which Petrarch's verses will eternally bear round the world.

The river Rhone runs so rapidly that the steamboat down the stream requires only one day between Lyons and Marseilles, while four days in all against the stream. I preferred the quick-rolling diligence, which started like the wild horses in the Leonore ballads, to the disagreeable steamer. The antique Roman theatre of Orange stood high above all the other newer buildings ; the Arch of Triumph of Septimius Severus, and all the rich works of Roman magnificence with which the banks of the Rhone are strewn, carried one's thoughts toward Italy. I had never before known anything of the grandeur of those Roman remains which the South of France here presents. The banks of the river became more and more various ; I saw towns with beautiful Gothic churches, and on the mountains old castles, lying there like huge bats. Beautiful, hovering suspension-bridges were stretched over the swift stream, against which the dirty vessel worked itself up. At length I arrived at Lyons, where the river Rhone takes up the Saône. From one of the most elevated streets there I discerned, many, many miles far to the northeast, a white shining cloud, rising over the even, green plain ; it was Mont Blanc : there was Switzerland ! So near was I now to that place, where I hoped again to drink in the air and feel new freedom in body and soul ; but the Swiss Consul would not *visé* my passport until the police of Lyons had given their signature, and the passport was declared irregular. I care, perhaps, too much about passports and *visés* when I travel, and my anxiety to have everything right is no doubt absurd ; yet for all that I am always the man among thousands of other travellers who meets with the most passport annoyances. Now they cannot read, then a subordinate clerk writes a wrong number on it so that it is not to be found again ; an Italian boundary-officer finds fault with the name " Christian," and thinks that it is a religious sect, calling themselves particularly by that name. In Lyons they told me that the passport should have been sent from the frontier directly to Paris to be verified there by the Minister of the Interior. I ran the whole day to and from the Préfecture de Police, until I threw myself upon the compassion of one of the higher police officers, to whom I declared that nobody had before claimed of me nor told me that I must send my passport to Paris, where I had no intention of going. They told me that it was necessary to return to Marseilles in order to let the Danish Consul get the passport in order for Switzerland. I declared that I could not bear the idea of travelling further, neither could I stay longer in hot Lyons, but must go to the mountains ! It was a polite, educated man I had to do with ; with the passport in his hand he examined me as to time and place, when I had been at the different places, where every *visé* was given, and soon was aware that nothing could hinder my departure, arranged everything in the best way, and the following day I could start.

In the evening I sat with a comfortable mind at the opera, which was a German one ; a company from Zürich performed in one evening Flotow's " Stradella " and Weber's " Der

Freischütz." There was no difficulty about getting through both, for we only got the music of " Der Freischütz," the dialogue was omitted ; they thought, I suppose, that the Frenchmen would not understand it ; but it seemed very funny, immediately after *Caspar's* drinking-song, to see *Max* seize his hat, nod, and go out ; while *Caspar* sang triumphantly as if he were sure of the game only by that song.

I reached Switzerland, and here also the heat was oppressive ; the snow at " The Virgin " on Mont Blanc itself was less than it had been for many years ; long, black stripes were to be seen in the rocks ; but here the air was more serene, and in the evening there was more coolness. I went immediately to Vevey ; here, on the lake-side, with Savoy's snow-covered mountains, it was a blessing to breathe and live ! Like red stars upon the black, rocky ground, the great fires, which the shepherds and charcoal-burners lighted on the opposite side of the sea, shone in the evening. I visited Chillon again. Byron's name, which he himself had carved on the pillar, had since the last time I was here, been molested, — somebody had tried to efface it by scratching over it. An Englishman had done it, but he was disturbed ; even if he had succeeded in erasing the name of Byron here, in the world it would not have been erased. Two new names were added, those of Victor Hugo and Robert Peel.

In Freiburg I saw the most bold, the most grand suspension-bridge I ever have seen ; it hovered high in the air over valley and river, and swung under the weight of heavy wagons. In the Middle Ages such a bridge would have belonged to the world of wonders ; science has brought our time into a region which before was supernatural.

At last we reached Berne, where Baggesen lived so long a time, married his wife, and spent happy days. Just as he saw them, so now also the Alps glistened with the same color of fire when the sun set. I spent a few days here and at Interlaken. I made trips to Lauterbrunnen and Grindelwald ; the refreshing misty spray that was carried by the wind from the waterfall of Staubbach, the chilly air in the caverns of Grindelwald's glaciers, made it paradisiacal after my travel through purgatory.

I went to Basle, and from there by railroad through France to Strasbourg. Steam navigation on the Rhine commenced here. The air lay heavily and warmly over the river; we sailed the whole day long; the steamer was at last crowded, mostly with Turners, who sang and made merry; they were ill disposed toward Denmark and all that was Danish: Christian VIII. had issued his proclamation. I was first informed of it here; it was not pleasant at all to travel through Baden; nobody knew me, and I would not have anything to do with anybody, but sat sick and suffering during the whole tour.

By way of Frankfort I reached dear Weimar, and here at Beaulieu's I was taken care of and got repose. I spent beautiful days at the summer castle of Ettersburg, where I was invited by the hereditary Grand Duke. In Jena I worked together with Professor Wolff at a German translation of several of my lyric poems; but my health was very delicate. I, who love the South so much, was obliged now to acknowledge that I was a son of the North, whose flesh, blood, and nerves have their roots in snow and storms. Slowly I returned homeward. In Hamburg I received from Christian VIII. the order of Dannebrog, which, as was said, had been destined for me before my departure, and therefore I ought to get it before I again reached my native country. I arrived there two days after.

In Kiel I met with the family of the Landgrave and Prince Christian, afterward called the "Prince of Denmark," and his wife; a royal steamer was sent for these high families, and I was invited to have the pleasure and comfort of going with them; but the sea-voyage was very disagreeable, the passage lasted two nights and days, and in mist and storm I landed at the custom-house of Copenhagen.

Hartmann's opera of "Little Christine," for which I had written the text, was during my absence brought on the stage and met with great success, which was ascribed to me. The music was appreciated, as it deserved, for it had the true Danish flavor, so peculiar, so touching. Heiberg had even taken a liking to it. I longed to hear and see that little work, and it happened that the very same day I arrived home "The Little Kirsten" was performed.

"I am sure you will enjoy great pleasure," said Hartmann. "People are very well satisfied both with music and text!" I entered the theatre, and was noticed ; I perceived this, and when "Little Christine" was finished there was applause, but also much hissing.

"That never happened before!" said Hartmann ; "I do not understand it!"

"But I do," answered I. "Do not be vexed, it does not concern you ; my countrymen, who saw that I had returned home, wished to give me a greeting!"

I was still suffering in health, and could not overcome the effects of my summer sojourn in the South ; only the refreshing winter coolness kept me up ; I was in a nervous, weak state, while my soul on the contrary was very active. I finished at that time the poem "Ahasuerus."

H. C. Örsted, to whom in recent years I had read all I wrote, acquired more and more influence over me by his lively sympathy and his spiritual judgment. As powerfully as his heart beat for the beautiful and good, so were his thoughts always searching in it indefatigably for the truth. One day I brought him a Danish translation I had made of Byron's "Darkness." I had been captivated by the grand, fantastic picture which the poet here has given, and was therefore astonished to hear Örsted declare it a total failure, because it was untrue all through, one addition in it more foolish than another. Örsted proved it, and I understood and acknowledge the truth of the words he spoke.

"A poet may think if he pleases," said he, "that the sun disappeared from heaven, but he must know that quite other results would follow than that of darkness and coldness ; those events are only crack-brained fantasies." And I felt the truth in it and I accepted already then the truths which in his work, "Spirit in Nature," he expresses for the poets of his age. As representatives of the advanced knowledge of the day, they ought to draw their images and expressions from science and not from a by-gone poetical armory ; but the poet, in picturing a past time, employs those representations and ideas of the world which would be familiar to the characters represented. The true and right thought, which Örsted afterward expressed so clearly in his work, was to my great astonishment not understood even by Mynster. One may find several thoughtful treatises in the work which he then read to me; when he had finished reading, we talked of it, and with his modesty he sometimes listened to an objection from me ; the only one I made was, that the dialogue form, which reminds one of Campé's "Robinson," had now grown obsolete ; that this form was used here, where there was no occasion for character-painting, merely the names of the speakers were required, and that without these the whole might be quite as clearly understood.

"You are perhaps right," said he, with all his amiableness ; "but I cannot immediately decide to alter that which for years has been presented to me in this form, but I will reflect upon your words and think of it when I write something more."

There was a fountain of knowledge, experience, and prudence which flowed forth from him ; he also possessed a lovely nature, something innocent and unconscious like the child ; a rare nature revealing the stamp of deity, and to this must be added his deep religiousness ; through the glass of science he saw that greatness of God which it is the beauty of Christianity to acknowledge even with the eyes shut. We talked often of the religious truths so profound and blessed ; we perused together the first book of the Pentateuch, and I heard the childishly religious man, the developed thinker, expounding the myths of old ages, and the traditions of the creation of the world. I always turned away clear in thought and rich in mind from the lovely and excellent Örsted, and in the most heavy hours of misjudgment and discouragement he was, as I must repeat, the one that sustained me and promised me better days.

One day as I left him with a suffering heart, occasioned by the injustice and hardness inflicted upon me from without, the old gentleman could not go to rest until, late in the evening, he had sought me in my home, and once more expressed to me his sympathy and consolation. That touched me so deeply that I forgot all my sorrow and deep feelings, and shed tears of thankfulness for his great kindness ; I again gained strength and courage for poetry and work.

By my " collected works," and by the different editions of my single writings, I became more and more known in Germany, and my works met with great favor; the stories, and "The Picture-book without Pictures" were most read; the first even found imitators. Many books and poems were sent me with kind and touching words. I received from Germany one: "With affectionate greetings from German children to the dear friend of children in Denmark, H. C. Andersen."

In the course of the year several of my writings, such as "The Bazaar," "Wonder Stories," and "The Picture-book without Pictures," were published in England, and were there received by the public and the critics in the same kind way as "The Improvisatore" before. I received letters from many unknown friends of both sexes, whom I there had won. King Christian VIII. received my works, richly bound, from the well-known London book-seller, Richard Bentley. One of our men of note told me that the King on that occasion expressed his joy at the reception I was getting, but also his astonishment at my being so often attacked and depreciated at home while abroad I was fully acknowledged. The kindness the King felt for me became greater when he read my Life.

"Now for the first time I know you!" said he kindly to me, as I entered the presence-chamber in order to bring him my latest book. "I see you very seldom!" continued he; "we must oftener have a little talk together!"

"That depends on your Majesty!" answered I.

"Yes, yes, you are right!" answered he, and now he expressed his joy at my reception in Germany, and especially in England; spoke of the story of my life, which he had understood clearly, and before we separated he asked me, "Where do you dine to-morrow?"

"At a restaurant!" answered I.

"Then come rather to us! dine with me and my wife: we dine at four o'clock!"

I had, as I have before mentioned, received from the Princess of Prussia a beautiful album, in which were several interesting autographs; their Majesties looked through it, and when I received it back again King Christian VIII. had written with his own hand the significant words: "To have acquired an honorable place by means of well-applied talent is better than favor and gift. Let these lines recall to you your affectionate   CHRISTIAN R."

It was dated the second of April ; the King knew that that was my birthday. Queen Caroline Amelia also had written honorable and dear words ; no gifts could have rejoiced me more than such a treasure in spirit and word.

One day the King asked whether I should not also see England. I answered yes, that I intended to go there the coming summer. "You must have some money from me !" said his Majesty. I thanked him and said, —

"I have no need of it! I have eight hundred rix-dollars from the German edition of my writings, and this money I shall spend ! "

" But," said the King with a smile, " you represent now the Danish literature in England, and you should therefore live a little more comfortably ! "

" That I also expect to do, and when I have spent my money I shall return home ! "

" You must write directly to me what you want !" said the King.

" O no, your Majesty, I have no need for it now ; another time I should perhaps be more in want of your Majesty's favor ; now I must not make use of it ; it is not right always to be importunate, — it is so unpleasant for me to speak about money. But if I might dare write to your Majesty without asking for anything ; write, not as to the King — for then it would only be a letter of ceremony ; if I might dare write to one who is truly dear to me !" The King granted my wish and seemed to be pleased with the manner in which I met his favor.

In the middle of May, 1847, I set out by land from Copenhagen. It was in the beautiful spring-time ; I saw the stork flying from its nest with wings stretched out. Whitsuntide was spent at old Glorup ; I witnessed at Odense the marksmen's celebration, which was one of the great days of my boyhood. A parcel of boys came, just as when I was a little fellow, carrying the target riddled with shot ; the whole crowd waved green branches, like the wood of Birnam coming to Dunsinane ; the same frolic, the same thronging — but how different it seemed to me now. A poor crack-brained young fellow outside my windows made a deep impression on me ;

he had nobly formed features and lustrous eyes, but there was something troubled in his whole person, and the boys made sport of him and chased him. I thought of myself, of my boyhood, of my insane grandfather. If I had remained in Odense, and had been put to an apprenticeship there ; if the powers of fancy, which I then possessed in high degree, had been blunted by time and circumstances, or if I had not learned to become fused with the society that surrounded me, how had I then perhaps been looked upon ? I don't know, but the sight of that unhappy fool chased about outside my windows made my heart beat violently ; my thoughts and thanksgiving flew up to God for all his mercy and love to me.

I travelled by the way of Hamburg, where I made the acquaintance of the author Glaszbrenner and his wife, the excellent actress Peroni-Glaszbrenner, who is so full of genius. A Copenhagen newspaper has said that the gay satirist had weakened my reputation as a romancer ; I do not know anything about it, but I have a poem from him by which I can see that the man is not so much against me !

After a visit with dear friends at Oldenburg, I proceeded to Holland. The diligence rolled us along over the brick-laid road, smooth and clean as the floor of a dairy. Houses and towns were the picture of wealth and cleanliness. In the fortress-town of Deventer it was-market day : there was a throng of people in spruce dresses ; in the market-place stood booths, like those I had seen in former days on the Deer-park hill at Copenhagen ; the chiming of bells sounded from the church-towers, the Dutch flag waved.

From Utrecht I came by the railway in an hour to Amsterdam, " where, like amphibious creatures, they live half on land, half in water ! " But it is not quite so bad as that, and it did not at all put me in mind of Venice, the beaver-city with the dead palaces. The first man I met in the street and asked the way, answered me so intelligibly that I thought the Dutch language must be very easy to understand ! but it was Danish that he spoke ; he was a French journeyman hair-cutter, who had been a long while with the hair-dresser Causse in Copenhagen, had learnt a little Danish, recognized me, and when I accosted him in French answered me in Danish as well as he could.

Shade trees stood on the banks of the canals ; variegated clumsy tug-boats, with man and wife and the whole family on board, glided softly by ; the wife stood at the rudder, the husband sat smoking his long pipe. It was striking to see in the crowded street a couple of small boys, whose clothes were in two colors ; half the back of the coat was black, the other half red ; the pantaloons also, each leg had its color. Now came by several small girls, who were also dressed in different colors, quite as convicts are distinguished at home. I asked what it signified, and I was told that they were orphan children, and were dressed here in that way.

In the theatres the plays were in French ; the National Theatre was closed during my stay here, which was very unfortunate, for otherwise I might have seen true Dutch customs : they smoke during the whole representation, and Jan, as almost all waiters in Holland are called, is going about, lights the pipes and brings tea, which is drunk out of great saucers ; the comedy is meanwhile still going on, the verses are sung, and tobacco-pipes are smoking, so that the smoke spreads out over the spectators and the stage. I heard this from different Dutchmen, and I dare believe that it was not exaggeration.

My first introduction in Amsterdam was in a book-store, where I went to buy a book of Dutch and Flemish poems. The man I spoke with looked in surprise at me, made a short apology, and ran away. I did not know what it could mean, and was about going when two men came out from the next room, who also stared at me, and one of them asked if I were not the Danish poet Andersen ! They showed me my portrait, that hung in the room ; it was by that they had known me ; the Dutch newspapers had already announced that I was expected.

A Danish gentleman, Mr. Nyegaard, who has lived many years in Holland, and is called there Van Nieweuhuis, had previously translated into Dutch all my novels ; not long before my arrival " The Story of my Life " and several of the stories (" Sprookjes ") were reproduced and published in Amsterdam. The editor of " De Tijd," the recently deceased Van der Vliet, had with great kindness made mention of my literary labors ; my portrait appeared in the " Weekly."

Thus I soon heard and perceived that I possessed many friends in Holland. H. C. Örsted had furnished me with a letter to Professor Fröhlich at Amsterdam, and by him I was introduced to the well known Dutch poet, Van Lennep, the author of "De Roos van Dekama" and "Haarlems Verlossing," which are reckoned among the most excellent novels in Dutch literature. In Van Lennep I learned to know a handsome, kind man, living in a comfortable, rich-looking house ; I was not received there as a stranger, but as a welcome guest in the family ; beautiful, kind-looking children gathered about me : they knew my stories ; "The Red Shoes" ("De Roode Schoentjes") especially made a deep impression on one of the boys ; it had so strangely affected him that he stood quite silently for a long time and gazed on me ; afterward he showed me the book where the story was, and there was a picture where the shoes were painted red, while the rest of the picture was uncolored. The oldest daughter, Sara, a very amiable and lively girl, asked me immediately whether the ladies of Copenhagen were handsome, and I answered her, "Yes, they are like the Dutch ladies!" She liked to hear me speak Danish, and I wrote down for her a few words of those which pleased her most. At the dinner-table Van Lennep asked me if I thought I could read Dutch, and then he presented me with a written sheet. It was a poem of his to me, and he read it aloud to the whole circle. I believe it is printed in "De Tijd."

From Amsterdam I went to Harlem by the railway. There was a place where we passed over a kind of bank between the open North Sea and the sea of Harlem, and I wondered at the grand enterprise of pumping out a lake, which had already fallen considerably. Harlem's mighty organ, the greatest in the world, was just sounding its eight thousand metal pipes beneath the beautiful timber vault when I entered the hall.

The language sounded very queerly, half Danish, half German, and I saw the inscription on several houses : "Hier gaat mair nit porren!"—"Here they went out to rouse the people." The chimes were always heard from the church towers ; the whole country seemed to me a great English park.

In company with Professor Schlegel and his wife, and Professor Geel, I set out to see the curiosities of Leyden, among others the mound raised by the Anglo-Saxons, when those under Hengist and Horsa went over to England. In the waiting-room of the railroad depot hung many pictures and placards ; the largest of those was one which announced Van der Vliet's " De Tijd " ; my name and portrait were accidentally there ; people became aware of the picture and of me ; I felt quite confused, and hastened to get into a carriage. I had bought a ticket for the Hague, and I read now on the paper they had given me, " 'SGravenhage," the Dutch name of the city ; I did not know it ; the train started, and I expected to come to quite another place than the one I meant. The first man I discovered from my window at the Hague in the street was an acquaintance, a friend from Rome, the Dutch composer Verhulst, whom I was said to resemble, if not in feature, yet in gait and movement. I nodded to him, he knew me, but did not dream of my being at the Hague. An hour after, going out to take a walk in the foreign city, the first one I met again was Verhulst ; what a welcome he gave me ! We talked of Rome, of Copenhagen ; I had to tell him of Hartmann and Gade, whose music Verhulst knew. He praised Denmark because it had a Danish opera. I believe that the Dutch only have French and Italian music. I accompanied him to his home somewhat out of the city ; from the windows we looked on fresh, green meadows and fields, so truly Dutch, and the chiming bells from the neighboring churches resounded at the same time ; a flock of storks passed by in flight, and here is their home ; even the coat of arms of the Hague is a stork.

I did not know Van der Vliet personally, but he had several times written to me, sent me translations and notices of my writings. I entered his room ; he was a young, kind-hearted man, appeared to be a true child of nature, who warmly applauded all that I had written, and was surprised at my unexpected visit, — almost overwhelmed by astonishment. He had expected to be informed of my arrival, and had planned to have me stay with him. He called his young wife ; she was even as young and kind as he, but she only spoke

Dutch ; yet when we did not understand each other we nodded kindly and pressed each other's hands. The good people did not know all the good they were doing me. Their only child, still a little boy, the father said, was named after me, and after the poor fiddler, " Christian." The extraordinary happiness my presence seemed to cause them touched me ; it was a little home full of love. As I, however, was to stay but a few days at the Hague, and as their house lay a little out of the way, I preferred to stay at the hotel, which was situated in the midst of the city. The husband and wife accompanied me to my door in order that we might so much longer be together.

How much pleasure it gives one in a foreign country to meet with kindness like this. My arrival was to them like a happy greeting, and our conversation was kept up in a lively fashion, with laughing and talking.

We separated, and on the staircase of the hotel where I was staying a gentleman dressed in black stood before me ; he told me his name ; I knew him, but how different this was from the laughter I just had separated from. Tears rushed from the gentleman's eyes ; it was Mr Hensel, the brother-in-law of Mendelssohn Bartholdy. He had just arrived from Berlin. The physicians desired him to travel, in order to turn away his thoughts from his grief which seemed to crush him. His excellent, highly gifted wife, Mendelssohn's sister, who so much resembled her brother, had suddenly died : she was a true musical genius, and possessed in her exterior kindred features and expressions. At Berlin I had often met her and her husband in society ; she was the life of the company ; she had her brother's spirit and boldness, and played like him with a dexterity and expression which charmed every one. Not long before she had left the dinner-table fresh and gay, and had retired to a bower, when she was heard to utter a cry and at the same time she expired. Her husband, who is a renowned portrait-painter, had painted her face as she looked in death ; he had brought his work with him, and had placed it upon the table in his room. I, who came from joy and the joyous, was affected at seeing that strong man so deeply troubled and in tears. The year after, as we now know, Mendelssohn died even as suddenly, and followed his intellectual and excellent sister.

I had been four days at the Hague; it was Sunday, and I intended to go to the French opera, when my friends besought me to give that up, and to visit some company that had gathered in Hôtel de l'Europe. "There must be a ball here to-night!" said I, mounting the staircase. "What's the matter?" I asked; "it looks very solemn!" My conductor smiled and answered: "There is a feast going on!" I entered the great saloon and was astonished at the large assembly.

"Here," they said, "are some of your Dutch friends, who have the pleasure of being together with you this evening!" During my short stay at the Hague, letters had been sent round in the country to the friends of my Muse, with whom Van der Vliet and others had arranged that they should be informed when I would accept their invitation. Even far up from the Zuyder Sea, the author of "Opuscules de Jeunesse," Van Kneppelhout, a rich man, came only for my sake, and in spite of the long journey. I found here many artists, as well literary celebrities as painters and actors. During the repast, at the large table adorned with flowers, toasts were given and speeches delivered. I was especially affected by a toast of Van der Vliet: "To the elder Collin at Copenhagen: that noble man who had adopted Andersen as a son." "Two kings," said he, and then turned himself toward me, "King Christian VIII. and Frederick William of Prussia, have each given you an order; when these shall be laid upon your coffin, then may God grant you for your pious stories the most beautiful order of all, the immortal Crown of Life." One spoke of Holland's and Denmark's connection on account of their language and history. One of the painters, who had painted beautiful pictures for my "Picture-book," proposed my health as an artist. Kneppelhout spoke in French of freedom of form and fancy. Songs were sung, humorous poems recited, and as I had no notion of Dutch comedies and tragedies, the renowned tragedian of the Hague, Mr. Peeters, played the prison-scene of Schrawemwerth's "Tasso." I understood not a word, but I felt the truth of his acting, the mimicry of which was as excellent as I ever had seen; it was as if the artist grew pale and red; it seemed as if he had power

over the very blood in his cheeks ; the whole assembly burst
out in vociferous acclamations.   Beautiful songs were sung,
and especially the national song, "Wien Neérlands bloed!"
stirred me by its melody and inspiration.   It was one of the
most notable evenings of my life.   It seems to me that the
expression of the greatest regard I have met, culminated in
Sweden and Holland.   God, who knows our hearts, knows
how humble mine was.   It is a blessing to be able to weep
for very thankfulness and joy.

I spent the next day in the open air ; Kneppelhout carried
me out " in Basch," where there was promenading and music ;
we passed by beautiful green meadows, over idyllic roads, and
by rich country-houses ; we saw Leyden stretching out before us.   We approached it, and then drove to the village of
Scheveningen,·which is protected from the North Sea by high
sand dunes and banks.   Here again a little circle of friends
at the table d'hôte in the Bath hotel drank toasts to art and
poetry, to Denmark and Holland.   Fishing-boats were lying
along the shore, the music sounded, the sea rolled ; it was
very homelike this beautiful evening.   The next morning as I
was about to leave the Hague, the landlady brought me a
number of newspapers, wherein already the feast given me
was mentioned.   A few friends accompanied me to the railway station.   They had become dear to me, and I left them
sorrowfully, uncertain whether we should ever again meet in
this world.

Rotterdam was for me the first really alive Dutch city
which I had seen, far more than Amsterdam was.   Many
large vessels were lying in the broad channels ; small Dutch
gayly painted yachts, where the wife stood at the rudder, — if
not with slippers and spurs, as in the song of "The Young
Mr. Pedersen," still at the rudder, and the good husband was
lying and smoked his pipe.   All seemed to be commerce and
traffic.

One of the oldest Dutch steamboats, a true steam-snail,
the *Batavier*, started the next morning for London, and I
took passage in it.   The ship was heavily laden, and high up
above the railing big baskets were piled filled with cherries ;
a great number of emigrants for America were deck passen-

gers. The children played gayly about: here walked a German, as fat as Falstaff, up and down with his lean, already
almost sea-sick wife, who dreaded the moment when we
should leave the River Maas and come out into the large
North Sea; her dog shivered like her, although he was
wrapped up in a blanket, tied with great loops. The tide
was falling, and it was eight hours before we reached the
North Sea; flat Holland seemed to sink more and more into
the grayish-yellow sea, and at sunset I went to bed.

When I came up on deck in the morning we were in sight
of the English coast. At the mouth of the Thames we saw
fishing-boats by thousands, like a huge flock of chickens, or
torn pieces of paper, or a great market, or a camp with tents.
The Thames surely proclaims that England is the ruler of the
sea; here its servants fly out, whole masses of innumerable
ships; every minute there come as couriers steamboat after
steamboat, — the courier with heavy smoke-veil in his hat,
from the top of which the red fire-flower flashes.

Swelling like swans, one great sailing ship after another
passed by us; we saw pleasure-yachts with rich, young gentlemen: vessel followed vessel; the further we advanced up
the Thames the more the crowd increased. I had begun to
count how many steamers we should meet, but I grew tired
of it. At Gravesend the Thames appeared as if we were
entering a smoking marsh on fire, but it was only the steam
of steamships and smoke of chimneys which lay before us.
A threatening thunder-storm was drawing over the country;
the blue lightning flashed toward the pitchy black sky; a
railway-train passed by, its steam waved, and the thunder-clap
echoed like cannon.

"People know you are here and wish to bid you welcome!"
said a young Englishman to me in joke. "Yes," thought I,
"our Lord knows it!"

The Thames became, one could not believe it possible,
still more a confusion of steamboats, rowing-boats, sailing-
vessels, a thronged street; I could not imagine how those
masses moved among each other without striking; the tide
was going down; the miry, slimy bottom appeared at the
banks; I thought of *Quilp* in Dickens's "Old Curiosity Shop,"
and of Marryat's descriptions of the life on the river.

At the custom-house, where we landed, I took a cab and drove and drove, thinking that I never should come to an end, through that endless city. The crowd was greater and greater, carriages after carriages in two streams up and down; all kind of vehicles : omnibuses filled within and without ; large wagons, that ought to be called boxes, advertising by placards pasted on them ; men with big signs on poles, which they lifted over the crowd, and on which one could read one thing or another that was to be seen or bought. All was in motion, as if half London was stirring from one part of the city to the other. Where streets crossed each other there was an elevated place, surrounded with great stones, where people rushed from one of the sidewalks through the nearest line of carriages, waiting here in that asylum for a chance to get through the other line and to the opposite sidewalk.

London, the city of cities! Yes, I felt immediately that it was so, and I learned to know it from day to day afterward. Here is Paris but with a mightier power ; here is the life of Naples but not its bustle. Omnibus after omnibus passes, — they say that there are four thousand, — teams, carts, cabs, hansoms, and elegant carriages are rattling, training, rolling, and driving away, as if they were going from one important event in the city to another. And this tide is always moving! always! When all those people we now see in such activity are in their graves, the same hurried activity will still continue here, the same waves of omnibuses, cabs, cars : the men walking with signs before and behind, signs on poles, signs on coaches, with advertisements of balloons, Bushmen, Vauxhall, panoramas, and Jenny Lind.

I reached at last the Hôtel de Sablonière in Leicester Square, which had been recommended me by H. C. Örsted, and got a room, where the sun shone upon my bed to show me that there also may be sunshine in London ; it was a little reddish-yellow, as if reflected through the glass of a beer bottle ; but when the sun had set, the air was clear and the stars sparkled down upon the streets, radiant with gas-light, and where the crowd always moved, rushed, or quietly hummed. Very tired I fell asleep, not yet having seen any acquaintance.

I had arrived here without any letter of recommendation ; the only one at home whom I had asked for one was a man of high rank, who had English connections, through whom I might be able to get a glance into the high life of London, but he did not send me any.

"You need no letter of recommendation here," said our Danish Ambassador, Count Reventlow, upon whom I made a call next morning ; "you are known and recommended in England by your writings. This very night a little select party is given by Lord Palmerston ; I will write to Lady Palmerston that you are here, and I have no doubt that you will get an invitation ! "

A few hours after I did receive one, and together with Count Reventlow I went to the house in his carriage. The highest nobility of England was gathered here : ladies in the richest toilets, silk and lace, sparkling diamonds, and beautiful bouquets of flowers. Lord Palmerston as well as Lady Palmerston received me very kindly ; and when the young Duke of Weimar, who was here with his. young wife, kindly greeted me and introduced me to the Duchess of Suffolk, who I believe spoke very civilly of my "Improvisatore, — "The first book on Italy ! " as she was pleased to express herself, — I was soon surrounded by the noble ladies of England, who all knew about the Danish poet, — knew "The Top and the Ball," "The Ugly Duckling," etc. Many generous words were said to me. I seemed to be no longer a stranger. The Duke of Cambridge spoke to me about Christian VIII.; the Prussian Ambassador, Bunsen, who at an earlier time had shown the Danes at Rome so many favors, was a friend of Reventlow, and met me very kindly. Many presented me their cards, and most of them offered me invitations. "You have to-night," said Count Reventlow, " made a jump into high life, which many would have required years to come into ! Don't be too modest ; here one must advance boldly in order to get ahead ! " and now with that gentleman's quick humor he continued in Danish, which was not understood by any of the company, " To-morrow we will look over the cards and choose the best one ! Now you have talked quite enough with him ; there you see another, with whom it will be more advantage to you to be acquainted ; at this gentleman's house you will find a good table ; with that, very select society !" and so he rattled on. At last I was so weary of moving over the polished floor, of the mental exercise of clambering over different tongues, that I did not know what I was about ; the heat was so exhausting that I was obliged to break away and go out on the corridor, to draw breath and to get a little rest, at least to lean up against the balustrade. As that evening so were all the others for three whole weeks ; it was in the season, the warm time of summer society, which we only know in the winter. I was invited every day out to dinner, for the evening, and after that to balls in the night ; there was a crowd everywhere that I went, in the saloons and on the staircases, and as I was engaged for a week ahead, I was obliged also to go out to breakfast. I could not stand it any longer ; it was just one long night and day for almost three weeks ; I have therefore been able to keep only a few moments and scattered incidents of that time clearly in my memory. Almost everywhere the same principal figures were presented, varying in gold, satin, laces, and flowers. In the decoration of rooms roses were especially employed. Windows, tables, staircases, and niches were covered with roses ; they were always placed in water, either in glasses, cups, or vases, but without looking closely the vessels could not be perceived ; to the eye they formed entire carpets, fragrant and fresh.

I lived, as I have mentioned, at Leicester Square, in the Hôtel de Sablonière, where also H. C. Örsted had lived, and who had recommended it to me ; but that lodging, said Count Reventlow, was not fashionable enough, and here all must follow the fashion ; he advised me not to say that I lived at Leicester Square ; that would be, he said, as if a stranger in Copenhagen were to mention in a fashionable society, "I live in Peter Madsen's Lane ;" I was to give out that I lived with him. And yet I lived near by Piccadilly, in a large square where the marble statue of the Earl of Leicester stood among green trees outside my windows ; six or eight years ago it had been fashionable to live here, but now it was not so.

The Chevalier Bunsen, Count Reventlow, and several of the ambassadors called on me here, but that was according to etiquette. In England every one must be obedient to etiquette ; even the Queen is dependent on it at her own house. They told me that one day, when taking a walk out in one of the splendid parks, and wishing perhaps to stay there a little longer, she was obliged to return home because the dinner-hour was precisely eight o'clock ; otherwise all England would have found fault with her. In this land of freedom one almost dies by etiquette ; but that is not worth mentioning where so much that is excellent is to be found. Here we find a nation, which in our time, perhaps, is the only religious one ; here is an esteem for good manners, here is morality ; we must not dwell upon single excrescences and offshoots, which always are to be found in a great city. London is the city of politeness, and the police themselves set good examples. In the streets you need only address one of the policemen, and he will immediately accompany and direct you ; in the stores you will always be answered in the kindest way. As to London's heavy air and coal-smoke, it has been exaggerated ; it certainly is the case in some of its densely populated old quarters, but its most growing part is airy and free, as much so as in Paris. I have seen in London many beautiful sunny days and many star-light nights.

It is, moreover, very difficult for a foreigner to give a true and faithful picture of a country and a city after a short stay there. One proves that best by reading other authors' descriptions and conceptions of our own home, where we are familiar with and know everything so well. The tourist writes down what some individuals relate, conceived from their special point of view, and he himself only looks through travelling life's wavering spectacles ; he paints landscapes and figures as on a railway flight, and the details are not even so true as there.

London is to me the city of cities, Rome only excepted. Rome is a microcosm, a bass-relief of the day. As for the rest, the topic of the day was here Jenny Lind, and only Jenny Lind. In order to avoid somewhat too frequent calls, and to live in the freshest air of London, she had hired a house at Old Brompton ; that was all the information I could get at the hotel, where I had at once inquired after her.

That I might find the place I went directly to the " Italian Opera," where she sung. Here also the policeman was my best guide ; he accompanied me to the cashier of the theatre, but neither he nor the different porters there would or could give me any information. I wrote then upon one of my visiting-cards some words to Jenny Lind ; I wrote that I had arrived, and told her where I lived, and asked her to give me her address without delay, and the next morning I received a joyful and kind letter " To her brother." I found out upon the map where Old Brompton was, took my place in an omnibus ; the conductor told me how far I was to go with him, and where I should turn to find the house of " The Swedish Nightingale." as he smilingly called her. A few days after I happened to go with the same omnibus ; I did not know the conductor again, but he knew me, and asked whether I had found " The Nightingale, Jenny Lind."

It was far out in a corner of the city where she lived, in a nice little house, with a low hedge shutting out the street. A crowd of people was standing without, and looking at the house in order to get a glimpse of Jenny Lind ; to-day they had a chance, for on the ringing of the bell she recognized me from the windows, and ran out to the carriage, shook both my hands, looked on me with sisterly affection, and forgot the people around who crowded about. We hastened into the house, which was pretty, rich, and cozy. It opened on a little garden with a large grass-plat and many leafy-trees ; a little, brown, shaggy dog trotted about, jumped up on the lap of his mistress and was patted and caressed.

Elegantly bound books lay on the table. She showed me my " True Story of my Life," which Mary Howitt had dedicated to her ; a large sheet lay on the table, it was a carica-ture of Jenny Lind, a great nightingale with a girlish face ; Lumley was shown putting sovereigns on the tail to get her to sing.

We talked of home, of Bournonville and Collin, and l told her of the Dutch feast given me, how they there had drunk the health of old Collin ; she clapped her hands and cried, " Was not that good ! " She promised me then that I should have a ticket to the opera every time she sang, but that I must not

speak of paying for it, because, she said, the tickets are fool-
ishly dear. " Let me there sing for you ; you may afterward
at home read some of your stories to me again ! " My many
invitations allowed me to make use of her ticket twice only.
The first time I saw her in *La Somnambula* which certainly is
her best part. The virginal purity that shines through her
imparts a kind of holiness to the stage. The manner with
which, in the sleep-walking scene in the last act, she takes the
rose from her breast, holds it up in the air, and involuntarily
drops it, had a charm, a beauty so strangely touching, that
tears came into my eyes. There was also such applause and
excitement as I have never seen even among the violent
Neapolitans ; flowers rained down upon her, and everything
was like a great festival. Every one knows how highly dressed
they are in the great opera at London ; the gentlemen on the
floor and in the first range of boxes come with white cravats ;
the ladies are dressed as for a ball, each of them with a large
bouquet in her hand.

The Queen and Prince Albert were present, as also the
hereditary Grand Duke of Weimar and his wife. The Italian
language sounded strangely from Jenny Lind's lips, and yet
they said that she was more correct than many Italians ; it was
the same in German ; still the spirit was the same as when she
sang in her beautiful vernacular tongue. The composer Verdi
had for that season and for Jenny Lind composed a new opera,
" I Masnadieri," the text after Schiller's " The Robbers." I
heard it once, but even Jenny Lind's acting and singing could
not give life to that hum-drum poetry. *Amelia's* part is closed
by her being at last killed in the wood by *Care* the Moor,
while the band of robbers is surrounded. Lablache played
the old Moor, and it was indeed highly comical to see the
robust, fleshy man coming out from the tower saying that he
was almost dead with hunger ; the whole house laughed when
he said it. That was at the same representation that I saw
for the first time the renowned dancer Taglioni ; she danced
in " Les Pas des Déesses." Before she appeared I felt a
throbbing of my heart, which I always have when my expectation is raised for something excellent and grand.

She appeared as an old, little, sturdy, and quite pretty

woman ; she would have been a nice lady in a saloon, but as a
young goddess — *fuimus Troes !* I sat cool and indifferent at
the graceful dancing of that old lady. There must be youth,
and that I found in Cerrito ! it was something incomparably
beautiful ; it was a swallow-flight in the dance, a sport of
Psyche, a flight ! that one did not see in Taglioni ; *fuimus
Troes !* The Danish dancer, Miss Grahn, was also in London,
and was highly admired of all, but she had a sore foot and
did not dance. One evening when " Elisire d'Amore " was
given, she sent for me to see her in her little box, where she
disclosed for me with liveliness and fun the world behind the
scenes, and gave me an account of each of the actors. She
did not seem to belong to the admirers of Jenny Lind. Of
course she had to suffer some opposition in the midst of the
applause of the day, but that is always the case with whatever
is great and good. Jenny Lind's presentation of *Norma*
as the afflicted, noble woman, which had deeply affected me,
did not generally please the English, who earlier, through Grisi
and her imitators, had conceived her as a passionate *Medea.*
Mr. Planche, the author of " Oberon " and of several other
opera texts, was a zealous opponent ; but those small blows
were lost in the glory of her popularity, and she remained
happy in her quiet home under the shadowy trees. One day
I came there fatigued and exhausted by continual invitations
and overpowering attention.

"Yes, now you have found what it is to be at a perpetual
feast ! " said she ; " one is so worn out ! and how empty, how
infinitely empty all those phrases one hears said ! "

When I afterward rode home in her carriage, people thronged
close up to it, believing that it was Jenny Lind, and they
perceived only me, who was to them a strange, unknown
gentleman. Old Mr. Hambro had through me invited the
artist to a *dinée* at his country-house, but I could not induce
her to accept, not even when it was left to her to fix the
number of guests, yes, even to be alone with the old gentleman
and me. She would not change her manner of living, but
allowed me to take the honorable old gentleman out with me
to see her ; that I did, and both agreed prettily together ; they
even talked of money affairs, and laughed at me, who under-

stood so little about those things, and how to change my talent into gold.

The young sculptor, Mr. Durham, wished to model her bust and mine ; neither of us had time to give him a sufficient number of sittings. Meanwhile the young man, by a few words from me, got permission to come for half an hour to her, and remodel the clay which he had already formed from what he had seen of her in the theatre. I allowed him an hour for myself, and in that time he produced, considering the brief space allowed him, a remarkably good bust. This bust, as also that of Jenny Lind, have both been at the exhibition in Copenhagen, but have been there criticised too severely ; for there was likeness and a spiritual conception in both of them, and I should like to know if any Danish artist in so short a time could have been able to do better than Durham did. After that time years elapsed before I again saw Jenny Lind ; she left England, as we know, in triumph and popular esteem, and went to America.

Count Reventlow presented me to Lady Morgan. He had already told me a few days before that the aged lady expected us, but that she had postponed our visit to a fixed day, be- cause, as he confided to me, she knew me very well by name, but had never read anything of mine, and now in a hurry was making acquaintance with " The Improvisatore," the stories, etc. She lived in a house with small decorated rooms, filled with objects of antiquity ; there was a French look about every- thing, and especially about the old lady, who was all life and merriment ; she spoke French, was entirely French herself, and dreadfully painted. She quoted from my books, which I knew she had read in a great hurry, but she did it always with the greatest politeness toward me. There hung on the wall a pencil drawing by Thorwaldsen ; it was that of " Night and Day," as we have them in bass-reliefs, and was given her at Rome. She told me that she would invite in my honor all the renowned authors of London ; that I should learn to know Dickens, Bulwer, etc. ; and the same evening she accompanied me to Lady Duff Gordon's, who had translated my story, " The Little Mermaid," and is a daughter of the authoress Jane Austen : here I might expect to meet with many celebrities,

and that was the case ; but I was received in a far more select
circle by another English authoress, to whom I was introduced
by my friend Jordan, the editor of " The Literary Gazette ; "
that was at the house of Lady Blessington.
She lived a little out of London, in her mansion Gore
House. She was a blooming, somewhat corpulent lady, very
elegantly dressed, and with sparkling rings on her fingers.
She received me as kindly as if I were an old acquaintance,
shook my hand, spoke of " A Poet's Bazaar," and said that
there was a treasure of poetry in it, which was not to be found
in many other books, and that she had mentioned it in her last
novel. We walked out on the great garden balcony, that was
richly overgrown with ivy and vines ; a big blackbird from
Van Dieman's Land and two white parrots balanced here : the
blackbird was caressed and must warble for me. Under the
balcony grew many roses ; there was a beautiful green sward,
and two pretty, drooping willows ; a little further away grazed
upon a green little meadow, only for show, a cow, — all looked
so country like. We wandered together down into the garden.
She was the first English lady whom I understood very well,
but she spoke also intentionally very slowly, held me by the
wrist, looked at me continually at every word, and then asked
me if I understood her ; she told me of an idea for a book
which she wished me to write, — an idea, which seemed to her
to belong to me. It was of a poor man, who only possessed
hope, and of a rich man, who possessed the real but not hope ;
and then it was to be shown how unhappy he was, while the
poor man was happy.

Her son-in-law, Count d'Orsay, the most elegant gentleman in London, entered, who, I was told, decided by his toilet
the English fashion. We went into his studio, where there
stood in clay a bust of Lady Blessington, nearly finished, made
by him, as also an oil painting of Jenny Lind as *Norma*,
painted by Count d'Orsay from memory. He seemed to be a
very talented man, and he was also very polite and amiable.

Lady Blessington now conducted me through all her rooms ;
the bust or portrait of Napoleon was to be seen in almost all
of them. At last we reached her work-room ; many open
books lay on the table, and, as I could see, all concerning

Anne Boleyn. We spoke of poetry and art, and she hinted at
my works in an appreciative way, saying that she found in
them much of that quality which had captivated her in Jenny
Lind, — a certain heartiness of nature. She talked about that
artist's representations of *La Somnambula,* the purity that was
manifested, and the tears stood in her eyes while she spoke
of it. Two young girls, her daughters I believe, presented
me a handful of beautiful roses ; Jordan and I were invited
to come there some day to dinner, and she would then make
me acquainted with Dickens and Bulwer. Coming at the
appointed time I found the whole house in festive splendor.
Waiters in silk stockings with powdered hair stood in the corridor ; Lady Blessington herself was in splendor and magnificence, but with the same mild and radiant face ; she told
me that Bulwer could not come ; he lived at that time but for
the elections, and was out getting votes. She did not seem
to like that poet much as a man, and said also that he was
very repulsive by reason of his vanity, and besides rather deaf
and very difficult to converse with. I do not know whether
she looked through a false glass, but otherwise she spoke
warmly, and that did all, of Charles Dickens ; he also had
promised to come and I should learn to know him.

I was just writing my name and a few words in the front of
" The True Story of my Life," when Dickens entered, youthful
and handsome, with a wise and kind expression, and long,
beautiful hair, falling down on both sides. We shook hands,
looked into each other's eyes, spoke and understood one another. We stepped out on the balcony. It was happiness to
me to see and speak with the one of England's living writers
whom I loved most, and tears came into my eyes. Dickens
understood my love and admiration. Among my stories he
mentioned " The Little Mermaid," which had been translated
by Lady Duff Gordon, in " Bentley's Magazine " ; he knew
also " The Bazaar," and " The Improvisatore." I was placed
near Dickens at the table, only Lady Blessington's young
daughter sat between us. He drank a glass of wine with me,
as did also the Duke of Wellington, then Marquis of Douro.
At the end of the table was a great picture, a full-length
portrait of Napoleon, strongly lighted by many lamps. Here

was the poet Milnes, here the Postmaster-general of England, authors, journalists, and noblemen, but for me Dickens was the first. I saw a great circle of rich and honorable men : the party consisted wholly of men, except the hostess' two daughters. No others came to Lady Blessington's house, and these frequented it without restraint. Count Reventlow and several others hinted to me that I must not tell in the great saloons of my going to Lady Blessington's, because it was not fashionable — she was frowned upon. I don't know whether the reason they gave was true, but they told me that her son-in-law, Count d'Orsay, liked better his mother-in-law's than his wife's company, and that the young wife, who was, to be sure, a step-daughter of Lady Blessington, had for that reason left husband, house, and home, and lived with a lady friend of hers, while her husband stayed behind.

Lady Blessington made a very pleasant impression upon me ; and in the great circles, when the noble ladies asked me where I had been, I could not abstain from naming Lady Blessington. Then there always was a pause ; I asked the reason why I was not to go there, or what was the matter with her, but I always got a short answer that she was not a good woman. One day I spoke of her personal amiability, and of her humor, and related how she was affected when talking of Jenny Lind's representation of *La Somnambula* and the womanly nobility she manifested ; I had seen her shed tears over it ! "The creature !" exclaimed an old lady indignantly ; "Lady Blessington weeping at the innocence of Jenny Lind !" A few years after I read of Lady Blessington's death at Paris. Count d'Orsay sat by her death-bed.

Among other literary ladies in London I must mention the Quakeress Mary Howitt who had introduced and made me known in England by her translation of my "Improvisatore." Her husband, William Howitt, is also known as an author ; they published at that time in London "Howitt's Journal ;" in the number which appeared just the week before my arrival, was given a kind of welcome for me, as also my portrait, which was to be seen in several shop windows. The first day I arrived I became aware of it, and entered a little shop to buy it. "Has it really any likeness to Mr. Ander-

sen ? " I asked the woman who sold it. " Yes, indeed, a striking likeness ! " said she ; " you will know him by the picture ! " but she did not know me, though she talked a long
time of the likeness. " The True Story of my Life," a translation of " Das Märchen meines Lebens," had recently been published by the Longmans ; the book was dedicated to Jenny
Lind, and was also afterward published in America. Immediately after my arrival Mary Howitt and her daughter visited
me, and invited me out to Clapton. I rode out there in an
omnibus, which was loaded outside and within ; the distance
was certainly more than two Danish miles, and I thought that
the journey would never come to an end. The Howitts lived
very comfortably ; there were paintings about them, and
statues, and a nice little garden. All received me very kindly.
A few houses from there lived Freiligrath, the German poet,
whom I had once visited at St. Goar on the Rhine, where he
sung his warm, picturesque songs. The King of Prussia had
granted him an annuity, which he refused, when Herwegh
mocked at him as a pensionary poet ; afterward he wrote
songs of liberty, went to Switzerland, then to England, where
he supported his family by working in a counting room.

I met him one day in London in the crowd ; he knew me
but I did not know him, because he had shaved off the thick
black beard he used to wear. " Do you not know me ? " said
he, and laughed ; " I am Freiligrath ! " and drawing me out
of the crowd toward a door, he said in joke, " You won't
speak to me in the crowd of people, you, friend of kings ! "
The little room looked friendly, my portrait hung on the wall ;
the painter Hartmann, who had painted it once at Graven-
stein, entered the room ; just then we talked about the Rhine
and of poetry, but I was suffering from London life and from
the excursion out here ; I trusted meanwhile that it would be
a cool evening, and took again a place on the omnibus, but
before I was well out of Clapton all my limbs gave way, I
felt very sick, and as weak as when at Naples ; I came near
fainting, and the omnibus every moment grew more thronged
and warm. On the top it was full ; booted legs hung down
before the open windows.

I was several times about to say to the conductor : " Carry

me into a house, where I can stop, for I cannot hold up any longer here." The perspiration poured out of every pore. It was dreadful ! we moved very slowly, and at last it seemed to me as if everything about me was becoming indistinct. Arriving finally at the Bank, I took a cab, and now, sitting alone, and with better air, I recovered and reached home, but I have seldom taken a trip more painful than that from Clapton.

Meanwhile I had promised to go out there again and stay a couple of days ; the length of the stay encouraged me to undertake again a similar journey in an omnibus. I had expected to find quiet and enjoyable days there, but friends often endeavor to make one have too good a time. They always will take one from what is near by to what is further away, and thus the very first day after dinner we started in a single-horse carriage, five persons within and three without, for a country-house of an old maiden lady ; the heat was oppressive, and the whole trip was just fit for a chapter of one of Dickens's novels.

At last we reached the old lady's, who no doubt was of the literary kind. In the middle of the grass-plat before the house were a crowd of children playing, that looked like a school of boarders ; they danced round a large beech-tree, and all were adorned with wreaths of beech or ivy on their heads ; they sang and ran about. They were called together, and were told that I was the very Hans Christian Andersen who had written the stories they knew, and all thronged round me and shook my hand, then ran away again, singing, to the green spot. Round about were beautiful hills and large groves, which threw upon the ground picturesque shadows. I looked upon it all from a hot bower, where we were placed, in the little garden. A deaf authoress came who wrote political things, and many poets I never had heard of. I became more and more exhausted, and was at last obliged to seek rest ; the whole of the afternoon I spent lying quietly in a room by myself unable to move.

At sunset the air was better, and I was glad that I could again take breath. On our way home to Clapton we saw London illuminated before us like a transparent gigantic plan. In fiery outlines, formed by the many gas-lamps, **we** perceived different winding streets ; some of them reached far out toward the distant horizon, a phosphoric ocean with thousands of fire-flames. The next day I was again in London.

I have seen "high life" and "poverty;" these are the two poles of my memory. I saw Poverty personified in a pale, famishing girl, with worn-out, miserable clothes, hiding herself in the corner of an omnibus. I saw Misery, and yet it said not a word in all its pitifulness: that was forbidden. I remember those beggars, men and women, carrying upon the breast a large piece of pasteboard with these words written : "I am starving! Mercy!" They dare not pronounce it, they are not allowed to ask alms, and so they glide by like shadows. They place themselves before a person and gaze at him with hungry and sad expressions on their pale, pinched faces. Standing outside cafés and confectionaries, they choose one among the guests whom they continually fix with a glance, — O such a glance as misery can show. She points at her sick child and at the written piece of paper upon her breast, where we read : "I have not eaten these two days." I saw many of them, and they told me that in the quarter of the city where I lived there were but few of them, and in the rich quarters none at all ; those quarters were shut out from that poor Pariah-class.

In London everybody is industrious, the beggar among them ; everything depends on who can best draw attention to himself, and I saw an arrangement by which this was fully accomplished. In the middle of the street-gutter stood a cleanly dressed man and five children, — who if they stood in the street or on the sidewalk would have stopped the passage, — one child smaller than the other, all in mourning, with a long mourning veil streaming from hat and cap, all cleanly dressed, and each of them holding a bunch of matches for sale ; of course they dared not beg. Another far more honorable and very profitable industry is that of a street-sweeper, and such a one, with his broom, is to be seen almost at any corner ; he sweeps continually the crossing from street to street, or keeps clean a certain portion of the sidewalk, and whoever will may give him a penny; there are quarters where in the course of the week they amass quite a little fortune. I believe it is Bulwer who has told of such a man, whose profession was not known to anybody in his quarter, how he became engaged and married to a young girl of the nobility; he was away from his house every day, nobody knew where, and every Saturday he brought home shining silver pieces. The family was anxious and restless, they believed him a counterfeiter, watched him, and discovered then that he was a street sweeper.[1]

It was the life of London I saw. I got an insight of " high life " in the rich saloons and in the crowds of the streets, the plaudits in the theatres, and, what is a part of the nation, the churches : it is in Italy that churches must be seen. The cathedral of St. Paul in London looks more impressive from without than from within ; it is little in comparison with the cathedral of St. Peter, and is not so solemn as that of Maria Maggiore or Del Angeli at Rome. It made the impression on me of a magnificent Pantheon with rich marble monuments. Everything, every statue, was covered with a black crape ; it was a veil of coal smoke, which penetrated here and gave to every statue a certain silky cover. Upon Nelson's monument stands a young figure, which stretches the hand toward one of the four inscriptions directing toward " Copenhagen." As a Dane I had a feeling as if he were going to efface that triumph.

Westminster made a much grander impression on me ; it is a truly great church both in exterior and in interior ! It is a pity that they have for English comfort here built in the interior of the great church a smaller one, where divine service is performed. The first time I entered Westminster Abbey through a side door, I stood in " the Poet's Corner," and the first monument I caught sight of was that of Shakespeare. I forgot for the moment that his dust did not repose here : I was filled with devotion and seriousness, and I leaned my head against the cold marble ; at one side is the monument or tomb of Thomson, at the left that of Southey, and under the large stones of the floor repose Garrick, Sheridan, and Samuel Johnson. We know that the clergy have not given permission

[1] Andersen has fallen upon a humorous story of Thackeray's. — ED.

to have Byron's monument placed here. "I missed it there!" said I one evening to an English Bishop, and spoke as if I did not know the reason. "How can it be that a monument made by Thorwaldsen for one of the greatest poets of England should not be placed there?" — "It has an excellent place elsewhere!" he answered evasively.

Among many other monuments in Westminster for kings and great men, there was one before which I always stopped, perceiving in one of the marble figures my own face, so wonderfully like and so much better than any sculptor or painter had been able to do it. Yes, it was strikingly like my bust. A number of strangers, who were accidentally standing there one day when I also was there, looked at it and at me, started and gazed astonishingly at me; it was for them as if the noble lord in the marble wandered alive in flesh and blood in my shape through the aisles of the church.

I have already mentioned before that it was just at the time of election I was at London, and that was the reason I could not meet Bulwer. Election time with all its arrangements and extravagances, which we in our country will certainly come to know, is full of interest and variety the first time one sees it. In several squares and streets were erected stands for speakers. Men went through the crowds with election-lists upon their breast and back, in order that the names might be read; flags waved, and were carried about in procession; from carriages filled with electors, handkerchiefs were shaken, and big flags with inscriptions. Many poorly dressed people, often with very showily dressed servants, came driving in elegant carriages, shouting and singing; it was as if the lords had sent for their most humble servants, as if for that old pagan feast where the masters served their own slaves. Round the stand is a thronging, surging crowd; here flew sometimes rotten oranges, yes, even carrion at the heads of the speakers. I saw in one of the more elegant districts of London two young, well-dressed men approaching the stand, but while one of them tried to mount, some one ran up, crushed both of their hats over their eyes, and turned them round; so they were pushed and tossed by the whole mass of people from one to another, away from the stand, yes, even out of the street, so

that they were not allowed to appear at all. In the vicinity
of London, several miles out, where I drove in a carriage a
couple of times, the excitement of the hour was still more
noticeable. I saw the different election parties coming in
great processions with large flags before them and the most
fierce inscriptions on them. The larger part were for Mr.
Hodges ; his name was especially seen ; one party had dark-
blue flags, the other light-blue, and inscriptions such as,
" Hodges forever ! " " Rothschild, the poor man's friend ! "
etc. Bands of music accompanied each procession, and were
followed by a motley crowd. An old, sick, palsied man was
carried in a wheelbarrow to give his suffrage. The collecting
of ballots took place at the market-place, which for the occasion was like a market-day, with booths and canvas tents,
where all things were exhibited for sale ; a whole theatre was
erected, and I saw them carry wooden scenes across the
street to that great Thespis-hall. What was especially poetical
was the neat peddler wagons, whole houses on wheels, — the
entire household upon one car, which was hung on two wheels
and drawn by one horse. It made a complete house with roof
and chimney ; it was divided in two compartments, of which
the hindmost formed a kind of room or kitchen with plates
and tin pans ; the wife sat before the door spinning upon her
distaff ; a little red curtain hung before the open window.
The husband and son were on horseback, but at the same
time guided the horse before the wandering house.

The present Baron Hambro had hired a country-house out
of the city of Edinburgh, at Stirling, where he spent the summer with his wife, who was an invalid and was trying salt-water
bathing. He wrote to his father that he should induce me to
visit him, as I had many friends in Scotland who would be
very glad to see me. I was afraid to undertake the long journey, as I did not speak English well enough to venture alone
so far up in the country. A renewed invitation and a letter
to his father asking him to accompany me, decided me to go,
and in company with the elder Hambro I now started on the
railway from London to Edinburgh. We divided our journey
into two days and spent the night at York. We went by an
express train at flying speed, and without as much stopping

as would allow us to alight a single time during the whole journey.

The old song runs: "Through valleys, over mountains;" here we might sing: "Over valleys, through mountains! We flew like the Wild Huntsman. The landscape rolled around us and under us; the country resembled that about Funen and Als: sometimes we passed through the earth, through endless, dark tunnels, where for ventilation they had made apertures over our head; we met many trains, which whistled by like rockets, and new views of more mountainous character appeared, interspersed with tile-kilns with fire flaming out of the chimneys. At the railway station in York a gentleman saluted me and presented to me two ladies: it was the present Duke of Wellington, who knew me, and one of them was his bride. We passed the night in the "Black Swan" at York; I saw the old city with its beautiful cathedral; I had never before seen such picturesque houses with carved work in gable-ends and balconies as were here. The swallows flew whistling through the street in great flocks, and my own bird, the stork, hovered over my head. The following day we went by the railway train to Newcastle, situated in a depth of smoke and steam. The viaduct and bridge near the town were not yet finished, and we were therefore obliged to go in an omnibus through the city to the railway beyond the town. All was bustle and in disorder here.

In England they do not give one tickets for baggage, as in other countries of Europe, and the travellers themselves must take care of their things; at those places where the luggage had to be shifted it was certainly a real plague. This day the crowd here was very great; there were many travellers, and early the same morning an express train of gentlemen had just started, who, with their hounds, were going a-hunting in Scotland. All the first-class carriages were already taken up, and so we were placed in second-class carriages, which are as bad as they can be, with wooden seats and wooden window-blinds, used only for fourth-class carriages in other countries.

The railway, passing over two deep valleys, was not yet finished, but still so far completed that we could pass over it. The timber-work of the bridges was placed upon mighty columns, and on this the rails were laid, but for the eye it was as if all wood-work was wanting, — as if we passed over the railings of a bridge ; we looked through the open frame-work down into the deep below us, where people were working on the banks of the river. We arrived at last at the river which marks the boundary between England and Scotland ; the realm of Walter Scott and Burns lay before us. Here the country was more mountainous ; we saw the sea ; the railway runs along the shore ; many boats were lying here, and at last we reached Edinburgh. The city is divided by a narrow, deep valley, like an immense dried up trench, into the old and new town, and down in the valley the railway from London to Glasgow passes. New Edinburgh has straight streets, and modern but tedious looking buildings ; one street crosses another or runs parallel with it ; the city possesses no other Scottish characteristic than that it has, like the Scottish plaid, its regular quadrangles ; but old Edinburgh is a city most picturesquely magnificent, so old looking, so gloomy and peculiar. The houses, which have in the main street two or three stories, have their rears on that deep cut which divides the old and new city, and here the same houses have from nine to eleven stories. When in the evening the lights are burning in the different rooms, story above story, and the intense gas-lights are beaming over the roofs of the other houses in the lofty streets, then it produces a peculiar, almost gala aspect, with lights high up in the air, and may be seen from the railway carriages, which pass at the base of Edinburgh. I arrived here with old Hambro toward evening ; the son met us with his carriage at the railway terminus ; the reception was a bright one, and soon we went on a gallop out of the city to their country-house, " Mount Trinity," where I was now to find in Hambro's family a home in Walter Scott's country, and Burns's mountains ! Many letters that had arrived for me, lay before me as a bouquet ; there was an air of elegance and comfort, such as one often finds in an English house ; I saw around me dear, kind people, who were most hospitably disposed. It was one of my life's happiest evenings. Our house was situated in the midst of a garden, surrounded with low walls ; the railway from Edinburgh out to the bay of the sea passed near by. The fishing-place here is a considerable town, but very like those of the Zealand fishers. The Scotch women's dresses were still more picturesque than the Danish ; a broad striped skirt very neatly tucked up showing the variegated petticoat.

The next day I already felt as if I had lived a long time in the family ; where we know that we are dear and welcome, there we soon feel as at home. I found here lively, amiable children whom the old grandfather loved tenderly. I could again enjoy a happy family life. The custom and manners of the house were in all respects quite English. In the evening the family and servants were gathered for devotions, a prayer was said, a chapter from the Bible was read. I saw the same thing afterward in all the families where I came ; and it made a beautiful and good impression on me. Every day was rich with variety for me. The first forenoon there began the making of calls and seeing and knowing all around me. I was certainly in great want of bodily rest, but how could I get it here where there was so much to be done ?

It was but a few minutes by the railway train to Edinburgh. The train stopped before a tunnel under the hill, on the top of which several of the new Edinburgh streets are situated. Most of the passengers alighted.

" Are we already there ? " I asked.

" No, sir," said my guide, as we again were moving, " but only a few passengers go farther, because they are afraid that the tunnel here is not strong enough ; that the whole street on the top may tumble down into the tunnel, and therefore most of them prefer to alight here ; I do not think it will tumble down while we are going through ! " — and we rushed into the long, dark vault — and that time it did not fall down, but it was not pleasant at all ; still I always passed through it when I visited Edinburgh by railway.

The view from the new city of the old one is imposing and magnificent, and offers a panorama which places Edinburgh, as to picturesque groupings, along with Constantinople and Stockholm. The long street — we may almost call it a quay, if the gap, through which the railway runs may be considered as a channel — has the whole panorama of the old city with its

castle and Heriot's hospital.   Where the city declines toward
the sea is the mountain, "Arthur's Seat," known from Walter Scott's novel, "The Heart of Mid-Lothian."   The entire old city itself is a great commentary upon his powerful writings.   Therefore the monument of Walter Scott is
fittingly placed here, where from the new part of the city the
panorama of old Edinburgh is seen.   The monument has the
shape of a mighty Gothic tower ; below we see a sitting statue
of the poet, his dog Maida reposing at his feet, and in the upper arches of the tower are seen the world-renowned characters
in his writings, *Meg Merrilies*, the *Last Minstrel*, and so forth.

The renowned physician, Dr. Simpson, was my guide in the
old town.   The main street runs along the ridge of a hill ;
its many side streets are narrow, filthy, and with houses of six
stories ; the oldest houses seemed to be built of heavy freestone.   We are reminded of the mighty buildings of the dirty
Italian towns.   Poverty and misery seemed to peep out of the
open holes which are used for windows ; rags and tatters were
put out to dry.   There was shown in one of those lanes a
dark, gloomy, stable-looking house, which once had been
Edinburgh's notable and only hotel, where kings used to put
up, and where Samuel Johnson had lived a long while.   I saw
the house where Burke had lived, where the unhappy victims
were enticed to enter and were suffocated, in order to be sold
as corpses.   In the main street was still to be seen, though
in a dilapidated condition, Knox's little house, with a piece of
sculpture representing him speaking from a pulpit.   Passing
by the old prison of Edinburgh, which does not attract attention by its exterior, but only by Walter Scott's novel, we
continued our researches down to Holyrood, which is situated
in the western outskirts of the city.   We saw here a long
hall with poor portraits, and other rooms, where Charles X.
had lived.   Not until we came to Mary Stuart's sleeping-
room had Holyrood any interest for me.   The hangings
here showed "The Fall of Phæton," which she might have
had always before her eyes, as if it was a prediction of her
own fate.   Into that little room near by was the unhappy
Rizzio dragged to be murdered.   Stains of blood are still to
be seen on the floor ; on either side was a dark tower-cham-

ber ; the church was now a beautiful ruin. Ivy, which in England and Scotland grows with an abundance I have seen only in Italy, covers here the walls of the church ; it looks like a great rich carpet, the eternal green winding up round windows and columns. Grass and flowers shoot up around the tombstones.

Do not call these pictures of Edinburgh passages from an account of a journey ; they are really sections of the story of my life. They are reflected so vividly in my mind and thoughts, that they belong there entirely.

There was a scene connected with this exploration of the city and buildings which made a strong impression on me. A large company of us visited George Heriot's hospital, — a grand building like a palace, whose founder, the goldsmith, we all know from Walter Scott's novel, "The Fortunes of Nigel." The stranger must bring a written permit, and then with his own hand write his name in the book at the entrance. I wrote my whole name, "Hans Christian Andersen,"[1] as I always have been called in England and Scotland. The old porter read it, and followed steadily the elder Hambro, who had a good, jovial face and silvery hair, showing him every attention, and at last asked him if he were the Danish poet.

"I have always thought him to have a mild face and venerable hair like yours."

"No," was the answer, pointing to me, "there is the poet!"

"So young!" exclaimed the old man : "I have read him, and the boys have read him also! It is remarkable to see such a man, for they are always so old or else dead, when we hear of them!" They told me of it and I went up to the old man and pressed his hand. He and the boys knew very well about "The Ugly Duckling" and "The Red Shoes!"

It surprised and affected me to be known here, and that I had friends among these poor children and those who surrounded them. I was obliged to step aside to hide my tears ; God knows the thoughts of my heart.

The editor of the "Literary Gazette," Mr. Jerdan, had furnished me with a letter to the well-known editor of the

[1] The reader may have noticed that in Denmark his name is always written "H. C. Andersen." — ED.

"Edinburgh Review," Lord Jeffrey, to whom Dickens has dedicated his "Cricket on the Hearth." He lived out of Edinburgh at his country seat, a truly old, romantic castle, whose walls and windows were almost covered with ivy. A great fire burned in the fire-place in the large saloon, where the family soon was gathered, and where young and old surrounded me. Kindly children and grandchildren came forth ; I was begged to write my name in different copies of my books which they had. We walked round in the great park to a point from which we had a fine view of Edinburgh, which resembles much that of Athens ; here we saw also a Lycabettos and an Acropolis. A couple of days after the whole family returned my visit ; they came to "Mount Trinity," and as they took leave Lord Jeffrey said, "Come soon again to Scotland that we may see each other ; I have not many years to live !" Death has already called him ; we did not meet again upon earth.

I met several renowned personages in social life at the house of the authoress, Miss Rigby, who has visited Copenhagen and written of it ; and at that of the excellent physician Mr. Simpson, I came to know the greatest variety of people. I met the joval critic Mr. Wilson : he was all life and humor, and called me jokingly " brother ; " the most opposite critical parties met to show me their good-will.

The Danish Walter Scott was the name of honor with which many unworthily honored me ; the authoress Mrs. Crowe brought me also into her novel "Susan Hopley," which has been translated into Danish. We met at Dr. Simpson's, where, at a large party, experiments with ether inhalation were made : it was to my mind not a nice thing to see ladies dreaming under the intoxication ; they laughed with open, dead eyes. It made me very uncomfortable, and so I said, confessing that it was an excellent and blessed discovery to be used at a painful operation, but not to play with ; that to make such experiments was wrong, and a tempting of God ; an old venerable man joined with me and said the same. It seems that I had by my remark won his heart ; and when a few days after we accidentally met on the street, where I had just bought as a souvenir of Edinburgh a copy of the Holy

Bible in a cheap, beautiful edition, he became still more drawn toward me, stroked me on the cheek, and said warm things in praise of my pious mind, which I did not deserve. Accident had placed me in a light which appeared to him so beautiful.

Eight days had elapsed and I wished to see a little of the Highlands. Hambro, who with his family, was going to a bathing-place on the west coast of Scotland, proposed to make me their guest on the journey through a part of the Highlands, and together with them to see those places which Walter Scott has painted for us in " The Lady of the Lake," and in " Rob Roy ; " we were not to separate before we came to Dumbarton.

On the opposite side of the Frith of Forth is situated the little town of Kirkcaldy, where on the woody mountain lies a magnificent old ruin ; gulls hovered over it, and plunged their wings with shrieks into the water. It was at first told me that that was the ruin of Ravenswood Castle, but an old gentleman from the town came forward, and explained that that was something they had invented to tell strangers, because the name had gained more than common interest through " The Bride of Lammermoor," but in itself the name of Ravenswood was only a fanciful name of the author. The event took place further up in Scotland. The name of Ashton, too, was a fictitious one, the real family living still, and called Star.

The ruin with its gloomy prison-vaults, its luxurious evergreen, which like a carpet covered the remnants of the walls, and grew in clusters down the projecting cliff, was most picturesque and peculiar, because the sea had just receded at the ebbing of the tide. The view of Edinburgh from here was very grand and memorable.

We went on a steamer up the Frith of Forth ; a modern minstrel sang Scottish ballads, and accompanied his song by playing upon his violin, which was in very poor tune ; thus we approached the Highlands, where the rocks stood like outposts, the fog hovered over them and lifted again ; it was like an unexpected arrangement to show us the land of Ossian in its true light. Stirling's mighty castle, situated on a rock, which appeared like a gigantic figure of stone, thrown out from the level plain, crowned the town, whose oldest streets are dirty, badly paved, and in quite the same style as in the days of yore.

It is said that the Scots like to tell stories about the history of their country, and out of Darnley's house there came a shoemaker up to us in the street, and gave us explanations, and anecdotes about Darnley, Mary Stuart, ancient times, and the exploits of the Scots.

The view is really grand from the castle over the historic plain where the battle was fought between Edward II. and Robert Bruce. We drove to the line where King Edward pitched his standard. Posterity has chipped off so many pieces of the stones among which it stood, that now, in order to prevent it, there has been laid an iron lattice over the stones. A poor smithy stands near by; we entered it: it was here that James I. took his refuge, sent for a priest and confessed; the priest hearing that he was the king, stabbed him with a knife through the heart, — the smith's wife showed us in her little room a corner, where her bed was standing, which was the very place of the murder. The whole country had besides a Danish appearance, but was poorer and did not look so advanced. The linden-tree was here in blossom, while at home it already bore its great seed-buttons.

Travelling in England and Scotland is very expensive, but one gets something for his money here; everything is excellent, one is well taken care of, and is comfortable, even in the smallest village-inns; at least so it appeared to me. Callander is nothing but a village, but we lived here as in a castle of a count; soft carpets were lying on the stairs and along the entries, the fire flashed in the grate, and it was needed too, though the sun shone and we saw the Scots going with bare knees, as they also do in the winter-time. They wrapped themselves up in variegated plaids; even poor boys wore one, if only a rag.

Out of my window a river could be seen winding round an old hill, like our Giant Mounds; there was an arched bridge covered with the most luxurious evergreen, and near by the rocks rose higher; the Highlands lay before us. Early in the morning we set out to reach the steamboat, on Loch Katrine. The road grew more and more wild; the sweet-broom

began to appear in blossom; we passed by some solitary
houses built of stone. Loch Katrine, long and narrow,
with deep, dark water, lay stretched between green mountain ridges. Heath and brush covered the banks, and as far
as I could see, the impression was: "If the heaths of Jutland are a sea in calm, the heaths here are a sea in storm!"
The great mountain waves are standing dull, but green, with
brush and grass. At our left lay in the lake a little island
overgrown with wood; it was Ellen's Island, from which "the
Lady of the Lake" had set out in her boat. At the opposite
side of the lake, at the extreme point where we landed, was a
poor inn, — a kind of sleeping-place, large and wide, bed set by
bed, I think almost fifty of them; the room was low-studded,
reed mats were on the floor, and the walls pierced by small
windows; it looked like a turf-house, where the travellers
coming over Loch Lomond from "Red Robin's" land could
get a shelter till the following morning, when the steamer
passed over Loch Katrine. We did not stay here very long;
all the passengers went away, most of them on foot, some
riding on horseback. Hambro had procured a little carriage
for me and for his wife, both of us being too weak to make
the fatiguing foot-journey through the heather. There was no
regular road, only a foot-path. We drove where the carriage
best could go, over high places and low, over knolls and stones,
which served as marks for a future road. The driver walked
by the side of the horse; now we rolled down the descent at
a rapid rate, and then went dragging slowly upward; it was
a peculiar pace. Not a house was to be seen; we did not
meet a man; all around was quiet, — dark mountains wrapped
in mist; all one and the same. A lonely shepherd, who,
stiff with cold, was wrapped up in his gray plaid, was the first
and the only living object we saw for miles. There was a repose over the whole landscape. Ben Lomond, the highest
top of the mountain, broke through the fog, and soon we discovered below us Loch Lomond. The descent to it was
so steep, although there was a kind of road, that it was a dangerous thing to come down with a carriage. We had to leave
it, and on foot we approached the well-furnished steamboat.
The first I met on board was a countryman, the excellent

geological author of the Island of Moen, Mr. R. Puggaard. We were all on board wrapped up in our plaids ; in rain and drizzle, in fog and wind the steamboat passed straight up to the most northern part of the lake, where a little river flows out ; passengers were coming and going ; we were now in the midst of the scenery of " Rob Roy," —

> " Land of brown heath and shaggy wood,
> Land of the mountain and the flood ! " —

as it is sung in " The Lay of the Last Minstrel." Here on the right, on our return down the lake, we passed Rob Roy's cavern. A boat arrived with a large company ; among them was a young lady, who looked fixedly and penetratingly at me ; a little while after one of the gentlemen came up to me and told me that she was a young lady who thought she knew me from a portrait, and asked me if I was not the Danish poet, Hans Christian Andersen ? " Yes," I said, and the young lady ran toward me, happy and affectionate, and like an old friend confidentially pressed my hand, and expressed naturally and beautifully her happiness at seeing me. I asked her for one of the many mountain flowers she brought with her from Rob Roy's rock, and she selected the best and most beautiful one. Her father and the whole family surrounded me, and urged me to accompany them to their home, to be their guest, but I neither could nor would leave my company. It pleased Mr. Hambro to see the respect that was shown me, and the attention of all the passengers was soon directed to me, and it was astonishing to see how large a circle of friends I had. There is a peculiarly happy feeling, when so far from home, in being so well received and made to belong to so many kind people.

We landed at Balloch, passed by Smollet's monument in his little native town, and arrived toward evening at Dumbarton, a real Scotch town near the Clyde. In the night a storm raged with long, gigantic gusts, and it was as if I continually heard the rolling of the sea ; there was a constant crash ; the windows rattled, a sick cat mewed all the time, it was not possible to shut my eyes ; but at dawn it grew calmer, — a sepulchral calm after such a night. It was Sunday, and that signifies something in Scotland, where all is at rest ; even railway trains were not going, except only that from London to Edinburgh,

but which does not stop, that it may not give offense to the
puritan Scots.   All the houses were closed, people were staying
at home, reading the Bible or getting drunk — so I was told.
It was entirely against my nature to stay in doors a whole day.
I proposed to take a walk, but I was told that it would not do
and would give offense.   Toward evening, however, we all
took a promenade out of town, but there was such a silence,
such a looking out at us from the windows, that we soon turned
back again.   A young Frenchman, with whom I spoke, assured
me that he had recently been out one Sunday afternoon
with two Englishmen with a fishing-rod, when an old gentleman passed by and with the most hard and angry words reproached them for their wickedness in diverting themselves on
Sunday, instead of sitting at home with their Bibles, and they
ought at least not to offend or excite others !   Such a Sunday
piety cannot be really true ; where it is, I honor it, but as an inherited habit it becomes a mask, and only occasions hypocrisy.
    I stopped at a little book-store with Hambro to buy books
and maps.
    " Have you the portrait of the Danish poet, Hans Christian
Andersen ? " asked Hambro, jestingly.
    " Yes, sir ! " answered the man, and added : " The poet is
said to be here in Scotland ! "
    " Should you know him ? "   The man looked at Hambro,
took my portrait, looked steadily at him, and said : " It
must be you ! " so faithful was the picture !   Hambro would
not let me remain unknown ; and when the good man in
Dumbarton heard that I was the author, he forgot all, begged
to know if he might call for his wife and children to come
and see and talk with me.   They came and seemed very
happy to meet me, and nothing would do but I must shake
hands all round.   I felt and understood that at least my
name if not I myself was known in Scotland.   " Nobody will
believe it at home ! " said I to Hambro, and added : " But let
it be so ; it is much more than I deserve ! "   I was touched, I
shed tears, as I always do when I am surprised by anything
unexpected, or when people see something too much in my
poetical nature.   It all went beyond my most daring youthful
dreams and expectations ; it often seemed to me that it was

only a dream, an empty dream, that I should not dare tell my friends when I awoke.   In Dumbarton I took leave of Hambro ; his wife and children went to a sea-side watering-place, and I by steamer up the river Clyde to Glasgow ; the parting made me very sad, for I had all the time in Scotland lived with these dear people.   Hambro himself had been as a kind, careful brother to me ; whatever he believed could please me that I received ; he anticipated my wishes, and his excellent wife was full of spirit and feeling ; the children also were trustful and lively.   I have not seen any of them since, and I shall see the mother only when I go to God, to whom she went from her dear ones here on the earth ; my thoughts fly toward her with thankfulness.   It is comforting and good to have dear friends on the earth and in heaven.

I had yet a struggle with myself before I left Dumbarton, whether I should go back to London, or return home, or prolong my stay in Scotland, thus going further north up to Loch Laggan, where Queen Victoria and Prince Albert lived, and by whom, as a letter told me, I should be graciously received.

My stay in Scotland was not such a rest as I had believed ; I was not much strengthened, after having spent about three weeks here, and no better than when I came up.   Besides, well informed people, as I believed they were, told me that there was no decent inn here for several miles ; that it was necessary for me to engage a servant ; in short, that I should live in better style than my purse would allow.   To write to King Christian VIII., who had kindly offered to support me, I could not bring myself to do, as I had verbally declined to accept that favor, and now weeks would pass before I could get an answer.   It was real torture !   I wrote a letter home, told them how I was, and that I thought it best for me to return home, as I also did, but I was obliged thereby to refuse various invitations which I received from some of Scotland's wealthy nobility to visit their homes.   I was deprived of the pleasure of seeing Abbotsford, to which place I had a letter of introduction.   Walter Scott's son-in-law, Lockhart, whose guest I had been in London, had received me very kindly and affectionately.   His daughter, the grandfather's darling, had told me of her dear grandfather.   At her house I had seen relics which had belonged to the great poet, — his magnificent life-like picture, as he sits with his dog Maida, gazing on me. Miss Lockhart presented me a fac-simile of him, who once was called the Great Unknown. Abbotsford had to be given up, as also Loch Laggan, and I returned homeward dejected, leaving Glasgow for Edinburgh.

I must tell an event, in itself very insignificant, but to me a new hint of that fortunate star which shines over me in what is little as well as great. During my last stay in Naples I had bought a plain cane made of palm, which had accompanied me on my travels, and thus to Scotland also ; when I drove with Hambro's family over the heath between Loch Katrine and Loch Lomond, one of the boys had taken my cane to play with, and when we came within sight of Loch Lomond he lifted it up in the air and exclaimed : " Palm, do you see the highest Scotch mountain ? Do you see there the wide sea ? " and so on ; and I promised that the cane, when it should again visit Naples with me, should tell his comrades about the land of mist, where the spirits of Ossian lived, — of the land where the red thistle-flower was honored, set sparkling in the heraldic arms, for people and land. The steamboat arrived sooner than we had expected, and we were called upon in a hurry to come on board. " Where is my cane ? " I asked. It had been left behind in the inn ; when the boat which brought us to the north end of the lake returned, I requested Mr. Puggaard when he went ashore to take the cane with him to Denmark. I arrived in Edinburgh, and in the morning I stood upon the platform at the depot waiting to go from there to London, when the train from the north arrived a few minutes before the departure of our train. The conductor alighted, came up to me, seemed to know me, and delivered me my cane, while he smilingly said, " It has travelled very well alone ! " A little label was attached to it with the inscription, " The Danish poet, Hans Christian Andersen ! " and they had taken such care of it, that the cane had passed from hand to hand, first with the steamboat on Loch Lomond, then with an omnibus conductor, after that by steamboat again, and now by a railway train, only by means of its little address label ; it reached my hands just as the signal was given

to start. I am still under obligation to tell the adventures of
the cane ; 1 wish I might some time do it as well as it made
its journey alone !

I went southward by way of Newcastle and York.   In the
carriage I met the English author Hook and his wife ; they
knew me and told me that all the Scotch newspapers had
mentioned my stay with the queen ! — I, who had never been
there at all ! the newspapers knew it, and one of them said
that I had read aloud my stories, yet not a word of it was true.
I bought at one of the stations the most recent copy of
" Punch." It was mentioned there ; it had a sally, a little
remark about a foreigner, a poet from abroad, being honored
by an invitation from the Queen, that had never been bestowed
on any English author.   That and various other reports of a
visit which never was realized, tormented me.   Speaking of
the witty paper, " Punch," one of my fellow-travellers said,
" That it was a sign of great popularity to be spoken of in it,
and that many an Englishman would pay his pounds to come
to that ! "   I would rather prefer to be exempt from it ; low-
spirited and depressed by the publicity, I arrived at London
almost sick.

I remained a couple of days in London.   I had still
not seen anything there but high life, and several of the
country's most excellent men and women ; galleries, museums,
and all such things were on the contrary new to me ; I had
not even had time to visit the Tunnel.   Early one morning I
decided to go to see it ; I was advised to go by one of the
many small steamers which are running up and down the
Thames through the city, but I felt so ill just as I started out,
that I gave up the long excursion to the Tunnel, and it may
be that my life was saved thereby ; for on the same day, and at
the very hour I was to have gone on board, one of the steamers,
the *Cricket*, was blown up with one hundred passengers.   The
report of the disaster was immediately spread over all London,
and although it was not at all certain that I should have gone
by just this boat, still the possibility, even the probability, was
so near, that I became solemnly and gratefully impressed and
thanked my God for the illness that overcame me shortly before the moment when I should have gone on board.

Society had now left London, the opera was closed, most of my best friends had left for different watering-places or for the Continent. I longed for Denmark, and for my dear ones there ; but before I took leave of England I was invited to spend a few days more in the country, at "Seven Oaks," at the house of my publisher, Mr. Richard Bentley. That little town, near by Knowle's renowned park, is situated not far from the railway to the English Channel ; it was for me then a very convenient and agreeable visit to make on my way home. I had been before at Seven Oaks, which is a pretty little town. This time I went by railway to Tunbridge, where Bentley's carriage was sent for me. Danish nature was all about me ; the country was varied with beautiful hills, on which here and there stood many old trees, that rendered the whole landscape like a park ; hedges or an iron fence formed the boundary. Elegant and comfortable rooms, roses and evergreen in the garden, close by the celebrated Knowle Park, whose old castle belongs to the Earl of Amherst. One of the possessor's ancestors was a poet, and in his honor one of the saloons is called the poet-saloon ; here is the portrait of that old, right honorable lord, the poet, in full length, and the portraits of other famous poets adorn the other walls as if for company for the reigning poet. In one of the neighboring houses was a costumer-shop, just like the old curiosity shop which Dickens has painted for us in " Master Humphrey's Clock." The day passed away like a feast for me among those kind people ; I became familiar with that genuine old English, excellent family life, where was found all the comfort that wealth and kindness can create.

How much I needed tranquillity and repose after the great exertion which my stay in England and Scotland had occasioned. If I was weary and exhausted, still I felt, and how could it be otherwise, a great sadness at leaving so many who had offered me so much pleasure and done me so much good. Among many of those whom I loved and should not see again, at least for a long time, was Charles Dickens. He had, since our acquaintance at Lady Blessington's, called upon me without finding me at home. We did not meet again in London ; I received a few letters from him, and he brought me all his works in a beautiful illustrated edition, and in every volume honored me by writing : " Hans Christian Andersen, from his friend and admirer, Charles Dickens." They told me that he and his wife and children were at the sea-side somewhere on the Channel, but they did not know where. I resolved to go from Ramsgate by way of Ostend, and wrote a letter to Dickens's address, hoping that it would find him, and told him the day and hour I expected to arrive at Ramsgate, and asked him to give his address in the hotel I was to stop at ; then if he did not live too far away I would come and see him and once more meet him. At the " Royal Oak " was a letter from Dickens ; he lived about one Danish mile from there at Broadstairs, and he and his wife expected me to dinner ; I took a carriage and drove to that little town near the sea. Dickens occupied a whole house himself; it was narrow and confined, but neat and comfortable. He and his wife received me in a very kind manner. It was so pleasant within that it was a long time before I perceived how beautiful was the view from the dining-room, where we sat ; the windows faced the Channel, the open sea rolled its waves beneath them. While we dined the tide ebbed ; the falling of the waters was very rapid ; the great sands where so many shipwrecked sailors' bones repose, rose up mightily, the lantern in the light-house was lighted. We talked of Denmark and Danish literature, of Germany and the German language, which Dickens meant to learn ; an Italian organ-grinder happened to come and play outside during dinner ; Dickens spoke Italian with the man, whose face was radiant at hearing his mother tongue. After dinner the children were brought in. " We have plenty of them ! " said Dickens ; there were no less than five, the sixth was not at home ; all the children kissed me, and the youngest one kissed his little hand and threw me a kiss. When the coffee was brought in, a young lady came as guest. " She is one of your admirers," said Dickens to me ; he had promised to invite her when I came. The evening passed very quickly. Mrs. Dickens seemed to be of about the same age as her husband, a little fleshy, and with such a very honest and good-looking countenance that one would immediately feel confidence in her. She was a great admirer of Jenny Lind, and wished much to have a bit of her handwriting, but it was very difficult to get. I had by me the little letter Jenny Lind had sent me on my arrival in London, to bid me welcome and to tell me where she lived ; I gave this now to Mrs. Dickens. We parted late in the evening, and Dickens promised that he would write to me in Denmark. But we were to meet each other again before my departure, for Dickens surprised me by coming to Ramsgate the following morning, and was on the quay when I went on board. " I wished to bid you farewell once more ! " said he, and accompanied me on board, remaining by me until the bell gave the signal for departure. We shook hands, he looked with his earnest eyes into mine, and when the ship started he stood on the very edge of the quay, so sturdy, so youthful, and handsome ! He waved his hat. Dickens was the last one who gave me a friend's greeting from the dear English coast.

I landed at Ostend. The first persons I met were the King of Belgium and his wife ; they received my first salutation, and reciprocated it kindly ; I did not know any other person there. The same day I went on the railway to Ghent. There, early in the morning, while I was waiting for the railway train to Cologne, several travellers came and presented themselves to me, saying that they knew me from my portrait. An English family approached me ; one of the ladies came up to me ; she was an authoress, as she told me, had been a few times in London in society with me, but I was then, she said, quite surrounded and monopolized ; she had besought Reventlow to present her to me, but he had answered, " You see that it is impossible ! " I laughed ; it really was the case. I was in the fashion as long as it lasted ; now I was entirely at her service. She was natural and kind, and I thanked my propitious star that I was so renowned. " How little it is ! " said I, and added, " and how long will it last ? " But still it has given me pleasure, although there is anxiety in being lifted so high, not knowing whether one can keep his place ! I was very thankful for all the honor and prosperity I had acquired ; through all Germany, where they had read of the honor I had found in England, great kindness and esteem was shown me. At Hamburg I met with countrymen of both sexes : —

"My God! Andersen, are you here?" was the reception; "nay, you cannot believe what immense fun "The Corsair" has made of your stay in England; you are represented with laurel-wreath and purses! My God, how funny it is!" I reached Copenhagen; a few hours after my arrival I was standing at my window, when two well-dressed gentlemen passed by; they perceived me, laughed, and one of them pointed at me, and said so loud that I could hear every word, —

"See, there stands our orang-outang so famous abroad!" It was rude — it was wicked — it reached my heart — and will never be forgotten!

I met also with sympathizing friends, — many who were glad of the honor which had been shown me, and the Danish nation through me, in skillful Holland and rich England. One of our older authors grasped me kindly by my hand, and said frankly and beautifully, "I have not before rightly read your works, now I will do it. People have spoken harshly of you, but you are something, must be something more than people here at home will allow; the manner in which you are received in England is such as would not befall an insignificant man! I honestly confess that I have now another opinion of you"

One of my dearest friends told me, however, something quite different, and proved it too in writing. He had sent to one of our prominent editors some English newspapers, in which mention was made of the honor I enjoyed in London, and also gave a very kind review of "The True Story of my Life." But the man would not print what was said about me, because, he said, "People would think that they made a fool of Andersen in England!" He would not believe it, and he knew that most of my countrymen would not believe it either. One of the newspapers reported that I had received money from the state for my journey, and therefore it was easy to understand how I could travel every year. I told King Christian VIII. what was written about me.

"You have — what I think few would have done," — said he, "refused my honest offer! They are unjust toward you at home! They do not know you!"

The first little book I wrote after my return, a volume of

stories, I sent to England ; they were published at Christmas time : " A Christmas Greeting to my English Friends; " it was dedicated thus to Charles Dickens : —

" I am again in my quiet Danish home, but my thoughts are daily in dear England, where, a few months ago, my many friends transformed for me reality into a charming story.

" Whilst occupied with a greater work, there sprung forth— as the flowers spring forth in the forest — seven short stories. I feel a desire, a longing, to transplant in England the first produce of my poetic garden, as a Christmas greeting ; and I send it to you, my dear, noble Charles Dickens, who by your works had been previously dear to me, and since our meeting have taken root forever in my heart.

" Your hand was the last that pressed mine on England's coast ; it was you who from her shores wafted me the last farewell. It is therefore natural that I should send to you, from Denmark, my first greeting again, as sincerely as an affectionate heart can convey it.

" HANS CHRISTIAN ANDERSEN.

" COPENHAGEN, 6*th December*, 1847."

The little book was extremely well received and flatteringly noticed. Yet what brightened my soul and heart like a true sunbeam, was the first letter from Dickens, in which he sent me his thanks and greeting. His affectionate nature shines forth and breathes a goodness toward me that makes me rich. Having before shown you all my best treasures, why should I not show you this ? Dickens will not misunderstand me.

" A thousand thanks, my dear Andersen, for your kind and very valuable recollection of me in your Christmas book. I am very proud of it, and feel deeply honored by it ; I cannot tell you how much I value such a token of acknowledgment from a man with the genius which you are possessed of.

" Your book made my Christmas hearth very happy. We are all enchanted by it. The little boy, the old man, and the tin-soldier are especially my favorites. I have repeatedly read that story, and read it with the most unspeakable pleasure.

" I was a few days ago at Edinburgh, where I saw some of your friends, who talked much about you. Come again to

England, soon ! But whatever you do, do not stop writing, because we cannot bear to lose a single one of your thoughts. They are too true and simply beautiful to be kept safe only in your own head.

" We returned some time since from the sea-coast where I bade you adieu, and are now at our own house. My wife tells me that I must give you her kind greetings. Her sister tells me the same. The same say all my children. And as we have all the same sentiments, I beg you to receive the summary in an affectionate greeting from your sincere and admiring friend,

" CHARLES DICKENS.

"To HANS CHRISTIAN ANDERSEN."

My poem, " Ahasuerus," appeared that Christmas in Danish and German. Several years before, when I entertained the idea of that poem, Oehlenschläger spoke to me about it. " How is it ? " said he : " they say that you are writing a drama of the world, with the history of all times ; I cannot understand it ! " I explained to him the idea as I have also expressed it earlier in these pages. " But in what form will you be able to do all that ? " he asked.

" I use alternately the lyric, epic, and dramatic, — now in verse and now in prose ! "

" You cannot do that ! " exclaimed the great poet passionately. " I also know something of making poems ! There is something which is called form and limit, and these must be respected ! Green wood has its place and burned coals theirs ! What answer have you for that ? "

" I certainly have an answer ! " said I kindly, although I was possessed to treat the matter jestingly. " I can certainly answer you, but you will become angry if I say what is in my mind ! "

" Indeed, I shall not take it ill ! " said he.

" Well, to show you that I really have an answer, I will keep to your words, — the green wood by itself and the burned coals by themselves. Now go on and say the sulphur by itself and the saltpetre by itself ; but then there would come one who mixed all those parts together, and — so he has invented gunpowder."

" Andersen ! it is dreadful to hear that expression, — to in‑ vent gunpowder ! You are a good man, but you are, as all say, too vain ! " — " But does not that belong to the trade ? " the frolicsome demon of humor prompted me to answer. " The trade ! the trade ! " repeated the good poet, who did not now understand me at all. When " Ahasuerus " was published he read it, and wishing to know if he now had altered his earlier opinion of it, he wrote me a very well meant and sincere letter in which he told me candidly how little the poem pleased him, and as his words at all times have an interest, and as several others have also looked upon my poem in the same way, I shall not conceal his judgment : —

" MY DEAR ANDERSEN, — I have always acknowledged and esteemed your fine talent in relating naturally and ingen‑ iously stories that have originality, as also in painting in the novel and in the account of travels the life which you meet with. I have been pleased, too, with your talent in the drama, for instance in ' The Mulatto,' although the subject was already given and poetically elaborated, and its beauties were mostly lyric. But a couple of years ago, when you read something to me, I gave you honestly to understand that the plan and form of the poem did not please me at all. Notwithstanding that, you seemed to be disagreeably surprised when I last talked with you, at my repeating it ; remarking that after all I only read a little of the book. I have now perused it with attention throughout, and cannot change my opinion. The book makes an unpleasant impression upon me : you must excuse my speaking so frankly. You ask me to tell you my opinion ; and I am obliged to tell it to you, when I would not put you off falsely with fair words. As far as I understand dramatic composition, ' Ahasuerus ' is no subject for a drama, and therefore Goethe wisely gave it up.

" The wonderful legend ought to be treated in a humorous manner as a wonder story. He was a shoemaker, but a shoemaker that went beyond his last, and was too proud not to believe what he could not comprehend. In making him an abstract idea of speculative poetry, you cannot make him an object of true poetry, still less of a drama. A drama requires necessarily a contracted, completed action, that may be held in the mind, and is expressed and unfolded by character. This is not the case with your piece. 'Ahasuerus' is presented throughout as a retiring and contemplating spectator. The other personages act as little ; the whole poem consists of lyric aphorisms, fragments, sometimes of narrative, all loosely combined. It seems to me that there is too much of pretension and too little of efficacy in the poem. It includes neither more nor less than the whole history of the world from the birth of Christ till our time. For those who profoundly and truly have studied history, with all its grand scenes and excellent characters, there can be no satisfaction in regarding those lyric aphorisms of hobgoblins, swallows, nightingales, mermaids, etc. Of course there are some beautiful lyric or descriptive passages, *e g.*, 'The Gladiators,' 'The Huns,' 'The Savages ;' but that is not enough. The whole is like a dream ; your natural propensity for writing stories is also visible here, because all images are represented almost as wondrous visions. The genius of history is not presented in its great variety ; thought has too little place ; the images are not new, nor are they original enough ; there is nothing that touches the heart ; on the contrary, in ' Barnabas ' there is something unnatural in the way he comes, after his crime, to honor and dignity, for no action nor development of character are seen in him ; we only hear it said that he formerly murdered an old woman, and then there is joy in heaven over his conversion. That is now *my* opinion ! Perhaps I fail, but I speak honestly on conviction, and cannot change my judgment for politeness or flattery ! Pardon me if I have innocently grieved you, and be assured that for the rest I acknowledge and regard you as an original poet, full of genius in other directions.　　" Truly yours,

" A. OEHLENSCHLÄGER.

" *December* 23, 1847."

There is much truth and justice in this letter about my poem, but I regard my work otherwise than the noble great poet has done. I have not called " Ahasuerus " *a dramatic poem*, and it ought not at all to be placed in that style of poetry; there is not and cannot be either the dramatic incident or its accompaniment of character-painting. "Ahasuerus" is a poem which in a changing form is intended to express the idea that mankind rejects the divine, but still proceeds toward perfection. I have tried to represent it shortly, clearly, and richly, believing that I should best attain that by changing the form ; the historical tops of mountain have served me as scenery. It should not be compared with a drama of Scribe or an epos of Milton : the aphoristic simplicities are like mosaic blocks ; the pieces taken together form the entire image. We can say of any building that we see it stone by stone ; each one may be taken separately, but it is not so that we should look at them but as an entirety produced by the combination of parts.

In later years many opinions have been expressed concerning the poem, which agree with my belief that it always will mark a transition-point in my poetic life. The first, and I must almost say the only one, who was immediately and highly touched by my poem, was the historian Ludwig Müller, who considered "Ahasuerus" and "Wonder Stories" as the two books which gave me position in Danish literature.

From abroad a similar acknowledgment has reached me. In "The Picture-hall of the World's Literature," where there is a considerable collection of lyric and dramatic poetry from all countries, — from Hebrew psalms and Arabian folk-songs to the troubadours and the poets of our days, — the section "Scandinavian" contained of Danish authors, besides scenes of "Hakon Jarl," "King René's Daughter," and "Tiber," a few scenes also from "Ahasuerus."

Just as I finish these pages, eight years after the first publication of the poem, a well disposed and profound critic of my collected writings has favored "Ahasuerus" in the "Danish Monthly" with a greater attention than before ; it is recognized as what I myself considered it to be, *a running on*, which points at my future development as a poet.

CHAPTER XIV.

THE year 1848 rolled up its curtain, — a remarkable year, a volcanic year, when the heavy waves of time washed also over our country with the blood of war. During the first days of January, King Christian VIII. was sick; the last time I saw him was on an evening; I received a note inviting me to tea, and asking me to bring something or other to read for his Majesty. Besides his Majesty I found here the Queen, a lady of honor, and a courtier. The King greeted me very tenderly, but was obliged to lie down on the sofa; I read for him a couple of chapters from my unfinished novel, "The Two Baronesses," and besides that two or three stories; the King seemed very animated, and laughed and talked in a lively fashion. When I took leave he nodded kindly to me from his couch, and the last words I heard him say were: "We shall soon meet again." But we did not. He grew very ill; I felt a restlessness and anxiety at fear of losing him, and went every day out to Amalienburg to ask after his state of health; we heard soon that he was surely going to die; I went in grief with the news to Oehlenschläger, who very strangely had not heard that the King's life was in danger; he saw my affliction and burst into tears; he was most intimately attached to the King.

In the forenoon of the next day I met Oehlenschläger at Amalienburg, leaning on Christiani, coming out from the antechamber. Oehlenschläger was pale; he did not say a word, pressed my hand in passing, and tears were in his eyes. The King was almost given up. The twentieth of January I went out there several times; I stood in the evening in the snow and looked up at the windows, where the King within was dying. At a quarter past ten he departed. The next morning people were standing before the palace: within Christian VIII. lay dead! I went home and wept bitterly and tenderly for him, whom I loved unspeakably, and now was lost for me in this world.

The whole city of Copenhagen was in motion ; a new order of things was developing. On the twenty-eighth of January the Constitution was announced. Christian VIII. lay on *lit de parade;* I came there, I saw him, and became so painfully touched that I was taken ill and carried into one of the side rooms. The twenty-fifth of February the King's corpse was brought to Roeskilde ; I sat at home and listened to the tolling of the church bells. Great changes were passing over Europe : the revolution broke out in Paris ; Louis Philippe with his family left France ; like heavy seas the revolt went through the cities of Germany ; at home we still only read of such things. Here only was a home of peace ! here we could still breathe freely and enjoy art, the drama, and all that was beautiful. But peace did not last long, the heavy swells reached us also. The uproar broke out in Holstein. Rumor struck here and there like a flash of lightning, and all was in motion. A very great mass of people was gathered in the large Casino-hall, and next morning a deputation waited upon the King : I stood at the open place before the palace and looked at the great multitude. The King's answer was soon known in the city, as also the dismission of the ministry. I became aware how differently the events were regarded in different circles. Great companies of people crowded the streets night and day, singing national songs ; no excesses happened, but it was rather unpleasant to meet those almost strange people, those unknown faces ; it was as if an entirely new race had come forth. Several friends of order and peace joined the crowd of people in order to lead them from wrong ways. I was appointed one of the committee of peace, and often, when the crowd cried out the name of a place where they perhaps would have committed some excess, a single one of us needed only to repeat " Straight forward ! " and the whole crowd would move forward ! The public sang in the theatres, and the orchestra played national songs. It was announced that the city was to be illuminated, and strangely enough, those who were the least well disposed toward the new ministry illuminated their houses, for fear of getting their windows cracked.

The Sleswick deputies came to Copenhagen ; the rage against them was great, but the King announced in his proclamation : " We trust to the honor of our Danish people the safety of the Sleswick-Holstein deputies ! " The students preserved peace ; they went round in the crowd and spoke friendly words. Soldiers were drawn up in the streets, that the deputies might safely walk down to the steamship ; the mass of people was here awaiting them, but meantime the deputies were led from the palace to the canal behind it, and from there to the custom-house, where without being observed they went on board.

Preparations for war were made by land and by sea. Every one aided as well as he could. One of our officers came to me and said that it would be well if I were to defend our cause through the English press, where I was known and read. I wrote immediately to Mr. Jerdan, the editor of the " Literary Gazette," where my letter, a true account of the tone and situation at home, was immediately published.

" COPENHAGEN, 13 *April*, 1848.

" DEAR FRIEND, — A few weeks only have elapsed since I wrote to you, and in the history of time lies a range of events, as if years had passed. Politics has never been my business ; poets have another mission ; but now, when convulsions are shaking the countries, so that it is almost impossible to stand upon the ground without feeling it to the very ends of the fingers, we must speak of it. You know how momentous it is in Denmark ; we have war ! but a war carried on by the entire animated Danish people, — a war where noble-born and peasant, inspired by a righteous cause, place themselves voluntarily in the ranks of battle ; an enthusiasm and patriotism fill and elevate the whole Danish nation. The false light in which the leaders of the Sleswick-Holstein party have for many years through German newspapers brought us before the honest German people ; the manner in which the Prince of Noer has taken Rendsborg, saying that the Danish king was not free, and that it was in his royal interest he acted, — all this has excited the Danes, and the people as one man have risen : all small matters of every-day life give place to great and noble traits. All is in motion, but with order and union ; contributions of money are flowing in freely from all ranks and classes, even the poor journeyman and servant-girl bring their share. It was heard that horses were wanting, and in a few days so many of them were sent from city and country that the Minister of War has been obliged to publish that he did not require any more. In all the houses women are picking lint ; in the upper classes of the schools boys are occupied in making cartridges ; most of those who are able to bear arms exercise themselves in the use of them. Young counts and barons place themselves as subalterns in the ranks of the soldiers, and you may comprehend that the soldiers' courage and enthusiasm are strengthened by the knowledge that all stand alike in love and defense of the father-land.

"Among the volunteers is also the son of the Governor of Norway, — a young man, who belongs to one of the first families. He was here on a visit last winter, and, carried away by our honest cause, he wished to share in the combat, but as a foreigner he could not be admitted ; he then immediately bought a Danish house, presented himself as a Danish citizen, put on the soldier's jacket, and marched off as a subaltern with one of the regiments, decided to live on his hard tack and his wages, twelve Danish shillings a day, and to share his comrades' lot. And like him Danish men of all classes have done the same ; the gentleman and the student, the rich and the poor, all go together, singing and rejoicing as to a festival ! Our King himself has gone to the army's headquarters ; he is Danish and honest-minded for his righteous cause. He is surrounded by his life-guard, consisting partly of Holsteiners ; those were at the departure exempted from going against their countrymen, but every one of them begged as a favor to be allowed to go, and it was granted.

"Until this moment and we hope further our Lord is with us. The army goes quickly and victoriously forward : the island of Als is taken, as also the towns of Flensborg and Sleswick ; we stand at the boundary of Holstein, and have taken more than a thousand prisoners ; the most part of them are brought here to Copenhagen, very enraged against the prince of Noer, who, notwithstanding his promise to sacrifice his life and blood with them, left them in the first battle, — left them when the Danes with gunshots and bayonets entered Flensborg by force. At the present time the storms of change sweep through the countries, but the one above all of them, the righteous God, does not change ! He is for Denmark, — that great Will which is right, and which shall and must be acknowledged ; truth is the victorious power of all people and nations.

" ' For the nationalities, their rights ; for honest and good men, all prosperity ! ' That is and must be Europe's watchword, and with it I look trustingly forward. The Germans are an honest, truth-loving people ; they will come to see more clearly into our situation, and their enmity will and must be changed into esteem and friendship : may that thought soon come ! May God make his countenance to shine over the countries !   " HANS CHRISTIAN ANDERSEN."

The letter was one among the very few that went through several of the newspapers abroad. I felt more than ever before how firmly I had grown to the native soil and how Danish was my heart ; I could have taken my place in the soldiers' ranks, and gladly have given my life an offering to victory and peace, but at the same time the thought came vividly over me how much good I had enjoyed in Germany, the great acknowledgment which my talent there had received, and the many single persons whom I there loved and was grateful to. I suffered infinitely ! and when sometimes one or another excited mind expressed itself in anger and harshness, seeking to break down that feeling in me, then it was often more than I could bear ! I will not here offer any examples of these words ; I hope the best, that all bitter words from that time may disappear, and the wound be healed between these kindred people ! H. C. Örsted here again raised my spirits, and predicted a new spirit toward me, which has come indeed. There was concord, there was love ; many of my young friends went out as volunteers, among them Valdemar Drewsen and Baron Henry Stampe. Örsted was strongly touched at the progress of events ; he wrote in one of our daily newspapers three poems, " The Combat," " Victory," and " Peace."

To put on the red jacket was in former days a step taken
only in desperation ; the soldier was then but a poor fellow :
now the red jacket came suddenly into esteem and honor ;
ladies in silk and gauze walked with the red-jacketed soldier.
The first one I saw of high rank was Lövenskjold, the Norwegian Governor's son, and also the young Count Adam
Knuth, who had very recently been confirmed. He lost one
of his limbs by a minie ball. Lövenskjold fell, as also the
painter Lundbye, but the last one died from an accidental
shot. I heard of it from an eye-witness. Lundbye stood
leaning in a melancholy manner on his musket ; some peasants
passed by where other muskets near him were placed, and
they happened to knock them down ; a shot was heard, and
Lundbye was seen falling to the ground ; he was shot through
the jaw, the mouth was torn open, and a piece of flesh with
the beard on shot away : he uttered some feeble sighs ; was
wrapped up in a Dannebrog-flag, and laid in the earth.

These young men's enthusiasm moved me to tears, and
one day, hearing a jest of some young gentlemen, who before
used to sport kid gloves, but now as pioneers were digging at
trenches with red, blistered hands, I rushed up and exclaimed
from my very heart, " I should like to kiss those hands ! "
Almost every day troops of young men were marching off. I
accompanied a young friend, and coming home I wrote the
song, —

"I cannot stay, I have no rest ! "

It was soon was taken up as a popular song and was really stirring to hear.

" The Easter bell chimed " — the unfortunate Easter Day
of Sleswick rose : the hostile forces divided ours ; heavy
grief was spread over the country ; but courage was not lost,
strength became more concentrated, men were knit closer to
one another ; this appeared as well in great as in small things.
The Prussians entered Jutland ; our troops, Als. In the middle
of May I went to Funen, and found the whole manor of Glorup
filled with our troops ; their head-quarters was in Odense. At
Glorup were forty men, besides several high officers ; General
Hedemann kept up maneuvers on the fields. The old Count
treated all the volunteers among the subalterns like officers,

and gave them places at his table. Most of the officers had been in the campaign, and related in a lively manner what they had seen pass. Their night-quarters had sometimes been in an open street of a village, where they slept by the side of the houses, with their knapsacks under their heads, in rain and storm ; sometimes they were stowed in small chambers, where their couch was often a high chest of drawers ornamented with brass work, which was very hard on the flesh, but the exceeding weariness saved them from feeling anything, and they slept soundly. A young surgeon told us of his march with the soldiers over the bare heaths ; he was assigned a church for a hospital, the altar-candles were lighted, but still it was half dark ; far off signal-shots were heard ; the enemy was coming ; the whole exciting scene of that night was brought as clearly to my mind as if I myself had seen it pass. The Prussians had pressed through Jutland ; they asked a contribution of four millions, and reports of another battle were soon heard.

All our thoughts and hopes were turned toward the Swedes : their debarkation was to take place at Nyborg, where everything was arranged to receive them in a solemn manner. The manor of Glorup received sixteen Swedish officers with their attendants, besides twenty musicians and subaltern officers ; among the Swedes were four men, supplied by the Duke of Augustenborg, or rather by his estates in Sweden, which were obliged to furnish them against their lord. The Swedes were received with rejoicing ; the true zeal shown by the stewardess of Glorup, old Miss Ibsen, was characteristic and beautiful ; the great quartering of soldiers on the manor gave her much to think of. " A great bed must be made for them in the barn ! " was said. " To let them lie in the barn upon straw ! " said she. " No, they shall have beds ! They are coming here to help us, and they shall certainly have a bed ! " and she had wood procured and bedsteads made for ten or twelve rooms. Feather-beds were also obtained; coarse but white sheets were shining in her " caserne," as she called it. I have later given a picture in the " Nordischer Telegraph " of the Swedish soldiers' stay in Funen, as I saw it at Glorup, and I think that a miniature of it would be in its right place here.

THE SWEDES IN FUNEN, 1848.

I must tell you a little of the Swedes in Funen! Their stay here is among the most beautiful and bright images of this summer. I witnessed their solemn reception in the small towns, the waving flags, the radiant faces ; many miles far up in the country, peasants were standing in crowds along the roads, old and young, asking, full of expectation, " Are the Swedes coming now?" They were received with eating and diinking, with flowers and hand-shakings. They were kind-hearted men, well-disciplined soldiers ; their morning and evening devotion was very solemn, as also their church-service every Sunday, all in the open air, after ancient warlike custom from the time of Gustavus Adolphus. The divine ser-vice on Sunday took place in the old mansion-house, where one of the highest commanding, officers and the whole band of music were quartered ; the band played, the troops marched into the large, square castle yard, and were here drawn up in order, the officers in front ; the singing of psalms commenced, accompanied by the music. Now the chaplain stepped forth on the large staircase, whose high stone breast-work was covered with a great carpet. I recollect well the last Sunday here : during the service, which had begun in gray, stormy weather, the minister spoke of the angel of peace, who descended as God's mild animating sunshine, and just as he spoke of it, the sun accidentally broke forth and shone upon the polished helms and the pious faces. Yet the most solemn of all was the morning and evening devotion. The companies were drawn up on the open road ; an under-officer read a short prayer, and now they intoned the psalms with accompaniment of music ; when the song was ended, through the whole rank was heard a profound " God save the King ! " I perceived many of our old peasants standing at the ditch and behind the hedge, with uncovered heads and clasped hands, joining silently in the divine service.

After the usual daily military exercise the Swedish soldier was seen faithfully assisting in the field in this year's rich harvest. At the manor, where we had the regimental band, there was playing every afternoon until sunset ; the long lin-

den-tree alleys in the garden were filled with people from the
whole neighborhood : it was a daily feast ; in the evening the
Swedish violin was tuned in the servants' hall, and dancing
commenced with mutual pleasure. As to the language, the
Funen peasant and Swedish soldier understand each other
soon. It was a real pleasure to observe the mutual affection,
and how every one gave with good-will according to his
abilities. " But did not the Swedish army come to fight ? "
will perhaps be said by one or another. Yes, but all the good
of the moment does not lie in the blow of the sword. The
esteem and friendship and harmony which of late years have
been established, especially among the younger ones in the
university cities, are now, by the Swedes' stay in Funen, brought
about for thousands of the people themselves : what did the
Funen or Swedish peasant know of the near relationship in
which one stands to the other ? The recollections of old hostile
times were still alive ; those are now dissipated, the neighboring people are drawn nearer to each other, a good understanding is laid, and good understanding is an herb of peace,
and one that brings blessings only. In the peasant's house,
in the parsonage, as well as at the manor, many an eye shed
tears at the departure. On the quay, at Nyborg, where the
Swedish and Danish flags waved, many a reciprocal visit was
agreed upon in the coming year of peace. The Dane will
never forget the Swede ; we have heard and felt his heart's
throbbing ; many a little Swedish town, that cannot boast of
riches, clubbed money together, " the widow's holy mite," for
the Danish brother. When the report of the Danish defeat at
Sleswick was spread over the country, far up in Sweden the
parishioners were assembled in their church, the minister
praying for king and father-land, when an old peasant rose up
and said : " Father, please to say a prayer for the Danes
also ! " That is one of those little traits that lift our hearts
from earthly things. The nations of the North understand,
esteem, and love each other ; may that spirit of unity and love
always hover over all countries !

The most of the summer I spent at Glorup. Being there both
in the spring and autumn, I was witness to the Swedes' arrival

and also their departure. I did not myself go to the seat of war; I remained at Glorup, where people daily arrived; some driven by curiosity, and relations also who went over to see their dear ones. All that I heard of honorable deeds at the seat of war, was lodged in my mind: I heard of an old grandmother, who with her grandchildren stood on the road when our troops past by; she had strewn sand and flowers for them, and cried out with the little ones: "God bless the Danes!" I heard of a freak of nature, that in a peasant's garden at Sleswick red poppies were growing with white crosses, displaying perfectly the Dannebrog colors. One of my friends visited Als, and then went over to Dyppel, where all the houses had chinks and holes made by cannon-balls and canister shot, and yet there remained still upon one of the houses the symbol of peace — a stork's nest with its whole family; the violent shooting, fire, and smoke had not been able to drive the parents away from their little ones when they could not as yet fly.

The mail from abroad brought me in the latter part of the summer a letter, written by an unknown hand; its tenor affected me much, and showed us also how events are often reported abroad. The letter was from a high functionary, the subject of a foreign sovereign; he wrote that, notwithstanding he had never seen me, nor had the least acquaintance with me, he believed yet, through my writings, especially "The Story of my Life," that he knew he could trust me; and then he said, that one morning the report had reached the city where he lived, that the Danes had made an assault upon Kiel and set it on fire; the young people were alarmed, and in the excitement of the moment his youngest son went with the other young fellows to help the hardly pressed citizens; the young man was made prisoner at the battle of Bau, and carried to Copenhagen on board a ship of the line, *Queen Mary.* He was among those who, after a long stay on board, were allowed to leave the ship; but as soon as they were ashore some of them committed excesses, so that only those who could procure a guarantee for their conduct from a citizen of Copenhagen were allowed to go ashore. The letter-writer did not know a single one at Copenhagen; I was the only one whom he knew, and that through my writings alone, and in me he had confidence and hope, and therefore he asked me if I would bail the son, who was a brave, kind-hearted man. He requested me also to find board for him in a Copenhagen family " that did not hate the Germans too much !' "

His confidence touched me, and I wrote immediately to one of my most influential friends in Copenhagen, inclosing the German letter, to enable him to see clearly the whole affair as it had been given me, and asked if the request could be granted upon my responsibility, and to any benefit for the young man. I knew that every hour which passed was an hour of confinement, and, therefore, I sent immediately an express with my letter to the nearest town. The next post-day I received an answer that we need not do anything, as all the prisoners had just been released and sent by steamship to Kiel. I was very glad on the father's account, and also glad at having immediately done what my heart told me to do ; but I did not answer his letter, that was not necessary ; the man has never heard of my sympathy. Now for the first time in the blessed days of peace I send him my greeting, which I have often thought of offering him ; and I dare add, that his letter touched me deeply, and I acted in the same.way as every one of my countrymen, if honored by the same confidence, would have acted.

I left Glorup in the autumn ; the approach of winter brought a cessation of hostilities ; the apparent tranquillity turned thought and activity for a while back on accustomed occupations. I had finished at Glorup, in the course of the summer, my novel, " The Two Baronesses," which, as regards the description of island nature, has certainly gained in freshness and truth by that summer sojourn.

The English edition was dedicated to my English publisher, the honored and well-known Richard Bentley. The book was issued, and, considering the time and circumstances, was pretty well received ; one of our newspapers, to be sure, confused the novel and the movements of time together in such a way that they did not find it just that the old Baroness, happy at her favorite the Chamberlain's contentment with London, should propose a toast for England ; and remarked that it was a little too early to let her do that, because England had not yet done anything for the Danes.

Heiberg read the book and wrote me some kind words, and gave a dinner to me and several of our friends and acquaintances. He drank my health with these beautiful words : " To that novel, which we leave as refreshed as after a wandering in the wood in the spring-time." It was the first really kind union, after many years, with that poet ; it made me a new man, and " the bitter was forgotten, the new sweet kept."

The centennial anniversary of the Danish Theatre was to be celebrated the eighth of December ; Heiberg and Collin both agreed in charging me with the writing of the prelude for the affair. Bournonville was to give a ballet on the same occasion, and gave " Old Memories ; " the most picturesque scenes from the ballets of the play-book were seen as through a magic lantern. My plan of the prelude received the approbation of the directors ; they liked my idea, which was based entirely on the present time. I knew with what feelings people at that time came to the theatre, and how little attraction it had for them, because their thoughts were with the soldiers in the war ; I therefore was obliged to let my poem go with them, and then to try to carry it back to the Danish stage. My conviction told me that our strength nowadays does not lie in the sword, but in intellectual ability, and I wrote " Denmark's Work of Art," as it is known, and is to be seen in my collected writings. On the festival evening it was received with great applause ; but it was a mistake to have it given to the subscribers of theatre-seats, and to be used as a prologue a whole week through. On the feast-day it was, as I said, received with great applause ; people were transported ; but now came the newspapers, and one of them blamed me for making the prelude contain a disgusting prattling of Denmark and Dannebrog ; that we ought to let others praise us and not do it ourselves, otherwise it would seem like Holberg's " Jacob von Thybo," etc. Another newspaper reported the prelude in such a manner that I could not well see whether the reporter had written in a spirit of folly or of malice. At the fourth representation it had already grown to be an old story ; they did not applaud any more ; and from that representation came the critique in "The North and South," whose reviewer was not satisfied with my poem: the poem made, however, an impression in due time, and I consider still the idea and its whole form as successful, and the only right one in those days when we were possessed by such national feelings.

In January "The Marriage at the Lake of Como" was brought on the stage, and now the composer Gläser, who had long been shown indifference, even injustice, was appreciated, and his music received with great applause. The criticism in the newspaper was warm and commendatory; his music and Bournonville's arrangements were highly praised, whereas I was not mentioned. Gläser, on the contrary, expressed himself warmly and kindly for the honor I had shown him.

Fredrika Bremer came at Christmas for the first time to Copenhagen. I was the only one she knew personally, and her other acquaintance was confined to having been in correspondence with the present Bishop Martensen. I had thus the pleasure of receiving her, of being at her service, and of taking her round in Copenhagen, which was as easy as it was pleasant with a woman of her position. She stayed here all winter and a great part of summer, during which she visited Ingemann at Sorö, and made an excursion to Svendborg and Moen's Klint; her heart was firmly fixed on the Danish cause, and that we can clearly see from her little book, the visible flower of her stay here, which is published in Swedish, English, German, and Danish, "Life in the North." Her heart and thought were for the Danes. The little book did not, however, find the appreciation, we may even say the gratitude, which she rightly deserved here; we always criticise, especially where we see that the heart acts a part. People dwelt upon the too exaggerated picture of the crowds in "East Street," which we were accustomed to, but not she, who had not yet seen London nor the great cities of America. Her little book shows a strong affection for Denmark, yet it did not get the acknowledgment which we owed it; but from its leaves there shine the sympathy, the tears I so often saw in her eyes; she felt deeply for the destiny of the Danish people and land.

The report that the ship of the line *Christian VIII.* had

blown up on Maunday Thursday, with all the troops on board, arrived here one evening in April ; people were in the theatre, the report found its way in, there was a hum through the multitude, the most part of course went out; it was empty within, the streets were filled, a grief pervaded all, deep and absorbing. All the theatres were closed ; it was a public grief. It was if one stood upon a sinking wreck. A single life saved from the ship was as a victory that had been won.

I met in the street my friend, the Captain-lieutenant, Chr. Wulff; his eyes sparkled, he pressed my hand. " Do you know whom I bring home?" said he : " Lieutenant Ulrich ! he is not blown up, he is saved, has fled, reached our outposts, and I bring him home!" I did not know Lieutenant Ulrich at all, but I burst into tears of joy. "Where is he? I must see him ! " — " He is now gone to the Minister of the Navy, and then he will go to his mother, who believes that he is dead ! "

I went into the first grocery shop, got a guide, and found out where Ulrich's mother lived. Arriving there, I was afraid that she still was ignorant of the whole ; I therefore asked the girl, who opened the door, " How is it in the house, — are they sad or glad?" Then the girl's face beamed : " They are glad ; the son is as if fallen down from the sky ! " and now I entered, without ceremony, the room where the whole family was sitting, dressed in mourning, — this very morning had they put on these dresses, — and the supposed dead son stood sound and safe among them ! I threw my arms round his neck, I could not do otherwise ; I wept, and they felt and understood that I came not as a stranger. Relating this story to Miss Bremer, which she has also mentioned in her book, she became quite as touched as I had been. Her soul is as tender as it is noble and great.

My mind was sick, I suffered in soul and body ; I was in the mood of the people around me. Miss Bremer spoke of her beautiful country: I had also friends there ; I decided on a journey either up into Dalarne or perhaps to Haparanda for the midsummer day. Miss Bremer's midsummer journey had induced me to it ; she was indefatigable in writing letters for me to her many friends through the whole realm of Sweden ;

in that country one needs such help, for one cannot always find inns to put up in, but must seek a shelter with the minister or at the manor. Before my departure she arranged a parting feast in Swedish style, such as we in Copenhagen do not know or like ; there was a mystification, many guests, and among them H. C. Örsted, Martensen, and Hartmann. I received a beautiful silver cup, with the inscription, "A souvenir from Fredrika Bremer !" a little poem accompanied it.

On Ascension Day I went over to Helsingborg. The spring was beautiful, the young birch-trees smelt refreshingly, the sun shone warmly, the whole journey became a poem, and thus it appears also in the description given in my book, "In Sweden."

Like a half English, half Dutch city, Göthaborg lay before me with its shining gas-flames, grand and lively : it is further advanced than other Swedish towns. The only theatre had made no progress, and the original piece they gave was dreadful — I will rather call it rough. They told me that the principal part was given by the author himself. What interested me was that the whole action turned literally about a real person still living. An old, learned Master of Arts, — who for fun was called " Arab," on account of his knowledge of the Oriental languages, — was represented in the piece as desirous of being married ; anecdotes of the man's life were here introduced ; the piece itself was made up of fragmentary scenes without action or character ; but the chief person was still living, and, as they said, was in the poor-house at Stockholm. The actor gave a true portrait of him, and there was a storm of applause. I went away after the second act : it is unpleasant to me to see a person made ridiculous when that is all that comes of it.

I believe that the harbor and the magnificent bath-house with its marble bathing tubs, are due to the clever and worthy Commerce-counselor, Mr. Wieck, in whom I also found a very amiable host, and in whose rich and comfortable home I made acquaintance shortly with the most important persons of Göthaborg, — among whom I must mention Miss Rolander, an accomplished novelist.

I saw again the great waterfall of Trollhätta, and have

tried since to paint it in words; the impression it makes is always new and great; but I have retained quite as freshly the impression that followed, — a meeting, namely, that took place outside of Wenersburg, where the steamer stopped for passengers. At the landing-place stood a little fifer, whom I had seen the year before with the Swedish troops in Funen; he saluted me in a happy, familiar fashion, and was quite astonished to see me again in his country. When the Swedish soldiers were stationed at Glorup, they went out one day to drill; the boy was not well, and the old stewardess would not allow him to go: the child must be physicked and have some gruel! The officer said that nothing ailed him. "I am his mother here!" she said; "the child is sick, and he shall not play the fife to-day!" The boy asked after the mistress and the old Count.

I arrived at Stockholm, and immediately changed my clothes that I might find our ambassador, from whom I expected to hear something of the war, which entirely occupied my mind. On the way there I was unfortunate enough to meet with Dr. Leo, a Danish-speaking German, whom I knew at Copenhagen, where I had received him kindly, and introduced him to Miss Bremer, who was then there on a visit; he has not dealt fairly with her and me in his "Characters out of my Scandinavian Portfolio," printed as a feuilleton in the "Novellen-Zeitung;" he gives a kind of caricature-portrait of me drawn from that meeting in the streets of Stockholm, where I immediately, as he says, after having left the steamer, appeared on the promenade in party dress, with white kid gloves, on in order to be seen, and that my arrival might be announced in the newspapers the next day. He has done me wrong in that, he has given me pain; but I will also remember that he has translated beautifully several of my books — has spoken in a friendly manner of me at other times and in other places. I hold out again my hand to him — and without "kid gloves."

Lindblad, whose beautiful melodies Jenny Lind has scattered about the world, was one of the first I met; he resembles her as much as a brother may resemble his sister; he has the same appearance of melancholy, but the features are more

powerful than hers ; he requested me to write an opera text
for him, and I should like to do it, that it might be carried by
his genius on the wings of popular song.   In the theatre the
Italian company gave one of its Italian operas, composed by
Kapelmeister Foroni, " Queen Christina ; " the text was by
the singer Casanova.   It seemed to have rather grand har-
monies than real melodies ; the conspiracy act was the most
effective ; beautiful decorations and good costumes were not
missing, and they had tried to make portrait likenesses of
Christina and Oxenstjerna ; the most peculiar thing of all
was, however, to see in Christina's Swedish capital, Christina
herself as a character on the stage.

Through the book-seller, Magister Bagge, I was introduced
into the " Literary Society," and at a feast there I was placed
by the side of the poet, Chamberlain Beskow ; Dr. Leo also
was a guest, and the president took occasion to propose
the health of "the two excellent foreigners, Mr. Andersen
from Copenhagen, the author of " The Improvisatore " and
" Wonder Stories told for Children," and Dr. Leo from Leipsic,
editor of " The Northern Telegraph."   Later in the evening,
Magister Bagge proposed a sentiment for me and for my
country ; he bade me tell my countrymen of the enthusiasm
and sympathy which the whole Swedish people bore toward
us.   I answered with words from one of my songs : —

> " Sharp as a sword lay Öresound
>   Between the neighbor lands,
> When a rose-bush branch one morn was found,
>   That joined the opposite strands ;
> Each rose breathed sweet of poetry,
>   That now to heal old wounds was eager :
> Who wrought this wondrous magicry?
>   Tegnér and Oehlenschläger ! " —

and added : " Several Skalds have since appeared as well in
Sweden as in Denmark, and by these the two peoples have
more and more learnt to understand each other, have felt the
throbbing of the hearts ; and the beating of the Swedish heart
has recently been felt deeply and tenderly by us, just as I feel
it in this moment ! "   Tears came into my eyes and hurras
resounded round about !

Beskow accompanied me to King Oscar, who received me very kindly ; it was almost as if we had often spoken with each other, and yet this was the first time we had met. I thanked his Majesty for the Order of the North Star, with which he had graciously honored me ; he talked of Stockholm's resemblance to Constantinople, of Lake Roxen's likeness to the southern part of Loch Lomond ; of the Swedish soldier's discipline and piety, and the King said that he had read what I had written of the Swedes' stay in Funen ; he expressed a warm and sympathetic feeling for the Danish people and friendship for the King. We spoke of the war ; I said that it was fixed in the character of the Danish nation to hold fast to what was right, whether it be a small or a great matter. I felt how noble a disposition the King had. I told him that the good which the Danes saw him do for them would bring him the whole people's gratitude. We talked of the hereditary Grand Duke of Weimar, whom he also loved ; after that his Majesty asked me, when I came back from Upsala, where I was about to go, to dine with him. " The Queen also, my wife," he said, " knows your writings, and would like to be acquainted personally with you."

After my return I was at the royal table. The Queen, who bears a strong resemblance to her mother, the Duchess of Leuchtenberg, whom I had seen at Rome, received me very kindly, and said that she had already long known me from my writings, and from " The Story of my Life." At the table I was seated by the side of Beskow, opposite the Queen. Prince Gustavus conversed briskly with me. After dinner I read for them " The Flax," " The Ugly Duckling," " The Story of a Mother," and " The False Collar." At the reading of " The Story of a Mother," I perceived tears in the eyes of the noble royal couple ; they expressed themselves with warmth and sympathy ; how amiable they both were, how straightforward and generous ! On my retiring, the Queen stretched out her hand to me, which I pressed to my lips ; she as well as the King honored me with a renewed invitation to come once more and read to them. A feeling of congeniality, if I may dare use the word, drew me especially to the amiable young Prince Gustavus ; his great, blue spiritual eyes possessed a kindness that exercised great power ; his unusual talent for music interested me ; there was something very attractive and confiding in his character, and we met on common ground, in our admiration for the Duke of Weimar ; we talked of him, of the war, of music and poetry.

At my next visit to the palace, I was, in company with Beskow, summoned to the Queen's apartments, for an hour before dinner ; the Princess Eugenie, the Crown Prince, and the Princes Gustavus and Augustus were there, and soon also the King came : " Poetry called him from business ! " he said. I read "The Fir-tree," " The Darning-Needle," " The Little Girl with Matches," and by request, " The Flax." The King followed me with great attention ; " the deep poetry that lies in these little narratives " — thus he was pleased to express himself — pleased him, and he said that he had read the stories on his journey to Norway ; amongst others, " The Fir-tree. All the three princes pressed my hand, and the King invited me to come on his birthday, the fourth of July, when Beskow should be my cicerone.

They wished in Stockholm to show me public honors. I knew how I should be envied for it at home, and be the object of malicious remark ; and I was disheartened, and became feverish at the very thought of being the hero of an evening's feast ; I felt like a delinquent, and dreaded the many toasts and the long evening.

I met there the famous and gifted Madame Carlén, — the writer under the fictitious name, " Wilhelmina," less known, but an excellent novelist; also the actress Madame Strandberg, and several other ladies who took part in the evening's entertainment. Madame Carlén invited me to walk with her ; but we dared not go into the garden, where I wished to walk, because I saw there were not so many spectators there ; and we had to walk in a particular place, because they said the public wished to see Mr. Andersen. It was a well-meant arrangement, but for me a little painful ; I saw in imagination the whole performance represented at home in " The Corsair " in wood-cut. I knew that Oehlenschläger, whom people used to look up to with a kind of piety, had been represented there surrounded by Swedish ladies, when he made his visit in

Stockholm. I perceived before me in the mall a whole crowd of children coming to meet us with a huge garland of flowers ; they strewed flowers for me and surrounded me, while a multitude of people gathered about and honored me by taking off their hats. My thoughts were, " You may be sure that at Copenhagen they will laugh at you: how many sneers you will have from them ! " I was quite out of humor, but was obliged to appear happy among these friendly, good people ; I turned the whole into jest, kissed one of the children, and chatted a little with another. At the supper-table the poet, Pastor Mellin, drank my health ; after having hinted at my poetic fertility, he recited some festive verses, written by the authoress " Wilhelmina," and now followed a beautiful poem by Mr. Carlén.

I replied that I considered the kindness shown me as a payment in advance, which I hoped that God would grant me power to return by a work in which I might express my affection to Sweden. And I have tried to redeem my promise. The writer of comedies, the actor Jolin, recited in dialect: " A Peasant Story from Dalarne ; " the singers of the Royal Theatre, Strandberg, Wallin, and Günther sang Swedish songs ; the orchestra played, and began with the Danish melody, " There is a Charming Land." At eleven o'clock I rode home ; glad at heart over these friendly souls, — glad, too, to go to rest.

I was soon on my way to Dalarne. One of Fredrika Bremer's letters introduced me at Upsala to the poet Fahlkranz, the brother of the renowned landscape-painter, and honorably known by his poems " Ansgar " and " Noah's Ark ; " I met with my friend, the poet Böttger, married to Tegnér's daughter Disa, — a happy couple, whose home seemed to be filled with sunshine and the poetry of family life. My room in the hotel bordered upon a large hall, where the students had just celebrated a sexa (feast), and learning that I was a neighbor, a deputation came and invited me to hear them sing ; there was frolic and gayety and beautiful singing. I tried to select one, judging from appearances, whom I might with pleasure join ; a tall, pale young man pleased me, and I learned soon that I had made a right choice. He sang beautifully and with great distinctness ; he was the most genial among all ; I afterward heard that he was the poet Wennerberg, the composer of "Gluntarne." Afterward I heard him, together with Beronius, singing his modernized " Bellman-songs ; " it was at the Prefect's, where I met the most eminent men and women of Upsala, and found a very kind reception. I met here for the first time Atterbom, the Skald of " The Flowers," he who sang of " The Island of Beatitude ; " there is, Marmier says, a kind of freemasonry among poets ; they know and understand each other. I felt and acknowledged its truth at the home of that amiable old Skald.

When travelling in Sweden one must have his own carriage ; I should have been obliged to buy such a one if the Prefect had not kindly offered me his carriage for the whole long journey ; Professor Schroeder furnished me with "slanter" (small coins) and a whip ; Fahlkranz wrote an itinerary, and I began now the for me very peculiar travelling life, not unlike what one gets in parts of America, where the railroad net has not yet reached. It was contrary to what I was used to, and almost like the travelling life of a hundred years ago. Wreaths were fastened to May-poles for Midsummer night, when I reached the Lake of Siljan, that lay spread out before me ; great willow-trees drooped above the quickly running Dal river, where wild swans were swimming ; beyond Mora, toward the boundary of Norway, the mountains appeared in bluish colors ; the whole life and stir, the picturesque dresses, the summer heat, all were so different from what I imagined it to be in the quiet, cold North ; and now what sport there was at the midsummer feast ! A multitude of boats arrived filled with nicely dressed church-people, old and young — even small babies ; it was a picture so lively, so grand, that I can but poorly present it in words. Professor Marstrand, influenced by my description, and later by my verbal account of it, undertook two years in succession to make a journey here just at midsummer time, and reproduced on canvas that gay picture with its lively colors very skillfully.

At Leksand the traveller could still find an inn, but not higher up ; at Rättvek I was therefore obliged to conform to the custom of the country, and put up at the minister's, and there make my lodging ; but before he heard my name I was already welcomed. Afterward there was a feast, and the following day, as I went with him to the neighboring watering-place, a crowd of children were standing at the bridge ; they swung their caps ; they knew him who wrote the stories. "Andersen is up here in Dalarne ! " was yesterday the news that one of the little chaps had to tell ! I thought that moment of my poor little friends at Heriot's Hospital in Edinburgh ; I thought of Scotland's bairns, and now I was standing in the midst of the happy circle of children here in Dalarne, and my heart grew humble and tender, thankful to God, whose forgiveness I asked for those sighs and pains I used to utter to Him in my heavy hours, in grief's bitter moments.

Old memories, the sunlight thrown by traditions and history over a country, have sometimes a greater power and significance than its picturesque beauty. What here is fixed in my memory is the faithfulness of the Dalkarle people, Gustavus Vasa's flight, and his whole demeanor ; here also, almost unaltered, is the scene of the romantic part of his life in all its grandeur and solitariness. As far as I was able, I have in the group of pictures " In Sweden " represented the impressions made upon me. Those immensely large and extensive wood-tracts, with solitary charcoal pits ; deep, clear, wood-lakes, where the linnæa blooms over the rocky stones, and where the wild swans are building their nests, were something new and marvelous to me ; I had a feeling as if I were moved back centuries of time. I visited Fahlun, with its copper-mines and its whole beautiful environs, and from here I recollect a little event, such as we count among accidents, but which by many people are yet placed upon a higher ground. Among my Swedish pictures I have given it the title: " What the Straws said." It is no invention, it is an event.

In the Prefect's garden at Fahlun sat a circle of young girls ; they took in sport four grass-straws in their hands and tied them two and two together at the ends ; when it happens that all the four straws form a coherent whole, the popular belief is that what the binder thought of shall be fulfilled. They could not any of them succeed in this, and they wished that I would try it. " But I don't believe in it ! " I answered :

nevertheless I took four straws, and promised that in case they came out right I would tell them what I wished. I tied, opened my hand, and the straws hung together; the blood involuntarily rushed up into my cheeks, I became superstitious, and directly against all reason I believed in it, because I wanted to do so; and what was the wish? they asked. I told it: "That Denmark might obtain a great victory and soon get an honorable peace!" — "May God grant it!" exclaimed they all; and the prophecy of the straws that day was — accidentally — a truth; there soon was reported in Sweden the battle of Fredericia!

By way of Gefle I returned again to Upsala and Dannemora, whose dizzy mines I beheld from above; I had before visited Rammel's mountain in the Harzt, Baumann's cave, the saltworks of Hallein, and the catacombs under Rome and at Malta; there was no pleasure in any of these places, gloomy, oppressing, a horrible nightmare. I do not like to go under the earth before my dead body is carried down there.

At Old Upsala I alighted to see the now excavated hills, which bear the names of Odin, Thor, and Freyr. When I was here, thirteen years ago, they lay still closed as they had been thousands of years. The old woman who had the key to the entrance of the hill, and whose deceased aunt then filled the horn of mead for me, was happy to hear my name, and now she would also, she said, illuminate for me, as she did for the noblemen who had been here from Stockholm. While she made her preparations I mounted the hill alone with prayer and thanks to God for all his goodness in the days gone by, since I was last here, and these words went from my lips, "Thy will be done toward me!" Thus do I go to church unconsciously, now in the woods, now upon the graves of former days, and now in my little solitary room. When I descended she had placed small tapers round about the gateway, and I saw the old urn containing, as she said, the bones of Odin, or rather the bones of his offspring, those of the "Ynglinga-generation." Round about were spread ashes of burnt animals.

After again greeting my friends at Upsala I drew near Stockholm, where I had been received in the house of the aged Madame Bremer as if 1 were her child, when the gifted but very sick Agathe was living, the sister of Fredrika Bremer, to whom all the letters from America are written, and who was dead on Fredrika's return. There was comfort and richness in the old mother's house, where I sometimes met with the great family circle, whose members belong to the best people in Sweden ; it was very interesting to me to see the real difference from all those stories that circulated in Denmark and abroad about this authoress's family and conditions. When she first appeared in public it was said she was governess in a noble family, when she was really proprietor of the estate " Aosta," free and independent.

In a foreign city I feel a necessity not only to pay my respects to the living men of genius and honor ; I must also visit the graves of those dear or famous who are dead, and carry them a flower or pluck one from their graves. At Upsala I had been at the grave of Geijer ; the monument was not yet erected ; the grave of Törneros was overgrown with grass and nettles. At Stockholm I went to the graves where repose Nicander and Stagnelius. I drove out to Solna, near Stockholm, and visited its little church-yard where Berzelius, Choræus, Ingelmann, and Crusell are buried ; in the larger one is the tomb of Wallin.

My principal home at Stockholm was indeed that of the poet, Baron Beskow, who was ennobled by Carl Johan ; he belongs to those amiable characters from whom there seems to radiate a mild lustre over life and nature ; he is kind-hearted and full of talent ; that one may see by his drawings and his music. The old man has a voice remarkably soft and fresh ; his position as poet is known, and his tragedies have also become popular in Germany by Oehlenschläger's translations ; he is loved by his king, and honored by all ; he is, besides, a man of exceedingly high cultivation, a faithful and dear friend.

The last day of my stay at Stockholm was King Oscar's birthday ; I was honored with an invitation to the feast ; the King, the Queen, and all the Princes were very kind. When I took leave, I was touched as if I were leaving dear ones.

Oehlenschläger mentions in his " Life," part IV., page 85,

Count Saltza, and one becomes curious to know who the man was, but the secret is not told Oehlenschläger says, " One of Bishop Münter's acquaintances once made me a call in those days. He was a tall, stout Swede, who, on entering, gave his name, but I did not hear it. As I was ashamed to ask him again, I hoped to hear it in the course of conversation, or perhaps to learn from what he said who he was. He told me that he had come to ask me how I liked the subject for a vaudeville which he intended to write. He gave it to me, and it was a very pretty one; I held on to that in my mind, and thought, of course, he must be a vaudeville poet. Then he spoke of Münter as an old friend of his, " For I must tell you," he continued, " I have studied theology, and have trans-lated the Revelation of St. John." A vaudeville poet, I now thought, who is also a theologian.   " Münter is a freemason, too," he continued ; " all his freemasonry he learnt from me ; because I am Master of the Chair."   I began mentally to reckon up : vaudeville poet, theologian, Master of the Chair. Now he began to talk about Carl Johan, whom he praised much, and said, " I know him well ! I have drunk many a good glass with him."   I said to myself, vaudeville poet, theo-logian, Master of the Chair, a bosom friend of Carl Johan. He continued, " Here in Denmark people do not wear their orders ; to-morrow I go to church and I shall wear mine." " That you may do ! " I answered ; and he went on, " I have them all ! "   I said to myself : vaudeville poet, theologian, Master of the Chair, bosom friend of Carl Johan, Knight of the Order of Seraphim. At last the stranger spoke of his son, whom he had taught to know that their ancestor was the first upon the walls of Jerusalem at its conquest. Now it was made clear to me that he might be the Count of Saltza. And it really was he."

So far Oehlenschläger.

Beskow presented me in the antechamber of King Oscar to the old Count Saltza, who immediately, with Swedish hospi-tality, invited me on my way home to visit him at his estate of Mem, if he was there when the steamboat passed ; if not, then at his estate at Saeby, near Linköping, which, further on my journey, was situated not far from the canal.   I re-

garded it as one of those kind words which we so often hear
and did not think to make use of his invitation ; but in the
morning on my journey home, when we left the Lake of
Roxen, and were going through the thirteen water-gates at
Wreta Church, whose royal tombs I have painted in " The
Picture-book without Pictures," the composer Josephson, with
whom I had lived, as I have before mentioned, in Sorrento
and at Capri, and lately had met at Upsala, came suddenly on
board the steamer ; he was Count Saltza's guest at Saeby,
and having calculated by what steamer I should come on
the canal route, he was dispatched to the locks here to fetch
me off in a carriage.   It was very kind of the old Count ; I
gathered my luggage together in a hurry, and in a violent rain-
storm we drove to Saeby to the castle, built in Italian style,
where the old Count Saltza resided with his cultivated and
amiable daughter, the widow-baroness Fock.
    " There is an intellectual relationship between us ! " said
the old man ; " that I immediately felt when I saw you ! we
were not strangers to each other ! "   He received me very
kindly, and the old gentleman with his many peculiarities became soon dear to me by his genius and loveliness.   He told
me of his acquaintance with kings and princes ; he had corresponded with Goethe and Jung Stilling.   He told me that his
ancestors had been Norwegian peasants and fishermen ; they
went to Venice, rescued Christian captives, and Charles the
Great made them princes of Saltza.   That little fishing-place,
situated where now St. Petersburg stands, had belonged to his
father's grandfather, and it is told me, that Saltza once had
said in joke to the Emperor of Russia, when he was at Stockholm, " That is really my ancestors' ground upon which the
Imperial city is built ! " and the Emperor is said to have
answered merrily, " Well, then, come and take it ! "   There is
a tradition that the Empress Catharine I. was Swedish, and
it is confirmed by Saltza's accounts and records ; he traces
the history of her childhood into the life of his father's grandfather ; the notes he has made about it are very interesting,
and he relates them thus.
    One day his father read a compendium of the history of
Russia, but he soon laid the book aside and said that it was

not as he read ; he knew much better about the Empress
Catharine, and then he told this story : " My father's grandfather was the General Hans Abraham Kruse, colonel of the
Green Dragoons. When he was lieutenant-colonel and lived
on the lieutenant-colonel's place, ' Broten,' it happened that
his valet de chambre, Jean Rabe, wished to marry his wife's
waiting-maid, Catharine Almpaph ; Madame Kruse, born Annike Sinclair, prepared a brilliant wedding, and even had
the nuptial bed edged with golden lace, the same that
Madame Annike, as lady at the court of Charles X.'s
queen, had worn on her purple robe ; it became afterwards
an adage of the family, ' As stately as Jean Rabe's nuptial
bed.' Jean became field-sergeant of Elfsborg's regiment, but
died, as also his wife, very soon after, leaving only one daughter, Catharina, who was brought to the old lady Kruse at
Hökälla, where she remained two years. Then it came about
that the cousin of Madame Annike, the Countess Tisenhusen,
came visiting and found Catharina, who was eight years of
age, to be a handsome and winning child, and therefore took
her home with her ; they spent the winter together at Stockholm, and in the spring they made a voyage to Pomerania,
where the Countess was to receive a great inheritance ; but
on arriving at the island of Rügen, a guard-ship which was
stationed there forbade them to go ashore, as the plague had
broken out there. They returned to Stockholm, and spent
the following winter in Government Street in the so-called
house Anchor Crown. An aunt of the Countess died at Re-
val, and she went over there in the month of May, notwithstanding the Russians just then often invaded and devastated
Esthland, which was the Countess's native place ; for this reason, also, she always spoke German and kept German help ;
Catharina was, of course, also obliged to learn that language.
They made a favorable voyage, and a stay of three days.
Catharina was sent out of town on an errand, and returning
home she found written upon the door of the house that nobody was allowed to enter as the plague was there. Catharina cried aloud ; the porter answered from within that the
Countess and nine other persons had already perished, and
he himself was shut in. Catharina ran weeping and in des-

peration up the street, when she met the minister, pastor
Glück of Majam, who had just come to the city in order to
get a nurse for his little son, who was to be weaned; the
minister saw the distress of the well-formed, ruddy girl, and
asked what was the matter with her. Being told her story,
and hearing that she had not been in the house, he engaged
her as nurse, and Catharina in her forsaken condition accepted the place, although she had before been accustomed to better life. She was soon a great favorite in the
parsonage, and the minister's wife at last could not do without her at all. Count Saltza's grandfather's father, when he
was hunting in that part of the country, passed a night at
the parsonage. After the battle of Norra, in the time of
Charles XII., Esthland was sacked by the Russians, who
were commanded by Anesen Laputschin; he set fire to
the church of Majam, took the whole tenantry on Saltza's
estate, and sent away the faithful vassals to Siberia; while
the parsonage stood in flames, he saw for the first time
Catharina, and kept her as his own share of the plunder.
Menschikow, having become prince and the favorite of the
Czar, remarked the beauty of Catharina when he saw her
at Laputschin's house, where she waited on them; the day
after she was sent to him as his bondwoman; he did not
care much about women, and considered her but a nice servant girl. One day she was scouring the floor, when the
Emperor entered, but as Menschikow was not at home, he
turned to go away again, when he saw upon the table the
plate of comfits, which was always set before him when he
came. He took of them; Catharina did not know him, and
continued to scour the floor; he looked at her and brushed
aside with his hand the hair on her forehead. 'You are a
beautiful girl!' said he; she blushed, he caressed her, gave
her a kiss and went away.

"Catharina, very much displeased, told Menschikow of the
unknown officer who had come, had eaten of the comfits, and
allowed himself to kiss her. When she had given a description of him, Menschikow understood that the Emperor had
been there, and took advantage of the meeting. Orders had
just then been given to wear a new costume of a different kind

from what had formerly been worn ; Catharina was dressed in one of those appointed for women, which was very becoming to her, and very elegant besides ; the head-dress resembled much that of the Dutch peasants. In this attire she was to deliver to the Emperor a plate of comfits, consisting of boiled fruits, together with a carefully expressed letter, insinuating that the Czar might not disdain the comfits and her who brought them." How she afterwards became the Czar's consort, the story goes on to tell.

The grandfather's father came back during her reign from his Siberian captivity, where he had been sixteen years. There was just then a great festival in the Imperial garden at Moscow ; he was invited to it, and came in attendance with the old Knight Gagarin, who, during his captivity, had been a true friend to Saltza. Herr Gagarin could not endure Menschikow, and when he entered and Menschikow did not acknowledge his salutation, he said : " Did you not observe that I saluted you ? " Menschikow did not answer, but smiled contemptuously, and the old man began then to use violent language. Menschikow called upon his people, who fell upon the old man and trod upon him. Saltza, defending his friend, was now also attacked. Catharina observed it from her elevated place, recognized the voice of her friend of earlier days, and cried to Menschikow : " If you dare touch a hair upon Saltza's head, your's shall to-morrow be put into the Kremlin ! " And the fight was ended.

Afterwards Saltza became president of the Board of Trade, and was always in favor with the Empress ; his family is still to be found in Russia. Old Saltza passes for one who sees ghosts. Carl Johan, who, according to Lenormann's prediction was to become king, placed great confidence in him, and the marvel is told that the king's day of death occurred upon the same date as Saltza had predicted. Here in that great hall of knights at Saeby, where now Saltza and I were seated, Carl Johan and Queen Eugenie had often dined : round about hung pictures of Saltza's knightly ancestors ; the furniture consisted of chairs and pieces in antiquated style ; the large hall was heated by two fire-places. Here I sat with the worthy old gentleman ; we talked of spirits, and he told me, with great seriousness and belief in its truth, how his grandfather had appeared to him in the night, asked him if he would go with him to see the heaven of God, and added : "'But then you· must first try to die.' He touched me," said the worthy old man, "and I fell as in a swoon. 'Is not death something else than this ? ' — 'No,' said my grandfather, and then I stood in the court of God's heaven. It was the most delicious garden."

The description of it was, as Saltza gave it, entirely of some earthly place ; I could not perceive anything new. He met there his brother and sister ; the latter was, when she died, only a little child ; he did not recognize her until she said who she was. "'It is very well you came now,' said she. 'To-day it is the anniversary day of Christ's name, and I shall go from the children's heaven into the great God's heaven ! '"

"But," replied I, "why does not the child go directly into God's great heaven, for so we are told in the Bible." — "Very good, but I have seen it !" said he. Yet what he told of God was very beautiful. "Standing there in heaven, I perceived a flash of light that I could not endure ; I threw myself down, there was a sound of music, such as I never had heard before ; I had a feeling of happiness, I felt an exceeding joy ! 'What is that ? ' said I. 'It was God, who passed by ! ' answered my grandfather." The old man told me all this with an earnestness and conviction that made a peculiar impression upon me. "There above I gained knowledge of all that shall happen !" said he ; "I know of the end of all things ; at the time I was only fifteen years old."

During my stay at Saeby the old Count's anniversary day, "Frederick's Day," occurred ; it was interesting to see the Swedish manner in which it was celebrated. In one of the rooms down stairs was erected an arch of beech-leaves, and above his monogram was placed a beautiful crown of beech-leaves, and roses instead of jewels. Sitting at the coffee-table we heard a report out on the lake ; one of the servants entered, and, with a loud voice, almost as if he had learned his words by heart, he announced, while he could not help at the same time betraying with a smile that the whole was a comedy, "A ship, the *North Star,* is riding at anchor without, and has foreign sailors on board!" They were now invited to come in ; shots were heard from the ship, the steward, his wife, and two daughters entered. These were the foreign sailors, who arrived from his estate on the other side of the lake. At the dinner-table were several other stewards and many other officers of his estates, and families from the neighboring estates came with their congratulations. Outside of the castle marched and were drawn up in ranks all the school children, girls and boys, each of them holding a little green branch ; they were conducted by the schoolmaster, who made a speech in verse to the old Count. He stepped out before them and was received with a resounding hurra. I observed that the schoolmaster got money, the children coffee and meat, and afterward were permitted to dance in the large front room, where a peasant played the violin ; the Baroness went kindly amongst them, showed the peasants the halls and rooms of the castle, and treated them plentifully with eating and drinking. Just then the mail arrived with letters and newspapers. " News from Denmark ; a victory at Fredericia ! " was shouted triumphantly ; it was the first printed and complete information about it ; all were interested in it. I seized the list of killed and wounded.

In honor of the Danish victory old Saltza opened a bottle of champagne ; the daughter had in a hurry contrived a Dannebrog flag, which was fastened up. The old man who before had spoken of the ancient hatred between Swedes and Danes, and preserved three Danish balls, — of which one had wounded his father, the second his grandfather, and the third had killed his grandfather's father, — now in the time of brotherhood raised his full glass for old Denmark, and spoke so kindly and beautifully of the honor and victory of the Danes that tears rose in my eyes. There was among the guests a German governess quite old. I believe she was from Brunswick. She had lived many years in Sweden, and hearing now what Saltza in his speech said about the Germans, she burst out weeping, and said innocently to me : " I cannot help it ! " When I had returned my thanks for Saltza's toast, the first thing I had to do was to give her my hand and say, " There will soon come better days ; Germans and Danes shall again grasp one another's hands as we now do, and drink a glass for the blessed peace ; " and so we clinked the glasses together.

The sympathy I found here for Denmark and the Danes was shown throughout the country, and as a Dane myself those expressions were dear to me. At Linköping I alighted at Professor Omann's, and was surprised to see in the garden so many young men assembled in order to give me a festive reception ; the poet Ridderstad had written three beautiful songs, the first written to the melody of " There is a Charming Land," brought me " A Greeting to Denmark." While they intoned the song the most splendid rainbow lighted up the firmament, as a token of peace. I was extremely touched by it, and now there sounded a song to " The Dannebrog." At intervals between the songs, affectionate speeches were delivered touching Sweden's love to Denmark and their joy at the victory ; among the speeches was one in honor of those killed at Fredericia ; I was moved to tears, I felt so Danish in mind. Swedish and Danish flags waved, and when I departed for Berg, where I was to go on board the steamer the next morning, Ridderstad and many other friends accompanied me with songs and greetings.

I intended to stay at Motala a couple of days ; all the way hereto may rightly be called " The Götha Canal's Garden." There is a beautiful blending of Swedish and Danish nature, rich beech woods bending over the lakes, rocks, and roaring streams. A young bachelor offered me, in the inn near the manufactory, his comfortable little room, and moved himself to a friend's, that I might find myself provided for, and that was the first time we had met. It was Mr. C. D. Nygren, since deceased, a man of a poetic nature, a friend of Fredrika Bremer, and an admirer of my poetry. The river Motala flowed below my windows, among leafy trees and pines, so swiftly, so green, and transparent that I could distinguish in the depth every stone, every fish ; upon the opposite bank of the canal is the tomb of Platen, which is saluted with cannon shots by all the passing steamboats. There in the country I had a kind, fresh letter from Dickens, who had received and read " The Two Baronesses ; " it was a white day for me ; most charming roses, brought for me, made a splendid show upon my table.

From here I made an excursion to the ancient Vadstena, whose rich castle is now but a large granary, — whose mighty monastery is a bedlam.   At my departure from Motala I was staying in the little inn down by the bridge ; I was to set out early in the morning and had therefore gone to bed early ; I fell asleep immediately, but awoke on hearing beautiful singing from many voices.   I got up ; it sounded deliciously ; I opened the door and asked the girl if there were any high guests here to whom the serenade was given.   " Of course it is for you, sir ! " she said.   " For me ! " I exclaimed, and could not understand it.   They sang : " There is a Charming Land ! " The song was for me ; I will not say for the poet Andersen, but for Andersen as a Dane ; it was love to the Danes that also here burst out in flower for me.   The mechanics at Motala had learned that I had returned here again from Vadstena, and that I was to start again next morning ; those good people had come to give me a token of their esteem and sympathy.   I now went out to them, and shook hands with the nearest of them ; I was deeply affected and thankful ; of course I could not sleep all the night after.

At each place I reached, every day was like a festival ! Everywhere was shown sympathy for Denmark so affection-ately, so faithfully, that the Danish people can hardly form an idea of it.   I met friends and hospitality ; even the little town of Mariestad would not let me go without it.   Everywhere I was invited to move into the houses of families and to be their guest ; they offered me carriage and horses, in short they showed me all attention possible.   I spent several days at Kinnekulle, in the society of the senior Count Hamilton ; and also at Blomberg, where one of the sons is married to the daughter of Geijer, who resembles very much Jenny Lind even in the sound of her voice ; she sung beautifully all her father's songs.   Little Anna, the only child of the house, usually bashful toward all strangers, came immediately to me ; we seemed to know each other at once. Wenersborg also offered me a circle of friends, who took me to the beautiful environs, and at Trolhätta the stay was prolonged for several days ;

here in the wood near the sluices I found a blessed home with Lieutenant-colonel Warberg and his wife ; they cared comfortably and kindly for me.

From Göthaborg I made an excursion to the island of Marstrand, where Fredrika Bremer visited her sister Agatha, when she made use of the baths. The many small rocky islands on the Swedish coast form excellent harbors with deep waters ; the wild rose bloomed upon those sun-heated rocks. The Italian opera troop from Stockholm gave concerts in the forenoon ; I found here the liveliness of a southern watering-place. Fredrika Bremer was going to America ; she accompanied me to Göthaborg ; on board the ship a company gathered around us and sang Swedish and Danish songs. " There is a Charming Land," seemed to be the favorite song of the Swedes ; it was sung again as a farewell to me.

A few days after I was again in Denmark. My book " In Sweden," perhaps the most carefully written of my works, gives the intellectual result of this journey, and I am inclined to believe that it displays better than any other of my writings those points most characteristic in me : pictures of nature, the wonderful, the humorous, and lyric, as far as the last may be given in prose. The Swedish paper, " Bore," was the first that gave a critique of the book.

At home, where the critics of late, not only had adopted a more decent tone, when my works were spoken of, but showed also greater attention to them and more true acknowledgment, my book was mentioned with praise and good-will, especially the chapter " A Story."

In England, where " In Sweden " was published at the same time as the Danish original, I met the same good-will, the same generous criticism, as almost always has been the case, until I met an attack, and that from a person from whom I least expected it, — from her who introduced my writings into England, and who received me there with such great friendliness, — Mary Howitt ; it surprised and grieved me, and was something so unexpected that I could scarcely believe it. I have before spoken of our meeting in London ; how, during my stay there, my friends who had an interest in me, so arranged it for me that my works, from the favor they had received in great England, might also bring me some advantage in pecuniary matters.

The estimable and clever book-seller, Richard Bentley, continued to be my publisher, and I was to send him from Copenhagen an English manuscript. I did this, and Mary Howitt did not translate either " The Two Baronesses " or " In Sweden ; " but that this should make her angry with me, and lead her to criticise me now most severely in her and William Howitt's work, — " The Literature and Romance of Northern Europe," — that I did not expect. All the Danish poets, great and small, are kindly mentioned in it, but not I, who once seemed to be her favorite ; she writes, having first spoken kindly of such of my books as she has translated : —

" But Andersen's subsequent productions have been failures ; those published in England have dropped nearly dead from the press ; and the reason for this is very obvious. Andersen is a singular mixture of simplicity and worldliness. The child-like heart which animates his best compositions appears to your astonished vision in real life, in the shape of a *petit maître* sighing after the notice of princes. The poet is lost to you in the egotist ; and once perceiving this, you have the key to the charm of one or two romances and the flatness of the rest ; for he always paints himself — his own mind, history, and feelings. This delights in a first story, less in the second, and not at all in the third ; for it is but *crambe repetita.* Perhaps much of Andersen's fame in this country arose from the very fact of the almost total ignorance here of the host of really great and original writers which Denmark possessed ; Andersen stood forward as a wonder from a country of whose literary affluence the British public was little cognizant, while in reality he was but an average sample of a numerous and giant race."

How entirely different had the same gifted lady conceived and mentioned me a few years before when I visited London ; then she wrote in " Howitts' Journal " a most cordial welcome of the Danish poet to English soil.

How shall I be able to compare those earlier judgments with the later, written by a lady of genius, and as it appears also of affection for me and my muse ? On Miss Bremer's return from America she passed through London, and I asked her about Mary Howitt, whom I knew she had visited.

"'The good Mary Howitt," she said," spoke so kindly of you, spoke with tears, saying, 'he will not have anything to do with me!'" How can I understand those words so generously spoken and those so harshly written. Well, they have perhaps their origin in a momentary bad humor, that we all may have ; she may perhaps also have changed her opinion of me, as she once did. There is no anger in my mind, and I stretch forth my hand as a friend desiring reconciliation.

The novel "The Two Baronesses" was nevertheless well received, and "In Sweden" not less. The very same year that Mary Howitt pronounced her severe judgment, the last book obtained even the honor of being made popular ; for in connection with "The Story of my Life," it was published in "The Popular Library," which is generally known under the name, "one shilling editions," and sold by thousands. The translation is excellent, and the translator, Kenneth MacKenzie, expresses himself in a postscript so warmly and generously, that Mary Howitt's sharp words are blunted. The "Athenæum's" criticism of the last book of mine published in England, " A Poet's Day Dreams," as they call my stories, indicates the same sympathy and favor : —

"By the form and fashion of this little book (dedicated to Mr. Dickens) it appears to be meant for a Christmas and New Year's gift. But it will be welcome in any month of flowers or harvests, or at the canonical time, —

'when icicles hang by the wall ; ' —

since it may be read and remembered by poets and by the children of poets long after this busy year and its busy people shall have been gathered to their fathers. Our antipathy to sentimentality (as the word is commonly understood) needs not to be again expressed. For what is false and sickly, be it ever so graceful, ever so alluring, we have neither eye, ear, nor heart ; but for sentiment, — as something less deep than passionate emotion, less high than enthusiastic faith, less wild than the meteoric extravagances of Genius, — we have a liking apart and peculiar, — and those who have not, relish Imagination only by halves.   For quaintness, humor, and tenderness, Mr. Andersen's little tales are unique.   Let those who desire warrant for our assertion read ' Good for Nothing,' ' Grief of Heart,' ' Under the Willow-tree,' and ' It is very true,' in this volume.   Let any who accuse these of being small, try to produce anything which shall be so complete, so delicate, and so suggestive.   They are on the most tiny scale, it is true, and mostly concern tiny things and trite affections ; but they are, nevertheless, real works of art, and, as such, deserve a warm welcome, from all who love art and its works."

The new year 1850 opened with a grief for me, — a grief also for Denmark and for all that is beautiful.   My first letter that year to Weimar announces it : —

" Oehlenschläger is dead ; he died the twentieth of January, the very day of the death of King Christian VIII. ; yes, almost the same hour of death.   I went out twice late in the night to Oehlenschläger, passing the palace.   I knew from the doctors that he was near death, and it was strange to me to look up at the dark windows of the palace and think, that two years ago I came here anxious for my dear king, and now I came again with similar feelings for a king — a poet-king.   His death was without pain ; his children stood around him, and he asked them to read aloud a scene from his tragedy, ' Socrates,' where he speaks of immortality and assurance of eternal life ; he was quiet, and praying that the agony might not be hard, laid down his head and died.   I saw his corpse ; the jaundice had given it the appearance of a bronze statue, and nothing showed death ; the forehead was beautiful, the expression noble.   On the twenty-sixth of January the people carried him to the grave, — the people in the true sense of that word, for there were public functionaries, — students, sailors, soldiers, all classes, who by turns carried the bier all the long way to Fredericksborg, where he was born, and where he wished to be buried.   The real funeral services took place in Our Lady's Church.   The funeral committee had requested two poets to write the cantata ; one was old Grundtvig and the other was myself.   The Bishop of Seeland gave the funeral address.   For the commemoration at the theatre there was appointed to be played his tragedy, ' Hakon Jarl,' and the scene of 'Socrates,' which was read to Oehlenschläger at the hour of his death!"

To my great joy Oehlenschläger became in his last years very mild and kind toward me, and warmly expressed his appreciation of my work. One day when I was a little grieved at some sneer against me in one of the papers, he gave me his little North Star decoration, which order I had received from the Swedish king on the burial day of Christian VIII. "I have worn that decoration," Oehlenschläger said ; " I give it to you as a remembrance of me! You are a true poet, I say, let others jabber as they will!" and he reached me the North Star decoration, which I own and keep.

The fourteenth of November, 1849, there had been a festival in his honor at the Marksmen's Hall, and it was but a short time after that this funeral commemoration followed. We know that the poet himself had requested the performance of his tragedy " Socrates ; " this, however, was not granted. It is strange that the great poet, when dying, should think of the honor to be paid him. I would rather wish that, like Lamartine's " dying poet," when reminded of his great fame here upon earth, he might have answered, " Do you believe that the swan, flying toward the sun, thinks of the little shadow its flapping wings throw upon the waves? " The theatre was crowded with people on the occasion, and all were dressed in mourning. The first rows of boxes were covered with mourning-crape, and Oehlenschlager's seat in the parquet was distinguished by crape and a laurel-wreath. "How good that is of Heiberg!" said a lady ; " it would touch Oehlenschläger himself, if he saw it!" and I could not forbear answering, " Yes, it would please him to see that he still had a seat! " When Heiberg entered upon his office as director of the theatre, all free seats for poets, composers, ci-devant directors, and different functionaries had been reduced to the end places and corners of each of the few benches we have in the parquet, and to those were also admitted all the singers, actors, and dancers, so that if all were coming, not the third part of them could get places even if they were standing up.

Oehlenschlager, while he lived, went to the theatre every night, but when it happened that he did not come punctually,

and that none of the persons seated would show him the attention of offering him his place, he was obliged to stand ; once
or twice he turned to me, and asked in a joking but pitiful
tone, " How dare I be here ? " To-night it seems he had a
place. It was the same seat he had appointed for himself
when he was one of the directors ; Thorwaldsen also had such
a seat. Heiberg may be excused, because the Diet ordered
him to reduce the number of free seats ; but for Oehlenschläger, the first dramatic poet of the stage, it seems to me that
he ought to have had a seat. A drop of bitterness went
through me at this commemoration, but it was not the first
time such had happened to me at the Danish theatre.

I now turn to another of our theatres, that of the Casino, or, as
expressed by one of our authors, " Only Casino ! " Copenhageners have had for the last two years a people's theatre, which
has grown up, we may almost say, without knowing it ; nobody
thought of it, at least of its making any progress. Mr. Overskou had, among many others, thought, spoken, and written of
such a theatre ; but that was only something on paper. At
that time we possessed a young and able man, endowed with
a remarkable talent of carrying out his projects, even though
he was not himself a man of means. He was a real genius
in his operations ; he knew how to contrive a " Tivoli " for
the Copenhageners, which may be compared with, and perhaps
still surpassed in design and plan all other similar places of
amusement ; he procured us also " Casino," where people at
cheap rates had music and comedy, and the city a large and
tasteful place for its most frequented concerts and masquer-
ades, — soon a place for the most popular amusements. That
man was George Carstensen : his name and ability come back
to us from America of late, as the one who, in connection
with Ch. Gildemeister, built the famous Crystal Palace in New
York. Carstensen was very good-natured, and that I believe
was his greatest fault ; he was very often ridiculed, called
" maître de plaisir ; " nevertheless his activity was of perma-
nent usefulness, and is so still. When the Casino building
was raised, the theatre was not looked upon as the main
thing ; that came about under the direction of the active Mr.
Lange, and little by little grew in the favor of the public, and

in its own strength. There was a time when the Casino shares stood so low that some of them, it is said, were sold for a glass of punch, but the whole soon took a great start.

The repertory was very limited ; no Danish author of celebrity had shown any desire or will to write a work for this stage. Mr. Lange proposed to me to show my sympathy, and my essay was successful beyond all expectation. I had read a story in " The Thousand and One Nights," — " The Story of Prince Zeyn Alasnam, the King of the Ghosts," — which I found very suitable for an opera text ; but although the subject interested me, I gave it up, as I knew that in this country operas relating to enchantment, even with the very best of music, are not understood or valued : I had a proof of this in " The Raven." On reading Gozzi, I found the subject treated as a comedy of enchantment ; but still better than this, and more suited to representation, was one by Raimund, in his " The Ghost-King's Diamond." I had earlier, as is known, essayed my ability in this style of comedy. I wrote for the Royal Theatre " The Flower of Fortune," which indeed was laid aside after its seventh representation, but it was applauded ; and I had the conviction that the talent which the world allowed me as a story-poet might be able to bring forth some flowers in that direction. I reproduced Raimund then in " More than Pearls and Gold," and this piece, I am bold to say, brought the Casino Theatre great credit ; all classes from the highest to the lowest came to see it. The Casino has seats for twenty-five hundred spectators, and in a series of representations, one immediately after the other, all the tickets were sold. It brought me great praise and good satisfaction. One hundred rix-dollars was the stipulated honorarium ; there was no theatre in this country at that time, except the Royal Theatre, which paid any author for his works ; that was therefore already something, and a further addition of one hundred dollars was sent me, as the piece steadily " filled the house," as they called it ; after that several other young authors followed my example. Hostrup, Overskou, Erik Bögh, Recke, and Chievitz, produced works of merit ; the actors improved year by year ; the demands of the public grew always higher and were constantly surpassed, for there were always some who of course

overlooked the care and endeavor shown by the actors. "Only
Casino," is said ; but when that is said by clever men, although
they never go near it, — as, for instance, when the author
of "A Hundred Years" in his poem speaks of the play in
Casino with scorn, — then it is unjust.

I had written a new piece for the theatre, the wonder comedy, "Ole Lukoie," the northern dream-god, to whom I had
already before in one of my stories essayed to give a body, —
to give him form and character ; I wished to bring him on the
stage, made alive to the eye, and let him express the truth,
that health, good humor, and peace of soul are worth more than
money. I mused on my poem and wrote it down. Director
Lange showed the greatest care, nay, love, in representing the
piece as respectably as possible on the little, narrow, confined
stage in Casino, — a piece that required a large stage. I was
pleased to deal with the actors, who were interested in the
poem ; they respected the author, they were not the all-impor-
tant, chief figures in the poem, such as I have met with at the
legitimate theatre. "Ole Lukoie" was brought on the stage
at Casino, and the house was crowded.

The evening of the representation arrived, and I observed
also in a few hours how that waving sea, the public, may criticise and judge what it has taken weeks to produce ; but the
same evening brought me both storm and calm. My poem
was not understood ; at the first act they laughed and became
noisy ; at the end of the second everything was ridiculed, several of the spectators went away at the beginning of the third
act, and said up at the club-house : "The whole thing is nonsense ! They are now in China, and God knows where his
fancy will carry them next !"

But at the beginning of the third act there was a moment's
calm ; before people all talked loudly, now they listened ; there
was more and more tranquillity, and as soon as the idea of the
piece seized them, a triumphant applause stormed through
the house. When the curtain dropped all were delighted,
they applauded and expressed their pleasure. I had never
before felt truly grieved at the misunderstanding, the mocking
and jest with which I was wont to be greeted, but now for
the first time I had a strong consciousness of the injustice

which I suffered. I felt angry as I faced that mocking crowd. I was grieved, and the applause, which now rushed toward me was empty, and had no meaning for me. When I went away several people came up to me and expressed their thanks, but I could not accept them: "They have scoffed and mocked — that I must first try to forget!"

The piece was played many evenings to great assemblies and received great attention. From the people themselves, — the common people, who are called the poorer classes, — I received thanks that no newspaper critique, no fine discrimination in different circles of society could equal. A poor tradesman stood one evening, at the end of the piece, with tears in his eyes, and going out of the door by me he seized my hand and said: "I thank you, poet Andersen: it was a blessed comedy!" Those words were more to me than the most brilliant critique. I must here mention one incident more: in a family of the official class, a house where I often visited, the lady of the house told me that she had been very much astonished in the morning to see the groom with an unusually delightful face when she spoke to him. "Has anything extraordinary happened to-day to Hans, since he is so unusually happy?" she asked one of the girls; and from her she learned that Hans had received one of the tickets yesterday which was not in use. Hans was what is called a real country bumpkin, who went drowsing about. "He is entirely changed," said the girl. "When he came home last night from the comedy, 'Ole Lukoie,' he was highly pleased with all that he had heard and seen. 'I have always supposed,' said he, 'that the rich and people of rank ought to be very happy, but now I see that we poor ones are quite as well off; that I have learned there at the theatre; it was like a sermon, only there was something to be seen, and something very splendid too!'" No judgment has pleased and flattered me more than that of the poor, uneducated fellow!

During the summer, which I spent at Glorup and at the beautiful Corselitze on Falster, I finished "In Sweden." It was the last of my writings which H. C. Örsted heard read, and it gave him great pleasure; the two sections, "Faith and Science," and "Poetry's California," both called forth by his ingenious and suggestive conversation, and by the conception of his " Spirit in Nature," became the subjects of many a talk between us. " They have so often accused you of want of study," he said one day in his mild, joking manner, " that perhaps you are going to be the very poet, who will do the most for science ! "

During my summer stay at Glorup he sent me the second part of " Spirit in Nature," and wrote of the book : " I dare not hope that it will make the same favorable impression upon you, as I had the pleasure to learn that the first part did, because this new volume is intended principally to explain more clearly the former ; yet it will not be wholly wanting in novelty, and I dare believe that the manner of thinking is the same in both of them ! " The book interested me much, and I expressed my pleasure in a long letter, of which I give the following extracts : —

. . . . " Your opinion is that this portion would not make the same impression on me as the first part did ; I cannot distinguish one from the other ; they are like one and the same rich stream ; and what above all makes me glad is that I here seem to see only my own thoughts. My belief, my conviction lies here in plain words before me. I have not only read for myself, but I have also read aloud to a few others, ' The Relations of Physical Sciences to various Important Subjects of Religion.' That chapter is especially suited for reading aloud. I could wish that I might read it to all mankind. I value the blind belief of the pious multitude of people, but I consider it to be far more blessed when they also know what they believe. Our Lord may well permit us to look at Him through that intellect with which He has gifted us ; I will not go to God blindfold ; I will have my eyes open ; I will see and know, and if I should not reach any other end than he who only believes, my thoughts have in any event grown richer. Your book pleases me very much ; for my own part I am also glad that the book is very easy to understand, so that it sometimes seems to me as if it were the result of my own reflection, — as if I might say to myself on reading it, ' Yes, I should have said exactly the same thing ! ' Its truth

has passed over into me and is become a part of myself. I
have, however, thus far read only half of the book ; the war
news drew me away from it ; and since, my thoughts have been
fixed on events at the seat of war ; yet I could not entirely de-
fer writing you and giving you my sincere thanks. . . . .
Eight long days I have not been able to do anything — I am so
overwhelmed. I forget the victory of our brave soldiers when
I think of all those young men who have sacrificed their lives ;
I knew several of them. Colonel Lässoe, you know, was a
friend of mine ; I have known him since he was a cadet, and
always thought that he would become a great man ; he had
a very clear judgment, a firm will, and was in possession of
knowledge and high education. He was so dear to me !
How often has he, though younger than I, overpowered me
with bold and hardy thoughts ; he rallied me jokingly, when
he perceived sickly sprigs in my fancy. On the way from his
mother's to the city, we had often talked of the present, of the
world, and of the future — now he is gone away ! His poor old
mother must certainly be deeply afflicted ; I don't know how
she can bear her sorrow. He fell on the same day as Schleppegrell and Trepka, in a little town near Idsted. It is said
that those of our soldiers who first entered the town were
treated to eating and drinking by the inhabitants ; those who
followed after felt safe, and arriving in the midst of the town,
the insurgents and inhabitants, men and women, rushed out
from doors and gates and commenced a heavy fusilade.
Our soldiers' steadfastness was admirable ; they advanced
through a deep moor against the enemies' fire, jumped from
knob to knob, and notwithstanding they fell before the grape-
shot like flies, their comrades followed and threw the enemy
from his secure position. Would that that battle were the
last, but we know not what still may be in store, and how
many dear lives may yet be thrown away. O God ! may truth
become truth, may peace again throw its light over the lands !
Sorrow now enters the houses of most : we have bitter, gloomy
days. I have half a mind to go and see that full, stirring life,
but I will not, for I know that I should be too much affected
by the sight of all the misery I should encounter there. If I
could only do something, if I could only comfort and quicken

some of the sufferers — but I cannot ! . . . . I bid you
a sincere farewell ! Yours affectionately,
"H. C. ANDERSEN."

When the tidings of the battle of Idsted arrived, I could
not partake in the common joy of the victory ; I was too much
cast down by Lässöe's death. In the night I wrote to his
mother ; I did not know what strength God was giving her to
endure such a heavy loss.

After the struggle and the victory, peace shone over the
land. The return of the soldiers made festival days, which
brightened my life and will always remain as a recollection
of beauty. I wrote a song for the Swedish and Norwegian
volunteers, with which they received the Danes at the
"Iron Gate" at Frederiksborg Avenue. Over the western
city gate was displayed as a greeting the inscription:
"The brave country-soldier has kept his promise !" All
the corporations met with their flags and emblems, a thing
which before we were used to see only in the theatre in the
drama "Hans Sachs;" many a poor man's mind was elated
at seeing what significance his class had in the city, each having its own banner. The music sounded ; "the golden apples"
in the fountain on "the old market-place" played, which
usually took place only once a year on the King's birthday.
Danish, Norwegian, and Swedish flags waved from all the
houses ; many inscriptions were ingenious and beautiful:
"Victory — peace — reconciliation," was read in one place.
All had a festival look, and I felt "Danish in mind." At the
arrival of the first soldiers, tears rushed down my cheeks.
The riding-school was transformed into a triumphal hall with
waving flags and garlands. The officers' table was placed
under three palm-trees covered with golden fruits ; the common soldiers were seated at long tables ; students and other
young men acted as stewards ; music, songs, and speeches followed gayly ; bouquets and wreaths rained down. It was a
pleasure to stay here and to talk with the plain, brave fellows,
who did not know they were heroes.

I asked one, who was a Sleswicker from Angeln, if they
had suffered a good deal in the caserns. He answered : " We

had a jolly time of it ; everything was so fine that we could not sleep the first night ; we lay upon mattresses covered with blankets. For three months we lived in that style, and the worst thing about the barracks was the bad smoke from wet wood. What fine times we are having here, and what gallant folks the Copenhageners are." He praised Flensborg as a true Danish town. " In the warm days they drove from there down to Sleswick and brought us wine and water ! That was a good thing ! " There was a modesty shown by the soldiers, especially the foot-soldiers ; they would point out the most valiant among their comrades, and would give the wreaths which were thrown into the crowd to those they thought most worthy. In the riding-school sixteen hundred men were entertained, infantry and hussars, and many speeches made. Mr. Lange, the director of the Casino, offered them a great number of tickets for the evening representations, so that a great part of the soldiers could go there without expense, and I was extremely glad that I could be of a little service to them there, by procuring them seats, speaking with them, and giving them information. I heard and saw many peculiarities on the occasion. Most of them had never seen a comedy, and had no idea at all what it was. The vestibule and the lobbies were adorned with green leaves and flags. Between the acts I met two soldiers on the lobby. " Well, did you see anything ? " I asked. " O yes, everything, and it was splendid ! " — " But the comedy — have you seen that ? " — " Is that something else to be seen too ? " said both of them. They had remained on the lobby and looked at the gas-lights and flags, and seen their comrades and people go up and down the stairways.

During these days of rejoicing still another festival was celebrated in private life — it may be called a family feast. The Privy-Counsellor Collin had two years previously retired from the administration of his office ; his jubilee occurred the eighteenth of February 1851 ; that was celebrated in the quiet of his family circle.

At the very time when our soldiers were returning home, while songs and words of joy were everywhere heard, there came heavy days of grief : Mrs. Emma Hartmann and H. C. Örsted died both in the same week. There was in that richly gifted woman a spirit of humor and liveliness, which were manifested wholly free from affectation. She was one of those beings who had drawn me into the circle of her genius, humor, and heart, and such always acted upon me as the sunlight acts upon the plant! It is impossible to describe that fountain of joy and sport, the tenderness which poured out from her. There was truth indeed in what the minister, the poet Boye, said at her coffin : " Her heart was a temple of God ; she filled it entirely with love, of which she received abundantly and gave plentifully not alone to her own but to many without, to the poor, the sick, and the sorrowful — as far as it could reach ! " — and always with a kind word, with some pleasantry, she gave to all the best she had. The testimony at her grave is true, that " Happy thoughts and merry feelings took their abode in her, and she let them freely flutter out, like winged birds, with song and merriment, making a friendly spring day at home for those who surrounded her ! " They warbled as they liked, and all went their way. It seemed as if words were ennobled when she used them ; she could say what she chose just as a child can, because one felt that it was served in a clean vessel. Many a jest, many a witty sally came from her lips, but she thought it excessively comical that people should put down on paper, nay, give from the stage such talk as, she said, she could give every day ; she could not understand how they dared offer a serious public such things as were said by the King of Spirits in " More than Pearls and Gold," and *Grethe's* replies about the stork, and her jest about standing in " stork thoughts." She went, to be sure, to the theatre to see this piece, as also " Ole Lukoie," but for a peculiar reason. One day it snowed very hard when her two eldest boys came home from school, but the third of them, a little one, was lost on the way home, far out at Christianshavn and as she sat in anxiety and fear ; I happened to come in, and promised at once to go and seek the lost child. I was not well ; she knew it, and was sorry that I should run out to Christianshavn ; but how could I do other than help her ? It touched her, and she told me that when I went away, she walked up and down the floor in anxiety but also in gratitude, and exclaimed : " He is really kind ! and I

will go and see his 'More than Pearls and Gold!' — if he
brings my dear boy I will also see 'Ole Lukoie.'" — "Yes, I
have made that promise!" said she, when I came back; "I
will go and see it, though it is horrible!" — and she did see it;
she laughed and was more amusing than both the pieces together. She was very musical, and several pieces of music of
hers, though without her name, have been published. With
her whole soul she conceived and understood Hartmann, and
when anticipating the acknowledgment and importance he
was to get abroad, she would become profoundly serious and
a brightness would flash out from her thoughts, — she, who
always was seen in laughter and full of fun. One of our last
conversations was about Örsted's "Spirit in Nature," and especially the part on the immortality of the soul. "It is so
dizzily grand, — it is almost too much for us human beings!"
she exclaimed. "But I will believe, I must believe it!" and
her eyes shone. In the same moment a joke passed over her
lips. Humor abides with us, poor mortals, else we might
think ourselves already quite like our Lord.

It was a sorrowful morning! Hartmann flung his arms
around my neck, and said with tears: "She is dead!"
"Where in the days of life the mother sat among flowers;
where, like the blessed fairy of the house, she nodded kindly
to husband, children, and friends; where, like the sunbeam of
the house, she spread joy around her, and was the binding
cord and heart of the whole, there now sat Sorrow."

In the same hour that the mother died, the youngest of the
children, the little girl, Maria, grew suddenly sick. In one of
my stories, "The Old House," I have preserved some traits
of her character; it was this little girl, a two-year old child,
who always, when she heard music and singing, must dance
to it; and entering one Sunday the room where the elder
sisters were singing psalms, she began to dance, but her musical sense would not allow her to be out of measure and tune,
and these were so long and slow that she was kept standing
first upon one foot and then upon the other, but she danced
involuntarily in complete psalm-measure. In the mother's
hour of death the little head drooped; it was as if the mother
had prayed our Lord: "Give me one of the children, the

smallest one, who cannot be without me!" and God listened to her prayer. The same evening the mother's coffin was carried to the church, the little girl died, and a few days after was buried in a grave close by her mother. Upon the bier the little child looked like a grown-up girl. I have never seen an image more like an angel, and its innocence displayed itself for me in those words, almost too child-like for this world, when I asked her in joke one evening when she was a very little girl, and was going to her bath : "May I go with you?" and she replied, "No, sir, I am too little, but when I am grown larger, then you may!"

Death does not efface the stamp of beauty in the human visage ; it often makes it more sublime ; it is only dissolution of body that is unbeauteous. I never saw any one in death so beautiful, so noble as the mother ; there was spread over her face a sublime repose, a sacred seriousness, as if she were standing before her God. Round about exhaled a fragrance of flowers. Over her coffin sounded words of truth : "She never wounded any man by her judgment when she judged the world and its doings ; she never lessened the honor and praise of the righteous ; she never permitted slander to go unpunished. She did not anxiously weigh her words ; she did not concern herself as to whether her speaking might be misunderstood by those who had not her frankness."

Close by the houses of the street that run by "the Garrison cemetery," just within the iron fence, is to be seen a tomb, always more adorned, and better guarded and kept, than the other tombs, — there reposes the dust of Emma Hartmann and little Maria.

Four days after that I lost H. C. Örsted. It was almost too heavy for me to bear. I lost in those two so infinitely much : first, Emma Hartmann, who by her humor, and life, and merriment, relieved my mind when I was depressed and afflicted, — she to whom I could go to find sunshine ; and now Örsted, whom I had known almost all the years I had been in Copenhagen, and who had become dear to me, as one of the most sympathizing in my life's weal and woe. During the last days I went by turns from Hartmann's to Örsted's, — to the friend who, in my spiritual struggles and trials, had by spiritual means kept me up, whom I was here for the last time to meet with. I did not, however, yet think so. Örsted was so youthful in heart, he longed and spoke so much of the coming summer in the pleasant house in the Frederiksborg's garden. The year before, late in the autumn, his jubilee was celebrated, and the city granted him and his family, while he lived, the summer residence that Oehlenschläger had lately occupied : " When the trees are budding and the sun comes a little forth, we will go out there ! " he said ; but already, the first days of March, he fell sick, yet he kept up good courage. Mrs. Hartmann died the sixth of March. In deep affliction I came to Örsted ; then I heard that his disease was dangerous ; he was suffering of inflammation in one of the lungs. " It will be his death ! " I was filled with this sorrowful thought, though he himself believed that he was recovering. " Sunday I will get up ! " said he, and that Sunday he rose before his God !

When I came there he was struggling with death ; his wife and children were standing around the bed. I sat down in the next room and wept — I was ready to sink. There was a quietness, a Christian's quiet repose, in that home !

The burial took place the eighteenth of March. I was physically ill, and it was a real exertion and struggle for me to walk the short way from the university to the church ; that slow walk was drawn out into two hours. Dean Tryde delivered the sermon, not Bishop Mynster: " He was not summoned to it," they said, excusing him ; but should it be necessary to ask the friend to speak of the friend ? I wanted to weep, but I could not ; it was as if my heart would burst !

Mrs. Örsted and the youngest daughter, Mathilde, remained in the house of mourning ; they heard the chiming of the bells through the many long funeral hours. The tones of the bassoons did the heart good. I went to them afterward, and we talked of the peculiar circumstance that Hartmann's funeral march was played in the church, that he composed for Thorwaldsen's funeral ; for the last time we heard it Örsted was with us, and Hartmann played it. At a little festival which Miss Bremer made for me, before my journey to Sweden, little Maria Hartmann, who now is dead, was then dressed as an angel, and bestowed on me a wreath and a silver cup. Hartmann played some pieces for us. Miss Bremer rose and asked for the funeral march ; she was strangely moved by it, and grasped my hand, saying that I must not consider it as having a sad meaning. " It signifies the going forward toward greater things ! " she said. Now it was played over Orsted, and over his coffin it sounded " Forward to greater things ! "

CHAPTER XV.

PEACE was hovering over the countries, the sun of spring shone. I felt a desire to travel, a longing to live again; and therefore I flew out of the city, out to the light-green wood, to dear friends at the bay of Praestö, to Christinelund (Christina's grove). The young people out there wished to have the stork build her nest upon their house, but no stork came. "Wait till I come!" I wrote; "then the stork will also come!" and just as I had said it, early in the morning of the same day they expected me, two storks came; they were in full activity building their nest when I drove into the yard. This year I saw the stork flying, and that signifies, says an old superstition, that I also was to fly away, to go travelling. My flight that summer was, however, but a short one; the spires of Prague were the most southerly points that I saw; this year's travelling chapter has but few pages, but the first of them, we see, has the vignette of flying storks, which build upon the roof in shelter of the recently budded beech wood. At Christinelund spring had itself drawn its vignette — a blooming apple-branch, growing at the side of a field-ditch. Spring itself was then in its most beautiful manifestation. The little story, "There is a Difference," had its origin from that sight. Most of my poems and stories have their roots thus from without. Every one will, by contemplating life and nature round about with a poetic eye, see and conceive such revelations of beauty, which may be called accidental poetry. I will here mention an example or two : — On the day that King Christian VIII. died, we know that a wild swan flew against the spire of Roeskilde Cathedral and bruised its breast; Oehlenschläger has, in his memorial poem of the King, preserved the incident. When they were fastening fresh wreaths on Oehlenschläger's tomb, and taking away the withered ones, they perceived that in one of these a little singing-bird had

built its nest. When once on a mild Christmas I was at
Bregentved, a thin fall of snow lay one morning upon the
broad stones at the obelisk in the garden ; I wrote thoughtlessly with my cane in the snow these words : —

> " Like snow is immorta'ity :
> No trace to-morrow doth one see."

I went away ; there came thaw, and after a few days again
frosty weather ; and then coming to the place, all the snow
was melted except upon a little spot, and there only remained
the word " immortality ! " I was deeply touched at the accident, and my fervent thought was : " God, my God, I have
never doubted ! "

My real summer sojourn that year was at dear Glorup with
my friend, the noble old Count Gebhardt Moltke-Hvitfeldt.
It was the last year we met there together ; God called him
the following spring ; but that summer stay crowned all the
dear days I had spent there. He planned a festival for the
soldiers who had gone from his estates to the war. I have
before spoken of the noble old gentleman's patriotic mind,
the vivid interest which he took in the agitations of the time,
and I have also spoken of the Danish and Swedish troops'
stay at Glorup. Now the bells of victory had rung, and he
wished the soldiers to have here a good time, a right happy day
and night. I was charged with the arrangement of the festival, which gave me much to do ; but it was successful, and
procured me great pleasure. On both sides of a great basin
in the garden two long lime-tree alleys extend ; in one of
them I pitched a tent forty yards in length, thirteen wide, and
eight in height ; the floor was laid with planed boards, giving
a room to dance. The trees in the alley served as columns ;
the trunks were wound about with shining red damask, that
once had been used as tapestry, and now was thrown away
in a corner ; the capitals were formed of variegated shields
and great bouquets. A rapeseed sail served as roof, and
under that, from the centre of the saloon, a canopy made of
garlands and Dannebrog shields stretched in each direction ;
twelve chandeliers with Danish colors lit the room. From
the red ground of the wall shone, surrounded with flowers, the

King's cipher, and upon variegated painted shields were the names of all the generals. Between the two entrances of the hall a large orchestra was placed under a canopy of Dannebrog flags; raised boxes were arranged at the sides, and uppermost in the hall, among blooming forget-me-nots, two vases with flame-fires, and mourning-crape, and small black shields, bore the names of the first and the last of the fallen officers : Hegermann Lindencrone and Dalgas. Two others bore the inscription, "The country soldier;" higher up, among shields which told of the victories, shone a mighty shield with a verse to the country soldier. A wreath of blood-beech leaves waved over it with golden crown and laurel branches. The whole had a great and peculiar effect upon those for whom it was arranged. "It is worthy to be seen by the King!" said a peasant. "It has cost more than a thousand dollars!" said another. "You may say a million!" said his wife. "That is the kingdom of heaven!" said an old paralytic man, who was carried to the festival. "Such splendor, such music! it is the kingdom of heaven!" For none of my poetic works did I ever get so unanimous an acknowledgment and praise as for my architectural talent, a thing which was very easy to me, who have seen so much of the kind contrived by Bournonville, and later by Carstensen.

The festival took place on the seventh of July, in beautiful weather. At one o'clock the soldiers came marching up, and were received in the castle-yard with a speech of welcome by the minister. At the sound of "The brave country soldier," the procession marched up to the dancing-hall, where the tables stood richly served ; cannon echoed from the little island, where flags waved ; the orchestra played, and joy and pleasure shone on all faces. His Excellency drank the health of the King, after that I read aloud a verse to the country soldier, and then my song was' sung. Among the many affectionate toasts, a soldier gave one for the man who had built the splendid hall, and another of them said innocently that I certainly ought to be paid a good shilling for it. The girls arrived in the evening. Each man was allowed to invite one girl, and the dance commenced in the brilliant dancing-hall ; the alley along the basin was illuminated ; a little three-masted vessel with variegated lanterns was floating on the water. Most of the cuttings for lamps and lanterns were made by myself.

"Next year I will again arrange such a festival," said his Excellency. "It is a pleasure to give such happiness to so many people, and they are so brave, so respectable too!" But alas! it was the last festival he gave : the next spring he was called to his God. That year, however, there was another celebration, that of the silver wedding of his children, and to that were invited only the peasants from all his estates. The soldiers' festival was meantime the chief affair of the summer day here, and all my exertions and interest had in them one reward. Those hours stand like a bright page in the story of my life.

The period of war lay between the present and my last stay in Germany. I had not yet visited the seat of war, because my feelings revolted against going there driven only by curiosity while other men were acting there. Now peace was concluded ; we could again meet, but my thoughts were full of all the bloody events, and my first wish was to go to those places where my countrymen had fought and suffered. One of my young friends travelled with me ; we met at Svendborg, and were carried by steamer to Als, where were still to be seen intrenchments and huts of earth ; at our sailing up the frith every tile-kiln, every projecting point of land, told us a story of the war. Our visit at Flensborg was to see the graves of our fallen heroes. The garden of death rises high over town and sea, and there was especially one grave here which I sought and found — that of Frederick Lässöe ; he lies between Schleppegrell and Trepka. I plucked here one green leaf for his mother, and one for myself, thinking of his short, active life and of his generous love for me. We approached soon the real field of battle. New houses, in place of those which were burnt, were now building ; but round about was seen the bare earth, where the rain of balls had ploughed the soil. My soul was filled with seriousness and woe. I thought of Lässöe and his last moment; I thought of the many who had expired here. It was sacred ground I passed over.

The town of Sleswick was still in a state of siege ; Helgesen was the commander there. I had never seen him before, and it happened that he was the first whom I met. Entering Mrs. Esselbach's hotel, his powerful figure drew my attention; his features put me also somewhat in mind of the portrait of him which I had seen; it ought to be the hero of Frederikstad. I went up to him and asked him if he was the commander: he answered yes, and giving him my name, he received me immediately very kindly. One of his officers accompanied me to Dannevirke, and gave me the information I desired. Queen Thyra's mighty earth-rampart seemed again to have risen. I saw an entire barrack-town still standing; the houses of the officers were furnished with windows of glass, and in one of those houses was now the soldiers' guard-room. I passed the evening with Helgesen. He was friendly, and a plain, straightforward man; in his look and manner he reminded me of Thorwaldsen; he named the one of my stories that had pleased him most, and it was, characteristically enough, "The Constant Tin Soldier." At the fortifications before Rendsborg Danish soldiers were standing. I nodded to them, and the honest fellows understood that Danes were sitting in the carriage; they smiled and nodded to me again. But the drive through the town of Rendsborg was very unpleasant; it was as if I drove through a pit of death; here it was that the insurrection had its root. Ugly memories came in my thoughts; the town had always seemed to me mouldy and oppressive, and now it was a smarting, unpleasant feeling for a Dane to come here. On the railroad I was seated by the side of an old gentleman, who, taking me for an Austrian, praised them, calling them my countrymen, and then spoke ill of the Danes. I told him that I was a Dane, and our conversation stopped; I fancied I saw evil looks round about, and only when all Holstein, and Hamburg too, were lying behind me did I breathe freely.

On the Hanover railroad I heard, in the carriage next to mine, a Danish song, from Danish-girl voices; a bouquet of flowers was thrown in to me; I sent them back again a bouquet, but in words only. Denmark and all that was Danish filled my mind, and surrounded me also at times on the other side of the river Elbe. I had never been so Danish before

when I travelled in the German country. Not until I came
to Leipsic and Dresden did I again find acquaintances and
friends ; they were unchanged, kind, and hearty. The hour of
our meeting was a dear one ; it was well for the mind that
the dark, gloomy interval had passed. Almost all acknowledged with heartiness the Danish people's power and unity,
and the strength that lay in it. Some of them exclaimed,
" The Danes are right ! " It is true that some were of another
opinion, but they did not express it. I had no reason to complain ; I saw and felt a friendly mind and a sympathy around
me ; yes, the accidental poetry, if I may repeat that word,
gave its poetry in honor of the Dane. I must relate a little
event :

Seven years had elapsed since I had seen the hospitable
family Von Serre, whom I have before mentioned as living in
beautiful Maxen, a few miles from Dresden. At that time,
on the evening before my departure, I found, on a walk which
I took with the lady of the estate, a little larch, so small that
I could carry it in my pocket ; it had been thrown away by
the roadside ; I picked it up, and found it was broken. " Poor
tree ! " said I, " it must not die ! " and I looked about upon
the rocky ground for a fissure with a little earth, in which I
could plant the tree. " They say I am a lucky hand ! " said
I ; " perhaps it will grow." At the very edge of the slope of
the rock I found a little earth in a stone crevice ; here I put
the tree down, went away, and thought no more of it. " Your
tree at Maxen is growing admirably ! " the artist Dahl told me
some years after at Copenhagen. He had come directly from
Dresden. I heard of it now at Maxen as " The Danish Poet's
Tree," for so it was called, and this name it had carried in an
inscription for several years. The tree took root, shot out
branches, and grew tall, because it had been cared for by Mrs.
Von Serre, who had caused earth to be laid about it ; after that
had had a piece of the rock blown away ; and lately a path
had been laid out close by it, and before the tree stood the inscription, " The Danish Poet's Tree." It had not been molested during the war with Denmark, but now " it is going to
die," they said ; " the tree will come to nothing." A mighty
birch-tree was growing close by, its large branches spread

themselves over the larch, and that alone was enough to check its growth and make it perish. But one day in the midst of the war there was a violent storm ; the lightning split the birch-tree and tore it from the rock, and — "The Danish Poet's Tree " stood free and untouched. I came to Maxen, saw my young tree, and near by the stump of the birch. A new plate bore the inscription. It was Major von Serre's birthday, and all the best people in Dresden were gathered here for the celebration. The workmen from the marble quarries and lime-kilns of the estate came with songs and flowers. It has always been a certain good fortune of mine on my travels to meet with something peculiar and interesting, and this was also the case on the railway between Leipsic and Dresden. In the compartment with me sat an old lady with a large market basket upon her lap ; at her side was her twelve-year old boy, Henry, who, tired of travelling all night and day, looked longingly after the spires of Dresden. Opposite me was a young, lively lady, who spoke boldly of art, literature, and music, with which she seemed to be very conversant ; she had been in England several years : they were all on their way from Breda. During the stopping of the train, I went out with two other travellers, and we guessed who she might be. I presumed her at first to be an actress ; another thought that she was governess in a very fine English family. On the way the old lady pushed me slightly and said, " That is a remarkable person ! "— " Who is she ? " I asked quickly. " Demoiselle "— she stopped suddenly, because the young lady, who was leaning out of the window, again talked with us. My curiosity was considerably strained. " Antoinette ! " the brother cried to her, " there is Dresden ! — Antoinette ! " When we stepped out of the carriage, I whispered to the old lady, " Who is that young lady ? " and she whispered mysteriously at parting, " Demoiselle Bourbon."—" And who is Antoinette Bourbon ? " I asked at Dresden, and they told me that she was the daughter of the well known watchmaker at Geneva, who claimed to be the son of the unfortunate Louis XVI. and Marie Antoinette ; that the children had lived for some time in England, were staying now in Breda, but sometimes came incognito to Dresden. An old French lady, who felt certain that they were the real Dauphin's children, lived with them and for them.   This was told me, and corresponded with the appearance of my travelling companions, and surely, Antoinette's face had a certain royal dignity ; she might well be considered the daughter of the Dauphin, or at least of a man who had the features of the Bourbons.

Weimar was deserted.   I knew that all my friends were scattered about.   The visit here and the continuation of my travel were therefore reserved for the following year.

I received at home in the autumn, the sixth of October, 1851, the title of Professor.   On the arrival of spring, and as soon as the wood put forth its leaves, I set out to tie fast the travelling-thread where I had lost it, and that was at my favorite Weimar.   My friends greeted me cordially ; the reception was as kind as ever, from the grand ducal palace to the many acquaintances and friends all over the city.   Beaulieu de Marconnay had, in the interval of our separation, become court-marshal and intendant of the theatre ; was married, had a happy home, where I, as in former days, was received as a friend, — I might almost say, as a brother.   Some sweet children were playing in the room ; they stretched their small hands toward me ; and the lady of the house stood there herself as the good guardian spirit of the house : happiness and blessings had here taken their abode.

The other thing that during my visit at Weimar this time offered itself to me as a new bouquet of memory was the intercourse I had with Liszt, who, as is known, had here an office as chapel-master, and had a great influence on the musical element of the whole theatre.   The problem he especially set himself was to bring out dramatic compositions of value, which perhaps otherwise would hardly have been introduced in the German theatres.   In Weimar has thus been given Berlioz's " Benvenuto Cellini," which, as regards the chief personage, has for the Weimarians a special interest through Goethe's " Benvenuto."   Wagner's music especially interests Liszt very much, and he is using every exertion to make it known, partly by bringing it on the stage, and partly by writing of it.   He has published in French an entire book concerning the two compositions, " Tannhäuser " and

" Lohengrin ; " the first one has, on account of its subject, great significance in Weimar, as it is associated with the Thuringian traditions. The scene takes place at Wartburg. Wagner is considered as the most remarkable composer of the present time, a position which I cannot in my plain, natural feeling well admit ; it seems to me as if all his music were composed intellectually. In " Tannhäuser " I must admire the exceedingly well-delivered recitative, as for instance where *Tannhäuser* returns from Rome and relates his pilgrimage, — that is charming ! I recognize the grand and picturesque elements in this music-poem, but I feel there is lacking the flower of music, — the melody. Wagner himself has written the text to his operas, and as a poet in this respect he occupies a high place ; there are variations, there are situations ; the music itself, the first time I heard it, sounded like a great sea of tunes which waved over me and affected me in body and mind. " What do you say about it now ? " he asked ; and I answered, " I am half dead ! " " Lohengrin " seems to me a wonderful tree, without flower or fruit. Don't misunderstand me, my judgment of music besides is of little consequence ; but I claim as well in this art, as also in poetry, the three elements : intellect, fancy, and feeling ; the last one is revealed in melodies ! I see in Wagner the thinking composer of the present time, great through intellect and will, a mighty breaker down of rejectable old-fashioned things ; but I do not feel in him that divinity which is granted to Mozart and Beethoven. A great and able party speaks as Liszt does ; the general public agrees with them here and there. I believe that Wagner has such a recognition at Leipsic, but it was not so before. One evening in the " Gewandhaus," several years ago, when I was there, after the execution of several pieces by different composers that were unanimously applauded, the overture of "Tannhäuser" was given ; it was the first time I heard it, the first time I heard the name Wagner. I was struck by the picturesqueness in the whole music-poem, and I burst out in applause ; but I was almost the only one. They looked at me from every side, they hissed, but I remained faithful to my impression of the music, applauded once more and shouted "Bravo ! " but in my heart I was overcome with bashfulness and the blood rushed up in my cheeks. Now, on the contrary, all applauded Wagner's "Tannhäuser." I told this to Liszt, and he and his whole musical circle rewarded me with a "Bravo" because I had given way to right feeling.

From Weimar I went to Nuremberg. The electro-magnetic thread kept along beside the railroad. My heart is as Danish as any one's! It throbs stronger at my country's honor! Thus I felt here on the railroad. A father with his son sat in the same compartment as I; the father pointed at the electro-magnetic thread. "That is," he said, "a discovery of a Dane, — Mr. Örsted!" I was happy to belong to the same nation as he.

Nuremberg lay before us. I have in one of my stories, "Under the Willow," given an impression of that old, magnificent city: so also the journey through Switzerland and across the Alps has supplied me with the background for the picture. I had not visited Munich since 1840, and then it stood, as I wrote in the "Bazaar," like a rose-bush that shoots forth every year new branches; but each branch is a street, each leaf a palace, a church, or a monument. Now the rose-bush had grown up to a large tree all in blossom: one flower is called Basilica, another Bavaria, and in that way I again expressed myself, when King Ludvig asked me what impression Munich made on me. "Denmark has lost a great artist, and I a friend!" said he, speaking of Thorwaldsen.

Munich is for me the most interesting city of Germany, and that is especially produced by King Ludvig's talent for art and his incessant activity. The theatre also is flourishing; it possesses one of Germany's most clever theatre intendants, the poet Dr. Dingelstedt. He goes every year to the most important German stages, and learns there what talent is coming forward. He visits Paris, and knows the repertoires and the wants of the theatres and the public. The royal theatre at Munich will soon offer a model repertoire; with us such "mise en scène" is entirely unknown: we for instance, in "The Daughter of the Regiment," where the scene is in Tyrol, have recourse to side-scenes with palms and cactuses; we let *Norma* in one act live in Socrates' Grecian room, and in another act in Robinson Crusoe's palm-hut ; they offer us day-scenes where the sun is shining in, while in the background one finds an open balcony and dark-blue starry sky ; all without thought and attention, and thus without any purpose. But who cares about such things, they say ; no paper complains of it. Munich's repertoire has variety ; there is pains taken to know the most important productions of the time in different countries ; the theatre intendant puts himself into relations with the best known authors there. A courteous letter which I received from him brought us into correspondence ; he wished information about the Danish repertoire as to original pieces, and mentioned in the same letter the present Bavarian king's knowledge of my writings and his gracious interest in me. The intendant Dingelstedt was thus the first person I visited at Munich ; he immediately assigned me one of the first boxes in the theatre ; it was during my whole stay at the disposal of myself and my travelling companion. He informed King Max of my arrival, and the next day I was invited to dinner at the hunting seat Stärnberg, where his majesty then sojourned. The Privy-Legation Counselor Von Dönniges came for me ; we travelled rapidly by rail, and arrived before dinner-time at the little castle, beautifully situated on a lake, bordered by the Alps. King Max is a young, very amiable man. I was received in the most gracious and friendly manner. He told me that my writings, especially " The Improvisatore," " The Bazaar," " The Little Mermaid," and "The Garden of Paradise," had made a deep impression on him. He talked of other Danish authors ; he knew Oehlenschläger's and H. C. Örsted's writings. He spoke with admiration of the spiritual, fresh life in art and science which stirred in my country ; from Von Dönniges, who had travelled in Norway and Seeland, he knew of the beauty of the Sound and our charming beech woods ; he knew what treasure we own in the Northern museum beyond other nations.

At the table the King honored me by drinking a glass to my muse, and rising from table he invited me on a sailingtrip. The weather was dull but the clouds were fleeting ; a large covered boat lay on the lake ; neatly dressed rowers appeared with their oars, and soon we were gliding smoothly over the water. I read aloud on board the story "The Ugly Duckling;" and amid lively conversation about poetry and nature we reached an island, where the king had just ordered to be built a beautiful villa. Near by a large hill was dug through; they thought it a giant grave, like those we have in the North; here were found bones, and a knife of flint-stone. The attendants kept themselves at a distance; the King invited me to take a seat at his side on a bench near the lake; he spoke of my poems, of all that God had granted me, spoke of the lot of man in this world and of that strength we had when we kept faith in our Lord. Near where we sat stood a large blooming elder-tree, which gave me occasion to mention the Danish Dryad as it is manifested in the story "The Elder-Mother." I told him of my latest poem, and of the dramatic application of the same person. Passing by the tree I asked his permission to pluck one of its flowers as a memento of these moments; the king himself broke one off and gave it to me. That flower I still keep, among pleasant souvenirs, and it tells me of the evening here.

"If the sun would shine," said the King, "you would see how beautifully the mountains here would look!"

"I have always good luck!" I exclaimed. "I hope it will shine!" and at the same moment the sun really burst forth, the Alps shone in beautiful rosy hue. On our way home again I read on the lake the stories of "A Mother," "The Flax," and "The Darning-Needle." It was a delightful evening; the surface of the water was quite calm, the mountains became of a deep blue, the snowy summits gleamed, and the whole was like a fairy tale.

I reached Munich at midnight. The "Allgemeine Zeitung" had an account of this visit under the title, "King Max and the Danish Poet."

From Munich I went to Switzerland, Lago di Como, and Milan, which city was still declared in a state of siege. When I was going to leave the city they could not find my passport in the police-office, and called for me to come up there : such an event was sufficient to disturb all my travelling-pleasure. An open letter from the Austrian Minister at Copenhagen, who recommended me to the civil and military authorities, became now of use to me. They were very polite, but my passport was not to be found ; but when they brought out all they had received, I discovered mine ; it had been put away according to its number, but the *gensd'arme* had written it down wrong, and the number did not correspond to that he had put upon my receipt, but it was soon all right; only it was my customary fortune to have more trouble with my passport than any one else when I always in travelling keep especial watch over it.

I returned by St. Gothard and the Lake of Lucerne, in whose charming environs I spent a few days. At ˙Schaffhausen I bid farewell to Switzerland, and travelled through the scene of Auerbach's "Dorfgeschichten" (village tales), the romantic " Schwarzwald." Black charcoal-pits sent out their bluish smoke, handsome men passed by, the mountain-way, "die Hölle" (the hill), was true Alpine-scenery.

I was witness to a touching scene at a railway-station between Freiburg and Heidelberg. A crowd of emigrants to America, old and young, stepped into the cars, their relations and friends took leave of them, with great crying and lamentation. I saw an old woman clinging fast to one of the cars, they were obliged to tear her away ; the train started, she threw herself down to the ground. We went away from those lamentations and shouts of hurra ; there was change for those going away, but for those who remained there was only want and sorrow, and everything reminded of those who had gone. I visited Heidelberg's castle-ruin on a fresh, warm summer day. Cherry-trees and elders were growing into the rooms and halls of the ruin ; birds were flying chirping about. All at once a voice called my name ; it was Kestner, the Hanoverian Ambassador at Rome, the son of Werther's Lotte. He was visiting Germany; that was our last meeting ; he died the year after.

The last of July I came back again to Copenhagen. Her majesty the widow-queen, Caroline Amelia, honored me with a gracious invitation to Sorgenfri (*Sans Souci*). I spent several days here, occupying the rooms of the deceased Privy-Counselor Adler. Many recollections of my life from boyhood,

from those bright and better days, went through my soul,
which turned thankfully toward the loving God. I became
better acquainted with the country round about, which I had
but slightly seen before. I learned to appreciate more the
pious, tender mind of that noble queen so tried by sorrow.

I had written the story-comedy, "The Elder-Mother," for
the Casino. The director and all the actors thought a great
deal of it. At the first representation it was received with
great applause, although some hissing was heard, but that
always happened of late to every new work. "Dagbladet" (a
daily paper) expressed itself in a friendly manner of it, but
"Berlingske Tidende" and "Flyveposten" ("Berling's Gazette" and the "Flying Post"), which at other times have always
spoken well of me, "broke their sticks" over the work, and
could not find any coherence in it. I answered by an analysis
which discovered a little story, carefully wrought. Meanwhile it
found acceptation with most of our poets. Heiberg and Ingemann, each of them, wrote me a beautiful letter ; the pastor
Boye expressed himself very warmly and tenderly ; and I
believe that "The Elder-Mother" was the only piece he ever
went to see in the Casino. But the newspaper critique in
general had its way, and cooled the interest of the people. I
felt convinced then that the most part of my countrymen have
not much liking for the fantastic ; they do not like to mount
too high, but would rather stay on the ground and feed themselves in a sensible fashion upon common dramatic dishes
made exactly according to the receipt-book. Director Lange
continued meantime to give the piece, and by degrees it
became understood, and was at last received with undivided
applause. At one of the representations it happened that I
was seated at the side of a good looking old man from the
country. Early in the first scene of the piece, where the
elemental spirits come forth, he turned toward me, whom he
did not know, and said by way of introduction, "Really,
that is a piece of damned nonsense they'll have to get out
of !" — "Yes, it is a little difficult," I answered, "but after
that it will be more intelligible : there will come a barber's
shop, where they shave and do a great deal of love-making !"

" Ah indeed! is that so?" said he. When the piece was finished he was very well pleased with it, or he had perhaps come to know that I was the author, for now he turned toward me and assured me "that it was an exceedingly good piece, and very intelligible ; that it was only in the beginning there were some difficulties to overcome ! "

" The Merman" was brought out in the Royal Theatre in February, 1853. Professor Gläser had made an abundance of melodies to flow over the poem. It was northern music that people heard, and that they appreciated.

I left Copenhagen at Whitsuntide and went out to Ingemann's in the fresh woody country, to that home where my heart, ever since I was a school-boy at Slagelse, drew me regularly every summer. There all things were unchanged, and there hearts remained the same. However far the wild swan may fly, it always returns to that old well-known place at the wood-lake ; and I have the wild swan's nature.

Ingemann is no doubt our most popular poet ; his romances, which criticism thought immediately to gnaw to death, live yet and are read ; they have made their way to high and low in the northern realms ; they are read by the Danish peasant, and through them he comes to love his country and its historic memories ; a deep harmony is heard in every poem, even in the smaller ones, and I will mention one of them, not very well known, "The Dumb Girl." In this it is as if the tree of poetry was stirred in its top by great movements that are gone in a second. They are movements we have all felt, and our grandchildren will hear them from the old people's mouth. Ingemann has, besides, humor and the eternal youth of the poet. It is a happiness to know a nature like his, and still happier am I to know that I have in him a tried and steadfast friend !

Here in the room hung with pictures, where the lime-trees outside throw shadows, and the lake shines bright and blue, everything almost is just as it was, when I, a scholar from the Slagelse school, came here on a beautiful summer day. And the memory of all that I have seen and experienced since then, indeed the whole story of my life, seems to be a garland that is woven here.

Spring, which commenced so beautifully that year, bade me welcome with green woods and the songs of nightingales ; and soon all that was only empty glory, — heavy, anxious days were rising. Cholera broke out in Copenhagen. I was no longer in Seeland, but I heard of all the horrors and fatalities of that disease. The first near and painful death-news that came to me was that of the poet, the pastor Boye. He met me in recent years so kindly and appreciatingly that he had become very dear to me.

One of the most painful ·and sorrowful days of that bitter period was a single day which should have been devoted to joy and merriment. I was at Glorup, where Count Moltke-Hvitfeldt celebrated his silver-wedding. I was the only stranger invited, and my invitation had been given a year and day before. All the peasants of his estate were guests. I presume that more than sixteen hundred were assembled here. Everything was rich and festive ; dancing and merriment went on, music was heard ; flags were floating, rockets rose in the air ; and in the midst of all that jubilation I received a letter telling me that two of my friends were taken away. The angel of death went from house to house ; now on the last evening he stopped at my home of homes, — at Collin's house. "We have to-day all moved from the place !" they wrote. "God only knows what will happen to-morrow !" It was as if I had got the message that all, to whom my heart had clung so fast, were to be taken away from me. I lay weeping in my room. Outside gay dancing-music and hurras sounded, rockets shone ; it could not be endured. New mourning-messages came daily. At Svendborg too the cholera had broken out ; my physician and my friends all advised me to remain in the country ; in Jutland more than one hospitable house was opened for me.

A great part of the summer was spent with Michael Drewsen at Silkeborg. I have given a description of that beautiful country, which reminds one in its nature of the woody tracts of the Black Forest and Scotland's grand solitary heaths, and I have given some of its memories and traditions. In the midst of that beautiful country and in a hospitable home, I went about deeply afflicted ; my heart was very sorrowful. I got into a nervous suffering state, and endured the torments of uncertainty. When the postilion's horn sounded, I ran away immediately to get letters and papers ; I was ready to sink down during the minutes I had to wait; I was tormented, depressed, and sick at heart ; and as soon as the disease at Copenhagen began to decrease so far that they thought I could return, I hastened to the dear friends whom I had thought never more to see again.

My publisher, Chancery-Counselor Mr. Reitzel, died in the spring, shortly before the epidemic broke out. We had, during my whole career as author, been associated with true sympathy, and that became fixed in friendship ; his last undertaking was the determination to bring out a cheap edition of my collected writings in Germany. Seven years before a collected edition had already been issued, followed by " Das Märchen Meines Lebens," — a sketch only, but one that was received abroad with hearty interest and sympathy.

I have found a like reception in England and America, where it was published in a translation by Mary Howitt. The happy fortune was now to be mine, of publishing, while yet young, my collected writings in Danish ; a matter of consequence, since I could then get in order, and also lop off one or another of the too leafless branches ; my autobiography would besides place the whole in its right light. I would not give the earlier sketch, but an entire fresh and full recollection of all that I had felt and enjoyed. An account of the many men of note whom I had come across in my path of life ; the impressions gained from my life and my whole circumstances ; everything which I thought, when noted down for a coming generation, might have the interest which attaches to contemporary history, as also a plain presentation of what God had permitted me to endure and overcome, that might fortify many a struggling soul.

The work was commenced in the fall of 1853, in the very month of October that, twenty-five years before, saw me receive my *examen* as a student. Of late the custom had prevailed for each section to celebrate its twenty-fifth *artium* feast, if I dare call it so. The most interesting part of the whole feast was the first meeting in the reception-hall, the seeing

again of so many whom we had not met with for so long a
time. Some of them were grown fleshy and unfamiliar looking ; others old and gray-haired ; but a youthful mind at that
moment shone in all eyes. This meeting was for me the true
bouquet of the feast ; at the table speeches were made and
several songs sung : one of them I had written, and it expresses
entirely my feeling then, and as it seemed that of the others
also as it appeared.

Professor Clausen made a beautiful and eloquent speech,
drinking a glass for Paludan-Müller and me, the two poets
who among the students of that year had maintained a very
distinguished place in literature.

A few days after I received the following printed cir-
cular : —

"At the meeting of the students of 1828, on the twenty-
second of October, wishes were expressed for a common undertaking, by which the remembrance of that year which had
brought us together might be preserved. After some consideration we agreed to act upon the suggestion of that year's ' four
great and twelve small poets,' and founding a legacy under the
name of ' The Andersen-Paludan-Müller Legacy,' which in
time, after annual contributions had increased it to a consider-
ble sum, should be applied to the support of a Danish poet
who had no public employment."

How far and to what this will develop, lies in the future ;
but the thought makes me glad, and it is an acknowledgment,
a homage shown by Danish students, by the comrades of one
and the same student-year.

Travelling-life is like a refreshing bath to my spirit and
body. I went away a few weeks in the following year, to
Vienna, Trieste, and Venice, to enjoy spring in its freshness.
Only three or four pictures of life having any importance are
noted down of this trip. The cherry-trees were in blossom in
the dear Saxon home at Maxen : the lime-kilns smoked ;
Königstein, Lilienstein, and all those miniature mountains
rose before me, and beckoned to me ; it was as if only a long
winter-night — but one disturbed by an ugly cholera-dream —
lay between the present and the time I last stood here. I
seemed to see the same blooming, the same skies and shad-

ows, the same hospitable home and dear friends. Upon the wings of steam I flew through mountains and over valleys. I caught sight of St. Stephen's Tower, and in the imperial city, after many years, I was again to meet with Jenny Lind Goldschmidt.

Her husband, whom I saw for the first time here, received me very kindly ; a sturdy little son gazed at me with his big eyes. I heard her sing again ; it was the same soul, the same fountain of music! Taubert's little song, "Ich musz nun einmal singen ich weisz nicht warum " ("I must sing just once, I know not why"), as formed by her lips was the song of a jubilating warbling-bird·; the nightingale cannot whistle like that, the thrush cannot quiver ; the soul of a child, the soul of thought must be in it, — it must be sung by Jenny Goldschmidt. Her power and greatness lie in dramatic delivery and truth, and yet it is only in the concert-hall that she permits us to perceive this in the arias and songs which she then gives. She has left the stage ; that is a wrong done her spirit : it is to give up her mission, the mission that God chose for her.

In trouble and yet happy, wonderfully full of thoughts, I hastened toward Illyria, that country which Shakespeare has chosen for many of his immortal scenes, — the country where *Viola* finds her happiness. There was a surprisingly charming view at sunset, as it was displayed to me, when suddenly from the high mountain-brow I looked far below upon the glowing Adriatic ; the brightness made Trieste look still more dark ; the gas-lamps were just lit, the streets radiated in outlines of fire ; from the carriage we looked down as from a balloon in its slow descent ; the shining sea, the gleaming streets, seen in those few minutes, remain in the memory for years. From Trieste we arrived in six hours by steamer at Venice.

"A sad wreck upon the water," was the impression it made upon me the first time I was here in 1833 ; now I came here again, seasick from the swells of the Adriatic. It seemed to me as if I could not get rid of it on land, but that I had only gone from a smaller to a larger ship. The only pleasant thing to me was that the silent city was fastened to the living continent by the railway mole. Venice seen in the moonlight, is a charming sight, — a wonderful dream well worth knowing. The silent gondolas are gliding like the boats of Charon between the high palaces, which are mirrored in the water. But in the day-time it is rather unpleasant here. The canals have dirty water, in which you see floating stumps of cabbage, lettuce-leaves, and all such things ; water-rats come out from the crevices of the houses ; the sun burns hotly down between the walls.

I was glad to leave that wet grave, and the railway steam brought me speedily over the endless dike bordered by muddy, slimy banks and sand-flats ; on the main-land the vine leaf hung in rich garlands, the black cypress pointed up toward the blue air. Verona was the end of my travel that day. Several hundred men were sitting upon the steps of the Amphitheatre ; they did not fill it up much ; they were looking at a comedy, performed in a theatre erected in the midst of the Amphitheatre, with painted side-scenes, illuminated with Italian sunshine. The orchestra played dance-music ; the whole had the look of a travesty, — an exhibition so piteously modern here upon the remnants of the old Roman times. During my first visit in Venice I was stung by a scorpion in my hand. Now in the neighboring city, as Verona has become by means of the railway, I had the same fate. I had stings upon my neck and cheeks that smarted and swelled. I suffered extremely, and in that state I saw the Lake of Garda, the romantic Riva, with its luxuriant valley of vine leaves, but pain and fever drove me away from here. We travelled the whole night in the clearest moonlight over a wild, romantic road, one of the most beautiful I have seen, — a picture of nature that Salvator Rosa's fancy could not create upon canvas. I have the impression of it as of a beautiful dream in the midst of a night of pains.

A little after midnight we reached Trient, which gave the traveller an epitome of all the discomforts. We were obliged to wait at the city gate till a *gendarme* of Italy came loitering along and asked for our passports ; those were delivered in a dark night into strange hands, with the promise that we should receive them back again early next morning, without any ticket or receipt, — nothing to rely upon in Austria, so strict about passports. Then they led us through long, pitch-dark streets to a palace-like but dead-alive hotel, where, after long knocking and crying, a drowsy, half-dressed cameriere came out and conducted us up cold, broad stairs, through long entries and dark corridors, into a large, high-studded, antique saloon with two made beds, each large enough for a whole family, children and all. A drowsy lamp stood upon a dusty marble table ; the doors could not be shut; we looked through them into large rooms, also with beds big enough for whole families. There were secret doors in the wall, privy stairs, and red wine spilt on the floor, looking very like blood-stains. These were my surroundings, and it was my last night in Italy. My wounds burnt, my blood burnt ; it was hopeless to think of sleep and repose. At last the morning dawned, the bells sounded from the vetturino's horses, and we drove from Trient and its naked mulberry-trees, — the leaves had been picked and carried to market. By the Brenner Pass we reached Munich, passing through Innsbruck. Here I found friends, care, and help. The physician of the King, the amiable old Privy-Councilor Gietl, cared for me most kindly ; and after fourteen somewhat painful days I was able to receive the royal invitation to the castle of Hohenschwangau, where King Max and his consort spent the summer time. A story ought to be written about the fairy of the Alpine rose, who from his flower flutters through Hohenschwangau's picture-crowded saloons, where he gets sight of something even more beautiful than his flower. Between the Alps and the River Lech lies an open, fertile valley with a transparent, dark-green lake at either end, one of them a little higher than the other ; and here, upon a marble crag, the castle of Hohenschwangau rises majestically. The castle of Schwanstein stood here before ; Welfs, Hohenstaufs, and Schyrs were once its lords ; their deeds live still in the pictures painted on the castle walls. King Max, as crown prince, has restored the castle and made it to be a state mansion. None of the castles on the Rhine are so beautiful as Hohenschwangau, and none has such surroundings, — the wide valley and the snow-covered Alps. The lofty, arched gate rises magnificently, where two chivalrous figures are standing with the arms of Bavaria and

Schwangau, — a diamond and swan. In the castle yard, where the water-jet is playing from the wall, which is adorned with the image of a Madonna, painted *al fresco*, three mighty lime-trees throw shadows ; and in the garden, amongst an abundance of flowers, where the most beautiful roses are blooming on the lawn, we might fancy ourselves to have found again Alhambra's lion-well ; the ice-cold spring, even at that elevation, sends its fountain forty feet up into the air. An armory, where ancient armor with helmets and spears seem living cavaliers, is the first place we enter ; and now opens a series of richly painted halls, where even the variegated window-panes relate legends and histories, where every wall is like a whole book, which tells us of times and men long gone by.

" Hohenschwangau is the most beautiful Alpine rose I saw here among the mountains ; may it be also always the flower of fortune here." These words I wrote in German in an album, just as they are in my heart, and ever will remain there.

Here I spent some charming, happy days ! King Max received me, if I dare say so, as a dear guest ; the noble, intellectual King showed me great sympathy and favor ; the Queen, a born princess of Bavaria, of rare beauty and lovely womanhood, was presented to me by his majesty himself. After dinner, the first day, I drove with the King in a little open carriage — a quite charming drive, certainly — a couple of miles, as far as into the Austrian Tyrol, and this time I was not asked for passport or stopped on the way. The country had a more picturesque look ; the peasants stood on the road-side saluting their King ; the carriages we met stopped while his majesty passed by. This charming drive lasted a couple of hours among the sunny lofty mountains ; and during all that time the King talked with me very kindly of " The Story of my Life," which he had recently read, and asked about several of those Danish persons mentioned in it ; saying, besides, how excellently all had turned out for me, and what happy feelings I ought to have after having overcome so much, and at last been fairly acknowledged as a poet. I told him that my life certainly very often seemed to me like a story, rich and wonderfully changing. I had known what it was to be poor and alone, and then to be in rich saloons ; I knew what it was to be scorned and to be honored, — even this hour, driving now by the side of a king among the sunny Alps, this was a chapter in the story of my life ! We talked of the most recent Scandinavian literature ; I mentioned Salomon de Caus, Robert Fulton, and Tycho Brahe, — how the art of poetry in our time brought forward these men of the time. Genius, heart, and piety shone through all the words of the noble King; it was and is still one of the most memorable hours I have spent here.

In the evening I read aloud to the royal pair the stories "Under the Willow " and " There is no Doubt." Along with Von Dönniges I ascended one of the nearest mountains, and had a view of the charming and grand scenery. Time passed too quickly. The Queen allowed me to write a few words in her album. I perceived there, among the names of emperors and kings, one from the realms of science, Professor Liebig, whose kind and winning nature I had learned to know and admire in Munich.

With tender heart and profound gratitude to the amiable royal couple, I left Hohenschwangau, where they told me that I should be welcome again. I carried with me a large bouquet of Alpine roses and forget-me-nots in the carriage, which brought me to Füssen.

From Munich my homeward journey took me through Weimar. Carl Alexander had begun his reign ; he was just then sojourning in the castle " Wilhelmsthal," near Eisenach, whither I went and spent happy days with the noble prince in that wonderfully beautiful country in the midst of the Thuringer wood.

The old Wartburg, on which the now reigning Grand Duke in the course of years has spent great sums of his own fortune, in order to restore it to its primitive style, was now almost finished, with fine pictures on the walls, that told the castle's traditions and history. Already the Minnesinger Hall was adorned in the grandeur of its time of yore with rows of columns ; and what a view there was here over woods and mountains, the whole scenery that existed in the minnesinger time — the Venus Mountain, where Tannhäuser disappeared ; the three " Gleichen ; " even the wood-solitariness, just as Walther von der Vogelweidet and Heinrich von Ofterdingen knew it. Tradition and history have here their whole unchanged plan.

On the little castle down in the town of Eisenach lives the Duke of Orleans's widow, with her two sons, the Count of Paris and the Duke of Nemours. I heard from the most different persons how much she and the children were loved by all there, how very much good she did as far as her means permitted, how kind-hearted and sympathizing she proved herself, — a true blessing to that little town. I met in the street the young princes with their teacher; they were plainly dressed, but looked wide awake and good; the Grand Duke of Weimar himself presented me to the Duchess. Quickly there passed through my thoughts, what she had suffered and endured, the whole change in her life, and involuntarily the tears came into my eyes, even before I had begun to speak. She remarked it, took my hand in a friendly way, and when I looked at her dead husband's picture on the wall, as young and blooming as when I had seen him at Paris at the ball at the Hôtel de Ville, and spoke of that time, tears burst from her eyes; she talked of him, of her children, and told me kindly that they knew my stories. There was a kindness, a sincerity, a sadness, and yet a womanly courage, such I had imagined might belong to Helene of Orleans. She was in her travelling-dress, intending to go by the railway train a few miles off. "Will you dine with me to-morrow?" she asked. I was obliged to answer, that I intended to leave the same day: "In a year I shall come back again here!" "A year!" she repeated; "how much can happen in a year, so much happens in a few hours!" and tears and thoughtfulness mingled in her eyes. On taking leave, she held out her hand to me, and I left that noble princess deeply affected. Her destiny has been heavy, but her heart is royally grand and strong in confidence toward God.

I was soon again in Denmark, and busily engaged not only with the edition of my collected writings, but also with the translation of Mosenthal's popular comedy, "Der Sonnwend-hof." During my stay in Vienna I had seen it at the Burg Theatre, and was much pleased with it. I drew the attention of State-Counselor Heiberg to it, but he took no notice of it. Director Lange, on the contrary, asked me if I could get it for the Casino, and through the intendant of the Burg Theatre I obtained the piece from Mosenthal, with privilege to treat it as I pleased. From its connection with Auerbach's "Village Tales," I chose the name, as more intelligible, "A Village Story ; " and when it was brought on the stage it had, as we know, a great success, and has been given repeatedly. I added besides several songs, which are necessary for any representation on the stage of the Casino. I had also made *Anna* in the last act, up in the Alpine cottage, take up a burning piece of wood, and by the brightness of that recognize *Mathias*, as she saw him when the Ilsang forge was on fire. Mosenthal afterward, by the aid of his Danish friends at Vienna, read my translation, and wrote me, immediately after, a letter full of gratitude and kindness ; and as to the few changes I had made in it, he added : " The songs are extremely well chosen ; the effect in the last scene, the brandishing of the burning wood, is so plastic, that we think of adopting it here in the representations."

My wonder stories [1] (*Eventyr*) were, as I have before mentioned, to be considered as given entire in the volume illustrated by V. Pedersen ; the new ones which followed, and were still to appear, were now brought together under the name " Stories " (*Historier*), which name I think, in our language, is the most appropriate for my wonder stories in their widest significance. The common speech of the people places the plain narrative and the most fanciful description under this title ; nursery-tales, fables, and narratives are called by the child, by the peasant, and among the people generally, by the short name, stories.

A few parts appeared in Danish and German, and were received very kindly ; an English edition, with the title, " A

[1] Some of these have recently been dramatized in Germany and brought on the stage there, as "The Swineherd," which, under the title "The Princess von Seedcake," has passed through a good many representations, and seems to have been brought out at the Children's Theatre by C. J. Görner. "The Little Mermaid" has been brought out as a fairy piece at the great theatre in Vienna.

Poet's Day Dreams," was published by Richard Bentley.   The
review in " The Athenæum," 1853, shows that Mary Howitt's
altered opinion of me has not had any influence on the
English critic's judgment.[1]   Just at this time, when my fiftieth
year is reached, and the collected writings published, the
" Danish Monthly " prints a review of them, written by Mr.
Grimur Thomsen.   The depth and warmth which this author
has before shown us in his book on Byron, are manifested
also in this lesser work ; he discloses a knowledge of and
feeling for the works he speaks of : it is to me almost as if
our Lord would that I should finish this chapter of my life
with the fulfillment of H. C. Örsted's trusting words to me in
the heavy days when I was misunderstood !   My home has
brought me a rich bouquet of appreciation and encouragement !

In Grimur Thomsen's review of my stories he has just
touched in a few words the right string, which gives a sound
from the depth of my poesy.   It is surely no accident that
the examples intended to show the general significance of my
work are taken from my stories, and what I have most lately
written in these last days : " The wonder story holds a merry
court of justice over shadow and substance, over the outward
shell and the inward kernel.   There flows a double stream
through it : an ironic over-stream, that plays and sports with
great and small things, that plays shuttlecock with what is
high and low ; and then the deep under-stream, that honestly
and truly brings all to its right place.   That is the true, the
Christian humor ! "   What I wished and tried to attain is here
clearly expressed.

The story of my life up to this hour lies now unrolled before
me, a rich and beautiful canvas, stirring my faith : even out
of evil came good, out of pain came happiness, a poem of
thoughts deeper than I could write.   I feel that I am fortune's
child, so many of the noblest and best of my time have met
me with affection and sincerity.   Seldom has my confidence in
men been deceived ! the bitter, heavy days bear also in them
the germ of blessings ! the injustice which I believed myself

[1] See page 367, *ante.*

suffering, the hands that stretch heavily into my growing life, — these have brought me still some good.

As we move onward toward God, what is bitter and painful vanishes, what is beautiful remains ; one sees it as the rainbow on the dark sky. May men judge me mildly as I in my heart judge them ! A confession of life has for all noble and good men the power of a holy shrift ; here, then, I yield myself, free from fear, openly and confidently : as if seated among dear friends, I have related the story of my life.

H. C. ANDERSEN.

COPENHAGEN, *April 2*, 1855.

The house in Monkmill Street where Andersen spent his childhood.
Watercolor by J. T. Hanck 1836

Hans Christian Andersen's house, Odense. Lithograph 1868

Drawing by Hans Christian Andersen 1833

Drawing by Hans Christian Andersen 1834

Paper Figures cut by Hans Christian Andersen

Hans Christian Andersen. From the Drawing by T. W. Gertner, 1845

Jenny Lind

Paper figures cut by Hans Christian Andersen

Charles Dickens

Victor Hugo

Hans Christian Andersen reading fairy tales. Drawing by
C. Hartmann 1845

*Finstern Grillen, auf, entflieht!
Sonnenschein ist morgen,
Lustig ist ein frohes Lebenslied
Kaum so lang wie Sorgen!*

H. C. Andersen

München 30 Juli 1856

Autographed German Verse

Paper figures cut by Hans Christian Andersen

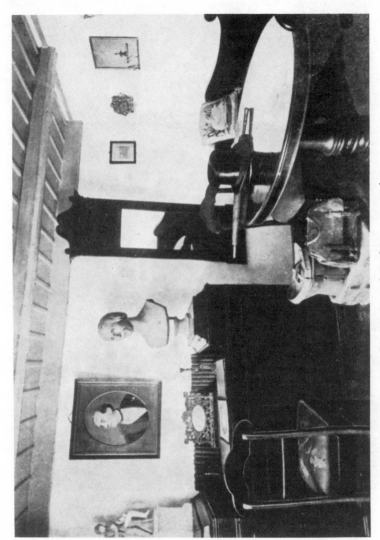

Interior from H. C. Andersen's Museum, Odense

Paper figures cut by Hans Christian Andersen

Wilhelm & Jacob Grimm

Paper figures cut by Hans Christian Andersen

Hans Christian Andersen in his room at Nyhavn

THE STORY OF MY LIFE,

CONTINUED FROM APRIL, 1855, TO DECEMBER, 1867.

—◆—

IN the Danish edition of my collected writings, "The Story of my Life" closed with my fiftieth birthday, April 2d, 1855; since then thirteen years, rich in experience and weighty, have gone by with their days of light and of darkness. What I have to tell of them is prepared to accompany the new American edition of my works, published by Hurd and Houghton in New York.

From my Danish home, Copenhagen, from this side of the great sea, which is made now by the telegraph thread to be nothing but a low wall separating neighbors, I tell my story for friends in the world's great country, tell it as I would for my own beloved Denmark ; and they will surely hear it with good will, judge it kindly, and understand that it is no vanity when I say aloud that I am the child of fortune, and with humble heart wonder that our Lord should bestow on me so much gladness and blessing.

It is far easier to write one's youthful life than to relate what has passed in one's later years ; just as in old age most people are long-sighted and see best objects that are far off, so is it also with what belongs to the soul ; with all recollection of what we have passed through and has stirred us, it is not quite easy to keep the scenes in the order of time which they had : yet in this also I am somewhat favored.

When the poet Ingemann died his widow sent me all the letters I had written him from my school-boy days till his death ; with these and her comments I have been able to give what unfolded itself in my life year by year since April, 1855, when I closed my autobiography.

And I may well begin with Ingemann and his wife. "The

Old People by the Forest Lake," [1] which he wrote on a picture
of their house at Sorö and sent me. I never, in any year, passed
there without spending some days with these charming people.
And so in the spring of 1855 my first visit was to the home of
the Ingemanns,' where I and where whoever came must feel
that here lived a man good and more than good. It was a
happy life they led, two loving souls ; they lived over again
the pretty tale of " Philemon and Baucis." Everything went
on in a quiet, happy way. Ingemann, I believe, never gave
parties ; people dropped in of an evening of their own accord,
and often the callers became quite a party ; but it was like a
table that set itself. All was as if ordered and carried out by
invisible little elves ; there was no anxious bustle to be seen,
but all made themselves agreeable with lively conversation.
Ingemann especially was the most quick and entertaining ;
particularly when he told the ghost stories that are commonly
connected with the monastery here and its neighborhood, he
told them with such a humorous smile that one who knew him
knew at once that the stories were made up at the moment,
suggested by one thing or another that came up in conversation ; frequently he borrowed the names of real persons to help
out his stories, but always good-naturedly. He snapped his finger at all the trivial topics of the day and twaddle ; he shook
by the neck all poor and ungenerous critics. A few of his
most read romances there were which became popular, but people have been unjust toward him, and of that I also can complain. The conversation one evening turned on this, and Ingemann told a pleasant story full of comfort and a moral for both
of us. The good old gardener of the academy, Nissen, used to
say very civilly, " You are in the right, and I thank you," but
he did not change his opinion for all that, but did as he liked.

" Do you know," asked Ingemann, " how this saying originated ? It is quite notable. When the gardener Nissen was
employed at the academy he displayed good ability in his
work, still he was obliged to swallow a good deal of talk about
it : one said the work should be done thus, another so, and
he took it hard, got into bad humor and went and fretted
about it. He met in the garden, one day, a little gray man
with a red cap on ; the little man asked him who he was.

[1] *De Gamle ved Skovsöen.*

"'I am Nissen,' answered the gardener.

"'Nissen?' said the little man. 'Yes, you are named Nissen, but I am the Nis (*Danish* Nissen) of the academy, the house Nis. Why do you look so depressed?'

"'O,' said the gardener Nissen, 'all that I do with my best endeavor, I get no thanks for; one says this, another says that. I cannot do anything to suit, and that troubles me: that is what makes me sad.'

"'I'll help you there,' said the little Nis, 'but you must serve me for eight whole days. I live over there back of the lake, where I have a garden that you shall take care of. I will meantime tell you beforehand there are a good many queer animals over there, kept in cages, — monkeys, parrots, and cockatoos, — that make a murderous noise, but they don't bite.'

"'Good!' said the gardener Nissen, and so he went with the Nis of the academy and took care of his garden for eight days. The small creatures were all the time screaming around him. When the week was finished the little fellow came, and asked him how it came that he saw him now in such good spirits and so well.

"'Did you get well because there was such a screeching going on?'

"'O, the screeching,' said the gardener Nissen; 'I let that go into one ear and out of the other; they scolded me and said that all I did was done wrong; but I laughed and nodded to them and said, "You are in the right; thank you," and so I minded my business: the screeching is not anything to lay to heart.'

"'Just so do you carry yourself over there in the academy garden, and mind your business.'

"The gardener Nissen followed the advice, kept his good humor, and the phrases 'You are in the right; thank you,' — 'Shouldn't we act just so?'" wound up Ingemann, with a roguish smile.

He was full of similar little stories, and very inventive. For the rest, his judgment was tender; the love of father-land, of the beautiful and the good, grew and flourished in this true poetic home, where I always had the delightful confidence, — Here am I a dear and welcome guest. Quickly passed the hours here with the two dear old folks by the wood lake. I could thoroughly enjoy this idyllic life, but I began to feel such a twitching in my wings that I must get on : the hospitable Basnös and Holsteenbörg threw open to me a manoi life, prosperous and happy. From there, the first thing in the summer, I went to Maxen, near Dresden, where a tree of my planting, which I had sheltered and taken care of, grew and flourished. An oak, no larger than I could span with my two hands, I planted in the garden in front of the house, grows now with large branches ; and a letter of mine to Ingemann will give more fully a picture of the journey and the stay there : —

"MAXEN, near DRESDEN, *July* 12, 1855.

" DEAR INGEMANN. — You remember in my autobiography my tree at Maxen, where my friends the Serres live. You will know, then, a little of the place where I now am. It is near Saxon Switzerland. It is very beautiful. My tree stands fresh and hearty, down to its very roots ; from the bench up here under the tree I have a bird's-eye view of a large village and a meadow where the hay stands stacked. The bluish mountains of Bohemia lie before me, and about me grow chestnut and cherry-trees. The sheep move about with bells till I think I am among the Alps. Serre's property contains besides, a fine old manor-house with arched passages and a great tower. Madame Serre is so good, so untiringly attentive to me. I hear fine music, and the reading of poems ; famous and notable people, and other gentlefolk flit in and out here, in this hospitable home, till it seems like an open inn. I certainly have entire freedom, and that one does not always get when he is to be an agreeable guest ; so I quite enjoy myself. Besides, I feel in this journey more than ever before the need of family life, — I care so much about being with people ; so that I care less and less every day about visiting Italy. I shall probably stay at home next winter. Now I am going to take a flying trip of eight days to Munich, and thence to Switzerland, where I expect to have a happy time touring among the Alps, if God will but give me health and a cheerful mind, — these blessings I have missed hitherto on this journey. This, to be sure, was only during the days, but they were painfully oppressive. Ham-

burg seemed to me an empty exchange on the hot summer
day ; the road to Berlin, was a dusty hot baker's oven.   I had
no wish to visit any one in Berlin, and hurried away to Maxen,
out in God's own country, to friendly people.   To travel is
to live !   Now do you think about setting out with your wife :
four hours from Stettin to Berlin, and then five hours more to
Dresden, where she longs to go and visit the picture galleries.
Forget the old time, the long journey it then was into the capital of Saxony ; now we fly on Faust's mantle.   The travel
by rail is the most poetic flight that our heavy-bodied people
can take safely and soundly."

In Munich I found a letter from Ingemann, which contained
kind words from him and my many friends over the book I
had then just published, " The Story of my Life."   The letter
closed as follows : —

"You have just left your flourishing tree at Maxen, and
your good friends that gathered about it ; but wherever your
story-bird has flown out into the world, there you will find a
fresh green tree, with friendly shadows and gentle eyes near
by.   If you go seeking such trees and such eyes on the Faust
mantle, you will entice me after you (it's more like the beast
that Dante rode by Virgil's side when he went through hell);
and I am too old and stiff for that.   Indeed, the world is beginning to rumble about me and our little monastery here, with
its steam and its whistle ; and when the mountains come to us,
we have as little need as Mohammed to go running after them.
The poet's house ought to be on wheels, so that it can go rolling off when the locomotive comes.   Every one to his taste.
Your house stands for the present by the locomotive's huge
dragon-tail."

I remained some little time in artistic Munich, and spent
many memorable hours with Kaulbach and his family.   At Professor Liebig's I heard Geibel read the first acts of his tragedy,
" Brunhilde ; " among the guests invited to hear the play was
the celebrated actress, Miss Seebach, who was to take the first
part in his drama.   I had enjoyed seeing her act in several
plays, and I knew that she was regarded with great respect
by those who knew her.   One thing I desire to say : There

is a poor custom by which the public, after the tragedy is over, call out the murdered heroine, and it is still worse to see her come out smiling and courtesying. A great actress should break up this evil custom, and not come out, no matter how loudly they called for her. Miss Seebach admitted that I was right, and I urged her to begin the reform.

The evening after, they performed " Cabal and Love," [1] where she appeared as *Louise;* and after she had drunk the poison, she was called out. She did not come. I was delighted. The call for her became louder, still she held out ; but the clamor and shouting rose into a very storm, she showed herself, and so I had made nothing in my attack on a dramatic vice.

It is a delight and indeed a necessity for me to travel a little out and about in the world ; economy and frugality at home have made this possible to me ; but I have often thought how much finer it would be if one were so rich that he could take a friend with him, and this has been permitted to me also a few times, in spite of my narrow means. I have several times received from princes presents of breast-pins and gold rings ; my noble donors will, I am sure, pardon me, and be glad that I sent these articles to the jewelers, got money for them, and so could say to a dear young friend who had never seen anything outside of his home : " Take a trip with me for a month or two, as long as the money lasts." The bright eyes I have then seen gave me far more pleasure than the glittering stones in the breast-pins and rings. This time there accompanied me from Munich, Edgar Collin, who, with his interest in all that he saw, his happy youthful spirit, and kind attention to me, made the journey very delightful. We went by Ulm and Würtemberg to Wildbad Gastein, where my friend, State-Councilor Edward Collin, with his family, was staying during the season.

The Black Forest, in which Auerbach's " Village Stories " had their origin, I visited for the first time. It was bright, sunny weather, and now began our happy life together. Then again I mounted the vapor dragon's back, as Ingemann called the railway train, for a greater country,— for Switzerland, with its deep lakes and lofty mountains. From Lucerne I wished to

[1] *Kabale og Kjærlighed.*

take the steamboat with my young companion to Fluellen; he
was taken sick on board, and felt worse and worse; so I determined to stop at the next landing-place, which was the
village of Brunnen. My young friend was well taken care
of in the hotel there, and on the next day was well enough to
want to read some book. The landlord brought him several,
and among them was a Swiss almanac. In it was a portrait
of Humboldt, as representative of science; and hard by it was
a portrait of H. C. Andersen, the fairy-tale poet.

"Here is your portrait!" cried Edgar. The landlord looked
at it and at me, gave me a friendly grasp of the hand, and at
once I found a friend in him, and friends, too, in his two sisters,
who managed the house. One of these, Agathe, was, like her
brother, very musical. She would give me a whole artistic
evening with her music. Always afterward, when I came to
Switzerland, I visited these friends, who still live there; they
are of old Swiss stock; in Schiller's "William Tell," their
name is given as Auf der Mauer.

The accident of the journey, Collin's illness, and the con-
sequent interruption of the whole trip there at the lake, really
was a sprout from which grew a great deal of pleasure for both
of us, and for me not only at the time, but in after years. At a
later visit I had a pleasure I had not dreamed of. The evening before the day I was to set out, there glided out in front
of the hotel a boat with torches and music; it looked charming to us. All the guests at the hotel came out on the balcony.

"What does it mean?" I asked Agathe.

"It is a greeting for you," said she.

"O, don't fancy such a thing," I replied — "music on my
account!"

"But it is," she replied.

"Nonsense!" said I. "It is all accidental; and if I were
to go out and thank them, how horribly ridiculous I should
appear, when it was not meant for me at all!"

"It is for you," she persisted. I felt myself uncertain, but
went meanwhile down to the shore, where several people had
gathered, and where the boat had now stopped. I spoke to
the first one who stepped ashore, saying, —

" That was fine music. Whom was it for ? "

" You," said he, and now I pressed his hand and that of a few others. Whether the whole celebration was a piece of courtesy toward me by Agathe Auf der Mauer, or whether I really have in this little town many musical friends of my poesy, is not yet quite clear to me. But certain it is that Brunnen has become for me a memorable Swiss town.

In Zurich lived the composer Wagner in exile. I knew his music, as I have before said. Liszt had warmly told me of the man himself. I went to his house, and was received in a friendly manner. Of the Danish composers he knew only Gade well ; we talked of his reputation, and then of Kuhlau, a composer for the flute, none of whose operas he had seen. Hartmann was known to him only by name. I got to telling him, therefore, of the great storehouse of Danish music, in strumental and vocal, all the way from Schultz, Kunzen, and the elder Hartmann to Weyse, Kuhlau, Hartmann, and Gade. I named several of these composers' works, and told of Schall's ballet composition, and Wagner heard me with great attention.

" 'Tis as if you told me a real fairy tale from the world of music, and rolled up for me the curtain that shuts off from me all beyond the Elbe," he said.

I told him of the Swede Belmann, akin to Wagner in this, that both themselves wrote the text for their music, but in other respects quite opposed to each other. Wagner impressed me fully as having a most genial nature, and it was a most happy hour, — such a one as I have never since had.

On the journey home, which led through Cassel, I called on Spohr ; he was living in his old place on the street that now bears his name. Since 1847, when we often met in London, I had not seen him, and now it was the last time ; a few years after the knell went through the country — Spohr is dead. How gay he was when I saw him at this last visit ! We talked of Hartmann's opera, " The Raven "[1] which he set a high value on, and wished to bring on the stage at Cassel ; he had even written to Hartmann about it, but it could not be brought about for want of a singer to take the part of *Armilla*.

From Cassel I journeyed to Weimar to see my friends, and

[1] *Ravnen.*

most cordially as ever was received at the court.   The interest
of the hereditary Grand Duke Karl Alexander and Kappel-
meister Lıstz in Hartmann's music brought "The Little Christine,"[1] to which I had written the text, to be studied under the
title of "Little Karin;" it received the greatest praise from all
the connoisseurs in music.

The last of the year I was again in Copenhagen, where I
prepared, for the Casino Theatre, Mosenthal's popular comedy,
"Der Sonnvendhoff," to which I gave a name better understood by us, "A Village Story."   I wrote for it a chorus and
songs, and the piece was a success.

With a few words from a letter which I wrote on the last
evening of the year I will close the record of 1855 : —

"Out of doors it is not wintry, but rather autumnal — rain
and sleet, dirty streets that make themselves look like the
Nile with their deep mud. So I feel a pleasure in this in-door
life, and if I continue in keeping with it, then perhaps I may do
something : I wish that 'The Story of my Life' was published ; then I may begin a new Life. I might produce a work
which would merit the name of 'a work.' I wish that like you
I might keep my freshness, and like you accomplish something."

1856.

Already, on the second day of the year, came Ingemann's
greeting and his thanks for the letter I wrote.   "It is right
good of you on New Year's Eve to stretch out your hand to
us here in Sorö, so that we here on New Year's morning can
see the hand in spirit. You are a steadfast, affectionate fellow,
and we know it."

The year was not so bright and happy as Ingemann had
wished it for me. One can have days in which all kinds of misfortune seem to come together, and it is very certain that one
also can have such years, and such was to me the year 1856.
The year's drop of water was, it seemed to me, full of small,
disagreeable animalculæ, — discomforts, vexations, annoyances,
which I will not place under the glass to show them ; for
now they look as small as grains of sand, or little insects

[1] *Liden Kirsten.*

that can fly into one's eye, and pain and burn one so long as they stay there, but get them out and look at them, and one says — the midge!

My whole thought and endeavor was to accomplish something worth while. I was not, as Sibbern had believed and said, a pious, dreaming child-soul; many religious struggles I had passed through to preserve faith and knowledge in the secret chamber of my heart. I wrote "To be or not to be," a romance of Danish life in war time. I made many studies for it, and read for it a great deal of what had been written on Materialism. It interested Ingemann to hear about it. I gave to him to read the remarkable book then just published, "Eritis sicut Deus." I attended Professor Esricht's lectures on Materialism.

Ingemann wrote to me a letter characteristic of himself and his opinion in these words : —

"When you favor me again with a letter, let me know what Esricht sets up against Materialism. He attacks it as if it were a personal living God, or a force of Nature ; the highest Lawgiver of the world's law, or an abstract Idea's idea, out of which his unknown laws are evolved, and which first appeals to man's consciousness as a dead first cause. In the last case you have that in your pious, ardent faith in God ; one can ask far more than what the knowledge of nature points out. Besides, we can surely always get some good from going to school to the students in nature, however old we may be."

In the summer I again was off on my journey, and once more at Maxen with my friends the Serres, where I wrote to Ingemann : —

"DEAR FRIEND, — I sent you a greeting from the station at Sorö while I paused there. Sorö had a most friendly aspect ; the lake shone with gold and purple. I am now at Maxen, where everything is clad in summer beauty ; the cherries are ripening, the roses are blooming, and my tree stands up hearty and strong on the edge of the cliff. We have here on a visit the author Gutzhow, whose latest play, ' Ella's Success,' [1] you know, as well as his celebrated romance, ' Ritter

---

[1] *Ella gjör Lykke.*

von Geiste.' If it had not been in nine parts, I should have read it. On Sunday my plan is to pay a visit in Weimar. The Grand Duke celebrates his birthday on the 24th of May. Goethe's 'Faust,' second part, is to be given, and I am very glad that I should have come here now."

In September I was again in Copenhagen : all my thoughts, all my time, were upon my romance, "To be or not to be," on which I myself set great store., It has seemed to me since, however, that all I had labored to gather and make my own touched me less than that one of God's gifts — the poetic thought in the book.

1857.

In April I wrote to Ingemann : "I have lately had a most welcome letter from Charles Dickens. He writes that he has this month finished his novel, 'Little Dorrit,' and is now a 'free man.' He has a pretty country seat between Rochester and London, where he moves with his family in the beginning of June, and he expects me there. I shall find a pleasant home and dear friends. I am delighted at the invitation to go, and I will see if I can make my route by Sorö the last of May, so as to be with you on your birthday, the 28th of May. In a week from now my romance, 'To be or not to be,' will be published. I have taken the liberty of dedicating it to the poet Ingemann and the philosopher Sibbern : you will believe I am grateful to you."

One of the first persons I read my new book to, when it was out, was her majesty the Queen Dowager Caroline Amelia. She and her royal consort have always been gracious and good to me. I spent this time several days in the beautiful, woody " Sorgenfri." [1] The forest put forth its leaves while I was there ; every evening I read some chapters of the romance, which relate to the heavy but yet exhilarating war ; [2] while reading I often saw the noble Queen deeply moved, and at the close of the book she expressed her thanks fervently.

The Queen Dowager belongs to that class of noble, thoughtful women whose high rank one forgets when he is with them,

---

[1] Or *Sans Souci.*   [2] The first war with Prussia, 1848.

and rejoices only in their noble humanity. One evening her majesty took an excursion through the wood and out on the "Strand road." I was in another carriage with two of the ladies of the court. As her majesty drove by a place on the road where a lot of children were playing, they recognized her, stood in a row, and cried, "Hurra!" A little after came the carriage in which I sat. "There is Andersen," cried the little things; "hurra!" After we had returned home, the Queen said, smiling, "I believe all the children know us two. I heard their shouts of hurra."

In the streets and from windows there often nodded to me a friendly child's face. I met one day a well-dressed lady walking with her children: the smallest boy broke away, ran over to me, and seized me by the hand. The mother called to him and said, as I afterward heard, "How dare you accost a strange gentleman!" but the little fellow replied, "It was no stranger, it was Andersen; all the boys know him."

It was this spring ten years since I had been in England. In this time Dickens had often given me the pleasure of his letters, and now I was accepting his friendly invitation. Fortunate indeed was I! The stay at Dickens's house must ever be a bright point in my life. I passed through Holland to France, and on the night of May 11, took the boat from Calais to Dover. In my "Collected Writings" is a detailed account of my most delightful visit, where the man Dickens showed himself as unfailingly kind to me as Dickens the writer. Here follows a brief account of what has been given in full.

In the early morning I reached London by rail, and immediately sought the northern railway that took me to Higham. Here was no carriage to be had, so I put myself under the guide of one of the railway porters, who took my bag, and we came to Gadshill, where Dickens had his pretty villa. He received me heartily, was looking a little older than when we last met; but this look of age was owing a good deal to his beard, which he had let grow. His eyes were as bright as ever; the same smile played about his mouth, the same pleasant voice sounded as kindly; in all this there was more heartiness than ever. Dickens was now in the prime of life, in his forty-fifth year, — so youthful, full of life, eloquent and rich in humor, that gleamed through his hearty affection ateness. I do not know how I can say anything more significant than the words I wrote of him in one of my first letters from his house : " Take the best out of all Dickens's writings to get a picture of a man, and you have Charles Dickens." And so as he stood before me in the first hour I was there, he was and continued to be unchanged all the weeks I spent with him, — always full of life, happy, and sympathetic.

Some days before my arrival a friend of Dickens, the dramatist Douglas Jerrold, had died : in order to secure a few thousand pounds for his widow, Dickens with Bulwer, Thackeray, and the actor Macready, joined together. A drama and several recitations were on the programme. All this active labor and business fell to him, so that he had to go oftener than others to London, and stay there whole days. I went with him a few times, and stayed at his comfortable winter residence in London. I accompanied him and his family to the Handel festival at the Crystal Palace ; we both saw for the first time the unapproachable tragic actress Ristori, as *Camma* and as *Lady Macbeth ;* it was especially in the last *rôle* that she impressed us ; there was in all her representation a psychologic truth ; terrible, and still within the bounds of beauty : it is impossible that ever before or since a more true and impressive picture could be given of this woman, so tremulous in soul and body.

I saw the grand and fanciful manner in which Director Kean, son of the famous actor, brought Shakespeare's plays on the stage : the first representation of the storm, where the *mise en scène* was carried to an exaggerated length ; the bold poetry was turned into stone in the illustration ; the living word vanished, one does not get the spirituality belonging to it, and then forgets it for the gold dish that it is served in.

A work of Shakespeare's artistically brought out, if only between three folding screens, gives me a greater pleasure than here, where it had all the accessories of beauty.

Of the representations that were given for the benefit of Jerrold's widow, that was a special treat in which Dickens with some of his family acted a new romantic drama, " The Frozen Deep," by Wilkie Collins, who himself took one of the principal characters, Dickens the other.

In Dickens's house dramatic representations were frequently given to good friends. Her majesty the Queen had long wished to see one of these, and now wished to honor it by her presence in the little theatre, "The Gallery of Illustration." There the only spectators were the Queen, Prince Albert, the royal children, and the young Prince and Princess, also his Majesty the King of Belgium ; besides this royal circle a select company of the actor's immediate friends was given admission ; from Dickens's house came only his wife, his mother-in-law, and myself.

Dickens performed his part in the drama with striking truthfulness and great dramatic genius ; the little farce, "Two o'clock in the Morning," was given with great vivacity by Charles Dickens and the editor of "Punch," Mr. Mark Lemon, who we hear, has since appeared in public with great success as *Falstaff.* After the performance I spent a good part of the night with all the actors and those aiding them, and bright hours they were, at the office of "Household Words ; " a festival afterward repeated in the country at the house of Albert Smith, who ascended Mont Blanc. At Dickens's country seat I saw England's richest lady, Miss Burdett Coutts, of whom every one speaks as one of the noblest and most benevolent of women ; it is not enough that she has built many churches, but she cares in the most rational and Christian manner for the poor, the sick, and the needy. She invited me to visit at her house in London ; I went there and saw an English house of the wealthiest sort, where yet the noble, womanly, excellent Miss Coutts was to me the most memorable part.

With all the variety and splendor of the life in London I was always glad to go once more to my own home at Gads-hil : it was so delightful in the little room where Dickens and his wife and daughters gathered around the piano. They were happy hours, and still there often came there heavy, dark moments, not from within, but from without. Once, I remember, when I was unhappy over some criticism on my last book, "To be or not to be," which had put me in bad humor, as it ought not, still just when I was most uncomfortable, I found that the very trial brought me a pleasure, by giving me an expression of Dickens's unfailing kindliness.

He had heard from his family how out of sorts I was, and he let off whole fire-works of jokes and witty words, and when that still did not make its way into my ill-humor's dark corner, he spoke in earnest so eloquently and with such warm appreciation that I felt myself uplifted, strengthened, and filled with a desire and longing to deserve such words. I looked into my friend's beaming eyes, and felt that I ought to thank my severe critic for having obtained for me one of the most delightful moments in my life.

The happy days at Dickens's house fled all too quickly. The last morning came, but I was yet, before I returned to Denmark, to see the apotheosis of Germany's poetic greatness. I was invited to the celebration in Weimar at the unveiling of Goethe's, Schiller's, and Wieland's statues. Early in the morning Dickens had his little wagon brought out, took his place as coachman, and carried me to Maidstone, from where I was to take the train to Folkestone ; he drew for me a map of all the stations as a guide. Dickens was lively and hearty all the way, and I sat silent and in poor spirits at the near approach of our parting. At the station we embraced one another, and I looked in his eyes so full of feeling, looked perhaps for the last time on one whom I admired as an author and still more as a man. A grasp of the hand, and he was carried away, and I was rushing on with the train. " All's over, and that happens to all stories."

From Maxen near Dresden I sent this letter to Charles Dickens : —

DEAR BEST OF FRIENDS, — At last I can write, and the delay has been long enough, all too long ! but every day, almost every hour have you been in my thoughts. You and your home are become as a part of my soul's life, and how could it be otherwise ? For years I have loved and honored you through your writings, but now I know you yourself. No one of your friends can hold more firmly by you than I. The visit to England, the stay at your house, is a bright spot in my life, therefore did I stay so long and find it so hard to say farewell ; certainly when we drove together from Gadshill to Maidstone, I was so disconsolate it was next to impossible

for me to carry on conversation; I was almost ready to cry.
Since then, when I think of the parting, I feel keenly how
hard it must have been for you, some days after, to go with
your son Walter on board his ship, and to know that you were
not to see him again for seven years. I cannot express myself, unless I write my letter in Danish, or I would say how
happy I was with you, — how thankful I am. I saw every
minute that you were my friend, and that you were glad to
have me with you. You may believe I value what that signifies. Your wife, too, welcomed me, a stranger, so cordially : I
can see that it could not have been so pleasant for your whole
family to have for weeks about them one like me who spoke
English so poorly, one who might be thought to have fallen
down from the sky. Yet how little I was allowed to feel
this. Give my thanks to all. ' Baby ' said to me the first
day I came, 'I will put you out of the window,' but afterward
he said that he would 'put' me 'in of the window,' and I
count his last words as those of the whole family.

" After having been in such a home, been so filled with happiness as I was, of course Paris could not be any stopping-place
for me. I felt as if I were in a hot hive where no honey is to
be found. The heat was oppressive ; I made haste to get
away, but by short days' journeys. Five whole days I took to
reach Frankfort ; not before the twenty-seventh did I reach
Dresden, where the Serres entertained me. The day was the
birthday of the master of the house, and it was spent at the
house of one of my lady friends, the celebrated pianist and
composer, Henselt, who lives most of the year at St. Petersburg, but in summer upon her estate in Silesia. I came here
to a merry festival. Yesterday for the first time we came here
to Serre's place in Maxen. In the early morning I am writing
this letter. It is just as if I myself were carrying it to you. I
stand in your room at Gadshill ; see, as I did the first day I
came, the roses blooming in the windows, the green fields that
stretch out to Rochester ; I see the apple-like fragrance of the
wild rose hedges out in the fields where the children played
cricket. How much will happen before I again see it in
reality, if indeed I ever do ! But, whatever time may disclose,
my heart will ever faithfully and gratefully thank you, my

great-hearted friend. Give me soon the pleasure of a letter ; tell me when you have read " To be or not to be," what you think of it. Forget kindly the cloudy side of me, which perhaps our life together showed you, and I will so live in good earnest with one whom I love as a friend and brother.

" Faithfully yours,

" HANS CHRISTIAN ANDERSEN."

I soon received a very kind letter from the noble, good Dickens, with a particular greeting from every one, even from the monument and the shepherd's dog there. Afterward letters came less frequently, and last year none at all. " All's over, and that happens to all stories."

In Weimar everything was in festive brilliancy : people streamed thither from all parts of Germany. I had at once the best, most cozy home with my friend the Court Marshal Beaulieu. Several of Germany's first dramatic artists were invited to take parts on the stage where Goethe and Schiller had labored and made their name. Scenes were given from Goethe's " Faust," second part, as well as a prelude suited to the occasion by Dingelsted, who was then intendant of the theatre. At the court were splendid receptions, princes and artists meeting together.

The unveiling of Wieland's as well as of Goethe's and Schiller's statues, took place in delightful sunny weather. When the veil fell from the forms of these two masters, I saw one of those accidents which seem poetically intended : a white butterfly flew over Goethe's and Schiller's heads, as if not knowing on which of them it should alight, — a symbol of immortality ; after a short flight flying about, it rose in the clear sunlight and vanished. I told this little incident to the Grand Duke, and to Goethe's widow and Schiller's son. I asked this last, one day, if there was any truth in what many at Weimar said, that I bore a likeness to his father, and he answered that it was the case, but the likeness lay most in my form, bearing, and gait. " My father," said he, " had a countenance quite different from yours, and red hair." I had not heard this before.

Liszt composed the music for the celebration at the theatre :

it brought out a storm of applause and he was called out. It
did not move me, but the fault was mine. It was like waves
of dissonances that rise into harmony, but not to carry me.
I felt vexed with myself that I could not be as the others
were, and unpleasantly embarrassed about Liszt, whom I honored as an artist, and looked up to as one having a moving
thought and human courage. The next day I was invited by
him to dinner; he received a company of his friends — all
certainly admirers; I felt that I could not honorably fall in
with the common applause; it grieved me, and I formed a
hasty resolve to travel the same day from Weimar; but it is
still a source of regret when I look back on it, and a grief to
me that I was remiss through being out of tune myself, and
that I did not give good-by to the prince of pianists. I have
never since met him who in his art belongs to one of the
great phenomena of the day.

The journey home was by Hamburg. The cholera was
there, and I went on to Kiel, where I heard that the disease
was also in Denmark, and most severe in Korsör, where I
was to go in the steamer. The weather was fair, the passage
all too short, and we reached the cholera stricken city several
hours before the departure of the train, and remained in the
waiting-room together with a part of the towns-folk, who were
very low spirited. In Copenhagen my doctor met me with
the inquiry what I was doing here, where several cholera
cases had shown themselves. I set off again into the country,
first to Ingemann, and from there to the hospitable Basnös,
but in the little place Skjelskör near by was also cholera: I
did not know it but felt strangely low-spirited. My mind
immediately recovered its balance, however, and then worked
out the scheme for a new wonder story comedy, — " The Will-
o'-the-Wisp." Ingemann thought well of the idea, but it only
got on paper as a slight sketch, and several years afterward
was given in quite another form and manner as the wonder
story, — " The Will-o'-the-Wisps are in Town."

The Director of the Royal Theatre urged me to write a
prologue for the theatre's centenary; the chief actor on the
stage was to deliver it, but he had of late years found it very
difficult to get anything by heart; he would forget and make

slips. I was afraid that this would be the case now, and it was the case. With his splendid resounding voice he declaimed the prologue, but made it so full of holes that for me it did not wave like a holiday banner, but like a ragged clout. The critics talked about the artist's fine delivery ; but that the prologue did not hang together well, it was of course the poet's fault and not the highly esteemed actor's. The day after I had the prologue printed that they might read it and understand it, but it was quite "the day after the fair." It has long since passed into the air, but Ingemann's letter to me remains as a poetic mark made over what was blotted out.

"SORÖ, *July* 2, 1857.

"A happy and blessed Christmas and New Year to you : no bitterness in the New Year, and no strain in the humor of the Copenhagenish or outer world's ephemeral cobwebs. Look at the milky way ; think of the great rich story of life through all the higher and higher places of existence till the final last great day of the world, and let us thank our Lord for immortality in that glory that He has prepared for us both here and hereafter : meanwhile we blow aside all the little planet's cobwebs with a gay, merry puff of breath. Poesy is still, God be praised, a better pleasure-boat than all the boasted balloon ships in which virtuosos daily go up and tumble down, according as the fickle and often mephitic popular breath distends or collapses the balloon of a day. When you get fast hold of your 'will-o'-the-wisp,' let him also take and free you from the spider-demon that spins and twists about us the airy cobwebs of a Liliput world ! I provided for it in my 'Four Rubies,' but the idea did not get sufficient expression. When one becomes old, poetical ideas become too poor, and wanting flesh and blood ; but one still cannot be without these in this world.

"Cordial greeting from my Lucia : some sin that has given her the toothache and swollen mouth, has tried to lessen our Christmas pleasure. There stands, besides, in our sitting-room a Christmas-tree with which the girl and the gardener's wife surprised us on Christmas Eve. From Madame Jerichau I have received Jerichau's medallion portrait of himself, and on the cover of the case she has drawn a pretty Christmas angel. There is still no little friendship and love in the world, and we were shamefully ungrateful when we were grumbling or low-spirited. That you, indeed, are not at bottom ; far from it, but those prologue trifles had wrongfully put you out of tune. Make us happy soon with the news that you are flying freely about in the poetic sky ! Your ever devoted

"INGEMANN."

1858.

Of late years it has so often been said to me that I finally have come to believe it, that when I myself read my Wonder Stories they are set forth in the best light. The greater the gathering the better delivery I am assured of, and still I always go to such a gathering with a doubting, anxious mind. The first time I passed a sleepless night, and when the evening came I was as one in a fever. It was no single, important person as hearer who disturbed my mind ; no ! it is the many, the multitude that make a mist, as it were, about me and depress me. And yet I have always been met with gladness and loud praise.

There was formed last year in Copenhagen a Mechanics' Association preceding the one now existing. Two of the men who showed a special interest in it by giving lectures and readings of an instructive kind, were Professor Dr. Hornemann and the Editor Bille. They applied to me to read before the association some of my Wonder Stories.

It was an uncomfortable, exciting time in Copenhagen.[1] There poured in far more people than there were places for in the great hall : the crowd outside pressed close up to the windows and clamored to have them opened : it was quite overwhelming to a nervous, timid soul, but as soon as I stood in the reading-desk my tremor disappeared.

I began with the following words, which at that time seemed necessary : —

"Among the instructive readings which are given at the Mechanics' Association there is one that it has been thought

[1] This refers probably to the ravages of cholera that had recently appeared in the city. — *Editor's Note.*

should not be omitted, and that is one from the poetic, the art that opens our eyes and our hearts to the beautiful, the true, and the good.

" In England, in the royal navy, through all the rigging, small and great ropes, there runs a red thread, signifying that it belongs to the crown ; through all men's lives there runs also a thread, invisible indeed, that shows we belong to God.

" To find this thread in small and great, in our own life and in all about us, the poet's art helps us, and it comes in many shapes.   Holberg let it come in his comedies, showing us the men of his time with their weaknesses, and their amusing qualities, and we can read much of these.

" In the earliest times the poet's art dealt most with what are called Wonder Stories ; the Bible itself has inclosed truth and wisdom in what we call parables and allegories.   Now we know all of us that the allegory is not to be taken literally by the words, but according to the signification that lies in them, by the invisible thread that runs through them.

" We know that when we hear the echo from the wall, from the rock, or the heights, it is not the wall, the rock, and the heights that speak, but a resounding from ourselves ; and so we also should see in the parable, in the allegory, that we find ourselves, — find the meaning, the wisdom, and the happiness we can get out of them.

" So the poet's art places itself by the side of Science, and opens our eyes for the beautiful, the true, and the good : and so we will now read here a few Wonder Stories."

And I read and was followed with close attention ; a single heartfelt burst of applause was heard.   I was glad and satisfied to have read.   Afterward I gave still a few more readings, and other authors followed my example.

In 1860 was founded with great *éclat* the Mechanics' Association that now exists, where almost every winter I have read and met hearty recognition ; several of our Danish poets and writers, as well as the most celebrated actors, have read their poems and dramatic works.

At one of the yearly celebrations of the anniversary of the founding of the Association, to which I was invited, an enthusiastic toast was drunk to that ornament of the Danish

stage, since dead, Michael Wiehe ; he was named as the first
who had broken the ice, the first who had brought the gift of
poesy to the Mechanics' Association, and when he had led
the way, the rest all followed.

In the Mechanics' Association of 1860, Mr. Wiehe certainly
had been the first who read, I believe, a poem of Oehlenschläger ; but two years before, when for the first time the
working classes were formed into an association, in 1858, I
was the one who broke the ice, and it is an honor I will not
let slip me !

In the Students' Union I had as a young student read my
first Wonder Story. The years have long since gone by. Now,
in 1858, I read again, and was so heartily received, so kindly
greeted, that certainly if my fright at reading before a great
company were not the chief thing, yet here and at the Association I felt and understood that I read before young, warm
hearts — men of nature, who made these evenings I have
spoken of as beautiful moments of festivity.

In the last year there was published at Christmas, or, little
later, in the spring, a little volume of Wonder Stories, on the
yellow cover of which was printed a picture of the storks as
they came flying with the Spring on their backs ; this last
volume contained for its longest story, " The Marsh King's
Daughter." Ingemann wrote of it : —

" SORÖ, *April* 10, 1858.

" DEAR FRIEND, — You are a lucky man ! When you scrape
up stones in a brook, you find pearls right away, and now you
have found a precious stone in the marsh. It is a benevolent
fancy that so holds up roses to our noses where it smells worst
in the world, and shows us royal splendor in the marsh ; that
she is beautiful I have already heard from others. It shall
be my pleasure to see her after the great washing, and the six
rinsings you have given her. I have so much affection for
her elder brothers and sisters, and so much confidence in her
washer's taste, and fine æsthetic light, that neither with her
nor half the kingdom she surely brings with her, does there
stick a single spatter from her father's whole state. In our

'whole state'[1] there is certainly some mud. If now your princess could only show us what good and beautiful thing can come out of such a kingdom. Happiness and blessing be on the new year of your life which you have begun. It is not logical, but I set a high price on the fact, that one is born as the condition on which all life depends, and it is the beginning that makes it worth while to live. Still I don't care much for birthdays.

"The second of April we remembered notwithstanding, with regard to the peaceful second of April's hero on the stork's back, which indeed is the vignette on your 'Wonder Stories and Tales.' The cross of the 'Dannebrogsmand'[2] had nearly come that day. We should have found that acknowledgment good and proper. Hearty greetings from us both.

"That the theatre had not killed Hauch was an agreeable piece of news to me. That position would kill me, and you, too, perhaps, although you indeed, when that shall be, can have practice as *packer*. I had that practice too, when I was Director, but it took all my strength and a whole year, and I have not yet got over it. Now I wish you a happy private life, and poet life, with fresh flying Psyche-wings that either fly over flowers, or run in their chariot through the marsh kingdom, again to fly over the world in sunshine and summer air.

"Your devoted friend, "INGEMANN."

In June I was already off on my travels, on a visit to the Serres and with some friends in Bremen. The pleasure of this travelling-life was soon ended. I happened to hear home news that made me tremble, filled me with sorrow, and which always comes back to me as painful and fearful, when friends from America invite me to their home, the other side of the world's sea. I have, in the first pages of "The Story of my Life," spoken of Admiral Wulff's house in Copenhagen, his wife and children, of the oldest daughter, Henriette, who always in dark days and bright took so constant an in-

---

[1] There was a party in Denmark then whose political watch-word was, "Whole State" (Heel-stat), referring to the union of Sleswick-Holstein and Denmark. — *Editor's note.*

[2] An order of knighthood.

terest in all that concerned me. After her parents died she
lived with her youngest brother, Christian Wulff, lieutenant in
the navy. Never has any one seen a more affectionate and
devoted brother. For her it was a necessity, one may say a
matter of health, to travel, and she loved the sea passionately ;
on several great journeys she accompanied her brother, visited
Italy with him, and went with him to the West Indies and
America ; on the, for her, last great voyage, they both were
aboard a vessel where there was infection of yellow fever.
The brother was seized, and she, the weak girl, was his nurse ;
sat by the fever bed, wiped with her handkerchief his hot,
clammy forehead, and wiped her own eyes with the same ; but
she became strong who was weak before the sickness, while
her brother sank under it and was buried.

Overwhelmed with grief she found a dear home at Eagle-
wood near New York, with the generous Marcus Spring and
his excellent wife Rebecca, whose acquaintance had been
made by the authoress Fredrika Bremer.

A year after Henriette Wulff came back again to Denmark ;
we saw one another nearly every day. The sense of her brother's loss was in many respects excessive. Her thoughts flew
often to the land where her brother's dust rested : she longed
to go thither once more, and was uneasy in the summer until
the journey. In the month of September she went by the
Hamburg steamer *Austria ;* from England her last letter came
to her sister : she said that there were a great many on board,
but no one toward whom she felt herself drawn, yet when they
came to England she felt such a great repugnance to the journey that she was almost resolved to go back, but shamed herself out of her weakness and remained.

Not long after we read the news that the steamer *Austria*
was burned on the Atlantic. I was overwhelmed ; her sister
and elder brother, her relations and friends were in an agony
of doubt. Soon there came descriptions of the fearful scenes
in the sudden disaster from those who only were saved : but
who were those ? Was she, with her little feeble form, among
them ? No certain intelligence came that she was at the bottom
of the ocean. If grief could find place in words, then surely
it could in what I wrote in the first moment of sorrow : —

HENRIETTE WULFF:

DIED ON THE STEAMER AUSTRIA, SEPTEMBER 13, 1858.

In the burning ship, on the rolling wave,
  In horrors we cannot bear to hear,
Thou hast suffered and died and found thy grave,
  But the cry of thy death never comes to our ear.

Thou bold and hardy soul that dwelt apart
  In feeble body ; little seemed the souls anigh,
And never chill took hold of thy warm heart —
  Here few there were that knew thee : many more on high.

Thou wert my sister, compassionate and strong,
  Uplifting still my soul when trampled in the dust ;
Thou knewest me — to thee it doth belong
  That often I sank not, when sink I felt I must.

False things and empty, jinglings of small bells
  Are guarded by the noisy crowd that float adown the stream ;
Thy course thou didst not change, — and so the sea-foam went,
  And so earth's life is spent, quick ended as a dream.

Farewell, my friend from childhood's days !
  To me thou hast been more than I was worth ;
Now is thy conflict o'er, thou seest thy brother's face,
  With whom was ever joined all that thou sought on earth.

Thy tomb was the sea, the wild rolling sea ;
  Our hearts bear the chiseled words of thy name ;
Thy soul is in heaven, and our Lord gives to thee
  A manifold bliss for the suffering that came.

In the burning ship, on the rolling wave,
  In horrors we cannot bear to hear,
Thou hast suffered, hast died, and found thy grave,
  But the cry of thy death never comes to our ear.

My thoughts, night and day, were filled with this matter. I
could think of nothing else, and many a night in the time of our
uncertainty I prayed God in my heart, if it be possible that
there is connection between the world of spirits and the world
of men, then grant me a glimpse, some least sign from it, if
only a dream of her ; but notwithstanding my waking thoughts
were wholly occupied with the friend of my youth, when sleep
with dreaming came, never did anything manifest itself or stir

my fancy that could seem to be such a communion. The constant thinking of this event so affected me that one day going out into the street the houses suddenly appeared to me as monster waves that rolled against one another ; I saw the motion, but at the same moment I was to that degree startled at myself, that with all the force of my will I burst this fixed thought upon one and the same thing ; I felt that it belonged to insanity.

There came a sudden peace in my mind, a trust in God, and sorrow spent itself in its lamentation. Ingemann wrote to me : —

"The greater has been that soul in the small weak body, the easier flight it had from the burning to the quenching element, and the freer flight to that great spirit world wherein we first rightly draw breath. But I need not paint for the poet who wrote 'The Dying Child' and 'To be and not to be,' the light side itself in the picture of the world's ruin where in a moment we are overwhelmed as by the most terrible thing. That you have yourself surely already done, and have at one and the same time given expression to the pain and the love in a farewell song to the released spirit ; so the affliction will have lost its sting when this little letter reaches you. Both my Lucie and I have felt sincerely and shared your grief by the thought and the picture of that fearful event ; but we know, God be praised, where and how you will seek and find, not trust only, but serene joy in what the highest love only still grants us. God bless you and give you strength, not only to find faith for yourself but to impart it to her sister."

Miss Wulff's eldest brother, Peter Wulff, a captain in the navy, wrote to one of the officers of the ship who was saved, and all that he learned was that Tette Wulff was seen at the breakfast-table ; after that, she used always, as was known, to go to her state-room and come from it again only to the dinner-table. It was between these hours that the disaster occurred : the ship was being fumigated by burning tar. The tar barrel upset, and the burning stuff gave out smoke and flame which soon enveloped the whole ship. It was presumed that she was suffocated by the smoke and died in her state-room, which is now her tomb at the bottom of the Atlantic Ocean.

1859.

Hartmann's melodious " Little Christine," which had been caught up in the people's singing, and for which I had written the text, was after a long, undeserved rest again brought on the stage and received a great deal of attention : my text even was praised ; the critics in " The Father-land " called it a true poem, an inspiration : ' une vere de l'ideal au milieu des tristes real-ites de la vie.' Beautiful lovely pictures glided past, speaking so naturally and innocently to one, and the working out of the language is so fanciful and plastic, that one cannot read the poem without being moved. There is a world written of in these pages, such as perhaps has never been and perhaps never will be ; but that matters not, since it has beauty in itself and remains in our heart as something we long for."

So kind an expression was granted to my poem, and Hart-mann's uncommonly beautiful music as well was praised with greatest appreciation.

Later in the spring was published a new collection of wonder stories and tales. Among these were " The Wind tells the Story of Waldemar Daae and his Daughters." This was dedicated to my friend the composer Hartmann.

The trees were putting out their leaves. The weather was warm and lovely ; King Frederick VII. was staying in the old splendid Frederick Castle, in the beautiful woody country, and sent for me to hear me read the new production. I was wel-comed with the open hearty candor which the King always showed, and spent two agreeable days in Christian IV.'s proud residence, which has had life given it in Hauch's poem, " Frederick Castle."

I saw all the splendor and the old glory, walked in these halls, sat at the King's table, which on the beautiful sunny day was spread below in the garden. When the tables were removed a sail was taken on the lake round about the castle, and out here in the open air the King wanted me to read what the wind told of Waldemar Daae and his daughters.

His majesty with his consort, the Countess Danner, took seats in the King's boat, where I too had a place : a few other boats with other guests followed. We glided over the blue water wherein the fiery sky at sunset was mirrored. And I read the story of how riches and happiness fled away, read the whistling of the wind " hu-u-ud away with you ! " There was a moment's silence as I ended the reading ; I myself felt strangely mournful, and one will understand that the recollection of these moments in the royal boat where the sea, the air, and the castle were beaming with delight, came vividly to my thought when in the year following the sad tidings came that Frederick Castle was in flames. — The summer called me to Jutland, the most picturesque part of Denmark. The recollection is preserved in " A Story from the Sand Hills," and a description of Skagen.

State Councilor Tang, proprietor of the old North Wosborg, where once the Knight Bugge's home stood, near Nyssum Fjord, had invited me to his house : a picture of the place, the building, and the people there is preserved in a letter to Ingemann : —

" On Monday I journeyed from Silkeborg westward. I thought I was going to a barren, almost uninhabited country, and I find everywhere cultivated fields, and a pretty garden up at the minister's house, where elder-trees and roses bloom ; there are many inhabitants here, and a noble people too. North Wosborg is a very old place, with deep moats and high ramparts close up to the very windows ; the sheltering thicket round about the garden has been clipped by the western storms as if it had been under the gardener's shears. The chapel of the place is turned into a guest chamber. Here I sleep. A white lady shows herself in the place, but she has not yet visited me : she knows well that I like jokes but not ghosts. On Wednesday, the 6th July, we celebrated here on the place the battle of Fredericia ;[1] six peasants who had been engaged in it were invited ; there was sport, drinking, and speech-making, the Dannebrog waved, and when I was asked to read a Wonder Story, I read ' Holger the Dane.' State Councilor Tang has shown great kindness to the peasantry, and we have visited among them. What a rich and pretty place it is here ! The kitchens look as if they were baby

[1] In 1848, in the first war with Prussia.

houses, and the whole ceiling was hidden in a mosaic of hams and sausages. The good people overwhelmed me with cakes, preserves, and drinks. They presented me with schnapps and several kinds of wine, Russian tea, and liquors, and when of course I could only sip of all the abundance they came with chocolate. 'That surely I could drink!' said they, and then they brought their old beer after that — they meant well.

"Yesterday we drove to Huusby sand hills near the Western Sea, three miles from here. We were several carriage loads, all with the Dannebrog flag ; we planted this on the sand hills ; a tent was pitched ; the sea rolled, and we sang patriotic songs. About two gunshots from the sand hills lies Huusby parsonage, with large pleasant rooms, a good library, and your portrait. In the garden large trees are growing, and there is a hedge of roses. But how sharply the wind blew as we drove home in the evening ; it cracked my lips and rasped my face. Yesterday there was a large company at North Wosborg on my account ; there were more than a hundred present, most from the peasantry : we drank tea in the garden, and afterward sat far into the night around the table in the great hall, singing and talking. It is a sturdy people, this peasantry, with their culture and their eagerness for knowledge and wisdom. They had a great desire here at the westward to have a railway : it will soon come. The country itself was once a grain and woodland country I am sure. But then the romantic heather grown fields will be gone with their loneliness, and their will-o'-the-wisp, and all the glory of the old times. Many legends have I heard over here ; several refer to North Wosborg. There in the cellar it is that the gipsy woman, Long Margethe sat. She had torn the fœtus from the wombs of five pregnant women to eat the warm heart of the child, and thought that only when she had eaten the seventh would she make herself invisible. To-day the wind howls as if it were autumn, and the sea listens. Give my warm greetings to your wife.   Your ever devoted,

"H. C. ANDERSEN.

"NORTH WOSBORG, *July* 11, 1859."

It was a charming stay here, and not so very short either.

At my departure the whole family accompanied me to Lemvig. Here, near the Liim Fjord, is Hamlet's grave, not Elsinor, where Shakespeare has placed his great dramatic poem. " Amlet's grave," says the West Jutlander. A solitary shepherd sits here frequently on the height, and blows his monotonous melody on the little flute he has fashioned out of an elder bough or a sheep's bone.

We reached Lemvig and put up at the inn : I soon saw the Dannebrog thrust out from the roof, and a little after at the opposite neighbor's appeared a Dannebrog's flag.

" Is there a celebration going on ? " I asked.

" It is in honor of you," said State Councilor Tang. We went together to see the town : kind eyes welcomed me, and from several houses the flags waved. I could not really believe that this was on my account, but when the next day in the early morning hour I came to the steamboat, I was made to understand that I had friends in Lemvig, from great people to small.

In the crowd of people there was a little boy well wrapped up. " Poor little fellow ! " said I, " up so early to go by the steamboat ! "

" That shall he not," answered the mother ; " he has had no rest or sleep, for I promised him he should come here in the morning to see Andersen set off : he knows all his Wonder Stories."

I kissed the little boy, and said : " Go home and to bed, my little friend ; good-by, good-by ! " I was as pleased as a child. I was warmed thereby and not frozen, like the little fellow in the cold, fresh, western morning on this coast. The steamer glided through Ottesund, where Germany's kings once planted its colors and willed that what was Danish should die. We came to Thisted, the witch-possessed town that Holberg tells us of.

We were by the landing-jetty ; I sat in the cabin ; the steam was sissing and whistling, when one came and called me up on the deck. Friends of my poetry stood at the jetty to give me a ringing hurra ! Later in the day I came to Aalborg : bright eyes welcomed me and I felt friendly grasps of the hand. My friend from student days, Kammerherre

Dahlström, who married Örsted's lovely daughter Sophie, took me to his home, the old Aalborg house.

Anders Sandö Örsted, brother to the discoverer of electro-magnetism, was here on a visit. He is a jurist of first rank, and an influential statesman. As we sat after dinner in the twilight, the servants announced that there were a great many people pouring into the place, and soon a deputation came into the room. The Aalborg Singing Club wished to give me a greeting song. I felt embarrassed that they should honor me and not Örsted. I could not stand by the open windows where he a few years since had stood and received a similar greeting. I went out into the place to the singers; the song began, and I pressed warmly the hands of as many as I could, with gladness and thankfulness. It was the first serenade at home. Swedish students had before, on my first visit in Lund, 1840, given me such a one.

From Aalborg I kept on my journey by Skagen, Denmark's northernmost point, where the North Sea and East Sea meet. The old Borglum monastery, where once the might of the Church gave more council than the King himself in his own kingdom, is now a manor-house. The *propriétaire* Rotboll is its owner. I had a friendly invitation from him to stay a while to see the country there, and perhaps one of the Western Sea's storms. I have in my historical narrative, "The Bishop of Borglum and his Kinsman," given a picture of the place, as follows : —

"We are now in Jutland, near the Wild Marsh ; we can hear the roar of the Atlantic Ocean, rolling hard by ; in front of us rises a great sand hill, and we are driving toward it, slowly driving through the deep sand. An old, large, rambling building crowns this sand hill : it is Borglum Monastery ; the largest wing is the church. It is late evening by the time we have ascended the hill, but the air is clear, the nights are bright, and we can still enjoy a prospect far and wide, over meadow and moor as far as Aalborg Fjord, over field and heath, till they are bounded by the dark-blue ocean.

"We are on the hill, we drive on through barn and shed, then turn round and pass through the gates, on toward the old castle-court, where lime-trees stand in a row along the walls ; here they get shelter from wind and weather, they thrive, and their leafy branches almost hide the windows.

"We ascend the stone winding-staircase, we tread the long corridors, under a ceiling of wood-work ; the wind whistles round us with such strange, wild notes, both within and without the building, and we begin to tell each other tales of the past — such tales as one remembers when feeling half-frightened. The forms of murdered men seem to our fancy to glide silently past us ; the wild wind, as it rushes through the church, still seems to sing mass for their souls ; the mind is thrown back into the days of old, pictures them, lives in them."

Then follows the narrative, which in its historic truth puts in its right light our age over that sung by poets, the happily vanished Middle Ages.

"Borglum is haunted !" had been said to me at Aalborg. "In a certain room there is an apparition of dead monks." One is assured that the Bishop of the Diocese himself had seen them. I do not venture to deny the possibility of intercourse between the world of spirit and of sense, but I do not believe in it with certainty. Our existence, the world in and about us, are all full of wonder, but we are so used to it that we speak of it as "natural ;" all is kept and controlled by the great laws of nature, the laws of reason, laws that lie in God's might, wisdom, and goodness, and I do not believe in any departure from them.

After the first night I had slept at Borglum monastery, I could not forbear asking the master of the house and his wife at the breakfast-table, in what apartment the Bishop had slept, and been visited by the spirits   I was asked if I had taken the alarm at anything in my chamber, and if the dead monks had shown themselves to me. The first thing I did now was to go and make thorough search from floor to ceiling, — yes, I went out into the place, examined carefully all the surroundings, climbed up to the windows to discover if the place was adapted to the getting up of ghost scenes.   I did not know but somebody here, as in another country-house happened in my early youth, might entertain himself with contriving some ghostly night scenes.   But I discovered nothing, and slept at night, and several nights afterward, in peace and safety.

One evening I went to bed earlier than usual and awoke at midnight with a strange cold shiver running through me : I felt disagreeably, and thought of the ghosts they had talked about, but said to myself how foolish such fright was, and for what reason should white monks show themselves to me. Had I not, when I was still living in ignorance of the death of Henriette Wulff, besought God earnestly that he would grant me, if a glimpse only were possible, to receive some sign of sight or hearing from the other world that she was among the departed ; but nothing showed itself ; I perceived nothing.

These thoughts raised me from my disturbed state, but at the same moment I saw in the farthest and darkest part of the room a misty shape like a man. I looked and looked, and it went through me like ice ; it was not to be endured. I was divided between fright and a necessity to know and understand it all : I sprang out of bed, rushed at the misty shape, and saw now when near by that it was the polished, varnished door, where three projecting parts receiving light from a mirror that through the window got light from the bright summer night, formed something like a man's shape. That was the ghost I saw at Borglum.

Since that I have come to have a share in a couple of ghost stories, and this will be the best place to record them.

It was a year afterward I was in another old country-house. I was going in broad daylight through one of the great halls, and suddenly I heard a loud ringing as of a dinner-bell ; the sound came from the opposite wing of the house where I knew the apartments were not occupied. I asked the mistress of the house what bell it was that I heard. She looked earnestly at me.

" You have heard it too ? " said she, " and heard it now in broad day ; " and she told me that was often heard, especially late in the evening when they were going to sleep ; yes, that the sound then was so loud that it could be heard by folks down in the cellar.

" Let us then look into it," said I. We went through the hall where I had heard the mysterious bell and met the master of the house and the clergyman of the place. I told about the sounding of the bell and protested as I went up to the window that "it was no ghost;" and while the words were spoken, the bell rang again still louder. At that I felt a shiver down my back, and said not quite so loud, "I don't deny it, but I don't believe in it."

Before we left the hall the bell rang once again, but at the same moment my eye fell accidentally on the great chandelier under the ceiling. I saw that the many small glass pendants were in motion: I seized a stool, stood upon it with my head against the chandelier.

"Go quickly and heavily over the floor here," I bade them; they did so, and now we heard all the loud bell sounds that had been ringing as if far away, and so the ghost was found out. An old clergyman's widow who heard about it, said afterward to me:—

"That bell was so interesting. How could you, who are a poet, bear to destroy it, and for nothing at all?"

Still another ghost story—the last. I was at Copenhagen. I woke up in the middle of the night and saw before me at the foot of the bed placed on the stove a chalk-white bust which I had not before noticed. "Surely it is a present," thought I. "Who could have given it?" I rose up in bed, and stared at the white shape, which at the same moment vanished. I shuddered, but got up, lighted the candle and saw by the clock that the hour was just one. At the same moment I heard the watchman call out the hour.

I wrote out the little incident and lay down again, but I could not get any rest, when it entered my head: "It must be the light of the moon that shines through the window upon the white wall." I again got up and looked out; the air was clear, the new moon must also have been long gone, all the street lamps were extinguished, nor could the light from one of them possibly have been seen.

The next morning I made search in the room and looked out over the street; over at the opposite neighbor's was a lamp. The light from it could, with the half-raised curtain and a sail in a vessel on the canal, form on the wall the shape of a human head. I went therefore when it was evening into the street and asked the watchman at what time he put out the lamp.

"At one o'clock," said he; "just before I call the hour." It was the reflection on the wall that I had seen and stared at ; the watchman had at the same moment put out the light and the ghost.

But to return to Borglum monastery, where more than one related nocturnal sights which I had not the fortune to see. As soon as I was on my way home going through Aalborg, I had to tell of the ghost and talk with the reverend gentleman who had seen the white monkish shapes. I undertook to discover whether the sight of these did not lie in some fault of the eyes, and he answered seriously : " It may be that there is something amiss in yours that you cannot see such ! "

Ten or twelve days were spent at Borglum, and during these I visited the little fishing town Lokken where there are quicksands in the streets quite up to several houses, but that I could make out to see still more effectively, they said, when I got to Skagen. The road thence led over Hjörring ; I reached it tired enough at evening, and was ready to go straight to bed ; but the landlord in the inn told me in confidence that I was to receive a visit in the evening, that several ladies and gentlemen were coming to call upon me, and the garden was to be illuminated.

Later in the evening there came indeed a deputation ; I was taken out into the garden, where I was received with a pretty song. Provost Djörup gave me a cordial address of welcome ; it was an evening full of enjoyment, the stars twinkled clearly, and I felt myself happy indeed.

In Fladstrand, also, where the railroad to Skagen begins, I found a cozy home with friends who sought to make my stay and journey as agreeable as possible. They looked out to get for me a steady driver who could drive me along the sea beach, where the surf was rolling. He was a well-to-do, excellent countryman, who knew well where there was safe ground and where the treacherous quicksands were.

They had shown him before my portrait, and said, " That is a great poet ! " and the countryman laughed a little and said, " No, it is a great lion." He would not enter into conversation at all with me on the way, nor tell me anything, but he laughed judiciously at what I said to him. He drove me well, however ; he was hospitable too, and I did not get leave to go from his place until I had been well treated with roast chickens, pancakes, wine, and mead.

We drove over pasture-land, heath, and moor-land ; we drove on the beach over the hard, burning sand. We came soon to the sand hills that lay like great snow drifts in winter-time. The shore was nearly covered with quivering, reddish-brown medusæ, large shells, and round, smooth pebbles. Wreck after wreck lay there ; we drove right through what was once a great three-master. Screaming sea-fowl circled above us. The tower of St. Laurentius' Church, half hidden in the flying sand, was seen, and there was the town of Skagen. It is formed of three villages, and the oldest part lies half a mile from the other two. It was to this that we drove.

The streets here are shifting ; they are marked also by a cable stretched from pole to pole, just as the quicksands may determine. Here is a house half buried by a pile of sand, there another ; here a dark, tarred, wooden house with straw thatch, there a few houses with red roofs ; in a little potato patch I saw a pig tied to a ship's figure-head : Hope leaning on an anchor. Here peeps from the gable of the house a colossal figure, — Walter Scott, a figure-head from some stranded vessel.

The desert here has its oasis also, a verdant plantation with beech, willow, poplar, fir, and pine. The sod covers the sand in the garden that otherwise would quickly get the mastery. I visited Skagen's extreme point, that is so small that one man can stand on it and have the waves from the North Sea wash over one foot and the waves from the Kattegat over the other. Countless sea-birds filled the air with their cry, and from the immense gulf of the sea the rolling and breaking of the ground swell gave out a deep roar. The view out over the level sea as it meets the sky makes one dizzy ; one unconsciously looks to see out here on the point if there is still solid ground behind him and that he is not out on the expanse of the sea, a worm only for these cloudy swarms of screaming fowl. Stumps of wrecks and of ships stand like mammoth's knuckles down in the clear transparent water that is turned, when a storm comes up, into foaming waterfalls that leap.over the ledges on the coast against the drifting sand heaps.

From Skagen I was driven over the deep sand of the dunes to old Skagen, that for years has always been moving back into the country ; the heavy waves roll where the last old Skagen lay. We came to an old church buried under the sand heaps, which Dutch and Scottish sea-captains had caused to be built and consecrated to St. Laurentius. In the course of years the sand heaped itself against the church-yard walls, and soon lay over them and over the graves and tomb-stones, quite up to the church's walls and windows. Still the parish came and held their service here, but soon one could not shovel it away. One Sunday when the neighbors and the priest came, an immense sand heap lay before the church door, then the priest read a short prayer and said, "Our Lord has now closed this his house, we must build Him a new one elsewhere."

The 5th of June, 1795, the church was by royal order closed, the tower alone to be preserved as a land-mark for sailors, and it still remains. The old inhabitants of Skagen would not give up the old church-yard : they all wanted to lie there by those who had gone before ; with great difficulty this was done until the year 1810, when the sand had so entirely covered the church-yard that a new one had to be laid out. I pushed my way through to the sand-buried old church, and give here the impression which is recorded in my sketch of Skagen : —

"One stands here by the buried church with a like feeling to that he has on the ashy heights over Pompeii. The leaden roof is broken off, the white, mealy sand, heated in the glaring sun, lies heaped upon the arches of the church ; all is hidden in the darkness of the grave, guarded and forgotten by men until some time when the western storms shall blow away the heavy sand heaps, and the sun's rays again shine in through the open arched window on the pictures in the choir, the long rows of portraits of Skagen's councilors and burgomasters, with their names and official seals. Perhaps a people coming from afar off enters this Pompeii of Skagen, and again gazes in wonder at the old curiously carved altar table with its Bible pictures. The warm sunshine again beams upon Mary and her Babe that holds in its hand the gilded globe. Now the dead sand waves lie here over the church, a desert of white thorn with their yellow berries growing in the sand ; wild roses too bloom here, and the wild brier.   One gets to thinking of the fairy tale about the sleeping beauty in the wood, where the castle is overgrown by an impenetrable thicket.   The mighty church-tower still rises for two thirds of its height above the sand hills ; the ravens build in it, a swarm of them hovering about ; their cry, and the crackling branches of the white thorn that we trod on to get forward, were the only sounds I heard in this sandy wilderness."

After a couple of days' stay here in the grand wild nature that with its screaming flock of birds suggested scenery for Aristophanes' " Birds," I turned again southward on my way home.   One of my Jutland friends and the minister's sister-in-law accompanied me.   The waves darting up were too heavy to permit us to drive on the shingle ; we were obliged to drive through the deep sand in the dunes, and go forward very slowly.   I talked and told about foreign lands I had seen, told of Italy and Greece, of Sweden and Switzerland.   The old post-boy listened, and said with a kind of astonishment : " But how can such an old man as you be content to roll round so ? " I answered with quite as much surprise. —

" Do you think me so old ? "

" You are indeed an old man," said he.

" How old do you think ? " I asked.

" Well on to eighty."

" Eighty ! " exclaimed I.   " Travelling has certainly aged me ; do I look sickly ? "

" Yes, you do look dreadfully lean," said he.   To be fleshy was his idea of good condition.

I spoke of the new beautiful light-house at Skagen.

" The king ought to see it ; " and I added, —

" I shall tell the king about it when I talk with him."   At that the old fellow smiled to my fellow-passengers.

" When *he* talks with the king ! "

" Yes, I have talked with the king " I answered, " and I have eaten with the king."   Then the old fellow laid his hand on his forehead, shook his head, and smiled knowingly.

" He has eaten with the king ! "   He thought I was a little cracked.

From Frederickshavn, whose environs are a most charming part of Denmark, with the heath, beech forests, cornfields, and open shore, I came often to Aalborg, lived again at Aalborg House, where I was honored with welcomes and singing ; it was like a dream, a lovely dream, which makes me happy, and for which I gave thanks to our Lord. Everywhere kind eyes, warm hearts, beautiful sunny weather in this varying Jutland country. On the way through Randers and Viborg, as we were driving, the song "Jutland" sprang from my heart, which our worthy composer Heise, set to music that is sung all over Denmark :

> Jutland twixt two bounding seas,
> Like a runic stone is laid ;
> The mighty Giant's Grave is there,
> Hid in the thick of woody glade.
> And on the heath between the tides,
> The mighty Tempest monarch bides.
>
> Jutland! dear to Danish heart!
> With thy wooded lonely heights,
> Thy wild-wind West with sand heaped hills
> That tower above in mountain flights.
> The Eastern Sea and North Sea stand
> And clasp their hands o'er Skagen's strand.

At Asmild-Closter, near Viborg, I was kindly entertained by friends, and enjoyed more merry days ; but the best, the most unlooked-for pleasure was on the morning of the day I left. I had gone about a mile on the road from Viborg when I saw by the way a young lady whom I had met at Asmild-Closter, and then another, and now my coachman reined in his horse, and I saw six young, pretty, child-like maids, who stood waiting for me with bunches of flowers. They had gone a whole Danish mile in the early morning to say the farewell to me which they would not say in the busy town. I was wholly taken by surprise and deeply moved, and did not show my thankfulness as I ought : in my surprise I only said : —

"My dear children, to come so far for my sake! God bless you. Thanks, thanks!" and called out in the same breath to the coachman, "Drive on! drive on!" I was so taken aback : it was not the way to show my pleasure and gratitude ; it was a piece of awkward embarrassment.

The result of my Jutland journey showed itself at Christmas, when I brought out a " Story from the Sand Hills," which was very well received ; but one reviewer of my book was of the opinion that one would certainly find himself deluded, if, after he had read these last descriptions and my sketches of Skagen, he should take a trip there and expect to find so poetic a country as had been pictured by me. I had meanwhile the pleasure of receiving a visit from Conference Councilor Brinck Seidelin, the man who could best judge of the truth of what I had written, and who had himself given an excellent sketch of Skagen in his description of Hjörring County ; he thanked me in the warmest manner for the accuracy and truthfulness with which I had represented the country. I had a letter from the clergyman of Skagen, expressing his thanks for the sketches of nature there, especially because they were so true. He added : " I shall now also believe and tell strangers when they come and stand on the mound of the sand-buried church, — ' Jörgen lies beneath there.' "

Christmas should have been spent at dear, home-like Bas nös ; but I must first, as always, visit Ingemann. I set out early in the morning of the 17th December; on the railway came the sorrowful tidings that the castle of Fredericksborg was in flames. The recollection of my last visit there came freshly to my mind, when, as I have related, I sailed in the royal barge, and while the sunset was burning in the sky, read what the wind told of Waldemar Daae. What wealth and glory vanished there !

At Ingemann's I received a letter from King Max of Bava ria. He wrote that when the year before, on the Stärnberg Lake, in the royal boat, I read some of my Wonder Stories, he resolved that I should be one of his Knights of Maximilian. The obstacles then in the way were now removed, and he sent me this high order. It was founded by the King, so well disposed toward art and science. On the order is a design of Pegasus when it is intended for poets and artists ; Minerva's owl when given to a man of science. I knew that in Munich it was bestowed on the poet Geibel, the artist Kaul bach, and the savan Liebig. I have been told that the two first foreigners who have received it were the Frenchman Arago and the Danish poet Andersen.

I was made happy by the noble, art-loving King's appreciation. Ingemann and his wife shared in my pleasure, and before I left their home came still another token, a Danish and splendid acknowledgment, which Ingemann had in a friendly way been regretting, because it did not come. Now I had it. Just after my return home from Jutland, I went one day out to the bath-house near Copenhagen ; on the way I met Bishop Mourad, who was the Minister of Public Worship : we had known each other for a long series of years ; as young students we lived in the same house, and he had asked me to visit him. Afterward when he was the minister at Falster, and I was on my way from the fine manor Coselitye, but on account of stormy weather could not get away from the island, I spent a couple of enjoyable, intellectual feast-days with him and family. We had not since met. Now he stopped me and said that the pension of six hundred rix-dollars which I had each year from the state was altogether too little ; that I ought to have a thousand rix-dollars, the same as the poets Hertz, Christian Winther, and Paludan-Müller. It was a surprise of pleasure, yet I was perplexed ; I pressed his hand and said, —

"I thank you. I do indeed need it ; I am growing old. The honorarium for authors at home is, as you know, very small — thanks, therefore, my heartfelt thanks ; but do not misunderstand me when I say, what you will yourself feel, that I shall never remind you of what you have said — I cannot do that." We parted ; for a long time I heard nothing further, until now, during my visit at Ingemann's, there came through the "Advertiser," in which the Rigsdag's proceedings were reported, the announcement that the pension of six hundred rix-dollars which had been granted me was to be increased by the yearly addition of four hundred rix-dollars. My dear Ingemann, in high spirits and joy, drank my health, and my friends sent me their congratulations ; I felt with deep humility that I was the child of fortune, always defended and sheltered, and it gave me a fear, such as I have often known, that such fortune could not always be by me, and there would soon come seas of trouble and days of heaviness.

On Christmas Eve I was at Basnös where the Christmas-tree was lighted not only for the guests of the house, but also there was one for the poor children on the estate. Their tree was quite as fine and brilliant as ours. Madame Scavenius had herself dressed it and lighted every candle. I had cut out and fastened figures which hung from the green branches; they spread a table about it with such Christmas gifts as would especially delight the mothers of the poor children, — cloth for petticoats, linen for underclothing, and many another useful thing. The poor women were well cared for and had a happy evening; we had many. The snow fell, the sleigh-bells jingled, the wild swans sang on the sea-shore; it was charming without, it was snug within. The young people danced till the morning light. From the neighboring place and from miles about, relations and friends were invited. From the neighboring place, Waldemar Daae's knightly house, the family and their guests came; among these was one I was especially glad to meet, the romance writer St. Aubain, by which pseudonym the author Karl Bernhard is widely known. His fresh, spirited sketches, and his character, so true to Danish nature, gave him a distinguished place. He was, besides, kind, ready to help, and always devoted to others; one could scarcely believe that he was up among the sixties, so youthful in appearance to outsiders; he was among the dancers, among the talkers, and with me open, hearty, laughing at the world's littleness, but happy too with the blessings he found there.

1860.

The sixth of January I was again in Copenhagen; it was the elder Collin's birthday, — a notable day for me, and for numberless others whom he had helped and aided a piece further over some rough road of life. At the beginning of this year there was started the idea of erecting a monument in honor of H. C. Örsted, the discoverer of electro-magnetism. The idea originated with Madame Jerichau; so, too, the idea of the monument already built to the poet Oehlenschläger came from Henriette Wulff, who, through her brother and other clever men, carried it oüt. Among the names of those who signed the call for Örsted's monument were, of states-

men, Privy-Councilor Tillisch ; of men of science, Forchham-
mer ; State-Councilor Suhr, to represent commerce ; and the
poet H. C. Andersen. The execution of the monument was
intrusted to Professor Jerichau, who for a fixed sum was to
have the statue cast in bronze by a certain date, and placed in
one of the public squares of Copenhagen.

Spring came and with it travel time. The woods were
green ; Ingemann wrote and bade me come. Soon I was at
Sorö, and a few days after in Rendsborg. Captain Lönborg
and his wife had invited me there. I spent a few delightful
days here, heard the praises only of whatever was Danish,
saw the Dannebrog wave, and had nothing to do with obstinate
people who declaimed against Danish things. There was quite
a show of military here, the officers honored me with a feast,
and when I was asked to stay a day longer, and give pleasure
to the soldiers by reading them some of my stories, I was of
course at once ready. A large club-house, the " Harmony,"
I believe, was selected for the reading, and decorated with flowers and the Danish flag. The King's bust stood above draped
with the Dannebrog. Officers and subalterns, besides many
ladies and some individuals of the citizen class in the town
who understood Danish, were given places ; the recruits filled
the gallery ; the band played between the reading of each
story. The sun was still shining when I went home to Lönborg's house, where several friends had met. " It was a
Danish day," they all said.

At midnight when I was in bed, I heard a noise outside ; I
became restless, and thought immediately, " Now some more
fun ; now follows a demonstration from the Germans." My host
and his wife thought the same. I lay listening a few seconds
when a song began given by beautiful voices, and I heard the
words, " Sleep well." It was truly a friendly greeting which
the Germans brought the Danish poet, whose Wonder Stories
and Tales they knew in translation.

In the morning the Danish military came and played outside our house, and when later in the day I went to the railway
station, the Dannebrog was flying over it. A deputation from
the soldiery brought me their thanks for the reading of the
day previous ; they stationed themselves in ranks, sang Danish

songs, and when the train started gave a ringing hurra for their good-by greeting.

It was my intention to travel once more in my life to Rome, and pass the winter in Italy. I made the journey through Germany by Eisnach and Nürnberg, and visited for the first time the old city Regensburg, and made an excursion out to the splendid Valhalla which King Ludvig had built as by enchantment on the rocky cliff.

In Munich good friends were expecting me. I spent charming hours there, rich in enjoyment, with the artist Kaulbach ; in his house one found such a fresh and home-like spirit ; several of Munich's famous names met there, Liebig, Seboldt, Geibel, and Kobbel. King Max and his noble consort showed me great kindness and favor. It was not easy to leave the artistic, hospitable Munich.

But an excursion of great interest called me for a few days out to the mountains to see the miracle-play at Oberammergau. Every tenth year they repeat the people's plays here, a relic of the mysteries of the Middle Ages. The celebrated Edward Devrient saw them in the year 1850, and he gave an interesting account of them. Now in 1860, they had begun the twenty-eighth of May, and would continue once a week until the sixteenth of September.

The inhabitants of Oberammergau live mostly by wood-carving. Now they rested from work for this was the festival year. Strangers came from afar to take part in it. The stream of people was continually increasing. Every one was received as a welcome guest, not as a stranger. Each was lodged for a very small sum, and entertained to the very best of their power and means. I was most excellently provided for ; my friends from Munich looked out for that. The priest of the place, Herr Daisenberger, who had written and published the history of Oberammergau received me with great hospitality.

There was life and stir in the houses and without ; the townsfolk and peasants bustled about, the bells rang ; cannon were fired, the pilgrims came singing on their winding way. The whole night long there was song and music, plenty of excitement, but no rioting. The next morning, Pastor Daisenberger took me to the theatre that had been built of beams and boards on the green plain outside the town.   At eight o'clock the miracle-play was to begin, and would continue, with only an hour's intermission, until five in the afternoon.   We sat under the open sky; the wind sighed above us, the birds came and flew out again.   I thought of the old Indian play in the open air where the Sakuntala was given; I thought of the Greek theatre; I saw before me the stage for the chorus, and the chorus leaders that entered with song.   Recitative and speech gave connection to the action.   The whole story of the Passion, illustrated by parallel passages from the Old Testament, was given in living pictures.   Behind the choir and choir leaders the stage was built, the real theatre with movable curtains, side scenes, and background.   The theatre itself was flanked on each side by a small structure with a balcony; in one of these was placed the High-priest, in the other Pilate; the dramatic action on the part of eachʳ took place on the balcony.   In each of the two mentioned buildings was an arched door, through which one could see into the streets of Jerusalem.   The entire, often threefold action was astonishingly well put on the stage.   One was with the High-priest, with Pilate; one stood with the people when they waved the palms and when they cried, " Crucify Him ! "   There was an ease and a beauty about it that must impress every one.   It is said that the persons whom the community unanimously appointed to the sacred *rôles* must be of spotless life, and that the one who represented Christ always, before the beginning of the Passion play, partook of the sacrament at the altar. Last year it was a young image-carver, Schauer; they say that the spiritual exertion possessed him in such a degree, that after the acting he was not able to partake of anything, or to speak with any one before he had recovered himself in solitude.

The whole play was like a church-going where the sermon was not merely heard but seen in living representation.   Certainly every one went away edified, his soul filled with a sense of that love which gave itself for unborn generations.   In 1870 the Passion play will again be given in Oberammergau.

My good hearted, well-read host said to me quite frankly

that he had never read anything of mine, but knew that I
wrote Wonder Stories; I saw a kind of smile playing about
his mouth — he did not read Wonder Stories. I had with me
a little volume of them translated into German, and I gave it
to him, and asked him to read occasionally a little in it; he
took it kindly, and honored me immediately afterward with
his description of Oberammergau. The day after as we were
going to the Passion play the hospitable man said to me, "I
have already read the little book you gave me yesterday. Call
them not Wonder Stories, — they are far beyond such. The
'Story of a Mother,' I shall be able to tell at a child's grave,
and carry faith by it to the bereaved."

From Munich I went by Lindau to Switzerland, up into
the Jura Mountains, to the little watchmaking town Le Locle,
where in 1833 I wrote my poem, "Agnete and the Mermaid."
At that time the journey up here was a laborious one, several
hours by diligence.; now one makes the trip by steam on the
railway, making a long ascent; then one comes to a stopping-
place; the locomotive is taken from the front and placed in
the rear, the last car becomes now the first, a new incline is
mounted to the next section, where again a locomotive waits
to send it up the next incline. It is a true "*Voyage en zigzag.*"

At the top the railway passes through one of the largest
tunnels, 4,200 metres long, and after one has just a peep of
daylight and a breath of fresh air one goes in a twinkling into
a lesser tunnel, half as long only, and then comes to the
pretty mountain-town of Chaux de Fonds, and soon in a deep
valley up at the top of the mountain, Le Locle. Here lives
and works my countryman and friend, Urban Jürgensen,
from whom every year a great number of watches are sent to
America.

Eighty years ago there was not a watchmaker in the country;
now in and about Le Locle 20,000 men support themselves by
this craft. There once came here by chance an English horse-
dealer, whose watch had become broken; he was directed to
the smith, Daniel Jean Richard, a skillful man, who certainly
never before had taken a watch to pieces, but now he ventured
it, put it together again so that it was in good order and went.
He took a fancy to make a watch for himself; he succeeded,

and from that hour he turned all his thought to watchmaking ; he taught his seven sons, and soon Le Locle was established as the first watchmaking place. It should raise a monument to the smith, Daniel Jean Richard.

My friend Jules Jürgensen was living, during this visit of mine, in the same old house where I had lived with his uncle Hourriet. I occupied my old room, visited again the under-ground water-mill, saw the Doub Fall, drove from the pine and birch woods to the French side where the beech-trees grow, where the sun shines far warmer than at Le Locle ; but warm hearts were there, sympathizing friends.

Jürgensen's oldest son, who with his brother are famous craftsmen in their father's art, have also no little literary skill. The single French translations of my writings did not seem to be very good, and my young friend wished to see if he could not produce better ones. With my coöperation during my visit here, a translation was begun. I read, and saw to my surprise how far ahead, as regards the expression of feeling and *tone*, the Danish language is of the French : they have often only one word where we have a large choice. I would call the French language plastic : it is akin to sculpture, where all is precise, clear, and well defined ; but our Danish mother tongue has a richness of color, a variety in expression that fits the varying tone. I was pleased at the wealth of my mother tongue, which is so supple and musical when it is spoken as it should be spoken. In Le Locle, on the Jura heights, it was that I made this discovery. Jules Jürgensen's translation of the " Marsh King's Daughter," and a few more of my Wonder Stories, was issued with the imprint of Joel Charbuliez in Geneva and Paris, in 1861, under the title of " Danish Fancies."

In Geneva I wished to spend some time : the way thither from Le Locle lay by St. Croix to Yverdun, through the loveliest part of the Jura Mountains, and where one from the heights has the most magnificent view of the Alpine range and the lakes of Neufchatel and Geneva. I saw the view in the wonderful evening light with the Alpine glow and the harmonious stillness. A good *pension* at Madame Achard's in Geneva was recommended to me : I had a room looking out on the lake. I made excursions out on the lake, had a delightful company of French and Americans about me, and I soon found friends and acquaintances in town : I was introduced to the Swiss poet Petit-Senn, a most excellent old man, — a Swiss Béranger. He had a pretty country-house outside the town. I dined with him, and found him very youthful and merry and full of spirits. Dinner over and the coffee drunk, he took his guitar, and like a Northern minstrel sang several of his songs.

One of the first days after I had moved to Madame Achard's I wished to visit one of the families I was introduced to, and I took a drosky at my door and showed the driver the address on the letter, the street and house I wanted to go to. I sat in the carriage and we drove and drove : it was a long way up street and down street, beyond the old abandoned rampart ; at length I was at the place. I got out of the carriage, looked about me and found myself in a street hard by the square from which I had driven all this long way. I saw Madame Achard's house from which I had set out.

" Are you a Swiss ? " I asked the driver. He answered " Yes."

" That cannot be true," said I. " I came from a long way off, from far up in the North, and there we have read of Switzerland and heard of William Tell, and the noble, brave Swiss people stand in high honor with us ; and now I come down here, so that I may tell people at home truly about these brave people, and then I take my seat in a carriage over there the other side of the square, show the address where I want to go, — it is only a few steps to drive, and I am carried all over town on a half-hour tour. It is a cheat, and no Swiss will cheat. You are not a Swiss ! "

The man at this was quite abashed : he was a young fellow, and burst out, " You shall not pay at all, or only pay what you please. The Swiss *are* brave folk." His words and voice touched me and we parted good friends.

During my visit at Geneva I received the news of the death of the poet Johan Ludvig Heiberg. I have, in " The Story of my Life," spoken of his distinction and of my relations to him. He had in his popular " Flying Post " brought forward my

earliest poems ; he had when I, as a young author, applied
for a travelling stipend, given me the striking testimonial that
in humor I was to be ranked with our eminent Wessel, the
most noted humorous poet in Denmark.   There came indeed
a time later when Heiberg opposed me, and wrote of me in
his book, "A Soul after Death," but soon there came again
an appreciation and perception of what God had bestowed
upon me.

The news of Heiberg's death came unexpectedly and affected
me greatly.   All the men of genius and power whom I had
known and loved were departing, one after another.

I stayed in Geneva until late in September.   The wind already blew cold and wintry from the Jura Mountains and sent
the yellow leaves whirling from the trees.   The reports from
Italy were not very encouraging.   I doubted whether I could
obtain agreeable winter-quarters in Rome, and the cholera
was in Spain.   I resolved to pass the winter in Denmark.   It
was cold as winter here in Geneva, yet before I drew near
home I was to have some summer in the luxury of the fruit
season.   By chance, as I was going by way of Basle to Stuttgart, I came upon a great agricultural fair.   People had
flocked thither from town and country.   Fruits of every kind
beautified the first part of the festival.   Heaps of corn and
hop-vines, pears and grapes, vegetables and fruits were displayed in arabesque splendor : ever since, whenever I look
back upon the country of Würtemberg, this autumn fruit-show
stands out in my thoughts.

With my young friend the painter Bamberg from Basle I
came to Stuttgart : he was received at the station by the
distinguished and busy book-seller Hoffman, who at once in
the heartiest way invited me also to stay in his house.   The
theatre intendant gave me a place in his box.

"You certainly can travel easily !" said friends in Copenhagen to me, when I came home and told of all the hospitality
and all the good fortune I had had.   A welcome fireside on
the Jura, in Stuttgart too, in Munich, in Maxen, — all the
way !   "You have your house on the locomotive dragon's
tail," Ingemann once wrote me ; and it was really almost so.

Christmas Eve I was not sitting in Rome as I had thought
to do, but was happy at Basnös.

In a number of " Household Words," Charles Dickens had brought together several Arabian proverbs and parables. Among them there was one which he referred to in a note : " ' When they came to shoe the Pasha's horses, the beetle stretched out his leg.' This is exquisite ; we commend it to the attention of Hans Christian Andersen." I wanted very much to make a Wonder Story of it, but it did not come ; and not till a year after, on the next to the last day of the year, during a visit at Basnös, where I accidentally read Dickens's words, the story of " The Beetle " suddenly found life. The day after I wrote the " Snow Maiden." This closed my literary work in 1860.

1861.

As soon as April came I felt my wings begin to creak. The bird of passage life came with the first warm rays of the sun. I wished once more in my life to see Rome, and carry out the journey which I had to give up the year before. This time there accompanied me my young friend Jonas Collin, son of Councilor of State Collin. We went by Geneva and Lyon to Nice ; here we rested, and from this point began the only new part of the journey as far as I was concerned, — the artistic, pretty Cornici road, between Nice and Genoa : one ought rather to travel it on foot or loiter along in a carriage, in order to enjoy the charming view that is discovered between cliffs and wooded tracts out over the rolling Mediterranean. There were palms here of a luxuriance which I have seen in no place in Italy ; every year palm branches are carried in great quantities to Rome, to be blessed by the Pope and distributed. The rocky little kingdom of Monaco lies, with its city and district, like a map drawn on the water ; it lay before us in the bright sunshine like a little toy kingdom, and one wishes to climb down there to it.

The journey from Nice to Genoa by diligence takes a day and night, but the road is far too beautiful a piece of art for us to allow half of it to be passed over in the night-time, so we made the journey in two parts, stopping over night half way, and securing our places in the diligence that was to go on the next day. Old memories were recalled in Genoa where I had

not been since my first visit there in 1833.   We took the steamboat, and had fair weather to Civita Vecchia.

On the whole journey thus far, not a soul had asked us for
our passport ; now in the Papal States began that passport
nuisance in the heaviest fashion ; no one was allowed to step
on shore until his passport had been dispatched ; every passenger must immediately at the landing place make his way —
and it was not at all a short way — to the town-hall, where he
did not get his passport but a sort of receipt for it, a permit
to go by rail to Rome ; in the middle of the journey the permit must be shown, and now at Rome one must through the
Danish Consul manage to get a residence card, and it was a
week before we got that.   Rome, that gets its great advantage
from the visits of foreigners, does not seem to think at all how
it can make such visits easy.

In the old Café Græcè, where the Consul for Denmark,
Sweden, and Norway, my friend Brovo, lived, I got apartments
for myself and my young travelling companion, and now we
went out into the great city, so familiar and so homelike.   I
once more saw and could point out to him all the famous
sights.   There had been no great change since I was last
here ; people talked a good deal, however, of the insecurity to
life and property in the streets of the city, but I myself saw
no signs of it.   Ruins, museums, churches, and gardens were
visited, friends and acquaintances sought out ; one of the very
first of these was my countryman Kuchler, now Pietro, a monk
in the convent near the ruins of Borgia's palace.   With his
tonsure, and dressed in a coarse brown monkish dress, he came
forward to meet me, embraced and kissed me and spoke with
the familiar " Thou."   He carried me to his *atelier*, a large
apartment with a most delightful lookout upon orange-trees
and rose bushes, to the Coliseum and over the Campagna to
the picturesque mountains beyond.   I was happy at being
with my friend, and in an ecstasy over the lovely view.

" It is wonderfully beautiful here," I exclaimed.

" Yes, here thou also oughtest to live, — to live in peace and
with God," said he with a quiet friendly smile that had a serious meaning.   But I answered quickly and decidedly, —

" For a few days I could stay here, but then I should need
to pass out into the world again and live there."

He was at work upon a copy after Domenichino, ordered by Mr. Pugaard of Copenhagen ; the money for it was of course to be paid to the monastery.

The Norwegian poet, Björnstjerne Björnson was in Rome, and I was glad now to make his acquaintance here, for I never had met him or seen him before. It was quite a long time at home in Copenhagen before I read the works of the gifted author ; several had said that his books would not suit my taste : It is best, I thought, to try that for myself ; so I read his story, " A Happy Boy." It was as if I stood in the open country, under the fresh sky, by the breezy birch woods ; I was captivated by it, and went immediately to all those who had told me that Björnson would not please my taste, and said to them that it was really a wrong done me, and I was astonished that they should believe me incapable of being glad and grateful for a true poet. Then one and another showed that they thought Björnson and I were so opposite in our nature that we should immediately be inimical to each other.

It so happened that on my journey from Copenhagen I was asked through a third person if I would not take out some books to him from his wife. I consented very willingly, and on calling upon her I told her how dear her husband was to me as a poet and I begged her to write to him that he must be prepared to like me when we met, for I thought a great deal of him, and we must be friends. And from our first meeting in Rome until the present hour he has been most kind and considerate toward me ; he was as ready to like me as I had asked and wished.

The Scandinavians had given an entertainment to our Consul Brovo in a rural outskirt of Rome ; I have given a picture of the place in my Wonder Story " Psyche " ; the entertainment was intended for me also, on this my fourth visit from the North to the Roman city. Björnstjerne Björnson read a pretty song he had written in my honor.

"Our sky is not so free,
A chill is on our sea,
Nor have our woods the palm-tree's sway,
As in the South, men say.
But the northern lights flash over the sky,
The woods whisper fairy tales airily,

And the sea doth bound
As the lingering sound
Of our fathers' song of victory.

" A traveller from that wonder land,
Thou bringest tidings in thy hand
Of winter's dreams by northern lights,
The pranks of the woods in their fancy flights ;
Aye, of a place so far away
That folks and beasts together play,
    And the veriest flower
    Will talk by the hour
So plain that a child its meaning can say.

" Where heaven itself in holy love
Bends as a Christmas-tree above,
And all goes on before God's face, —
Tidings thou bearest from that place,
And comest to sirocco-laden Rome,
Breathing of beech and birch from home,
    With melody
    And witchery
From the north land's faerie."

I was only one month in Rome this time. Among the acquaintances which I made, one is especially dear to me, the
American sculptor Story. He took me to his studio, where I
was delighted with a statue of Beethoven and an allegorical
representation of America ; he introduced me also to his wife
and children at his apartments in the Barberini Palace. He
brought together there one day several American and English
friends, with all their flock of children. I sat in the midst of
the circle of children, and read with unpardonable boldness in
English, which I did not know at all well, but I read, at request, the story of " The Ugly Duckling ; " the children gave
me a wreath of flowers.

Mr. Story took me to see the English poetess, Elizabeth
Barrett Browning ; she was ill and suffering greatly, but she
looked upon me with her lustrous gentle eyes, pressed my
hand, and thanked me for my writings. Two years afterward
I heard from Lytton Bulwer's son how kindly and tenderly
Mrs. Browning thought of me ; her last poem, too, " The North
and the South," written in Rome in May, 1861, on the day of

my visit, closes the volume of her writings called " Last Poems," that appeared after her death. I lay the fragrant flowers between these leaves.

THE NORTH AND THE SOUTH.

I.

" Now give us lands where the olives grow,"
  Cried the North to the South,
" Where the sun with a golden mouth can blow
  Blue bubbles of grapes down a vineyard row ! "
  Cried the North to the South.

" Now give us men from the sunless plain,"
  Cried the South to the North,
" By need of work in the snow and the rain
  Made strong and brave by familiar pain ! "
  Cried the South to the North.

II.

" Give lucider hills and intenser seas,"
  Said the North to the South,
" Since ever by symbols and bright degrees
  Art, child-like, climbs to the dear Lord's knees,"
  Said the North to the South.

" Give strenuous souls for belief and prayer,"
  Said the South to the North,
" That stand in the dark on the lowest stair
  While affirming of God, ' He is certainly there,' "
  Said the South to the North.

III.

" Yet O, for the skies that are softer and higher,"
  Sighed the North to the South ;
" For the flowers that blaze and the trees that aspire,
  And the insects made of a song or a fire ! "
  Sighed the North to the South.

" And O for a seer to discern the same ! "
  Sighed the South to the North ;
" For a poet's tongue of baptismal flame
  To call the tree or flower by its name ! "
  Sighed the South to the North.

IV.

The North sent therefore a man of men
As a grace to the South ;
And thus to Rome came Andersen :
" Alas ! but must you take him again? "
Said the South to the North.

The sun already burnt with fervent rays ; people were going out to the hills, and Collin and I started on our home journey. We visited Pisa, and spent a week at Florence.   From Leghorn we took steamer for Genoa.   The weather was stormy, the sea rolled heavily, and we were all sea-sick ; in the morning the rain came pouring down.   I felt very unwell, and so worn out that when we drew near Genoa I could think of nothing but how to reach my destination and go that day to Turin. As we drew near to land, volleys from cannon announced the sad news that Cavour was dead.

The following day I still felt unfit for travelling, yet hoped that by setting out in the morning we might be able to reach Turin in season to attend Cavour's funeral.   We reached there in the afternoon and heard that it had already taken place the evening before.   His picture hung in all the picture shops, and I bought the one that was said to be the most like him.

Later in the week we came to Milan, and from the cathedral roof, in the midst of beautiful statues of saints carved in marble, we saw the sunlit Alps ; and before the diligence carried us over the Simplon, we spent a few days of sunshine and moonlit nights at Isola Bella in Lago Maggiore.   Our stay in Switzerland was longest at Montreux.   Here was wrought my Wonder Story " The Ice Maiden." The sad accident that befell the young bridal pair ,on their honeymoon, when they visited the little island by Villeneuve, and the bridegroom was drowned, I took for the fact that should be the basis of a story in which I would show the Swiss nature as it had lain in my thought after many visits to that glorious land.

At Lausanne we received intelligence from home that old Mr. Collin lay on his death-bed : it was presumed that God would already have called him away when we should receive our letter, and so we were bidden not to hasten our journey home. We kept on northward, and spent a few days with friends Auf der Mauer at Brunnen, and met there the Librarian of the monastery at Einsiedeln, Father Gall-Mosel, a lovely and spiritual man. The monastery itself is the most esteemed in Switzerland, and much visited by pilgrims and strangers from Germany and France. Einsiedeln lies about a mile away from the high-road between Brunnen and the Lake of Zurich. Collin and I were unwilling to pass it by, and reached it just on the day of the celebration of the one thousandth year of the establishment of the monastery.

The little town was filled with strangers, who gathered in the church, which was gayly dressed with flowers and candles and inscriptions. Many collected outside in the place by the bubbling springs and drank of the water of each, for the saying goes that Christ once was in Einsiedeln and drank of the water, but of which spring no one knows, and so people drink of them all.

We visited my acquaintance, the Librarian, who was very friendly, and accompanied by several young ecclesiastics took us to see the notable things in the convent, and carried us to the church, where the flower-decked sarcophagus of the Founder was seen, bearing beautiful memorial inscriptions written by our learned guide. We saw the treasures of the library, and for one thing an old Bible in Danish translation, and when a wish was expressed for a newer one, I promised to furnish it, and there it now is.

From holiday bright Einsiedeln we came to Nuremberg. Here also was a festival; flags were waving in all the streets. There was a musical festival going on, not of Minnesingers, but of the choral societies of our time. All the music associations of the different Bavarian towns were met here to give an immense musical festival. The people from the neighborhood all flocked to it, and it was not easy to find a place at the hotels : but as always, I was in luck ; I found the snuggest little chamber in the world. From Nuremberg we came to Brunswick, and here too the flags were flying from the houses : garlands hung round about, and the streets were bestrewn with flowers. The town was celebrating its birthday, a cus-

tom reaching back a very long way. I believe this was the
thousandth year. It seemed as if our return journey was to
be taken only through towns that were celebrating some festival.

At the Sorö station Collin and I separated, he to go to
Copenhagen, I to Ingemann's. Here I got intelligence of
the dear old Collin's death. " During his last days he lay in
perfect quiet, recognizing no one ; you would scarcely have
known him," they wrote. I went immediately to town to be
with the bereaved ones.

> The fire is out on the hearth at home,
> And sorrow sits in the family room ;
> Through Jesus to God thy life did aspire ;
> Here, a handful of ashes — there, the flaming of fire.

So I sang ; many and better songs there were, but surely
none more deeply felt than mine : so many recollections of
deeds and words moved through my mind.

I went into town, and would gladly have been alone, but
all the carriages were filled, except one in which sat two
ladies ; I took my place there. The elder one sat still, half
asleep in the corner, the younger had stretched herself out
on the other seat, occupying the width of the carriage, and
enjoyed her fruit and luncheon : she looked like a Spanish
girl ; her black eyes shone and carried on an entire conversation before she began to speak.

" I believe I know you," said she in French. I said the
same to her and asked her name.

" Pepitta," she answered. She was a Spanish *danseuse* who
the year before had been overwhelmed with flowers at the
Casino Theatre. I gave her my name, and she told the elder
one, her companion, that I was a poet, and that she had at the
Casino acted a part in one of my pieces, where she spoke
French and carried on a Spanish dance. It was the comedy
" Ole Luköie." She told her companion the contents of the
piece in very few words. " There is a young chimney-sweep
in love with a Spanish *danseuse*, and the whole thing is a
dream."

" *Charmant*," said the old lady. But I was not in the mood
to carry on a lively conversation. At the first station I looked

for a place in another carriage, and excused my leaving them by explaining that I had found friends with whom I wished to travel.

I drew near Copenhagen, and went to that home of homes where were gathered the children and children's children of that father and grandfather who lay in his deep sleep of death: the day of burial followed and I wrote to Ingemann : —

"I found all of Collin's family in the old home ; they were all quiet, but profoundly sad. My old friend lay in his coffin : he looked peaceful, and as if in sleep ; a sweet calm spread over his face. I dreaded much the day of burial, fearing that I should be too much overcome in the church, but I felt stronger than I should have dared believe. Bishop Bindesböll's discourse did not satisfy me : it dwelt too long upon his political life and on King Frederick VI. Pastor Blödel afterward spoke a few words at the grave : they formed an excellent supplement to the Bishop's discourse, giving there just what should be said. The rest of the day I spent quite alone, and a sad time it was to me. I missed that which I had been so used to for a long series of years, the daily seeing of old Collin and talking with him. The house is now strangely lonesome. Since I came home two acquaintances besides have died, — the composer Glæser and the artisan Gamst : it is strange to see the ranks so broken in upon : now am I myself in the first ranks of the march."

Time passed on toward Christmas : I had during my journey and after my return home worked industriously, and when Christmas came there was published a new volume of my stories. "The Ice Maiden," as well as "The Butterfly," were both written in Switzerland ; "Psyche," however, during my stay in Rome. An incident that occurred on my first visit there in 1833–34, came to my mind and gave me the first suggestion ; a young nun was to be buried, and when her grave came to be dug there was found a beautiful statue of Bacchus. "The Snail and the Rosebush" was also written in Rome, and belongs to the class of my earlier Wonder Stories. I dedicated the book to Björnstjerne Björnson.

Christmas was spent at Holsteinborg, where I wrote the following letter to Ingemann : —

" DEAR FRIEND, — My chamber is right up against the church. I can walk through my door straight to the pulpit. The organ is playing, the singing of psalms is borne in upon me as I write this letter. There is a pleasant Christmas festival here, and last evening there was great delight among the children. All the little folks were most happy over Christmas and its glory. I also had my Christmas-table with many things on it that served to expound my stories. The cat sat on the ink-stand, the Nis danced with the penholder, the butterflies flew in Florentine mosaic on the paper weight ; my little girl with matches also I found there. I had many thoughts yesterday of my Christmas times in childhood, the richest in memory I have ever spent, even though the chamber was so small and I had no Christmas-tree. But grits, geese, and apple-pie were never lacking, and in the evening there were two candles on the table. A half century of Christmas memories have I ! How wonderfully am I still borne along. Thanks for the two happy days spent with you and your wife. Give my greetings to Sophie also : she had certainly dressed a Christmas-tree for you and concealed it down in the cellar : 'You should stay till Christmas Eve,' she said to me.

" God knows whether I shall be in Sorö next Christmas ; my wish is to travel to Spain in the new year. I must always have my Christmas dreams, and they are of travel. I think of Italy or of Spain. The weather is mild, but I would rather have clear cold air and signs of snow. Last year it was so, with glittering snow and ice-clad trees ; then I wrote my story of 'The Snow Man.' This year my muse will not visit me. May a good and happy New Year fall upon all of us — no war, no cholera ! Peace and health abound ! So live well and heartily.   Your faithful and devoted

                              " H. C. ANDERSEN."

1862.

Immediately, as soon as the year began, while I was still out in the country, I received from Ingemann a letter full of hearty good-humor. Ingemann and H. C. Örsted, who both were fond of me, stood in their poetic nature quite opposite to one another, Örsted demanding of right strict truth, even when it was contained in the form of fancy.

" The rational in rational things is Truth, the rational in fancy is Beauty, the rational in feeling is Goodness." So he once wrote to me and firmly believed. In the " Monthly Journal of Literature," Örsted had handled most severely Ingemann's fanciful poem, " Ole Navnlös " (" Ole Nameless "), so severely indeed that the kind-hearted philosopher Sibbern went to the defense in a paper, " Örsted and Ingemann ; " these two amiable men never knew or met each other, or they would certainly have felt their kinship of nature. I used to repeat to each the sayings of the other, so that they came thus to have a mutual esteem. Örsted had now been dead several years.

In a letter which I received from Ingemann when I was in the country, he writes : " I was this morning out at the railway station and went under the telegraph wires when they began to hum. What is the matter ? Can't I have leave to go on thinking ? what does H. C. Örsted want ? The wires buzzed and talked. What in the world is going on up there ? Then I felt it run through me. Örsted knows that I am going to write to Andersen to-day and so he is saying, Greet him for me ! So you see I have a greeting for you from H. C. Örsted."

It was the last letter I had from my dear Ingemann, and in the greeting he sent me I perceive the communion and affectionate intercourse which there really was between these two souls. God willed that they soon should meet. For the rest, the year began happily for me. The stories published at Christmas brought me many words of appreciation, and here are two instances.

King Frederick VII. always preferred to hear me read my stories, not only at Fredricksborg, as I have related, but several times I was summoned to Christiansborg. Early in February I read thus to the king and a little company whom he had collected about him the four stories. " The Ice Maiden " especially interested and moved him, for he had himself when a prince spent a good deal of time in Switzerland. A few days after the reading I received the following letter from his majesty, written by his own hand : —

"MY GOOD ANDERSEN, — It is a pleasure to me to send you my thanks for the happiness you afforded me by reading your delightful stories the other evening, and I can only say thus much, that I congratulate my country and its king that they have such a poet as you.   Your well wishing,

"FREDERICK R.

"CHRISTIANSBORG, *February* 13, 1862."

I was exceedingly pleased with this kind, royal letter, which I treasure among the best of my souvenirs. With the letter came at the same time a gold box with his majesty's name engraved on it.

I received a letter from Björnstjerne Björnson in Rome. He was much pleased with the dedication, and with every single story, especially with " The Ice Maiden."   He wrote : —

" ' The Ice Maiden ' begins as if it were rejoicing and singing in the free air, by the pine-trees, and the blue water, and the Swiss cottages. You have sketched such a boy as I would gladly have for a brother, and all the scenery is so distinct with Babette, the miller, and the cats, that it is as if I had crossed the country and seen them all with my own eyes.   I was so stirred that I must needs cry aloud, and had to make several stopping places. But, thou dear, gentle man, how could you have the heart to make such a violent ending for us to this lovely picture !   The thought that fashions the last portion has something divine in it, — so it impresses me, the thought that two people should be separated at the very highest point of their happiness ; still more that you showed clearly how as when a sudden breeze ruffles the still water, so there dwelt in the souls of both that which could overthrow their happiness ; but that you should have the courage to do this with these two of all people ! "   The letter closes, " Dear, dear Andersen, how much I have loved you, yet I believed confidently that you neither rightly understood me nor cared for me, although with your good heart you would gladly do both ; but now I see clearly what a happy mistake I made, and so I have been deceived into doubling my affection for you ! "

I was exceedingly pleased over Björnson's letter, happy at his friendship and affection for me, which he expressed in such lively terms. I may hint, too, at another letter which I had from a young unknown student from one of the Provinces, because of the poetry and *naïveté* of the letter. There was inclosed in it a four-leaved clover, dry and pressed. He wrote of this that when he was a little boy and read for the first time my stories, he was delighted with them ; and his mother told him that Andersen had known dark days and gone through much, which so saddened the little fellow when he heard it that he immediately went into the fields and found a four-leaved clover, which he had heard brought good luck with it ; so he bade his mother send this to Andersen that he might be happy. The clover was not sent ; the mother put it away in her psalm-book. "Now several years have gone by," read the letter ; "I am become a student ; my mother died last year, and I found the four-leaved clover in her psalm-book. I have just been reading your new story 'The Ice Maiden,' and I read it with the same pleasure as when in my childhood I read your stories. Fortune has favored you, and you do not need the four-leaved clover, but I send it to you and tell you this little incident."

This was about the substance of the letter, which I have lost. I do not remember the young man's name, and have not been able to thank him, but now in late years, perhaps he will read here my thanks and my remembrance of him.

I sat reading and writing one evening late in February, when the newspaper came and I read : "Bernhard Severin Ingemann is dead." I was overwhelmed, and this letter bore my grief : —

"DEAR BLESSED MADAME INGEMANN, — I first heard this evening by the paper what God had willed. I am grieved, but in grief only for you ; you are so lonely, for he has gone away from you. It must be to you as a sad dream, from which you long to wake and see him again by you. Our Lord is so good, only what is best for us comes to pass, — that I believe ; I cannot let go the faith. I would that I might have seen him once more and have talked with him ; we were both of us so young, and yet now all at once after these years old enough to go with him. I long for him. There is a life after this ; there must be if God be God. There is a happiness for our thoughts, so that I cannot be grieved except for you, my dear noble friend, if I may dare to call you thus. Do not be at the pains to answer this letter ; you have no mind for that now ; I know that you think kindly on me. Greet Sophie, your maid ; she, too, is affected, I know, for she was so attached to him and he to her. God give you strength, and raise you through days of peace to him, who is your dear, kind, never to be forgotten one.   " With fervent sympathy,

" H. C. ANDERSEN."

Early in March the fields lay white with snow, but the sky was charmingly clear, the sun shone, and I took the cars out to Sorö, for it was the day of burial. I stood in that home, where, from my school days at Slagelse until now an old man, I had spent such happy hours, where our talk had gone on in earnest and in jest. Madame Ingemann sat quiet, meek in sorrow, while the old, faithful maid, Sophie, burst into tears on meeting me, and spoke of her beloved dead, his kind words and gentle talk.

From the academy the coffin was carried to the church, a great procession of mourners accompanying it, being representatives of all classes of the community. Many peasants followed : for them he had indeed spread open the history of Denmark ; his writings so told that story that the heart beat quicker on learning it.

The coffin sank into the grave amidst the twittering of little birds, as the sun shone down. We have a picture of the funeral, and I wrote these words :

" BERNHARD SEVERIN INGEMANN.

" By his cradle stood the Genius of Denmark and the Angel of Poetry, who looked through the child's gentle eyes into a heart that could not grow old with his years ; the soul of the child would never depart, but he was to dwell as a gardener in the garden of poetry in our Danish land, and they gave him a greeting and a consecration by a kiss.

" Wherever he looked there fell a sunbeam ; the dry branch which he touched put forth leaves and flowers ; he broke forth in song as the birds of heaven sing in gladness and innocence.

" From the field of popular faith, from the moss-grown graves
of decaying time he took his seed-corn, and placed it by his
heart and brain ; the seed thus planted grew and thrived till
it became great in the peasant's low cottage, wound itself about
under the roof like the St. John's wort, and put out broad
leaves ; every leaf was a leaf from history for the peasant, that
stirred in the deep winter evening over the listening circle ;
they heard of the old times in Denmark and of the Danish
mind, and then their Danish hearts were lifted in gladness and
love.

" He laid the seed-corn behind the sounding organ pipes, and
the tree of singing cherubs wafted its branches, and the hymn
sang itself — peace in the heart, gladness in God.

" In the dry soil of every-day life he planted the flowering root
of the wonder story, and it burst forth, unrolling in variegated
beauty and striking oddity. He travelled with the storks to
King Pharaoh's land, learned their morning and evening song,
and understood every single word. Whatever he planted
grew, because it had struck root in the hearts of the people.
He spoke in their tones, in the Danish speech ; his native
land's soul was the might of his sword, and his pure thoughts
are like the fresh blowing sea-breeze. He has had his last
Christmas. His life on earth is ended, his body is like cast-off
clothing ; he was borne away, yet still he held fast by the hand
of one — he could not let go that, the faithful hand of his wife,
and he knew that it was wet with tears, and in that moment
she was with him, to be with him when he should awaken.

" Awake is he now, but she sits alone in that home where
every one who entered grew gentler and better ; she sits in
longing for him : the hour until the time of meeting comes is
as one of our minutes ; that she knows ; ' thanksgiving and
love ' rise from her lips, and from the young hearts of the
Danish people.

" That which may disappear and decay is laid in the grave,
under the sound of church-bells and the singing of psalms
and the tears of love ; what never can die is with God ; what
He planted is with us for our joy and blessing."

My spring-time began early in May, when my manor home-

life began. I was at the homelike Basnös, dear Holsteinborg,
and the music loving Lerchenborg. Great plans of travel
were laid, for I felt a strong desire to visit Spain : once had
I stood at the entrance, but the summer heat and sickness had
kept me back. Now I looked for a better season. I had in
jest said to my young friend Jonas Collin, that if I were to
win the prize in the lottery, then we should travel together to
Spain, and even slip over to Africa ; but I did not win it and
never should, but must get my share in another way. My
Danish publisher, Reitzel, said to me one day that my collected
writings were sold out : he would give me a new edition ; for
the first I had received only three hundred rix-dollars, but now
he offered me three thousand. It was as unexpected as a lottery prize ; it was just as welcome, too, and Collin and I set
out.

I took the morning train out to Sorö to spend an-hour or
two with Madame Ingemann. She looked unwontedly bright,
and felt strengthened, she told me, by a delightful dream which
God hath sent her the night before. She had seen Ingemann
looking so young and beautiful and exceedingly happy, and
then they had talked with one another. Her eyes shone as she
spoke of it. All in the room, for the rest, was as of old ; it was
as if Ingemann had gone out only for a walk and every moment he might come home again. She talked to me of the
forthcoming edition of his writings, his biography from the
time of his student life, which I had prepared for one volume. She asked my advice in one thing and another, but
when we talked of the days when they had their life together,
the tears would come into her eyes.

I went to the church yard. Just at the entrance was a grave
where upon the stone was written a name well known in Danish
literature — Christian Molbech. In " The Story of my Life "
I have spoken of him ; he was severe in his judgment of my
books and also of the Ingemann romances. Time changed
all that bitterness, and we have come to understand each
other. A little incident which Ingemann told me came into
my mind. Shortly after Molbech's death, Ingemann went out
in the evening in Sorö, going home slowly after some company.
The church-door was open and in the doorway stood the priest
Zeüthen, in full priestly dress.

" I am waiting," said he, " for the funeral of old Molbech ;
it is to come in a few minutes to the church." Just then came
along an ammunition wagon, and two young men clad in their
capes followed ; they were Molbech's sons. The coffin was
borne into the church ; Zeüthen and Ingemann followed after
the sons ; that was all the procession. Zeüthen spoke a few
words over the coffin, and Ingemann was glad that he was
there. With the same feeling I now stood here, and so I made
my only visit to the church-yard where Ingemann's grave was.
On the stone is his medallion portrait. One often sees, they
say, little children lift one another up to kiss the poet's mouth :
a painter might make a pretty picture from this incident.

From Corsör began my journey with Jonas Collin. We
were to take the route that lay by Flensborg, because the next
day, July 25th, the monument over the fallen soldiers was to be
dedicated in the cemetery ; it was the celebrated lion done by
Bissen. There was a great gathering of men under waving
Dannebrog flags. I had earlier visited the graves of the fallen
heroes. These had now been made level, but no boundaries
disturbed. A great mound had been raised in the centre,
and a memorial stone bore the names of the fallen ; here also
stood Bissen's lion, not yet unveiled. I took my place among
the grave-stones. Students from the Danish high-school were
collected and sang a song. The weather was fine, the sun
shone, but it almost blew a gale. It was for me as if the departed souls were sighing in the tree-tops. Twenty-five guns
were fired, the veil fell, and the lion stood uncovered, looking
out over the graves. What if an enemy were ever seen here
by us — was the thought that suddenly passed through my
mind.

We approached Brunnen by Frankfort, and there we were to
meet Collin's parents and sister, who were staying here on their
way to Italy. At the Lake of Lucerne we were overtaken by
one of those mighty Swiss storms. A *föhn* came down from
the mountains and lashed the lake into great waves. The
captain could not bring the boat to her wharf, the breakers
dashed over the side, and so a strong boat rowed by several
men came out to take us to land, a little way from the town,
where a river emptied into the lake and there was a little har-

bor.   But before we could reach it we had quite a long passage to make where the breakers were tumbling.   The water
dashed upon the shore, and we did not dare approach till we
were just opposite the mouth of the river ; then we came
nearer and nearer, till we were on the breakers, where the men
plied their oars, which creaked and bent, but in a moment afterward we were in still water in the river, and received by
friends, acquaintances, and strangers.

Days hot as African ones afflicted the usually fresh and
pretty Brunnen.   Auf der Mauer had given up his hotel to a
stranger, and was living with his sister in a pleasant place near
the town.   I heard Agatha sing again ; her brother and Father
Gall-Mosel, the librarian from Einsiedeln, accompanied her.

With Collin's family we took the route over the Brunnen
Pass to Interlaken.   As we rose, the air became fresher and
the fields were green as in early spring.   Giessbach was visited
and the glacier at Grindelwald.

In Berne there was living an ecclesiastic who was a son of
the Danish poet Baggesen and Sophie Haller, daughter of the
Swiss poet.   Every time I have travelled through Berne I
have been wont to visit the friendly old man, who has great
sympathy for Denmark, though he cannot speak the Danish
language in which his father sang his beautiful and his witty
songs.   Our longest stay in Switzerland was, however, to be at
Montreux.   The beauty of nature thereabout I have recorded
in a poem, or rather a letter to the poet Christian Winther at
Copenhagen, who intended to bring out a New Year's annual
from the Danish writers, and wished a contribution from me
also.

MONTREUX, *August* 30, 1862.

A poem askest thou ?   I've none to give,
Else would I send my very best.
Here in Montreux the laurel grows, but poems — none ;
The last was Byron's — Byron's on Chillon.
Nature herself is here the poem,
And in my heart she rhymes anew.
I cannot paint the evening on the lake,
Where the water shimmers in purple and blue —
An airy rose-leaf with the sky for a gold ground.
Like mighty choral seats in church,
The crags rise high, crags upon crags,

'With wooded slopes for drapery ;
And far away the highest towers
A mount[1] with lasting snow for altar cloth.
Here is a peace, an evening charm,
A color play no painter gives.
And yet for all this splendid show
My harp hangs voiceless and unstrung,
Nor can the upland air awake its tones ;
Vain is my heart's touch on its strings ;
They lie as though in slumber deep,
Sleeping to gather strength for sounding forth
With mightier voice and newer tones.
When I shall enter soon the glorious land,
Where glowing pomegranates shine midst laurel leaves,
Growing in wildness 'neath the Southern sun, —
That land of the Cid, Cervantes's father-land, —
There pray I God to grant poetic grace
That shall awake the silent strings
And carry music home to our green isles,
Where the beech casts its shade over giant graves ;
Fata Morgana from the garden of Granada.

Spain was our destination. As soon as we entered French
territory, Jonas Collin and I separated from his parents and
sister, who went by Chambery to Italy; we by Lyons, Nismes,
and Narbonne to Spain. On the sixth of September, the very
day when I first came to Copenhagen, the first also that I
came to Italy, on this day was I to enter Spain also. I had
not so arranged it ; circumstances had ordered it should be só,
and so the sixth of September has become one of the white
days of my life.

What I saw, felt, and experienced I have written under the
title " In Spain," and here I give only a few short notes. From
Gerona we went slowly by rail in the evening to Barcelona, with
its glittering cafés that quite outdo anything of the kind that
Paris has to show. The great Inquisition house stood looking
grimly ; the monasteries, as everywhere in Spain, have been
changed into warehouses or hospitals. I saw for the first time
a bull-fight, not bloody, however, as afterward I saw in the
South, where the bull thrust his sharp horns into the belly of
a horse and ripped it up so that the entrails rushed out — a
sight that made me faint. In Barcelona I was witness to the

[1] Dent de Midi.

tremendous power of a rain storm; the mountain streams swelled into tearing floods that broke down every boundary, and washed over railway and highway, and swelled through the town gates over Barcelona's principal street with whirls of water that filled the houses; in the churches the priests stood up to their waists in water singing the mass.

For more than a mile out to sea I saw the water of a coffee color from the freshets that poured in. In delightful sunny weather we went by steamer over the quiet sea to Grao, a suburb of Valencia. We were as in a great orchard. The whole plain about Valencia was fragrant and beautiful with groves of lemon and apple-trees; crowded vineyards too, with rich bunches of grapes, flourished here in the warm, ruddy earth. A few days' stay here, and the same in Alicante, and we travelled to the palm-tree town, the high, romantic Elche, where we saw for the first time the gypsy folk as they live in Spain, and as they appear in the neighborhood of Murcia.

It was the last of September, and the sun still burned as if it would have the grain all thoroughly cooked. In Cartagena, whence we were to go by steamer to Malaga, there was no relief; the air was red-hot, the wind was red-hot; the rain that we had to mingle these was gentle, lukewarm rain; all nature and mankind were beautiful indeed — and red-hot. My balcony overhung the narrow street, so near the neighboring houses that the nearest one touched it, and I involuntarily looked straight into it, and immediately put what I saw into song.

The night before we were to take the steamer to Malaga, there blew such a gale that the trees were torn up by the roots. I felt a good deal of concern about the passage, but the steamer's departure and arrival were fixed things, and I had no choice, so I went on board with Collin. Indeed I am Fortune's child, and this I said before we left port; for the waves subsided, the sea was as quiet as a piece of silk, and so in the most delightful night we slipped over the bright water, and in the early morning came in sight of Malaga, with its white houses, its great cathedral, and its lofty Gibraltar, once the Moors' fastness.

In towns that lie by the sea-side I always feel myself at once at home, and how much here filled and possessed my mind! — the sweet Moorish memories, the eternally youthful, charming country, and all the beauty of the Andalusian women. We can be transported at a grand statue, a lovely picture ; how much more then at that picture in womanhood which comes straight from God. I was amazed, and stopped in the street to look at these royally moving daughters of beauty, their eyes shining beneath the long black eyelashes, their delicate hands playing gracefully with the fan. It was beauty from God shown in humanity — a fairer thing to see than statue or picture.

One day our Danish Consul took Collin and myself out to the Protestant burial-ground at Malaga: it was a paradisiacal spot. I would not, however, have mentioned this visit again, were it not that the sketch which I gave of it in my book, " In Spain," called forth a singular correction. I wrote, " In the centre of all this vegetation was a neat small house, within which refreshments were to be had ; pretty children with laughing eyes were playing there."

It was for this passage, after my book was published and translated into English, that I received a setting right that astonished me exceedingly. A lady in London had read the book, and felt herself disagreably affected by the rather incorrect translation of " Refreshments were to be had within : " she had written to a relative in Malaga for an explanation of it ; the person written to addressed himself to one of the gentlemen whom I had known ; and he in turn applied to the Danish Consul, who spoke to the family in the pretty little house at the cemetery, and asked if any one here had for pay furnished refreshments to a stranger ; and when it appeared that none had been thus sold, I was bidden to strike out in the next edition of my book, " In Spain," what I had before written, " Refreshments were to be had within." The words flowed from my pen ; I had no thought of these being an offense to any one.

I remember distinctly that visit to the cemetery. The air was warm ; I was tired and thirsty, and asked our guide, therefore, if it were not possible to get something here to refresh one ; he took me into the little house, and the kind man there

gave me fruit or ice-water, I forget which, but it certainly was
not paid for.   I ought to have added that in my book and so
not have scandalized the pious lady, nor, what concerns me
more, have caused the good man who had compassion on me
to be annoyed by an investigation into this thing.

Collin and I spent a week in Malaga, from which place we
desired to go back again to Gibraltar ; but first Granada was
to be visited, where people had made great preparation to receive the Queen, who was entering Andalusia for the first time.

Granada with its Alhambra was to be the bright spot in our
Spanish journey.   The evening came ; we sat in the diligence
drawn by ten mules with jingling bells ; the whip cracked, we
started off by the Alameda, along the bed of a stream and up
the heights, from which we looked off on to Malaga, shining
with its many lights.   The air became heavy, sharp lightning
flashed, and just then a couple of armed men looked into the
coach.   I thought at once of an attack, but it was only our
guard against highwaymen, — gens d'armes who saw us safely
over the dangerous parts of the road.   Passing by Loja we
came the next forenoon to Granada, where we had previously
engaged apartments.

From my countryman in Barcelona, Herr Schierbach, I
brought a letter to his Spanish brother-in-law, Colonel Don
José Laramendi, a lively, amiable man, unwearied in his attentions to Collin and myself.   We went with him to see and study
beautiful and interesting things, which otherwise we should
never have been allowed to see.   The Alhambra received our
first attention ; but we came at an unfortunate time, for the velvet trappings and tasteless decoration hung there, on the occasion of the Queen's near visit, made it lose its peculiar beauty.

The ninth of October the Queen made her entrance into
Granada, and never since the time of Isabella I. had there
been here any such affair ; for six nights and days Granada
was indeed a fairy town.   The church-bells rang ; dancing girls,
with castanets and curious instruments, went dancing through
the streets ; bands of music played everywhere ; the banners
waved : " Long live the Queen ! "   Roses were torn leaf from
leaf and fell from the balconies like a shower of flowers over
the Queen, who could be told for a queen right away by every

child, for she wore a gold crown and was dressed in purple. In the evening and night it was as if there hung over the streets a cloud of variegated humming-birds.

After the Queen's departure to Malaga, and the festivities were over, Collin and I moved our quarters to the Alhambra, in the "Fonda de los siete Suebos," which is close by the walls of the Alhambra, hard by the walled-up gate through which the Moorish king Boabdil rode out to do battle against Ferdinand and Isabella, who conquered him and drove him out with his Moorish people.

I read Washington Irving's "Alhambra" here for the third time: the dead became living; the departed came again. I could every day visit the Moorish halls, and wander in the Sultan's court. There was a scent of roses here, like a poem strayed from those old times: the clear water fell with the same rush and roar, the ancient mighty cypresses, dumb witnesses to the voice of speech and song, stood with fresh green leaves in the sunlit air which I was breathing.

Through tears, as when I first left Rome, I took my leave of the Alhambra, where I had been happy, and where I had felt a profound melancholy, passing through many swingings to and fro in my soul, feeling myself afflicted and grieved, at what? — Yes, these very memories are now leaving me: it is good to forget, better often than to remember, yet best of all to come to a true understanding.

I marked my departure by these words: —

ALHAMBRA.

Like an Æolian harp broken in two,
But hanging still on Darro's hilly banks,
I see thee rich in ornament and grace,
Alhambra! though thy greatest beauty lies
In the soul-stirring memories of the past.
What tones still issue from thy fragile strings?
Sweet tones of love, mingling with warlike sounds,
Clashing of swords that to siroccos swell.
Ah! broken is that harp, but still it hangs
Yonder, amidst the weeping cypresses, —
It is Alhambra; glorious in decay.

When we came to leave, our countryman, Visby, and Colonel

Laramendi were on hand to bid us good-by, and my little friends, Laramendi's children, were also there to cry, "Adois! Vaya usted con dois!"

Again we were in Malaga, and when I was putting my things in order for leaving, I met with a strange misfortune. I carried with me my decorations of order in miniature, and among them one North Star, the one that Oehlenschläger had worn, and once when I was much cast down by a too severe criticism, had given me with the most sympathetic and confident words, " The north star never goes out : you shall have mine when I am called away." Now it was stolen from me ; all my orders were taken, and I did not recover them, though I advertised both in the Malaga and in the Granada journals.

In the evening, Collin and I went on board our steamer ; at daybreak we saw the Gibraltar rock, and soon we were on English ground, in a good hotel, where the Danish Consul, Mathiesen, had already engaged rooms for us. Here, with him, we spent a few delightful days, visited the impregnable fortress, mounted the highest point of the rock, and saw thence to the west Teneriffe, Europe's most southern point, and south of that Ceuta, on the African coast.

On the second of November, a beautiful sunny day, the sea rolled in from the Atlantic, and Collin and I went over to Tangier, where the English minister resident, Drummond Hay, who had married a Danish lady, had given us a cordial invitation to his house. My letter announcing our coming had been given several days before to a fisherman, but it had not yet reached them when we got there, — strangers in a strange town, in a new part of the world. We went, meanwhile, through the narrow streets, full of people, to the minister's hotel. The whole family was in the country, a few miles from Tangier, at their country-seat, Ravensrock.

The Secretary of the embassy was fortunately at the Legation, and he quickly provided horses for us, and mules to carry our luggage, and so, quite a caravan, we drove through the town's narrow main street, which was full of Moorish Jews, Arabs, beggar women, and naked children. Out beyond the fortified part we came suddenly upon a whole encampment of Bedouin Arabs and their camels.

Passing through a wild open country we reached Ravensrock, a strong castle in the midst of green fields. Drummond Hay, his wife, and daughter, received us most heartily ; the Danish tongue was heard, and all was sunshine and delight about us. From my room I looked out over Tangier to blue mountains. I could see over to Europe, caught sight of Gibraltar's rock, the town of Teneriffe, and in the evening, Trafalgar's Light.

There was a loneliness here, and yet a strong life in nature by the rolling ocean. We wished to know something, also, of the town life ; and therefore the whole family, a week later, moved back with us to their great, well-ordered residence in Tangier.

Sir Drummond Hay introduced us to the Pasha, who received us in a friendly manner in the paved court of the castle, which reminded us of the Alhambra. Tea was brought ; we each had two great cups of it, and would have had a third, but I prevented it by saying that it was against our religion to drink three cups, and so we got off. The Pasha accompanied us afterward to the castle's outer gate, where he shook hands with us with much cordiality.

In Drummond Hay's house we found English comfort : it was cozy and well-ordered, and most charming in its amiable inmates. From the balcony of the house one looked out over oleander shrubs and palm-trees quite to the Mediterranean. The time passed here all too quickly.

A French war steamer was expected from Algiers, and we were to go by this to Cadiz. It was hard to say farewell to the dear friends in this charming African home ; the visit here was quite the most interesting part of the whole journey.

At sunset we went on board. In the middle of the night, when we lay sound asleep, the vessel struck on a sand bank in the bay of Trafalgar. I hurried upon deck ; the vessel lay as if on one side. My fancy painted the greatest peril, but it was scarcely a quarter of an hour before the ship righted itself, and we slipped over the rolling sea in the clear moonlight. When the sun rose, we cast anchor in the roads before Cadiz, the town of towns for neatness. Flags were flying, and in the harbor lay ships of all nations : it was a pretty sight that burst on us. For the rest there is not much to see here, — no notable churches, or ruins, or galleries. The romantic one must look for in the view out over the sea, and in Andalusian eyes that shine in the mantled beauties that walk the Alameda.

The railway by Xeres de la Frontera runs to Seville, one of the most romantic of Spanish towns, adorned with beautiful churches and immortal pictures. The memories of olden times and great names were linked with this place. Every day we visited the majestic cathedral where is the Moorish bell-tower La Giralda, the highest in the land. Troen stands winged, shining in the sunlight. We visit the castle of the Moorish king, the gay Alcazar, that gleams with gold and colors as in its time of splendor. The garden was filled with oranges and roses : the summer of the south had still a place here. In Murillo's native town, in the presence of a wealth of his beautiful pictures, it came over me how great he was ; yes, often I exclaimed, " He is the greatest of them all ! " One must travel to Spain, especially to Seville and Madrid, to see what he has put upon canvas.

With the well known genre painter John Phillips, who is now dead, and the Swedish painter Lundgreen, we saw for the first time the Murillo Hall, which includes in the Academy of Art at Seville the richest display of his glories. We saw next his beautiful painting of " Moses in the Bulrushes," which is found in the church La Caridad, next the monastery, which now is a hospital for old and infirm men, established by Don Juan Tenorio, who died a monk here in the monastery and wrote his own epitaph : —

" Here lies the worst man in the world."

The story of Don Juan Tenorio was for the first time dramatized by the Spanish poet Tirso de Molina : his piece was used by Molière, and written again as a text for Mozart, to be carried by immortal music through time and generations.

We came after some hours by rail to Cordova, once a principal seat of the Moors, where, when the manufacture of cordovan [1] was in full activity, an academy of music flourished. The most elaborate of Moorish mosques is here, possessing relics of the Prophet himself ; now it is a quiet, deserted town,

---

[1] A peculiarly dressed leather made in Cordova.

where the spirit of desolation seems to have spread a wide
robe of forgetfulness over so much grandeur. The grand
mosque of Cordova, now a Christian church, is the only splendor of Cordova. A thousand and eight marble pillars support
the roof; it is like a plantation of pillars to look upon, and
in the midst rises a richly gilt church, where the great hymn
resounds in honor of Jesus and the Virgin Mary, between
walls that bear on their arches in Arab characters, " There is
only one God and Mohammed is his prophet."

From Cordova to Madrid the larger part of the railroad
was not yet finished and we must again try how uneasy we
could be in a Spanish diligence. At evening we came to
Andugas, and later in the night to the German colony Caro-
lina, around which the country was of a wild beauty. Sierra
Morena afforded us great variety and delight. Here, too, in
this outlawed land, where every other tourist tells of robbers,
attacks, and murders, I was in good fortune : I believe that if
I had travelled with an open pocket-book in my hands, not a
soul we met would have given any trouble. Shanty towns
thatched with cactus had sprung up along the route of the
railway on which the men were working ; here at least was life
and bustle.

After about four or five hours' wild riding we came to the
little place Santa Cruz de Mudela, a town with poor, mean
houses, the streets unpaved and covered with an offensive
mire. The fonda near the station, which had been recommended to us, was a great filthy tavern with straw strewn on
the floor ; the sleeping chambers had no panes of glass in the
windows, but wooden shutters. Tired as I was, I would not
stop here. The train to Madrid was to start immediately, and
after ten hours' journey we came at midnight, quite worn out,
to Madrid, where in the well known plaza Puerta del Sol we
found a good hotel, " Fonda del Oriente," where we got good
meals and wine from the blushing hostess, good beds and good
rest. It was cold here, snow was falling, and the town gave
me little pleasure. There was nothing characteristically Spanish, and no great memorials of the Moorish times. Still one
thing gives Madrid a preëminence among capitals, — its splendid gallery of paintings of Europe's greatest masters, especially

the works of Murillo and Velasquez. Here I spent hours,
— most happy hours; and that we might refresh our Spanish
memories and see the peculiar Spanish nature, Collin and I
spent a few days in a journey to the picturesque, interesting
Toledo. The road led by orange groves, which reminded us
of Danish nature and wooded shades. Toledo makes the impression of a great memorable ruin, and is surrounded by
naked crags, where the Tagus, in a succession of falls, rushes
down and turns little water-wheels that are very picturesque.
The Alcazar, with its proud colonnade and ruined arches,
makes a great impression on one, as it rises royally over the
waste about it, still keeping some of its ancient glory. One
wing only of the castle remains habitable. The soldiers of the
Cordova regiment are quartered there.

The cathedral and the church of San Juan de los Reges,
ah! that is a Spanish church to see! even after one has seen
the cathedrals of Malaga, Seville, and Cordova. With a
glory like that of Solomon, but buried and hemmed in, stand
the two Jewish synagogues, now christened by the names of
Nuestra Señora del Transito and Santa Maria la Blanca. In
the artistic decoration of the walls there is inwoven in a
broidered scroll the words in Hebrew: " Solomon's temples
stand here still, but Israel's people are departed, — the people that keep the law. There is one only true God."

It is lonely and quiet here in the town, and still more in all
the surrounding country; there are only three signs of life:
the sound of the church-bell calling to mass, the beating of
the hammer in the making of Damascus blades, the only remaining memory of old times, and now the locomotive, —

> Which comes and blows its blast;
> Then stillness reigns again,
> And all about is waste and bigness.

In Madrid, where we went again to stay some weeks, perhaps through Christmas, the author Don Sanibaldo de Mas,
formerly Spanish Ambassador to China, arranged in one of
the Madrid hotels a reception for me, where I might become
acquainted with some of the writers of the day. I met here
Don Rahael Garcia y Santesteban, author of " El Romo de
Artigas," and several zarquellas. I found in the capital of

Spain several eminent men who came cordially and apprecia-
tively to me, while they knew but little of my writings ; the
only ones that had been translated were " The Match Girl "
and " Holger the Dane." I became warmly attached to the
poet Hartzenbusch, of German extraction but of Spanish birth,
— a well known dramatist and writer of wonder stories ; his
" Quantos y Fabulas " were upon every one's tongue : people
were so polite as to say we resembled one another in our writings. He came most kindly to me, and wrote generous words
in the copy of his " Quinlar y Fabulas," which he gave me as
a souvenir. One other name, noted in Spanish politics and
in recent literature, I may mention, the Duke of Rivas ; I was
taken to see him and was well received. We were old acquaintances, he reminded me, for we had met before at Naples
when he was ambassador there.

I did not remain in Madrid over Christmas. The climate
was intolerable. There was rain, snow, and cold as severe as
in Denmark at the same time of year. Occasionally there
came a change of temperature, but it was a wind that was dry
and piercing, irritating the nerves, and not to be endured. I
made up my mind to go north into France, and so toward
Denmark ; but on my departure in the cold evening when the
snow fell, I became very warm at heart on seeing in the cold
waiting hall so many who had shown good-will toward me,
and who were dear to me, I found, when we came to separate,
— his excellency, the venerable Swedish Minister Bergmann,
several young Spanish poets, and one of the most affectionate
and unwearied during my stay here in his attentions to me,
Jacobo Zobel Zangroniz, from Manilla. I offer him here,
should he ever see this writing, my greeting and thanks.

The train went rushing away in the storm. The wind
howled and a snow-storm broke over us at the Escurial, and
here already the train stopped. We were crowded into a diligence and obliged to ride in that till the morning. A fellow-
traveller ran his elbow through the window pane, the snow
blew in, a child kept up a steady crying, the vehicle was
always on the point of upsetting, there was no thinking of
sleeping or resting, we only thought of broken arms and bones.

At San Chidrian we again came to the railroad, but the

first train did not go for several hours after our arrival, and all that time we had to wait, sitting in a cold, ill-appointed station. At last the hour struck, and at noon we were in Burgos, where Spain's hero, the much sung Cid, lived, and where he and his noble wife Ximene rested in the Benedictine monastery San Pedro de Cardoña. We saw in the cathedral the chest filled with stones, with which he deceived the Jews, a very characteristic relic of that time, but held in little honor now.

Collin and I stayed here in Fonde del Rafaello; it was a hard, severe winter. The window panes were covered with frost, snow lay on the ground, and we were furnished with an iron pot filled with burning charcoal, to keep us warm. We put this outside the door before we went to bed, but the door hung so loosely by its hinges that there were wide cracks, and the fumes came in so that I was awakened in the night by the sensation of a nightmare which arose from the smoke; it was as if I had a hood tightly pulled down over my head. I called out to Jonas Collin; he answered strangely as if dreaming. I repeated "I am sick." He did not answer at all, and I sprang out of bed, staggering, got the balcony door open, and a blast of wind sent a drift of snow on me. It was an hour in that cold air before Collin and I fairly came to our senses; that night in Burgos came near being our last on earth.

From Burgos there was a railway to Olozagoitis where we again took the diligence. The snow lay all about us, the night was dark, and by daylight we crossed the Pyrenees to St. Sebastian, which lies picturesquely placed on the Basque bay. It was winter here, but when some hours later we came near the French boundary, the sun shone out, spring had come, the trees had buds, the violets were blooming. We came soon to Bayonne and spent our Christmas here; a small wax candle stuck in a champagne bottle was lighted for a Christmas light, and healths were drunk for Denmark and all our dear ones.

The famous watering-place, Biarritz, on the Bay of Biscay, lies, as is known, very near Bayonne; here we spent several days, and from the heights we could see the snow covered mountains of Spain. The breaking of the sea upon the rocky coast resounded like the firing of cannon. The sea spirted like great whales over the projecting rocks, that lay like basking seals. The eye looks out over the waters of the world's ocean, whose nearest shore is America. New Year's Eve we were in Bordeaux, where countrymen of ours and French friends welcomed us heartily.

1863.

Bordeaux pleased me greatly ; I felt myself specially attracted by the theatre, where the opera was in full flower. There for the first time I heard Gounod's " Faust," and I repeated my visits. There were voices ! and dramatic song and fine decorations ! I have forgotten the names of the singers, but not the strong impression they made on me, nor my vexation over the otherwise charming actress of *Margaret's* part, to see how thoughtless an actress sometimes can be. In the third act, where *Margaret* in a maidenly and pious way, with her psalm book in her hand, comes home from church, she takes out her spinning and sits and sings the ballad of the " King of Thule ": *Margaret* seated herself, but as she had no longer any use for her psalm-book, she tossed it like an old rag behind the side scenes, as *Margaret* in reality, or, so to speak, in the kingdom of beauty, certainly would not have handled the church book. Every time I heard " Faust " this happened, and it was only after hearing more music and real acting that I could again enter into this character.

The cathedral was visited, the remains of the Roman amphitheatre, the old foundations of the town. The weather began to be warm and fine, violets in great multitude were out in the meadows, the fruit-trees were in blossom. Our Danish Consul took us to a pretty villa out in the country close by the river side. Here we saw fresh young spring as if it were ready to follow us on our journey northward.

In Angoulême we stopped for a day, but stayed longer at Poictiers, where Collin had a friend : he took us about the town, which stands high and has a noble cathedral which dates back to the time of the Moors : here are also some very old build, ings, and not less than two-and-thirty monasteries.

The weather meanwhile was not more spring-like than in Bordeaux. We were forced again to hear the wood crackle in the fire-place. Some 'little turtles which Collin brought from Tangier were as cold as we were, and we shoved them up to the fire till they were nearly burnt.

From old Poictiers we came to the pretty town of Tours, with its immense suspension bridge and great cathedral, its broad streets and gay shops ; here was spring again, and sunshine, flowers, and green things. We went to see the old house where Louis XI.'s infamous executioner, Tristan the Hermit, had lived. The garden was adorned with decorations and inscriptions ; from the tower one looks over town and river far into the country. A part of the churches lie in ruins, single ones being put to profane use, — as one for a stable, another for a theatre.

From Tours our journey led to Blois : every town, like every man, has its own countenance ; they have a common likeness and yet are different ; one keeps in his mind all their peculiar touches ; so it is with me as regards the towns of Southern France ; they are like little vignettes of my journey ; and not the least vivid is my recollection thus of Blois, with its crooked narrow streets and the shaded promenade by the bank of the river. I remember well wandering up to the cathedral, where the street rises so steeply that they have had a parapet made for one to hold on by as one climbs up. Never shall I forget the old castle turned now into barracks, but well preserved too. The whole building, and the memories that cluster about it, make an impression upon one that calls up dark mysteries. The red-painted open balcony arches before every window seem like mouths one has run a tongue out of so as not to tell what has been done there inside. Here was the Duke of Guise murdered ; we saw the apartment, and the hole in the tapestry through which Henry was an eye witness.

Two days were spent in Orleans, a time all too short for seeing its beautiful buildings and monuments. There is a monument to Jeanne d'Arc in the square Napoleon III., full of beauty and poetic thought. She is represented on horseback, and round about on a pedestal are large bronze bas-reliefs, which contain representations quite close to the conception in

Schiller's tragedy ; from where, watching her sheep, she saw the Virgin reveal herself, to that last moment where she stands in flames at the stake. A lesser statue, modeled by King Louis Philippe's daughter Maria, and presented to the town, has a place in the town hall garden ; we saw also on the bank of the river an older statue erected to Jeanne d'Arc. We saw the house she lived in, and Diana of Poictiers's residence, and the splendid mansion which Charles VII. had built for his beloved Agnes Sorel.

From Orleans one soon comes to Paris, where we were now to stay two months, the first in the year, the most full of enjoyment to strangers, where many have more pleasure than they could wish for. It was not the first time in my life that it had been granted me to be here, and I would enjoy this sunshine of life, and I enjoyed it as I had before enjoyed the whole romantic journey through Spain to Africa's coast and back ; great pleasurable pictures of memory were granted me, but the days and months are not all made of silk, and every day's life has its rough prickling yarn. There is an old saying, " Men are not so good as they ought to be ! " and I belong to the ranks of men. " Forgive us as we forgive our debtors " — that's in the Lord's Prayer.

Björnstjerne Björnson was in Paris, on his way home from Italy. At his suggestion, the Scandinavians made a pleasant feast for me at a restaurant in the Palais Royal. The table was adorned with flowers, and at the lower end of the hall was arranged a large picture representing H. C. Andersen surrounded by his " Wonder Stories." " The Angel " floated above ; " The Wild Swans " flew past ; here was " Thumbling," here " The Butterfly," " The Neighboring Families," " The Little Sea-maid," " The Constant Tin Soldier," — not one was wanting of the mice that told of " Soup made of a Sausage-stick."

Björnson made a hearty speech, and in his kind feeling toward me placed me beside Baggesen, Vessel, and Heiberg in popular wit and satire. I replied that it was to me as if I were dead and lay in my coffin, and people were saying over me the prettiest and best things they could think of, and everything was put in the strongest light ; but I was not dead. I hoped there was still some future remaining to me, and I heartily wished it might be given to me to make good all that they had been saying.

A Swedish song was now sung, and then was read a letter to H. C. Andersen from the poet P. L. Möller, who had lived for several years in Paris, but was prevented by sickness from taking part in the festival. I read for my friends a few of my Wonder Stories : "The Wind tells of Waldemar Daae," "It is certainly true," and "Children's Prattle." There was most hearty and happy accord, and I look back upon it as one of the bright evenings of my life.

Late in March I left Paris, and our journey home lay by Düsseldorf, where some pleasant days were spent with the Norwegian painter Tidemand, in whose studio there then stood partly finished his remarkable picture, "A Fght at a Feast in Norway." The knife ends the quarrel. One man lies stretched dead ; another, mortally wounded, is cursed by the grandmother of the dead man. It is a powerful picture, with masterly handling of the light ; it streams from the fire and from the dawn which comes through the open roof.

On my birthday, the second of April, I was again in Copenhagen, but soon the forest put forth its leaves, and I started out again to visit my friends at Christinelund, Basnös, and Glorup. At these places I wrote out from notes, which I brought home from my journey, the book "In Spain." Nearly all of June I was at the delightful manor-house, Glorup, with Count Moltke Hvitfeldt, where I always had found a home. The garden had been, as it were, transformed in beauty since I was last here ; the old French part had been beautified with a fountain, which cast its bright jets up among the great trees ; the newer part had been turned into an English park, with lawns and fine groups of trees.

At the close of August I was again back in my little room in Copenhagen. They gave at the Casino my comedy, "Elder Mother." The talented young Carl Price played very naturally and pleasantly the simple minded young lover's part, sang delightfully the little songs. He and the piece were received with great applause, and from that time it became one of the little pieces which are regularly seen with great acceptance, much more than at the first representation. I have before spoken of the time when it was only poets like Heiberg, Boye, and Thiele who then felt the worth of the piece, not the critics. What a change now! I wrote this autumn for the Royal Theatre the play, " He is not well born," and for the Casino Theatre, " On Long Bridge."

I had, in turning over the pages of Kotzebue's dramatic works, found a drama I did not know: it was written after the well known pretty tale, " Still Love," of Musæus. I took this piece and let it tell its story as Musæus gives it, but gave it in my mind a very Danish action. Bremen Bridge is Copenhagen's Long Bridge. The whole story was very home-like ; songs were introduced, and I had a good deal of pleasure from it. All was happiness and sunshine ; but now was coming a tempest ; dark days were at hand, and a heavy, bitter time. The storm burst, not over me alone but over land and kingdom, for now came Denmark's time of trial.

King Frederick VII. made his residence in Sleswick, at the castle of Glücksborg : there came alarming rumors of the state of his health. It was Monday, the fifteenth of November. I was with the Minister of Public Worship, Bishop Monrad, who was plainly uneasy. The weather was raw and gloomy. The damp air oppressed me ; I seemed to myself to be in a house of mourning. I thought of the King and felt troubled, and when a few hours afterward I went to see some friends in the house where the Minister Fenger lived, I met the telegraph director, who himself brought the dispatch. I waited anxiously on the steps until he came back, and asked if I might see what was written. He answered only, " We must be prepared for the worst." I went in to the Minister. He said to me, " The King is dead." I burst into tears. When I went out into the street the people stood in groups and showed the sorrowful news in their faces. I was overcome, and longed to see some friend, so I went to Edward Collin. Here people came in who had been at the theatre, but when the play was to begin, a voice was heard in the parterre saying that " When the King lies at the point of death, it was not proper to play comedies," and the public was bidden to go. The curtain soon rose, and the actor Phister stepped forward and said that it was very natural that people under these circumstances

should have no pleasure in seeing comedies, and the actors
certainly had no more pleasure in giving one. The play was
therefore given up.

In the Casino Theatre a couple of acts were played when the
sorrowful news came of the King's death. A sob went through
the house, and the people immediately went quietly out; the
play was broken off.

The next forenoon the air was thick and heavy, as if in
keeping, and I went out to Christiansborg Castle. The square
was filled with men. The President of the Council, Hald,
stepped out on a balcony of the castle and proclaimed " King
Frederick VII. is dead. Long live King Christian IX." Hurras resounded all about. The King rose, and while the clamor
continued he came forward again and again. From the happy
family life, with its quiet and gladness, he was elevated now
to the trial of dark days which God had willed should pass
over us all. I felt sick in body and soul and quite cast down.
In the evening I wrote : —

Sad tidings through the Danish country sped :
" King Frederick the Seventh, our Danish king, is dead ! "
Sound the dirge over Thyra's mighty mound.
On Danish shield his broken heart was found.
God sent that heart to Danish land and folk,
Nor any truer man the Danish language spoke.

From heather plain to stormy coast,
No man for Denmark greater love can boast ;
Thou that hast kings' meaning spoke,
Art blessed with love of common folk.
Thanks for thy love, for all thy nature gave,
And, giving thanks, we weep beside thy grave.

In the evening of Wednesday, the second of December, the
King's corpse came to Copenhagen. From my dwelling in
Newhaven I saw the sarcophagus vessel glide quietly over the
water to funereal music and the ringing of church-bells. The
words " Castrum Doloris " were inscribed on the Christiansborg
Castle ; people were streaming from there, and I was troubled
for the crowds that had pushed on foot by foot, and were now
so hemmed in that they could not escape until the whole
procession was over. Alone with my thoughts, this tingled my

nerves ; I could not go that way, and gave up going ; but when
the time for admission was gone by, I was sorry that I had
not been there. I felt that I must once more get near the
good friendly King and stand by his coffin. It was granted
me, and I got there with great ease. The lamps were still
burning in the chamber of mourning. The workmen were
taking away the last pieces of the catafalque and inscriptions :
the white satin canopy still decorated the Hall of State, the
lights were burning in the candelabra ; the escutcheons were
in their place ; only the *tabourets* with orders and insignia were
gone. I came just as the lid was lifted from the open coffin
to make ready for the lowering of it. I saw the inner black
wooden box lined with lead which inclosed the corpse ; I
bowed myself over the coffin, the odor from which was so strong
as to send me to the open window. In the room close by
were laid wreaths from Sleswick ; I held in my hand the flower-
less moss wreath which some poor people had brought. I
saw garlands of Christ's - thorn from Flensborg — all these
wreaths were to go into the king's grave.

The Singing Union of Copenhagen were to give in chorus
a farewell song to the departed king, when his dust was borne
to Roeskilde, and I was charged with the writing of the words.
The day of burial came ; the time was toward evening. The
procession halted at the west gate while the song was sung ;
the insignia of the corporations waved, the cannon flashed
and boomed, the smoke swelled into little clouds that floated
up toward the sun. Sorrow and grief held our hearts and
thoughts.

The bloody waves of war were again to wash over our father-
land. A kingdom and an empire stood united against our
little country. A poet's way is not by politics ; he has his
mission in the service of Beauty ; but when the ground trembles
beneath him so that all threatens to fall at once, then has he
only thought for this which is a matter of life and death : he
does not stand on one side of occurrences, but knows full well
their significance and has his serious thoughts concerning
them. He is planted in his father-land as a tree ; there he
brings forth his flowers and his fruit ; and if they are sent
widely through the world, the roots of the tree are in the

home soil and perceive what shapes that, what issues from it to death.

The Duke of Augustenborg's eldest son appeared as laying claim to the dukedom of Holstein and the Danish dukedom of Sleswick. Germany was ready to maintain his right. The whole reading world saw that it would be for Denmark a heavy, bitter conflict. The Danish soldier is uniformly brave, fair, and honest. "The brave Johnnies," the soldiers are called in the popular tongue. A girl's "John," they say, is one who is marked as especially liked by women. With song and shout they moved away to protect Denmark at the *Dannevirke*, the old ramparts which Gorm the Old, Thyra Dannebod, had raised a thousand years ago to shield our land against the German invasion. This time had passed, and now was to come the overwhelming might. In the early morning I was awakened several times by the song and tramp of the soldiers as they came from the barracks past my dwelling. I sprang out of bed, opened my window, and with moist eyes prayed God to bless and keep the young, joyous defenders. On one such occasion, deeply moved, I wrote, —

A SONG OF TRUST.

No mortal knows what to-morrow shall bring ;
None knows or sees save God our King ;
But when comes Denmark's darkest day,
Then comes from God deliverance alway.

When rent and racked the country lay,
Niels Ebbesen's courage was her stay ;
God led us in his own great way,
And Denmark saw a brighter day.

O'er the white capped waves the black winds sweep,
Our vessel rocks on the stormy deep ;
But God our Lord in the tumult stands,
And, wiser than man, gives his commands.

No mortal knows what to-morrow shall bring ;
None knows or sees save God our King ;
But when comes Denmark's darkest day,
Then comes from God deliverance alway.

This was printed in the " Dagblad." The evening after, I received a letter signed " Only a Woman," which read : —

" If Herr Professor should again feel himself disposed to give the people faith respecting the impending campaign, it might be well to choose another form for inspiring our departing brothers with, than to quiet them ; our present condition, as far as the eye can see, is like a stormy night, in which our little vessel puts out into the deep. The Danish warrior who goes away, glad and proud, to fight for our righteous cause, cannot understand that there is any occasion for gloomy thoughts over the present times."

I still believed in a deliverance from God, but sometimes was filled with anxiety, yet never have I more fervently felt how fast I clung to my native land. I did not forget how much affection, good fellowship, and courtesy I had met with in Germany, how many dear friends, men and women, I there had, but now a drawn sword was between us. I do not forget those who have served me, or my friends ; but my country is as a mother to me, and she is first. Yet how heavily it all lay on my heart ; it seemed to me that I could not bear it. Never has Christmas appeared so dark and gloomy as this year. As the year departed, on New Year's Eve, I stood filled with grief at what the next year might bring. God was almighty — I trusted in Him. He would not fail Denmark.

1864.

New Year's morning was a tingling, frosty day. I thought of our soldiers at their posts, and in the cold barracks. I thought, — Now the frost bridge is thrown over the water for the enemy, a whole army of people can cross it. What will happen ? I had not the strong confidence which so many about me had, that the Dannevirke could not be taken. I knew indeed how far more extensively they could array their soldiers than we, even if every soul went. I knew that from great Germany the railways could hurl against us soldiers, as the sea in a storm casts its waves against the strand. I asked one of my countrymen who was high in office, " Should the Dannevirke be taken, how could our soldiers then approach Dyppel and Als without being fired upon ? "

"How can a Dane," he burst out, "ask such a thing! how can he think of the Dannevirke being taken!" So strong was the confidence in God Almighty and what we sang and felt — our brave soldiers.

Every day soldiers left for the seat of war, young men, — singing in their youthful gayety, going as to a lively feast. For weeks and months I felt myself unfitted to do anything; all my thoughts were with the men. On the first of February the telegram came that the Germans had crossed the Eider. Operations had commenced. By the end of the week we heard the evil tidings that Dannevirke was abandoned. General Meza with our troops had, without the blow of a sword, retired from the frontier and were moving northward. I thought I was dreaming a horrid dream! How crushed I was, and many, many were like me. Wailing crowds went rushing through the streets. What an evening it was! what a time! It was a day of fiery trial for us all; but in this was our steadfast trust, — Father-land, the soldiers — our defense.

There was exhibited great ingenuity in raising funds for the sick and wounded, and for the families and orphans of those who died. Every one gave more than his share, — he gave all he could scrape together. The theatres stood every evening as good as closed, for no one was in the mood to go there. My previously named piece at the Casino, "On Long Bridge," it was believed, would as a novelty draw some spectators, and it proved to be so; it took well, and people came for a few evenings.

The sixteenth of February the enemy crossed King River, but we still held Als and Dyppel. God would not forsake us was my steadfast thought. The Queen's mother died just at this time, and I was appointed by the King to write a psalm which should be sung over her grave in Roeskilde cathedral. Some days after I was summoned to the Queen, who thanked me most kindly for my words. We stood by the window, music struck up, soldiers went by to join the army, to give their young life blood. Large tears started from the Queen's eyes, — farewell tears for the Danish children. Foreign war had about it something to relieve it, — its moments of lightness but now we stood here singly against a multitude, and had only our trust, — God can abase, but He raises again.

Collin's daughter's son, Wiggo Drewsen, whom I had danced upon my arm when he was a child, and to whom I had sung one of my best known songs, "Little Wiggo," was badly wounded at Dyppel, and lay there among the dead and wounded until the battle was ended, and the Prussians bore him to their hospital. Who in this country had not some relation, some dear friend, for whom they went, as I for him, in mournful unquietness.

The second of April, Sönderborg was fired by the enemy. All Jutland was soon occupied by armed men, who crowded over Liimfjord and drew near Skagen. I had in faith and hope sung, while the soldiers were fighting from the half destroyed fortifications, —

> A little band with trust in God
> And Right, holds out to th' end.

But what avails a little band against well appointed great armies ? I had a misgiving that my father-land would be severed piece by piece, and bleed to death, that my mother tongue would be washed away, only sounding as an echo from the Northern coasts. Our old songs themselves would not come to the lips ; they sounded like the shoveling of earth upon the coffin :

> And shall we never sing again,
>   " To Denmark meadows green belong ? "
> The heart is dead in singing men,
> For cruel Winter chased it when
> There came not to us that one friend
>   For whom we watched so long.
>
> The Summer blows its gentle wind,
>   The whitethorn blooms, and the cuckoo sings ;
> All as of old is fair and kind ;
> The birdies chirp with their wonted mind,
> And flowers with old bright hues we find,
>   Only man's heart to sighing clings.
>
> There is no gain in grief's dark mood ;
>   To weep, to mourn, no fortune makes
> What shall be has eternally stood,
> Writ by His hand who is wise and good, —
> Who His people has led by field and by flood, —
>   Great King of kings who counsel takes.

Not yet has our old ship bade adieu.
Up! on the deck, then, every man!
A piece of the gunwale has gone, it is true,
For the sea did brew, and its white foam flew
Up to the Dannebrog fast held by the clew, —
God held that fast in his mighty hand.

Never shall trust vanish in air
Till hearts have burst with sorrow;
And ever the people saith in prayer,
Denmark in God's own love hath share, —
He is our God, we are his care,
And the sun shall shine to-morrow.

But no sunshine fell upon us. Ships brought the wounded
and mangled to Copenhagen. They were lifted out and
borne through the streets to the hospitals. Some, like Captain Schack died on the way thither. Several of the bodies
of officers slain were brought to Copenhagen. I saw some
friends among the dead; most lay in their uniforms: there
was a rest, a calm spread over their countenances, as if they
had, wearied of the conflict, lain down here for quiet, to
awaken strengthened and refreshed

How heavily and drearily the time passed. The sun shone
warmly, the trees and bushes stood fresh in the spring-time.
I felt as if it were an added grief that all should seem so
charming, — as if all things on earth were at peace. I could not
think of there being joy or any happy future. During this
grievous time, my play, " He is not well-born," which I had
written and brought out just before the beginning of the war,
was to be performed at the Royal Theatre. Now I had no
thought for it, nor any care to see it tried. The day when the
piece was to be given in the evening was indeed a great funeral day. Thirteen bodies of our fallen brave men were to
be buried: there were ten officers and three privates. From
the garrison church, dressed with flags and flowers, the coffins
were borne, garlanded with flowers. A great procession accompanied them, headed by the King and Landgrave. I
joined the ranks, but was so overcome that I was soon forced
to leave it and go into a friend's house. Thus cast down, I
was forced in the evening to go to the representation of my
piece. It was a felicitous affair, but I could not, as before, ask

our Lord for a good result; there was far weightier things to
ask of Him. The piece, meanwhile, was received with great
applause. The public's favorite, our distinguished actor,
Michael Wiehe, played the principal part with a truthfulness
and ardor that carried all with him. It was his last *rôle;*
some months after God called him away, and no one since has
ventured to assume this part, for he elevated it and gave it its
real character. The critics were well-disposed toward my work,
but I felt no real pleasure ; that had no home with me for the
moment, and I lost all hope of a happy future.

My neighbors, friends, and acquaintances were as dispirited
as I : every one was penetrated by the feeling : one common
ground we all had — love for our father-land. Daily, our youth
still marched away. Als was attacked : soon came one evil
telegram after another. France and England stood neutral.
Als was taken, gone ! gone ! I could not weep ; the worst had
come, the people fled from Middelfart. In Funen they awaited
the enemy. I lost, for the moment, my hold of God, and felt
myself as wretched as a man can be. Days followed in which
I cared for nobody, and I believed nobody cared for me. I
had no relief in speaking to any one. One, however, more
faithful and kind, came to me, Edward Collin's excellent wife,
who spake compassionate words and bade me give thought to
my work. Another older and steadfast friend, Madame Neergaard, took me to her pleasant home in the wooded Sölleröd,
by the shining, quiet lake. Kind eyes shone on me, popular
melodies sounded about us. She had a mother's love for me
as a poet and a man. The year after, when God called her, I
drew her picture in a few lines : —

> A Christian wert thou like apostles of old,
> Filled full with faith that flowered in actions right ;
> A very Dane at heart, thy soul took flight
> To Heaven's throne, where in thy meekness bold
> Thou bendest knee and prayest for Denmark there, —
> " O let her grow in right and wisdom fair."

Surely her first prayer in heaven would be, " Be gracious
and good to Denmark."

There was a merry gathering when I came there. The little
garden was illuminated by torches and variegated lights, a

most cheering greeting to the heartsick. It was indeed a pleasure to see the affectionate and lively company that gathered about her. It was here that I learned especially to know the gifted philosopher Rasmus Nielsen. Madame Neergaard bade me put my thoughts into some new production. My dear old friend, Professor Hartmann, likewise so urged me, and I wrote the words for a five act opera, " Saul."

It was my determination that when peace, which was now concluded, brought back comfortable times to Denmark, I would go to Norway, where I never yet had been ; see the roaring cataracts, the deep quiet lakes, the country where my mother tongue resounds with a metallic ring from the mountain : with us it is a waving speech, as if from the bending beech boughs. I wished to visit Munch and Björnstjerne Björnson. Affectionate letters, full of heartiness and trust, were sent to me during our heavy days of trial. With what friendliness Björnson estimated me, may be seen in a few lines which he wrote in his " Sigurd Slambe, " and sent me : —

> " Fancy thou gavest wings
> To fly over strange things and great ;
> But poesy gavest thou to my heart
> That knows things little and plain.

> " When my soul was heavy with child,
> Thou gavest me strength with growing thought ;
> And since my child has also grown,
> Thou feedest me with thinking too."

The peace did not have a very certain sound, and I did not go to Norway. God only knows whether I ever shall go.

Epiphany Eve I was at Madame Ingemann's house in Sorö. In the rooms all was the same save the empty chair ; but outside, how changed ! The castle gardener had certainly beautified the place exceedingly. The academy garden was thrown open, with plots outside the academy, but half of Ingemann's garden had to be taken away for it. This included the choicest part ; a little hill with great trees upon it had disappeared.

Madame Ingemann had the right to have nothing changed after her husband's death, but they asked her permission, and the good woman answered at once, Yes. " It is indeed a kind-

ness that I should be asked," said she, " a favor that I should
continue to live here." At my departure I received a great
bouquet, which came from Madame Ingemann, and from Sophie the maid, as well, who had added to it from flowers that
grew in the pots in her window. My year closed at Basnös,
the darkest, gloomiest year of my life.

1865.

New Year's Day opened with clear, still cold. Every one
at Basnös drove to church, but I had more need to stay alone.
In a churchly frame of mind I went into the garden, where
there was a peacefulness in nature, a sacred quiet. I felt no
anxiety for what the year should bring, nor yet any anticipation. This New Year's morning is the only one I know when
I did not with the Basnös' folk have a wish ready to ask. Like
a sombre night of terror, the past year lay behind me.

We were all invited to dinner at a neighboring place, the
Espes. I begged to be allowed to remain at home, and then
suddenly in my solitude there came a rush of thoughts which
developed into a dramatic poem, " The Spaniards were here,"—
a romantic play in three acts." I could, when the others returned late in the evening, have related the movement of the
action, scene by scene. My thoughts had again got their elas-
ticity : I was absorbed in my intellectual labor, and my soul was
lighter. The first act of my new play was produced at Basnös,
the other two afterward in Copenhagen. I had given myself
the problem that the chief character, the Spaniard, should not
appear in person at all. I would not let him talk Danish like
the others in the piece. One heard his Spanish song behind
the scenes, and heard the shaking of the castanets ; his whole
personality, meanwhile, was to stand out clear, fine, and noble,
without his being visible : we were to accompany him in his
love, his flight, and peril, confident that a year and a day would
bring the hour of meeting his fortune and love.

The piece was undertaken at the Royal Theatre, where the
then manager, State Councilor Kranold, interested himself especially for its success. My friend, Professor Hoedt, who had
great influence in the theatre, showed a like sympathy. When
the evening of the representation came there was quite a full

house. Their majesties, the King and Queen, were present at the performance, but from the first moment there rested an inexplicable heaviness on the spectators, so that I had a feeling as if I were at some funeral gathering. The talented young actress, Miss Lange, who took the part of the romantic young mistress, was, contrary to all custom, very strongly censured. Madame Södring, the public's special favorite, had made out of the court lady *Dame Hagenau* a character rather strongly marked, but not upon the first representation ; only afterward was she fully estimated, and this *rôle* is now named as amongst her most notable ones. Jastrau sang the Spanish ballads remarkably well ; but he also, whose singing usually met with enthusiastic applause, got none of that now. At the fall of the curtain, clapping and hissing were mingled.

At the second representation, and always afterward, undivided applause attended it. The actors deserved all praise, and especially, Madame Södring. The public is sometimes like wet kindling-wood that will not catch fire. The fault can lie in the dramatic work, too. It is difficult to pronounce an opinion when one's self is a part of the case, but it has been my experience that several of my compositions have suffered their severest condemnation at the first representation.

For more than a year and a day had I written no wonder story, my soul was so burdened ; but now, as soon as I came out into the country to friendly Basnös, to the fresh woods by the open sea, I wrote " The Will-o'-the-Wisp is in the town," in which was told why it was that the wonder stories had been so long unwritten : because without was war, and within sorrow and want that war brought with it. The scene was laid at Basnös. Every one who has been here will remember the great alleys, the old grave-stone which once lay in Skjelskjör over a councilor and his six wives. A new story still came forth, the week after, here at pretty wooded Frijsenborg. Since my former visit the enemy had been here, but now there was again rest and happiness : the entire castle, the new wing and the old part, was occupied. In the princely apartments, in the blooming garden, with kind hearted people in the midst of all the happiness which well doing and well wishing can offer one, several weeks flew by, and I wrote the Wonder Story " Gold Treasure," as well also as " In the Nursery."

My summer journeying closed in Zealand with friends at Christinelund, where I wrote the story, " The Storm shakes the Sign-boards : " the ink was not dry on the paper when I read it to the family, and just as I closed the reading, there came a violent blast : the trees bent, the leaves were sent scattering ; it was as if Nature in this wild storm were playing a fantasia on my new story. When, a few days afterward, I left Christinelund, there lay still by the road-side great trees which had been torn up by their roots. It was a storm that might well shake the sign-boards. The poet is just ahead of his time, they say ; I was certainly here just ahead of the storm.

I was soon in Copenhagen, in my little room, among my pictures, books, and flowers. The owner of the house was an excellent, practical, and cultivated woman, with whom I had now lived eighteen years, and from whom I had never thought of going away ; but I was nearer that than I supposed. I had just at this time received a letter from my Portuguese friend, the Danish Consul at Lisbon, George O'Neill, who with his brother, when they were both children, was brought up in Denmark in Admiral Wulff's house, where I was a daily visitor. George O'Neill and I had lately been corresponding ; he invited me to visit him, see his beautiful country, stay with him and his brother, and enjoy myself as well as they could make me. I felt a desire to make the visit, a longing to meet the friends of my youth again, but the recollection of the discomforts I had experienced in my journey to Spain made me reluctant. One morning, however, my excellent landlady came in quite cast down, and said that we must separate, and that in a month's time. Her son had become a student, and she had promised him that if he passed a good examination he should have a better apartment than formerly ; she had moreover given a promise to take in a young boarder, and needed thus my chamber. It was very disagreeable to me. I had spent eighteen changing years with these friendly people : I was a neighbor here, also, to my friend the composer Hartmann, whom I daily visited. All this was now to be changed. I took it as an indication from God that I should take the journey to Portugal, and it settled the matter. Meanwhile it was reported in the papers that the cholera was in Spain, and had broken

out in Portugal. I wrote a letter to George O'Neill about it.
His kind answer was that he would not urge me to come, but
would be exceedingly happy if I decided thus myself, and that
I was to stay just as long as I liked.   The cholera was spread-
ing in Spain, but only a single case had shown itself in Portugal.   I decided to take the journey, but not to go south at once.
I wished to delay and to go to Stockholm, where I had not
been for a long time, and where my dear friends, the authoress Fredrika Bremer and the writer Baron Beskow, lived.   It
was in the charming after-part of summer that I set out.

The first time that I visited Stockholm I made my journey
by diligence, and was a whole week about it.   Now Sweden
had the railway: at two o'clock in the afternoon the train
started from Malmö, and in the evening one is at Jönköping,
where there is a good hotel, and as well managed as if it
were in Switzerland: the next morning one takes his place
in a carriage, and is at Stockholm in the afternoon.   How
changed! what a flight!   Our children and children's children
live in the time of conveniences.   We old folks have had the
line of trouble midway between the two generations : we stand,
so to speak, with one leg in one generation and one in the
other, but that is very interesting.

Beskow was out in the country when I got there, as also
Miss Bremer, but both were expected shortly ; meanwhile
I wished to go to Upsala.   I did not go alone ; a kind Danish family, Henriques, whom I had lately learned to know and
to feel myself at home with, were in Stockholm, and they
accompanied me to Upsala.   Here I again saw my friend
Bötticher, who married Tegnér's daughter Disa, author of many
sweet songs, which, set to Lindblad's music, had been carried
by Jenny Lind out into Europe's world of song.   I met again
Count Hamilton and his amiable wife, the poet Gejer's daughter.   He was now Chief Proprietor, and lived in the romantically placed old castle.   I also saw again the composer Josephsön, who was Jenny Lind's godson, when he was christened.
His songs sound as melodious as the lay of the thrush in the
northern birch woods.   I went to see him.   He lived in the
house of Linnæus, Sweden's world-renowned botanist of former
days.   I passed a charming musical evening with Josephsön,

and the most cordial welcome was given to the gifted musician, Madame Henriques, from Copenhagen. In the evening we returned to our hotel. The Henriques had their room near mine, and I had already lain down, when I heard a noise in the street — a charming song, a serenade. Was it for me? — I knew the good-will my young Swedish friends bore me — or was it given to Madame Henriques? I sprang out of bed, went to the window, and sat behind the curtain. The singers turned their faces all toward my neighbors' windows. So doubtless Madame Henriques got it! I received from the students at Upsala an invitation to a festival to be given in the summer hall, which was adorned with flags, especially the Danish one. The Chief Proprietor and several of the older members of the University took part in it. The author Björck, son of the Bishop of Götheborg, a true poet of great genius — God has since called him to Himself — greeted me with a pretty poem that did me too much honor.

The song was sung; the conversation was very lively and hearty. I read three of my Wonder Stories, — " The Butterfly," " The Fir-tree," and " The Ugly Duckling," and received loud applause, and then was escorted amidst singing by the students to my home. The stars shone, the new moon was glimmering, it was a lovely, quiet evening, and up in the north the horizon was flaming with Northern Lights. When the next day I came to Stockholm, I found in the hotel an invitation to visit the King at his pleasure castle, Ulriksdal, which is situated a few miles from Stockholm, in the midst of woods and rocks, on a bay running in from the salt sea. After a lowering sky, the rain poured down and there was a great storm, so that I was obliged to get to the castle immediately, without seeing anything of the picturesque environs. As I sat a moment alone in the fine large hall, a gentleman stepped in, reached out his hand to me, and gave me a hearty welcome. I pressed his hand in return, but while I talked it came out that it was the King himself. For a moment I had not known him. He took me himself about the castle, and before sitting at table presented me to the Queen, who in her appearance reminded me of the noble — now dead — Grand Duchess of Weimar, whose relation she was. The young and not yet confirmed Crown Princess Louise shook hands with me in a friendly way and thanked me for the pleasure she had had in reading my stories. She made a very pleasant impression upon me by her naturalness, her trustworthiness, and child-like affection. She is now the Danish Crown Prince Frederick's betrothed, and soon will be our Crown Princess. God bless the young couple. A lively conversation was carried on at the table. The King and Queen and all about were cordial and kindly disposed toward me. When coffee was brought in, the King took me to his smoking room and presented me with the latest books of his own writers. It was a charming day, one full of happiness, that spent with my royal patron.

A few days after I was called to an audience and dinner at the Queen Dowager's at Drotningholm, where also Prince Oscar with his family lived. I went out there by steamer, and was surprised at the splendid castle with its garden! I was reminded of the villa Albano at Rome, but Drotningholm has more beauty; it lies on an arm of Lake Malar. I had not seen her majesty since her husband King Oscar died. How much had there not passed in the world between that time and this. She seemed to me just as before, lively and kind. We talked for a long time together, when she was simple and gracious, open and cordial. Before dinner one of the gentlemen of the house took me around the garden; there was something very bright and sunny about all of Drotningholm. When her majesty said good-by after dinner, she added, — " You came by the steamboat, but that is gone; but here is a carriage at your service whenever you yourself wish to order it." She gave me in charge to one of the chamberlains, who was to show me the halls of the castle. As we began our walk Prince Oscar came up, and showed me the historic and artistic treasures, and took me into his private garden, where he showed me his children and a little oak also. He told me that he was betrothed to his wife on the Rhine, and that when they went there a year after, an acorn then planted had grown into a two-leaved tree, which they took up and transplanted in a little flower pot and set out here in the garden; it was now higher than I. When I was taking a leaf from the nearest tree as a souvenir of my visit at Drotningholm, the Prince

gave me a branch from this tree. Lake Malar was before
the castle, and quite hanging over the water was a great
willow-tree. It was when Drotningholm was put in order,
in the- time of Charles XII.'s mother, and the quay was
built, that many trees and bushes were taken away. Popular
belief said then that this tree lived and put forth its leaves
with the kingly race. When King John lay sick the tree withered and came near dying, the old kingly race was near dying
out ; but when King John's grandson, Sweden's present king,
was born, the old willow grew green again. It was almost
dark night when I left hospitable Drotningholm ; as I stepped
into the carriage, the composer Wennerberg, came up, Sweden's Bell man of our time, both in music and words. We
pressed one another's hands and separated with the warm
feeling which is natural to Sweden's skalds and thier youthfulness.

The next evening, when in Stockholm, I visited the River
Garden, which the little island under the bridge is called which
joins the castle holm to the north holm, where there is a café,
and in the evening an illumination and music. I was in company with a number of young and old authors and artists ; the
highly gifted and very genial dramatic writer Blancha came
in ; he was greeted with great delight and brought to me.
"Art thou there, brother?" he cried with a bright face, and
embraced and kissed me. I mention it, because while I was
surprised at the feast which gave me so much pleasure, I knew
that we never had drunken *Thous* to each other.

In Sweden it is so common that I can well understand that
when young or old men with mutual interests in intellectual
matters come together, all titles are thrown away, and they
express themselves naturally with the confidential *thou ;* so
that after a time of festivity or lively meeting one easily, when
years have gone by and he sees me again, is sure that we
know one another, are friends, and even that we have most
certainly drunk *thou* to each other. This the vivacious
Blancha now believed, and I held my peace and answered
with a *thou*, and clinked glasses with my Thou brother. That
will never again occur, for he also belongs to the great ones
who have left us. In 1868, at a festival, when Charles XII.'s

monument was to be dedicated, Blancha suddenly fell dead in
the street.

Miss Bremer was in the country at her estate Årsta. As
soon as she heard of my coming she invited me there for a
long visit, but when this could not be managed on my part
she came to Stockholm. I had not seen her or talked with
her since she with our American friends, Marcus Spring and
his wife, visited Denmark. So much meanwhile had happened! We talked about the Springs, and about Henriette
Wulff's death in the burning ship on her voyage to America :
we talked of Denmark's sorrowful days of trial. The tears
fell down the cheeks of the noble, compassionate woman.
We talked of Jenny Lind, of much that was now gone by.

" I am always a steadfast friend, Andersen," said she, and
her delicate hand grasped mine. It was the last time for this
life : with Christmas came the sorrowful tidings, — Fredrika
Bremer is dead. She had taken cold in church, had come
home, and passed quietly into the sleep of death. Another
of my faithful friends was lost to me for this world. In her
letters I have a treasure and a memory.

The writer Baron Beskow had come to town, and had for
my gratification invited a select company, whom I was to
meet. I have his letter that gives the programme : —

" TUESDAY, *October* 3, 1865.

" DEAR FRIEND, — I went to see you yesterday, to name
those who are to come to our little dinner party to-morrow,
namely, the Librarian of the Royal Library, Rydquist (our
Jacob Grimm), the Antiquary Hildebrandt (our Thomsen),
the keeper of the archives Bovwalius (our Wegener), the
Skald (talis qualis) Strandberg (the translator of Byron), C. G.
Strandberg (the translator of Anacreon), Tander, who is personally known to you, and Dahlgren (who is the author of a
national drama, which has been given one hundred and thirty
times ; the translator, also, of Calderon, etc.). You see the
guests are not many but they are select. You will be welcome to-morrow at four o'clock, by your old friend,

" BESKOW."

It was a cozy party, with a spirit of intellectual freedom and heartiness about it.

It was twenty-five years since I had been in Sweden's university town of Lund. In 1840 I received here the first public reception that was ever given me ; the students came with music and speeches. I have told about it in " The Story of my Life," and have said how overcome I was at this expression of regard. It seemed to me then as if I dared not come here again in years to come — that such a feast could never again be given me. Five-and-twenty years had gone by since that. I should meet a whole new generation. The journey home carried me close by ; I wanted to spend a day or two in the town so friendly to my youth, to visit the old church, see the new college building which I had never seen. Some friends in Upsala had given me letters to a few of the Professors in the University, when I said that I was now a stranger in Lund.

The long journey by rail was still a play of color in the woods ; the yellow birch, the dark-green pines, and vermilion thorns, wooden houses with black roofs and white chimneys, the stony soil, the bold cliffs, and the great full sea were constantly appearing in turn. I reached Lund in the evening ; I knew nobody, and believed that nobody knew me. I sought the hotel and went early in the evening to bed, weary from my journey. Soon I heard singing ; some students were having a supper at the hotel in honor of some who were leaving. The singing sounded sweetly, and soon it sounded just outside my door. The young friends knew I was here, but when they heard that I had lain down to rest they went back again.

I was commended to Professor Ölde, and Linngreen gave me also a pleasant dinner with an intellectual company ; during the dinner there came an invitation from the students, who had hastily decorated a hall to give a feast to me, with a youthful enthusiasm such as their fellows at Upsala had also shown toward me.

At seven o'clock in the evening Professor Linngreen took me there. The hall was splendidly decorated. The walls were dressed with the arms of the provinces, and over each waved a Swedish and a Danish flag ; at the stand also was planted the flag which the ladies of Copenhagen had worked for the

students of Lund. The hall and apartments were filled with
the old and young members of the University ; after the eating came the speech-making, and I was welcomed from the
stand by the spokesman of the students. I have kept the
memory of what was said, but not the very words in which it
was said : " Five-and twenty years ago the students of Lund
gave me a welcome and greeting. The current was still the
same, but it was another generation ; exactly a generation had
grown up under my writings, which had been to them spiritual
sustenance, for which they owed me thanks and love."

Singing followed, and a young poet, Wendel, read a pretty
poem to me, and I expressed my gratitude by reading three of
my Wonder Stories, — " The Butterfly," " The Happy Family,"
and " It is certainly so."   Each one was received with shouts
of applause, and now there followed in quick succession Danish and Swedish songs, which were so familiar, so full of young-
hearted warmth, that it was again an evening of fortune which
shines in my memory. The whole gathering followed me to the
hotel where I was staying, arm in arm ; the procession marched
out to the sound of singing from the college building past
the old church ; we stopped for a moment by Tegnér's monument, and then moved on with song through the quiet streets
emptied of townsfolk. When I stood at my door they gave
me nine cheers. Moved to deep gladness, I expressed my
thanks, and reached my little chamber, humble and yet lifted
up in heart, when there sounded still from the street a song
which was the very melody that five-and-twenty years before
had been sung at my festival in Lund in 1841. God grant
every one of these young friends that gladness of life which I
felt this evening.

As soon as I came to Copenhagen I went into a hotel, for I
was still a traveller and about to go to Portugal ; but the route
thither by sea from France was not attractive in the stormy
autumn ; in Spain it was unquiet. The paper spoke of Prim's
troops that were in movement on the border near Badajos, — the
very route I should have to take if I went by land. I decided
to wait here at home some time and see how things turned out.

The pleasantest picture which my memory holds of this
time is a short and charming visit at Fredensborg. The King

was so gracious as to receive me. Two apartments in the castle were given me, and I found, as always, the most cordial, if I dare use the expression, most friendly reception. The King's family wished to hear me read my last written stories. I have seen all the King's children grow up, and always from their childhood they have given me the hands of friends. To know this family is to be drawn to them, — it is such a charming household, full of affection and a temperate life. The Queen has great good sense, and an inborn talent for painting and music ; of the King's noble heart and amiable character one sees many beautiful traits. All the King's children have heard me read my Wonder Stories, — the Crown Prince Frederick and his brother, now King of Greece, the princesses Alexandra and Dagmar. Now there sat here the two youngest children, Princess Thyra and little Valdemar, who had this evening got a promise that he should stay up half an hour longer so that he could hear a part of the reading.

The next day I made a few pleasant calls. Off in the garden of the castle, in one of the buildings, lived my friend, the poet Paludan-Müller, of whom I have previously spoken. He is master of the Danish tongue, as Byron and Rückert were masters of their mother tongues, so that he made music of it. Every one of his poems discovers a profoundly poetic soul. " Adam Hama," " The Marriage of the Dryad," " The Death of Abel," will always be read and admired. As a man Paludan-Möller has something so naïve, frank, and good that one immediately feels drawn toward him.

Still another happy house I was to visit in Fredensborg was that of my friend the rare artist and ballet-writer August Bournonville, who has raised his kind of art on the Danish stage, so that it occupies a worthy place among the best of all arts. In Paris they have more distinguished dancers than we, more decorations and extraordinary arrangements intermingled with the dancing, but such richness in truly poetic ballet composition as Bournonville has given, only Copenhagen possesses ; there is a beauty, a noble purity, something very refined and characteristic in the great circle of ballets which he has given us. It would be a complete repertoire if we were to mention all that one or another has

pronounced excellent, but most will certainly agree in naming
" Napoli," " Kermesson in Bruges," " The Conservatory," and
" A Folk Story." Bournonville can perhaps rightly blame us
if we do not also here mention a couple of his historic ballets,
" Waldemar," with popular and beautiful music by Frölich, and
" Valkyrien," which has the grand music so full of melodies,
by J. P. E. Hartmann.

Bournonville, who is the creator and manager of the ballet
of our day on the Danish stage, has at the same time a father's
interest in all those who take part in his works. He is of a
warm, affectionate nature, and a good comrade. When one enters his homelike house he finds it full of sunshine, and sees
his pretty lively wife and well-behaved children.

I saw the familiar home life in the King's castle; I saw it
also in two smaller homes, equally full of sunshine, those of
my friends Paludan-Müller and Bournonville. To the latter I
had just now dedicated my latest Wonder Stories which I read
to the King's family. Bournonville took me to his arms and
expressed his hearty thanks, just as he had often encouraged
me by word and by writing, giving me confidence and lifting
my soul when one and another called friends had made me
discontented.

At Copenhagen I was as restless as a traveller who cannot
reach his destination. The cholera was in Paris, and how that
would affect my health and peace in Spain I could not get informed, but I hoped to learn it immediately after the new year.
Circumstances must determine my journey, and show how far
south I should go. Christmas and the first days of the new
year I spent at Holsteinborg and Basnös. There I received a
letter filled with the perfume of violets. George O'Neill sent
these as greetings from the spring which awaited me at Lisbon.

1866.

At Amsterdam I have two prosperous and excellent fellow-
countrymen, the brothers Brandt; I received from both of
them a cordial letter, with an invitation to stay during my entire visit with the elder of the brothers, who is gifted, as I
came to know, with one of the noblest, most thoughtful women

of Holland for a wife. Only once before had I been in Holland, in the year 1847, when I first visited England. I then met at the Hague so much good-will and attention that I received a constant feast of good things, of which I have before spoken.

The first of the friends who then came to see me was now dead, the publisher of " De Tijd," Van der Vliet, but I remembered the names of dear friends who looked for my coming ; such were the old, highly honored writer, Van Lennep, the distinguished composer Verhulst, the author Kneppelhout, and the remarkable tragic actor Peters. Now I could for a longer time be with these, and see what especially belongs to Amsterdam, and enjoy the pleasures of family life there.

The last of January I left Copenhagen by the evening train. It was winter time ; the water was open, but it was cold. I was, it seemed to me, well provided with travelling luggage. It seemed to one of my friends, however, that this was not the case, for he came in the morning and left a whole lot of well lined travelling boots spread out on the floor ; the largest and best pair was to be his good-by souvenir. I mention this little incident, and could in my life name numberless others of like character, the acts of individual friends. The words of sympathy and willingness to serve me which he expressed so earnestly showed me clearly what a friend I had, and how large a place I was made to have in his noble home circle. I shall hereafter come to speak of this home, when at the close of these pages I speak of the week-day and Sunday homes which I have, so to speak, in my father-land.

From Korsör by Funen through the Grand Duchy we went in rapid journey. At Haderslev I saw the Prussian soldiery. I felt in an unhappy mood and depressed. I occupied the coupé with a young Prussian officer and his still younger wife, obliging people. I did not know them, nor they me. Later in the evening, at Altona station, while I stepped out of the carriage, there came an older man with a little girl, who looked at me and said in German to the child, " Give your hand to that man. It is Andersen, who has written the pretty stories." He smiled at me, the child reached out her hand, and I patted her cheek. This little incident put me in good humor, and soon I was in my old home in Hamburg, the Hôtel de l'Europe.

The next day I drew near Celle, where I had only been in 1831, on my first journey. I wished to visit the unhappy Queen Mathilde's grave, and the castle where she spent the last years of her life. In the " French Garden " there is shown a monument of her made of a block of marble ; there was a wooden penthouse over it to keep off the winter snow ; it looked like a barrack.

In one of the apartments of the castle there hung a large portrait of Queen Mathilde, very different from the earlier one I had seen in Denmark. The picture I saw was beautiful, and the expression reminded me of Frederick VI.

I left Hanover by the Westphalian Gate, and came by rail to Rheine, approaching the Holland border. It was late evening and a storm raged. Nearly all the lamps in the carriage had gone out, and it was black night within and without. I thought to myself, if this turns out well it is a good thing. We whizzed away as if driven by the storm, and when we drew near the station at Rheine, it seemed as if here also all the lights had been blown out. A man stumbled ahead with a lantern : that was to light us while we crossed the iron rails and eyed the procession that was in motion behind and before us. I came to the hotel which was pointed out ; it did not look very inviting outside, and proved very frugal, with low-studded rooms, slow attendance, with black and sour bread. I felt as if I had gone back thirty years, and was travelling in a little town. Many call that the time of romance ! I prefer the time of modern conveniences — our time.

The next day I entered Holland ; the carriage contained also a gentleman wearing decorations, a Hollander. In the course of conversation he heard that I was from Denmark. " You will meet with a distinguished countryman of yours in Amsterdam," said he ; " Andersen is there." I doubted that, and said that I was Andersen.

At the station in Amsterdam the brothers Brandt met me, and took me to my new home with the oldest of the brothers. It was a large, fine house, with garden and trees, outside by the canal called Heerengraacht, in the prettiest part of the town.

I was received as an old friend by people whom I saw for the first time. The mother and sons in the house spoke excellent Danish ; they both made a good impression upon me. The master of the house himself was full of animation and attention to my wants. I had at once the delightful sense of being blessed with good friends. Here, as in England and Scotland, there is a pleasing patriarchal custom with household and servants, of having a religious season morning and evening. The whole household is gathered for the reading of the Bible, which is followed by a psalm that gave a restful feeling to my soul. There was much sociability here. The evenings passed with music, song, and reading. Many more than I had supposed spoke Danish. I read nearly every evening a few of my Wonder Stories and Tales ; if the company was large, they were given in French, English, or German translation. The elder Mr. Brandt was quite good at giving on the spot a Dutch translation of the Danish book which he had before him.

Soon after my arrival I received an invitation from the management of the Stadt Theatre, three of the most eminent actors, among whom was the distinguished tragedian, Mr. Peters, to occupy any place which I might prefer during my entire visit. I had individual friends in Amsterdam of long standing whom I must visit. The town itself I became more familiar with than before. This time it was no flying visit which I made, but a stay of several weeks.

Amsterdam is not Holland's capital, but its chief city, the most extensive and active town in the country, — a very Venice of the North. The town is built upon piles in mud and water. The learned Erasmus characterized it when he said, " I have come to a city whose inhabitants live like crows on tops of trees." Many an overflowing grain depot has given way when the foundation was not strong enough to sustain it ; many a house pitched uneasily toward the street, only held in place by its stronger neighboring dwellings. There is a net-work of canals, as in Venice ; but they are made wider, and have streets on both sides, where wagons rumble, — a thing which Venice does not know. The principal street of the town, Kalver Straat, stretches small and crooked from the Amstel up to the square where the Town Hall stands, on ground resting on piles, and where the Exchange, with its rows of Grecian pillars, is the noticeable point of the town. What always shocked my eye in Amsterdam was the striking costume worn by the children in the Orphan House; perhaps the disagreeableness for me lay in the fact that one only sees a similar dress on our criminals in Denmark, who work in servitude, — the one side of their clothes being gray, the other brown. In Amsterdam the poor orphans go about, girls and boys, with one side red, the other black. The boys' jackets and trousers, and also the girls' waists and skirts, are two sorts, black and red.

I visited a few of the schools for the poor, and heard the singing of the children. I saw the Jews' quarter, the Art Gallery and Museum, and what was especially new and wonderful to me, the Zoölogical Gardens — that was the most interesting of any I know. In summer there is music here: now one could only hear the fearful beasts' howl; the shrieking parrots and cockatoos made their noises; a little blackbird had learned to say a few Dutch words, which it repeated incessantly. There was a grand collection here of wolves, bears, tigers, and hyenas; the kingly lion and the clumsy elephant. The llamas cast their spittle at us; the eagle looked with its human, wise — much too wise — glance at us; what splendid dress of feathers he wore! In such a collection of feathered fowls one learns to despise what the dyer's art can do. Black swans swam in the basins; seals came out and sunned themselves; but the most interesting, because most novel to me, were the hippopotamuses, male and female, in their deep water ponds. They raised their ugly heads several times above the water, and displayed their great mouths with big teeth far apart. Their skin reminded me of hogs' skin without the bristles. There had just been born a young one. The keeper had to watch night and day for the coming of the little creature to secure it before it should be killed by the male. The young fellow had his own house provided like his parents. He ducked under the water when I entered. The keeper knew how to poke him out; he was as big as a fattened calf, had dusky eyes, and a reddish yellow hide that looked like a fish skin minus its scales. His future was already provided for, for he had been sold to the Zoölogical Garden at Cologne.

The days flew by all too rapidly in Amsterdam ; there was so much to see, so many acquaintances to visit. The three oldest ones I had, dating from my first stay here, were the honored old writer Van Lennep, the composer Verhulst, and the actor Peters. My dear friend Van Lennep was an old man, with silver white hair like Thorwaldsen. He spoke jestingly of the likeness of his face to Voltaire, and said it was more wrinkled and satiric now. He said that he was at work upon the since completed romance, "The Seven Stars." A few of his best known dramatic works have recently been put upon the stage, and he promised that during my stay here I should see acted his tragedy, " De Vrouwe van Wardenburg."

The composer Verhulst, whom I next visited, met me with rejoicing. His first question was about our common friend Niels Gade, who of all contemporary composers he placed the highest. He showed me how thoroughly he studied his compositions ; he showed me these, and among them the " Hamlet Overture," which the week before I came had been given at the Amsterdam Musical Union, where Verhulst was director. He mourned that Holland, unlike Denmark, had no national opera. In the following week there was again to be given a grand concert, and he promised that, notwithstanding there had been given at the two last concerts pieces by Gade, namely the " Hamlet Overture " and " In the Highlands," I should still hear some of Gade's works.

The evening came. I was present at the concert, when was given one of Gade's symphonies, and this was especially applauded, and people looked at me as much as to say, — " Carry our enthusiasm to your gifted countryman." There was an elegantly dressed audience ; but it was unpleasant to me not to see a face of the people, whose men in our time are those who have given us the most remarkable musical works, the people who gave us Mendelssohn, Halévy, and Meyerbeer. I did not see a single Jew, and mentioned my surprise, and it was still greater when I heard — would I had misunderstood my ears! — that they were not admitted here. On several occasions I received the impression that there is a strong division here between men in social, religious, and artistic relations.

In Denmark one meets on the stage the most remarkable artists, men and women, moving in the best circles, but not here in Amsterdam. I spoke of this, and named a person whom I wished to meet, and was answered that here it was contrary to custom and usage ; but it is not good custom and usage. In Denmark, God be praised, we do not know such distinctions. At the King's palace on reception evenings, when the most eminent are invited, the famous actors are not excepted.

The Stadt Theatre at Amsterdam, which I visited frequently, gave nearly every evening a representation in Dutch ; but once a week there came from the Royal Theatre at the Hague the French opera and ballet; Meyerbeer's "L'Africaine" was given, and the ballet "Biche en Bois." The opera had good vigor, beautiful voices, and was well received ; the ballet was, in respect to composition and beauty, far below what the Danish stage has. I saw a few tragedies, such as Schiller's "Maid of Orleans" ; the principal *rôle* was taken finely and with understanding by the first actress on the stage, Miss Kleine Gartmann ; and of still greater interest to me was her rendering of "De Vrouwe van Wardenburg." The piece is a dramatic poem in three acts. First one sees her as the strong, passionate woman, who herself leads the defense when her town is stormed ; later she comes forward as an older wife ; and finally she is the aged matron in a time when all the former relations and opinions are entirely changed, when her daughter's son is a Protestant and leads to the altar the daughter of a workman. She awaits the bridal party in the knightly hall, where they are to receive her blessing ; her hand rests upon her grandson's head, but when she is to lay it upon the head of the bride, born in poverty and meanness, her last strength leaves her and she drops dead. It is a strong and absorbing picture from historic times. With my friends' (the Brandts) explanation I understood the whole movement, and was especially taken with Miss Kleine Gartmann's masterly acting. I heard later that it was a copy of Ristori's representation of *Elizabeth*, which I have not seen ; but it was certainly well done and a piece of genuine acting which was exhibited in "De Vrouwe van Wardenburg." I saw the piece a few times ; it is certainly a remarkable production upon the Holland stage, but if it were to be given in a strange country I have my doubts about it. Here it was given well mounted and with great refinement. Between the acts, however, there was something out of place. The orchestra played modern dance music : I was for my part zealous for Verhulst and Petters. The gallery on the occasion was filled with a noisy, restless people, who shouted at the music and whistled an accompaniment. It was a poor custom too, I thought, that in the evening the spectators drank their tea and lager in the parquet ; but every country has its own customs.

On my former visit to Holland I did not see Ten Kate, who is perhaps the most eminent writer of the country, but now we were to meet and become friends. His-son-in-law, the merchant Van Hengel, had a few years before with his young wife been in Denmark ; they visited me there, and brought a greeting from the poet. Now he gave this for himself at the table of his son-in-law. There was met here a large company, and most of them understood Danish. Ten Kate proposed my health, and then that of my father-land, Denmark, which should live and blossom forth after all its heavy trials. He spoke warm words, that were uttered with such fervor as to bring tears to my eyes. I proposed Ten Kate's health and then Holland's, and finally read in Danish two of my stories, " The Most Charming Rose of the World " and " The Butterfly," which had been faithfully and poetically rendered, and included in my collected works.

He improvised a poem in Dutch to me, which I answered in the same way in Danish. It was most hearty and lively, and the little snug room was certainly one of gayety. The table was decorated with a large confection representing Fortune. She held the Danish flag, on which my name was inscribed, and Holland's flag with the name Ten Kate : I have still as a souvenir this flag. Ten Kate keeps the Danish one. The entire piece was quite covered over with small storks, my favorite bird, and, I believe, the arms of the Hague.

Our Danish Consul, Völdsen, gave a similar dinner, where I was the honored guest, and where Ten Kate gave me a delightful and charmingly expressed welcome from the children of Holland. He read also his versified translation of my story, "The Angel." I was obliged then to tell *vivâ voce* in Danish the story of "The Swineherd."

One evening in my home with the Brandt family, there was a large and select company, when I heard for the first time the old white-haired poet Van Lennep recite with great youthfulness and dramatic action a long poem of Van Bilderdijk, Holland's old and honored poet.

Five weeks had I spent in this hospitable and happy home, and now came the day of departure. The brothers Brandt accompanied me to the station, but I was not going farther than to Leyden, where good friends awaited me. The sun shone warmly, a thin sheet of snow still lay on the earth; but at the last station the snow had melted, and from this time we entered spring, for there was no more snow or cold.

At the railway station in Leyden I was met by my friend the poet Van Kneppelhout, and taken by him to his pretty house, where I was to stay a few days. His excellent wife called us to dinner, and here I found gathered a large part of the professors of Leyden University, with their wives. We talked in French, English, and Danish. A large printed story by Van Kneppelhout, "The Swallows and Leeches," was given to the guests in remembrance of this dinner. I met again my old friend, the well known Professor Schlegel, and learned to know the celebrated astronomer Keiser, visited his great observatory, and would have seen the sun spots, but the clouds would not give me a chance.

In an open carriage, one beautiful sunny day, I drove with Van Kneppelhout and his wife out to the dunes, where a new immense sluice-way conducts the Rhine to the sea; and thus the Rhine does not, as my geography taught me when I was at school, "lose itself in the sand." The way led through picturesque villages; in the grounds were long beds filled with crocuses, hyacinths, and tulips.

We got out of the carriage in front of the sand dunes and climbed over the wet sand, where the sun, as long as we were on the lee side, burned with hot rays. The sea lay stretched out before us; only a solitary ship was to be seen. We went to the sluices where the Rhine is conducted into the North Sea; it is a cyclopean work built in our day. The wind blew icily cold, and sent the flying sand into our eyes: it was late in the afternoon before we returned to our home in Leyden.

Meeting and separating, however happy one may be, or however much he may enjoy himself, is the beating of the pulse in travel. At the Hague, whither my route now lay, I should in a few days only see again my excellent host and hostess, and meet with friends and acquaintances. I had there our Danish Ambassador, Baron Bille-Bröhe, whom I had known from his student days ; and there too was Fredrika Bremer's relation, my friend Baron Wrede, the Swedish Ambassador.

In the carriage which took me the short distance to the Hague, I sat with a young couple, who asked if I was not the Danish writer Andersen. They thought they knew me from the portrait they had seen in Amsterdam. At the hotel Oude Doelen, where I had stayed before, I received a cordial shaking of hands.

How delightful it is, a real blessing from God, to be out in the world, to sit down in a great city all unknown, an entire stranger, and yet know with certainty that only meet there with some misfortune and one suddenly discovers that he has friends, real and true. I soon felt myself quite at home at the Hague. I saw here, at a great dinner given by Van Brienen, all the distinguished world, learned to know many excellent people, and went away again south by Rotterdam to Antwerp.

The fire burned in the chimney-place, the sun shone into the cozy room. One of my first visits was to the celebrated painter Keiser, the director of the Academy. He lives at the Musæum, where I found him in his study, and was received as if I were an old acquaintance. He showed me the colossal work which was occupying him at the time, and can be finished only after several years' labor, — a painting which is to cover the walls in a great hall of the Musæum, — a representation of all the history of Flemish art. There are more than a hundred portraits in full length, to say nothing of lesser allegorical pictures, as of Philosophy, Poetry, History, marked by busts of Plato, Homer, and Herodotus.

The good man himself took me about the Musæum, which

is rich in the best paintings of Rubens, Van Dyck and others. In Antwerp also had I a hospitable Danish home with my countryman the merchant Good and his wife. I saw with him a large part of the city, the fine churches and monuments. What especially interested me in this place was an artistic memorial; it was not the statues of Rubens and Van Dyck, only a tablet sunk in the wall at the entrance of the cathedral — the likeness of Quentin Matsys, who died in 1529. The inscription tells how " in Sijnen Tijd grossmidt en daernais Tamens schilder." Therein lies a whole romance. Out of his love for a painter's beautiful daughter, he threw aside his anvil and hammer and took up brush and pallet. Love inspired him and carried him on, and as a painter of repute he gained his young bride. One of his greatest pictures has a place in the Musæum, and on the tablet stands in Latin, " Love made the smith into an Apelles."

I passed through Brussels to Paris. Our Danish Crown Prince Frederick was here, staying at the Hôtel Bristol, on the Place Vendôme. He spoke graciously with all. One heard his praises everywhere. He received me with his wonted kindness, and on the first Sunday afterward I spent a delightful day in his company. He invited me to accompany him to the races at Vincennes. At one o'clock we set out in three carriages, every one with four horses and out-riders. Our route lay by the Boulevards, and we passed all the other carriages. People stood and gazed with all attention at the Crown Prince : " Cést lui ! cést lui ! " they cried. Arrived at the place, the Prince was received by one of the town officials, who took him to the imperial tribune, while the rest of us followed on. There was a great apartment there with fire burning in the grate, soft chairs and sofas : shortly after a son of Murat came in, an elderly man, and his son followed after ; they were the only ones here of the emperor's family. Below a great crowd was singing ; all eyes were turned toward the imperial tribune. I sat there enjoying the scene, and full of thought, too, of the changes in my life. I thought of my childhood in poverty in the little house at Odense, — and now here !

On the way home people stood by the road to see the Danish

Crown Prince. At dinner that day with him, he remembered that the day after, the second of April, was my birthday, and he drank the health of my new year that was to begin on the morrow.

The festival day, which my friends among men and women always make so bright when I am in Denmark, with flowers, books, and pictures, blossomed about me now in my room ; I expected it would be very different in a strange land, but this was not the case, for from home there came in the morning many letters and telegrams from the Collins in Copenhagen. All my dear friends were thinking of me, and later in the day Denmark's Crown Prince honored me with a visit. I dined with our consul, where I found a company of many of my countrymen who drank my health.

When I came home to my hotel late in the evening, there sat there awaiting me a countryman residing in Paris with a great bouquet of flowers from Madame Melchior of Copenhagen. He had received a letter in the morning telling him to bring me such a one, but the whole day passed with his inquiring for my lodgings, which he did not find till evening. I was happy as a child, and in the midst of my pleasure there came, as so often with me, the thought : I have too much happiness ! it must some time slip away, and heavy trials come — how shall I then bear those ? There is an uneasiness in being so lifted up and endowed with such wealth of fortune.

I heard for the first time Christina Nilsson ; she appeared in " Martha." I was pleased with her dramatic gifts and enraptured with her delightful voice. I paid her a visit, and found we were not strangers to one another. When I read in the papers of her first appearance, the fortune which rained down on the young Swedish maiden, born so poor and yet so rich, I felt great interest for her, and wrote to one of my friends in Paris that when he met Mlle. Nilsson he must mention me to her, and say that when I should go there I should ask the privilege of visiting her. She replied that we were already old friends ; that she lived with a Norwegian family where I had been one day with Björnstjerne Björnson, and had heard me read a few of my Wonder Stories, and that she had been introduced to me as a young Swedish girl who was studying music and would one day go upon the stage; yes, I had given her a little cutting of paper, when I was snipping out something for some children who were in the room. At hearing that, I suddenly recalled a morning visit in Paris, where I had read and had cut out some paper things. I remembered talking there with a young lady who was some time to appear in opera, but it had escaped my mind; I did not remember more of her; but now I stood before her and was received gladly, as a friend; she gave me her portrait, and wrote in French some generous, kind words.

A letter of introduction took me to Rossini, whom I had not before this seen or conversed with. He was so polite as to say that he was well acquainted with my name, that I needed no letter of introduction. We talked about Danish music; he had heard Gade's name, he said. Siboni he had known personally, and his son, the composer, had visited him. He asked me next if I would translate for him a piece from a newspaper which the Austrian Minister had sent him, in which it was mentioned that on the fifteenth of April there would be given at Vienna a concert, on the occasion of laying the corner-stone of a monument to Mozart, and that there would be brought out two new pieces of music by Rossini, — "Christmas," and, if I remember rightly, "The Battle of the Giants." During our conversation a new caller came, and to him he spoke in Italian. I heard him say that I was "una poeta Tedesco!" I corrected him to "Danese," when he looked at me and continued, "but Denmark belongs to Germany!" Then the stranger interrupted with the explanation: "The two lands have lately been at war with one another." Rossini smiled good-naturedly, and asked me to forgive his ignorance of geography. He gave me his portrait card, wrote his name on it, and asked me to write mine and my address, when he would give me an invitation to one of his musical evenings.

The King of Denmark's birthday, the eighth of April, I spent with my countrywoman, Madame the Viscountess Robereda, daughter of the deceased Danish Minister of the Marine Zahrtmann. I learned, in making my way thither, how much difference it may make in a great populous city if one suddenly turns to the right or to the left. The place to which I was to go lay

by the Porte Étoile, on the left side. I went from Place de la
Concorde an hour before the time, in order to look at the multitude promenading the Champs d'Elysées The crowd pressed
on along the broad road, passing on both sides : one carriage
followed another, — elegant equipages from the drive in the
Bois de Boulogne. They increased all the way up to the Porte
Étoile, where it seemed to me impossible to cross without being
run over, and yet I must get over to the opposite side. For a
whole hour I hunted for a good crossing-place. Here and there
a man accomplished the act, but I dared not venture. I could
see the house where I was to go in, but I could not see any possibility of getting across to it. The clock had already passed
the appointed time, when my good genius again came to me,
or rather it was sent, — a heavily laden wagon drawn by six
horses, that was going across at a slow pace, and so made a
bulwark, as it were, against all the dashing equipages, and I
walked on the lee of this very safely, and so got across to
where I wanted to be.

As we sat at table a great storm sprang up, and soon the
lightning flashed so that all the lights in the room lost their
power. It was a magnificent sight to look out over Paris,
which now lay shrouded in darkness, and then suddenly
blazed as with a dart of sunlight. The rain did not lessen.
It was impossible to get a carriage, and the storm promised
to hold far into the night. All the omnibuses were full, all
the carriages taken up, — so said the servants and porter.
A guest chamber was offered me, but I was quite certain
I myself could find a carriage, so I ran across the place and
into the broad drive-way, but no carriage was to be found, and
on all the omnibuses was the word *complet*. The rain poured
down, and it was half after one before I reached my hotel ;
there was not a dry thread upon me. I was as wet as if I had
gone through the Seine.

My able fellow-countryman, the artist Lorenz Frölich, who
as an artist has also in France a well known and honored
name, had just begun upon some illustrations for a number of
my later stories which had lacked pictures. He worked with
great pleasure on the book. He had a happy home, a noble
wife, and a charming little girl, the original of " Baby," in the

picture-book,[1] which all France knows well. At his table I met the writer Sauvage, who said that he would give dramatic treatment to the idea contained in the Wonder Story, "The Galoshes of Fortune," and show the falsity of the position taken by so many, that the old times were better than the new. He showed me a letter he had received from Jules Sandeau, in which were the words, "You are fortunate in dining with Andersen ; he is a poet full of grace, and a true Prosaist ! He is like Haydn in music. I am delighted with what I know of his, and, to name a single one, with 'The Little Sea-maid.'"

Before I left Paris, I was permitted a great pleasure, — an honor I received from Vienna, sent by the Emperor Maximilian in Mexico, — the commander's order of Notre Dame de Gaudeloupe ; the letter which accompanied it said that the order was bestowed upon me in recognition of my poetic writings. The noble, richly gifted, and soon so ill-fated Emperor had remembered me and wished to give me pleasure. I remembered an evening many years ago, when in the Emperor's palace at Vienna with his mother, the Archduchess Sophia, I read some of my stories ; two young men came in who were very friendly and talked to me : it was Prince Maximilian and his brother, now the Emperor of Austria.

The thirteenth of April I left Paris, and in the afternoon reached Tours. The whole journey long the spring greeted me with blossoming fruit-trees ; and when the day after I came to Bordeaux, there was a luxuriant display in the Botanical Garden. All the trees, southern and northern, were in their glory, the blossoms gave forth their fragrance, the gold-fish sported by hundreds in the canal. I was again in my accustomed Hôtel Richelieu, and saw once more my countrymen and my French friends, among whom I especially received great attention and kindness from the littérateur George Amée, and the musician Ernst Redan. I spent a few lively evenings with them. Redan played from Schumann ; Amée read in French several of my stories and the entire " Picture-book without Pictures " ; a young Frenchman who listened was so overcome that tears flowed down his cheeks, and, to my surprise, seized my hand and kissed it.

[1] In its English form the book is *Rosy on her Travels.*

Through George Amée I received an invitation from the commander, General Dumas, who had formerly served in Africa, and has in the " Revue de deux Mondes " written in an interesting way of Algiers and the Arabs. He spoke warmly and appreciatingly of the Danish soldiers' bravery, which did my heart good, as when one hears his own kin praised. He invited me to share his box at the opera, and I was there several times and enjoyed his kindness.

On the twenty-fifth of every month a steamer leaves Bordeaux for Lisbon. I had already announced my coming to O'Neill by the vessel which would reach there the twenty-eighth of April. The weather meanwhile was very stormy. I knew the Spanish sea offered no pleasure excursion, but it was not much better to go through uneasy Spain, where the railway between Madrid and the border of Portugal was not yet completed. Then I heard that Ristori was at Bordeaux, and would appear one of the first evenings as *Medea*, and also as *Marie Stuart*. I have previously mentioned how she enraptured me when I saw her in London as *Lady Macbeth*. I must see her again, give a few days to a stay in Bordeaux, give up the sea voyage, and go through Spain to Portugal.

Ristori's *Medea* was magnificent, never to be forgotten ; equally so her *Lady Macbeth*.

My departure was arranged, and the journal " La Gironde," which afterward came to hand, spoke very courteously of me and my stay in Bordeaux. When I left I received from the learned Frenchman Michel, who had known my celebrated countrymen Bröndsted and Fiin Magnussen, his rendering in French of the Basque popular tales, which I thus could read on my journey through the Basque country. Tunnel followed tunnel ; it was wild and lonely, with single places here and there, and small black towns. We came by Burgos to Madrid. During my former visit the city did not attract me, and still less did it this time ; I felt myself alone and unhappy. The government forces had got the better of the revolutionary movement, but how easily and how soon this might break out ! and so it did but a few weeks after I had reached Lisbon. The telegrams announced bloody fighting in the streets and lanes. I was exceedingly desirous to get away, but the railway to the Portuguese boundary was not yet open, and to engage a place in the mail wagon I must wait five days.

Thursday evening, the third of May, I finally took my leave. A young lawyer from Lisbon was my only travelling companion : he spoke French a little, and was very kind and considerate.   It was a moonlit night.   We went over the campagna, — past single, solitary ruins.   A never-to-be forgotten romantic character belonged to it all.   In the early morning we passed the river Tagus, and later in the day pretty wooded tracts ; it was nearly evening before we began to cross the mountains, and we dined at Truxillo, Pizarro's birthplace.   At the post-houses one could not be sure of getting anything but chocolate, and my companion and I therefore carried wine and provisions with us, so that we lacked nothing but rest at night ; that was not to be thought of, so broken up was the way.   The carriage stuck and swung about, we went over great stones and into deep ruts, and at last at Merida we came to the railway, reaching it early in the morning before the sun was up.

My travelling companion took me through a number of streets and lanes to see some ruins which had come down from the time of the Romans.   I was so fagged out, so very indifferent to seeing any shows, that I went along reluctantly with stumbling steps, and looked with sleepy eyes on the old stones ; it was much more delightful to hear the locomotive's whistle and see the steam curling up.   We had only a short distance to go, and we were in the large Spanish border town Badajos. Here, in a good hotel and with an irreproachable breakfast, I got my vigor back, and after a few hours' rest we were able to continue the journey, and so we came to Lisbon early in the morning.

To go from Spain into Portugal is like flying from the Middle Ages into the present era.   All about were whitewashed, friendly looking houses, hedged about by trees ; and at the larger stations refreshments could be had, while in the night we found a chance to rest in the roomy railway carriage.

We were a day and night reaching Lisbon.   My attentive travelling companion procured a carriage for me, and bade the coachman take me to the Hôtel Durand, where I would be close by Tolades O'Neill's offices. So far all was very well; but not when I came to the hotel, for all the rooms were taken, and I heard that O'Neill's establishment and offices were not his lodging place ; that he had his home half a mile (Danish) outside of Lisbon, at his country-seat " Pinieros." It was Sunday, and no one came to town on that day. Tired as I was, I must take a carriage and drive out there. It was on one of the heights by the Alcantara Valley, hard by the great aqueduct, " Arcos dos Aquas Livres."

I was most cordially welcomed by the friend of my youth, and by his wife and sons. They had so confidently expected me by the French steamship that they had gone to meet it. The Danish ships that lay in the Tagus had raised the Danne-brog as a greeting to me.

The garden was still in full flower, with roses and gerani-ums ; climbing plants and passion-flowers hung over the walls and hedges. The elder-tree's white blossoms against the red pomegranate's gave me the Danish colors ; in the grain appeared the red poppy and the blue chicory, so that I could fancy I saw a piece of field from home, but here it was hedged about by high cactus and solemn cypresses. The wind whistled nearly every night as at home in the autumn time. " It is the coast wind that blows and makes Portugal blessed and healthy," they said.

I had read of Lisbon's narrow, crooked streets, where wild dogs feasted on the carcasses left to rot. I saw a light, hand-some town with broad streets, and houses whose walls were often decorated with shining slabs of porcelain.

One of the most noted of the living authors in Portugal is Antonio Feliciano de Castilho ; he has married a Danish lady, Miss Vidal. I had thus a fellow-countrywoman and a great writer to visit. George O'Neill took me to them.

Castilho was born at the beginning of this century. In his sixth year he caught the small-pox and lost his sight by it ; but he was seized with a fervent desire to study ; his rich endowment helped him, and he devoted himself especially to grammar, history, philosophy, and Greek. When not quite fourteen he wrote Latin verse which won high praise, and shortly after followed writings in his mother tongue ; but he devoted himself most to the study of botany. With his brother, who was eyes for him, he wandered in the charming country about Coimbra and took in all the beauty of nature, so that he sang of it in his poem " Spring." At Coimbra too he wrote the poem " Echo e Narcisso," which in a few years ran through several editions. He translated " Ovid," and showed great poetic power. A young lady, Maria Isabel de Buena Coimbra, was educated at a Benedictine nunnery near Oporto, where she remained some time after her education was completed. She was acquainted with classic and modern authors ; she read the poem " Echo e Narcisso," and wrote, without giving her name to the author, " Should Echo be found, would you then resemble Narcissus ? "

With this began a correspondence between Castilho and the unknown writer. After a time he asked if he might venture to inquire her name. She gave it ; the correspondence continued, and in the year 1834 they were betrothed and married. Three years afterward she died. The poem which he wrote to her memory, is placed by his countrymen beside the best things in their literature. He afterward married Charlotte Vidal, whose father was consul at Helsingör. By her aid Castilho translated into Portuguese several Danish poems, such as some from Baggesen, Oehlenschläger, and Boye.

I was received into his house as an old acquaintance and friend. The good poet talked with great vivacity, he was full of youth and freshness. He was at work now upon a translation of " Virgil." His son, also a writer, aided his blind father. The daughter has fine eyes, that shine with the light of the south. I improvised a poem on them ; stars by day they were, brighter than the stars of night. Castilho and his family soon gave me the pleasure of a return visit at Pinieros. I received from him one or two letters, dictated in French, and signed by his own hand. My letters to him I wrote in Danish ; he says, therefore, in one of his, — " We talk with one another like Pyramus and Thisbe — my wife the wall." With Madame Castilho's help, Danish letters and literature were imparted to the blind poet.

I had been several weeks at Pinieros and felt myself at home with these dear Portuguese friends. Madame O'Neill

gave interesting reminiscences of her childhood, dating from
Don Miguel's time ; the oldest of her sons, George, played
the piano well, read much, and took great interest in nature ;
the younger, Arthur, was a bright, handsome boy, quick at
vaulting on his horse and riding away, and both of them were
very attentive to me. The father, my friend George O'Neill,
spent the whole day at his counting-room ; he was at the head
of the house Tolades O'Neill, and Consul for Denmark and
other greater countries.   In the evening we saw him at home,
always happy and lively ; we talked Danish together, of our
old times in Denmark ; then the guitar was taken down, or
his son George took his place at the harpsichord, when the
brothers sang with fine rich voices out of " Martha " and
" Rigoletto."   I put confidence in O'Neill ; it seemed to us as
if we were fellow-countrymen and brothers.

   We had been here already a month together ; I wanted now
to see a still more fertile and more beautiful portion of Portugal.   Carlos O'Neill had invited me to his pretty villa, Bonegos, near Setubal.   His brother George with his wife and sons
accompanied me.   We went by steamer across the broad Tagus, and then took the railway straight to Setubal, which lies
right on the ocean among orange groves and hills.

   Carlos O'Neill's carriage took us from the railway station to
his villa.   It was the old highway from Lisbon to the southern
part of the country which we were passing over, and it wound
quite like a road in Spain ; soon it was so small that only a
single carriage could go, then it was wide enough for four
carriages ; it rose on rocky ground and then sank for a long
distance in deep sand, set with flowering aloes.   Before us
rose the fortress of Palmella, like a great ruin ; nearer, under
shady trees, was the desolate, lonely monastery Brancana, and
hard by was O'Neill's villa.   Here I stepped into a well ordered, happy home.   Every view from my balcony window
looked out on palm-trees overshadowing fountains ; the
ocean lay before the terrace, with its rich diversity of color ;
the pepper-trees stood like weeping willows above the reser-
voirs of water, where gold-fish swam about among the water-
lilies ; further on was an orange grove, and beyond that, still
further, was the vineyard.

I looked out over the town of Setubal and the bay with its ships, and the white sand hills were set against the blue ocean.   After every warm day, there was a breeze at evening that brought rest and coolness.   Darkness fell, but the stars came forth and shone wondrous clear, and then the countless fire-flies darted about over trees and bushes.

They were affectionate, home-loving people with whom I lived, and they showed me the greatest attention and consideration.   The son, young Carlos, a fine fellow with dark blue eyes and coal-black hair, was my faithful guide and escort on all my expeditions to the hills, he on his horse, I on an ass. He had had one sister; it was only a few months since that God had called her to Himself; she was fourteen years old, the joy of the household.   The loss of her had clouded the sunshine in what had been her father's merry home.

We lived very quietly, but for me, there was a rich variety. Young Carlos and I rode through lemon groves, where pomegranates and magnolias were brilliant with flowers; we visited a few deserted monasteries, and took a view from Palmella out over the great cork groves to the Tagus, Lisbon, and the Cintra mountains.   We took a sail out over the open sea to the grotto at Mount Arabida, and visited the town of Troja, now buried under sand hills.   The Phœnicians founded it; the Romans afterward dwelt there, and made salt in the same way as it still is obtained: the great remains show that.   The sand hills were covered with a growth of bushes, thistles, and flowers that with us flourish in greenhouses.   Where we stopped on the shore great heaps of stones were piled up, ballast for ships, which here in the bay had exchanged their lading for salt; stones from Denmark, Sweden, Russia, China: quite a wonder story might be written about that.   We walked about in this desolate place, and climbed the sand hills and looked out on the ocean.   I looked over the water — the nearest coast was America.   I thought of my friends there, Marcus Spring and his good wife; of Longfellow, the great poet of "Hiawatha" and "Evangeline;" I thought of what America had given us in Washington Irving and Cooper, — wine of the soul from yonder hemisphere: I never shall go there, I have such terror of the water; but my thoughts went thither from the dunes at Troja, the Portuguese Pompeii.

I saw a bull-fight at Setubal, innocent and bloodless by the side of Spanish ones. I saw too the popular St. Anthony's feast, with torches in the streets, singing and processions. I spent a delightful month, full of lively occupation in this beautiful Setubal. The visit here and at Pinieros had already occupied half the time I had devoted to my stay in Portugal, and I desired also before I left to visit Coimbra and Cintra. I must leave or I should be spending the whole winter.

The journey by diligence through the burning-hot, unquiet Spain was not advisable ; it was more sensible to go by steamer from Lisbon to Bordeaux, but I dared not set out till the equinoctial storms were over. How would the journey from France be arranged ? What dimensions would the war in Germany take ? Would France enter it ? I saw that the journey home would be full of uneasiness, and I came near spending the winter in Portugal, but to travel far away from friends and live in a hotel were not at all pleasant to think of, while to stay as a guest several months — I thought of the old proverb : " The welcome guest becomes tiresome when he sits too long in the strange house." I came therefore to the conclusion to try the sea voyage, and see what a war-vexed time would bring to pass. In the middle of August a steamer came from Rio Janeiro to Lisbon, and went immediately on to Bordeaux ; so I determined to take that after a visit to Coimbra, and a stay of a week or two in charming Cintra.

It was hard to leave pleasant Bonegos, and the amiable people there. Carlos O'Neill, father and son, accompanied me to Lisbon, and from here, with the brothers George and José O'Neill, I made a journey first to Aveiro, and thence to the romantically placed Coimbra, the university town of Portugal. It lies up on the side of a mountain, one street above another, several of the houses rising three or four stories over those below. The streets are narrow and crooked ; steep stone steps lead between separate buildings from one street up into the next. Here are a great many of the shops and bookstalls. Everywhere I saw students, all dressed in a kind of mediæval costume, — a long black gown, a short cape, and a Polish cap hanging down. I saw a company of the lively youths setting out with guitar or gun over the shoulder, bound for the woods and the mountains.

The university, an extensive building, occupies the highest point of the town ; from it one looks out over groves of oranges, cypresses, and cork-trees.   Far down below, a great bridge of masonry led over the Mandego River to the nunnery of Santa Clara and La Quinta dos lagrimas ; the castle lies half in ruins where the beautiful, unfortunate Inez de Castro and her innocent child were murdered.   The fountain still bubbles in the garden where Inez and her husband, Don Pedro, so often sat under the tall cypresses that still cast their shade.   On a marble tablet is written the verse about Inez which Camoens wrote in his " Lusiad."

During my visit at Coimbra, there was a festival at the university ; a young man got his " Doctor's hat."   The Professor of the History of Literature had heard that I was in Coimbra, and he honored me with a visit.   He took me to the festival, and I saw almost all the buildings, — the beautiful chapel, the great hall, and the library.

From Coimbra I returned to Lisbon, in order to go to Cintra, the prettiest, most enthusiastically praised part of Portugal. " The new paradise," Byron called it.   " Spring has her throne here," sings the Portuguese Garret.

The road thither from Lisbon leads over a poor country, but suddenly rises before one a part of Armidas, — the enchanted garden of Cintra, — with its umbrageous, mighty trees, its rushing waters, its romantic country fields.   One says rightly, that every nation finds here a bit of its own country. I found Danish woods, clover, and forget-me-nots.   I believe that I found also many familiar reminders of other countries, — England with its green sward ; the Brocken's wild rocks hurled about ; now I saw Setubal's flowers with their rich variety of color ; and again, far up in the North, Lecksand's birch groves.   From the road one can look out over the little town, with the old castle, where the reigning King Louis lives.   One sees the champaigns, and the distant cloister Maffra.   A beautiful and picturesque place high up on the hill, is the summer residence of King Fernando, once a monastery.   The road, began among cactus, chestnuts, and bananas, ends among birch and pine, growing among wild rocks that lie tossed about. You can look far out to the mountains beyond the Tagus, and away over the great ocean.

My friend José O'Neill had his country-seat in the paradisaical Cintra ; I was his welcome guest, and I had another friend here in the English Consul, Lytton, son of Bulwer Lytton. I had in Copenhagen made the acquaintance of young Lytton, who is himself a graceful writer. He came to see me in the most cordial manner, and made my stay here very pleasant. With him and his lovely wife I saw much of the charming country about Cintra.

I had also the pleasure of meeting with my noble countrywoman, Madame the Vicountess Roberda née Zahrtmann, whom I had visited in Paris on my way hither. She invited me to the house of Count Armeida, and I found myself in a circle of friendly and good people, from whom it was hard for me to tear myself away, as well as from my affectionate friend José ; but time was passing on, the steamer for Bordeaux would in a few days touch at Lisbon, and thither must I go. Stormy weather delayed the arrival of the vessel, and I was forced to wait a few days, with no pleasurable anticipations of my sea journey.

Early in the morning of Tuesday, the fourteenth of August, we were informed that the steamer *Navarro* had arrived, and was taking goods and passengers on board. It was an exceedingly large vessel, — the largest I had ever been on, — a great floating hotel. George O'Neill introduced me to the captain and a few of the officers, bespeaking the best attention for me, laughed, and jested, and pressed my hand as we left ; I was sorrowful indeed "but we should see each other often ! "

The signal was given, the anchor was raised, the steam whistled, and soon we were out on the Atlantic Ocean ; the ship rose and fell, the waves rolled greater and greater. The storm had ceased its movements, but not the sea. I took my place at the table, but at the same moment must needs rise quickly and get out into the fresh air, where I sat suffering from the motion of the ship, which I had every reason to expect would be worse in the Spanish sea.

It was soon evening, the stars came out, the air was very

cold. I dared not venture into my state-room, but entered the dining saloon, where toward midnight I was the only one remaining. The lights were put out ; I knew the rolling of the sea, the movement of the machinery, the sounding of the signal bell, and the answer that came. I thought upon the might of the sea, the might of fire, and I had quite too vivid recollections of the friend of my youth, Jette Wulff's fearful death on her voyage to America. And as I lay there a sea struck us midship ; it was as if we suddenly were stopped, as if the steam held its breath. It was only a moment, and again the engine gave its wonted sound and trembling motion ; but involuntarily there was pictured in my thoughts, and that more and more forcibly, a shipwreck, with the water upheaving, and we sinking and sinking. How long would consciousness and the death agony last ? I had all the torment of it, as this fantasy took possession of me. I could no longer endure it, and rushed up upon deck, pushed the sail aside at the gunwale, and looked out upon what splendor ! what majesty ! — the rolling sea shone as if on fire ; the great waves gleamed with phosphorus ; it was as if we went gliding over a sea of fire. I was so overwhelmed by this grandeur that in a moment my fear of death had vanished. The peril was not greater nor less than it had been all along, but now I did not think of it. Fancy had taken another direction. " Is it really so important," I asked myself, " that I should live any longer ? Were Death to come to-night, in what majesty and glory he would come." I stood for a long time in the starry night, and looked out on the grand, rolling world's sea, and when I again sought the saloon for rest, my soul was happy and refreshed by resignation to God's will.

I slept, and when the next morning I went up on deck I felt no more sea-sickness, and began to take pleasure in looking out on the swelling water. Toward evening this seemed to grow less ; and next morning, when we were in the midst of the Spanish sea, which I had especially dreaded, the wind died down ; the water lay like a piece of silk stretched out ; it was as smooth as if we were on a lake. Surely I was Fortune's child : such a voyage I had not expected nor dared to think of.

The next morning, the fourth day I had spent on board, we sighted the light-house on the rocky heights at the mouth of the Gironde. We had heard at Lisbon that the cholera was in Bordeaux, though this was said doubtfully. The pilot who came aboard assured us that the condition of health there was excellent: it was the first greeting we received, and was a very joyful one to us.

The passage up the river took several hours ; it was seven o'clock in the evening before we reached Bordeaux. The porter from the hotel where I had stopped before knew me ; the coach was in waiting, and I was soon to see dear friends. The excellent, quick minded Amée I met afterward with Redan, Amiat, and several gifted French friends. Music, reading, and animated conversation, made the time pass quickly.

With one of my countrymen, I went one day through one of the smaller streets, and saw there at a book-stall the French translation of "The Picture-book without Pictures." I asked the price. "One franc," answered the man. "That is what a new copy costs," said I, "but this is an old, worn one."

"Yes, but this book is sold out," said the book-seller. "It is very much inquired after ; it is quite a famous book, by Andersen, who is now in Spain ; there was a commendatory piece about him and this book in 'La Gironde' day before yesterday." At that my friend could not keep back, and said that I was Andersen, and the book-seller made a low, civil bow, as his wife did also.

My friends urged me to extend my stay here, and to give up Paris, where the cholera was ; that I would gladly have done, but the shortest way home led by Paris. I went to the Grand Hotel on the Boulevard, said to be the healthiest quarter ; but remained only a day and night, visited no one, and did not go to the theatre, but kept quiet, and then the next evening set out by rail through France, where they said that the cholera was in nearly every town, and came to Cologne, where nobody spoke of the cholera, for the town was quite free from it.

I went to Hamburg, where I believed myself quite beyond the plague, and there I stayed a few days for rest, went to the theatre, and was hospitably entertained at a supper just before the morning of my departure. I heard accidentally, and read afterward the confirmation in the papers, that at this very time the cholera was at its height here ; that men were dying by the hundred every day, while in great Paris, which I had hurried away from, the deaths were not more than fourteen a day. I was most disagreeably affected, and immediately began to diet, had pains in my stomach, and an unquiet night, and early the next morning I fled through the Grand Duchy, and in the afternoon was in Denmark and in my native town of Odense.

My first visit was to the Bishop's house, to my noble, learned friend Bishop Engelstoft, where I knew I should find the most cordial welcome. With him I saw the old landmarks, — the house where I had spent my childhood, and St. Knud's Church, where I stood for Confirmation, and where, in the church-yard, my father lay buried. Many friends in my native place followed me in the afternoon to the station, as I wished to be at Sorö that evening, when I would surprise good Madame Ingemann with an unexpected visit ; but at the station I heard that only an hour or two before she had come by the train from Copenhagen, where this old, deaf, and almost blind lady had undergone an operation on her eyes, and seemed exhausted and depressed. I gave up the visit, and took up my quarters at the little inn by the station. They knew nothing of mattresses for beds, but had only oppressively hot feather beds ; so I put one at the bottom, covered it with a straw sack, and put my plaid on top of that, and so made comfortable, I slept till the early morning, when I took the train to Roeskilde, to my friends Hartmann and his wife. The day after I was in Copenhagen.

My travelling was over, and again I was to grow fast in the home soil, drink in its sunshine, feel the sharp winds, live in the hubbub, and know nothing of wandering except perhaps in a wonder story ; but I was also to live among the great things of the good, the true, and the beautiful, with which our Lord has gifted my native land.

My faithful friends, the Melchiors, received me at the station and took me to their country-seat " Rolighed " (Quiet), just outside the town. Above the door were flowers woven into the word "Welcome!" the Dannebrog flag waved. From the balcony before my room I looked out over the Sound, which was filled with sail and steamships. I met my friends, men and women. A few evenings were so mild and quiet, as if in southern latitudes, that the candles were lighted on the table under the high trees in the garden: multitudes of fire-flies were here, and I could easily have fancied myself at Bonegos, in Portugal. All the kindness which fortune and affection could give one was given me here; they were charming days, and I have renewed them since.

Among the distinguished men whom I met here was a young man whose genius I esteemed and admired, the painter Carl Bloch. We had, during my last visit in Rome, met a single time, and at home I came to appreciate his renown as an artist and his estimable character as a man. At Rolighed our friendship was knit more closely, and the new stories which appeared at the close of the year were dedicated to him. In the copy which I sent him I wrote, —

CARL BLOCH.

It was an Exhibition time at Charlottesburg,
And everything was new, charming, and fair.
A picture took my fancy, — a monk stood, young and clever,
And looked upon two married folk, who homeward rode,
Mounted on asses, and both with happy faces;
And the young monk's soul and passion thoughts
Grew dark with sorrow looking on the scene, —
And one felt sure this painter had a heart.
Each year came forth a new and glorious work;
Samson we saw, set midst the Philistines;
We saw "The Barber," and "The Roman Boy;"
The grief of life and humor truly shown.
And now "Prometheus" came, and from men's eyes
Melted the snow — how great that picture was!
My happiness I shared with Copenhagen.
And then we met. Thou wert just what I thought:
A child in soul and yet so manly-wise;
Modest, and doubting of thy own great strength,
Yet very sure of what our Lord had bade thee,
For otherwise such work could ne'er be done.
And since I found thy love, take thou my flowers
That tell my pleasure and my heart's good-will.

One of the first days after my arrival home, I was graciously and cordially, as ever, received by the royal family, — at the end of the very week when the king's noble and amiable daughter Dagmar left Denmark and became Russia's Grand Duchess. I had one more talk with her in her ancestral home.

As she left, I stood in the crowd of men on the wharf where she, with her royal parents, went on board. She saw me, stepped up to me and shook my hand warmly. Tears started from my eyes: they were in my heart for our young princess. Everything promises for her happiness; an excellent family like that she left, is that she has' entered. A fortunate pair are she and her noble husband.

I had not yet since my return home seen good Madame Ingemann. I hastened out to her. She was overjoyed at the recovery of her sight; how glad too she was in thought at the anticipation of a still better sight, the meeting again with Ingemann. From Sorö I went to Holsteinborg. One day the lady of the place took me to see a poor paralytic girl, who lived near by in a neat little house by the road-side, but had a very poor view, since the house was situated on low ground and a high bank was thrown up before it. The sun never shone into the room because the window looked north. This could be helped, thought the kind lady of the castle. She had the poor paralytic brought up to the manor one day, and meanwhile sent masons to the house, and had them break the wall through to the south, and insert a window there, and now the sun shone into the room. The sick girl came to her home and sat there in the sunshine; she could see the woods and the shore, the world grew wondrous large, and this just by one word of the gracious lady.

"That word was so easy, the act so little," said she, and I too expressed my pleasure as I accompanied her who had done this and many another Christian act. I placed this among my small stories and called it "Kept close is not forgotten."

On my return to Copenhagen I moved into my new apartment upon the King's New Market Place, Copenhagen's greatest and finest square, with the Royal Theatre, one of the least beautiful buildings, just before me; but it is good inside, and bound to my affection by many memories. Perhaps it may please one and another of my friends on the other side of the water to hear of my home in Copenhagen.

The house stands, as I said, on Kongen's Nytorv ; in the building is one of the largest and most frequented cafés of the town ; in the first hall a refreshment room, and in the second a club-room. On the story with me a lawyer lives, while overhead is a photograph atelier; so it will be seen that I have meat and drink near by, have no want of society ; I cannot die away from a lawyer, and a photographer is at hand to secure my picture for posterity. I am certainly very well placed ; my little apartment — I have only two rooms — is snug and sunny, and adorned with pictures, books, statues, and what my lady friends especially provide for me, flowers and something green, which are always there. In the Royal Theatre, at the Casino, I have every evening my pleasant seat. All classes of the community are kind and friendly in receiving me into their circles.

In Copenhagen it is the custom in several families that on a certain day in the week they see their friends at dinner or in the evening, but one is nevertheless free and can accept another invitation. I have almost from my student days so spent my noons. I will give here a short sketch of my varying seven days of the week, and cut a silhouette picture of a few of my most intimate circles of friends.

Monday calls me to some friends of many years' standing, — friends through good and evil days, State Councilor Edward Collin and family. Of him, his wife, and his children I have often spoken in " The Story of my Life ;" I will only add what the excellent Fredrika Bremer once said with great truth : " Madame Collin was the first Danish lady I saw and spoke with in Copenhagen, and she is the type to me of the noblest and best women that Denmark possesses.

Tuesday takes me out of town to a half-country like place ; near to the shore lives the Drewsen family. Drewsen is the son-in-law of Collin's father. I have spoken before of his sons, and have sung of little Wiggo. The mother, Madame Ingeborg Drewsen, was always a steadfast, sympathetic sister to me, from the first time her father opened his house to me : a youthful, fresh spirit, a sparkling humor, and a fervor and depth are the gifts she has received from our Lord.

On Wednesday I go to that home which early received me, even before my student days, and has continued thus to this time, while one after another of those I met there were called away to God, — Hans Christian Örsted's house; he himself, the bright, gentle sun within, is gone; his wife and richly gifted youngest daughter Mathilde are now the only ones left. From the earliest time I always read there whatever new thing I had written, or now write: it is as a memory of the days gone by.

Thursday was the day at home at the elder Collin's house. I used to gather with all his children on that day. He too is gone, and this day takes me now to a home where the affection for me is likewise strong and considerate, where husband, wife, and children treat me as if I belonged to the family of Melchior.

Friday also takes me back to a home full of early remembrances, which I have with Henriette Wulff's sister, Madame Ida Koit. We have the same memories clustering about her parents' house. I have seen her as a child, as a mistress at home, and now as a loving grandmother; and I have in her children and grandchildren devoted friends.

Saturday was the day of meeting at Madame Neergaard's, where she was truly Danish and Christian in thought and good deeds that shone over her circle. God has called her away, and given me a home akin to this with the family at Basnös.

Sunday I can describe by pointing back to my visit at Upsala and the serenade there, which was not for me but for the wise and musical Madame Henriques: her hospitable husband throws open his house to all that is good and worthy, while cordiality and music invite the guests.

There! there are the seven days of the week, and should it be noticed that it is the mother of the house whom I always put first, one will understand my thoughts — she is the very one who makes the table beautiful and spreads sunshine over the room.

1867.

One evening late in January, at the Students' Association, where hitherto I only had read my stories, two of these,

"The Butterfly" and "The Happy Family" were recited by Professor Hoedt, and received most hearty applause. The carefulness, the humor, and the dramatic manner with which he gave these little stories were qualities of good work.

When Professor Hoedt was still a young student he appeared on the royal Danish stage as *Hamlet* and *Solomon de Caus ;* in what I recall most vividly as *Toby,* in "The Deputies," and as *Harlequin* in Heiberg's comedy, "The Invisible." At the social supper table at the Student's Association, where he had recited the two Wonder Stories mentioned above, he gave a *viva* for me, and said in the toast he offered that his first appearance as an actor had been at the Students' Association, and that in a student comedy by H. C. Andersen ; therefore had he this evening, when after many years he stood again on the boards here, wished to recite a wonder story of Andersen's who had continued to be a member of the association, fresh and young, — yes, perhaps even younger than when first admitted.

We got out now the old play bills that showed the representations given by the students, and among these was found my comedy, "Long Bridge," which should not be confounded with my later drama, "On the Long Bridge." The first is a sort of reverie over all that in the course of years had transpired at Copenhagen, in the councils of literature, art, and the drama. The piece is quite akin to the French reverie style, which has since, with great effect, been introduced among us by Herr Erik Bögh ; but when I used it, it was a kind of art of which we at home knew nothing. I myself knew nothing of it ; it was an idea that came to me, a room into which I had admitted whatever had especially impressed me in the years that had passed and in the people who lived in them.

Professor Hoedt was, as I have said, the first, with the exception of myself, who had read my stories at the Students' Association ; but from the Royal Theatre, as well as from the Casino and from other private theatres, for some time back, a number of my stories had been recited. The first who ventured it was the highly honored actress Miss Jürgensen, whose dramatic faculty was so great, that while one evening she appeared with tragic majesty as *Queen Bera* in Oehlenschläger's tragedy,

" Hagbarth and Signe," one was amused the next evening with her equally humorous rendering of the governess *Miss Trumph-mayer*, in Heiberg's " April Snares. " The most celebrated artist in comedy on the Danish stage, Instructor Phister, the Proteus of manifold *rôles*, created a complete dramatic work when he told the story of the " Emperor's New Clothes."

The actor Nielsen, who took the part of *Hakon Jarl* and of *Macbeth*, recited in private circles, and upon his tour in Sweden and Norway, several of my stories. Our well known Michael Wiehe gave with an ardor, a naïveté, and a humor unequaled by any, " It is certainly so," "Tip top," and " Jack the Dullard." Very like him, and touched with a child-like nature, was the distinguished actor at the Casino, Christian Schmidt. Recently and very often it is the royal actor Mantzius who has especially contributed to make my stories popular by his excellent dramatic talent. The gifted philosopher, Professor Rasmus Nielsen, in the days just before these, unfolded by his reading at the university the meaning in my two stories " The Snow Man," and " What the Good-man does is sure to be right."

On my birthday, the second of April, my room was made delightful with flowers, pictures, and books. There was music and speaking at my friends' the Melchiors ; the spring sun shone without ; within in my heart there was shining too. I looked back over the years that had fled : how much happiness had there not been granted me, but always rises the anxious doubt. I must think upon the old story about the gods who could be jealous of men, when they were exalted too much by their fortune, and so destroyed them. Yet that was in heathen times : now we live in Christian days, and " God is love."

The great Exhibition at Paris had just opened. People from all lands were streaming to it. Fata Morgana's castle had been reared on the Champs de Mars, which had been transformed into the most beautiful garden. I must go there and see the fairy tale of our time. By the eleventh of April I was in the train, going past Funen, through the Grand Duchy and Germany, hurrying toward Paris.

The exhibition palace had been built, but was still constantly growing. The buildings about it, complete gardens laid out with canals, grottoes, and water-falls were in busy preparation. Every day one saw a great progress. It all took possession of my soul. I came here almost daily, and met acquaintances and friends from different countries of the world. It was as if a great rendezvous had been appointed here.

One day as I went out there, there came an elegantly dressed lady with her husband, a negro. She addressed me in a mixed speech of Swedo-English-German. She was born in Sweden, but had lived abroad of late ; she knew who I was from my portrait, she said, and introduced me to her husband, the famous actor, the negro Ira Aldridge, who was just now playing to the Parisians at the Odeon, where he took the *rôle* of *Othello.* I pressed the artist's hand, and we exchanged some friendly words in English. I confess it gave me great pleasure that one of Africa's gifted sons should greet me as a friend. There was a time when I should not have ventured to speak of such a thing, but my surroundings are now such that it is no mark of vanity, but of my pleasure in all that God has granted me, — the book of fortune indeed, and that my friends in distant lands will quickly understand.

One of the gentlemen in the English department of the ex-hibition building invited me one day to dine with him at the Grand Hotel de Louvre, where I met the Englishman Baker, the discoverer of the source of the Nile. He was here with his faithful wife, who had accompanied him on that perilous journey, and had lent him faith, courage, and fortitude. To me was assigned the honor of taking Lady Baker in to dinner.

King George of Greece was in Paris. I had the pleasure of seeing again the young King, whom I had known from his childhood in his royal father's house, where he had listened to my stories. A visit from him was expected at the Exhibition. The Grecian division stood by chance next to the Danish ; by a single step one went from Greece to Denmark. The passage was adorned with Greek flags upon the Grecian side and with the Danish flag upon the Danish. I was asked to write an inscription, and I wrote upon the spot a little verse, which was soon waving in large letters among the flags and banners.

In the Danish division there were many photographic portraits from Copenhagen, and a fine collection of busts in clay of eminent Danes. Many strangers had inquired for my picture and bust, without finding it. But this was no fault of the committee. The President, Chamberlain Wolffhagen told me that he had written repeatedly to Copenhagen, asking especially for two busts, one of the deceased State Councilor, the antiquarian Thomsen, and one of H. C. Andersen. The reply came that the busts which he desired did not exist in marble ; then they were asked for in plaster, and there were sent Thomsen's bust and that of the Norwegian writer Björnstjerne Björnson, not Andersen's.

Among my countrymen in Paris was Robert Wall, young and vivacious, yet one of those who have experienced heavy trials in youth, and it was this which especially interested me in him. His father had owned a place in Jutland, was well to do, and gave his children an excellent education. Circumstances were changed, and at their father's death the children had to look out for themselves. Young Robert found a place in a merchant's counting-room in Aarhuus, when a letter came from his uncle, who lived in Melbourne, in Australia, who wished him to come and be a son to him. The young man immediately set out with high hopes and travelled thither safely, but on his arrival his uncle had lost his property and had suddenly become a poor man, so that Robert stood destitute, a stranger in a strange land. But his heart did not fail ; he tried various situations, all honorable, but all poor : travelled as a driver, washed in the gold mines, and when he had gotten together as much money as would take him back to Denmark, he hastened thither, where he described in a lively way Australian scenes, and wrote sketches of travel as a feuilletonist in " Dagbladet." All this, carried on with spirit and a fresh youthfulness, won my interest, and my heart wishes for him a bright future.

On the twenty-sixth of May, the silver wedding day of the royal pair, I wished to be in Copenhagen, and I desired to make my journey home lie by way of Le Locle in Switzerland. Before I left Paris I received an invitation from countrymen and Swedish and Norwegian friends to meet with them in a

Scandinavian gathering. It was a repetition of the feast which Björnstjerne Björnson brought about for me when we last met here. The northern flags waved, King Christian's and King Carl's portraits were decorated with fresh flowers. Chamberlain Wolffhagen proposed a health to the northern kings, and songs were sung. I read Wonder Stories and proposed a toast to northern poetry.

From Paris to Neufchâtel it is only a day's journey by rail. At sunset I came to the boundary of Switzerland. The Jura Mountains, clad with oak, beech, and pine, rose before me. The way led now through tunnel after tunnel ; in many places the iron rails passed close by steep precipices ; one could look down far below and see houses and towns. The lights trembled there, the stars shone far above, and in the evening I was at Neufchâtel, and soon up on the heights at Le Locle with my friend Louis Jürgensen.

The beech-trees stood with their fresh leaves, the bushes were green, but the snow fell, and every bush looked like a blossoming whitethorn. The cold increased, and I could not travel nor get to Copenhagen in time for the festival. A song of welcome, written from my heart, I sent home in a letter to the Crown Prince Frederick, who graciously delivered it to his royal parents. " From William Tell's land to the land of Palnatoke " flew my thoughts, with the best wishes of my heart. Jules Jürgensen raised the Dannebrog, and in the bubbling champagne we drank a toast in honor of the silver wedding of King Christian IX. and Queen Louise.

A few days after I left my dear friends at Le Locle and was soon in Copenhagen. At the King's silver wedding, many were honored with honorable mention or with order. The King had graciously bestowed upon me the title of State Councilor. I tendered his majesty my profound thanks. The royal family was at Fredensborg. Princess Dagmar, now the Grand Princess of Russia, was here on a visit to her royal parents. I went out there ; it was not an audience day, but I was nevertheless received, and that with great warmth and kindness. The King asked me to stay to dinner, where I met and talked with the amiable, noble Princess Dagmar. She told me that she had read a Russian edition of my stories, which she knew so well before in Danish, and so I had spent another delightful day with the King's family.

It was warm summer, and not at all pleasant to be in the heated streets of the town. I became the guest of my friends the Melchiors, at Rolighed, and wrote there "Godfather's Picture-book" and the story of "The Greenies," but there was always coming up in my thoughts a desire to give in a wonder story my impression of the Paris Exhibition, the wonderful wonder story of our time, which is called so material. I needed to fix some point of departure for it, when suddenly there came to me a reminiscence of my visit to Paris in the spring of 1866 when I was travelling to Lisbon. I stayed then at the Hôtel Louvois, in the Place Louvois, by the Royal Library. There is a little garden there surrounding a fountain. One of the great trees had died, and so it had been torn up out of the earth and thrown aside ; near by was a heavy cart with a large vigorous tree brought in from the country to be planted here. "Poor tree! poor Dryad!" thought I ; "thou camest from thy pleasant, fresh country air here, to drink in the gas and the lime dust and find thy death." There was a suggestion for a poem here, and it accompanied me to Holsteinborg, Basnös, and Glorup. I began to write it down, but was not satisfied with it. I had only seen the Exhibition at its beginning, and it was only now that it could be seen in its completeness. I felt a strong desire to go there again, but to journey to Paris twice in a summer was a little too much — when one is not rich ; I must get over it some way.

While I was at Holsteinborg in August, Copenhagen was visited by a number of young and old French journalists. Their reception was so cordial, so much a matter of popular feeling, it was as if one had announced, "Here are faithful friends who come, children of France, our old ally." I heard through the papers of the entertainments given them and of the jovial days that passed, but it was not expedient for me to go to town and take part in the festivity.

Just as the last French visitors were departing from Copenhagen I entered the station and talked there with Edward Tarbé now director of " Le Gaulois," and with the author Victor Tournel, who has since written an interesting and well con-

sidered work, "Le Danemark contemporain : Études et Souvenirs d'un Voyageur." He was acquainted with several of
my writings, and at his departure I expressed the hope that
we might soon see each other in Paris. And this was the
case. I could not longer resist the impulse to travel and to
see the Exhibition in its complete magnificence before it
should disappear, and then I could finish my story of "The
Dryad."

The first of September I set out. Robert Watt also desired
to see the Exhibition again, and see it in its full flower, so we
went together. The thunder rolled the lightning flashed, it
was a most striking journey. At Corsör we went on board
the boat, which was loaded down with freight. In the rain and
darkness one reeled over the deck, and flash succeeded flash.
At daybreak we came to Kiel, and flew through Germany to
reach Paris, but stopped to rest at Strasbourg. We reached
there at evening. The tattoo beat so that the old timber work
house in which we were shook. The old cathedral stood before us and cared very little about our visit in the morning :
it had had a visit from the great world's storm king, his wife,
and children, who had left their name carved upon the old
bells so that they might ring it out to the world. The evening was fine ; I felt happy at once more being in France ; I
was young again, as I always feel on a journey. "Two and-
sixty years old," says the baptismal record ; "Two-and-sixty
seconds," Eternity says.

It was market day in Strasbourg, and it was not easy to
press through the crowd to the church, so splendid with its fila-
gree work in stone, as if it were all cast in a foundry, a beautiful picture of Gothic art. "Master Bloodless" stirred within
in the great clock. The clock struck ten just then, and the
figures started out. Death struck the strokes ; the old hour
went and the new hour came and stood still and waited till
the last stroke had sounded, when it began its own course.
A crowd of strangers about us looked on ; among them I discovered my good friend from Bordeaux, Francis Michel, the
translator of the Basque folk-lore.

We were soon in Paris, and again in the Aladdin's castle
of our time, the wonderful Exhibition Palace, with a Fata

Morgana in reality; the garden of enchantment, — with its flowers from South and North, the great aquaria where one, as if in a glass diving-bell in the sea or at the bottom of fresh water lakes, stood in the midst of a Hall of Fishes. I was filled with astonishment at all I saw. In a café where Danish papers could be found I read in one of them a letter describing the Exhibition, in which it was said that no one except Charles Dickens was enough of a writer to compose an artistic picture from this splendid performance. There was truth in that, and I began to mistrust myself in regard to the work I had undertaken, and soon, while I was in Paris, I gave up the whole thing. The advantage I was to find, and for which I had travelled here a second time, was now lost, and I had myself to laugh at. I had not felt myself at home before in Paris; but this year the Exhibition's fascination had extended over the whole, and I felt myself borne along with the town of pleasure.

The genial feuilletonist, the intellectual Philaret-Chasles, invited me to Mendon where he has a pretty country-seat with a cozy little garden. I met here a few of the French journalists who had visited Copenhagen. There was life and spirit here! Toasts were drunk; one speech followed another, like butterflies flitting over the table. Philaret-Chasles afterward, at a lecture to the students in Paris, spoke warmly and highly of me and my stories.

Several of those who had visited Copenhagen invited me and a few Danes to a supper. The editor of " La Situation " was there and several distinguished members of the press; Edmond Tarbé, director of " Le Gaulois," who, beside his singular journalistic capacity, has a decided musical talent, an inheritance surely from his mother, who must rank among the best composers at Paris. Edmond Tarbé played on the piano for us " The brave Soldier-boy," and then the Danish popular piece " Roselil." There was a Danish character to the feast thus that made it very pleasant.

I was in Mabille for the first time the next evening. I never before had been there. It was finely illuminated, and lights hung on the weeping-willows over the little ponds, while the moon shone softly, and there was a multitude of people. One of my young friends swung a Mabille beauty toward me and asked, "What do you say to such poetry as this — such a sight as this?" I pointed to the moon which shone in all its glory, "I think that everlasting sight is better." "Monsieur!" exclaimed the justly offended beauty. I stayed a quarter of an hour, and have in "The Dryad" given the impression of what I felt and saw.

The time for departure from Paris drew near, and I left at the close of September. On the way home, I spent a few days at the gambling town of Baden Baden. In Mabille there was gayety; I knew what it was; at Baden Baden there was a fine show, but the place had an unhappy, demoniacal look. The great, quiet gaming-hall, where the gold pieces rolled, was to me as if Satan himself were there invisibly; there was silence and gloom. As soon as I had returned home to my hotel after my first visit, I wrote out my mood in a little poem : —

THE GAMBLING-HOUSE.

Could lights and pictures only call,
　They'd say, "Come to the feast, my friend!"
But silence dwelt in the splendid hall,
　One heard but the gold its message send.
Young women sat with feverish breath
　And threw the gold, and staked their all ;
There came a laugh like the laugh of death, —
　" I want a life in the gambling-hall."
Splendor and quiet in the silent place,
Dumb gold and throbbing pulse kept pace.

Still, around the gambling-house, the baths, and the town, are mountains and woody charms, a great and noble castle ruin, — large trees growing in the knightly hall ; one sees from the hanging balconies, far out over the winding Rhine into France, to the Vosges Mountains.

My journey home was a hasty one, and it was only in Odense that I took a day and night for rest. The Dannebrog waved from the houses, new soldiers were to arrive. In the Riding-house there were preparations making for their reception. I was invited. The tables were loaded down with meat and drink. The ladies and their daughters in the town,

all appeared there as ready to serve. The soldiers came, gave
a hurra, and sang songs, and made speeches. How changed
for the better! how bright and pleasant a time as compared
with the old time which I knew. I spoke of this, and remarked that when I was last here, in the Riding-house, a
long time ago indeed, I was quite a little boy, and I saw a soldier run the gauntlet; now I came and saw the soldiers, our
defenders and guardians, greeted with song and speeches, and
sit beneath the waving of flags. Blessed be our time!

A few of my friends said to me that I must come back here
at least once a year, and not always go flying through my birthplace; that it would make a celebration for me, and that I
should certainly get an invitation in November. I had no
inkling how great it was to be, to what a summit of fortune in
my life I was to be raised. I answered that I was truly glad
at their kind expressions, but added, — " Forget it then till
1869, on the fourth of September, when it will be half a century since I left Odense for Copenhagen. The sixth of September I was there, and that is the great day of my life, but
it is not likely that any one would think of that. Rather let
me come over here to Odense upon the semi-centennial of my
departure."

" It is all of two years till then," they answered. " One
ought not to put off any good pleasure. We will see in November."

And so it came about. The old prophecy, made when I
was a poor boy, going out from Odense, that the town would
one day be illuminated for me, was fulfilled in the most beautiful shape. Late in November I received in Copenhagen a
communication from the Common Council in Odense.

" In the Odense Common Council: We herewith have the
honor to announce to your Excellency that we have elected
you an honorary burgher in your native town; permit us to
invite you to meet with us here in Odense on Friday, the sixth
of December next ensuing, upon which day we desire to deliver to you the certificate of citizenship." Then followed the
signature. I replied: —

" Last night I received the communication of the honorable
Common Council, and hasten to present my sincere thanks.

My birthplace proffers me, through you, gentlemen, a mark of esteem greater than I ever dared dream of receiving.

"It is this year forty-eight years since I, a poor boy, left my native place; and now, rich in happy memories, I am received in it as a dear child is received in his father's house. You will understand my feelings. I am lifted up, not in vanity, but in thankfulness to God for the heavy hours of trial and the many days of blessing He has granted me. Accept the thanks of my whole heart.

"It will give me great pleasure on the day appointed, the six December, if God grant me health, to meet with my noble friends in my beloved native town.

"Your grateful and humble

"H. C. ANDERSEN."

On the fourth of December I went to Odense. The weather had been cold and stormy; I had a cold and suffered from toothache, but now the sun shone and it was quiet, pleasant weather. Bishop Engelstöft met me at the station, and took me to my home at the Bishop's house by Odense River, which I have described in my story of "The Bell's Hollow." Several of the town officers were invited to dinner, which went off pleasantly and with great liveliness.

Now came the important sixth of December, my life's most beautiful feast. I could not sleep at night. I was oppressed in body and soul. I felt pains in my breast and my teeth ached, as if to remind me, — In all your honor, you are yet a child of mortality, a worm of the dust; and I felt it not only in my body's aches, but in the humility of my soul. How should, how ought I to enjoy my incredible fortune! I knew not. I was all in a tremble.

I heard in the morning of the sixth of December that the town was beautifully decorated, that all the schools had a holiday, because it was my festival. I felt cast down, humble, and poor, as if I were standing before my God. There was a revelation to me of every evil thing within me, every fault and simple thought, word, and deed. Everything sprang forth strangely clear in my soul, as if it were the Day of Judgment, — and it was the day of my honor. God knows how mean I felt myself to be, when men so exalted and honored me.

In the forenoon came the Chief of the Police, State Councilor Koch, and Burgomaster Mourier, and escorted me to the
Guild Hall, that I might receive my diploma of honorary citizenship. From almost all the houses in the streets through
which we drove the Dannebrog waved. There was a great
concourse of people from the town, and from the country, citizens and farmers. I heard the shouts of hurra, and before the
Guild Hall I heard music ; the citizen's chorus was drawn up,
and they sang melodies to my songs, "Gurre" and "I love
thee, Denmark, father-land !" I was overcome, and one can
understand that I said as I must say to my two escorts, "What
must it be to be carried to the place of execution ! I believe
I understand the sensation now."

The hall was filled with richly dressed ladies, and town
officers in uniform and decorations. I saw citizens and peasants there.

The "Funen Advertiser" gave the same day a sketch of
the scene, as follows : —

"At ten o'clock in the morning the poet H. C. Andersen
was presented in the Guild Hall with the diploma of an honorary citizen. The Town Council, with whom the idea originated, summoned him, by three gentlemen of their number,
from the Bishop's house, where he is staying during his visit
here. The police force was drawn up before the Guild Hall,
and the music played "In Denmark was I born."

"The remaining members of the council received the poet
at the entrance, when he was escorted by the Burgomaster
into the hall, which had been decorated with flags, flowers,
and his own bust, while the ladies rose at his entrance. The
Burgomaster, Councilor of Justice Mourier, spoke in behalf
of the council, of the occasion upon which they were met, and
assured the poet of the feelings of esteem and gratitude which
the Danish people in general, but the inhabitants of Odense
especially, bore toward the man who by his wonder stories,
songs, and stories, had delighted and strengthened both young
and old, not only in days of peace, but in time of war, and
had brought honor and renown to Denmark's name in foreign
lands.

"He delivered the diploma with the wish that the poet

might for many a year receive strength to increase the treasures with which he had enriched Danish literature.

"A hearty three times three hurra for the honorary citizen showed that this wish found a response with all. In his reply the poet expressed himself nearly as follows : —

" 'The great distinction which my native town has bestowed upon me overwhelms me and makes me proud. I must think of Oehlenschläger's *Aladdin*, who when by his wonderful lamp he had built his grand castle, stepped to the window and said : "Down there I walked a poor boy." So has God granted me such a spiritual lamp — Poesy ; and when its light shone over other countries, and men were pleased at it and gave it their praise, and said, that light shone from Denmark, — then my heart beat with happiness. I knew that at home I had sympathizing friends, and surely in the town where my cradle stood ; and it gives me on this day so honorable a proof of its sympathy, by bestowing upon me a distinction so overwhelmingly great, that I can only speak my thanks from the bottom of my heart.' "

I was near to sinking, overcome by the whole scene. Only on the way back to the Bishop's house did I have eyes for the friendly countenances which greeted me. I heard the congratulations of the multitude ; I saw the waving flags ; but in my heart the thoughts knocked : What will the people everywhere say to such a celebration being given me — how will the papers talk of it ? I felt that I could bear well enough any remark, that it was too great a thing to bestow on me ; but I could not bear that any unfavorable or unkind opinion should be spoken against my native place for so honoring me.

It was, therefore, I confess, an unspeakable pleasure to me to see soon that all the newspapers, great and small, spoke with warm feeling of my festival in my native town. Even as soon as I had returned from the Guild Hall to the Bishop's house, I heard the first voice, one of the most eminent journals in Copenhagen, which had just come by the post, and brought me a heart greeting, and had only praise for my native town. It did me good, and gave me peace of mind and readiness for the great part of the celebration which yet awaited me during the day and evening. In "Dagbladet" of December sixth there read : —

"State Councilor H. C. Andersen enjoys to-day a special honor, since he is presented in Odense with a diploma as honorary citizen in that his native town. It is seldom in our country that such a distinction is given ; but Odense has good reason to honor the poor workingman's son who went out from her, has won for himself a name which is mentioned with honor far beyond the narrow boundaries of his father-land, and so in return he has honored his country and the town where he was born. Many, certainly, whose thoughts to-day turn to the festival at Odense, will receive a prominent place in H. C. Andersen's ' Story of my Life,' and they send the poet their greeting and thanks for all that he has done for them and for us all."

With more freedom than I had in the morning I drove now with the committee of invitation to the Guild Hall, and I had eyes for the first time to see the tasteful decorations. The band played melodies which belonged to my songs. The Funen "County Times," in its issue the next day, gave an account of the celebration, and its report is accurate and full : —

"In the finely decorated hall of the Guild Hall the bust of the honored guest was placed on a pedestal in the centre of the room, surrounded by medallions, with the inscriptions : 'April 2 ' (the poet's birthday), 'September 4, 1819 ' (the day he left Odense), and ' December 6, 1867.' In the afternoon, at four o'clock, as many men and women of different ranks were assembled as could find room (in all 250). The speaking opened with some words by the Burgomaster, Councilor of Justice Mourier, who gave the health of his majesty the King, reminding them that there was a good old custom in Denmark of al ways first drinking the King's health at every festive gathering The following song was then sung : —

> " ' Like the swan flying back to the place
>   Where the nest of the baby bird lay ;
> And its fellows had little of grace
>   For the poor little thing dressed in gray ;

> " ' Where it dreamed, lying hid all alone
>   In the bushes that no one might see,
> And, strange among birds, made its moan,
>   And sighed like its fellows to be.

"'They knew not its lineage, nor recked they
    That the dreaming had truth and gave might;
And soon o'er the sky 'twould be winging its way,
    In the luminous, musical swan flight :

"'That wide o'er the land in its flight it should go,
    And wider by far should fly its renown,
Till all the round world the dear name should know,
    And honor come back to the old native town :

"'That deep in all hearts its music should chime,
    In the great and the small holding sway,
Since always in memory it kept close the time
    When it too was little and gray.

"'So thanks to thee, singer of magical art,
    For thy visit to childhood's old home ;
It is proud of its son, and forth from each heart
    The musical thanksgivings come.'

"Mr. Petersen said, — 'About fifty years ago a poor boy left his native town to begin the struggle of life. His departure was quiet and unnoticed, for no one knew him or thought anything of him. Two women, indeed, his mother and grandmother, accompanied him a little way on the road, but their wishes and prayers followed him the whole journey. His first object was to reach the capital : there would he struggle to attain the great end of his life. In the great city he stood alone without friends or kinsmen ; but he began his struggle and he had in it two powerful supports : trust in Providence, that He would help him as there was need, and confidence in his own strength. The struggle was hard and bitter, and brought with it many wants ; but his strong will persistently carried him forward, and just this struggle and this want gave birth to his wonderful fancy with its exuberance and its lofty flight. The boy has become a man and stands to-day in the midst of us ; his name has in these latter days been upon all men's lips. Now has the conflict issued in victory : he stands here honored by kings and princes, but what is more, honored and esteemed by his fellow-citizens. As a poor testimony to this, the Common Council has elected him an honorary citizen of his native town, and has thereby gratified a cherished wish which grew out of an unusual harmony of feeling in the agreement to take this

step, and the strong desire which has shown itself on the part
of all to take part in the festival in his honor, but which, alas !
all could not share. But, in the name of all, the speaker would
thank the honored guest for the warm, living words which
came crowding from his heart, and thank him for words which
he had sent forth into the world, and for all that he had given
his father-land. However much he had wandered, he never
had forgotten *that*, — never had forgotten he was a Dane, and
that his cradle stood here in our town. So then a *viva* for
our honorary citizen, the poet Hans Christian Andersen.'
(Tumultuous applause.)

"State Councillor H. C. Andersen thanked them, deeply
affected. He had come back here willingly to think upon the
days of his childhood and the memories that flowed from them.
Three memories especially centred about this hall in his mind.
The first of coming as a boy and seeing a wax figure exhibition ; he was greatly astonished then at seeing the kings and
princes and the world's celebrated men represented. Another
time he saw a festival in the hall ; an old town musician took
him to see it. It was a celebration of the King's birthday, and
from the orchestra in the brightly illuminated hall he looked
out upon the dancers, among whom he recognized several. The
third reminiscence dated from this day, when he himself now
stood as a guest in the hall, and met with so much unexpected
cordiality. It all came to him as a wonder story ; but he had
indeed learned that life itself is the most beautiful wonder story.

"After a double quartette had sung the song, ' In Denmark
was I born : there have I my home,' Bishop Engelstöft took up
his parable : —

" ' The poet's charming words in this song, and many other
of his pieces, carry our thoughts out from this assembly into
the greater public of which our circle is only a little part : but
both have the same stamp, the spirit which gives a unity without and within. All history teaches that it is the spirit which
is the chief spring in the lives of people as well as of individuals. It was just this spirit which bore Denmark's name into
the world and gave it honor, from Tycho Brahe and Ole
Römer down to H. C. Örsted, from Holberg to the great
man of our day. This spirit gave the little nation strength to

bear heavy fate and to stand against assaults made on its very existence, power to hold out and to join again what had been separated by violence, but stamped with the same spirit of the nation. So in peaceful contests this spirit had given Denmark honor, and confidence gave promise of a blessing which this spirit would bring about assuredly in the time to come ; and when we remember with thankfulness all the mighty power of a national spirit, let us wish then that our father-land may find many honored sons who will offer all their strength and fire to this end. Fortune and blessing abide on old Denmark.'

"State Councilor Koit wished to propose a health to H. C. Andersen's wife. Ah, he saw very well that people opened their eyes, that they knew quite positively that Andersen was not married. But he had for all that a wife. Was it asked how she looked ? On one side it might be very correctly answered that she only existed in his poetic fancy ; on the other, that she was in a thousand, yes a hundred thousand specimens, and every lawful husband believes that he is in possession of the one right person. That is quite true, because all the wives say with Andersen in his story, — 'What the good-man does is sure to be right!' How often does it not happen to us, as in the Wonder Story, that we barter a good horse away and at last come home to the mother with a bag of rotten apples, and get the promise of being called blockhead when we shall get home ; but the mother proves to be good, and looks at the best of the thing. So a health for Andersen's wife, — for her who creates a paradise for us all our life long and grows always more beautiful.

"H. C. Andersen returned thanks for the health, reminding them of the old-fashioned custom that wreathed the cup with flowers : so he could wish to adorn his books with a wreath, and let the leaves bear the names of all the noble women who were present.

"Colonel Vanpell then spoke : 'It is quite true, as the previous speaker has said, that a beautiful rose garland of women surrounds our honored guest ; but what shall one say of the children, for there are many of them here. We soldiers think a good deal of children, and they think a good deal of us. We see that when we come to our quarters. But An-

dersen's children we love most of all ; they always seem to
lead us the right way.   When we knew not how far we dared
go, then Andersen sang : " I cannot stay ; I have no rest; I
must away to the war."   He called on us ; he called on
friends in the North, while he sang, —

"One folk are we, of Scandinavian name."

Andersen is of Palnatoke's kin from the same isle, and he
shows us what we should fight for.   He tells us of " Holger
the Dane ; " yes, he is our travelling companion to the end.
There is joy when he sends us a Christmas greeting ; as the
child opens a box with tin soldiers, so do we open every new
book, sure to find in it a new " Tin Soldier."   There is a joy
every time there is a " Barselstue "[1] at H. C. Andersen's
house ; and so a health to his children who are already born,
and to those yet to come ? '

" The School Inspector Möller desired to bring the children's thanks to the poet.   The speaker gave this offering, both
because he was himself a great admirer of Andersen's stories,
and because he was naturally a representative of the children.
He had been going about this year among the schools, and
had told the sixteen hundred children who came under his in-
spection about the man whom we honor to-day.   He had
told them that this man had sat upon the same school bench
as they, and he had advised them to follow his illustrious
example.   In the children's name the speaker gave thanks,
because Andersen had shown us what faith was, and taught
us to see the spirit in nature, and the spirit in men's lives.
Our times were skeptical, and the material held sway ; but there
still could be born a man who told us of ' Thumbling,' of the
' Sea-maid,' of ' Agnete,' and who through these opened our ears
for the music of nature.   Andersen had been pretty severe.   He
had chastised affectation, and whipped folly and vanity (which
the speaker demonstrated by citing several of Andersen's stories) ; but he had told the truth : he had shown that nobility
could be hidden in poverty (' She was good for Nothing ' and

[1] Referring to one of Andersen's comedies, suggested by a play of Holberg's, and based on an old custom by which one room in the house was
set apart as a lying-in chamber, where the new mother received the congratulations of friends.

'The Tin Soldier '), and therefore ought thanks to be given by the children, to whom he had given the most beautiful gifts in life.

" Procurator Chancellor Petersen recited a poem in Andersen's honor, and addressed himself to the poet as the friend of his youth and schoolmate. He thanked him for his continued friendship, and proposed again to empty a glass to the poet's honor.

" County Provost Svitzer would turn his thoughts to that which lies nearest to us. It does our town honor that Andersen should go forth from it, and he is now bound fast to us by still tighter bonds. It is an honor to the town that it has such a man for a citizen ; but it is also an honor to the town that it has elected him to that place and that all should come to the festival, for it showed that they had a regard for the good and the beautiful. It is an honor to be a citizen of Odense ; it is always going forward ; it does not know what standing still means. He hoped that this progress might continue in the future, and this hope he would express in a *viva* for Odense's citizens.

" Then Andersen said he could compare his life with a building, and he ventured then to name two men, Collin and H. C. Örsted, who had stood steadfastly by him and helped him forward. Now he could say that the building was ready, and as people were wont to place a garland on a building when completed, his should be a return of thanks to the Common Council and to the Odense Commonalty, in which he saw with pleasure that not only material things, but goodness and beauty also blossomed with flowers. He would fain address some chosen words to all who had afforded him his great pleasure this day, and his thanks should be all summed up in a *viva* for Odense town.

" With that the ceremonies closed, and shortly after the young people began to come. Before the dancing was begun, the children sang a welcome to the poet H. C. Andersen : —

> " ' There, where the street turns round,
> A little house is found,
> And there, say the wise men,
> The stork brought Andersen.
> Ole came, the lively fellow,

And hoisted his umbrella ;
While dreams about the baby flocked,
His cradle the Nis gladly rocked.

" ' Here he sat by the river side,
And mermaids, mermen there he spied ;
And when on the mossy bank he walked,
With Elder Mother then he talked.
Christmas came, blustering, raw,
And the Snow-queen white he saw, —
Whate'er it was that charmed his heart,
He let us freely have a part.

" ' Thanks for every hour we've had
Round the table he makes glad.
The lamp burns bright while mother sews,
And father reads what every one knows ;
Prince and Princess, King and Queen,
Forth they come upon the scene ;
Dance the elves, the troll alarms,
Tin-soldiers stand and shoulder arms.

" ' With fairy shoes thy feet were shod,
And so in royal homes they trod ;
While still thy name the children know
Wherever Tuk and Ida go.
Take, thou poet of the children's play,
Take the youngsters' thanks to-day ;
We cannot grasp with a very big hand,
So take our *both* as here we stand.'

" In the course of the evening H. C. Andersen gave the persons present great pleasure by reading two of his stories. During the dancing there was received from his majesty the King the telegram given below, which was received with unbounded applause.

" A great torch-light procession, in which all the córporations of the town with their colors took part, and which numbered a hundred and fifty torches, marched about eight o'clock to the Guild Hall, and brought H. C. Andersen the congratulations of the united craftsmen on the occasion of his nomination to honorary citizenship in our town, and expressed the hope that for many a year he might labor for his own prosperity and for the honor of old Denmark. H. C. Andersen begged the deputation to convey to the gathering a hearty greeting and thanks from him for all the honor they had shown him. In his childhood it had been predicted, he said, that his native place would one day be illuminated in his honor, and when he now cast a glance over the square and saw the many burning torches, he must perforce see in this the fulfillment of the prediction. The deputation then handed him the song which the workmen wished to sing to him there in the square.

"After it had been sung there was a long live the honored guest and poet! which was followed by a prolonged hurra. At that H. C. Andersen stepped forward to an open window and thanked the workmen for the honor they had shown him, saying that this day and evening would hold their place as the dearest recollections of his life. Thereupon the torches were all thrown in a heap on the pavement and the procession disbanded.

"During the festivities several congratulatory telegrams came to Andersen. Among them we should especially mention the following : —

"From his majesty the King : 'To the distinction shown you to-day by the citizens of your native town, I and my family add our sincere congratulations. Christian Rex.'

"From the seniory of the Students' Association : 'The Students' Association sends its greeting to the poet H. C. Andersen on his day of honor, with thanks for the past and best wishes for the future.'

"From Slagelse : 'The Slagelse Workingmen's Union, which holds a special meeting this evening in honor of the distinguished men who graduated from Slagelse Latin School, sends you, dear Hon. State Councilor, as one of those, the heartiest and most affectionate greeting.'"

Such was the pleasure throughout the country over my rare and beautiful festival ; and needs must there have been in my heart profound feelings and varying movements. How could people dream that so much should be granted me — that was the thought which constantly pressed upon me and cast a shadow over all the splendor and pleasure, which I ought to have been enjoying every moment. Then came the first telegram, from the Students' Association, lifting my heart. I saw that the academic youth shared my pleasure and did not envy me it. Then came a dispatch from a private circle of young students in Copenhagen, then from the association at Slagelse. It will be remembered that I went to school there, and thereby was attached to the town. Soon there followed messages from congratulatory friends in Aarhuus, in Stege ; telegram after telegram came from every quarter. One of these was read aloud by State Councilor Koch ; it was a congratulation from his majesty the King and the royal family. The assembly broke forth in applause : " How fine it is ! how hearty ! " Every cloud and shadow in my soul vanished. Now began the children's part. An arm-chair was placed for me in the middle of the hall, and two by two came gayly dressed children, who danced in a ring about me and sang their song. How happy I was, and yet — up to heaven's height man dare not exalt himself. I should and must feel that I was only a poor child of humanity bound by earthly frailty. I suffered from a dreadful toothache, which, with the heat and the excitement I was in, became excessive, but I read a wonder story for the little friends. Then the deputation came from the corporations of the town, who with torches and waving banners came through the streets to the Guild Hall.

I was to fulfill the prophecy which the old woman made when as a boy I left my birthplace, — Odense should be illuminated for me. I stepped to the open window ; there was a blaze of light from the torches, the place was quite full of people. They sang, and I was overcome in my soul. I was physically overcome indeed, and could not enjoy this summit of fortune in my life. The toothache was intolerable ; the icy air which rushed in at the window made it blaze up into a terrible pain, and in place of fully enjoying the good fortune of these minutes, which never would be repeated, I looked at the printed song to see how many verses there were to be sung before I could slip away from the torture which the cold air sent through my teeth. It was the pitch of suffering ; when the flames of the torches piled together sank down, then my pain decreased. How thankful was I to God. Gentle eyes looked upon me from all sides, every one wished to speak to me, to press my hand. Wearied out, I reached the Bishop's house and sought rest, but I did not get it until the morning hour, so filled to overflowing was I.

I wrote at once to his majesty the King and expressed my deeply felt thanks ; I wrote to the Students' Association and to the Workingmen's Union, and now I received many visits. Especially must I mention an old widow who as a child had been a boarder for a short time with my parents ; she wept for gladness over my life's career, and told how she had stood in the evening with the torch-light procession on the square and seen the parade : " It was just as it was for the King and Queen when they were here." Then she had thought of my parents, and upon me as a little boy ; she had talked about it with several old people who stood by her ; she had wept and they had wept, that the poor boy should so turn out and be honored like a king.

In the evening there was a large company at the Bishop's house, at least a couple of hundred people. I read a wonder story to them, and afterward the young people danced.

The day after I went to each of the Common Council, and sought out and found a number of acquaintances whom I had known as a child. There was still living one of the poet Hans Christian Bunkeflod's daughters, Susanne. I went to the old house where I had passed my childhood. A picture of this was shortly after the festival given in the " Illustrated Times." I went to the charity school where I had learned my lessons when I was a little boy.

The Odense Musical Society invited me to a concert at the Guild Hall. I was given the place of honor. In the " Funen Advertiser," the account ran : —

" The last public mark of respect on the occasion of the poet's reception as an honorary citizen of Odense took place on Saturday evening in the Guild Hall Sáloon, at the Musical Society's first concert of the season. The management had invited the poet to this assembly, and a more fitting close could not have been thought of, nor could any act have been more graceful," etc. " As many people had crowded to the concert as the hall would contain, nearly five hundred. At

about eight o'clock the honored guest entered, and was received with a blast of trumpets, while the whole assembly
rose and the chorus sang a welcome to the poet."

The day before my departure occurred the yearly feast in
the so-called Lahn's Institution for Poor Children, girls and
boys, who are here educated and clothed until their Confirmation. I was among those invited. The feast was for me a
very significant knot that tied all together in the speaking that
was there done. Lahn's portrait hung adorned with flowers
on the wall. Who was Lahn? many asked. He was born in
Odense, a poor boy who learned to sew gloves, went out into
the country and sold them, and so got to Hamburg; and the
Odense Lahn gloves became soon an article much inquired
after. He came to great position, was a rich man, built himself a house in Odense on Nether Street, never was married,
but did much good, and when he died he bequeathed a legacy
for the education and clothing of poor children and gave his
house for the Institution. He lies buried in the Virgin's
Church grave-yard in Odense. The tombstone says, " Here
lies Lahn whose monument stands on Nether Street."

Upon the wall in the school-room there hung another picture by the side of Lahn's, a portrait of an old woman; she
had many years had her little stand on the street and sold
apples, but now had been some time dead. As a child she
had until her Confirmation been an inmate of Lahn's Institution ; and when she died it was found that by great simplicity
of life and frugality she had hoarded a few hundred rix-dollars, which she bequeathed to Lahn's Institution, and so her
picture now hung there by the side of Lahn's.

A young and talented man, the School Inspector, Pastor
Möller, made a speech to them at the festival, and spoke of
all the famous men and women in Denmark, concluding with
the words : " You all know whose festival it is that has been
celebrated here the last few days. You have seen how a man
from our town has been welcomed and honored, and he has
sat upon just such a bench for poor children as you sit on.
He is here among us."   I saw the eyes about me moist with
feeling, and then I bowed to the company, and took the hand
of some of the mothers, and as I left I heard several exclaim,
" God make him happy and bless him ! "

It was a festival for Lahn ; it was a blessed one for me. It was as if one sunbeam after another shone into my heart. I could not comprehend it.   In such a moment one clings to God as in the bitterest hour of sorrow.

Now came the day of departure, the eleventh of December. People come crowding into the railway station, so that it was filled with them.   My lady friends brought me flowers.   The train came which I was to take, and it stopped only for a few minutes.   The Burgomaster, Herr Mourier, bade me good-by. I uttered my farewell ; the loud, repeated hurras rang forth, they were lost in the air as we moved away, but still from single groups of people in the town and near by the shouts continued to be sent up.   Now first as I sat quite alone, did there seem to rise into one great account all the honor, gladness, and glory which had been given me by God in my native town.

The greatest, the highest blessing I could attain was now mine.   Now for the first time could I fully and devoutly thank my God and pray, —

" Leave me not when the days of trial come."

Copenhagen, *March* 29, 1869.

THE END.